BEST REFERENCE BOOKS

THE REFERENCE BOOK

BEST
REFERENCE BOOKS

Titles of lasting value selected from

AMERICAN REFERENCE
BOOKS ANNUAL
1970-1976

Bohdan S. Wynar, editor

1976

LIBRARIES UNLIMITED, INC.

Littleton, Colo.

LIBRARIES UNLIMITED, INC.
P. O. Box 263
Littleton, Colorado 80160

REF
II
B465

Library of Congress Cataloging in Publication Data
Main entry under title:

Best reference books.

    Includes indexes.
    1. Reference books—Reviews. 2. Reference
books—Bibliography. I. Wynar, Bohdan S. II. A-
merican reference books annual.
Z1035.1.B535   011'.02   76-45781
ISBN 0-87287-163-0

TABLE OF CONTENTS

Chapter 1
General Reference Works

Chapter 2
Librarianship and Library Resources

Chapter 3
Social Sciences and Area Studies

Chapter 4
History

Chapter 5
Archaeology

Chapter 6
Genealogy and Heraldry

Chapter 7
Political Science

Chapter 8
Law

Chapter 9
Geography

Chapter 10
Education

Chapter 10—Education (cont'd)

Chapter 11
Recreation and Sports

Chapter 12
Sociology

Chapter 13
Urbanology

Chapter 14
Anthropology and Ethnology

Chapter 15
Statistics and Demography

Chapter 16
Economics and Business

Chapter 17
Fine Arts

Chapter 18
Applied Arts and Hobbies

Chapter 22
Religion

Chapter 23
Philosophy

Chapter 24
Mythology, Folklore, and Popular Customs

Chapter 25
Linguistics and Philology

Chapter 25–Linguistics and Philology (cont'd)

Chapter 26
Journalism

Chapter 27
Literature

Chapter 27—Literature (cont'd)

Chapter 28
Science and Technology—General

Chapter 29
Mathematics

Chapter 30
Astronomy

Chapter 37
Earth Sciences

Chapter 38
Psychology

Chapter 39
Medical Sciences

Chapter 40
Agricultural Sciences

Chapter 41
Engineering and Technology

Chapter 42
Military Science

Indexes

INTRODUCTION

Best Reference Books provides a careful selection of 818 substantial reference titles, chosen from seven volumes of *American Reference Books Annual*. It is well known that *American Reference Books Annual* provides a comprehensive reviewing service for reference books published in a given year. The seven volumes of ARBA published since 1970 have provided reviews of a total of 12,339 titles. The reference books reviewed in ARBA can be categorized as follows: 1) Dictionaries, encyclopedias, directories, bibliographies, guides, concordances, atlases, and other types of "ready reference" tools are reviewed in each volume of ARBA; coverage in this category is nearly complete. 2) General encyclopedias that are updated annually, yearbooks, almanacs, indexing and abstracting services, and other annual or serial publications are reviewed at intervals of three, four, or five years. 3) ARBA reviews foreign reference titles that have an exclusive distributor in the United States. 4) Government documents and reprints are reviewed on a selective basis. Certain categories of reference books are usually not reviewed in ARBA as a matter of editorial policy: reference books of fewer than 48 pages; reference books produced by vanity presses; reference books produced by the author as publisher; and certain types of reference materials published by library staffs for internal use.

Best Reference Books offers the library profession our selection of 818 titles produced from 1969 through 1975. In our judgment, these are titles of lasting value that can be safely recommended as substantial reference books for libraries of all types. Works selected include those of a specialized nature, which will be of particular value to larger libraries, as well as those of wider appeal, which will be useful in smaller as well as larger libraries.

Reviews for the titles included in this volume were prepared by 175 reviewers for ARBA; some have been slightly re-edited for this compilation. Prices have been updated, and, if necessary, notes about new editions have been added. Unsigned reviews are by the editor. Reviews signed by two contributors are in most cases composite reviews, which have been prepared from two reviews pertaining to two different editions or two separate volumes of a particular work. We have retained citations to reviews in other media, and we have indicated, for the first time, the outstanding reference books of the year selected by the committee appointed from the membership of the Reference and Adult Services Division of ALA. The results of this selection are published in *Library Journal*, usually in the April 15 issue. Our form of citation here is "ALA 71," "ALA 72," etc. It is interesting to note that only 22 of the titles selected by the ALA committee as outstanding reference books from 1969 through 1975 are not included in this volume, although our selection obviously includes many additional reference titles.

Excluded from our selection for *Best Reference Books* are all serial publications (e.g., *Books in Print*) and all general encyclopedias that are updated annually. In the next few years we hope to offer our readers a separate volume devoted exclusively to serial publications. Also excluded from our selection are all travel guides reviewed in ARBA (there are simply too many of them), how-to-do-it books of reference value, and, in the area of literature, reference titles that cover only one author. These restrictions stem from a need to keep this volume to a manageable size and thus make it more readily available to smaller libraries.

Even though this is a selection of "best reference books," critical comments provided in the original ARBA reviews have been retained. Thus, this volume follows the same policy as ARBA, providing a critical appraisal of a given volume, since even titles that are basically satisfactory can at the same time be deficient in one respect or another. On many occasions, the reviews evaluate and compare a work in relation to works of a similar nature.

Acknowledgments are due to all the fine ARBA contributors whose reviews appear in *Best Reference Books*. The list of these reviewers and their affiliations begins on page xix. Thanks are also extended to all those Libraries Unlimited staff members who contributed their talents to this volume: Peggy Jay, Christine Wynar, Ann Harwell, Eugenia Greenfield, and Toni Stephens.

September 1976   BOHDAN S. WYNAR

LIST OF CONTRIBUTORS

RICHARD AKEROYD, Director, Department of Planning, Audit-Review and Research, Connecticut State Library, Hartford

WALTER C. ALLEN, Associate Professor, Graduate School of Library Science, University of Illinois, Urbana

ROBERT H. AMUNDSON, Loretto Heights College, Denver

FRANK J. ANDERSON, Librarian, Sandor Teszler Library, Wofford College, Spartanburg, S.C.

MARGARET ANDERSON, Assistant Professor, Faculty of Library Science, University of Toronto

CHARLES R. ANDREWS, University Librarian, Southeastern Massachusetts University, North Dartmouth

MARTIN ANDREWS, Assistant Professor of Psychology, St. John's University, Collegeville, Minn.

THEODORA ANDREWS, Pharmacy Librarian and Professor of Library Science, Purdue University, Lafayette, Ind.

HENRY T. ARMISTEAD, Head of Technical Services, Scott Memorial Library, Thomas Jefferson University, Philadelphia

ANDREW D. ARMITAGE, Chief Librarian, Owen Sound Public Library, Ontario

JUDITH ARMSTRONG, Director of the Library, Drury College, Springfield, Mo.

RAYMOND PAAVO ARVIO, Lecturer in Home Economics, Department of Home Economics, Queens College, City University of New York, Flushing

THEODORE M. AVERY, JR., Gift and Exchange Librarian, Brooklyn Public Library, N.Y.

EDWARD J. BACCIOCCO, JR., Post-Doctoral Research Fellow, Hoover Institution, Stanford, Calif.

JULIE BICHTELER, Assistant Professor, Graduate School of Library Science, University of Texas, Austin

ALEXANDER S. BIRKOS, Mount Shasta, Calif.

MARTY BLOOMBERG, Director of Library Operations, California State College, San Bernardino

JAMES E. BOBICK, Coordinator of Science Libraries, Temple University, Philadelphia

NANCY G. BOLES, Curator of Manuscripts, Maryland Historical Society, Baltimore

VLADIMIR T. BOROVANSKY, Head, Science and Engineering Reference Services, Arizona State University, Tempe

WILLIAM BRACE, Associate Professor, Graduate School of Library Science, Rosary College, River Forest, Ill.

PAUL BREED, University Bibliographer, Wayne State University Library, Detroit

DAVID W. BRUNTON, Assistant to the Director, Englewood Public Library, Colo.

CHARLES R. BRYANT, Curator, Southeast Asia Collection, Yale University Library, New Haven, Conn.

RICHARD M. BUCK, Assistant to the Chief, Performing Arts Research Center, New York Public Library at Lincoln Center

BROWER R. BURCHILL, Chairman, Division of Biological Sciences, University of Kansas, Lawrence

DWIGHT BURLINGAME, University Librarian, University of Evansville, Ind.

HELEN M. BURNS, Chief Law Librarian, Federal Reserve Bank of New York

JOAN E. BURNS, Principal Art Librarian, Art and Music Department, Public Library of Newark, N.J.

KAREN BURT, Cleveland Institute of Music, Ohio

JUDY G. CARAGHAR, Staff, Libraries Unlimited, Inc.

CHING-CHIH CHEN, Associate Professor, School of Library Science, Simmons College, Boston

FRANCES NEEL CHENEY, Professor and Associate Director, School of Library Science, George Peabody College for Teachers, Nashville

CECIL F. CLOTFELTER, Technical Services Librarian, Eastern New Mexico University, Portales

MARY CLOTFELTER, Part-Time Instructor, Library Science, Eastern New Mexico University, Portales

HARRIETTE M. CLUXTON, Librarian, Noah van Cleef Medical Memorial Library, Illinois Masonic Medical Center, Chicago

PAUL B. CORS, Chief of Technical Processing, University of Wyoming Library, Laramie

ROYLENE G. CUNNINGHAM, Loan Services Librarian, Norris Medical Library, University of Southern California, Los Angeles

WILLIAM J. DANE, Supervising Art and Music Librarian, Public Library of Newark, N.J.

DONALD G. DAVIS, JR., Assistant Professor, Graduate School of Library Science, University of Texas, Austin

DÉSIRÉE DE CHARMS, Music Librarian, Kent State University, Ohio

DOMINIQUE-RENÉ DE LERMA, Music Librarian, Indiana University, Bloomington

WINIFRED F. DEAN, Reference/Bibliographer, Social Sciences, Cleveland State University Libraries, Ohio

ELIE M. DICK, formerly Assistant Professor, Department of Mathematics, Louisiana State University, New Orleans

ROBERT K. DIKEMAN, Assistant Professor, School of Library Science, Louisiana State University, Baton Rouge

AMITY DOERING, Librarian I, Social Science and Technology Department, Northeast Regional Library, Free Library of Philadelphia

PETER DOIRON, Woodbridge Public Library, N.J.

PAUL Z. DUBOIS, Director, Roscoe West Library, Trenton State College, N.J.

DAVID EGGENBERGER, Publications Officer, U.S. National Archives and Records Service, Washington

JULIA M. EHRESMANN, Instructor, William Rainey Harper College, Palatine, Ill.

DONALD EMPSON, Reference Librarian, Minnesota Historical Society, St. Paul

G. EDWARD EVANS, Associate Professor, Graduate School of Library Service, University of California, Los Angeles

EDGAR EVERHART, Professor of Physics and Astronomy, University of Denver

CHARLES FARLEY, Reference and Readers' Advisor Librarian, Plaza Library, Kansas City Public Library, Mo.

SHARON PAUGH FERRIS, Massillon Public Library, Massillon, Ohio

P. WILLIAM FILBY, Director, Maryland Historical Society, Baltimore

GREGORY T. FOUTS, Assistant Professor, Department of Psychology, University of Denver

MARILYN GELL, Library Projects Manager, Washington Metropolitan Council of Governments, Washington

EDWIN S. GLEAVES, Director and Professor, School of Library Science, George Peabody College for Teachers, Nashville

RICHARD A. GRAY, Littleton, Colo.

SUZANNE K. GRAY, Coordinator of Science, Boston Public Library

LAUREL GROTZINGER, Professor, School of Librarianship, Western Michigan University, Kalamazoo

LEONARD GRUNDT, Professor and Chairperson, Library Department, Nassau Community College, Garden City, N.Y.

DORIS L. GUSTAFSON, Branch Librarian, New Lots District Library, Brooklyn, N.Y.

LAURA GUTIÉRREZ-WITT, Head Librarian, Latin American Collection, University of Texas, Austin

ELIZABETH C. HALL, Senior Librarian, The Horticultural Society of New York

DONALD P. HAMMER, Executive Secretary, Information Science and Automation Division, American Library Association, Chicago

ROBERT P. HARO, Associate University Librarian, University of Southern California, Los Angeles

PATRICIA C. HARPOLE, Assistant Chief Librarian, Minnesota Historical Society, St. Paul

ANN J. HARWELL, Editorial staff, Libraries Unlimited, Inc.

ROBERT J. HAVLIK, Associate Director for Technical Services, University of Notre Dame Memorial Library, Notre Dame, Ind.

ROSEMARY HENDERSON, Director of Library Services, Coffeyville Community Junior College, Kansas

PETER HERNON, Ph.D. candidate, Graduate Library School, Indiana University, Bloomington

SHIRLEY B. HESSLEIN, Associate Health Sciences Librarian, State University of New York, Buffalo

GEORGE V. HODOWANEC, Director, William Allen White Library, Emporia Kansas State College

MARJORIE P. HOLT, Director of Reference and Research, Brooklyn Public Library, N.Y.

SHIRLEY L. HOPKINSON, Professor, Department of Librarianship, California State University, San Jose

JOHN PHILLIP IMMROTH, Associate Professor, Graduate School of Library and Information Science, University of Pittsburgh

DAVID ISAAK, Reference Librarian, University of Victoria Library, Victoria, B.C.

CLARA O. JACKSON, Associate Professor, School of Library Science, Kent State University, Ohio

MILES M. JACKSON, Professor, Graduate School of Library Studies, University of Hawaii, Honolulu

JOHN C. JAHODA, Assistant Professor of Biology, Bridgewater State College, Mass.

PEGGY JAY, Denver, Colo.

MARCIA JEBB, Associate Reference Librarian, Cornell University, Ithaca, N.Y.

THOMAS L. JENKINS, Manager of Planning, Orange County Transit District, Santa Ana, Calif.

IVAN L. KALDOR, Dean, School of Library and Information Science, State University College, Geneseo, N.Y.

MARGARET KAMINSKI, Librarian, Public Relations Department, Detroit Public Library, and Co-editor of *Moving Out*

DORIS FLAX KAPLAN, Reference Librarian, Raymond H. Fogler Library, University of Maine at Orono

SHARAD KARKHANIS, Associate Professor and Coordinator, Library Instruction Program, Kingsborough Community College, Brooklyn, N.Y.

RICHARD J. KELLY, Assistant Reference Librarian, University of Minnesota Library, Minneapolis

LOUIS KIRALDI, Documents and Map Librarian, Dwight B. Waldo Library, Western Michigan University, Kalamazoo

DONALD J. LEHNUS, Associate Professor, Graduate School of Librarianship, University of Puerto Rico, San Juan

DOROTHY E. LITT, Assistant Branch Librarian, Douglaston Branch, Queens Borough Public Library, N.Y.

DAVID W. LITTLEFIELD, Near East Subject Cataloger, U.S. Library of Congress, and Near East Librarian, Georgetown University, Washington

H. ROBERT MALINOWSKY, Associate Dean of Libraries, University of Kansas, Lawrence

MARY D. MALINOWSKY, Owner and Manager, Apple Valley Farm Antiques and Crafts, Lawrence, Kans.

THEODORE MANHEIM, Librarian, Education Division, Wayne State University, Detroit

CHARLES W. MANN, Chief of Rare Books and Special Collections, University Libraries, and Associate Professor of English, Pennsylvania State University, University Park

GUY A. MARCO, Dean, School of Library Science, Kent State University, Ohio

DENTON MAY, Department of English, Loretto Heights College, Denver

STEVEN J. MAYOVER, Head, Special Services Department, Northeast Regional Library, Free Library of Philadelphia

JAMES P. McCABE, Librarian, Allentown College of St. Francis de Sales, Center Valley, Pa.

STANLEY JOE McCORD, Reference Librarian, University of Texas Health Science Center Library, Dallas

LAURA H. McGUIRE, Documents Librarian, Eastern New Mexico University Library, Portales

JIM WAYNE MILLER, Professor of German, Department of Foreign Languages, Western Kentucky University, Bowling Green

JOSEPH H. MOREHEAD, Assistant Professor, School of Library and Information Science, State University of New York, Albany

JOHN M. MORGAN, Reference Librarian, University of Toledo, Ohio

SUZINE HAR NICOLESCU, Assistant Professor and Chief of Technical Services, Medgar Evers College Library of the City University of New York

DENNIS NORTH, Head Librarian, Dayton Memorial Library, Regis College, Denver

MARSHALL E. NUNN, Reference Librarian, Glendale College, Calif.

ELLIOT S. PALAIS, Reference Librarian, Arizona State University Library, Tempe

C. GERALD PARKER, Music Cataloger, Boston Public Library

ROBERT PARSLOW, Assistant Professor of Linguistics, University of Pittsburgh

JOHN G. PECK, JR., Librarian, Westminster Choir College, Princeton, N.J.

SHARON S. PETERSON, San Diego, Calif.

JANICE J. POWELL, Assistant to the University Librarian, University of California, Berkeley

GARY R. PURCELL, Director, Graduate School of Library and Information Science, University of Tennessee, Knoxville

BERNARD D. REAMS, JR., Assistant Professor of Law and Law Librarian, Washington University School of Law, St. Louis

ALAN M. REES, Professor, School of Library Science, Case Western Reserve University, Cleveland

JOHN R. RITER, JR., Professor, Department of Chemistry, University of Denver

WILLIAM C. ROBINSON, Assistant Professor, Graduate School of Library and Information Science, University of Tennessee, Knoxville

A. ROBERT ROGERS, Professor, School of Library Science, Kent State University, Ohio

DAVID ROSENBAUM, Reference Librarian, Education Library, G. Flint Purdy Library, Wayne State University, Detroit

JUDITH K. ROSENBERG, formerly Children's Librarian, Ayers Branch, Akron Public Library, Ohio

KENYON C. ROSENBERG, Associate Professor, School of Library Science, Kent State University, Ohio

RICHARD H. ROSICHAN, Chief Librarian, Heed University, Hollywood, Fla.

STEVEN RYBICKI, Reference Librarian, Macomb County Community College Library, Warren, Mich.

JULIA SABINE, Special Assistant to the Director, Munson-Williams-Proctor Institute, Utica, N.Y.

WILLIAM Z. SCHENCK, Assistant to the Head, Acquisitions and Bibliography Department, Yale University Library, New Haven, Conn.

R. G. SCHIPF, Science Librarian, University of Montana, Missoula

LORRAINE SCHULTE, Associate Director of Libraries, USC Health Sciences Campus, University of Southern California, Los Angeles

ELEANOR ELVING SCHWARTZ, Associate Professor, Coordinator, Library Science Program, Department of Communication Sciences, Kean College of New Jersey, Union

LeROY C. SCHWARZKOPF, Government Documents Librarian, McKeldin Library, University of Maryland, College Park

RALPH L. SCOTT, Reference Librarian, East Carolina University Library, Greenville, N.C.

JESSE H. SHERA, Professor and Dean Emeritus, School of Library Science, Case Western Reserve University, Cleveland

GERALD R. SHIELDS, Assistant Professor, School of Information and Library Studies, State University of New York, Buffalo

BRUCE A. SHUMAN, Assistant Professor, Graduate Library School, Indiana University, Bloomington

SAMUEL L. SIMON, Director, Finkelstein Memorial Library, Spring Valley, N.Y.

JACQUELINE D. SISSON, Head, Fine Arts Library, and Associate Professor of Library Administration, Ohio State University, Columbus

ANN SKENE-MELVIN, formerly Consultant, Dominion Glass Reserve Library, Brampton, Ontario

DAVID ST. C. SKENE-MELVIN, Consultant, Brampton, Ontario

STANLEY J. SLOTE, Assistant Professor, Department of Library Science, Queens College, N.Y.

MILUSE SOUDEK, Assistant Professor, Northern Illinois University Libraries, DeKalb

LAWRENCE E. SPELLMAN, Lt. Col. U.S. Army (Ret.), Curator of Maps, Princeton University Library, N.J.

BERNARD SPILKA, Professor, Department of Psychology, University of Denver

JOSEPH W. SPRUG, Director of the Library, St. Edwards University, Austin, Tex.

JERRY E. STEPHENS, Associate Law Librarian, University of Kansas, Lawrence

ROLLAND E. STEVENS, Professor, Graduate School of Library Science, University of Illinois, Urbana

ELMA M. STEWART, Assistant Science and Technology Librarian and Assistant Professor, Eastern Michigan University, Ypsilanti

DENNIS THOMISON, Assistant Professor, School of Library Science, University of Southern California, Los Angeles

PEGGY M. TOZER, Assistant Director, Library, Eastern New Mexico University, Portales

DEAN TUDOR, Chairman, Library Arts Department, Ryerson Polytechnic Institute, Toronto

NANCY TUDOR, Assistant Head, Cataloguing Department, Metropolitan Toronto Central Library, Toronto

ROBERT VAN BENTHUYSEN, Library Director, Guggenheim Memorial Library, Monmouth College, West Long Branch, N.J.

ALBERT C. VARA, Senior Assistant, Business Library, Temple University, Philadelphia

MARY JO WALKER, Reference and Special Collections Librarian and University Archivist, Eastern New Mexico University, Portales

DEDERICK C. WARD, Head of Science Libraries, University of Colorado, Boulder

JON M. WARNER, Librarian, Hunter College of the City University of New York

HANS H. WEBER, Assistant Director for Technical Services, University of Houston Libraries, Texas

ROBERT L. WELKER, Professor of English, School of Humanities and Behavioral Sciences, University of Alabama, Huntsville

JOHN ROBERT WHEAT, Reference Librarian, Austin Public Library, Texas

WAYNE A. WIEGAND, Assistant Professor, School of Library Science, University of Kentucky, Lexington

SARA LOU WILLIAMS, Chairman, Reference Department, Gene Eppley Library, University of Nebraska at Omaha

PAUL A. WINCKLER, Professor of Library Science, Palmer Graduate Library School, Long Island University, C. W. Post Center, Greenvale, N.Y.

JOHN H. WINKELMAN, Associate Professor, School of Library and Information Science, State University College, Geneseo, N.Y.

GLENN R. WITTIG, Ann Arbor, Mich.

FRANCIS J. WITTY, Professor, Graduate Department of Library Science, Catholic University of America, Washington

IRVING WORTIS, Humanities Librarian, Trenton State College, N.J.

ANNA T. WYNAR, Ethnic Heritage Studies Development Program, Cleveland

CHRISTINE L. WYNAR, Editorial staff, Libraries Unlimited, Inc.

LUBOMYR R. WYNAR, Professor, School of Library Science, and Director, Center for the Study of Ethnic Publications in the United States, Kent State University, Ohio

SALLY WYNKOOP, Denver, Colo.

STEVE WYNKOOP, Environment and Natural Resources Reporter, *The Denver Post*

WILLIAM CURTIS YOUNG, Lawrence, Ks.

SAMIR M. ZOGHBY, Assistant Head, African Section, U.S. Library of Congress, Washington

JOURNALS CITED

FORM OF CITATION	JOURNAL TITLE
AL	American Libraries
BL	Booklist
Choice	Choice
C&RL	College & Research Libraries
LJ	Library Journal
LRTS	Library Resources & Technical Services
NYTBR	New York Times Book Review
PW	Publishers Weekly
RQ	RQ
SLJ	School Library Journal
SMQ	School Media Quarterly
SR	Saturday Review/World
Unesco	Unesco Bulletin for Libraries
WLB	Wilson Library Bulletin

CHAPTER 1

GENERAL REFERENCE WORKS

BIBLIOGRAPHY

BIBLIOGRAPHIC GUIDES

1. Orton, Robert M., ed. **Catalog of Reprints in Series**. 21st ed. Metuchen, N.J., Scarecrow, 1972. 922p. $27.50. LC 61-13547. ISBN 0-8108-0438-7.

Orton began this irregular annual in 1940 with the H. W. Wilson Company. His purpose was, and is, to identify books, articles, fiction, and poetry which have been reprinted in a recognizable series. He defines reprints in three ways: 1) straight reproduction from original plates; 2) resetting with minor corrections, if any; 3) collection of readings from diverse sources. A series is a group of titles related by one or several factors—price, size, series name, subject, purpose, etc.—so ordinary reprinters are omitted.

Part one of this catalog is an author/title alphabet—main entries being the author portion. Bibliographic technique suits the intentions: author, title, publisher, series and number, reprint date, paging, paperback, translator, illustrator, original title, price, contents if anthological. Part one also includes breakdown by type (e.g., poetry) for anthologies. Omnibus volumes are cross-referenced. Most convenient is the part which groups series under the publishers, although some publishers are not included (e.g., Faucett). — Peter Doiron. [R: ARBA 73, item 3]

2. **The Reader's Adviser: A Layman's Guide to Literature. Volume 1: The Best in American and British Fiction, Poetry, Essays, Literary Biography, Bibliography, and Reference**. 12th ed. Ed. by Sarah L. Prakken. New York, R. R. Bowker, 1974. 808p. index. $23.50. LC 57-13277. ISBN 0-8352-0781-1. ISSN 0094-5943.

The 11th edition of *The Reader's Adviser*, published in 1968, was expanded at that time from one to two volumes. The 12th edition will be published in three volumes.

Volume 1 consists of 16 chapters. The first four cover general background, bibliography, reference books, and anthologies. Chapters 5 through 9 discuss British and American poetry, by period, and Chapters 10 through 14 cover fiction. Essays and criticism and literary biography and autobiography conclude the volume.

Another innovation in this 12th edition is the selection of a number of subject specialists to be responsible for individual chapters. This has resulted in some unevenness in coverage, which is indirectly acknowledged in the preface: "Because each chapter was revised by a different person, small individual differences of approach may be detected from chapter to chapter" (p. xi). In all, there are 16 contributing editors.

A comparison of the 11th edition and the first volume of the 12th edition reveals that most of the material has been substantially updated and certain chapters (e.g., Modern American Poetry) also show considerable revision. The general structure of the volume remains the same, including some of the previous weak-nesses of *The Reader's Adviser*. In spite of the claim that "in the general bibli-ographies at the head of each chapter and in the reading lists about an individual author our editors have been highly selective, choosing only *la crème de la crème*" (p. xviii), bibliographies and other reference books are traditionally rather poorly represented. As an example, Aliki Dick's *Student's Guide to British Literature: A Selective Bibliography of 4,128 Titles and Reference Sources from the Anglo-Saxon Period to the Present* was selected by ALA as one of the Best Reference Books of 1972; nevertheless, it somehow did not pass the editorial criteria for *The Reader's Adviser*. The section on rare book prices does not even mention Mandeville's *The Used Book Price Guide*, which lists 74,000 books. However, it does include *Bookman's Price Index*, which lists 32,000 titles, and *American Book-Prices Current*, which lists 28,000. Because *The Reader's Adviser* is used by many bookstores and secondhand dealers, coverage of this subject should be more balanced.

These critical comments do not belittle the overall general usefulness of the volume. The selection of representative editions for individual writers is the strong-est point of *The Reader's Adviser*, being usually sound and well balanced. Although deficiencies remain—omission of the year of publication for certain titles, incon-sistencies in prices, and no pagination for monographic works—they will not deter the user who is already familiar with the format of bibliographic citations in *The Reader's Adviser*. With the publication of the remaining two volumes of this 12th edition, this standard tool will be substantially enlarged in its scope. Volume 2 will cover drama and foreign literature in translation. Volume 3 will cover general biog-raphy and autobiography, general reference books, Bibles, world religions, philos-ophy, psychology, science, social sciences, history, government and politics, the lively arts and communication, folklore and humor, travel, and adventure. Both are expected to be published late in 1976. —Bohdan S. Wynar. [R: ARBA 75, item 1314]

3. Sheehy, Eugene P., comp. **Guide to Reference Books**. Eighth Edition, Second Supplement, 1967-68. Chicago, American Library Association, 1970. 165p. index. $4.00pa. LC 66-29240. ISBN 0-8389-0073-9.

4. Sheehy, Eugene P., comp. **Guide to Reference Books**. Eighth Edition, Third Supplement, 1969-70. Chicago, American Library Association, 1972. 190p. index. $4.50pa. LC 66-29240. ISBN 0-8389-0115-8.

The second supplement to Constance M. Winchell's *Guide to Reference Books* (1967) includes about 1,200 entries, most of them published during 1967 and 1968. Occasionally there are some older imprints not included in the first supplement (published in 1968) or in the main volume.

The listings in this second supplement, coded to the main volume, contain occasional citations to reviews published in ALA publications: *Choice, College and Research Libraries*, and the *Booklist and Subscription Books Bulletin*. References to published reviews in such reviewing media as *Library Journal* and other non-ALA publications would be even more helpful. A cumulative index covering both supplements is an improvement. In terms of titles represented, one can assume that the present supplement covers not more than 20-25 percent of reference titles actually published in both years in this country. This figure pertains only to new titles and substantially revised editions. The book does not include most annuals, directories, and other serial publications, since this category of materials is usually listed only once, and there appears to be little effort to update these listings, even if certain serials considerably change their structure or contents.

The general policy for compilation of the third supplement remains the same as for the second. The third supplement includes approximately 1,200 titles, most of which were published during 1969 and 1970. There are a few works with 1968 or earlier imprint dates, as well as a very few 1971 publications. Together with the main volume and the first and second supplements, the guide now has a total of about 10,900 entries. The list of reviewing media has been considerably expanded; there are references to *Library Journal*, *New York Times Book Review*, *Library of Congress Information Bulletin*, and even *Papers of Bibliographical Society of America*— a total of 15 journals, compared to four in the second edition.

Omission of important titles is, as ever, a problem. The first area selected for examination was philosophy. This third supplement provides 11 titles; all but three were published abroad. Omitted are important works with both American and foreign imprints: Jon Wetlesen's *A Spinoza Bibliography* (Oslo, Universitetsforlaget, 1968; distributed here by Humanities, 1970) and, more importantly, John Lachs's *Marxist Philosophy: A Bibliographical Guide* (University of North Carolina). The section on religion has more entries (a total of 39). Among other things, there is an entry for the well-known *Sacramentum Mundi: An Encyclopedia of Theology* (Herder and Herder), a six-volume work published simultaneously in English, German, French, Italian, and Dutch. The editor for this work, however, is not indicated. In addition, some of the works not included are *Dictionary of Comparative Religion*, edited by S. G. I. Brandon (Scribner's, 1970) and the monumental *Broadman Bible Commentary*, published in 12 volumes and edited by Clifton J. Allen. This project started in 1969, with six volumes published during that year. The listing of important omissions can be continued in such broad areas as history, literature, and education.

Winchell is simply too important to limit a review to laudatory comments, as is traditionally done in library literature. One can question, for example, both its structure, with a minimum of critical comments, and its criteria for selection, which do not necessarily reflect some of the dynamic changes in informational needs. In other words, Winchell may offer too little, considering the quality and quantity of reference resources available today.

In addition to problems already noted, government publications are slighted. In this respect, Winchell provides only token coverage of GPO imprints, not to mention foreign government publications. For the latter, in general, Winchell's percentage of coverage is considerably lower than coverage of domestic material. From the quantitative point of view, humanities and social sciences receive more balanced coverage (linguistics is one exception), while sciences are not as well represented. Technology is probably the weakest part in Winchell. The coverage of national bibliographies, obviously the most important type of publications for guides like Winchell, is inadequate.

For materials which are listed in Winchell, the bibliographical data are usually accurate, but information about reprint editions is seldom indicated. Most annotations are brief; they are descriptive, but seldom critical. Particularly for more important works, there is a need to provide critical comments and comparisons. If this were done, Winchell would be much more likely to succeed in reaching its stated objectives.

One last comment of a general nature. Many titles listed in the main volume of Winchell have only a sentimental value. They could be safely removed into a "historical volume," which would allow the much-needed expansion and updating of this reference guide. —Bohdan S. Wynar. [R: LJ, Aug 70; AL, July-Aug 70; WLB, Oct 70; ARBA 71, item 7; ARBA 73, item 5]

5. Walford, A. J., ed. **Guide to Reference Material. Volume 3, Generalities, Languages, the Arts, and Literature.** 2nd ed. London, Library Association; distr. New York, R. R. Bowker, 1970. 585p. index. $14.50. LC 66-71608. ISBN 0-85365-222-8.

The first edition of this standard work was published in 1959, and its supplement in 1963. This third volume completes the set in its new edition. Volume 1, *Science and Technology*, was published in 1966 (483p.) including 3,000 entries arranged by the Universal Decimal Classification. Volume 2, *Philosophy and Psychology, Religion, Social Sciences, Geography, Biography and History* (543p.), was published in 1968, with about 3,300 entries. The present volume has annotated entries for about 5,000 reference books, constituting a 50 percent increase in corresponding sections of the first edition and its supplement.

Walford's *Guide* is, for all practical purposes, a British counterpart to our Winchell, and some comparison might be in order. Winchell and its two supplements list 9,700 entries, compared to 11,300 in Walford (a combined total for the three volumes). Secondly, beginning with this new edition, Walford provides in its annotations references to related works—e.g., in the first volume one finds 1,000 such "subsumed entries," while the second and third volume each contain 1,500. These subsumed entries are also listed in the index. This combination of main entries and subsumed entries substantially increases the coverage of reference titles found in Walford; in this respect, Winchell offers much less.

In examining several sections of the third volume, we have the impression that Walford covers practically the same number of American imprints but that his coverage of British titles, reference books published in Europe, or even non-European titles, is about twice that offered by Winchell. With respect to government publications, the coverage of American imprints in Walford is much more comprehensive and their descriptions more up-to-date. Both Winchell and Walford offer descriptive annotations; Walford's annotations occasionally are somewhat longer. In the preface, it is stated that "in general this volume contains entries for items published up to the end of October 1969. Some later material has been noted at galley-proof stage, as far as possible up to March 1970, including announcements of forthcoming books." Unfortunately, this is not always true; we are more inclined to say that many 1969 American imprints are not included. It should be noted that Walford frequently provides information about existing reprints (usually published before 1969)—a policy that would be desirable for Winchell. Obviously, even with some omissions of 1969 imprints (this fact per se is not important, and we examined this particular aspect only because of the statement in the introduction), it seems that Walford is a somewhat better balanced work than Winchell, and it is certainly much more comprehensive. —Bohdan S. Wynar. [R: RQ, Fall 71, p. 84; WLB, Apr 71, p. 789; ARBA 72, item 6]

6. Wynar, Bohdan S., ed. **Reference Books in Paperback: An Annotated Guide.** Littleton, Colo., Libraries Unlimited, 1972. 199p. index. $7.50; $4.75pa. LC 74-189257. ISBN 0-87287-046-4.

WLB provided an "A" rating for this book; we quote the review in its entirety: "*Reference Books in Paperback* is a classified, annotated list of 675 reference works available in paperback. All subject fields and levels of sophistication are represented. The annotations provide descriptions of the works, as well as pointed critical comments and indications of potential uses. Reviews in reviewing journals are frequently cited. For most uses greater selectivity might have improved the work (e.g., *Flowers of Point Reyes National Seashore* seems somewhat out of place here). However such a guide has been needed for a long time, and this one will be useful to libraries attempting to build economical reference collections and to reference librarians helping patrons choose inexpensive reference tools (a sizeable home reference collection could be tailored to the needs of a family for the price of an encyclopedia)." [R: WLB, Dec 72, p. 364; LJ, 1 Jan 73, p. 52; ALA 72; ARBA 73, item 6]

NATIONAL AND TRADE BIBLIOGRAPHIES: UNITED STATES

7. **A Checklist of American Imprints, 1820-1829. Title Index. Author Index.** Comp. by M. Frances Cooper. Metuchen, N.J., Scarecrow, 1972, 1973. 562p. 172p. $17.00 (Title Index); $7.00 (Author Index). ISBN 0-8108-0513-8 (Title Index); 0-8108-0567-7 (Author Index).

8. **A Checklist of American Imprints for 1831.** Comp. by Scott Bruntjen and Carol Bruntjen. Metuchen, N.J., Scarecrow, 1975. 429p. $15.00. LC 64-11784. ISBN 0-8108-0828-5.

It is 18 years since the first volume of *American Imprints*, familiarly known as Shaw and Shoemaker, appeared. The aim of its initial compilers, Ralph Shaw and Richard Shoemaker, was to fill the gap in American national bibliography by continuing the work begun by Charles Evans. Shaw and Shoemaker's first volume covered the year 1801 and their series continued to cover each year through 1819. At this point, Shaw dropped out of the project and Shoemaker continued the work. As each volume from 1820 to 1825 appeared, Shoemaker modified the original precept of the project, which had been to depend solely upon printed sources and catalogs for compiling entries. This policy had led to numerous duplications of titles and the listing of nonexistent ones. From the 1821 volume and continuing, in addition to noting author, title, place of publication and publisher, selected locations of books were added and, for rare titles, actual copies were examined. This approach resulted in improved reliability and usefulness of the *Checklist* as a reference tool. Shoemaker died in 1970, before he could complete the volumes for 1828 and 1829. These volumes and that for 1830 were seen through the press by Dr. Gayle Cooper. The series is now in the hands of Scott and Carol Bruntjen. The work will be continued until it covers the years through 1875, when it will be complete.

The *Title Index* for 1820-1829 was compiled by M. Frances Cooper and published in 1972. It affords easy access to the more than 41,000 entries in the *Checklist* for the years covered. The *Author Index*, also compiled by M. Frances Cooper, was published in 1973 and follows the example set by Shaw and Shoemaker in their index to *American Biography*. Over 500 corrections deal with duplicate entries, multiple listings, misdatings, etc.

The volume for 1831, compiled by the Bruntjens, was published in 1975 and follows the format of previous volumes. The compilers have examined few of the items listed in the *Checklist*. Nevertheless, this series has long been considered an important tool in American bibliography and this volume is no exception. [R: ARBA 73, item 11; ARBA 76, item 8]

9. Shipton, Clifford K., and James E. Mooney. **National Index of American Imprints through 1800: The Short-Title Evans.** Worcester, Mass., American Anti-quarian Society and Barre Publishers, 1969. 2v. 1028p. $45.00. LC 69-11248. ISBN 0-8271-6908-6.

This compilation is a great boon to all students of American culture. It is a by-product of the Early American Microprint Project, which undertook to reproduce on micro-card all non-serial works printed in America before 1801. The basic guide or index for this project was Charles Evans's *American Bibliography*, which listed 39,162 items for this period. But the percentage of "ghosts" listed by Evans was estimated to be 1 in 10 and, in the intervening years since its publication, an additional 10,035 titles had turned up. The project underlined the need for a less cumbersome and more trustworthy and timely index than that provided by the 13 volumes of Evans. Finally the Microprint cards themselves provided the means by which such an index could be produced.

The *National Index*, handsomely bound on good paper and supervised by the leading authority in the field, is, in essence, an inventory. The compilers' rigid insistence on examining the books directly has laid many ghosts and has enabled the compilers to correct title mistranscriptions, remove faulty attributions, and incorporate much new information. The 49,197 entries are arranged in a single alphabetical list, including short titles, places of publication, dates, a single location, the Evans number, and, in many cases, a brief note on attributions, imperfect copies, or unlocated items. Of course, more titles will turn up for this period, but "not in Evans" will now be superseded by "not in the *National Index*," thus paying tribute to a work which measures up to the standards we associate with the American Antiquarian Society. —Charles W. Mann. [R: ARBA 71, item 14]

10. Thompson, Lawrence S., ed. **The New Sabin: Books Described by Joseph Sabin and His Successors, Now Described Again on the Basis of Examination of Originals, and Fully Indexed by Title, Subject, Joint Authors and Institutions and Agencies.** Troy, N.Y., Whitston, 1974. 1v. in 2 pts. $25.00(pt.1); $10.00(pt.2). LC 73-85960. ISBN 0-87875-049-5(pt.1); 0-87875-050-9(pt.2).

In 1868, Joseph Sabin inaugurated his *Dictionary of Books Relating to America*, which became the most important bibliographical monument in American historiography. This two-part volume is the first of a projected series that will expand Sabin's earlier work to include entries from additional and specialized listings in other bibliographic works (both American and foreign). It lists items in the modern bibliographic form, following the practice adopted by the Library of Congress. All the entries given in the first part have been inspected by the compiler, either in the original or in microfilm form.

The second part of Volume 1 provides index access to these same entries, allowing one to search by "joint author," title, subject (drawn primarily from the entries on the LC cards), institutions, and agencies. This index, to be cumulated as new volumes appear, is regarded by the compiler as *The New Sabin*'s most important innovation, and it may be so regarded by the user as well, since it facilitates the scholar's bibliographic tasks. —Jesse H. Shera. [R: Choice, Oct 74, p. 1114; ARBA 75, item 5]

PERIODICALS AND SERIALS

11. Katz, Bill. **Magazines for Libraries: For the General Reader, and School, Junior College, College, and Public Libraries.** 2nd ed. New York, R. R. Bowker, 1972. 822p. index. $24.50. LC 72-6607. ISBN 0-8352-0554-1.

12. Katz, Bill. **Magazines for Libraries: For the General Reader, and School, Junior College, College, and Public Libraries.** 2nd ed. **Supplement.** Berry Gargal, science ed. New York, R. R. Bowker, 1974. 328p. index. $16.50. LC 72-6607. ISBN 0-8352-0761-7 (suppl.).

Some 4,500 titles are annotated in this new edition, as compared to approximately 2,400 titles represented in the first edition, which was published in 1969. As the author indicates in the preface, "unless out of business, all magazines included in the first edition are included in the second with updated information. . . . Most annotations in the first edition were carefully checked with the editor and/or publisher for accuracy and fairness. The editor was asked also to comment on the evaluative or descriptive statements. His or her comments were or were not followed, depending on the opinion of the compiler." Apparently the greatest amount of revision was in price (the editors claim an overall increase in price of 30 percent, sometimes more), along with obvious factual data. In addition, there are some new features in this edition, all of them enumerated in an informative introduction. For example, where possible, the word "sample" is included in the bibliographic information to indicate that the publisher is willing to send a free sample of his magazine for examination.

The professional standards of the second edition have been retained in the supplement, which lists 1,800 periodicals and journals. The supplement and the main volume together, then, provide a guide to the contents of 6,300 journals and periodicals, compared to the checklist of some 55,000 titles found in *Ulrich's*. In addition, a combined index to both volumes is found at the end of the supplement, a timesaving device for locating desired information. A number of subject headings used in the main volume have been revised, and there are also some changes in basic arrangement. Most foreign titles published abroad were grouped together in the main volume; in the supplement, however, they are entered under the appropriate subject heading, an obvious improvement. Another innovation consists of brief introductions to sections (e.g., Folklore) to indicate changes in publishing trends. Such introductions are promised for all sections in the third edition. For the most part, the supplement lists new journals and magazines published since the cut-off date of the second edition (i.e., Spring 1972) and up to Spring 1974. In addition, certain titles omitted in the second edition are also listed. There is a list of 54 periodicals that the editors and contributors consider to be among the best published since 1971, plus modifications of the second edition's "recommended" list of indexing and abstracting services.

As indicated in the review of Farber's *Classified List of Periodicals for the College Library*, *Magazines for Libraries* offers many more titles, but then Katz aims at all libraries. In comparing the two books, it should be pointed out that their approaches differ somewhat. Katz offers much more complete bibliographic information and his annotations reflect more recent changes in editorial policy, frequently making comparisons to other magazines of a similar nature. Farber's work, obviously more selective in coverage, offers more information of an historical nature—indicating how a given magazine was started, its first editor, major stages in its editorial growth, etc. Thus, if we can use an oversimplification, the two guides complement each other—providing both an historical perspective and a more "formal" treatment (Farber) and some interesting and occasionally "subjective" insights (Katz) as to the current editorial trend. —Bohdan S. Wynar. [R: ARBA 73, item 25; LJ, 15 Dec 69; WLB, Dec 69; ARBA 75, item 171; LJ, 15 Dec 74, p. 3187]

13. **New Serial Titles: A Union List of Serials Commencing Publication after December 31, 1949; 1950-1970 Cumulative.** Washington, U.S. Library of Congress; New York, R. R. Bowker, 1973. 4v. $220.00. LC 53-60021. ISBN 0-8352-0556-8. ISSN 0028-6680.

The third edition of the *Union List of Serials*, published in five volumes in 1965, contained 156,499 entries for serial titles held by 956 libraries in the United States and Canada. The information was current up to 1949. In 1950 the Library of Congress conceived a plan for putting records of serial holdings on punched cards and the compilation of *New Serial Titles* was first issued in 1951. Today there are more than 800 cooperating libraries in the United States and Canada. Some types of material—such as government documents, annual reports, and house organs—that were not listed in the *Union List* are included in *New Serial Titles*. The serials are arranged alphabetically according to title. The basic publication is issued monthly, with quarterly and annual cumulations, as well as cumulative volumes for the years 1950-60, 1961-65, and 1966-69. This new cumulation supersedes not only the above-mentioned cumulations, but also the quarterly issues for 1970. In addition to this material already available in printed form, the Library of Congress added for this cumulation 43,000 cards containing 13,000 revisions and 200,000 additional library holdings.

Serials are listed under entries prepared in accordance with the rules in the *A.L.A. Cataloging Rules* . . . (2nd ed., 1949) or the *Anglo-American Cataloging Rules*, following generally the form used in the *Union List of Serials*. It is indicated in the introduction that "since the entries for inclusion in this publication often may be prepared prior to their official establishment for cataloging records, new corporate entries appearing in this list may not always agree with the established form adopted subsequently. In such cases, the entries which are affected are revised so that their next appearance in a cumulative issue will be under the heading officially adopted (p. vii). Thus, this cumulation contains a "Changes in Serials" section, covering the 1950-1970 period and including some 25,000 entries.

The following bibliographic data are provided "whenever the information is readily available" (p. vii): title, issuing body (in parentheses following the title in title entries), place of publication, beginning and ending dates, Dewey Decimal

Classification number, library locations and holdings, ISSN, and code for country of publication. Entries for serials published monthly or quarterly also include frequency, address of publisher, and occasionally annual subscription price in the United States. It should be noted, however, that the statement "whenever the information is readily available" means just what it says. Over 50 percent of the entries for serials published quarterly or monthly do not show their frequency, and at least 40 percent of the entries for serials do not show their first year of publication or a closing year. There are adequate cross references—a total of 65,000, according to the description provided on page ix.

In all, this cumulative set has many advantages over the previous cumulations. It will be an indispensable reference tool for larger libraries for years to come—provided, of course, that its binding holds up; the binding, unfortunately, is of rather poor quality for such a heavy set. For a more detailed investigation of the book's physical aspects, see the thorough comments in the *Booklist* review.   —Bohdan S. Wynar. [R: BL, 15 Oct 74, p. 253; Choice, July-Aug 74, p. 740; WLB, May 74, p. 765; ARBA 75, item 41]

14. **New Serial Titles 1950-1970 Subject Guide.** New York, R. R. Bowker, 1975. 2v. $138.50. LC 75-15145. ISBN 0-8352-0820-6. ISSN 0098-2237.

New Serial Titles: 1950-1970 Cumulative has been described as an indispensable reference work for years to come. The same general characterization clearly applies to the present work. However, the *Subject Guide* serves entirely different purposes.

The *Subject Guide* is arranged in modified DDC order. As a requirement of computerization, it was necessary to establish Dewey "ranges." Hence, under 150, Psychology, we are told that this number encompasses DDC numbers 150-159, including behaviorism. Headnotes preceding major number ranges helpfully list "see also" and "see" references by subject and number. Under each subject, entries are arranged first by country alphabetically and within country by title. A main entry for a serial consists of: title, ISSN, one or more DDC numbers, descriptive cataloging, and publication history. Note that entries do not include library locations, for which it is still necessary to consult *New Serial Titles*, in any of its several formats.

Indexing and other user aids include: Country Names and Codes; Subject Headings, Numerical Sequence; Subject Headings; Alphabetical Sequence; Index to Subject Headings; Correlation Table of Dewey Numbers to Subject Headings; Statistical Summaries (by subject and by country).

The reference uses to which this compilation may be put are the verification of a truncated or garbled citation to a serial whose subject or subjects are, however, known; and the identification of pertinent 1950-1970 serial titles as possible information sources. Acquisitions uses include cooperative coordination of purchasing among groups, networks, or consortia of libraries.

It lends itself beautifully to compilation of subject bibliographies, particularly those with a strong orientation to country of origin. It will serve as a research data book. Because of the prominence of the country of origin approach, it provides the raw data from which inferences—potentially significant in several fields of study—can be drawn; as measured by the launching of new serials, how active or productive are the various national groups in identifiable fields of scholarship and research?

In geological sciences, for example, how do the British compare with the French, or the West Germans? The *Subject Guide* is an indispensable resource in attempting to frame answers to such questions. —Richard A. Gray. [R: LJ, 1 Dec 75, p. 2235; ARBA 76, item 26]

PUBLISHING AND BOOKSELLING

DICTIONARIES

15. **The Bookman's Glossary**. 5th ed. Jean Peters, ed. New York, R. R. Bowker, 1975. 169p. bibliog. $10.50. LC 74-28432. ISBN 0-8352-0732-3.

The fourth edition of this work, issued in 1961, had a total of 212 pages, as compared with 169 in the current edition. Pruned from the fifth were all foreign book trade terms. The general orientation remains as it was in previous editions: to record those terms frequently encountered in the American book trade and publishing community. Terms used previously in specialized subfields of that community (e.g., librarianship, printing) are included only to the extent that they have had general adoption by the book world. [R: Choice, Nov 75, pp. 1139-40; C&RL, July 75, p. 318; RQ, Summer 75, p. 350; LJ, 15 Mar 75, p. 570; ARBA 76, item 46]

16. Collins, F. Howard. **Authors and Printers Dictionary**. 11th ed. Rev. by Stanley Beale. New York, Oxford University Press, 1973. 474p. $8.00. ISBN 0-19-211542-1.

The fact that this work is now in its eleventh edition attests to its usefulness and popularity. It has frequently been revised and amended since its first appearance in 1905. Beale has completely revised and updated this edition to make it more useful for the contemporary researcher. The type has been reset and the printing is sharp and clear.

This is a dictionary of usage rather than a dictionary of definition. The entries are in double columns, with boldface roman type for English words and boldface italic type for foreign words and phrases. At the end of each alphabetical section is a blank page for the user's own notes. American and English spellings of words are indicated. A lengthy section under "punctuation" is divided into 15 subsections, which explain the function and usage of all punctuation marks.

This is a very useful work, not only for authors and printers, but for anyone (student, scholar, secretary, etc.) involved in the preparation of typewritten or printed copy. —Frank J. Anderson. [R: ARBA 75, item 51]

PRICE GUIDES

17. **American Book-Prices Current; A Priced Summary of Literary Properties Sold at Auction in England, the United States, and in Canada: Index 1965-1970 for Volumes 72-76**. New York, Columbia University Press, 1974. 2v. $100.00. LC 3-14557. ISBN 0-231-03822-4.

ABPC, whose coverage began in 1895, is a very valuable tool for those trying to establish reasonable prices for older, out-of-print, rare, or collectible works. The catalog is published annually, and every five years there is a cumulated index—an abridgment, in that it is designed primarily as a guide to prices. Included are books, broadsides, serials, maps, charts, autographs, and manuscripts. Items sold at less than $10 are not included; as another footnote to inflation it may be noted that during the period covered in this index (1969-70) the minimum for inclusion was raised from $10.00 to $20.00.

ABPC is in two parts, with autographs and manuscripts in Part 2. There are about 129,000 entries, based on 661 sales from 10 auction houses (Parke-Bernet, Sotheby, etc.) in England, Canada, and the United States. Broadsides and maps, formerly in separate parts, are now incorporated into Part 1. Books are arranged by author (or by title for serials and anonymous works), with the form of entry conforming to relevant national catalogs: the BM, BN, NUC, etc. There are a few entries under notable presses or illustrators, and cross references are used in all problem areas. The preface provides statistical information as well as notes on significant trends and sales of the period. A complete statement on bibliographical policy is contained in the introduction.

The index can be used independently of the annual volumes, but primarily as a guide to prices alone. Details on sales, the auction house, purchaser, bibliographical descriptions, etc., can be found only in the annual volumes. Typography and layout continue to be very good. —Joseph W. Sprug. [R: Choice, Dec 74, p. 1453; ARBA 75, item 61]

18. Bradley, Van Allen. **The Book Collector's Handbook of Values.** New York, Putnam, 1972. 569p. illus. $17.50. LC 75-136795. ISBN 0-399-10905-6.

Bradley, the author of two well-known books, *Gold in Your Attic* (1958) and *More Gold in Your Attic* (1961), has prepared a fairly comprehensive guide to the values of o.p. and rare books. The handbook lists some 15,000 British and American titles published after 1800. Generally speaking, only books with a retail price of over $25.00 are included, and the emphasis is on books in fine condition with original binding. All titles are listed in one alphabetical sequence (under the author, if possible), and entries provide the following information: author's name, title and subtitle, edition statement, place and date of publication, pagination, and the price range.

Since Mr. Bradley uses the title page as his final authority, the user may face some problems in locating a desired item, especially in the case of anonymous and pseudonymous works. In order to establish a reasonable price range, the author has searched and examined catalogs of leading American and British booksellers, as well as the book auction records of the major galleries. (The auction price is indicated with an "A," followed by the auction season concerned.)

All in all, it is a handy compilation for libraries that cannot afford such standard sources as *Bookman's Price Index* or *American Book-Prices Current*. The only serious drawback of this work is the omission of the publisher's name—and it is hoped that this obvious error will be corrected in the next edition. —Bohdan S. Wynar. [R: LJ, 1 Jan 73, p. 65; RQ, Spring 73, p. 311; Choice, Mar 73, p. 56; WLB, Feb 73, p. 520; BL, 15 Jan 73, p. 454; ALA 72; ARBA 74, item 59]

19. Heard, J. Norman, and Jimmie H. Hoover. **Bookman's Guide to Americana**. 6th ed. Metuchen, N.J., Scarecrow, 1971. 368p. $11.00. LC 73-149997. ISBN 0-8108-0397-6.

As in the previous editions, this useful alphabetical compilation of book prices is based on recent catalogs of U.S. dealers in out-of-print Americana. The 7,425 entries do repeat titles from previous editions, but all price quotations are new. The compilers have fashioned a workman-like, middle-brow listing, which, for the most part, does not list those books that find their way to the auction rooms to be duly recorded in *American Book-Prices Current*. In addition, this guide is not confined to the strict, no-nonsense, don't-bother-me-with-the-run-of-the-mill approach of Wright Howe's *US-iana*. The comparatively low price, as contrasted with *US-iana* and *Bookman's Price Index*, is a good feature. BPI is based on the catalogs of 54 dealers in the United States and abroad, whose specialties vary a great deal. Of the 39 dealers whose catalogs are drawn upon by Heard and Hoover, ten are also found in BPI. *Bookman's Guide to Americana* is a good source of prices for thousands of books in the lower-to-medium price range. —Charles W. Mann. [R: WLB, Dec 71, p. 369; RQ, Winter 71, p. 176; ARBA 72, item 54]

20. Mandeville, Mildred S. **The Used Book Price Guide: An Aid in Ascertaining Current Prices**. Kenmore, Wash., Price Guide Publishers, 1972, 1974. 2v. $45.00/set; $37.00/set pa. LC 63-24123. ISBN 0-911182-72-1.

Most order librarians are familiar with *American Book-Prices Current* or *The Bookman's Price Index*. *The Used Book Price Guide* serves a similar purpose, but offers more entries. Some 74,000 books are listed here, with prices based on quotations found in dealers' catalogs (American and some Canadian) for the period 1967 to 1972 (for letters A-K) and 1968 to 1973 (for letters L-Z). Each entry pr 'ides the following information: author, title, place of publication, date, size, type of binding, condition, dealer's code number, and price. Smaller libraries may still use Bradley's *The Book Collector's Handbook of Values* (Putnam, 1972), which lists some 15,000 British and American titles published after 1800 with a retail price of over $25.00. [R: LJ, 15 June 74, p. 1692; WLB, June 74, pp. 850-51; ARBA 75, item 62]

BOOK COLLECTING

21. Tanselle, G. Thomas. **Guide to the Study of United States Imprints**. Cambridge, Mass., Harvard University Press, 1971. 2v. index. $40.00. LC 79-143232. ISBN 0-674-36761-8.

This comprehensive work, prepared in the tradition of McMurtrie's record of American imprints, will serve as a standard guide to the study of the principal material dealing with printing and publishing in this country. The material is arranged in nine broad subject categories: regional lists (imprints of particular localities); genre lists (arranged by types, e.g., accounting books, almanacs, architecture books); author lists (subdivided by localities); copyright records; catalogues; book trade directories; and "supplementary studies" listing studies of individual printers and publishers, general studies, and checklists of secondary material. The appendix provides a listing of 250 titles that constitute a basic collection on this subject. As one would expect in a work of this type, the basic approach is chronological, and the bibliographical description of all titles listed is, of course, complete. There is an excellent index to facilitate the use of this work, which should be of interest to many libraries as well as to scholars of American civilization as represented in the printed word. Needless to say, the enormous value of this guide is only emphasized by the fact that, in spite of the great bulk of research in this field during the last decade, there is nothing comparable to this guide, which was prepared in accordance with sound principles of scholarship. —Bohdan S. Wynar. [ALA 72; ARBA 72, item 55]

ENCYCLOPEDIAS

22. **The Cadillac Modern Encyclopedia.** Max S. Shapiro, exec. ed. William Jaber, managing ed. New York, Cadillac Publishing Co.; distr. Secaucus, N.J., Derbibooks, 1973. 1954p. illus.(part col.). maps. index. $24.95. LC 73-81377. ISBN 0-87445-000-4.

Designed for schools or homes, the *Cadillac Modern Encyclopedia* emphasizes "subjects most often included in American school curricula at all levels, from junior high school through college" (Preface). Most of the 18,000 entries are brief (100 words or so), but a few survey-type articles are a little longer. The well-designed page layout, which is clear and easy to read, consists of two columns, with entries in bold-face capital letters. Cross references are in small capital letters. A 300-page "Special Reference Section" contains tables that cover everything from philosophers (a comparative life-span chart) to logarithms of trigonometric functions. This section is the only indexed part of the encyclopedia. Some articles have bibliographies (usually only two or three citations); none are signed. [ARBA 75, item 73]

23. **The Lincoln Library of Essential Information.** 35th rev. ed. Columbus, Ohio, Frontier Press, 1972. 2v. illus.(part col.). index. $59.95. LC 24-14708.

Since its establishment in 1924, the Lincoln Library has had two aims—to be a self-instruction device for general cultural information, and to serve as an effective, fundamental daily reference for basic information.

Articles are grouped by specific subject fields into 12 divisions. An explanatory note setting forth the scope, importance, and usefulness of a subject precedes each major topic. Within the large divisions material is organized either chronologically, geographically, or topically. Specific points and supplementary information can easily be located through the detailed "Cross Reference Index." The editors claim that the subject arrangement avoids the duplication of material which is inherent in an alphabetical arrangement.

Fourteen editors and some 75 contributors are responsible for the Lincoln Library's articles; although the articles are not signed, the areas of contribution of each author are clearly defined.

Information is clearly and concisely presented in the text, with many charts, diagrams, and tables. The indexing system includes 76 pages of approximately 25,000 entries. To supplement each major section, there are several thousand review test questions useful for measuring comprehension. Definitions of terms are included with many subjects.

The quality of some 1,000 illustrations is not very good. Many of the plates are duplications of works which were used during the early 1900s. The color lacks quality in detail and clearness, as do many of the black and white photographs.

The Lincoln Library has particularly strong sections on literature and the fine arts, including a full exposition on music and a valuable major section on education. The biography section discusses over 4,000 of the world's most noted men and women. Also included are valuable charts and lists, such as Nobel Prize winners, tables of literature, and genealogy of royal families. For condensation, and often for side-by-side comparison, a tabular presentation of information is used. The Lincoln Library frequently uses this method not only for statistical data, but for other facts which may be grouped to indicate relationships or chronological sequence. All in all, this is an excellent two-volume encyclopedia. —Bohdan S. Wynar. [R: ARBA 73, item 206]

24. **The New Columbia Encyclopedia**. 4th ed. Ed. by William H. Harris and Judith S. Levey. New York, Columbia University Press; distr. Philadelphia, J. B. Lippincott, 1975. 3052p. illus. $79.50. LC 74-26686. ISBN 0-231-03572-1.

Since the publication of its first edition in 1935, the *Columbia Eneyclopedia* has been committed to the ideal of an accurate, current volume of general reference. Until the fourth edition, however, it did not attempt to provide information for specialists in their areas of expertise—no one-volume work could possibly do that—it does now offer far more detailed expositions of scientific processes and theories than it did in editions one, two, and three (1935, 1950, and 1963, respectively).

In their introduction, the editors claim to be current as of January 1975. In general, this claim is validated by sample testing. Articles on Vietnam, Watergate, U.S.-Chinese relations, and Nobel prizes are current as of the end of 1974. Bibliographies are equally current, although citations are not as complete as librarians usually wish them to be.

Maps, placed as close as possible to relevant textual material, are clear and illuminating, as are diagrams, charts, and tables.

This edition is an excellent home reference work, but it is important as a library reference tool as well. Its subject entries are discrete and precise and its brief discussions serve effectively as a first-order entree into a field of study both for the reference librarian and for the library user. —Richard A. Gray. [R: Choice, Dec 75, p. 1292; LJ, 1 July 75, p. 1309; WLB, Nov 75, p. 263; ARBA 76, item 60]

DIRECTORIES

25. **Awards, Honors, and Prizes. Volume 1, United States and Canada. Volume 2, International and Foreign.** 3rd ed. Paul Wasserman, managing ed. Detroit, Gale, 1975. 2v. index. $38.00 (v.1); $48.00 (v.2). LC 75-4632. ISBN 0-8103-0376-0 (v.1); 0-8103-0377-9 (v.2).

These volumes list more than 7,000 awards, honors, and prizes in advertising, art, business, government, finance, science, education, engineering, literature, technology, sports, religion, public affairs, radio and television, politics, librarianship, fashion, medicine, law, publishing, international affairs, transportation, architecture, journalism, motion pictures, music, photography, theatre and performing arts.

Excluded are scholarships, fellowships, study grants, awards given for entering or winning a contest, and dynastic and family orders.

In the first volume, awards are listed under name of awarding organization, under distinctive name of awards, and under subject. The latter list is copiously cross-referenced. The second volume has three main sections: international awards, national awards, and indexes. The international section is arranged in classified order, duplicating that of Volume 1. National awards are arranged first by country and then by broad field—e.g., art, culture, history, etc.

Information for both volumes is obtained from the sponsor and, sometimes, from secondary sources. The information provided varies, but it usually includes address, exact title of award, purpose, form (medal, money, etc.), frequency, and date of establishment. A few discontinued awards are retained with date of discontinuance given.

The editor acknowledges that his second volume is seriously incomplete, but argues that this is inevitable in a first attempt to document awards on an international basis. [R: ARBA 76, items 71-72]

26. **Encyclopedia of Associations. Volume 1, National Organizations of the United States. Volume 2, Geographic and Executive Index. Volume 3, New Associations and Projects.** 9th ed. Margaret Fisk, ed. Detroit, Gale, 1975. 3v. (Vol. 3 issued periodically, looseleaf.) index. $55.00 (v.1); $38.00 (v.2); $48.00 (v.3). LC 74-22265.

Of the 14,563 entries in Volume 1, the basic volume, more than 12,600 contain full descriptions of active organizations. The remaining number are listings for inactive or defunct groups. Active organizations are arranged in 17 subject categories: Trade, Business and Commercial Organizations; Agricultural Organizations and Commodity Exchanges; Governmental, Public Administration, Military and Legal Organizations; Scientific, Engineering and Technical Organizations; Educational Organizations; Cultural Organizations; Health and Medical Organizations; Athletic and Sports Organizations; Labor Unions; Public Affairs Organizations; Fraternal, Foreign Interest, Nationality and Ethnic Organizations; Religious Organizations; Veterans, Hereditary and Patriotic Organizations; Hobby and Avocational Organizations; Social Welfare Organizations; Chambers of Commerce; and Greek Letter Societies. Information in each entry includes the group's name, address, chief executive, phone number, purpose and activities, membership, publications, convention schedule, etc.

Volume 2 is divided into two sections. The Geographic Index rearranges the entries in Volume 1 by state and city, providing access to associations on a geographic basis and listing addresses, phone numbers, and names of executives. The Executive Index lists all the executives who appear in Volume 1, arranging them alphabetically by surname and including their titles, names of the organizations they head, addresses, and phone numbers. Each entry in each section of Volume 2 is cross-referenced to the main informational entry in Volume 1.

Volume 3 updates Volume 1 on a periodical basis, providing the same information found in Volume 1 for new organizations. [R: ARBA 71, item 165; ARBA 73, item 196]

27. **The Foundation Directory**. 5th ed. Ed. by Marianna O. Lewis. New York, The Foundation Center; distr. New York, Columbia University Press, 1975. 516p. index. $30.00. LC 60-13807. ISBN 0-87954-005-2.

The fifth edition of *The Foundation Directory* was prepared from a computer file; this marks the first time that a volume in this series has been prepared in such a way. Due to computer assistance, it is anticipated that new editions of the *Directory* will appear biennially.

This edition lists 2,533 foundations—2,921 entries fewer than in the fourth edition, a reflection of changes in criteria, which have increased the amounts of assets and expenditures a foundation must have in order to qualify. A foundation is defined as "a nongovernmental, nonprofit organization, with funds and program managed by its own trustees or directors, and established to maintain or aid social, educational, charitable, religious, or other activities serving the common welfare, primarily through the making of grants. Both charitable trusts and corporations are included. Excluded are organizations . . . whose primary purposes are other than the awarding of grants . . . [which act] as trade associations for industrial or other special groups; or which are restricted by charter solely to aiding one or several named institutions; or which function as endowments set up for special purposes within colleges, churches, or other organizations and are governed by the trustees of the parent institution." There are three general criteria for inclusion: 1) the organization must meet the Center's definition of a foundation and, if it qualifies, in the year of record, it must 2) have assets of one million dollars or more, or 3) have made total contributions of one-half million dollars or more. These last two criteria have substantially decreased the number of foundations that qualify, as mentioned above. In the fourth edition of the *Directory*, assets had to be $500,000 or more and contributions had to be $25,000 or more; the comparable sums for the fifth edition are $1,000,000 and $500,000, respectively. Private operating foundations also have grant-making programs, and community foundations are also included if they meet the general criteria.

Arrangement is by state, and there are four indexes: by field of interest, by cities within states, by donors, trustees, and administrators, and by foundation name. Information provided for foundations includes: name, address, donors, purpose and activities, assets and expenditures, names and titles of officials, field(s) of interest, and limitations. There are two primary sources of information for the *Directory*: 1) reports voluntarily submitted directly to the Center by foundations, and 2) Internal Revenue Service files of information returns submitted annually by private foundations. Information gleaned from the latter source is subject to a one and one-half year processing period before it becomes available, so it may be outdated by the time it is available in the *Directory*. Four supplements to the fifth edition are planned before issuance of the sixth edition in 1977. —Peggy Jay. [R: ARBA 73, item 197 (4th ed.); ARBA 76, item 620 (5th ed.)]

28. Hudson, Kenneth, and Ann Nicholls. **The Directory of World Museums**. New York, Columbia University Press, 1975. 864p. bibliog. index. $65.00 LC 74-21772. ISBN 0-231-03907-7.

Before reading the editors' delightful introduction, this reviewer had no clear idea of how extraordinarily difficult it is to define "museum" in a logically satisfying way. On reflection, however, it is obvious that numerous criteria intrude to deflect the cause of rigorous definition. Among these are permanence (of staff, of establishment, of collections) and animation versus physicality (e.g., are zoos and botanical gardens museums?).

The editors report beautifully on their struggles in the realm of defining logic, and then they give us six precisely defined negative criteria. The 22,000 institutions that survived the exclusionary thrusts of the following are the ones included: 1) no museum without a permanent collection; 2) no zoos or botanical gardens; 3) no historic houses without appropriate furnishings; 4) no historic site which is only a historic site; 5) no collection which exists solely for purposes of propaganda (e.g., The Turkish Museum of Greek Atrocities in Cyprus); 6) no collection without a serious collection (e.g., Ripley's "Believe It or Not" Museums in the United States).

Entries are arranged by country, then by city, and then alphabetically by *English* name. Specific informational elements in each entry are address, brief characterization of holdings, and hours of opening. Most country sections are preceded by a brief essay describing or explaining the state of museums in that country.

This directory had the full cooperation of the International Council of Museums in Paris. It is certainly the most comprehensive directory of its kind ever to be issued. Moreover, its reference value is greatly enhanced by a lengthy and minutely detailed classified index of specialized and outstanding collections, according to which it is possible to identify museums by every conceivable field of special collecting interest.

The work is subject to negative criticism on only one ground. The basic arrangement is by country, then by city. This principle of arrangement works well for most countries—there is, after all, only one London, one Paris, and one Nuremburg. But applied to the United States (itself a massive section containing about one fourth of the 22,000 entries), it causes inconveniences. A case in point is Rochester. There is, as it happens, a Rochester in Michigan, one in Minnesota, and still another in New York. The result is that all museums in all three cities are interfiled in one alphabetic sequence. It would appear that U.S. entries require a modification of the arrangement scheme—to state and then city. Irritating though it may be to users, this is a minor flaw in an excellent reference book. —Richard A. Gray. [R: WLB, May 75, p. 673; LJ, 15 Apr 75, p. 746; Choice, Oct 75, p. 980; ARBA 76, item 67]

HANDBOOKS

29. Bauer, Andrew, comp. **The Hawthorn Dictionary of Pseudonyms.** New York, Hawthorn Books, 1971. 312p. $12.95. LC 73-107900.

A reference handbook providing nearly 10,000 entries for real names and pennames, pseudonyms, cognomens, abbreviations, latinizations, etc., of prominent writers, public officials, philosophers, artists, and some scientists.

A typical entry will illustrate the treatment employed in this handbook: "Mehta, Rustam Jehangir (1912–). Indian writer, whose pseudonyms are Roger Hartman, R. Johnson Martin, and Plutonius." The coverage is adequate, with the possible exception of Eastern-European writers, primarily in the Soviet Union. We are referring here to the "intellectual underground" and works published in *Samizdat*, frequently under pseudonyms. The reader will find practically nothing about these writers, some of them rather prominent and well known in the West. [R: ALA 71; ARBA 72, item 1314]

30. Sharp, Harold S., comp. **Handbook of Pseudonyms and Personal Nicknames.** Metuchen, N.J., Scarecrow, 1972. 2v. $30.00. LC 71-189886. ISBN 0-8108-0460-3.

31. Sharp, Harold S., comp. **Handbook of Pseudonyms and Personal Nicknames: First Supplement.** Metuchen, N.J., Scarecrow, 1975. 2v. $35.00. LC 71-189886. ISBN 0-8108-0807-2.

A retired professor of library science at Indiana State University, known to reference librarians for his *Index to Characters in the Performing Arts*, has assembled this list of pseudonyms and personal nicknames. It includes in one alphabetical sequence approximately 15,000 real-name entries and about 25,000 nicknames and/or pseudonyms, most of them from the Western world, ranging in time from Aristides (c.530-468 B.C.) to Willie Mays. No authority is cited for the information given for the real names, and since the work must have extended over some years, a few dates of death are not noted, as in the case of E. L. Arnold, 1856– , and Frederick A. Atkins, 1864– , surely no longer with us. If the letter A is an adequate sampling, about a third of the main entries are authors, while among the rest are actors, musicians, popes, saints, kings, statesmen, bullfighters, military men, and many sports figures. Occasionally conflicting information will be found, as for Ira Albridge (c.1810-67) and Ira Aldridge (c.1810-66), both identified as Negro tragedians, both with the nickname "The African Roscius," though only the latter is listed under "African Roscius" or "Roscius, The African," in this otherwise heavily cross-referenced handbook. The compiler laments the "substantial number of discrepancies in the birth dates as reported by various standard reference sources." This is the only clue to sources used, though it is obvious that many of the entries were found elsewhere. But in spite of these rather picky criticisms, this will be a ready source for pseudonyms used by dime novelists, for the many nicknames given to Hiram Ulysses Grant, better known as Ulysses S. Grant, and for the real names of many contemporary figures in the performing arts. Though Winchell lists Shankle's well-known *American Nicknames*, as well as about 40 reference books on the authorship of anonymous and pseudonymous books, no one volume is as comprehensive as this. The supplement lists 18,000 real names and some 30,000 nicknames or pseudonyms. –Frances Neel Cheney. [R: Choice, May 73, p. 433; WLB, Apr 73, p. 703; ALA 73; ARBA 74, item 117 (main vol.); ARBA 76, item 451 (suppl.)]

32. Showers, Victor. **The World in Figures.** New York, Wiley, 1973. 585p. illus. bibliog. index. $16.50. LC 73-9. ISBN 0-471-78859-7.

A valuable digest of significant, authoritative, and comparative statistical data presented in over 40 tables and covering about 250 countries, 1,600 cities, and 2,000 other geographic and cultural features. The first part, a "world's records" section, includes comparative statistical data on the largest, longest, or highest natural and man-made features in the following categories: continents, countries, cities, seas, islands, rivers, natural lakes, waterfalls, mountains, buildings, bridges, tunnels, dams, universities, and libraries. It provides comparative demographic data on the amount and density of population, and the highest and lowest birth and death rates and life expectancy. It presents comparative climatic data on the warmest, coolest, driest, and wettest cities. For some categories, data are provided by continent and individual countries.

The second part consists of tabular gazetteers, with the following data for individual countries, grouped by continent: area, latest population count and density; trends in population since 1800; vital statistics on birth, death, and life expectancy; transportation data on highways and railroads. A second section provides the following data on leading cities arranged by continent and country: date of settlement, current population and trend since 1800; geographic and climatic data (including latitude and longitude, temperature, and precipitation).

Measurements are given in both English and metric units, and temperature in Fahrenheit and centigrade. Conventional names in English are used, but these are supplemented by official names, if they are different. Alternate and former names are also given, which is another useful feature.

The title should perhaps be "World in Numbers," since the work emphasizes presentation of numerical data in tabular form. Indeed, the author uses the term "figure" in the text to designate and number his 37 illustrations, which are charts and, primarily, photographs. —LeRoy C. Schwarzkopf. [R: BL, 15 Nov 74, p. 352; Choice, Mar 74, p. 64; ARBA 75, item 86]

ALTERNATIVE INFORMATION SOURCES

33. Danky, James P. **Undergrounds: A Union List of Alternative Periodicals in Libraries of the United States and Canada.** Madison, State Historical Society of Wisconsin, 1974. 206p. illus. index. $12.95pa. LC 74-8272. ISBN 0-87020-142-5.

Some 2,500 to 3,000 periodicals are listed alphabetically by title, with cross references from alternative titles and, occasionally, from the publisher.

The list was compiled from lists provided by 180 cooperating libraries and from 20 bibliographies. The Wisconsin Historical Society has the largest collection of alternative periodicals. Danky's definition of the term is purposely broad—"one that is politically and culturally to the left of center; i.e., a publication that expresses views not normally presented in the daily press."

Most entries provide at least one location. However, some give only a citation from one of the bibliographies, such as Noel Peattie's *Sipapu.* There is no indication of library holdings, publishers' addresses, etc.

There is a geographical index by state and city for the United States; by province and city for Canada, in a separate alphabet; and by country and city, in a third alphabet, for the rest of the world. There are about 250 publications listed for countries outside the United States and Canada. Many of these have English titles and are apparently American servicemen's or ex-patriots' publications.

This is without a doubt the most complete list of alternative publications available and, as such, is of great importance. One wishes, though, that the dates of holdings of the libraries could have been shown, at least in a general way. —David W. Brunton. [R: AL, Oct 74, p. 498; ARBA 75, item 99]

34. Muller, Robert H. and others. **From Radical Left to Extreme Right.** 2nd ed., rev. and enl. Vol. 1. Ann Arbor, Mich., Campus Publishers, 1970. 510p. $14.75; $13.75pa. LC 79-126558.

35. Spahn, Theodore Jurgen, Janet M. Spahn, and Robert H. Muller. **From Radical Left to Extreme Right: A Bibliography of Current Periodicals of Protest, Controversy, Advocacy, or Dissent, with Dispassionate Content-Summaries to**

Guide Librarians and Other Educators. Vol. 2. 2nd ed. rev. and enl. Metuchen, N.J., Scarecrow, 1972. 504p. index. $13.50. LC 79-126558. ISBN 0-8108-0470-0.

The first edition of this title was published in 1967. The scope of this second edition is indicated by the subtitle above. Volume 1 describes 402 periodical titles and Volume 2 covers an additional 272; entries are arranged under broad subject categories (e.g., Marxist-Socialist Left, civil rights, peace, anarchist, anti-communist, women's liberation, etc.). Each entry includes most of the following information: name of publication, editor, address, frequency, date publication began, circulation, format, and issue(s) examined in preparing the "content-summaries." Each article gives a detailed description of contents, comments on editorial policy, and "feedback" information from the publication's sponsor who has commented on the bibliographic information and "content-summaries" prior to publication in this book. In this respect, the directory is as reliable as one can make it, considering the type of material covered. Each volume has two indexes: a geographical index and an index of titles, editors, publishers, and opinions. The geographical index is confined to periodicals reviewed in the particular volume. The main index in Volume 2 repeats the titles (but not the editors, etc.) of periodicals that were reviewed in Volume 1. Many important titles, primarily those published in languages other than English by ethnic minorities in this country, are not included.

Some of the editorial work was supported by a faculty research grant from the Horace H. Rackham School of Graduate Studies of the University of Michigan, and all of the editors and a number of contributors have graduate degrees in library science. This is the best publication on the subject; it serves as a good model for similar compilations. [R: WLB, Oct 70; AL, May 72, p. 557; WLB, June 72, p. 928; ARBA 71, item 45; ARBA 73, item 26]

36. **The (Updated) Last Whole Earth Catalog.** 16th ed. Sausalito, Calif., Whole Earth; distr. Baltimore, Penguin Books, 1975. 442p. illus. index. $6.00pa. LC 75-22894. ISBN 0-14-003544-3.

This sixteenth edition updates *The Last Whole Earth Catalog* (distr. New York, Random House, 1971) to June 1975; it is cross-referenced to the *Whole Earth Epilog* (distr. Baltimore, Penguin, 1974); and it adds a combined index to these two.

Major sections of *The (Updated) Last Whole Earth Catalog* include: Whole Systems, Land Use, Shelter, Industry, Craft, Community, Nomadics, Communication, and Learning, with the usual photographs, sketches, descriptions, reviews, and access information for the items included. This catalog does not re-evaluate items, but it does update access information (addresses, prices, etc.). New items have been added, but defunct items remain, in most cases. The index covers subjects, articles, titles, and individual items. Format remains nearly the same, with only minor changes. This edition's "work of drama" is "Divine Right's Trip" by Gurney Norman.

The New Earth Catalog (New York, Putnam, 1973) represents one attempt to cash in on the success of the Whole Earth series. While it is an interesting collection of information, it seems to lack any unity of purpose, so the result is something of a hodgepodge. [R: ARBA 76, item 81]

GOVERNMENT PUBLICATIONS

37. Andriot, John L. **Guide to U.S. Government Serials and Periodicals.** 1971 ed. McLean, Va., Documents Index, 1971. 4v. (in 3). index. $60.00pa. LC 75-7027.

First published in 1962, this annual publication is probably familiar to all documents librarians. The 1971 edition is different in many ways from earlier editions. Volume 1, "U.S. Government Agencies, An Authority File and Superintendent of Documents Classification Outline," is called a "bonus to subscribers of the 1971 edition" (Introduction, Vol. 1). The first section contains an alphabetical listing of 2,216 government agencies, committees, etc., with a brief history of each. The publishers expect this to be expanded and sold separately in the future. Volume 2 lists serial publications of current government agencies. Volume 3 lists those of agencies which have been abolished or superseded. These two volumes are arranged by Su-Docs numbers. It should be noted that there is no designation for serials which have ceased publication (see entry for *World List of Future International Meetings*). Volume 4 contains an agency and title index. Many typographical errors and unevenness in the amount of information given per entry are drawbacks. It is hoped that more careful editing in future editions will improve this worthy contribution to bibliographical control of government documents. —Sally Wynkoop. [R: ARBA 72, item 203]

38. **Bibliography of Publications Issued by Unesco or under Its Auspices; The First Twenty-Five Years: 1946 to 1971.** Paris, Unesco, 1973; distr. New York, Unipub, 1973. 385p. index. $9.90. ISBN 92-3-001037-5.

"This bibliography lists all works known to have been produced throughout the world with the assistance of Unesco, whether published by the organization itself, or under its auspices, from the foundation of Unesco in 1946 until the end of 1971" (Preface). There are 5,475 entries (for works of more than 16 pages) in classified arrangement. Categories of publications included are 1) works published by Unesco under its own imprint; 2) works issued by other publishers under contract with Unesco (in the original version or in translation); 3) works compiled and published by non-governmental organizations in receipt of a subvention from Unesco (the works are in the Unesco archives); and 4) works issued by national commissions under agreement with the Unesco Secretariat (these are mostly translations of publications issued by Unesco).

Citations contain the following elements (where applicable): author or editor, title, subtitle, joint author or editor, compiler, translator, edition, place of publication, publisher, year, frequency, number of volumes, number of pages, illustrations, series, price or o.p. statement, reference number for other language versions, and annotations. Entries follow Anglo-American Cataloging Rules as they are used in the Unesco library. Titles are arranged according to the Universal Decimal Classification and by alphabetical order within each subject group. Materials covering more than one subject are entered under the primary one.

It should be noted that not all (in fact, very few) entries are annotated. For those that are, the annotations are primarily statements about availability or co-publishers rather than contents. Title and author indexes are included for easier access to the entries.

This bibliography is a boon to documents and reference librarians. It is hoped that other U.N. agencies will compile similar lists and keep them up to date with periodic supplements. —Sally Wynkoop. [R: Choice, Oct 74, p. 1116; ARBA 75, item 111]

39. Buchanan, William W., and Edna M. Kanely, comps. **Cumulative Subject Index to the Monthly Catalog of United States Government Publications, 1900- 1971.** Washington, Carrollton Press, 1973– (in process). 15v. $900.00. LC 4-18088. ISBN 0-8408-0001-0.

This landmark publication in federal documents bibliography indexes more than one million publications listed in the *Monthly Catalog* from 1900 to 1971. As the title indicates, this is primarily a cumulative "subject" index to the *Monthly Catalog*. It does not contain the following entries included in the source indexes: names of persons who were beneficiaries of individual "relief" measures, and "personal authors." The latter entries have been cumulated by Edward Przebienda in two decennial and two quinquennial volumes covering the years 1940-1970 (published by Pierian Press; see entries 43, 44, and 45). However, the following types of entries contained in the source indexes have been cumulated: government agency "author" entries, and title entries.

This cumulation represents a massive merging of entries in all previously published official cumulative indexes to the *Monthly Catalog*: 49 annual indexes (calendar years 1900-1905, 1935-1940, and 1961-1971; and fiscal years 1908/09- 1933/34); the two decennial indexes; and one six-month index (July-December 1934). Original indexing was done for the 30 monthly issues that were not indexed, and the entries were merged. The compilers did not include the years 1895-1899, since the *Monthly Catalog* was not indexed during this early period. In view of their commendable effort to close the 30-month gap mentioned, their failure to do original indexing for this earlier five-year period is a regrettable, but not serious, oversight.

Although this compilation will increase the use of the *Monthly Catalog* for the period 1900-1940 and will make searches more convenient and complete, it will not eliminate the need for the *Document Catalog*, which is more comprehensive and includes many additional documents. Its indexing is generally better and in greater depth. The *Document Catalog* is also a combined catalog-index. Arranged by subject, the entries provide complete bibliographic information, and the user must look only in one place and need not consult both index and catalog listings. In those cases in which the user can narrow the search to a short time frame, the *Document Catalog* might still be preferred. However, most documents reference work concerns more recent publications, and this cumulative index is warmly welcomed since it fills a serious gap for the period 1961-1971.

Due to variations in terminology and indexing rules that have occurred over this span of 72 years, the compilers have been forced to make certain arbitrary, but eminently reasonable and practical, editorial decisions. Subject headings appear intact under their original spellings. However, this problem has been alleviated by merging many *see* and *see also* references that had disappeared over the years. The problem of subject headings in both singular and plural form, often widely separated, has been solved by combining them under either one or the other heading. In the case of series and certain types of reports, chronological and numerical listings are used rather than straight alphabetical listings.

The complete set is being published in attractive, folio-size, case-bound volumes. The price may appear to be prohibitive, but when judged by its value in practical use, in time saved for librarians and other users of federal documents, and in the more exhaustive searches which it allows and encourages, the set is quite inexpensive and is considered to be an outstanding bargain. —LeRoy C. Schwarzkopf. [R: ARBA 75, item 102]

40. **Checklist of United States Documents, 1789-1970: Indexes.** Comp. by Daniel and Marilyn Lester. Washington, United States Historical Documents Institute, 1972. 5v. $160.00.

These indexes are part of the dual media collection referred to as Checklist '70. The fourth edition of the Checklist has been needed for a long time (see Boyd and Ripps, 3rd rev. ed., 1953) and here it is—complete with indexes. Checklist '70 (on 118 microfilm cartridges) lists 1.2 million government publications in shelf list arrangement. It is available with indexes for $2,550.00. The indexes are: 1) by SuDocs number with government authors and organizations; 2) an alphabetical list of 3,000 government authors (both current and inactive); 3) by key word of cabinet level departments subdivided by individual publishing agencies which are also listed alphabetically; 4) a list by titles of 18,000 series; and 5) the master key word index to the publications-issuing agencies. Each index entry gives both SuDocs and microfilm reel numbers. Volume four of the indexes is being enlarged by the Lesters and will be published as *Bibliography of U.S. Government Serial Publications, 1789-1970.* These indexes are useful even without the microfilm. Especially valuable is volume two, which brings together all SuDocs numbers for any government author.

No depository library can afford to be without the fourth edition of the Checklist and its indexes. Medium-sized collections will find the indexes alone valuable in servicing documents. The publisher and the compilers should be congratulated on this monumental work. —Sally Wynkoop. [R: ARBA 73, item 219]

41. **The National Union Catalog of United States Government Publications Received by Depository Libraries as of December 1973.** Washington, Carrollton Press, 1974. 4v. index. $285.00. LC 74-78464. ISBN 0-8408-0025-8.

In the introduction to *New Serial Titles*, one finds the following statement: "No holdings are shown for United Nations and United States Federal and State serial documents. United Nations and United States Federal documents are held by depository libraries." To fill this gap, at least for federal publications, this four-volume work (known by its acronym NUC/GP) records the "Item" holdings of all United States government depository libraries. Each of these depository institutions subscribes to some percentage of over 3,000 Items, or categories of documents; 44 regional depository libraries must accept all Item categories.

NUC/GP was compiled from information in the Office of the Superintendent of Documents, where records (in the form of Item cards) are maintained of Items selected by each of the depository libraries. About once a year the Superintendent issues a *List of Classes of United States Government Publications Available for Selection by Depository Libraries*, arranged alphamerically by the classification system of the Public Documents Department Library. This organization became the framework for the NUC/GP volumes, which give for each classed Item those individual depository libraries, by state, that subscribe to the Item. Because the

Office of the Superintendent assigns a number to every depository library, NUC/GP identifies the subscribing institutions by that number. A list of depository libraries, by state and within state by assigned number, precedes the main text in each volume.

Thus, it must be emphasized that the "union" aspect of NUC/GP refers to the Items, or categories, rather than to the many individual publications within those categories. Moreover, subscription to an Item as of December 1973 provides no clue as to the retrospective depth or strength of holdings for that series. To be sure, the list of libraries marks the date the institution became a depository, but that implies nothing concerning the broken or unbroken aspect of the subscription. The compilers of NUC/GP, acknowledging this limitation, note in the foreword that "the year during which each library was designated a depository appears in the library locator list on page ix and may offer some indications along these lines in certain cases." It is tempting, but misleading, to trust the date of designation as a truly reliable indication of holdings.

Several useful parts of NUC/GP accompany the main union listing: a User's Guide, the aforementioned list of depository libraries by state and number, and a list of classes. Volume 4 has an Item Index, arranged by Item number referencing the SuDocs class number, and a "bestseller" list showing, in ranked order, the 300 series selected by the largest number of depository institutions.

The limitations of NUC/GP have nothing to do with the organization of the volumes, which is admirable. As a list of holdings, NUC/GP will have value as time goes by. It must be kept in mind that, except for the 44 regional depositories, a partial depository may cancel or add Items at any time. Moreover, they may discard material after five years, upon approval of the regional institution. Therefore, an effective record of holdings will emerge only after NUC/GP becomes a well-established annual or biennial series.

In their prefatory remarks, the compilers have given no indication of projected periodicity. An annual revision, or at least a biennial edition, is necessary to record the continuity and discontinuity of union Item holdings. If the NUC/GP is to have a promising future, this sort of supplementation is crucial. —Joseph H. Morehead. [R: ARBA 75, item 105]

42. **United Nations Documents Index: United Nations and Specialized Agencies Documents and Publications, Cumulated Index, Volumes 1-13, 1950-1962.** Millwood, N.Y., Kraus-Thomson, 1974. 4v. $240.00. ISBN 0-527-91530-0.

The cumulated edition was prepared by transcribing indexes from the annual volumes of the *United Nations Documents Index* (UNDI) and by merging the files, through the use of computer programs, into one alphabetical sequence. Major headings and cross references have been largely correlated, but some minor variant formats still exist. The user is advised to search carefully in the immediate vicinity of major headings before being assured of catching synonymously-related headings in variant forms.

The years covered by this set constitute a logical segment in the bibliographical history of United Nations and agency documentation. The predecessor to UNDI, *1950-62* was the *Check List of United Nations Documents* (ST/LIB/SER.F), which was to be a complete list of the documents and publications issued by the Main Organs and some of the subsidiary bodies for the years 1946 through 1949. Unfortunately, some of the parts in this series were never issued, notably those for the

General Assembly and the Secretariat. From 1950 through 1962, UNDI listed all the documents and publications received by the Documents Index Unit of the Headquarters Library from both the United Nations *and* the specialized agencies, with the exception of restricted materials. But the agencies found this responsibility too burdensome; moreover, the librarians at the Headquarters Library found their editorial chores increasingly difficult. Finally, beginning in 1963, UNDI dropped all the specialized agencies from the index. This decision was hailed in the *Report of the Headquarters Library and the Geneva Library, 1963* (p. 6) as a "step backward in the long-range effort to provide bibliographic control of documentation within the United Nations family."

Thus, even for these years the *Cumulative Index* must be supplemented by the various agency lists, guides, and bibliographies, for a publication may exist, but may simply not have been reported by the agency to the Documents Index Unit. Kraus plans to issue another cumulation covering the years 1963 to 1973, when UNDI—in its backward leap—underwent several crucial transmogrifications. It will be welcomed, as this set is welcomed, for the convenience to the users of these valuable materials. —Joseph H. Morehead. [R: BL, 15 Oct 75, pp. 322-23; ARBA 76, item 85]

43. **United States Government Publications Monthly Catalog: Decennial Cumulative Personal Author Index, 1941-1950.** Ed. by Edward Przebienda. Ann Arbor, Mich., Pierian Press, 1971. 276p. $29.95. LC 4-18088. ISBN 0-87650-007-6.

44. _____ : **Decennial Cumulative Personal Author Index, 1951-1960.** Ed. by Edward Przebienda. Ann Arbor, Mich., Pierian Press, 1971. 351p. $29.95. LC 4-18088. ISBN 0-87650-008-4.

45. **United States Government Publications Monthly Catalog: Quinquennial Cumulative Personal Author Index, 1961-1965.** Ed. by Edward Przebienda. Ann Arbor, Mich., Pierian Press, 1971. 293p. $24.95. LC 4-18088. ISBN 0-87650-009-2.

From 1947 through 1962, personal authors were not indexed in the *Monthly Catalog*, although they were included in individual entries. Documents librarians and others having frequent recourse to government documents are aware that sometimes the only way to locate citations is through personal authors. These indexes now make this possible. The three volumes are computer produced. Citations are to year and entry numbers after September 1947, when entry numbers were first used; prior to that, citations are by page number. For personal names appearing before September 1947, the index designates whether the name appeared once or more than once. The 1941-50 volume also indexes the *Monthly Catalog* supplements for 1941-42, 1943-44, and 1945-46. Citations include abbreviations indicating the author's relationship to the publication (such as BIB, "bibliography by," or EDIR, "editor"). —Sally Wynkoop. [R: ARBA 72, items 209-211]

46. Wynkoop, Sally. **Subject Guide to Government Reference Books.** Littleton, Colo., Libraries Unlimited, 1972. 276p. index. $11.50. LC 72-83382. ISBN 0-87287-025-1.

WLB said the following about this work: "*Subject Guide to Government Reference Books* is a selective list (1,050 citations) of government publications in a wide range of subjects. Emphasis is on comprehensive works and serial publications, including atlases, bibliographies, directories, indexes, dictionaries, guides, statistical works, manuals, and catalogs. Arrangement is by broad subject headings, each sub-divided by specific subjects, with a detailed subject index in the back of the book. Price, Library of Congress card number, Superintendent of Documents classifica-tion, and a brief annotation is included for each item. Frequency of publication is indicated for serials. Some works published 1968-1971 are included, but most are earlier publications. For more recent publications, users are referred to the biennial series *Government Reference Books*, by the same author and publisher. A useful tool for locating sources of information in government documents, this may also have limited use as a buying guide in building a documents collection." [R: WLB, Oct 72, p. 200; ARBA 73, item 230]

ABBREVIATIONS

47. Buttress, F. A. **World Guide to Abbreviations of Organizations**. 5th ed. Detroit, Gale, 1974. 470p. $24.00. LC 74-13530. ISBN 0-8103-2015-0.
The fifth edition of this standard British work has added close to 6,000 addi-tional entries to the 12,000 that appeared in the fourth edition. Of these, almost 5,000 relate to bodies, official and unofficial, of the European Economic Community. Hence Buttress's *World Guide* is becoming increasingly international—or at least in-creasingly European. Because of Britain's EEC connection, the new edition abounds in the abbreviations of terms and phrases in Dutch, German, Italian, Flemish, French, and Danish. It is a decided advantage for American libraries to have all such EEC terms assembled in an English language work. [R: LJ, Aug 75, p. 1404; ARBA 76, item 89]

48. Crowley, Ellen T., and Robert C. Thomas, eds. **Acronyms and Initialisms Dictionary: A Guide to Alphabetic Designations, Contractions, Acronyms, Initial-isms, and Similar Condensed Appellations**. 4th ed. Detroit, Gale, 1973. 635p. $27.50. LC 73-568. ISBN 0-8103-0500-3.

49. Crowley, Ellen T., ed. **New Acronyms and Initialisms; 1975 Supplement to Acronyms and Initialisms Dictionary (Cumulates the 1974 Supplement): A Guide to Alphabetic Designations, Contractions, Acronyms, Initialisms, and Similar Condensed Appellations**. Detroit, Gale, 1975. 131p. $30.00pa. LC 73-568. ISBN 0-8103-0501-1.

50. Crowley, Ellen T., and Robert C. Thomas, eds. **Reverse Acronyms and Initial-isms Dictionary**. Detroit, Gale, 1972. 485p. $27.50. LC 71-165486. ISBN 0-8103-0514-3.
The fourth edition of *Acronyms and Initialisms Dictionary* (AID) has 103,000 entries, a 25 percent increase over the third edition. Terms are arranged in alphabeti-cal order by acronym. For acronyms having more than one meaning, the various meanings are included, arranged alphabetically. Revised material includes the updat-ing of New York Stock Exchange terms and the addition of new ones and appro-priate changes in Selective Service classifications. New material includes additional slang expressions, the addition of English translations to many listings for inter-national organizations and foreign phrases, and the incorporation of abbreviations.

Following a publishing pattern established with the second edition of AID, supplements to the current edition will be published annually. Titled *New Acronyms and Initialisms* (NAI), these supplements are to provide new terminology and updating of terminology in rapidly changing fields and are to cumulate previous supplements to the same edition. Thus, the 1975 supplement cumulates all entries in the 1974 supplement and adds several thousand terms—a total of 19,000 entries. However, this supplement is also attempting to record acronyms retrospectively (e.g., World War I terminology). The introduction states this intention, but does not indicate any criteria for selection, which is rather haphazard. If the publishers are serious about developing systematic retrospective coverage of acronyms, they ought to be more explicit about their approach. A bona fide historical acronymic dictionary, beginning at least with those prolific coiners of acronyms, the Romans, would be a very useful tool.

The first edition of *Reverse Acronyms and Initialisms Dictionary* (RAID) rearranges the 80,000 entries in the third edition of AID in alphabetical order by complete words or terms, using the acronyms as "definitions." [R: ALA 72; ARBA 72, item 182; ARBA 73, items 211, 212; ARBA 74, item 95, ARBA 76, item 90]

BIOGRAPHY

BIBLIOGRAPHIES

51. Slocum, Robert B. **Biographical Dictionaries and Related Works: Supplement.** Detroit, Gale, 1972. 852p. index. $25.00. LC 67-27789.

The main volume of Slocum's international bibliography of collective biographies and related works, published by Gale Research in 1967, is a standard reference tool in this area. The subtitle describes the scope of the work: "An international bibliography of collective biographies, bio-bibliographies, collections of epitaphs, selected genealogical works, dictionaries of anonyms and pseudonyms, historical and specialized dictionaries, biographical materials in government manuals, bibliographies of biography, biographical indexes, and selected portrait catalogs." The main volume contains 4,829 entries, and the supplement adds 3,442 more. Entries provide complete bibliographical descriptions plus short notes describing contents. The work is divided into three main sections: universal biography, national or area biography, and biography by vocation. There are three indexes—authors, titles, and subjects—which constitute a generous portion of the volume (nearly 300 pages). [R: ARBA 73, item 231]

INTERNATIONAL

52. **Atlantic Brief Lives: A Biographical Companion to the Arts.** Ed. by Louis Kronenberger. Boston, Little, Brown, 1971. 898p. $15.00. $4.95pa. LC 73-154960. ISBN 0-316-50451-3; ISBN 0-316-50457-2pa.

This is a truly useful addition either to the library's reference shelf or to one's home collection. It contains 1,081 brief biographies covering 1,103 personages important in the literature, art and music of the Western world. Living figures are excluded. Besides these succinct, factual accounts of the biographees, 211 were selected for extended essays which follow the regular biography and which explicate those individuals' *oeuvres*.

Among the contributors who have written these essays are Jacques Barzun, Stanley Kunitz, Lewis Mumford, Mark Schorer, and John Updike. Useful inclusions, in the brief biographies, are the subject's major works with their dates and a selective bibliography of critical and biographical studies. There are no indexes except a pair of alphabetical listings, the first keying the essayists to their subjects and the second doing the inverse. —Kenyon C. Rosenberg. [R: LJ, 15 Oct 71, p. 3312; ARBA 72, item 213]

53. **Chambers's Biographical Dictionary.** Rev. ed. Edited by J. O. Thorne. Edinburgh and London, Chambers, Ltd.; New York, St. Martin's Press, 1969. 1432p. index. $20.00. LC 76-85529.

First published in 1897, this is one of the standard British biographical dictionaries. The major revision was undertaken in 1961, and at that time the editors reviewed most of the entries. The entries vary in length, depending on the relative importance of a given person, and most of them, in addition to the usual biographical data, include published works of the biographee, important critical works about him, with an editorial policy "of clothing the bare facts with human interest and critical observation, listing in its archives the infamous along with the worthy." The present edition includes some 15,000 biographies as against some 11,000 in the previous edition.

There are two major criticisms of this otherwise satisfactory work. Some bibliographic references are rather sketchy, lacking complete bibliographical description. Secondly, there is some tendency to elaborate on contemporary political personalities out of proportion to their relative historical importance. For example, the Soviet politician Shepilov received nine lines, while Shevchenko, the most prominent Ukrainian poet of the nineteenth century, received seven lines. Many American modern poets and writers are also omitted. But, all in all, this is one of the best one-volume biographical dictionaries; it shows improvement with every new edition published. [R: SR, 6 Dec 69; LJ 1 Jan 70; ARBA 70, v. 1, p. 34]

54. Ireland, Norma O., ed. **Index to Women of the World from Ancient to Modern Times: Biographies and Portraits.** Westwood, Mass., F. W. Faxon, 1970. 573p. index. $16.00. LC 75-120841. ISBN 0-87305-097-5.

Approximately 13,000 women are listed in this index, in which 945 collective biographies, a few magazines, general compilations and compilations in special fields have been analyzed. Most reference books have been omitted, with the emphasis on "circulating books" published in the United States and Canada. A few books for younger readers may be found. The editor has not tried to duplicate *Biography Index*, but older books not in this series are indexed. *Celebrity Index* and *Current Biography*, however, are included.

There is a lengthy introduction in which each of the following areas is discussed: Women as Pioneers, in History, as Patriots and Military Leaders, in Religion, in the Fine Arts, in Literature, in Science and Invention, and the Future of Women, although there is no such breakdown in the names listed. This is followed by the list of collections analyzed, index to abbreviations, and key to symbols.

The name of each woman listed has, in parentheses, birth and death dates when known, her field, and references to sources for information, with paging and illustrations if included.

It is a straight alphabetical arrangement, and a breakdown into the field of activity would have made the volume more useful. However, it is timely.
—Marjorie P. Holt. [R: WLB, Mar 71, p. 695; ALA 71; ARBA 72, item 215]

55. **The McGraw-Hill Encyclopedia of World Biography**. David I. Eggenberger, editor-in-chief. New York, McGraw-Hill, 1973. 12v. illus.(part col.). index. $250.00 (for schools and libraries); $300.00 (for individuals). LC 70-37402. ISBN 0-07-079633-5.

According to the introduction, this encyclopedia "has been designed to meet a growing need in school and college libraries as well as in public libraries. Written entirely by academic authorities and other specialists, and enriched with illustrations, bibliographies, Study Guides, and Index, this work, we believe, combines more useful features for the student than any other multivolume biographical encyclopedia" (Vol. 1, p. v). In other words, EWB was conceived primarily for the use of students. The editors have provided 5,000 biographies, averaging about 800 words in length, with a curriculum orientation. Each article is signed, and each concludes with a "further reading" section, consisting of references to Study Guides in Volume 12 and to related articles in other volumes. An annotated bibliography of English language books is appended to each article. Access to the material is enhanced by the 100,000-entry index located in the last volume; the last volume also contains a list of contributors, showing their institutional affiliation.

It is almost impossible to provide a formula for selection of 5,000 biographees who might be "universally appealing" to students. Inclusions (or exclusions) can be debated. With respect to politicians, Beria, head of the Soviet secret police until his execution, is included (although with an inadequate bibiliography), as is Trotsky (who is provided with much better coverage). Benesh, however, the president of Czechoslovakia from 1935 to 1938 and 1940 to 1948, is treated in less detail. A comparison of the EWB with *Dictionary of Scientific Biography* shows that the coverage of famous scientists who have popular appeal is quite adequate.
—Bohdan S. Wynar. [R: ALA 74; ARBA 74, item 106]

56. **The New York Times Obituaries Index 1858-1968**. New York, The New York Times, 1970. 1v. (unpaged). $75.00. LC 72-113422.

Brings together, in a single alphabetical listing, all the names entered under the heading "Deaths" in the issues of the *New York Times Index* from September 1858 through December 1968, augmented by entries for the years 1907 through 1912, for which the indexes are still in preparation, and by names from the period 1913 through 1925, not listed in the published indexes. Each listing consists of the name and the reference (by year, month, day, and column) to the item that appeared in the *New York Times*. Pseudonyms and nicknames, if any, are in parentheses. It should be noted that entries are made for news stories only, not for paid notices. Entries for stories other than the obituaries themselves, such as stories about funerals, memorial services, etc., are included in many cases and appear in parentheses between the name and the date reference for the obituary. An impressive total of 350,000 names is included in this index. [R: LJ, 15 May 70, p. 1826; WLB, Jun 70; ALA 69; ARBA 72, item 219a]

57. Webster's Biographical Dictionary. Springfield, Mass., G. & C. Merriam, 1972. 1697p. $12.95. LC 72-85. ISBN 0-87779-143-0.

Since its first appearance in 1943, there have been many editions of this work, although they should perhaps be called reprintings, since few changes were made from one edition to another. This fact has been pointed out in many reviews.

The present edition, unlike the 1970 or 1971 edition, has indeed been updated. It contains some 40,000 biographical sketches—approximately the same number as in the 1943 edition. Nevertheless, there are still some glaring omissions. For example, there are no entries for Golda Meir, Ian Smith, or Suharto. The coverage of American public figures could also stand some improvement. Examples: no entry for George Wallace; a relatively long article on Humphrey, Duke of Gloucester and Earl of Pembroke (1391-1447), the youngest son of Henry IV—but the two-liner for Hubert Humphrey does not even indicate that he was a candidate for president of the United States.

The editors point out in the preface that "the length of a biography is no measure of the relative importance of the person treated, but rather an indication of editorial judgment of material most likely to prove useful to consultants" (pp. v-vi). This editorial judgment seems to be in need of revision. Compared to previous editions, the 1972 edition shows a considerable amount of improvement. Nevertheless, it still has serious shortcomings; it is hoped that most of them will be eliminated next time. *Webster's Biographical Dictionary* is a fine universal dictionary, but it should be better. —Bohdan S. Wynar. [R: RQ, Summer 73, p. 411; ARBA 74, item 108]

UNITED STATES

58. Dictionary of American Biography, Supplement 4, 1946-1950; With an Index Guide to the Supplements. John A. Garraty and Edward T. James, eds. Published under the auspices of The American Council of Learned Societies. New York, Scribner's, 1974. 951p. index. $40.00. LC 44-41895. ISBN 0-684-14126-4.

The *Dictionary of American Biography*—or DAB, as it is widely known—is not in need of an introduction here. The main set, completed in 1936, was published in 20 volumes plus an index. Supplements one, two, and three were published in 1944, 1958, and 1973, respectively. The fourth supplement adds 561 biographies of significant figures who died between 1946 and 1950. To facilitate location of names in all three supplements, a cumulative index is appended at the end of this volume. [R: BL, 1 July 75, p. 1141; WLB, Apr 75, p. 594; ARBA 74, item 110; ARBA 76, item 106]

59. Garraty, John A., ed. **Encyclopedia of American Biography.** New York, Harper & Row, 1974. 1241p. $22.50. LC 74-1807. ISBN 0-06-011438-4.

A handy, one-volume biographical directory containing 1,000 entries for notable Americans from the earliest period to the present day. Each biographical sketch consists of two parts: a factual chronological summary (about 350 words) of the biographee's personal data, and an interpretive essay of his achievements. All the essays are signed.

Although this directory and Van Doren's *Webster's American Biographies* overlap somewhat in coverage, their different approaches keep them from being competitive; they can be used together. The average user might find Garraty's compilation more interesting, primarily because of the evaluative interpretations provided after the biographical sketch. The selection criteria for the two works were practically the same; both include Americans in all professions, living and dead, aiming at more popular figures who will be of interest to the general reader. —Bohdan S. Wynar. [R: NYTBR, 1 Dec 74, p. 100; WLB, Dec 74, p. 313; ALA 74; ARBA 75, item 124]

60. **Notable American Women 1607-1950: A Biographical Dictionary.** Edward T. James, ed. Cambridge, Mass., Harvard University Press, 1971. 3v. $75.00; $25.00pa. LC 76-152274. ISBN 0-674-62731-8; ISBN 0-674-62734-2pa.

This biographical dictionary, the first large-scale scholarly work in its field, was prepared under the auspices of Radcliffe College. A total of 1,359 biographical sketches is included and the entries are patterned after the well-known *Dictionary of American Biography*, which includes some 700 biographies of women out of a total of nearly 15,000 entries.

According to the preface, "for each biography the editors endeavored to find an author with special knowledge of the subject or of her field. Seven hundred and thirty-eight contributors were enlisted, the scholarly community making a generous response in time and effort for which the modest honorarium was a purely token recompense. The few unsigned articles are the product of editorial collaboration. The length of the article varies according to the importance of the individual, the complexity of her career, and the availability of the material: the two longest (more than 7,000 words) are the biographies of Mary Baker Eddy, founder of the Church of Christ, Scientist, and author Harriet Beecher Stowe; the shortest is the 400-word sketch of the Colonial printer Ann Timothy." It should also be pointed out that "only one group of women, the wives of the presidents of the United States, were admitted to *Notable American Women* on their husbands' credentials. For the others the criterion was distinction in their own right of more than local significance." It is worth noting that of the 706 women who appear in the *Dictionary of American Biography*, 179 were omitted in this biographical dictionary—"mostly individuals who seemed to have lost significance with the passage of time or . . . marginal figures about whom so little material was available that there seemed no point in attempting a fresh sketch."

Articles are evaluative and are accompanied by bibliographies that list both primary and secondary material. A classified list of selected biographies is appended, including names of 17 librarians. An authoritative scholarly work for women's history. [R: ALA 72; ARBA 72, item 221]

61. **Sibley's Harvard Graduates: Biographical Sketches of Those Who Attended Harvard College in the Classes 1764-1767; Volume XVI.** By Clifford K. Shipton. Boston, Massachusetts Historical Society, 1972. 598p. illus. index. $20.00.

In 1873, John L. Sibley commenced the monumental task of compiling biographical sketches of Harvard graduates from 1642. Almost 100 years later, the sketches have advanced 125 years and have reached 16 volumes. Under the authorship of Clifford Shipton, formerly Director of the American Antiquarian Society, the graduates are lovingly commemorated. He has been in charge of the work for the past 40 years and 13 volumes. The present volume, like Mr. Shipton's others, is a monument of erudition, with the lightness typical of the author, and with a succinctness not always achieved in biographical works. The series is definitive; it is a "must" wherever historians study, and genealogists should not neglect it as a primary source. —P. William Filby. [R: ARBA 74, item 112]

62. Van Doren, Charles, ed. **Webster's American Biographies.** Springfield, Mass., G. & C. Merriam, 1974. 1233p. $15.00. LC 74-6341. ISBN 0-87779-053-1.

Includes biographies of 3,000 prominent Americans, dead and alive, who made significant contributions in all fields. Thus, it provides more comprehensive coverage than Garraty's *Encyclopedia of American Biography*, which has 1,000 entries. The information is usually factual, and the reader will find very little here in the way of opinionated statements. Van Doren's work is also much stronger in covering artists and writers. Both works, however, made special efforts to cover minorities, women, etc., thus catering to the interests of contemporary readers. A choice between the two is difficult, since each offers a different approach. [R: NYTBR, 1 Dec 74, p. 100; WLB, Dec 74, p. 313; ARBA 75, item 127]

CHAPTER 2

LIBRARIANSHIP AND LIBRARY RESOURCES

GENERAL WORKS

63. Cheney, Frances Neel. **Fundamental Reference Sources**. Chicago, American Library Association, 1971. 318p. index. $9.95. LC 73-151051. ISBN 0-8309-0081-X.

There are very few people better known to the library profession at large than Frances Neel Cheney, formerly author of a separate column on reference books in *Wilson Library Bulletin*. After several decades of teaching (Peabody Library School), Mrs. Cheney decided to have her own text on teaching basic reference sources, sharing her rich experience in this area with other library educators. To use her own words, "*Fundamental Reference Sources* is an introduction to selected sources of bibliographical, biographical, linguistic, statistical, and geographical information, intended to acquaint the beginning library school student with their general characteristics and uses."

The brief introductory chapter discusses the nature of reference and information service, not only incorporating basic definitions, but also introducing the student to other guides to reference material. The following six chapters discuss in some depth different types of information sources: bibliographies, sources of biographical information, dictionaries, encyclopedias, sources of statistics, and geographical information. There is also a rather substantial appendix containing proposed guidelines for reviewing specific types of reference materials—e.g., atlases, bibliographic reference sources, etc.

The well-balanced and clearly structured text progresses from general to more specific. This is quite evident in, for example, the chapter on encyclopedias. The brief historical introduction, with references to existing literature on this subject, is followed by a clear step-by-step presentation of "the making of encyclopedias." The main section of this chapter presents a detailed evaluation of the most important encyclopedias, including representative foreign works. The chapter ends with a section on the future of encyclopedias, where a number of helpful generalizations provide the student with proper perspective for understanding those "monumental syntheses of knowledge."

There have already been several reviews published about this work, but somehow no comparison was made to similar works. In 1969 William Katz published a two-volume set, *Introduction to Reference Work* (McGraw-Hill). Mr. Katz's book covers much more ground, since he did not limit himself to basic reference sources but also included social sciences, humanities, and to some extent even sciences. Mr. Katz's book is more suggestive, if one can make such a generalization, while Mrs. Cheney tries to be more informative. Mr. Katz's chapter on encyclopedias (which also includes subject encyclopedias) has 41 pages, while in Mrs. Cheney's book we have 52 pages of discussion limited to general encyclopedias. Similar comparisons can be made regarding other chapters. Mrs. Cheney covers basic information sources in more depth and provides more detailed organization of material. Both books are first-class textbooks. [Mr. Katz's book is now in its second edition. See next entry.] –Bohdan S. Wynar. [R: RQ, Winter 71, p. 172; LJ, 15 Sept 71, p. 2746; WLB, Sept 71, p. 84; ARBA 72, item 104]

64. Katz, William A. **Introduction to Reference Work. Volume I: Basic Information Sources. Volume II: Reference Services and Reference Processes.** 2nd ed. New York, McGraw-Hill, 1974. 2v. index. $9.95(v.1); $8.95(v.2). LC 73-8658. ISBN 0-07-33353-X(v.1); 0-07-033354-8(v.2).

The second revised edition of this work has been almost completely rewritten and updated to the early part of 1973.

In the first volume, the author discusses the basic reference sources, following the traditional arrangement of different types of reference sources: bibliographies, indexing and abstracting services, general and subject encyclopedias, general and subject almanacs, handbooks and statistical sources, biographical sources, geographical reference publications, and government documents. Each chapter includes challenging and meaningful discussion of the reference publications from the viewpoint of the librarian and user of library resources. The author stresses that only basic works are considered, and no effort is made to cover "the vast and growing area of subject specialization and bibliography" (Preface, p. xi). It should be pointed out that the author includes in his chapters references to various library publications that deal with reference services and sources, thus broadening the basis of his own interpretation.

The second volume exposes the student to the basic concepts of reference services and processes; it covers such topics as channels of communication, the reference interview, the reference search, definition of reference process, special reference forms (print and nonprint material), automation, evaluation of reference sources and services, and other relevant topics. Through diagrams, Katz provides a solid graphic illustration of conceptual analysis of reference problems and information retrieval systems as well as the anatomy of the reference interview and search. Katz's presentation is, in general, quite clear.

Since the author addresses his textbook to the library student, several questions and critical comments are in order. The author's classification of "reference forms" into primary, secondary, and tertiary sources (p. 14) is rather questionable. According to his definition, primary sources constitute "original material which has not been filtered through interpretation, condensation or evaluation by a second party" (ibid.). This category also includes "daily newspaper reporting, monographs, dissertations," etc. The author's use of the historical terms of secondary and primary sources is not justified in the in-depth analysis of reference forms.

Katz is correct in stating that "another breakdown by the sources may be made by considering the scope of the works. Scope is either general or particular" (p. 18). In his text he emphasizes general reference sources and, to a certain extent, subject reference publications. Unfortunately, Katz does not include in his discussion some major reference subject guides, which constitute the general reference sources for individual areas of human knowledge. For instance, there is no discussion of White's basic *Sources of Information in the Social Sciences* and other important subject guides. In any future edition the author should consider devoting a section to basic and comprehensive subject bibliographical guides. There is one unfortunate omission in Katz's second edition—namely, foreign national bibliographies; the author ignores all non-English national bibliographies. Such an omission constitutes a very serious gap within this textbook. On the other hand, there is a brief section on foreign-language encyclopedias (pp. 121-27). It seems that Mr. Katz is highly selective and has adopted his own special criteria in evaluating basic foreign reference tools.

In the opinion of this reviewer, Mr. Katz's first volume would be helpful as an auxiliary textbook in an undergraduate curriculum, and the second volume may be used in a graduate intermediate reference course. The author's suggestion that the volumes may be used independently is sound. —Lubomyr R. Wynar. [R: RQ, Fall 74, p. 64; Choice, Oct 74, p. 1110; LJ, 15 May 74, p. 1371; ARBA 75, item 245]

65. Rogers, A. Robert. **The Humanities: A Selective Guide to Information Sources.** Littleton, Colo., Libraries Unlimited, 1974. 400p. index. (Library Science Text Series). $11.50. LC 74-78393. ISBN 0-87287-091-X.

For some time the library profession has recognized the need for a comprehensive text covering all important aspects of the humanities, to update Asheim's well-known work, *The Humanities and the Library* (Chicago, American Library Association, 1957). Although the present work has a different structure and takes into consideration recent developments in the humanities it is hoped that it will serve the same purpose as Asheim's older work.

After two introductory chapters—one on research problems in the humanities and the other, contributed by Cynthia McLaughlin of the State Library of Ohio, on the computer and the humanities—Dr. Rogers presents separate sections covering Philosophy, Religion, Visual Arts, Performing Arts, and Language and Literature. Each section consists of three chapters: the first discusses trends in the area under consideration; another discusses accessing information that pertains to the discipline; and the third chapter considers the principal information sources. Leading figures, landmark works, major organizations and associations are discussed, and the bibliographic chapters list and annotate introductory works, bibliographies, indexes, abstracts, dictionaries, encyclopedias, directories, annuals, histories, biographies, periodicals, and other information sources. [R: WLB, Oct 74, p. 184; Choice, Nov 74, p. 1286; ARBA 75, item 174]

DIRECTORIES

66. Ash, Lee, comp. **Subject Collections: A Guide to Special Book Collections and Subject Emphases as Reported by University, College, Public, and Special Libraries and Museums in the United States and Canada.** 4th ed., rev. and enlarged. New York, R. R. Bowker, 1974. 908p. $38.50. LC 74-19331. ISBN 0-8352-0435-9.

The first edition of this work, issued in 1958, contained 17,000 entries, whereas the fourth contains 70,000 entries. If these statistics (the author's own—Introduction) are accurate, the growth rate does show an impressive improvement in the efficiency of the author's data-gathering machinery. As in earlier editions, this work is based on a questionnaire sent out to all libraries listed in the *American Library*

Directory. An innovation in this edition is the inclusion of selected museums. Inevitably, some institutions failed to return their questionnaires, hence their collections are not represented.

The work is arranged by modified LC subject headings under which are listed the libraries (with full addresses and name of unit head) that have collections in the field denoted by the subject heading (e.g., Art, Cambodian, or Botany—History). The collections themselves are characterized in the briefest terms.

As a device for locating special collections, this work has one serious limitation. Unlike a properly constructed library catalog, there are no cross-references among subject headings. This curious lapse indicates that the subject analysis of collections has been superficial and that there has been no effort to link interlocking headings in a systematic way. It must be clarified that there are "see" references (e.g., Aborigines—see Ethnology) but there are no "see also" references. This is a serious deficiency.

As constructed, the book is exceedingly wasteful of space, with endless repetition of identical entries. Economy and compression could be achieved by listing all special collections first and then supplying a detailed subject index thereto. Such an arrangement would serve an additional purpose—that of offering an overview of the totality of a given library's special collections. This is an insight and a perspective that Ash's book does not provide at all. —Richard A. Gray. [R: C&RL, July 75, p. 319; RQ, Summer 75, p. 349; WLB, Apr 75, p. 597; LJ, 1 Feb 75, p. 271; ARBA 76, item 131]

67. **Directory of Special Libraries and Information Centers.** 3rd ed. Ed. by Margaret Labash Young, Harold Chester Young, and Anthony T. Kruzas. Detroit, Gale, 1974. 3v. $55.00 (v.1); $35.00 (v.2); $57.50 (v.3, for 4 issues). LC 74-3240. ISBN 0-8103-0279-9(v.1); 0-8103-0280-2(v.2); 0-8103-0281-0(v.3).

This is a substantial revision of the standard directory of special libraries. The scope and format are the same as in the second edition, which was published in 1968. It covers all types of special libraries, in the broadest sense of the word— e.g., special collections in university or public libraries, governmental libraries, company libraries, specialized libraries of associations and institutions, etc.

Volume one provides an alphabetical approach, listing U.S. and Canadian libraries in two separate sections. As an exception to this straight alphabetical arrangement, all libraries associated with a company or agency are grouped under the official name of the parent organization; thus, all departments and agencies of the U.S. government are listed under "U.S." Each entry provides the following information: name of sponsoring institution, name of library (if distinctive), address and telephone number, name of person in charge, founding date, size of staff, subjects represented in the collection, size and composition of holdings, number of serial titles, services available, publications, special catalogs, and names and titles of professional supervisory staff. There are about 4,000 new entries in this volume, plus considerable updating of addresses, names, etc. A subject index concludes the volume.

Volume two serves as a geographic-personnel index. The geographic section lists by state or province all the institutions included in the first volume. The second section provides an alphabetical listing of the names of library personnel. Each person is identified, with professional title and affiliation.

Volume three is a supplement that is to be published every six months in order to keep subscribers up to date on new libraries or important changes.

This new edition is by far the most comprehensive directory of special libraries and information centers; its execution reflects high professional standards.
—Bohdan S. Wynar. [R: WLB, Nov 74, pp. 250-51; Choice, Dec 74, p. 1462; ARBA 75, item 164]

68. Downs, Robert B. **American Library Resources: A Bibliographical Guide. Supplement 1961-1970.** Chicago, American Library Association, 1972. 244p. index. $15.00. LC 51-11156. ISBN 0-8389-0116-6.

The present volume is the second supplement to *American Library Resources: A Bibliographical Guide*, published by ALA in 1951. The general structure of this volume is identical to that of the first supplement; it provides listings of printed library catalogs, union lists, description of special collections, surveys of library holdings, and calendars of archives and manuscripts. The total number of items listed here is 3,421, substantially higher than the number for the first supplement (2,818). The main volume had a total of 5,578 items covering a 75-year period (from 1875 to 1950). [R: WLB, Oct 72, p. 202; ARBA 73, item 73]

69. Downs, Robert B. **British Library Resources: A Bibliographical Guide.** London, Mansell Information; distr. Chicago, American Library Association, 1973. 332p. index. $25.00. LC 73-1598. ISBN 0-8389-0150-6.

British Library Resources, like the author's *American Library Resources*, is a bibliography of publications concerning library collections, including published catalogs, checklists of special collections, calendars of manuscripts and archives, directories, union lists of serials, and guides to individual libraries and their holdings. These publications range in size from an eight-page list of art libraries to the monumental British Museum *General Catalogue*. Many entries are articles from journals such as the *British Museum Quarterly*, the *Bodleian Library Record*, and Bibliographical Society *Transactions*. Such a bibliography serves the important purpose of identifying published descriptions of the resources of a nation's libraries. It is a bibliographical complement to a directory of libraries and, as such, it may be used by scholars to locate strong collections in their field of interest. The finding aids listed here locate valuable scholarly resources hidden in obscure institutions or organized as special collections in better known ones, and many of them locate copies of rare books both in Britain and in the United States.

BLR covers all types of libraries, all subject areas, and all categories of library materials. As the author points out, it is the first work of its kind for Great Britain, and like any pioneer effort of such broad scope, it is incomplete. A comparison was made with the bibliographical entries found in two library directories, both of which are cited in BLR: R. Lewanski's *European Library Directory* (Olschki, 1968); and *Aslib Directory* (1970). These works provide information on published guides to collections, although they lack the full bibliographical descriptions that are such a valuable feature of Downs's work. A sampling showed that the following titles are listed in *Aslib Directory* but not in BLR: King's Lynn Public Library, *Stanley Library, 1854-1964*; Wiltshire Archaeological and Natural History Society, *Guide Catalogue to the Neolithic and Bronze Age Collections*; Barnsley Public Library, *Bibliographical List of Books . . . Connected with Barnsley* and South Staffordshire

College Librarians, *Union List of Periodicals*. Similarly, titles found in the *European Library Directory* but omitted from BLR are: Royal Observatory, Crawford Library *Catalogue*; and the University of London, Huguenot Library, *Bibliothèque de la Providence*. A more painstaking examination of these directories would probably reveal other titles. BLR also fails to record many of the calendars published by the Royal Commission on Historical Manuscripts, a complete list of which is available in H.M.S.O. Sectional List No. 17. Moreover, some of the calendars that are cited are not indexed under the heading "Great Britain—Historical Manuscripts Commission." These relatively minor defects should be corrected in the first supplement to this useful and well-planned reference work. —Elliot S. Palais. [R: Choice, Sept 74, pp. 908-910; LJ, July 74, p. 1782; AL, July-Aug 74, p. 368; BL, 1 Nov 74, p. 300; ARBA 75, item 148]

70. **World Guide to Libraries; Internationales Bibliotheks-Handbuch.** 4th ed. Munich, Verlag Dokumentation; distr. New York, R. R. Bowker, 1974. 2v. index. $59.50. ISBN 3-7940-1788-9.

Previous editions of this directory were published in 1966, 1968, and 1970. The third edition listed 36,000 libraries in four volumes. The present edition has been somewhat enlarged in scope, identifying 36,932 libraries in 157 countries; it is now published in two volumes. The first volume covers Europe and America (20,000 libraries in 34 European countries and 12,155 libraries in 37 countries of North and South America); the second volume covers Africa, Asia, and Oceania, and it also includes the index.

According to the preface, national libraries, university and college libraries, and public libraries are included if they have holdings of 30,000 volumes or more, and special libraries with holdings of 3,000 volumes and more. Each entry provides the following information: name of the library, address, year of establishment, holdings, letter code to identify the type of library, and specialization (identified by number code). The information was obtained from a questionnaire administered by the publisher. Entries are arranged by country, and within countries by the location and the name of the library.

The index, which takes up more than three-fourths of the second volume, provides listings of public libraries (subdivided by country), "national or state" libraries, research libraries, and university libraries. The latter two categories overlap somewhat; the term "research library" is not defined, and many special or public libraries are also research libraries. In the category of "research library," only 34 entries are provided for the United States,

In spite of its deficiencies, the *World Guide* is of value. It is more comprehensive than A. P. Wales's *International Library Directory* (3rd ed., 1968). For American institutions, it is neither as comprehensive nor as accurate as the *American Library Directory*, which is indispensable. The *World Guide* is the only work of its type, even though it is not a finished product, editorially speaking, and it should definitely be used with caution. Some libraries might be interested in acquiring this publication simply because there is nothing better on the market with such comprehensive coverage. —Bohdan S. Wynar. [R: AL, Dec 74, p. 613; ARBA 75, item 168]

ENCYCLOPEDIAS AND DICTIONARIES

71. **Encyclopedia of Library and Information Science.** Allen Kent, Harold Lancour, and Jay E. Daily, executive eds. New York, Marcel Dekker, 1968– . $40.00/v., subscription. LC 68-31232. In progress.

Projected for 18 volumes, 13 of which have been published to date, the *Encyclopedia of Library and Information Science* is the first attempt in English to provide encyclopedic coverage for library science. The purpose is clearly stated in the preface to the first volume. "The emphasis has been, throughout, on depth of treatment. While the contributors were urged to stress basic information, they were likewise encouraged to express their evaluative opinions as well, wherever possible, to suggest and indicate future trends as they saw them. . . . The editors are . . . committed to a 'one world' concept of their science. To this end the approach has been strongly international. . . . A more accurate description of the basic editorial policy would be that this work is not so much inter-national as it is non-national, although, admittedly, this has not been easy to accomplish."

In general, the editors have kept their promise. There is an impressive number of foreign contributors, a number of good articles on individual countries (.e.g, Brazil), and many excellent pages devoted to certain aspects of library science or library development. Nevertheless, the material is of uneven quality. Articles vary in length, not necessarily reflecting the relative importance of a given topic. Some articles are quite chatty, others provide only a minimum of factual data and occasionally read like observations made by tourists visiting libraries in some strange countries. Such articles are not, unfortunately, limited to those on libraries in Botswana or the British West Indies. A good example of this treatment is found in a long article on the National Library of Austria. Much factual information is somehow lost in its chatty style, and the facts that can be ferreted out are not always accurate. There are many books and hundreds of articles about this library, but no bibliography is included with this article. Obviously, not all articles dealing with the national development of libraries are so inadequate, but, nevertheless, more editorial attention in this particular area will eliminate embarrassment.

Articles on the "home scene" are much better, although there are exceptions. For instance, an article on bookmobiles stretches out to 57 pages while, by contrast, an article on bibliography is crammed into 12 pages. Obviously, the value of printed material is measured in terms other than number of pages, but such a dramatic difference seems worth pointing out. There is a wealth of information in this encyclopedia and its purpose is to be applauded and supported, but the lack of editorial supervision remains evident. The most harmful result of this neglect of supervision seems to be that the volumes are filled with a certain amount of trivia.

The final volume will contain a detailed analytical index for the entire work. When the set has been completed, it will be re-evaluated. —Bohdan S. Wynar.
[R: Choice, Apr 73, p. 164; RSR, Jan/Mar 73, p. 20; ARBA 71, item 101; ARBA 72, item 86; ARBA 73, item 81; ARBA 74, item 129; ARBA 75, item 152; ARBA 76, item 129]

72. Harrod, Leonard Montague. **The Librarians' Glossary of Terms Used in Librarianship and the Book Crafts**. 3rd rev. ed. New York, Seminar Press, 1971. 784p. $19.50. (Grafton Library Science Series). LC 71-158511. ISBN 0-12-843250-0.

The author was right in his decision to revise this work, because much has happened in library science since the publication in 1958 of the second edition. Since there are about ten definitions to a page, they are brief—occasionally too brief. It is evident that some attempt was made to incorporate new concepts, especially in such areas as documentation and information retrieval, with definitions of hardware, new organizations, etc. Nevertheless, the author is more at home within the traditional framework of librarianship, and this shows in his entries for Information Scientist or even Information Retrieval. There is no entry for Information Science. In the brief description of ALA Information Science and Automation Division, the author tries to incorporate some American concepts, terminology, etc., but only on a limited scale. Essentially this is a handbook of British terminology and it is for a British audience.

There is a rather sarcastic review of this book by Paul Dunkin in *Library Journal*, and we think this book deserves a more objective treatment. The reviewer could not find many American terms, is not pleased with some definitions, and feels that some entries are not necessary (e.g., Adequate Description, Principle of). With some of his comments we may agree, but there is no need to ridicule the handbook. There is nothing like it for American terminology. Why has the ALA glossary not been revised? Simply because it is not an easy task. The price is too high. If Mr. Dunkin will look at current pricing of Bowker publications and will take into consideration a few facts—e.g., the relationship of price to potential market—he may reconsider. Last year we made similar comments about the first volume of *Advances in Librarianship* because we felt that comments made in *Reference Quarterly* were not fair. We seldom do this, and it is possible that we may be dead wrong in using this approach. —Bohdan S. Wynar. [R: LJ, 15 Nov 71, p. 3579; ARBA 72, item 88]

SELECTION AIDS

GENERAL

73. **The New York Times Book Review Index, 1896-1970**. New York, New York Times and Arno Press, 1973. 5v. $600.00. LC 68-57778.

The *New York Times* re-issued the entire *Book Review* series (from October 10, 1896) in 125 bound volumes. This index was designed to accompany those volumes and to provide the means for their effective use. It covers virtually everything that was printed in the *Book Review*, including reviews, essays, biographical sketches, letters to the editor, brief commentaries, notes, and anecdotal items; it can be used with either the bound volumes or the microfilm copies of the *New York Times*.

Volume one is an author index (with author defined as the person who wrote the book, not the one who wrote the review). It is arranged alphabetically and lists main authors, associate authors, corporate bodies, editors, illustrators, translators, and authors of prefaces or introductions. The title is given in parentheses after the author, followed by the name of the reviewer (preceded by R) and the citation (e.g., 1934, Je 3, p 18). Bonus features of this volume are the inclusion of pseudonyms (sometimes with cross-references to legal name and sometimes with duplicate entries), and the addition of birth and death dates or titles of nobility when they are necessary to avoid confusion. If many titles by the same author are listed, they appear in alphabetical, not chronological, order.

Volume two contains the title index. Entries are made under titles, collective titles of multivolume works, and subtitles. Furthermore, permuted title entries provide access through each significant word in the title. Every significant mention of a title is indexed; if the book is reviewed, mentioned in an essay or referred to in a letter to the editor, it is indexed. The author's name and citation follow the title.

Volume three, entitled "Byline Index," indexes reviews, essayists, columnists, and writers of letters to the editor. For reviews, the personal name is followed by the title of the work, the author, and the citation. For other items, the person's name is followed by a brief abstract and the citation.

Volume four is a subject index. The subject entries conform to *The Times Thesaurus of Descriptors*, with exceptions and modifications where necessary. This volume indexes primarily essays, reviews of non-fiction works, and comments and letters. The introduction states that "reviews of fiction may be included [in the subject index] under certain circumstances," but these circumstances are not explained. Thus, the user should not rely on this index as a subject approach to fiction.

Volume five is entitled "Category Index." In this volume works are classed by the following genres: anthologies, article and essay collections, children's fiction, children's nonfiction, criticism and belles lettres, drama, humor and cartoons, mystery, detective and spy fiction, nature and wildlife books, poetry, reference works, science fiction, self-help books, short stories, travel books, and westerns. Entries under these headings, arranged chronologically by year and date of the *Book Review* issue, are limited to reviews only. "General fiction, biography, history, and the descriptive or analytical literature on current affairs were excluded from this listing. Since these have always been the principal fields [of books reviewed], a separate listing here would not have revealed anything new and would have been largely redundant." Users of this index may not agree with that. Historical fiction is not one of the categories included, nor is it discussed as one purposely omitted. Certainly the genre is an important one that should not have been overlooked.

The New York Times Book Review Index is one of the major reference works of recent years. The *Book Review* section of the *New York Times* reflects the literary, political, social, artistic, and scientific trends in American life and this comprehensive index provides the key to that vast source. We can look forward to the annual supplements and future 10-year cumulations. —Sally Wynkoop. [R: Choice, May 74, pp. 413-14; WLB, Mar 74, p. 593; ARBA 75, item 172]

COLLEGE LIBRARIES

74. **Books for College Libraries: A Core Collection of 40,000 Titles**. 2nd ed. Chicago, American Library Association, 1975. 6v. index. $60.00pa. LC 74-13743. ISBN 0-8389-0178-6.

The present work, known as BCL II, is, of course, the successor to BCL I (Chicago, American Library Association, 1967). The number of 40,000 titles (the actual count is 38,651) was chosen because it represents four fifths of the 50,000 minimum that the 1959 ALA Standards require for even the smallest four-year academic library. The remaining one fifth, or 10,000 titles, each individual college is expected to choose in accordance with its own particular curricular needs.

The authority for the selections rested in a group of teaching scholars, specialist librarians, and staff members of professional associations, many of whom were *Choice* reviewers. Working from BCL I as a base, the BCL II team expanded, pruned, and modified the list as necessary. In most cases, final selections represented a consensus of contributor opinion.

The editors admit to a liberal arts bias, an admission that was absolutely necessary, given the extreme thinness of the offerings in science and technology. Part of the reason for this comparative neglect of science is the stress that BCL II places on monographs. There are no periodicals and only a scant few serials. Since science, even at the undergraduate level, places its prime reliance on serials, the science sections are inevitably meager.

The arrangement is by modified LC classification. A modification was used to effect a coherent structure of the bibliography in five paperbound parts: I, Humanities; II, Language and Literature; III, History; IV, Social Sciences; V, Psychology, Science, Technology, Bibliography (LC's "Z" class). Volume VI is an author and a title index. The entries are LC catalog cards in *run-on* style, hence the elements or fields are identical to those of LC cards.

The root questions, of course, are: how good is selection? And has ACRL really identified four fifths of the 50,000 titles that every four-year academic library worthy of the name must have?

On prima facie grounds, the effort itself seems presumptuous. Therefore, one is justified in viewing the results with skepticism. It was noted above that the editors concede the thinness of their science offerings; however, the situation is worse than even they imagine it to be. There are serious gaps in basic science monographs, particularly in reference works. Because of the decision against including serials, no abstracting and indexing services are cited, an omission which for science reference is almost fatal. Serials aside, the number of monographs cited in the various "Z" categories relevant to science is suspiciously low.

The books cited under the several subheadings of library science are both insufficient in number and unbalanced. Under Z678-686 (Library Administration), there are precisely four titles, two of which deal with library architecture. Other library science sections, Z675 and Z710-715 (Reference Circulation), not only contain citations to books that are inappropriate to the small college library (e.g., Wilson and Tauber's *The University Library*) but neglect titles of high relevance. Section Z710-715 lists only one book on reference, Gates' *Guide to the Use of Books and Libraries*. The selection of professional literature is definitely not appropriate to the needs of the managers and staff members of libraries with collections in the 50,000-volume range. —Richard A. Gray. [R: ARBA 76, item 141]

SCHOOL LIBRARIES

75. Brown, Lucy Gregor. **Core Media Collection for Secondary Schools**. New York, R. R. Bowker, 1975. 221p. index. $16.95. LC 75-8792. ISBN 0-8352-0643-2.

Brown's core collection contains a selection of 2,000 non-print media (16mm films, filmstrips, filmloops, phonodiscs, audiotapes, kits, study prints, transparencies, specimens, slides, and models) that have been favorably evaluated in 65 professional journals and selective bibliographies. Titles chosen were produced between 1965 and 1974. The three major sections are: Media Indexed by Subject; Media Indexed by Title; and Producer/Distributor Directory. Complete entries are provided in the Media Indexed by Subject section. Entries give title, medium, producer/distributor, date, collation, order number, price, grade level, recommending sources, Dewey number, and contents. Annotations are not provided for all entries and only a small number of the annotations are longer than one line. The subject arrangement of the first section is based on Sears headings, with "see" and "see also" references as needed. There is no break-down of number of entries by type of medium, but it is clear that filmstrips and filmloops predominate, and very few 16mm films are included.

A "core collection" is generally accepted as the basic items that are essential for providing minimum service in a particular type of library. Selecting a basic collection of non-print media for secondary schools is more complex than selecting a basic book collection. The same curricula may be implemented in a wide variety of ways and with different instructional media, depending on the philosophy of the school and the individual approaches adopted by teachers. It is doubtful whether any non-print selection at this time can be accurately described as a core collection for secondary schools. Brown has performed a great service by identifying a manageable number of proven instructional materials. The collection, with its DDC arrangement and full cataloging information, is reminiscent of H. W. Wilson Company's *Filmstrip Guide*. It is a convenient source for locating media on frequently asked-for topics, although the selection will not satisfy requirements for a variety of media on a subject. The entries cited under Great Britain, for example, include nine items, all of which are filmstrips; under Classical Mythology, 35 items are listed (27 filmstrips and 8 phonodiscs). In summary, a welcome addition to the reference shelf which is useful for collections dealing with instructional media. —Christine L. Wynar. [R: WLB, Nov 75, pp. 261-62; ARBA 76, item 156]

76. Library Committee of the National Association of Independent Schools. **Books for Secondary School Libraries**. 4th ed. New York, R. R. Bowker, 1971. 308p. index. $10.95. LC 68-17858. ISBN 0-8352-0424-3.

The NAIS booklist has been published under several titles since its first edition in 1961. The fourth edition is a recommended selection of 4,000 titles considered by the NAIS Library Committee as a basic collection for use by college-bound students.

The guide is arranged by Dewey Decimal Classification numbers. Entries give author, title, publisher, date, price, DDC number, and LC subject headings, but provide no annotations. Separate sections cover fiction and story collections. A directory of publishers and an author, title, subject index conclude the volume.

The preface indicates expansion of the list in areas such as ecology, race relations, space travel, professional tools, reference works. The index is said to be more detailed, bringing together authors and titles, as well as subjects. The six-member Library Committee, chaired by Ronald W. Warden, is identified in the preface.

A list covering all subjects that is limited to 4,000 titles cannot be without serious omissions. In nearly every section there are important books that should be included. To suggest, as the *RQ* reviewer did, that first purchase items should be indicated, encourages even more limited collections. Other criticisms are valid (e.g., books appear in odd classifications).

More comprehensive lists aimed at the more typical high school reader are the *Senior High School Catalog* (Wilson), Dorothy McGinniss' *Guide to the Selection of Books for Your Secondary School Library* (Baker and Taylor), and the *High School Library Book Program* (Xerox) which lists about 10,000 titles. The NAIS list, which concentrates on a small number of titles for college-bound students, would be a better aid to the librarians and teachers it serves if more professional tools, especially subject bibliographies, were listed. The fourth edition is improved and is a welcome supplement to other selection aids for school use. [Editor's note: The fifth edition ($14.95), published in 1976 by R. R. Bowker, contains 6,291 numbered entries for nonfiction books. Fiction is no longer included.] —Christine L. Wynar. [R: RQ, Winter 71, p. 172; ARBA 72, item 168]

77. Wynar, Christine L. **Guide to Reference Books for School Media Centers.** Littleton, Colo., Libraries Unlimited, 1973. 473p. index. $17.50; $10.00pa. LC 73-87523. ISBN 0-87287-069-3; 0-87287-157-6pa.

The guide contains 2,575 annotated entries arranged under 53 subjects. The first two sections describe 182 basic tools for locating print and non-print media and for evaluation and selection of media. Entries give full bibliographic descriptions and prices plus descriptive and evaluative annotations. References to reviews in major reviewing media and standard recommended lists and catalogs are appended to the annotations. A full author-title-subject index provides access to all entries and to hundreds of related titles mentioned in the annotations. The guide suggests reference books for use by students K-12 and for the professional needs of teachers and librarians in elementary and secondary schools. It is updated by biennial supplements. [Editor's note: The 1974-75 Supplement ($8.00) was published in 1976.] [R: ARBA 74, item 173; RQ, Summer 74, pp. 370-71; WLB, Feb 74, p. 508; SMQ, Summer 74, p. 365; BL, 1 Feb 74, p. 558; AL, Feb 74, p. 81]

BIOGRAPHY

78. **A Biographical Directory of Librarians in the United States and Canada.** 5th ed. Lee Ash, editor. Chicago, American Library Association, 1970. 1250p. index. $45.00. LC 79-118854. ISBN 0-8389-0084-4.

The fifth edition of this standard work contains biographical listings of some 20,000 librarians, archivists, and information specialists in both countries, plus librarians employed abroad by U.S. governmental agencies. All entries provide basic biographical data, including a list of positions held, memberships and publications, etc. In terms of information provided, there is practically no change from the previous editions, although there are obviously more entries. Since the representation of information specialists is not adequate, the user might be well advised to use other biographical directories for information in this area.

The editorial work was done by Shoe String Press for the ALA. The questionnaire was administered several years ago, and, unfortunately, the information has not been updated—even for some of the more prominent librarians. There is very little evidence of editorial work in certain areas. Many entries seem "padded" while others, even for some of the most important writers in the library profession, do not provide adequate information. Terms of eligibility were printed on the questionnaire: "Active members of the library profession, archivists or information scientists associated with all types of libraries in the United States and Canada." The term "active members" is somewhat hard to define, and this reviewer is under the impression that all librarians that received professional education (and the questionnaire) are included. This, of course, is fine, and the directory, for all practical purposes, serves as a "finding list," telling who is employed where—providing, of course, that the position has not changed in the last four years.

We may still need a biographical directory with more clearly defined selection criteria, possibly patterned after the *Directory of American Scholars* or other biographical guides of this nature. Our profession is large enough to support a more selective biographical "who's who." —Bohdan S. Wynar. [R: RQ, Summer 71, p. 350; AL, Mar 71, p. 320; ARBA 72, item 131]

CHAPTER 3

SOCIAL SCIENCES AND AREA STUDIES

BIBLIOGRAPHIC GUIDES

79. White, Carl M., and associates. **Sources of Information in the Social Sciences: A Guide to the Literature**. 2nd ed. Chicago, American Library Association, 1973. 702p. index. $25.00. LC 73-9825. ISBN 0-8389-0134-4.

The first edition of this bibliographical guide (1964) gained a deserved recognition among social scientists and bibliographers. The present updated and revised edition is similar in structure to its predecessor. This guide includes separate chapters on social science literature, history, geography, economics and business administration, sociology, anthropology, education, and political science. Each chapter consists of two basic parts—a subject introduction, written by a subject specialist, that introduces the user to the historical development and subject structure of the discipline, and a strictly reference-bibliographical section, usually prepared by the subject bibliographer. All reference entries contain adequate descriptive or critical annotations. The chapter on geography is new to this edition, and the present index shows a marked improvement over that of the first edition. In his preface, Dr. White states that the main objective of this edition is "to make it easier to get at knowledge and information of importance to us all . . . to throw light on the workings of the social science information system, and to support subject bibliography as a branch of the study" (p. xiii).

In general, the editor accomplished his objectives. However, a few critical remarks are in order. White's guide is international in scope—but the history section's emphasis on English publications renders it rather parochial. The bibliographical section is also confused and not adequately updated. The section on "Specialized Guides" (B320-B337) includes both *Guide to the Records in the National Archives* and Miller's *The Negro in America*. There should be a separate section on archival reference publications and on minority and ethnic groups in the United States. In the section on "Reviews of the Literature" (pp. 108-109) there is no listing of Long's comprehensive chronology, *The Civil War Day by Day* (1971), or H. Bengton's *Introduction to Ancient History* (1970). The list of omissions is endless. Again the auxiliary historical sciences, except for skimpy coverage of genealogy and heraldry, are omitted. A more representative and balanced selection of relevant titles is needed in future editions. Despite its shortcomings, this is an important guide.
—Lubomyr R. Wynar. [R: C&RL, Sept 74, pp. 372-73; Choice, Apr 74, p. 240; WLB, Apr 74, pp. 675-76; ARBA 75, item 284]

AFRICA

80. **African Encyclopedia**. New York, Oxford University Press, 1974. 554p. illus. maps. index. $13.00. ISBN 0-19-913178-3.

This is a comprehensive compilation of 1,850 articles by 137 contributors, copiously illustrated and blessed with a 4,000-item index. A major contribution of the work is that it is Africa-oriented: illustrations are presented in an African context, and the work provides a continental view of Africa.

There are some minor shortcomings that could be corrected in a future edition. Not all changes in city names have been included. The general map shows Fort Lamy, and not N'Djamena, while the Chad map (p. 121) shows Sarh. The general map and the Gambia map (p. 220) show Banjul, while the Senegal map (p. 450) shows Bathurst. The dates of all historical and contemporary figures should be added. It is confusing to see an entry for Usuman dan Fodio, with appropriate dates, when there are no dates for his brother Abdullahi and no dates for President Barre, Bai Bureh, Hamad of Macina, Kayira, and many others. An effort should be made to include the synonyms of African language names. "Fulfulde" is included in the index, but the more correct "Bamana" is not. "Mɔre" is commonly written "Moré" and not "Moore" (p. 156). If Aimé Césaire is cited, shouldn't Léon G. Damas be included? He was one of the founders of Negritude, and he played a role in the formative stages of African politics. Ali Mazrui is as important on today's scene as his forefathers were on theirs (p. 333). There are some confusing typographical errors: Ibrahim al-Salahi becomes Salami (p. 65) and Egangaki appears as Ekangani (p. 366). The picture of the Beirut harbor seems to belong to the 1920s (p. 299). And finally, each article should be signed by the contributor.

In spite of these details, the *African Encyclopedia* is a useful, balanced, continent-wide, and Africa-centered reference tool of particular importance to the high school and undergraduate university audience. —Samir M. Zoghby.
[R: LJ, 15 Sept 74, p. 2139; BL, 1 Oct 74, pp.195-196; ARBA 75, item 314]

81. Duignan, Peter, ed. **Guide to Research and Reference Works on Sub-Saharan Africa**. Comp. by Helen F. Conover and Peter Duignan. Stanford, Hoover Institution Press, 1972. 1102p. index. (Hoover Institution Bibliographical Series: 46). $19.50; $8.95pa. LC 76-152424. ISBN 0-8179-2461-2.

According to the preface, "the purpose of this volume is to describe African library and archival material important in reference, research, and teaching. . . . For the librarian it should be not only a reference source but also a guide to building an African collection." The coverage is Africa south of the Sahara, excluding Morocco, Algeria, Tunisia, Libya, and Egypt. There are four major parts to the book—guide to research organizations, libraries, and archives; bibliographies for Africa in general; general subject guide (here the material is arranged by subject—e.g., geography, history, law, economics, etc.); and "area guide" to the regions and countries of Africa, grouped under the former colonial powers.

The coverage is more comprehensive than that found in Miss Conover's older work on this subject (*Africa South of the Sahara*, published in 1963), with a total of 3,127 entries. Most entries have adequate descriptive annotations and Western European countries having reference books on this subject are well represented. It should be noted that the first two parts were essentially closed in 1968 and contain only minor updating with respect to material published during 1969-70. Parts III and IV contain more revisions, including more recent imprints.

Although the work is modestly called "a preliminary version," it is well balanced and professionally structured. —Bohdan S. Wynar. [R: LJ, 15 Nov 72, p. 3690; ARBA 73, item 250]

82. Duignan, Peter, and L. H. Gann. **Colonialism in Africa, 1870-1960. Volume 5, A Bibliographic Guide to Colonialism in Sub-Saharan Africa.** New York, Cambridge University Press, 1974. 532p. index. $27.50. LC 75-77289. ISBN 0-521-07859-8.

The two authors, both Senior Fellows of the Hoover Institution, have compiled a massive and thorough bibliography that should serve both librarians and researchers. The authors preface the work with an interesting introductory essay on the development of historical research into colonialism, and on the institutions established by the European powers to study Africa. The bibliography itself is divided into three sections. Part I, "Guide to Reference Materials," lists organizations concerned with African studies, general guides to African research, and library and archive collections that are important to the study of African colonialism. Collections in Western Europe, America, and Africa are included. The section concludes with a collection of bibliographies on Africa. The second part, "Subject Guide for Africa in General," an annotated list of important works on Africa, is divided into 15 subject areas (demography, economics, education, etc.). This section is quite selective, listing only the more important titles. The third part, "Area Guide," contains a much more detailed annotated list of works relating to all aspects of colonialism. This section cites bibliographies, serials, atlases, and reference works arranged by colonial power, region, and country (British Africa—West Africa—Nigeria). There is an extensive index that includes author and title information to all cited works.

Although 1969 was the original cut-off date for inclusion, important works published up to 1972 are included. Because of its interdisciplinary approach to the study of colonialism, this is a valuable book for all major fields of study that are concerned with Africa from 1870 to 1960. The inclusion of works in all Western European languages makes this work valuable for even the most sophisticated researcher. The scope, organization, access, and 2,500-plus annotations combine to make this book an important and very useful addition to the field of African studies.

Other volumes in the *Colonialism in Africa, 1870-1960* series include: Volume 1, *History and Politics of Colonialism, 1870-1914*; Volume 2, *History and Politics of Colonialism, 1914-1960*; and Volume 3, *Profiles of Change: African Society and Colonial Rule.* —William Z. Schenck. [R: Choice, Oct 74, p. 1108; ARBA 75, item 288]

83. Musiker, Reuben. **South African Bibliography: A Survey of Bibliographies and Bibliographical Work.** Hamden, Conn., Archon Books, 1970. 105p. index. $6.50. LC 73-16088. ISBN 0-208-00391-6.

This book is intended to serve as a companion volume to D. H. Borchardt's *Australian Bibliography* (2nd ed. 1966). The material is arranged under eight major subject categories: retrospective national bibliographies, current national bibliographies, subject bibliographies, periodicals and newspapers—indexes and lists, theses and research, official publications, archives and manuscripts, and bibliography in South Africa. Each chapter is presented in the form of a bibliographical survey, with bibliographical description of reference works listed in footnotes. The chapter on subject bibliographies is based on South African Library's *Bibliography of African Bibliographies* (four editions at the time of this compilation), but it also updates the listing of this guide since the last edition was published in 1960. This competent work on the subject can serve as a much-needed model for other regional bibliographical guides. —Bohdan S. Wynar. [R: WLB, Nov 70; LJ 1 Dec 70, p. 4158; ARBA 71, item 241]

84. Rosenthal, Eric, comp. and ed. **Encyclopaedia of Southern Africa.** 6th ed. New York, Frederick Warne, 1973. 662p. illus.(part col.). maps. index. $15.00. LC 75-114791. ISBN 0-7232-1487-5.

This is a most detailed and informative encyclopedia on South Africa, despite the compiler's somewhat emphatic claim that "this is an encyclopaedia of *Southern* not merely *South* Africa." The bibliography includes about 5,000 abundantly illustrated entries. It contains 11 colored plates, seven maps, a number of photographs, and 22 main topical articles.

The compiler's claim is not substantiated; about 680 entries relate to white South Africans or individuals identified with the country, while there are references to only about 50 Bantu Africans, 51 white and three black Rhodesians, three Zambians, two black Mozambicans, three personalities from Botswana, and two from Swaziland. There are approximately 1,295 references to geographical locations in South Africa proper or territories under its control, and only 28 for Botswana, 13 for Lesotho, 84 for Rhodesia, 27 for Zambia, and 14 for Swaziland. The author has also cleverly woven the history of white settlement into the notes on the various geographical locations in South Africa. There are 41 references to African tribes within the South African orbit, but only four from Rhodesia and two from Mozambique. A number of hardly important towns and villages are cited, such as Umbumbulu with a population of "60, including 30 Whites." The complex question of South West Africa is treated in a relatively cavalier way. The paternalistic attitude toward blacks comes through in a citation about a Bantu leader, which reads: "Mr. Justice de Waal described Champion as 'in many respects a remarkable man' " (p. 107).

If one adopts the premise that this is an encyclopedia on South Africa, and on a given segment of its society, then this work is indeed a remarkable one. —Samir M. Zoghby. [R: BL, 1 Mar 74, p. 702; ARBA 75, item 319]

ASIA

GENERAL WORKS

85. Birnbaum, Eleazar, ed. **Books on Asia from the Near East to the Far East: A Guide for the General Reader.** Toronto, University of Toronto Press; distr. Buffalo, N.Y., University of Toronto Press, 1971. 341p. index. $17.50. LC 75-151361. ISBN 0-8020-1683-9.

This bibliographic guide consists of four main divisions—Asia as a Whole; The Islamic World; India, South and Southeast Asia; and The Far East, including China, Japan, and Korea. The main divisions within each of these four parts are similar, e.g., reference works, general works, history, social sciences, etc., but the subdivisions vary considerably according to the nature of the material and the number of books available. All entries provide adequate bibliographical description: author, title, edition, and imprint, but no pagination. In general, the coverage is well balanced and most materials listed here will appeal to the non-specialist. Some expensive works or more specialized works have been omitted and, according to the preface, most books listed here should still be in print. Annotations are brief and descriptive; obviously critical annotations are not necessary in a compilation of this type. It is a well-executed work.   [R: ARBA 72, item 232]

86. Gillan, Donald, comp. **East Asia: A Bibliography for Undergraduate Libraries.** Williamsport, Pa., Bro-Dart Publishing Co., 1970. 130p. index. $8.95. LC 78-116140. ISBN 0-87272-010-1.

This computer-produced bibliography offers a sound selection of 2,114 books on East Asia which are suitable for inclusion in an undergraduate library collection. They are almost all in English. The work is divided into seven categories—East Asia General, China, Japan, Korea, Taiwan, Hong Kong, Overseas Chinese—each of which is subdivided into topics such as bibliographies, journals, reference books, geography, history, and fine arts and architecture. Each entry gives full bibliographical information for the work cited, and a comprehensive author index complements the main section of the book. The usefulness of the work is further enhanced by a system of classifying books as to their "degree of essentiality for undergraduate collections." In addition, there are references to annotations and reviews of each work. Revisions at periodic intervals would be desirable. —John H. Winkelman. [R: ARBA 71, item 234]

CHINA

87. **An Annotated Bibliography of Selected Chinese Reference Works.** 3rd ed. Compiled by Ssu-yü Teng and Knight Biggerstaff. Cambridge, Mass., Harvard University Press, 1971. 250p. glossary. index. (Harvard-Yenching Institute Studies, 11) $8.00pa. LC 77-150012. ISBN 0-674-03851-7.

The original *Annotated Bibliography of Selected Chinese Reference Works* was published in China as monograph no. 12 of the *Yenching Journal of Chinese Studies*, 1936, subsidized by the Harvard-Yenching Institute. The second edition appeared in 1950 as the second volume of these Harvard-Yenching Institute Studies. This third edition, bearing the same number, is substantially revised and enlarged, adding nearly 200 new titles, including 25 written in Japanese. Some 100 titles that appeared in the second edition have been dropped because they have been superseded by newer works. The format of the second edition has been retained and the material is arranged under eight broad subject categories: bibliographies, encyclopedias, dictionaries, geographical works, biographical works, tables, yearbooks, and Sinological indexes. All entries provide complete bibliographical description with excellent annotations that should serve as a model for critical evaluation of foreign reference works. The emphasis is on new material, since *Contemporary China: A Research Guide*, by Peter Berton and Eugene Wu (Hoover Institution, 1967) covers reference works published during the 1950s and 1960s. All in all, this is an excellent bibliographical guide that will be of substantial assistance to subject specialists in this area.   [R: ARBA 72, item 249]

88. **Biographic Dictionary of Chinese Communism, 1921-1965.** Donald W. Klein and Anne B. Clark, eds. Cambridge, Mass., Harvard University Press, 1971. 2v. $35.00. LC 79-12725. ISBN 0-674-07410-6.

This biographical directory is a selected listing of 433 biographical sketches of prominent leaders of the People's Republic of China. Sketches vary in length, depending on the relative importance of a given individual and, as one might expect, the availability of information. Appended to the biographical sketches the reader will find a list of sources used—occasionally even interviews, but primarily secondary sources (books and articles in many languages, including Russian). There is also a selected bibliography and a glossary-name index, which lists 1,750 persons found in the text. The many appendixes show that all information gathered in this work is current to 1965. Thus, the events of the Cultural Revolution are not included. This is truly a work of significant proportion—the first such undertaking in the West.

This work is obviously not as detailed as the monumental *Biographical Dictionary of Republican China*, and its biographical sketches often lack the wealth of documentation provided by its counterpart on Republican China. But again, at this point in our study of Chinese Communism, it might be impossible to prepare such a work, since so much information is simply not available. In the meantime this is by far the best biographical source on this important subject. —Bohdan S. Wynar. [R: Choice, Nov 71, p. 1162; LJ, 15 June 71, p. 2071; ARBA 72, item 222]

89.   Boorman, Howard L., ed. **Biographical Dictionary of Republican China.** New York, Columbia University Press, 1967-1971. 4v. map. bibliog. index. $27.50 (v.1&2); $30.00 (v.3); $35.00 (v.4). LC 67-12006. ISBN 0-231-08955-4 (v.1); 0-231-08956-1 (v.2); 0-231-08957-0 (v.3); 0-231-08958-9 (v.4).

This comprehensive directory is the most important biographical work on Republican China available in English. Chinese personal names are romanized according to the Wade-Giles system and alphabetically arranged in the Chinese style—i.e., surname first. However, a few biographies (e.g., Chiang Kai-shek) appear under the name most familiar to Western readers. For the few biographies of Japanese subjects, the Hepburn romanization system is used.

Each biography begins with a brief summary of the subject's most recognized contributions or attainments. Biographies include both personal and career information, but emphasis is on the latter. Articles are not signed and bibliographies are not appended. However, the bulk of Volume IV is the bibliography for the set. Names are listed in the same sequence in which they appear in the text and the bibliography for each is given, including both works by the subject of the article, if any, and sources used in preparing the article. More than ten years in preparation, the *Biographical Dictionary of Republican China* is executed according to sound traditions of modern scholarship; it will remain for years the standard source on the subject. [R: WLB, Mar 70; Choice, Sept 70; ARBA 71, item 206; ARBA 72, item 223]

90. Fairbank, John K., Masataka Banno, and Sumiko Yamamoto. **Japanese Studies of Modern China: A Bibliographical Guide to Historical and Social-Science Research on the 19th and 20th Centuries.** Rutland, Vt., Tuttle, 1955; repr., Cambridge, Mass., Harvard University Press, 1971. 331p. index. (Harvard-Yenching Institute Series, No. 26) $7.00pa. LC 74-134948. ISBN 0-674-47249-7.

A reprint, with minor corrections, of an excellent annotated bibliography of over 1,000 Japanese studies of modern Chinese society. These studies, in the form of monographs and articles, are the core of Japanese research on modern China published up to 1953. A companion volume to cover the period since 1953 is currently being prepared.

The entries, organized into nine subject categories, are subdivided by subject again under each of these. Comments precede each section and sub-section and each item has an incisive annotation, often with references to other works in the *Guide*. The ninth category is Reference Works, a particularly helpful section for those who wish to find works to assist in the comprehension of an item at hand or a bibliography for additional material.

Each item has a three-digit code number. The first digit denotes the category; the second, the sub-category; and the third, the item. The name of the author and the title of the work are given in romanization according to the Hepburn system, followed by the Japanese script—as are all other names and items in both these respects. Each title is translated into English. The collation for each item gives complete information, including publisher and date of publication, number of volumes and pages, edition, illustrations, maps, and other useful information.

There are three indexes, which give access to virtually all information in the *Guide*. The first of these is a romanized general index containing an alphabetic list of all authors, editors, compilers, and titles of books and articles in the work. The second is a character index of authors in which each character entry is followed by the romanized version. This index is arranged by the radical scheme used in the 1931 edition of *A Chinese-English Dictionary* by R. H. Mathews, with supplementary information on Japanese characters from Ueda's *Daijiten*. The third index is to frequently cited names and abbreviations.

The introduction is an absorbing essay on the development of the study of modern China in Japan and, to a lesser degree of detail, in the United States. —John H. Winkelman. [R: Choice, June 71, p. 530; ARBA 72, item 250]

91. Skinner, G. William, and others, eds. **Modern Chinese Society: An Analytical Bibliography.** Stanford, Calif., Stanford University Press, 1973. 3v. $35.00(v.1); $38.00(v.2); $32.00(v.3). LC 70-130831. ISBN 0-8047-0751-0(v.1); 0-8047-0752-9(v.2); 0-8047-0753-7(v.3).

This is the most comprehensive bibliography on China published so far, with a total of about 31,500 entries. The volumes are divided on the basis of language: Vol. 1 covers publications in Western languages (1644-1972); Vol. 2, publications in Chinese (1644-1969); and Vol. 3, publications in Japanese (1644-1971). The project was initiated in 1963 by the Social Science Research Council's Subcommittee on Research on Chinese Society. The purpose of the project was to cover the modern period (1644 to the present) of Chinese history, concentrating on writings in Western languages, Chinese, and Japanese. The voluminous writings in Russian and the excellent Russian bibliographies are not included. [R: Choice, Sept 74, p. 918; WLB, May 74, p. 767; ARBA 75, item 302]

92. Wu, Yuan-li, ed. **China: A Handbook**. New York, Praeger, 1973. 915p. illus. maps. tables. index. (Handbooks to the Modern World). $35.00. LC 72-101683. ISBN 0-275-33050-8.

A three-part compendium of information on contemporary China, edited by a well-known scholar whose special area of interest is the Chinese economy. Part one consists of 29 essays (each of which is about 20 to 30 pages in length) on the physical characteristics of the country and its people, government, economy, educational system, and amusements. These essays, many by outstanding authorities, are informative and well written and include documentation as well as selected annotated bibliographies. Part two consists of 10 significant political documents including The Constitution of the People's Republic of China, 1954; The Constitution of the Chinese Communist Party, 1956; Outline of the First Five-Year Plan, 1955; and Lin Piao on People's War, 1965. Part three consists of tabular information on a wide range of topics including population, energy resources, agriculture, public health, and education. The 17 line-maps bound into the text at appropriate places add a considerable amount of information to the work. The only weak point in this work is the index, which is made up of proper nouns. Subject headings, which could have bound the three sections of the work together, are included only under some of these proper nouns. Nevertheless, this very useful work could serve the needs of a wide range of persons and institutions interested in contemporary China. —John H. Winkelman. [R: NYTBR, 23 Sept 73, p. 40; Choice, Nov 73, p. 1362; WLB, Sept 73, p. 85; LJ, 15 June 73, p. 1905; ALA 73; ARBA 74, item 278]

INDIA

93. **Dictionary of National Biography**. Ed. by S. P. Sen. Calcutta, Institute of Historical Studies; distr. Columbia, Mo., South Asia Books, 1972. 4v. $110.00 (sold only as a set; standing order arrangement). ISBN 0-88386-030-9.

According to the preface, this four-volume dictionary is "the first attempt of its kind in India, on the lines of similar works in other countries." The four volumes cover the period 1800 to 1947 and include about 1,400 entries for Indians and for foreigners who made India their home and who "made some tangible contribution to national life." Articles of varying length cover living as well as deceased individuals and are signed. Most of the 350 contributors are historians in Indian universities. Selected bibliographies are appended to longer articles and emphasize Indian language materials. The work is extensively cross-referenced. An important contribution in an area where nothing comparable exists. [R: Choice, June 73, p. 596; ARBA 74, item 116]

94. Sharma, H. D., S. P. Mukherji, and L. M. P. Singh. **Indian Reference Sources: An Annotated Guide to Indian Reference Books**. Varanasi, Indian Bibliographic Centre; distr. Columbia, Mo., South Asia Books, 1972. 313p. index. $12.00.

This guide describes some 2,200 reference books published in India in recent decades. The organization is similar to that found in Walford or Winchell—namely, reference books are listed by broad subject categories subdivided by types of materials (e.g., bibliographies, dictionaries, handbooks, etc.). There are four major sections: general works, humanities, social sciences, and pure and applied sciences. The bibliographic description for all listed works is complete, including the price in addition to the usual data. Most entries are annotated. Annotations, which vary in length from one sentence to seven or eight lines, are descriptive but not critical. It should be emphasized that coverage is limited to reference books published in India (in several languages), which is probably the only serious weakness of this otherwise satisfactory guide. It is to be hoped that the next edition will include some important reference materials published about India in a number of foreign countries, since this would add to the research value of *Indian Reference Sources*. [R: ARBA 73, item 4]

JAPAN AND KOREA

95. Shulman, Frank J., ed. **Japan and Korea: An Annotated Bibliography of Doctoral Dissertations in Western Languages 1877-1969**. Chicago, American Library Association, 1970. 340p. index. $6.95pa. LC 71-127675. ISBN 0-8389-0085-2.

The bibliography expands and updates an earlier list, *Unpublished Doctoral Dissertations Relating to Japan, Accepted in the Universities of Australia, Canada, Great Britain, and the United States, 1946-1963*, compiled by Peter Cornwall and issued by the University of Michigan Center for Japanese Studies in 1965. There are 2,586 entries (2,077 for Japan, 509 for Korea) in English, French, German, Russian and other European languages. All dissertations are classified in broad subject arrangement and within each subsection the arrangement is chronological by date of completion rather than alphabetical by author. There are three indexes— an alphabetical listing by author and main entry code number, an index by degree-awarding institution, and a register of all dissertations that are primarily biographical in nature. With the exception of those dissertations in the Russian language, the coverage in this bibliographical guide seems to be quite comprehensive; entries offer a complete bibliographical description and, in most cases, brief descriptive annotations. Several well-known Soviet guides to dissertations apparently were not consulted (see *Guide to Russian Reference Books*, v. 1, p. 47-50), so the coverage of Russian materials is rather weak in this otherwise useful and well-executed bibliographical guide. —Bohdan S. Wynar. [R: WLB, Nov 70; ARBA 71, item 247]

THAILAND

96. Thrombley, Woodworth G., and William J. Siffin. **Thailand: Politics, Economy, and Socio-Cultural Setting; A Selective Guide to the Literature**. Bloomington, Indiana University Press, 1972. 148p. index. $7.50 LC 75-126218. ISBN 0-253-35850-7.

This selected and annotated bibliography of English language literature on Thailand in the social sciences includes dissertations and unpublished papers as well as books and major articles. Entries are arranged by general subject in eight chapters. The annotations are concise and critical, and the most important studies are further brought out in the very brief, but informative, bibliographic essays that precede each chapter. A ninth chapter lists "Other Sources of Information," including American academic centers with programs focused on Thailand, other organizations concerned with research and documentation on Thailand, English language periodicals and newspapers published in Thailand, major international journals in which future research on Thailand is likely to be published, and bookstores that specialize in Southeast Asian materials. It is a most useful guide for the scholar, student, and librarian and should serve as a model for similar bibliographies on other countries in Southeast Asia and the third world. —Charles R. Bryant. [R: Choice, Nov 72, p. 1116; ARBA 73, item 260]

AUSTRALASIA AND OCEANIA

97. **Australian Dictionary of Biography.** Victoria, Melbourne University Press; distr. Portland, Ore., International Scholarly Book Services, 1966– . $27.90/v. (v.1, 3); $29.70/v. (v.2, 4, 5). ISBN 0-522-83516-3(v.1); 0-522-83705-0 (v.2); 0-522-83909-6(v.3); 0-522-84061-2(v.5).

The *Australian Dictionary of Biography* is planned to be a 12-volume work plus a general index volume. Rather than following a straight dictionary arrangement, the work is first divided into three chronological sections: 1788-1850, 1851-1890, and 1891-1939. Each of these sections lists individuals who flourished during the period covered, arranged alphabetically. The first section, 1788-1850, is complete in two volumes (A-H, I-Z); in the second section, 1851-1890, three of the four volumes have been published to date (A-C, D-J, K-Q), leaving one volume (R-Z) yet to be published; all six volumes of the third section have yet to be published. "This chronological division was designed to simplify production, for over six thousand articles are likely to be included."

Entries are not limited to Australians. Although no specific selection criteria are mentioned, the preface states, "Many of the names were obviously significant and worthy of inclusion. . . . Others, less notable, were chosen simply as samples of the Australian experience. . . . Most authors were nominated by the Working Parties" (committees throughout Australia). Brief bibliographies are appended to the articles. This scholarly reference work is based on consultation and cooperation "and the burden of writing has been shared by university historians and by members of historical and genealogical societies and other specialists." The completed work will represent the effort of more than 2,000 contributors who are listed at the beginning of each volume in which their articles appear, although identification other than name is not given. [R: Choice, May 75, p. 367; ARBA 74, item 115; ARBA 76, item 108]

98. Day, A. Grove. **Pacific Islands Literature: One Hundred Basic Books.** Honolulu, University Press of Hawaii, 1972 (c. 1971). 176p. bibliog. index. $7.50. LC 70-151452. ISBN 0-87022-180-9.

Here is one book that delivers far more than is claimed in its title! The author, now Senior Professor Emeritus of English, University of Hawaii, taught a course in "Literature of the Pacific" for 10 years prior to his retirement. His book reflects a wealth of background knowledge from which to make judicious selections. He has chosen 100 authors, given brief biographical information, highlighted the leading work, and then commented on other books by the same author or other works related to the subject. Annotations are sometimes critical. They range in length from less than half a page for J. R. Ullman's *Where the Bong Tree Grows* to 10 pages for *The Journals of Captain James Cook on His Voyages of Discovery*. Between 500 and 1,000 additional titles receive comment in the text of the annotations. The rationale for the arrangement of the book is not immediately apparent, despite its table of contents. Thus, the description by the author is helpful: "The arrangement by number is chronological, based on the date of the first episode in any series of events. The first items cover prehistory, folklore, and general works; then . . . the Magellan story, which is followed by writings about other voyages and adventures, and so on to more recent times."

There is a supplemental bibliography in the back and an alphabetical "Index of Pacific Names and Places." Only first editions are mentioned. Literary quality, rather than current availability, was the criterion for selection. Day has not attempted to compete with comprehensive works like C. R. H. Taylor's *A Pacific Bibliography* (2nd ed., 1965), but he has compiled a thoughtfully prepared guide to the most important works in the voluminous literature of this field. —A. Robert Rogers. [R: ARBA 73, item 271]

99. **Encyclopaedia of Papua and New Guinea.** Peter Ryan, gen. ed. Victoria, Melbourne University Press; distr. Portland, Ore., International Scholarly Book Services, 1972. 3v. illus. maps. index. $99.00. ISBN 0-522-84025-6.

Published by Melbourne University in association with the University of Papua and New Guinea, this comprehensive work covers all important subjects relating to Papua New Guinea. The official name of Papua New Guinea was adopted following unification of the two former territories at the time this encyclopedia went to press. It was decided to retain the original title because the work covers the time when these areas were under separate names.

All entries are arranged in one alphabet, and authors of the signed articles are identified in the third volume. Most entries are lengthy comprehensive discussions of the topic. For example, see Education, which covers nearly 50 pages and includes sections on the history of education, education of indigenous groups, influence of religious missions, etc. The article on art is very well balanced, including numerous photos (unfortunately all in black and white). Almost every entry contains bibliographic citations. There are entries on all aspects of Papua New Guinea, such as persons, animals, diseases, economics, customs of the peoples, law, etc. One serious drawback is the treatment of the indigenous peoples: "Abau. People of the Central District," followed by a bibliographic source. In other words, these specific entries tell virtually nothing about the various indigenous groups; one finds more detailed information on them in the broader headings such as Initiation or Education.

The encyclopedia itself is in two volumes. Volume three (83 pages) contains a chronology of 1971 events, a gazetteer of place names, an index (only

50 pages), a fold-out map, and other supplementary data. One hopes that the incomplete index can be improved for the next edition. An essential work on this subject. [R: LJ, 15 Nov 72, p. 3696; ARBA 73, item 275]

100. Learmonth, Andrew T., and Agnes M. Learmonth. **Encyclopaedia of Australia.** New York, Warne, 1969. 606p. illus. $10.00. LC 69-11019.

Primarily designed for young adults and students, this handy volume includes over 2,700 entries with 50 main articles supplemented by color plates, black-and-white photographs, line drawings and some 20 maps. Articles incorporating information and commentary cover such subjects as the arts, biography, history and geography. Many articles provide references to additional readings and the volume is current to 1968. Libraries that cannot afford the more comprehensive 10-volume *Australian Encyclopedia* (Michigan State University Press, 1958) will find this one-volume compilation useful. [R: LJ, May 69; ALA 69; ARBA 70, v.1, p. 28]

CANADA

101. **Canadian Serials Directory, 1972.** Buffalo, N.Y., University of Toronto Press, 1972. 961p. $65.00. ISBN 0-8020-4502-2.

This volume presents by far the most comprehensive listing of periodicals and series published at the present time in Canada. French-language entries are described in French; all other entries are described in English. The present edition lists in one alphabet some 8,000 titles, providing the following information: title, publisher and address, editor, sponsor, type of publication (e.g., scholarly or popular), language, frequency, circulation, price, and occasionally other data (e.g., available as gift, information on advertising, etc.). The following categories of serial publications are included: periodicals, annual reports, and yearbooks; journals, serial memoirs, proceedings, and transactions of associations; numbered monographs (parts of series); and serially published technical reports and government documents (including also provincial and municipal documents). Also included in the directory are newspapers of special interest, such as religious, ethnic, etc. Excluded are some house organs, company reports, school and university calendars, telephone directories, and similar material. Following the main body, one finds a list of publishers with their addresses, a list of indexing and abstracting services, a subject index, a list of international serial numbers, and an addenda section for serials not listed in the main body.

As the introduction indicates, all titles listed have been verified to remain current in 1972; the information was based on a questionnaire. The new edition (or supplement) will add some 2,000 titles for which information was unavailable for this edition. *Canadian Serials Directory* offers much more comprehensive coverage of Canadian serials than any other publication to date. —Bohdan S. Wynar. [R: Unesco, Jan-Feb 73, p. 45; LJ, 1 Nov 73, p. 3237; Choice, Sept 73, p. 942; ARBA 74, item 32]

102. **Dictionary of Canadian Biography: Volume III, 1741 to 1770.** George W. Brown, David M. Hayne, and Francess G. Halpenny, general eds. Toronto and Buffalo, University of Toronto Press, 1974. 782p. bibliog. index. $20.00 ISBN 0-8020-3314-8.

The *Dictionary of Canadian Biography* (DCB) is not being published in sequence. Volume I, covering subjects who died before 1701, was published in 1966; Volume II, for the period 1701-1740, appeared in 1969; Volume X, for the decade 1871-1880, was published in 1972. The University of Toronto Press is now returning to the main chronological sequence with the issuance of Volume III.

There is a major difference between DCB and the DNB and DAB, on which it is closely modelled; the first is being produced on the premise that coverage of a segment of time creates the most coherent frame for the consideration of a nation's major figures. In contrast, DNB and DAB were, in their main volumes, issued in straight alphabetical order. Their supplementary volumes, however, are appearing on a time segmental basis.

Editorial policy is stated in the preface, including the "Directives" supplied to contributors: "Each biography should be an informative and stimulating treatment of its subject, presented in readable form. All factual information should be precise and accurate, and be based upon reliable (preferably primary) sources. Biographies should not, however, be mere catalogues of dates and events, or compilations of previous studies of the same subject. The biographer should try to give the reader an orderly account of the personality and achievements of the subject against the background of the period in which the person lived and the events in which he or she participated."

To reinforce the delineation of the background of 1741-1770, the editor has included two clearly written historical review essays on the French forces and the British forces in the Seven Years War, written by W. J. Eccles and C. P. Stacey, respectively. These essays are particularly apposite because most of the 550 figures who died between 1741 and 1770, and are therefore treated in this volume, were in one way or another involved in that eighteenth century struggle between Britain and France for commercial dominance of the North American continent.

Persons qualified for inclusion are those who took an active part or exerted major influences in that part of North America which later became Canada. Thus, we find many prominent French officers (e.g., the Marquis de Montcalm), British officers (e.g., General James Wolfe), and Indian chiefs (e.g., Pontiac).

Examining sample biographies, it is clear that the editors have accomplished their main goal: the sketches do indeed "give the reader an orderly account of the personality and achievements of the subject against the background of the period."

The DCB is being issued simultaneously in a French edition under the title *Dictionnaire biographique du Canada* and published by Les Presses de l'Université Laval. Some American libraries may prefer to purchase the French language edition.

Because of the close, intense, and protracted interactions between Canada and the United States, the DCB is as important for U.S. history as it is for the history of Canada. —Richard A. Gray. [R: ARBA 76, item 109]

103. **Directory of Associations in Canada 1975**. Prep. under the direction of Brian Land. Toronto and Buffalo, University of Toronto Press, 1975. 550p. $37.50. LC 73-85085. ISBN 0-8020-4519-7. ISSN 0316-0734.

Canada is small enough to have a thorough directory of the association that exist within its boundaries. Unlike Gale's *Encyclopedia of Associations*, which is a guide to national and international associations in the United States only, the present work includes associations of all kinds and interests at the following geographical levels: international, national, interprovincial, provincial, regional, metropolitan, and local (there are 48 entries beginning with the place name, Montreal).

The work is bilingual throughout, beginning with the title page, where its French title is given as *Répertoire des associations du Canada*. There is a long and detailed subject index arranged by English language rubrics; the other main section is in straight alphabetical order. Associations that are officially bilingual are entered under their English forms with cross references from their French forms. Associations that are exclusively French are entered directly under their names.

As is essential in a bilingual work, there is a "Guide to the Subject Index/ Comment Consulter l'Index des Sujets." This section is needed by French users as a guide from French descriptors to their English equivalents that are actually used in the subject index. Examples: Acier voir Steel; Balle au mur voir Handball.

The information components for each association are three: full official name in English or French with an added French form if bilingual, name of chief administrator, and address.

Excluded are governmental departments and agencies, profit-making corporations, and some minor local groups, such as ratepayers' associations, cooperatives, credit unions, private clubs, and labor unions (locals).

The definitive work for Canadian associations. —Richard A. Gray. [R: ARBA 76, item 65]

104. Lochhead, Douglas, comp. **Bibliography of Canadian Bibliographies**. 2nd ed. rev. and enl. Buffalo, N.Y., University of Toronto Press, 1972. 312p. index. $20.00. LC 76-166933. ISBN 0-8020-1865-3.

The first edition of this standard work on the subject was published in 1960, with three supplements to cover the years 1961 to 1965. This new edition incorporates the material from the supplements and brings the coverage up to June 1970. Some changes have been made in this edition. First, all entries are now given in one alphabetical sequence, regardless of subject, and a detailed subject index provides the reader with the subject access. In addition, the index provides an author approach (by compiler or corporate body), and the material in French has been noticeably enlarged. There is a total of 2,323 entries; as was the case with the first edition, they are not annotated. Nevertheless, this bibliographical guide, in its enlarged edition, is an important reference book on Canada. [R: Choice, Sept 72, p. 792; ARBA 73, item 270]

105. Ryder, Dorothy E., ed. **Canadian Reference Sources: A Selective Guide**. Ottawa, Canadian Library Association, 1973. 185p. index. $10.00. ISBN 0-88802-093-7.

106. Ryder, Dorothy E., ed. **Canadian Reference Sources: Supplement.** Ottawa, Canadian Library Association, 1975. 121p. index. $7.00pa. ISBN 0-88802-106-2.

According to the introduction, the purpose of this work is "to provide librarians and students with a guide to Canadian reference material. It is a selective guide only, and does not aim at completeness. The material covers Canada in general, the ten provinces, the territories, and three cities—Ottawa, Montreal, and Toronto. No geographical area smaller than a province, with the exception of the three cities named, is considered" (p. iii).

The arrangement and, as a matter of fact, the treatment of material are quite similar to what is found in Winchell: complete bibliographical information, plus brief descriptive annotations. No price is indicated and there are no references to published reviews. Although this work is very useful, a more comprehensive approach would be an improvement.

The *Supplement* to *Canadian References Sources* adds new works and editions published up to December 1973. The work follows the same format as the previous volume. The scope has been enlarged to include "a few personal bibliographies and material dealing with areas smaller than the provinces" (p. i). Four pages of corrections and additions to the main volume are provided. While this new supplement adds greatly to the already useful *Canadian Reference Sources*, it is hoped that a new edition incorporating both volumes and future additions will be forthcoming. —Bohdan S. Wynar and Chester S. Bunnell. [R: LJ, 1 Dec 73, p. 3532; Choice, Oct 73, p. 1159; AL, Oct 73, p. 553; RSR, July/Sept 73, p. 11; Choice, Sept 75, p. 815; ARBA 74, item 8; ARBA 76, item 6]

CONTINENTAL EUROPE

GENERAL WORKS

107. **Directory of European Associations: Part 2, National Learned, Scientific and Technical Societies.** I. G. Anderson, ed. Beckenham, Kent, England, CBD Research Ltd.; distr. Detroit, Gale, 1975. 315p. index. (A CBD Research Publication). $45.00. LC 74-25410. ISBN 0-900246-17-0.

CBD Research has carved a unique monopoly for itself in the compilation of directories. Although there are national directories of both learned and trade associations for several European countries, no other work assembles this information on a continental basis. The two volumes under review have an identical format and organization. Each is officially tri-lingual, English, French, and German. Each is arranged by a consecutively numbered series of subject headings. Alphabetizing is in accordance with the English alphabet. The introduction in each is in English only, but the "how to use the directory" section appears in French and German translations. There are lists of subjects (i.e., *Sachverzeichnis* and *Table Alphabétique des Matières*) in German and French as would be mandatory in a book of this kind, since subjects appear in the English order.

These directories exclude Great Britain and Ireland since CBD Research has covered those countries in its *Directory of British Associations*. Under each subject entries are arranged by country alphabetically in the order of the international country designation scheme—e.g., "D," Deutschland; "E," España; but oddly "A" and not "O" for Austria (Österreich). A full entry contains the following components: name, authorized translation of name into other languages, acronym for name, foundation date, address, telephone, membership, activities, publications, former names, if any. Many entries are far from full. The compilers relied on a questionnaire. When questionnaires were not returned, the compilers had to piece together fragmentary descriptions from secondary sources.

The indexes are models of completeness. They incorporate all pertinent entries in English, French, and German as well as in the language of the association itself. A valuable, well-executed work. —Richard A. Gray. [R: Choice, Dec 75, pp. 1288-90; ARBA 76, item 66]

108. **Guide to European Foundations.** Prep. by the Giovanni Agnelli Foundation. Milano, Italy, Franco Angeli Editore; distr. New York, Columbia University Press, 1973. 401p. index. $17.50. ISBN 0-231-03701-5.

The first edition of this work, published in 1970 under the title *Directory of European Foundations*, was prepared by the Giovanni Agnelli Foundation with the cooperation of the Russell Sage Foundation; it was distributed by Basic Books. Out of 1,662 foundations contacted for that edition, some 56 percent responded (834); of these, 301 were selected for inclusion.

The present edition uses similar criteria for inclusion (that is, non-governmental and non-profit organizations). It describes 296 foundations, but the information is much more detailed than in the previous edition. There is an excellent introduction that not only provides information on collecting of data (as was done for the first edition), but also indicates the breakdown by country (16 countries covered), describes fields of activity, foundation size, etc. Appended to the volume are: a good selective bibliography, an index by field of activity, an index of persons, and an index of foundations by country and name. All in all, this valuable reference book is much improved over the first edition. —Bohdan S. Wynar. [R: ARBA 72, item 597; ARBA 74, item 70]

EASTERN EUROPE AND THE SOVIET UNION

109. Bakó, Elemér. **Guide to Hungarian Studies.** Stanford, Calif., Hoover Institution Press, 1973. 2v. illus. index. (Hoover Institution Bibliographical Series, No. 52). $35.00. LC 79-152422. ISBN 0-8179-2521-X.

This massive, two-volume guide offers 4,426 bibliographical entries describing special reference works, periodicals, monographs, and journal articles devoted to Hungarian history, culture, and economics. A brief sketch of the history of Hungarian intellectual life (pp. 3-21) is followed by a two-part chronology of Hungarian political, military, cultural, economic, and social history (pp. 25-145). Preliminaries also include a useful list of Hungarian abbreviations, with English equivalents for each term (pp. 147-151). Bibliographical entries in the main body of the work fall into 20 categories: 1) History of the Hungarian Book; 2) Cultural Life and Institutions; 3) General Works; 4) Statistical Research; 5) The Land; 6) The People; 7) History and Historiography; 8) Constitution and Legislation; 9) Government and Politics; 10) Social Life; 11) Economics; 12) Religion and Church Affairs; 13) Language; 14) Literature; 15) Fine Arts and Music; 16)

Education; 17) Science; 18) Press and Publishing; 19) Hungarians Abroad; 20) Hungary and the United States.

A system of cross references facilitates access to works devoted to more than one subject. Two indexes—one to periodical titles and another to personal names—close the second volume. The bibliography section includes sources in Hungarian, English, French, German, and Latin. Hungarian titles are followed by their English translations. The Bakó work, like other recently published, excellent reference books in the area of Hungarian studies (Paul L. Horecky's *East Central Europe: A Guide to Basic Publications* and Albert Tezla's *Hungarian Authors: A Bibliographical Handbook*), should become a most significant addition to Hungarica collections. —Ivan L. Kaldor. [R: Choice, Sept 74, p. 907; ARBA 75, item 304]

110. Fischer-Galati, Stephen. **Rumania: A Bibliographic Guide**. Washington, Reference Dept., Slavic and Central European Division, Library of Congress, 1963; repr. New York, Arno, 1969(c.1968). 75p. index. $5.50. LC 63-60076. ISBN 0-405-00057-X.

The first issue in a series of concise bibliographic area guides sponsored by the Slavic and Central European Division of the Library of Congress. The first part is a well-written bibliographic survey covering 11 major subject areas, exclusive of medicine and the natural sciences. The second part presents a detailed bibliographic listing, alphabetically arranged and consecutively numbered, of the 748 publications mentioned in the survey. The majority of books and periodicals listed in this guide are in the Rumanian language, although the most important publications issued in other languages have also been incorporated. An essential work for area programs and specialists. [R: LJ, 1 Sept 69; ARBA 70, v.1, p. 42]

111. Horecky, Paul L., ed. **East Central Europe: A Guide to Basic Publications**. Chicago, University of Chicago Press, 1969. 956p. index. $27.50. LC 70-79472. ISBN 0-226-35189-0.

112. Horecky, Paul L., ed. **Southeastern Europe: A Guide to Basic Publications**. Chicago, University of Chicago Press, 1969. 755p. index. $25.00. LC 73-110336. ISBN 0-226-35190-4.

With these two companion guides to the standard sources for two East-European geographical areas, Dr. Horecky provides the library profession with the most comprehensive guide ever attempted. He was assisted in this difficult task by a number of well-known subject specialists, responsible for individual sections, whose names and professional positions are listed in both volumes. In terms of scope and organization of material, the volumes are almost identical.

The first volume, *East Central Europe*, covers Czechoslovakia, East Germany (including a separate section on Lusatians and Polabians), Hungary, Poland, plus a general section dealing with the publications "which pertain either to two or more countries of the area or to subjects for which a consolidated rather than separate presentation by countries seemed indicated." In this general section, the reader will find such topics as general reference aids and bibliographies, general works on Slavic language or literature, Jewish problem, etc. The material for each country is presented under uniform subject categories: general reference aids and bibliographies, the land, the people, history, the state, the economy, the society, and intellectual and cultural life. Coverage is international, with emphasis on monographic material, but important serial publications and occasionally articles of special significance are also included. All entries are annotated, frequently with critical comments and references to similar works.

The second volume, *Southeastern Europe*, covers Albania, Bulgaria, Greece, Romania, and Yugoslavia and has identical arrangement. Both volumes list over 6,000 entries, but the main value of this work is not its quantity, but the well-designed criteria for selection. In this respect, the two volumes omit very little. The third part of the first volume is an index of authors and publishers, with rather unique information for scholars.

Dr. Horecky, Assistant Chief of the Slavic and Central European Division of the Library of Congress, is to be congratulated for this substantial contribution. Both volumes, along with his earlier guides, *Basic Russian Publications* (1962) and *Russia and the Soviet Union* (1965), will serve the academic community well as standard sources of information. —Bohdan S. Wynar. [R: WLB, June 70; LJ, July 70; Choice, July-Aug 70; ARBA 71, items 237, 237a]

113. Pundeff, Marin V. **Bulgaria: A Bibliographic Guide.** Washington, Reference Dept., Slavic and Central European Division, Library of Congress, 1965; repr. New York, Arno, 1969(c.1968). 98p. index. $5.50. LC 65-60006. ISBN 0-405-00059-6.

This well-designed bibliographic guide follows the pattern of Fischer-Galati's bibliography on Rumania (1963). The first part is a narrative bibliographic survey of major sources, in subject categories: general reference works, land and people, language and literature, history, politics, government and law, economy and social conditions, and intellectual and artistic life. The second part is an alphabetical listing of 1,243 sources discussed in the first section. Science and technology are not covered; as some reviewers rightly point out (e.g., *Slavic Review*, Sept. 1969, p. 532) the inclusion of at least the history and philosophy of science would greatly improve this pioneering work. No comparable bibliography has been compiled since *The Balkans: A Selected List of References* (Library of Congress, 1943). [R: LJ, 1 Sept 69; ARBA 70, v.1, p. 43]

114. **Ukraine: A Concise Encyclopaedia. Volume 2.** Prepared by Shevchenko Scientific Society. Edited by Volodymyr Kubijovych. Toronto, Buffalo, published for the Ukrainian National Association by University of Toronto Press, 1971. 1394p. illus. (some col.) maps. index. $60.00; $94.50/set. ISBN 0-8020-3261-3 (v.2).

A Concise Encyclopaedia is a revised and substantially enlarged version of the three-volume work published in Ukrainian in 1949 by the Shevchenko Scientific Society in Munich. The first volume, published in 1963, covers physical geography and natural history, population, ethnography, language, history, culture, and literature.

The present, concluding volume provides information on law; Ukrainian church; education and research institutions; libraries, archives, and museums; book publishing and the press; the arts; music and choreography; theater and cinema; national economy; health, medical services, and physical culture; and military science. There is also a separate chapter on Ukrainians abroad. Several hundred noted scholars cooperated in this project; all articles are signed, with appended bibliographical listings of additional sources of information. The material is arranged under broad subject categories as noted above, with numerous subdivisions, and some 800 illustrations are integrated with the narrative.

The first volume of this work, which is probably the most authoritative single source on the Ukraine and its history in the English language, received most favorable reviews in many professional journals, including *Slavic Review*. The second volume retains the distinguished tradition of its predecessor, providing a well-balanced and impressive presentation of the subjects covered. Both volumes offer a wealth of information. [R: ARBA 72, item 270]

115. **Who Was Who in the USSR: A Biographic Directory Containing 5,015 Biographies of Prominent Soviet Historical Personalities.** Comp. by the Institute for the Study of the USSR. Metuchen, N.J., Scarecrow, 1972. 687p. index. $42.50. LC 70-161563. ISBN 0-8108-0441-7.

This biographical directory covers important Soviet persons no longer living. According to the preface, "it includes a certain number of biographies of people who actively campaigned against the Soviet regime or were later exiled or put to death by the Soviet authorities." Criteria for selection are stated in the preface: "contains 5,015 biographies of prominent individuals who made major contributions to the political, intellectual, scientific, social and economic life of the country." Thus, this is a sequel to some of the Institute's other publications, such as *Biographic Directory of the USSR* (Scarecrow, 1958), two volumes of *Who's Who in the USSR* for 1961-62 and 1965-66 (International Book and Publishing Co., 1962 and 1966), *Prominent Personalities in the USSR* (Scarecrow, 1968), and *Party or Government Officials of the Soviet Union 1917-1967* (Scarecrow, 1969).

Biographical sketches vary in length, depending on the relative importance of the biographee and, of course, on the availability of sources. Thus, we find a fairly lengthy article on M. S. Grushevskiy (which should actually be Hrushevskyi), but rather inadequate treatment of Mykola Khvylovyi (real name Fitilov and not Fitilyova), a Ukrainian writer who committed suicide in 1933. We find much better coverage of Russian personalities, including some of only minor importance— e.g., F. K. Mironov, military commander; diplomat A. I. Plakhin; or the Russian critic Adrian I. Piotrovskiy, to name only a few. Occasionally the editors have problems with English terminology (e.g., M. M. Pistrak is called an "educationist," rather than an "educator"). The treatment provided for L. G. Kornilov, one of the co-founders of the Russian Volunteer Army, is rather inadequate, in spite of the fact that there are many biographical studies about him. And occasionally the editors take official Soviet material at face value—see the biography of I. P. Kripyakevich or, an even better example, the noted literary historian V. N. Peretts.

Summing up, the coverage is uneven. However, considering the magnitude of the undertaking, this biographical directory is among the best works compiled by the Institute. —Bohdan S. Wynar. [R: LJ, 15 May 72, p. 1799; Choice, Sept 72, p. 795; ARBA 73, item 246]

GREAT BRITAIN

116. **The Dictionary of National Biography: 1951-1960.** Edited by E. T. Williams and Helen M. Palmer. New York, Oxford University Press, 1971. 1150p. index. $32.25. ISBN 0-19-865206-2.

DNB hardly needs an introduction. The present volume includes 760 biographies describing "the lives of men and women who for a significant period of their careers were British subjects and died between 1 January 1951 and 31 December 1960" (Prefatory Note). The main dictionary to 1900, edited by Sir Leslie Stephen and Sir Sidney Lee, was published in 63 volumes from 1885 to 1900. It was completed to 1900 by the issue of a supplement, and was reissued in 22 volumes by Oxford University Press in 1938. The main set is supplemented by "The Twentieth Century D.N.B.," each volume of which covers approximately 10 years. The present volume is the sixth in this series of supplements, with a cumulative index for all previous volumes—that is, for the years 1901-1960. [R: Choice, Mar 72, p. 42; WLB, Jan 72, p. 454; C&RL, Jan 72, p. 42; ARBA 73, item 239]

117. **Directory of British Associations & Associations in Ireland: Interests, Activities and Publications of Trade Associations, Scientific and Technical Societies, Professional Institutes, Learned Societies, Research Organisations, Chambers of Trade and Commerce, Agricultural Societies, Trade Unions, Cultural, Sports, and Welfare Organisations in the United Kingdom and in the Republic of Ireland.** 4th ed., 1974-5. Beckenham, Kent, England, CBD Research; distr. Detroit, Gale, 1974. 399p. index. $30.00. ISBN 0-900246-15-4.

There are many directories for Great Britain, as evidenced by Henderson's *Current British Directories: A Comprehensive Guide to the Directories of the British Isles with Commonwealth and International Sections*. The present volume, now in its fourth edition, is one of the best. Based on a questionnaire administered by the publisher, it lists in one alphabet major associations, trade organizations, etc., as indicated in the subtitle. The scope of DBA is basically limited to national organizations located in the British Isles. Not included in this directory are friendly societies, building societies, benevolent societies in aid of specific occupational groups, and similar organizations.

A typical entry includes the full name of the organization, date of establishment, validity indicator (whether or not the questionnaire was returned), address of the headquarters or secretary, telephone number, membership data, activities, type of association, publications, and other pertinent information (e.g., previous names, information on branches or affiliated organizations, etc.). Abbreviation and subject indexes conclude this volume.

The present edition has been substantially enlarged; in conjunction with such fact-finding books as *Directory of European Associations*, also published by CBD Research, it will help larger libraries locate desired information. It is not, however, so well executed as the well-known *Encyclopedia of Associations*, which covers a similar field for the United States. What is lacking in the CBD work is a more detailed description of activities, although this obviously results from the failure of the organizations to cooperate in providing information. Some aspects of the problem of obtaining cooperation are explained in the preface. —Bohdan S. Wynar. [R: ARBA 75, item 80]

118. Pemberton, John E. **British Official Publications**. 2nd rev. ed. New York, Pergamon Press, 1973. 328p. index. (Library and Technical Information). $9.00. LC 73-16231. ISBN 0-08-017797-2.

This new edition of Pemberton's exemplary text and reference work reflects some institutional changes and includes a chapter on non-H.M.S.O. publications, which were accorded only one paragraph in Chapter 17 of the first edition. Chapter 14, "Science, Technology and Medicine," has been dropped from this revision and its matter relocated in other chapters. What remains is essentially the same, in up-dated fashion: a pellucid treatise for the beginning student and a valuable source book for the practitioner by virtue of its detailed index.

The text begins with a brief, but adequate, overview of British parliamentary government. Following are an explanation of the classification and indexing appa-ratus, a discussion of the proceedings and journals of the parliament, Commons and Lords papers, Command papers, Royal Commissions, bills, debates, acts, administrative tribunals, so-called non-parliamentary papers (that is, statutory instruments and "Green Papers"), reference works of significance, statistics, docu-ments in the National Archives, and information on how to obtain H.M.S.O. and non-H.M.S.O. publications.

The second edition has wisely continued the practice of supplying specimen pages of lists, tables, and indexes illustrating the salient access tools. Pemberton's text, along with Ford's *A Guide to Parliamentary Papers* (3rd ed., 1972) and Olle's *An Introduction to British Government Publications* (2nd ed., 1973) is a standard guide to British government publications. —Joseph H. Morehead. [R: Choice, July-Aug 74, pp. 741-42; ARBA 75, item 110]

119. Pollard, Alfred W., and G. R. Redgrave. **Short Title Catalogue of Books Printed in England, Scotland, and Ireland, and of English Books Printed Abroad, 1475-1640**. London, Bibliographical Society, 1926; repr. New York, Oxford University Press, 1970. 609p. $9.95. LC 47-20884.

This bibliography was originally intended to provide a preliminary list for the preparation of a more complete catalog. It lists about 26,500 items. Arrange-ment is alphabetical by authors and other main entries. Entries give author, brief title, size, printer, date, reference to entry of the book in the Stationers' registers, and location of copies in libraries. This important feature includes a listing of all known copies of very rare items and a representative selection of British and American libraries having copies of the more common books. One hundred thirty-three British and fifteen American libraries are represented. Cataloging rules of the British Museum were followed. The varied methods used to enter anonymous works and to indicate cross references make the bibliography difficult to use. Omissions from abridged titles are not indicated. The original punctuation of titles is not always followed. In spite of inaccuracies and inconsistencies, however, this bibliography is very valuable as the most comprehensive list of English books for the period. —Bohdan S. Wynar. [R: ARBA 71, item 20]

120. Ward, William S. **British Periodicals and Newspapers, 1789-1832: A Bibli-ography of Secondary Sources**. Lexington, University Press of Kentucky, 1972. 387p. index. $21.00. LC 74-190536. ISBN 0-8131-1271-0.

This is a sequel to Ward's *Index and Finding List of Serials Published in the British Isles, 1789-1832*, which was published in 1953. In the present work the author attempts to "provide a bibliography of the books and articles that have been written about the newspapers and periodicals listed in that *Index*." Recorded here are all sorts of writings that deal with the history of these newspapers and periodicals, with the men who wrote for them or who edited them or produced them, and with the "public that read them and the government that was concerned with their impact upon the times."

The work contains a unit that lists general bibliographies and bibliographical studies and general studies, both arranged alphabetically by author. This is followed by units on periodicals, arranged under name of journal; people, arranged by surname; and places, arranged by place-name. The final unit includes material on printing, production, advertising, freedom of the press, etc. There are some brief annotations for a few of the entries. The indexes are most complete and are arranged in three units: authors, subjects, and library catalogs and union lists.

A specialized, but useful, guide whose aim is to "disentomb as many of these memoirs and books and articles as possible and thereby make it easier for those who come hereafter to discover what others have already said and done." —Paul A. Winckler. [R: Choice, May 73, p. 434; ARBA 74, item 30]

121. Woodworth, David P., ed. **Guide to Current British Journals**. 2nd ed. London, The Library Association, 1973; distr. New York, R. R. Bowker, 1974. 2v. index. $37.50. ISBN 0-85365-356-9(v.1); 0-85365-097-7(v.2).

The first edition of *Guide to Current British Journals* was published in 1970. This new edition lists 4,706 journals, which is 1,848 more than the first edition. It includes those published in England, Wales, Scotland, Northern Ireland, the Isle of Man, and the Channel Islands.

The directory is arranged by the Universal Decimal Classification system. Entries provide current title, former title (if any), first year of publication, circulation figures, subscription rates, frequency of issue, name and address of publisher, level of appeal (i.e., popular, technical research, trade/professional, society, or house organ), and notes describing special features such as book reviews, obituaries, legal notices, etc. Those journals indexed in *British Education Index*, *British Humanities Index*, *British Technology Index*, and/or *Internationale Bibliographie der Zeitschriften-literatur* are so noted.

Three useful appendixes contain handy lists. The first provides details of those journals carrying abstracts of the literature of their field, the second lists discontinued journals, and the third lists societies and their publications. Volume one also contains a subject/title index. Volume two, a directory of publishers of journals, provides their addresses and a list of the titles they publish. [R: BL, 15 Apr 74, p. 889; LJ, 15 June 74, p. 1682; LJ, July 74, p. 1796; ARBA 75, item 28]

LATIN AMERICA

122. Comitas, Lambros. **Caribbeana 1900-1965: A Topical Bibliography**. Seattle, University of Washington Press, 1970 (c.1968). 909p. $15.00 LC 68-14239. ISBN 0-295-73970-3.

A unique bibliography of twentieth century publications on the non-Hispanic Caribbean islands and mainland territories. Unannotated, it is deliberately unselective, except for the requirement of a minimal level of scholarly value. The 7,000 references include books, monographs, reports, periodical articles, unpublished theses, and "authored" government documents. Entries were drawn mainly from the scholarly libraries and special collections of New York City (locations are cited). Supplementary searching was done in various libraries and collections in the West Indies, London, and Canada. Nothing was included without examination, even references from the nearly 700 periodicals. The compiler's limited claim to have included "most of the scholarly writings" in this field is perhaps modest, but probably just (given that the large and important class of agency-produced documents is intentionally omitted).

The arrangement consists of ten major themes subdivided into topic-chapters (sixty-seven in all). It has virtually no subject limitations, covering all topics of possible interest to social scientists (the primary audience). The expected topics are all here under cultural, historical, political, socioeconomic, and environmental science categories, but there also are such imaginative topic-chapter headings as: Values and Norms; Cultural Continuities and Acculturation; Ethnohealth and Ethnomedicine; West Indians Abroad; and Theory and Methodology.

There are author and geographic indexes, but no subject index (or keyword or catch-title index). Some help is provided by the coding of the unannotated entries to bring out additional subject aspects. There are other useful codings and marginal cues, part of a splendid format. —David Rosenbaum. [R: ARBA 71, item 232]

123. Delpar, Helen. ed. **Encyclopedia of Latin America**. New York, McGraw-Hill, 1974. 651p. illus. $29.95. LC 74-1036. ISBN 0-07-055645-8.

Many hard-to-find facts on such topics as population, political parties, trade, communism, transportation, etc., are included in this alphabetically arranged encyclopedia. All the information is in a very concise form; most articles are less than half a page in length, but some run to two or three pages. The 1,600 articles are signed and many are accompanied by bibliographies. There is a general article on each of the 18 Spanish-speaking republics, plus Brazil, Haiti, and Puerto Rico; these articles cover history, geography, industry, and culture. The encyclopedia seems to be particularly rich in biographies; included are political figures, writers, musicians, and artists of all kinds, both living and dead. According to the editor, "efforts were made to include . . . every vital subject or person related to each country's history and position in the world." This can be considered as an excellent one-volume reference work for identifying Latin Americans and as a source for current statistics on many aspects of Latin America. —Donald J. Lehnus. [R: ALA 74; ARBA 75, item 316]

124. Gropp, Arthur E. **A Bibliography of Latin American Bibliographies: Supplement**. Metuchen, N.J., Scarecrow Press, 1971. 277p. index. $8.50. LC 68-9330. ISBN 0-8108-0350-X.

This bibliography supplements and updates the author's 1968 edition. Both of Gropp's works, the 1968 edition and this supplement, are based on the 1942 compilation by Cecil K. Jones and J. A. Granier. This supplement must be used with the 1968 edition, since its 1,400 entries, excepting 432 imprints dated prior to 1965, do not attempt to cumulate the earlier work. In essence, this book continues both the organizational format and bibliographical objectives initiated by Cecil K. Jones's work.

Items are arranged by subject with geographical subdivisions; entries are listed alphabetically by author within these subdivisions. There are subject subdivisions, where appropriate. If there is too little material or if it is too specific to be accommodated under a broad subject or geographical division, arrangement is alphabetical by author under a main heading.

On the whole, the supplement is successful, well organized, and quite valuable. Forty sources are listed for the Latin American bibliographies—rather authoritative, considering that this is just a supplement. The subjects with the greatest number of entries are biography, education, periodicals, and library catalogs. There is a good table of contents, an abbreviation guide and a 66-page index, alphabetically arranged by author and subject. Brief, but useful, comments are listed under a very few of the citations. Unfortunately, the format and printing, quite aside from the few typographical errors, leave something to be desired.

As an access tool to the literature on Latin America, it is a basic work to have. The index is extensive and easy to use, particularly for providing intellectual access where a definite work or specific area of interest may be vague in the user's mind. —Robert P. Haro. [R: ARBA 72, item 242]

MIDDLE EAST

125. Adams, Michael. **The Middle East: A Handbook**. New York, Praeger, 1971. 633p. maps. bibliog. index. (Handbooks of the Modern World). $25.00. LC 77-134528.

Another volume in the well-known "Handbooks of the Modern World" series. The structure of this volume is quite similar to that of the previous volumes. Part I provides general background; Part II is an alphabetical listing of individual countries with brief information on geography, population, government, recent history, and mass media. In Part III, Political Affairs, a number of well-known authors discuss such problems as Arab nationalism, political forces in the Middle East, etc.—a total of five topical articles. Part IV deals with economic affairs; Part V with social patterns; and Part VI with the Arts and Media.

How does it compare with similar Europa publications? First, it might be noted that chapter bibliographies are somewhat dated, but statistical information is quite recent (usually stops with 1968). Praeger's handbooks provide more information on certain topics common to a number of countries—e.g., an article on art in the Arab states of the Middle East. The Europa annual presents more factual data, including historical statistics. Consequently, it might be fair to say that the two publications are supplementary, serving different purposes. —Bohdan S. Wynar. [R: LJ, Aug 71, p. 2480; ALA 71; ARBA 72, item 275]

126. **Encyclopaedia Judaica**. Jerusalem, Encyclopaedia Judaica; New York, Macmillan, 1972. 16v. illus.(part col.). index. $500.00. LC 72-177492.

The history of *Encyclopaedia Judaica* was detailed in the February 28, 1972, issue of PW, and we will not repeat this information here. It is sufficient to say that it started in the late 1950s. There are 25,000 entries, 11 million words, and over 8,000 illustrations in color and black and white, plus hundreds of maps, charts, tables, diagrams, and other illustrative material. In addition to the 2,000 contributors, there are many divisional and departmental editors. The editor in chief was Professor Cecil Roth, until his death in 1970; he was succeeded by Dr. Geoffrey Wigoder, who served from 1966 to 1970 as deputy editor in chief. All articles are signed with initials, and identification is provided in the first volume, where one also finds a lengthy introduction, an index, and other supplementary material.

The criteria of selection are discussed in the introduction. The goal was comprehensive coverage of all subjects and areas related to Jewish problems. Thus, there are many long articles on modern and historical Israel, Zionism, arts and sciences, philosophy, the Bible, Yiddish literature, Jews and their contributions to individual countries, etc. There are a number of so-called "capsule" entries— "to expand the scope of biographical entries, especially covering the participation of Jews in world culture" (p. 7). It should be noted, however, that many biographies found in other encyclopedias (even in the more popular *Universal Jewish Encyclopedia*) have been omitted in the *Judaica*. Longer articles are subdivided by specific topics; thus, "Synagogue" (Vol. 15, pp. 579-630) has eight main subdivisions plus some 30 sections, all represented in an outline preceding the article. There are extensive bibliographies appended to each article, and, in most cases, the coverage is well balanced.

Probably the only serious drawback to this encyclopedia is its index (some 250,000 entries), which is incomplete and hard to use. In addition, compared to the rest of this lavishly produced encyclopedia, it is not easy to read and it contains a number of typographical errors. In general, the treatment of most subjects is highly authoritative and well balanced. Occasionally, there are some ideologically inspired colorings, especially with respect to more recent political events or the history of Jewish minorities in individual countries (notably in Eastern Europe). But this is probably to be expected, since this is, after all, a national Jewish encyclopedia; even scholars are entitled to their opinions. All in all, this is a monumental work; it will be envied by the many nations that do not have anything even close to it. —Bohdan S. Wynar. [R: LJ, Aug 72, p. 2562; Choice, Oct 72, pp. 948-49; WLB, June 72, p. 933; PW, 28 Feb 72, pp. 46-47; ALA 72; ARBA 73, item 274]

127. **Encyclopedia of Zionism and Israel**. Edited by Raphael Patai. New York, Herzl Press and McGraw-Hill, 1971. 2v. illus. bibliog. $44.50. LC 68-55271. ISBN 0-07-079635-1.

Recent years have witnessed a number of scholarly reference materials about Israel and Jewish problems in general, including such notable works as *Encyclopaedia Judaica*. The present work deals primarily with the Zionist movement and, with its nearly 3,000 signed articles written by some 285 contributing authors, it constitutes probably the most authoritative single source on this subject. The history of this interesting project is described in some detail in the Preface. Originally, some 12 years ago, it was envisioned as a "Zionist Encyclopedia." Gradually, during the process of preparation, its scope was substantially enlarged and it was agreed that since "Zionism and Israel were so closely intertwined, the nature of material to be covered in the encyclopedia required that they be given equal attention." Thus, both subjects receive adequate coverage and the reader will find here not only a well-documented presentation of the history of the Zionist movement in various countries, but also a description of Zionist institutions in Israel integrated with Israel's political and social history, cultural customs, governmental agencies, Jewish immigration, etc. In addition to articles that, generally speaking, may be described as topical (e.g., "Belgium, Zionism in," or "Architecture and Planning in Israel"), there are a number of biographical articles, primarily on Zionist leaders and Israeli statesmen and public officials. The third category consists of articles of a geographic nature, describing major cities, towns, regions, etc. Most of them are rather brief.

To this reviewer, some of the best documented articles are "Crime in Israel" and "Foreign Aid Program in Israel," while, on the other hand, such topics as "Assimilation" or even "Anti-Semitism" seem to be rather brief, considering the availability of material on both subjects. For most major countries (e.g., Germany, Russia, the United States), the encyclopedia presents well-written surveys of interrelations between Zionism and Israel. There are separate articles for immigrants from various countries (e.g., Bulgarian Jews in Israel, German Jews in Israel). It is probably unfortunate that even the major articles do not contain bibliographical listings referring the reader to additional sources of information. A selected bibliography is appended at the end of the second volume but, as one might expect, it is limited to monographic works. The text is accompanied by many black and white illustrations.

On the whole, *Encyclopedia of Zionism and Israel* is a modern reference work that presents a wealth of information and a well-balanced treatment of the different subjects. It is one of the best sources available on this subject today. —Bohdan S. Wynar. [R: RQ, Fall 71, p. 74; LJ, 1 Nov 71, p. 3594; ALA 71; ARBA 72, item 268]

128. Wigoder, Geoffrey, ed. **Encyclopaedic Dictionary of Judaica.** Jerusalem, Keter Publishing House; distr. New York, Leon Amiel, 1974. 673p. illus.(part col.). index. $29.95. LC 74-12588. ISBN 0-8148-0598-1.

In recent times we have witnessed an unparalled flourishing of Jewish scholarship. In the United States the 10-volume *Universal Jewish Encyclopedia* was published from 1939 to 1943 and was reprinted by KTAV in 1969. *Encyclopaedia Judaica* (New York, Macmillan, 1972; 16v.) is being updated regularly with yearbooks. Planned as a complementary volume to the 16-volume *Encyclopaedia Judaica*, the *Encyclopaedic Dictionary* contains some 15,000 entries covering broad aspects of Jewish culture, history, and literature. Most articles represent a condensed treatment of subjects found in *Encyclopaedia Judaica*, with special emphasis on topics of current interest, such as Jewish contributions to world culture, population statistics, Jewish customs, and, obviously, all aspects of Israel. The volume is intended as a mini-encyclopedia on Jewish subjects for school and home use. Well indexed and well illustrated, the *Encyclopaedic Dictionary of Judaica* is professionally executed and is highly recommended for its intended audience. —Bohdan S. Wynar. [R: ARBA 75, item 320]

CHAPTER 4

HISTORY

GENERAL WORKS

129. Poulton, Helen J. **The Historian's Handbook: A Descriptive Guide to Reference Works.** Norman, University of Oklahoma Press, 1972. 304p. index. $9.95; $4.95pa. LC 71-165774. ISBN 0-8061-0985-8.

Intended for students of history as a conveniently arranged handbook to basic source material, this work should provide substantial assistance for the uninitiated. The following topics are covered: the library and its catalog; national library catalogs and national and trade bibliographies; guides, manuals, and bibliographies; encyclopedias, dictionaries, and chronologies; almanacs, yearbooks, statistical handbooks, and current surveys; serials and newspapers; geographical aids—including bibliographies, indexes, gazetteers, etc.; biographical materials; primary sources and dissertations; legal sources; and government publications. The material is presented in the form of bibliographical essays, with some 970 titles mentioned in the text. The coverage is international, and the reader will find here a good sampling of basic reference materials pertaining not only to the United States but also to Great Britain, Latin America, the Soviet Union, the Far East, etc. Unfortunately, Western European countries and the Soviet Union receive rather sketchy coverage, which is probably the only serious drawback of this otherwise satisfactory handbook. —Bohdan S. Wynar. [R: LJ, 15 May 72, p. 1789; WLB, June 72, p. 928; RQ, Fall 72, p. 94; ALA 72; ARBA 73, item 301]

WORLD HISTORY

ENCYCLOPEDIAS

130. Dupuy, R. Ernest, and Trevor N. Dupuy. **The Encyclopedia of Military History.** New York, Harper and Row, 1970. 1406p. illus. bibliog. indexes. maps. $20.00. LC 74-81871.

A monumental reference work covering the world's history of armed conflict and associated military matters from 3500 B.C. to the present, compiled by two of America's most renowned and prolific professional soldier-historians (*Compact History of the Civil War*; *Brave Men and Great Captains*; *Military Heritage of America*; etc.). The entire gamut of world military history is examined both chronologically and by physical region, and is arranged in orderly, readable form. An advisory staff of esteemed academicians and retired military officers assisted the Dupuys to insure accuracy and an uncommon degree of definitiveness. The result

is the most comprehensive and current volume of its kind in the English language today. Arrangement is by 21 separate periods of time with a chapter covering each from the standpoint of contemporary military trends, famed leaders, state of the art or science of administration, equipment, organization, logistics, tactics and strategy. Significant conflicts are surveyed chronologically and are also treated regionally to explain causal factors and each war's outcome as influenced by (and influencing) peoples and/or nations within the region. Buttressing the text are more than 80 black and white drawings and photographs plus over 160 maps. Some of the latter are too small to read easily; others, particularly those illustrating battle plans, sometimes neglect to incorporate a scale. The bibliography is in two parts: one is general in nature, the other lists works considered most appropriate to a particular period or type of warfare. Although not exhaustive, it does include most of the major U.S. and British trade books on the subject of war published since 1900. The outstanding feature of the work is the indexes. There are three, all voluminous, exhaustively compiled and excellently cross-referenced. The reader may gain access to desired information either by (1) a general index which incorporates events, subjects and persons mentioned in the text, (2) a specific index of battles and sieges or (3) an index of wars, including rebellions and civil and colonial conflicts. For the benefit of lay readers a glossary of military terms might well have been included.
—Lawrence E. Spellman. [R: Choice, Oct 70; ARBA 71, item 317]

131. Langer, William L. **An Encyclopedia of World History: Ancient, Medieval, and Modern, Chronologically Arranged.** 5th ed. rev. and enl. Boston, Houghton Mifflin, 1972. 1569p. illus. maps. genealogical tables. index. $17.50. LC 68-14147. ISBN 0-395-13592-3.

The outlines in this work provide a historical chronology for important events that occurred in various places throughout the world from prehistoric times through 1970. The broad periods are subdivided geographically, and events are concisely described. The fourth revised edition (1968) was a major revision in which more material was added to the prehistory section, including information on new dating techniques, and sections on art, literature, thought, and science and technology were also incorporated. Cross references were improved and better genealogical tables were prepared. Lists of emperors, popes, and rulers are included. Fifty-seven outline maps and 104 genealogical tables are included in the fifth edition.

The fifth edition (1972) brings the chronologies up to January 1, 1971, incorporating events in the Middle East, Southeast Asia, the cultural revolution in China, the emergence of Japan as a prime industrial power, the increase in the number of states gaining their independence, the youth revolt and drastic changes in educational systems, and race conflicts. An extensive index supplies access to names of events, places, and people mentioned in the text. It should be noted that Langer's *New Illustrated Encyclopedia of World History* (1975) in two volumes varies from the work above only in its lavish illustrations. There is no evidence of textual revision.
—Christine L. Wynar. [R: ARBA 73, item 309; ARBA 76, item 300]

132. Morris, Richard B., and Graham W. Irwin, eds. **Harper Encyclopedia of the Modern World: A Concise Reference History from 1760 to the Present.** New York, Harper and Row, 1970. 1271p. $17.50. LC 73-81879. ISBN 0-06-013072-5.

This book should be very useful in reference work and for study or review. It resembles Langer's *An Encyclopedia of World History* in its general make-up but, because their field is limited to the past two centuries, the editors can bring in more detail and at the same time give a clearer description of events than Langer was able to do.

The encyclopedia is arranged in two parts: I, Basic Chronology, in which political and military history is summarized; and II, Topical Chronology, which includes the social, intellectual, and cultural developments of the period under review. One of its most commendable qualities is the amount of attention to the history of Asia, Africa, and Latin America, as well as to those events and developments more immediately connected to Europe and North America. Another is the amount of space devoted to non-political and non-military history in part two, almost half the encyclopedia. There are 52 maps scattered through the text; all but a few are political or military. A few statistical tables are provided, but no genealogical tables or lists of world leaders. From time to time the continuity of an account of a government, a war, or a cultural development has to be broken off, in order to maintain some semblance of a chronological arrangement; a note at the end of the article gives the page on which the subject is continued, which is helpful, but equally useful notes on the last previous treatment of the subject are not provided. The index has been prepared with care and professional skill and its use is mandatory if all information on a given subject is to be located.   —Rolland E. Stevens. [R: ALA 71; ARBA 71, item 318]

CHRONOLOGIES

133. Storey, R. L. **Chronology of the Medieval World, 800-1491**. New York, McKay, 1973. 750p. index. $15.95. LC 72-90909.

This work is the third volume of an untitled series edited by Neville Williams. Other volumes in the series cover the modern world from 1492 to 1965.

Actual political events that can be dated, at least to the year, are listed on the verso pages; social and cultural happenings are listed under six categories on the recto pages; 1) law and politics; 2) economics, science, technology, and discovery; 3) religion and education; 4) art, architecture, and music; 5) literature, philosophy, and scholarship; 6) births and deaths. The work is very fully and accurately indexed, with numerous cross references and a preliminary guide to the subject headings used. The only difficulty noted in the index was the entry of Thomas Aquinas as "Aquinas, St."; other saints are cited in the usual fashion.

Headings at the top of each page are an aid to the occasional "skimmer" who wants a bird's-eye view of the Middle Ages. The specialist may note lacunae, but the reviewer was quite pleased with the comprehensiveness and accuracy of the work. Although Europe predominates in the listing of events, other continents that have left records are not neglected. The volume is tastefully printed, with dates, headlines, and subjects in heavy type for ease of reference.   —Francis J. Witty. [R: ALA 73; ARBA 75, item 353]

134. Williams, Neville, comp. **Chronology of the Expanding World 1492-1762**. New York, McKay, 1969. 710p. index. $12.50.

A chronology of dates arranged in tabular form, providing a month-by-month approach to significant events. The left-hand pages chronicle the political and military highlights of a particular year and the right-hand pages, major events in sciences, religion, arts and economy, etc. This volume was reissued in conjunction with a new edition of *Chronology of the Modern World 1763 to the Present*. Both works were best described by a reviewer in *Saturday Review* as an "amply stocked historical cafeteria," with a rather poorly designed index. Nevertheless, most public libraries will find such a compilation handy for ready reference purposes, since nothing similar exists. [R: SR, 6 Dec 69; ALA 70; ARBA 70, v.1, p. 55]

ATLASES

135. Darby, H. C., and Harold Fullard, eds. **The New Cambridge Modern History: Volume XIV, Atlas.** New York, Cambridge University Press, 1970. 319p. maps. bibliog. index. $37.50; $12.95pa. ISBN 0-521-09908-0.

The *Atlas* was designed to accompany *The New Cambridge Modern History*. However, it can stand alone as a useful adjunct to the study of modern history, whatever text might be used. Darby is Professor of Geography and Fullard is the Cartographic Editor for George Philip & Son Ltd.

The compilers have done an excellent job of presenting a balanced coverage, and the atlas depicts the world as it was at various times in the modern era. There are maps of Europe, North America, Latin America, Africa, the Far East and Australasia. The 288 maps are essentially political, but thematic maps are also included, and all have been newly compiled for this atlas, with reproduction done by a lithographic process that gives them a sharp and clean appearance. Typography is well selected and is crisp and sharp; the color work is pleasing and excellently registered. Maps within groups are arranged in chronological sequence and are reproduced on the same scale so that the user can make meaningful comparisons. Projection is not indicated for every map, but the editors have selected those projections which were most useful for the presentation of particular data.

A 31-page short subject index facilitates access to the cartographic data, and a three-page short title bibliography will be useful to scholars. There is no text.

The only criticism that might be leveled would be the size of the volume, which had to be scaled to match the other volumes in the set. It is difficult to print a minutely detailed map on a 6 x 9 inch page, and a folio volume would have been preferred. On the other hand, the compact size makes it easy to handle. —Frank J. Anderson. [R: ALA 71; ARBA 71, item 320]

136. Gilbert, Martin. **Recent History Atlas: 1870 to the Present Day.** Cartography by John R. Flower. New York, Macmillan, 1969. 121p. maps. $4.95. LC 69-17102.

Supplements and complements the well-known *Shepherd's Historical Atlas*, which covers world history from 1450 B.C. to 1964, but in some areas it is not as comprehensive. Gilbert's atlas concentrates on the last 100 years of world history, providing detailed coverage of both world wars, the after-war period of cold war, the Korean conflict, and Vietnam. Arrangement of the 120 black-and-white maps is chronological and there is adequate explanation. Martin Gilbert is the author of

several atlases, among them *British History Atlas and American History Atlas*.
[R: LJ, 15 May 69; ALA 69; ARBA 70, v.1, p. 57]

137. Shepherd, William R. **Shepherd's Historical Atlas**. 9th ed., rev. and updated.
New York, Barnes & Noble, 1973 (c.1964). 115p. illus. maps. index. $17.50. LC
Map 64-26. ISBN 0-06-013846-7.

Beginning with the Old through New Kingdoms of Ancient Egypt (ca. 3000-
525 B.C.), Shepherd's superb atlas progresses in chronological arrangement to the
European community in 1973, covering all periods and continents. All maps of the
seventh edition (1929) have been reprinted and eight more, prepared by C. S.
Hammond & Company, have been appended to cover the period 1930 to 1973.
However, it would be more accurate to limit this latter date to the mid-1960s, as
one map of Europe cannot suffice to convey world history between then and 1973.

The Index and Index-Supplement provide thorough and detailed references
to the maps. Locations are coded to correspond to latitude/longitude grids, as well
as to page numbers for the maps. Variations in names, including classical and medieval Latin, and spellings of localities are noted or cross-referenced. The two indexes
together list names that appear in the original edition and those that are omitted
from it, and update the work to 1929. The indexes do not cover the eight new maps.

Typography is generally quite excellent, only occasionally fading, shadowing,
or being inadequately revised (as apparent on the map, "Central Europe about
1786"). Color and cartography are superior, especially in the basic work. There is
no text. —Peggy Jay. [R: WLB, May 74, p. 767; ARBA 75, item 352]

UNITED STATES HISTORY

GENERAL WORKS

138. Adams, James Truslow, ed. **Album of American History**. New York, Scribner's,
1969. 6v. illus. index. $120.00. LC 74-91746.

James Truslow Adams was one of America's most noteworthy historians and
essayists. He edited the well-known *Dictionary of American History* and *The Atlas
of American History*, and now an updated edition of *Album of American History*
is also available.

The first edition of this work was published in 1944-49 (5v.). Many scholars
cooperated in the preparation and organization of the articles. To obtain the pictorial material used in these volumes the editors have searched museums, libraries,
private collections, and public institutions of the country.

Volume one covers the colonial period. Around 1,600 pictures are presented,
many of them previously unknown. In reissuing this volume, the editors have revised 62 of the pages, providing improved pictorial treatments of the original subjects. The second volume illustrates the years 1783 to 1853, roughly the period of
westward expansion. In some 1,300 pictures of various types, with brief text, it
presents a chronological panorama of American politics, economic development,
social life, and customs. The third volume covers 1853-1893 and volume four
1893-1917. The fifth volume, which presents the pictorial history of the United
States between the years 1917 and 1953, was originally published after an interval

of 11 years. The sixth volume contains pictures illustrative of various phases of the years 1953 to 1968; it was edited by J.G.E. Hopkins. Like the previous volumes, it provides a pictorial chronicle of this period, covering in five chapters various aspects of American cultural and political life. This last volume also contains a general index to volumes one through six. An excellent work printed from new plates with some 6,300 pictures. —Bohdan S. Wynar. [R: ARBA 71, item 323]

139. Commager, Henry Steele, ed. **Documents of American History**. 9th ed. Englewood Cliffs, N.J., Prentice-Hall, 1973. 2v. index. $17.50/set. LC 73-11490. ISBN 0-13-217018-2(set).

Though it has been more than five years since the last edition of this basic reference tool was published, the ninth edition adds little in content. In fact, the first volume of the seventh edition, which this reviewer had at hand for comparison, duplicates exactly Volume I of the ninth edition. Volume II of the ninth differs from Volume II of the eighth only in that several documents (focusing mainly on civil rights and civil disobedience) have been dropped in order to make room for documents of the period from 1965 through mid-1973.

But for these exceptions, the ninth edition is almost a carbon copy of its predecessors. Commager still includes documents of an official/quasi-official nature, which he calls part of the country's "official record." Each document is preceded by a brief background note and an even briefer suggested bibliography. Treatment is chronological, beginning in Volume I with the "Privileges and Prerogatives Granted Columbus" on April 30, 1492, and ending in Volume II with Miller vs. California, the June 21, 1973, Supreme Court decision on obscenity. Volume II also repeats the Constitution in an appendix. —Wayne A. Wiegand. [R: WLB, Nov 74, p. 249; ARBA 75, item 354]

BIBLIOGRAPHIES

140. **Harvard Guide to American History**. Rev. ed. Ed. by Frank Freidel, with the assistance of Richard K. Showman. Cambridge, Mass., Belknap Press of Harvard University Press, 1974. 2v. index. $45.00. LC 72-81272. ISBN 0-674-37560-2.

The last edition of this standard work was published in 1954. This new edition has been expanded into two volumes. Volume one includes sections on research methods and materials, biographies and personal records, comprehensive and area histories, and histories of special subjects. Volume two is arranged chronologically, beginning with "America to 1789" and ending with "Twentieth Century." It should be noted that the cut-off date for inclusion of both books and articles was June 30, 1970.

The first chapter, "Research, Writing, and Publication," includes essays on history as a literary art, research, writing for publication (including guidelines for style, proofreading, and indexing), and book reviewing. In this chapter, a discussion of bibliographies notes the elements that should appear in bibliographical citations. But the entries in this work do not follow their own guidelines. Neither place of publication nor publishers' names are included in citations. (The 1954 edition did include place of publication, but not publisher.)

Some inconsistencies are still evident in this edition, and the updating seems to have been done on a random basis. In the section on government publications, *Checklist '70* is included, but *CIS/Index* and *Government Reference Books*, two serial publications that began in 1970, are not. Similar examples can be found in other sections.

The two volumes are indexed by authors and subjects. More detail in the subject index would have been helpful. A specific example is the list of individual biographies arranged by names. These names are not indexed. A title index would also have been a helpful feature.

As a standard general orientation guide, the *Harvard Guide to American History* is impressive. Nevertheless, one hopes that future editions will be published at more frequent intervals, and that more bibliographic detail will be provided in entries. —Sally Wynkoop. [R: WLB, Nov 74, p. 249; Choice, Dec 74, p. 1456; ARBA 75, item 355]

DICTIONARIES AND ENCYCLOPEDIAS

141. Boatner, Mark Mayo, III. **Encyclopedia of the American Revolution**. Bicentennial ed. New York, McKay, 1974. 1290p. illus. maps. index. $20.00. LC 73-91868. ISBN 0-679-50440-0.

Colonel Boatner, a noted military historian, author of *Civil War Dictionary*, *Landmarks of the American Revolution*, and other historical works, has prepared another outstanding reference work on the American Revolution. The encyclopedia, which covers the period from 1763 to 1783, contains alphabetically arranged articles on people, issues, and events of the American Revolutionary period. The volume contains a number of maps, diagrams, and genealogical charts, which increase the reference value of this encyclopedia. The author thoroughly covers the political, military, and diplomatic aspects of the Revolution and provides a reliable presentation of all important historical events. Many encyclopedic entries constitute biographical sketches of statesmen, diplomats, and officers. All entries contain necessary cross references. The author also provides a useful bibliography and a short-title index. —Lubomyr R. Wynar. [R: Choice, Dec 74, p. 1453; ARBA 75, item 365]

142. Carruth, Gordon, ed. **The Encyclopedia of American Facts and Dates**. 6th ed. with a supplement of the 70s. New York, T. Y. Crowell, 1972. 922p. index. $9.95. LC 72-78262. ISBN 0-690-26302-3.

The main text of this sixth edition has not been updated since the fifth edition (1970). Material continues to be presented in chronological order in four roughly parallel columns: (1) politics and government, war, disasters, vital statistics; (2) books, painting, drama, architecture, sculpture; (3) science, industry, economics, education, religion, philosophy; (4) sports, fashions, popular entertainment, folklore, society. The detailed index refers to appropriate year and column, rather than to page.

A supplementary section covers events from 1970 through 1971. The index to the supplement follows the format of the main index. These 31 additional pages of text and index have spared the publisher the expense and trouble of making new plates, but may not justify the purchase of this new edition. —Bohdan S. Wynar. [R: ARBA 73, item 323]

143. **Encyclopedia of American History.** Enlarged and updated. Edited by Richard B. Morris. New York, Harper and Row, 1970. 850p. maps. charts. $9.89. LC 73-95647.

The updated fourth edition of this historical encyclopedia follows the basic chronological arrangement of its previous editions (1953, 1961, 1965). The encyclopedia is designated "to provide in a single handy volume the essential historical facts about American life and institutions." The volume consists of four main parts: I, Basic Chronology (covers mainly political history of the United States); II, Topical Chronology (nonpolitical aspects of American life—economy, science and invention, thought and culture, expansion of the nation); III, Updated Supplement (basic and topical chronology for the years 1965-1969); IV, Four Hundred Notable Americans (biographical section).

The scope of the volume is broad and its presentation accurate, brief and easy to read. However, its arrangement and the index do not facilitate use of this reference compendium. It should be stressed that the new material in the "Updated Supplement" is contained in a separately paged section, along with an "Index to Updated Supplement." There was no attempt to integrate this new material and index into the main body of the encyclopedia. In order to use the topical chronological section, the user must check two places—the main "Topical Chronology" and the "Updated Supplement" and two indexes.

In the reviewer's opinion, the fourth part of the encyclopedia, devoted to biographical sketches of "Four Hundred Notable Americans," is of questionable value. Even the editor admitted that "making selection involved some arbitrary choices." As a consequence, there are many omissions of notable Americans. Biographical sketches are informative; however, the biography of Martin Luther King is divided and listed on pages 738 and 809, and the biography of Richard Nixon is not listed in alphabetical order under "N" but is located after "Zworykin."

Outstanding features of this encyclopedia include 36 maps and charts and a listing of leading court decisions. It is hoped that the future "completely revised" edition will eliminate the above-mentioned shortcomings, and that the "Updated Supplement," which now has separately paged signatures, will be integrated into the main body of the encyclopedia. —Lubomyr R. Wynar. [R: LJ, 15 Dec 70, p. 1442; RQ Winter 70, p. 174; ARBA 71, item 331]

144. Hurwitz, Howard L. **An Encyclopedic Dictionary of American History.** Rev. and updated. New York, Washington Square Press/Pocket Books, 1974. 913p. illus. maps. index. $1.95pa. LC 68-18511. ISBN 0-671-48757-4.

Originally published in 1968 as a ready reference work for the non-specialist in American history, this revised edition includes in a 30-page "Contemporary Supplement" items of national importance occurring between January 1969 and November 1973. Except for this "Supplement," the 1974 edition varies little from its predecessor.

The key to the tool is a 108-page index, which serves both text and "Supplement" and which lists under broad subject headings (e.g., "Indians" and "slavery") the cross references excluded from the body of the work. It is preceded by a section containing 30 maps, most of which are arranged chronologically, showing the nation's boundary changes. Still featured are complete texts of the Declaration of Independence and the Constitution.

The work includes 400 brief biographies—not to emphasize the importance of the lives of certain Americans, but to supply focus for cultural aspects difficult to pinpoint by a specific term. The length of each entry is determined by the author's judgment of the subject's relative importance in American history. An additional special feature provided on the inside of the front and back covers is a list of entries (without page numbers) relevant to the American Revolution, arranged under five broad chronological headings covering the years 1763 to 1789. —Wayne A. Wiegand. [R: ARBA 71, item 332; ARBA 75, item 367]

145. **Webster's Guide to American History: A Chronological, Geographical Survey and Compendium.** Editors: Charles Van Doren and Robert McHenry. Springfield, Mass., G. & C. Merriam Co., 1971. 1428p. illus. $14.95. ISBN 0-87779-081-7.

This is one of the better one-volume compendiums to American history. The material is divided into three main sections. The first section presents a compact chronology from 1492 to the end of the 1960s. Alongside the chronology of events appear quotations from the primary documents of the past that bear upon one or more of the particular events noted on the page. Part two consists of a collection of maps and tables (some maps in color), and part three includes 1,035 biographical sketches of notable Americans. One can always question the selection criteria in a work of this type, but, in general, it is a well-balanced compilation with good editorial execution. —Bohdan S. Wynar. [R: LJ, 15 May 71, p. 1697; WLB, May 71, p. 885; ARBA 72, item 305]

ATLASES

146. **Atlas of the American Revolution.** Map selection and commentary by Kenneth Nebenzahl. Narrative text by Don Higginbotham. New York, Rand McNally, 1974. 218p. illus.(col.). maps. index. $35.00. LC 74-6976. ISBN 0-528-83465-7.

This is a large, lavish, and colorful recapitulation of the Revolutionary War, its antecedents, actions, and outcome. Map commentary is by Kenneth Nebenzahl, internationally acclaimed rare map expert, and narrative text by Don Higginbotham, professor of history at the University of North Carolina and author of *The War of American Independence*.

The work is woven around a germane selection of over 70 superbly reproduced maps/map insets originally drawn during or very shortly after noteworthy military events of the period (e.g., Bunker Hill, Bemis Heights, Yorktown). These are arranged chronologically by theater of war to depict and accentuate their tactical or strategic import from the standpoint of what happened and how it influenced the colonial struggle for self-rule. Each map is accompanied by cogent notes on its cartographic information content. All are interconnected intelligibly by a sprightly 40,000-word account of the times, concentrating on the activities of individual political and military leaders. The source of each map is indicated. More than 100 illustrations of contemporary portraits, views, cartoons, broadsides, and other printed items exert an impact on the reader that is both stimulating and instructive.

Maps, text, and illustrations are printed on quality stock and are positioned with an aesthetic sense of visual balance and contrast that is rarely encountered in volumes of this type. An appendix lists alphabetically all major American, French,

British, and Hessian participants. The index contains approximately 600 entries keyed, as appropriate, to Higginbotham's text, Nebenzahl's map observations, and/ or the maps themselves. The sole drawback of the atlas is the omission of a bibliography or suggested reading list. Summation: outstanding political, social, and military portrait of the American Revolution limned by mapmakers of the period with significant appeal to both browser and researcher. —Lawrence E. Spellman. [R: LJ, 15 Nov 74, p. 2691; WLB, Dec 74, p. 314; ARBA 75, item 364]

BIOGRAPHY

147. Vexler, Robert I. **The Vice-Presidents and Cabinet Members: Biographies Arranged Chronologically by Administration.** Dobbs Ferry, N.Y., Oceana, 1975. 2v. index. $50.00/set. LC 75-28085. ISBN 0-379-12089-5(v.1); 0-379-12090-9 (v.2).

This two-volume work is a significant reference tool deserving consideration as an essential acquisition for all libraries. Biographical sketches of Vice Presidents and Cabinet members from the administration of George Washington to that of President Ford present basic, concise, and detailed information concerning the public and private lives of each individual. The editor has established December 31, 1974, as the concluding date for information contained therein. As an aid to the researcher, bibliographic references are cited to guide one's search to more detailed sources. These volumes have been planned by the publishers to be used with their "Presidential Chronology" series through a system of cross-checking. The editor has diligently cited the most accurate dates and other pertinent information through consultation with diaries and original documents. The appendix includes a listing of members of the various presidential administrations by term. This work appears to be more comprehensive and scholarly (albeit less entertaining) than Sol Barzman's *Madmen and Geniuses: The Vice Presidents of the United States* (Chicago, Follet, 1974). —Bernard D. Reams, Jr. [R: ARBA 76, item 340]

148. Warner, Ezra J., and W. Buck Yearns. **Biographical Register of the Confederate Congress.** Baton Rouge, Lousiana State University Press, 1975. 319p. illus. bibliog. $15.00. LC 74-77329. ISBN 0-8071-0092-7.

In their introduction, the compilers acknowledge that the Confederate Congresses were, for the most part, impotent, almost ceremonial gatherings. So inconsequential did Confederate Congressmen consider their legislative service that, after the War, surviving members often suppressed accounts and memoirs. Certainly no member rose to fame and prominence *because* he was a senator or representative.

Nonetheless, this scholarly volume, with its alphabetically arranged series of biographies of all men who served in the three Confederate Congresses (the Provisional Congress in five sessions from February 4, 1861, to February 17, 1862; the

First Congress in four sessions from February 18, 1862, to February 17, 1864; and the Second Congress in two sessions from May 2, 1864, to March 18, 1865) fills a gap in our knowledge of Southern Civil War history.

Each biographical sketch is itself a solid piece of historical research. Moreover, because of the fact already alluded to that ex-members were not proud of their legislative service, the research effort was extraordinarily difficult. All possibly relevant primary and secondary sources were combed for clues. Often the only source that yielded hard biographical data was the 1850 Census, the first census to record heads of households by name.

Sources are cited at the end of most sketches; those that lack source citations were compiled from such standard sources as the *Biographical Directory of the American Congress*. The latter work was particularly fruitful because many of the men who served as Confederate legislators had previously served in the U.S. Congress.

The work concludes with four appendixes (Sessions of the Confederate Congress, Standing Committees, Membership, and Maps of Occupied Confederate Territory, 1861-1864), and a bibliography of the manuscripts, newspapers, government documents, and other materials used as sources. —Richard A. Gray. [R: ARBA 76, item 341]

ETHNIC HISTORY

149. Katz, William Loren. **Teachers' Guide to American Negro History**. Rev. ed. Chicago, Quadrangle Books, 1971. 192p. illus. index. $6.95; $2.65pa. LC 68-13459. ISBN 0-8129-0059-6; 0-531-06457-3pa.

First published in 1968, this guide offers "a framework for the full-scale integration of Negro contributions into the existing American history course of study."

The first chapter discusses basic concepts and attitudes needed to successfully integrate black history in traditional, white-oriented junior and senior high school history courses. Suggestions for a teacher's reference library, specific teaching goals, planning, AV materials, committee work and evaluation procedures are included in the second chapter. The third chapter, the bulk of the book, provides an introduction and annotated bibliography for 26 major units in American Negro history. Each one- or two-page introduction opens with a brief list of important dates and summarizes the contributions of blacks for the period covered. The last chapter is a list of sources of inexpensive or free materials. Included in the appendixes are a reading list on race, a directory of libraries with Negro history book collections, and a directory of museums of Negro history and places of interest.

While it is not a syllabus, or even an outline for a history course, the simply written guide provides the most essential information for integrating and improving high school history courses. More specialized bibliographies are now available, but Katz's work remains highly recommended as an introductory guide for secondary school teachers. —Christine L. Wynar. [R: ARBA 72, item 313]

151. Toppin, Edgar A. **A Biographical History of Blacks in America Since 1528.** New York, McKay, 1971. 499p. $7.95; $5.95pa. LC 70-107402. ISBN 0-679-50240-8; 0-679-30014-7pa.

This book grew out of an ETV course prepared by Mr. Toppin and a series of his articles that appeared in *The Christian Science Monitor* in 1969.

The first half of the book consists of the 15 expanded articles covering chronological periods: prehistory to 1591 (African background) through 1955-1971 (Civil Rights revolution and new militancy). Well written and balanced in treatment, these short historical surveys are informative and stimulating reading. While it will be most useful at the high school level and up, younger readers are able to use the book as a reference source. At the end of part one is a 19-page brief listing of additional reading arranged by chapter. Paperbacks are starred. The bibliography includes o.p. titles as well as 1969 imprints.

The second half, newly prepared, consists of 145 biographical sketches of historical and contemporary men and women. One of the more noticeable omissions is that of Countee Cullen. These are arranged alphabetically and give name, dates, vocation, and a 200- to 300-word sketch. Preceding the alphabetical section, the biographies are listed under 20 vocational areas and under five historical periods. Presented from a black viewpoint, but successfully maintaining a good balance in handling some emotional issues, this is a useful and eminently readable reference source. [R: ARBA 72, item 314]

152. Washburn, Wilcomb E. **The American Indian and the United States: A Documentary History**. New York, Random House, 1973. 4v. illus. map. index. $135.00. LC 72-10259. ISBN 0-394-47283-7.

Wounded Knee "II" was a symbol of the long-standing conflict between the American Indians and the government of the United States, not just the Sioux Nation and the United States. Dr. Washburn draws together, in four impressive volumes, the documentary evidence relating to this conflict, which has yet to be resolved. He uses five sources to illustrate how the problem(s) developed: 1) reports of Commissions of Indian Affairs (Vols. 1 and 2), 2) congressional debates on Indian affairs (Vols. 2 and 3), 3) acts, ordinances, and proclamations (Vol.3), 4) Indian treaties (Vols. 3 and 4), and 5) legal decisions (Vol.4).

Each section is arranged in chronological order with a one- or two-page introduction by Dr. Washburn. The introductory statement provides an overview of the material and some indication as to how items were selected for inclusion. Every entry has a brief paragraph that provides the basic background about the item. All major aspects of the five types of documents are covered, and there are interesting sidelights that provide a fuller view. While individuals may disagree with some items selected for inclusion, the total result is excellent. One could not hope to find a better overview of the situation.

It must be pointed out that this *is* a documentary history, which means that it presents the case of the United States government—and *not* the Indians' case. The Indians' point of view is frequently indicated in Dr. Washburn's opening paragraph for an entry—for example, on page 81: "Commissioner Dole's report for 1862 discussed the problems in the Northern Superintendency caused by the depredations of the Sioux, who had been goaded to an outbreak by an insensitive Government."

Access to this very important work is provided by a 92-page index. No matter what limitations can be identified for this set, the fact remains it must be considered *the* best basic general reference work on the subject. —G. Edward Evans.
[R: BL, 15 Oct 74, pp. 248-49; LJ, 15 Apr 74, p. 1116; WLB, May 74, pp. 766-67; ARBA 75, item 369]

AFRICAN HISTORY

153. Freeman-Grenville, G. S. P. **Chronology of African History**. New York, Oxford University Press, 1973. 312p. index. $16.00. ISBN 0-19-913174-0.

The purpose of this extensive and well-researched reference work is to provide a time framework for African history. Starting around 1000 B.C., the volume lists in tabular form all important events that occurred in Africa. The starting date has been set arbitrarily to avoid duplicating previous chronologies on Egyptian history. From 1000 B.C. to A.D. 599, four columns are listed, giving comparative dates for Egypt, the Sudan and Eastern Africa; Northern and Western Africa; Western Asia; and Europe. From A.D. 600 to 1399, the columns change to reflect the development of Africa, listing Egypt and the Sudan, Northern Africa, Africa South of the Sahara, and other countries. After 1400, when knowledge of African history becomes more extensive, there are six columns (three per page), dividing Africa into its four geographic regions, plus Central Africa and other countries. The last column is included in each time period to give better perspective to events in Africa.

The majority of entries in this book are after 1500, when the author could rely on independent sources for verification of dates. Entries before this time are limited due to lack of verification methods and the still limited knowledge of early African history. An excellent index helps to make this a useful volume for both the casual student and the advanced researcher. —William Z. Schenck.
[R: Choice, Sept 74, p. 910; ARBA 75, item 391]

ASIAN HISTORY

154. Burgess, James. **The Chronology of Indian History: Medieval & Modern.** Delhi, India, Cosmo Publications, 1972; distr. Portland, Ore., International Scholarly Book Services, 1973. 483p. index. $19.50.

One of the encouraging trends in Indian publishing in the late 1960s and early 1970s has been the reprinting of outstanding works that have been out of print for several years. These two volumes of *Chronology of Indian History* are a result of that trend. Volume 1, which covers the period from the earliest times to the sixteenth century and which was written by C. Mabel Duff (Mrs. W. R. Rickmers), was first published in 1899. James Burgess's second volume, covering the medieval and modern period, was originally issued in 1912.

In view of the complexities of Indian history, the extensive Hindu literature, and the accumulated material scattered through hundreds of English and foreign volumes and periodicals, one must admire the authors for their scholarship and hard work in giving us this systematic chronology of Indian history. Volume 1 begins with the year 3102 B.C. and ends with 1530 A.D.; Volume II picks up from 1492 A.D. and concludes with 1894 A.D. Within entries, civil material is given first, then literary dates. When several events occur under the same date, they are roughly grouped according to their relative importance. Events in Northern India generally take precedence over those of Southern India. Each entry is accompanied by references to the sources from which it is derived. A 50-page appendix in Volume I contains a rare collection of lists of the dynasties ruling throughout India, giving the names of the rulers in a chronological order. To facilitate use, each volume has a detailed index.   —Sharad Karkhanis. [R: ARBA 74, item 328]

155. Lu, David John. **Sources of Japanese History.** New York, McGraw-Hill, 1974. 2v. index. $9.95/v.; $6.95/v.pa. LC 73-6890. ISBN 0-07-038902-0(v.1); 0-07-038903-9(v.2).

This is a two-volume compilation of primary source materials for the study of Japanese social, intellectual, economic, and political history. The first volume covers the period from the prehistoric, mythological era through the middle of the Tokugawa regime (early eighteenth century). The second volume covers the period from the decay of the Tokugawa system during the early years of the nineteenth century to the present time, with emphasis on the events of the past 125 years. The compiler, a professor of history and director of the Center for Japanese Studies at Bucknell University, has done a thorough job of selecting representative writings to reflect the spirit of each age and to portray the life-styles of its people.

In the first volume, chapter introductions give background information on the period and on subjects illustrated by the readings. The compiler has carefully avoided duplication of existing sources available in this country, and more than three-fourths of the documents have been translated into English for the first time. Some were written by commoners and minor officials and record everyday matters and business transactions. A number are excerpts from religious works and government directives. Some are folk tales and poems. An appendix to the first volume translates Japanese weights and measures into both metric and U.S. equivalents, and a brief glossary translates Japanese terms and names into English.

In volume 2 the documents, or excerpts from documents, are arranged in eight chapters, each portraying a particular period in time; a ninth chapter contains the Nobel lecture of Kawabata Yasunari, given in 1968. The documents and writings range from imperial edicts, constitutions, and treaties to wartime diaries of students and housewives, public opinion surveys, and questions from a qualifying examination for a position in a newspaper company. Complete bibliographical citations for all documents are given in footnotes that accompany each chapter. The compiler's introductions and supplementary notes add greatly to the usefulness of the material, and the introductions provide a running commentary and serve to tie all the material together.

This carefully prepared work will be of primary interest to students and teachers of Japanese history and civilization. Its arrangement and detailed index will make it useful also as a quick reference tool for information on many subjects within its overall scope. —Shirley L. Hopkinson. [R: ARBA 75, item 392]

CANADIAN HISTORY

156. Thibault, Claude. **Bibliographia Canadiana**. Don Mills, Ontario, Longman Canada, 1973. 795p. index. $25.00.

The 25,660 entries in this classified bibliography make it *the* Canadian history bibliography. Entries are up to date through 1970 for books and 1969 for periodical articles.

Two main criteria were used: the first was that genealogical, biographical, local, or provincial works were to be omitted; the second was that the works should indicate "the trend of interpretation which had taken place in Canadian history since the middle of the nineteenth century." The arrangement is primarily under three main chronological headings: "The French Colonial Regime," "British North America, 1713-1867," "The Dominion of Canada, 1867-1967." The first section, "Tools of Research," is divided into 1) primary sources (i.e., guides to manuscript and archival collections, collections of printed documents, government publications), 2) general secondary sources (e.g., bibliographies, encyclopedias, atlases), and 3) historiography. [R: ARBA 75, item 394]

EUROPEAN HISTORY

157. **Bibliography of British History: Stuart Period, 1603-1714**. 2nd ed. Mary Frear Keeler, ed. Issued under the direction of the American Historical Association and the Royal Historical Society of Great Britain. New York, Oxford University Press, 1970. 734p. index. $16.00.

The first edition of this standard work on the subject, edited by Godfrey Davies, was published in 1928. The introduction to the first edition has been reprinted here, since in it Davies explains in some detail the preparation of this monumental undertaking.

There are 14 main chapters: general reference works, political history, constitutional history, legal history, ecclesiastical history, military and naval history, economic history, social and cultural history, local history, and colonial history—

plus separate chapters on Wales, Scotland, and Ireland. There are numerous subdivisions under all subjects, and the reader will find some changes from the first edition—e.g., the elimination of a separate chapter on voyages. In general, the following order is maintained: bibliographies, occasionally with references to manuscript collections; source materials; and then selected later works.

The Davies plan of adhering to a chronological order according to the date of the first edition has been replaced by alphabetical order in most of the sections, although for works published during the Stuart period the order is generally chronological. In several sections in which geographical areas are of primary importance, the arrangement is according to area names.

This edition has eliminated from most of the bibliographical descriptions those items relating to size and format. Also omitted are most of the references to London as the place of publication. If no place of publication is given, London is to be understood. References to periodical literature now provide more complete information—in most cases, numbers for volumes, pages, and year of publication. All major sections are updated. The reader will find especially significant the additions in economic history, local history, cultural history, and various aspects of intellectual history, especially those aspects pertaining to the non-English areas.

Other titles of this series include: *Bibliography of British History to 1485* (2v.); *Bibliography of British History, Tudor Period, 1485-1603*; *Bibliography of British History, 1851-1914.* —Bohdan S. Wynar. [R: ARBA 72, item 327]

158. Elton, G. R. **Modern Historians on British History, 1485-1945: A Critical Bibliography, 1945-1969.** Ithaca, N.Y., Cornell University Press, 1970. 239p. index. $8.50. LC 77-137676. ISBN 0-8014-0611-0.

This critical historical bibliography was prepared by a well-known historian and author of several monographs on English Tudor history. It constitutes an updated and extended bibliography that appeared in *Historische Zeitschrift Sonderheft* (No. 3) in 1969.

The bibliography is arranged chronologically and topically. Within each chronological division (from 1485 through 1945), the author arranged his materials topically, including sections on such topics as general history, political history, social and economic history, culture and civilization, church, foreign affairs. Separate topical chapters cover reference works, historical sources, social history, history of ideas, Scotland, and Ireland. The critical commentaries on included works are brief and to the point. Excluded are materials dealing with the history of British expansion and possessions overseas and with the historiography of the Empire and Commonwealth. Altogether, the author lists 1,351 works, mainly by British historians, with a few listings of German, French, and Italian publications.

The weakest part of this useful bibliography is the author's subject index. Many important subjects are excluded (e.g., "Welsh," "Emigration," "Nationalism," "Chronology," and others). Also, major Soviet and East European publications dealing with British history are not listed. A valuable feature is the references, in many of the entries, to other reviews. —Lubomyr R. Wynar. [R: ALA 71; ARBA 72, item 328]

159. Gilbert, Martin. **Russian History Atlas**. New York, Macmillan, 1972. 1v.(various paging). index. maps. $8.95. LC 72-80174.

Martin Gilbert is known as the compiler of several atlases. In his introduction to the *Russian History Atlas*, he states that he has "designed this Atlas in the hope that it is possible to present within the span of 146 maps a survey of Russian history from the earliest times to the present day." To a large extent, Mr. Gilbert has succeeded in his objectives; compared to A. F. Chew's *An Atlas of Russian History*, this represents a step in the right direction.

Black and white sketch maps, with simple explanations, cover not only political history but also historical geography, economic development, and some topics of special interest (e.g., "The Jews and Their Enemies, 1648-1917"). Occasionally the notes provide a rather simplistic explanation. For example, on the map showing "The Russian Revolution, November 1917-March 1918" we read "Occupied by German troops in March 1918, as a result of the Bolshevik-German treaty of Brest-Litovsk." But the Brest-Litovsk Treaty was never signed by the Bolsheviks. They walked out, in accordance with Lenin's instructions. This treaty was signed on February 1, 1918, by the newly created Ukrainian National Republic, on one hand, and Germany, Austria-Hungary, Bulgaria, and Turkey, on the other.

Nonetheless, as we have already indicated, Gilbert's *Russian History Atlas* is much better than Chew's work and will probably be an adequate source for a beginning student of Russian history. —Bohdan S. Wynar. [R: LJ, 1 Nov 72, p. 3571; ALA 72; ARBA 73, item 346]

160. **The New Century Italian Renaissance Encyclopedia**. Ed. by Catherine B. Avery. New York, Appleton-Century-Crofts, 1972. 978p. illus. $29.95. LC 76-181735. ISBN 0-390-66950-X.

Comparison with *Dictionary of the Renaissance*, edited by Frederick M. Schweitzer (New York, Philosophical Library, 1967) reveals similarity in scope, but the encyclopedia covers most topics in much more depth and detail from Dante's birth to the close of the 16th century. Biographical entries predominate in both works. *New Century* is also well illustrated. In addition to numerous black and white reproductions in the text, there are 12 color plates and 32 pages of black and white plates. The latter are arranged in groups to give a chronological survey, but are not directly keyed to pages in the text. This did not prove to be a problem with the items sampled because the text contained entries for all the artists in the normal alphabetical sequence. When more than one form of a name has been used in the past, cross references are provided to the form chosen. Resumes of some literary works are included. There are also general articles of some length on topics like architecture (five pages), painting (five pages), and sculpture (four pages). The one area apparently neglected is music. No entries were found for "music," "musical instruments," "madrigal," "motet," or "polyphony," and only the briefest treatment of "ars nova." Apart from this and the lack of a bibliography, the book is a superb reference tool. —A. Robert Rogers. [R: RQ, Fall 72, p. 85; LJ, 1 Feb 72, p. 485; ALA 72; ARBA 73, item 348]

161. Pushkarev, Sergei G., comp. **Dictionary of Russian Historical Terms from the Eleventh Century to 1917.** Edited by George Vernadsky and Ralph T. Fisher, Jr. New Haven, Yale University Press, 1970. 199p. $15.00. LC 73-81426. ISBN 0-300-01136-9.

The dictionary is "designed to assist English-speaking readers to understand the specialized terms they encounter in Russian historical sources and in English-language works on Russia." It includes approximately 2,000 terms from areas of political, ecclesiastical, military, economic, social, legal, and cultural history. Excluded are biographical data and geographical names.

It should be pointed out that the terms in this dictionary are not limited only to Russian history. In many instances they are related to Belorussian and Ukrainian history. In the Preface, Professor Pushkarev states that he has "labeled terms from the Grand Duchy [of Lithuania] as West Russian (W.R.)." This designation is impossible to justify on a contemporary historical source basis because the terms "West Russian" and "West Russia" were not used during the Grand Duchy period.

In the reviewer's opinion the compiler should present a clearer and more objective concept of historical terminology and periodization of Russian, Belorussian, and Ukrainian history. Considering that this is the first attempt to compile such a dictionary in English, however, there is no reason to doubt that it will assist American historians and graduate students in their research. —Lubomyr R. Wynar. [R: LJ, July 70, p. 2451; Choice, Nov 70; ARBA 71, item 399]

162. **A Source Book for Russian History from Early Times to 1917.** Ed. by George Vernadsky, sr. ed., and Ralph T. Fisher, Jr., managing ed. Alan D. Ferguson, Andrew Lossky, and Sergei Pushkarev, comps. New Haven, Conn., Yale University Press, 1972. 3v. $15.00 ea.; $40.00/set. LC 70-115369. ISBN 0-300-01602-5(set).

The purpose of this comprehensive work is to provide in English translation representative excerpts from primary sources pertaining to Russian history from early times to March 1917. The arrangement of material combines chronological and topical groupings, following the usual presentation of Russian history in most textbooks. Thus, the first chapter opens with introductory comments on pre-Kievan beginnings, by George Vernadsky, followed by excerpts from Procopius, Jordanes, Mauricius, etc., and concluding with Nestor's *Primary Chronicle.* Chapter two, "Kievan Russia, Tenth to Twelfth Centuries," provides excerpts from the *Laurentian Chronicle* concerning Oleg's establishment in Kiev in 882 and the campaign against Byzantium in 907. This is followed by the treaty of Oleg with Byzantium, as transmitted in the *Laurentian Chronicle* for 911. All in all, the three volumes contain some 700 distinct sources pertaining to political, legal, and administrative history; economic history; social, cultural, and intellectual history, etc.

In addition to Russian history, the editors present some documents related to the history of the Lithuanian state and to Ukrainian history (primarily in the first volume). It should be noted that about 75 percent of the material has not been previously published in English translation, which means that the present work will be invaluable for all students of Eastern Europe.

The only major criticism concerns certain terminology used by the editors. The introduction points out that a companion volume, *Dictionary of Russian Historical Terms* (compiled by Sergei Pushkarev and published by the Yale University Press) provides explanations for the Russian terms that appear in the book.

Both Pushkarev and the *Source Book* use the term "Kievan Russia" instead of "Kievan Rus." Even such well-known Soviet historians as Grekov (see his work *Kiev Rus*) and Tikhomirov (*The Towns of Ancient Rus*) use "Rus" as the political designation for the above-mentioned period. Pushkarev is, of course, aware of this, and we are somewhat at a loss to understand some of the political implications presented in this otherwise excellent work. —Bohdan S. Wynar. [R: ARBA 73, item 349]

163. **Writings on British History 1901-1933: Volume V, 1895-1914. Appendix (Parts 1 and 2).** Compiled by the Royal Historical Society. New York, Barnes & Noble, 1970. 2v. $45.00. ISBN 0-389-01367-6.

The fifth volume of the series *Writings on British History* was edited for the Royal Historical Society by the late Professor H. Hale Bellot. A most comprehensive bibliography, it covers books and articles on the history of Great Britain from about 450 A.D. to 1914, published during the years 1901 to 1933. Excluded are items published by learned societies of Great Britain.

This international bibliography is arranged by various types of histories and by special subjects. The bibliographical description of book entries excludes the name of the publisher. The first part covers political, economic, social, cultural, ecclesiastical, science and military history. Special sections list publications on foreign relations (subdivided chronologically), English local history, British Empire (divided by geo-political units) and historical sources. Part 2 includes a biography (collective and individual), an appendix containing a select list of publications in the years 1914-1933 on British history since 1914, and an author index.

Previous volumes cover *Auxiliary Sciences and General Works* (v.1, 1968), *The Middle Ages, 450-1485* (v.2, 1968), *The Tudor and Stuart Periods, 1485-1714* (v.3, 1968), and *The Eighteenth Century, 1714-1815*, 2 parts (v.4, 1969). —Lubomyr R. Wynar. [R: ARBA 71, item 385]

LATIN AMERICAN HISTORY

164. Griffin, Charles C., ed. **Latin America: A Guide to the Historical Literature.** Austin, University of Texas Press, 1971. 700p. index. (Conference on Latin American History, No. 4). $25.00. LC 71-165916. ISBN 0-292-70089-X.

This comprehensive guide contains 7,087 entries providing full bibliographical description of titles listed plus brief evaluative annotations. The basic organization of material is chronological, with main divisions devoted to the colonial, independence, and post-independence periods. Within these major parts, separate sections deal with the various geographical areas. The major parts are preceded by sections that include reference materials and works of a general nature. The organization of these sections and of Part II, International Relations, is topical and geographical rather than chronological.

It should be noted that this guide has a long history, having originated at a meeting in the Library of Congress jointly sponsored by the Hispanic Foundation and the Joint Committee on Latin American Studies of the American Council of Learned Societies and the Social Science Research Council in April 1962. At that time, a group of invited specialists discussed the general structure of this undertaking; most of the suggestions were later adopted by the editor and advisory editorial board. As a result we have at our disposal a cooperative work of high professional caliber, which will serve for years to come as the standard guide to the historical literature of Latin America.   [R: ARBA 72, item 340]

CHAPTER 5

ARCHAEOLOGY

165. Bray, Warwick, and David Trump. **The American Heritage Guide to Archaeology**. New York, American Heritage, 1971 (c. 1970). 269p. illus. $6.95 LC 77-122588. ISBN 0-07-007348-1.

A general guide to archaeological terms and concepts with approximately 1,600 entries, more than 200 figures and drawings, and over 100 maps and photographs, designed for the layman. The disproportionate preponderance of English sites included in text, maps, and photographs is to the detriment of Asian, classical, medieval, and New World material. Appropriate figures and drawings are referred to within the text, whereas photographs more effectively draw the reader's attention by bold marginal notations. The book concludes with a selection of line maps. [R: Choice, June 71, p. 530; LJ, 15 May 71, p. 1696; ALA 71; ARBA 72, item 346]

166. Charles-Picard, Gilbert, ed. **Larousse Encyclopedia of Archaeology**. Trans. by Anne Ward. New York, Putnam's, 1972. 432p. index. illus. $25.00. LC 76-179972. ISBN 0-600-75451-2.

The *Larousse Encyclopedia of Archaeology* was first published in France in 1969. Designed as an authoritative reference book for students of archaeology and for laymen, it discusses archaeology as a field of study and surveys archaeological sites throughout the world.

The book is beautifully illustrated with 40 color plates and 600 monochrome photos. At the end are a bibliography for further reading (subdivided by topics) and an index to names, places, and subjects, with italics referring to illustrations. The two main parts of the encyclopedia are Archaeology at Work and The Recovery of the Past. Part one contains six chapters defining archaeology, explaining the survival of relics, how sites are located and excavated, and how scientists date and restore finds and publish the collected data. Part two, geographically arranged, describes the work and discoveries of famous archaeologists in various parts of the world. These 12 chapters cover work in prehistoric archaeology, ancient Western Asia, the Nile, the Aegean world, Greece, the Etruscans, the Romans, Europe, the Americas, India, Southeast Asia, and China. All articles are signed by specialists. [R: ARBA 73, item 351]

167. Cottrell, Leonard. **The Concise Encyclopedia of Archaeology**. 2nd ed. New York, Hawthorn Books, 1971. 430p. $16.95. LC 70-130701.

This work brilliantly conveys the romantic, passionate, and human appeal of archaeology. The book has been compiled with the intelligent amateur in mind.

A great many archaeological discoveries are described, such as the Tomb of Tutankhamen, Ur of the Chaldees, Jericho, Knossos, the ship burial treasures of

Sutton Hoo, and the tomb treasures of Ziwiye. Short descriptions are provided of ancient languages, the evolution of man, artifacts and fossils, and great monuments such as Stonehenge. Articles cover places and peoples, cities and civilizations, trends and techniques, ancient languages and their decipherment. Each article has been prepared by an acknowledged expert on the subject. In all, 48 eminent authorities have contributed to the work. The field covered is worldwide, although there are few references to the archaeology of classical Greece and Rome, since these topics have been extensively discussed elsewhere. The main criteria in selecting topics are the intrinsic interest and importance of the subject and the unfamiliarity of the subject to the general as distinct from the specialized reader.

The value of the encyclopedia is enhanced by the inclusion of a short essay (17 pages) by Leonard Cottrell on "What Is Archaeology?" This essay reveals both Leonard Cottrell's mastery of the subject and his capacity to convey the fascination of the subject to lay audiences. A classified list of topics is provided to assist those wishing to study a particular area or topic in more detail. Typical topics are: Archaeologists and Historians, Early Man and Geological Periods, Egypt, India, the Middle East and the Far East. In addition, ten regional maps show the location of principal archaeological sites. —Alan M. Rees. [R: LJ, 1 Oct 71, pp. 3112-13; Choice, Sept 71, pp. 807-808; ARBA 72, item 348]

CHAPTER 6

GENEALOGY AND HERALDRY

GENERAL WORKS

168. Filby, P. William. **American and British Genealogy and Heraldry: A Selected List of Books.** Chicago, American Library Association, 1970. 184p. index. $10.00. LC 75-106200. ISBN 0-8389-0079-8.

For the genealogist (professional or amateur), the librarian, and the historian, P. William Filby has compiled a bibliography of American and British genealogy and heraldry, which will prove to be a valuable reference source. The more than 1,800 titles can only begin to list the wide range of material available on heraldry and regional and ethnic history in the United States, Canada and Great Britain, but Mr. Filby and his consultants have put together a very basic list for any genealogically oriented researcher. Because of the complete and often annotated citations, the work serves an additional function as a purchasing guide. Each state has approximately 20 to 25 entries, listing major histories, biography collections, published censuses, atlases, military rosters, bibliographies, gazetteers, church records, and vital records whenever available. A comprehensive index to author, keyword title and general subjects completes this most useful reference tool. [Editor's note: The second edition was published in 1976.] —Patricia C. Harpole. [R: Choice, Oct 70; LJ, 15 Nov 70; WLB, Oct 70; AL, June 70; RQ, Winter 70, p. 174-5; ARBA 71, item 410]

GENEALOGY

GENERAL

169. Kaminkow, Marion J., ed. **Genealogies in the Library of Congress: A Bibliography.** Baltimore, Magna Carta Book Co., 1972. 2v. $125.00. LC 74-187078. ISBN 0-910946-15-9.

This is the most comprehensive bibliography of family histories, superseding *American and English Genealogies in the Library of Congress*. The coverage is, of course, international. In addition to published materials, it also covers unpublished manuscripts, microforms, etc., including all the entries from the family-name index in the Local History and Genealogy Room of the Library of Congress (to mid-1971). All entries are arranged alphabetically by family surname, with some 20,000 cross references to help in locating variations in spelling. [R: LJ, July 72, p. 2376; ALA 72; ARBA 73, item 355]

170. Schreiner-Yantis, Netti. **Genealogical Books in Print**. Springfield, Va., the Author, 6818 Lois Drive, 1975. 311p. $4.00pa. LC 75-4225. ISBN 0-89157-015-2.

This is a "catalogue of in-print genealogical titles, useful and interesting to those doing genealogical research; including prices and complete ordering information for over 5,000 items." This subtitle tells it all, and with this book's publication much of the frustration has been taken from anyone in the field—researcher, family historian, and most of all, librarian. Over 1,100 vendors are listed, from the over 500 titles of the Genealogical Publishing Company to only one by many family historians. Although not every publisher answered the author's request, this first edition is sufficient to enable most books of genealogical importance to be found with a minimum of trouble. All the reader has to do is to look for the book needed; if it is in print, complete information (price, publisher, and address) is supplied. The compiler proposes to update the work as often as required; indeed, a reprint, making a few corrections, has already been published. It is one of the best reference works in the genealogical field to have been published in the last decade. —P. William Filby. [R: WLB, Nov 75, p. 262; RQ, Fall 75, pp. 80-81; LJ, 15 Nov 75, pp. 2133-34; ARBA 76, item 421]

UNITED STATES

171. Greenwood, Val D. **The Researcher's Guide to American Genealogy**. Baltimore, Genealogical, 1973; distr. New York, Scribner's, 1974. 535p. illus. $14.95. LC 73-6902. ISBN 0-8063-0560-6.

Books and records available anywhere in the country are listed here and examined in detail; areas and states are fully covered. The author is not satisfied with merely listing records; he generally gives basic background for their presence and discusses methods of research. Milton Rubincam, himself the author of genealogical manuals, comments in his eulogistic introduction that the guide has long been needed and that "Mr. Greenwood delves deeply into the historical background of our records systems, providing us especially with an understanding of the legal aspects of genealogical research." The only objection to this important book is its unwieldy size—large octavo, 535 pages! —P. William Filby. [R: ARBA 74, item 357]

GREAT BRITAIN AND IRELAND

172. Hamilton-Edwards, Gerald. **In Search of British Ancestry**. 3rd ed. Baltimore, Genealogical, 1974. 296p. $15.00. LC 74-9346. ISBN 0-8063-0628-9.

In 1967 Mr. Hamilton-Edwards brought out a book that was of great assistance to those wishing to trace British forebears and that has become the standard book for American research. The third edition adds items that were suggested to the author or that he has discovered in his own researches.

All types of records are discussed, with details of the record offices in Ireland, Wales, and Scotland. To the average researcher and also to the professional, the records held by the Public Record Office in London are of particular value, but they are not easy to find or to understand, largely because so many were the products of the established church. One, for instance, the Prerogative Court of

Canterbury, collected vital papers for years. Their value is scarcely known to American researchers, yet with the thousands of names in wills, marriage lists, inventories, etc., they are of prime interest. These and many other idiosyncrasies are discussed. Above all, the bibliography is certainly the finest to be found in any book of genealogy; nothing has escaped the author. It is also an excellent study of British history. —P. William Filby. [R: ARBA 75, item 438]

173. Hamilton-Edwards, Gerald. **In Search of Scottish Ancestry**. Baltimore, Genealogical, 1972. 252p. illus. $10.00. LC 72-86. ISBN 0-8063-0506-1.

Mr. Hamilton-Edwards' new book on Scottish ancestry is, without question, the best book on Scottish genealogy for the researcher yet to be produced. The author deals extensively with basic places of research and shows himself to be adept in the use of all types of registers.

There are chapters on surnames and Christian names, tax and census lists. Genealogists working on Scottish records will meet with words and phrases not seen elsewhere, and the glossary will be of great value to Americans who must delve into commissariat and other early lists. Nonconformist and other parish lists are equally difficult to find and to understand, but with this outstanding work, which overlooks no aspect of Scottish genealogy, the American will find his work made more easy. There is also an introduction to Scottish history. This outstanding bibliography is the best produced so far. —P. William Filby. [R: ARBA 73, item 380]

HERALDRY

174. **Boutell's Heraldry**. Revised by J. P. Brooke-Little. New York, Warne, 1970. 343p. illus. $20.00. LC 63-19183. ISBN 0-7232-1708-4.

The Rev. Charles Boutell, a great heraldic authority, brought together his knowledge in *The Manual of Heraldry* in 1863, and added English heraldry in 1867. For the next 60 years, various authorities revised Boutell's works, and in 1931 Wheeler-Holohan produced a book entitled *Boutell's Manual of Heraldry*, in which he combined the two works. He also added 32 color plates. Finally, in 1950, Scott-Giles revised the whole work and, although much of Boutell's original work remained, the whole was edited realistically and was revised four more times in the next 16 years.

J.P. Brooke-Little, Richmond Herald of Arms, a co-editor for a few years, has now taken over the task of the 1970 revision. It includes 28 plates in color and over 400 text figures. He has added a new feature on trends and developments in the heraldic world, and there is a comprehensive glossary and index to the terminology of heraldry. It is a beautifully printed book and probably the most up-to-date manual available. —P. William Filby. [R: ARBA 71, item 448]

175. Brooke-Little, J.P. **An Heraldic Alphabet**. New York, Arco, 1973. 224p. illus. (part col.). $8.95. LC 72-95468. ISBN 0-668-002941-2.

A dictionary of 1,000 terms, with drawings accompanying many of the definitions. One of the best features of this book is the sensible manner in which Brooke-Little (Richmond Herald of Arms and, therefore, a top authority) has attempted to solve the orthographical questions. For the beginner (and the professional), many heraldic words make little or no sense, partly because of the peculiar spelling. While Brooke-Little does not claim to have solved all the problems, his anglicizing of many endings will be useful.

The chapters that precede the alphabet concern heralds and the birth of heraldry, the development and law of arms, and the grammar of heraldry. As might be expected, all of these are authoritative and useful. One of the best points about the book is its size. Heraldists always expect a weighty tome—and they usually get it—but Brooke-Little has deliberately cut the book to smaller size without sacrificing anything of value. —P. William Filby. [R: WLB, Nov 73, p. 264; LJ, Aug 73, p. 2261; ALA 73; ARBA 74, item 381]

176. Fox-Davies, Arthur Charles. **A Complete Guide to Heraldry**. Rev. and annotated by J.P. Brooke-Little. New York, Barnes & Noble, 1969. 513p. illus. color plates. $30.00. ISBN 0-389-01208-4.

First published in 1909, with a revised edition by C.A.H. Franklyn published in 1949. Fox-Davies died in 1928 and this edition is now revised by J.P. Brooke-Little, an authority on heraldry.

This comprehensive and authoritative work covers the history of armory, including such matters as regalia, seals, badges, cadency, the law of armorial bearings, etc., arranged in short chapter form. Most of the material has been updated, providing details of new rulings and developments in heraldry since the time the old edition was written. A new concluding chapter is concerned with such matters as coats-of-arms of the younger members of the Royal Family, corporate arms, Commonwealth heraldry, current fees, and a general guide to procedure for those who wish to apply for a coat-of-arms. Well illustrated. [R: ARBA 70, v.1, p. 76]

177. Franklyn, Julian, and John Tanner. **An Encyclopaedic Dictionary of Heraldry**. New York, Pergamon, 1970. 367p. illus.(part col.). $32.00. LC 69-19596. ISBN 0-08-013297-9.

Franklyn and Tanner have added to the corpus of works on heraldry a work which, at first sight, would seem superfluous, since there are so many books that are described as dictionaries or glossaries. While each of them is good and useful for the average heraldry student, Franklyn and Tanner have the edge over all others. Foreign heraldry is included, and Violetta Keeble's very fine illustrations add much to the book. Though expensive, it is an indispensable work. —P. William Filby. [R: ALA 70; ARBA 72, item 373]

PERSONAL NAMES

178. Smith, Elsdon C. **American Surnames**. Philadelphia, Chilton, 1969. 370p. bibliog. index. $9.95. LC 71-85245. ISBN 0-8019-5263-8.

A study of 2,000 most common American surnames, listed in order of their frequency, and with an estimated number of the people bearing each name. The book is divided into six parts: classification of surnames, surnames from the father's name (patronymics), surnames from occupation or office, surnames from description or action (nicknames), surnames from places, and surnames not included elsewhere. On the whole, this reference book offers a thorough examination of the roots and derivations of American surnames today, including Jewish and Negro surnames, and immigrant alterations. Mr. Smith is a recognized authority on the subject, author of the well-known *Dictionary of American Family Names* and the founder of the American Name Society. [R: LJ, Sept 69; SR, 6 Dec 69; RQ, Winter 69; ALA 69; ARBA 70, v.1, p. 78]

179. Smith, Elsdon C. **New Dictionary of American Family Names**. New York, Harper and Row, 1973. 572p. $13.95. LC 72-79693. ISBN 0-06-013933-1.

In 1956 Mr. Smith published a definitive study that included 10,000 American family names. It was hailed then as the most complete dictionary of American names, but in the intervening years Mr. Smith has found many more.

The present work is three times as large as the first edition, and if it is not as complete in explanations as some of the earlier attempts by British scholars, it will completely satisfy American users. The original edition was faulted for its lack of references, roots, etymological origins, and early forms of the words from which the surnames were derived. Perhaps so, but such a work would be too unwieldy and, therefore, these references are still omitted. However, explanations of surnames are emphasized as are "the meaning of the words and the manner in which they were used to evolve into hereditary family names, rather than the technical etymology of the words from which the names were derived." The result is a book that answers the question: "How did my surname originate?" It is a definitive study. —P. William Filby. [R: Choice, June 73, p. 603; ARBA 74, item 388]

180. **Webster's Dictionary of Proper Names**. Geoffrey Payton, comp. Springfield, Mass., G. & C. Merriam Co., 1970. 752p. $9.95. ISBN 0-87779-083-3.

Based on the British publication *Payton's Proper Names*, this dictionary is not a simple adaptation but rather a skillfully revised work that will meet the needs of an American audience. Many British names were dropped, and some 2,000 were added for this American edition. The total of 10,000 entries constitutes a comprehensive and well-balanced listing of a wide variety of proper names.

In comparing the two editions one gets the impression that the American edition is somewhat superior to its British counterpart, not only in terms of binding or typeface (as was indicated by the reviewer in *Library Journal*), but in its scope as well. Its few inconsistencies are minor and do not detract from the excellence of this work. —Bohdan S. Wynar. [R: RQ, Fall 71, p. 85; WLB, May 71, p. 886; LJ, 1 May 71, p. 1598; ARBA 72, item 381]

CHAPTER 7

POLITICAL SCIENCE

GENERAL WORKS

181. Robert, Henry M. **Robert's Rules of Order, Newly Revised**. A new and enl. ed., by Sarah Corbin Robert and others. Glenview, Ill., Scott, Foresman, 1970. 594p. index. $8.50. LC 71-106451. ISBN 0-673-05714-3.

This new revision (first major revision since 1915) of the authoritative manual of parliamentary procedures is almost completely rewritten, especially the chapters Voting, Mass Meetings, Disciplinary Procedures. There is a substantial revision in the second chapter on the Conduct of Business in a Deliberate Assembly. [R: LJ 1 June 70; ARBA 71, item 469]

DICTIONARIES

182. Laqueur, Walter, ed. **A Dictionary of Politics**. Rev. ed. New York, Free Press, 1974. 565p. $14.95. LC 74-9232.

The purpose of this rather comprehensive dictionary is to present concise and up-to-date information about the important political events, the changes in terminology, and the historical background of contemporary politics, including some biographical sketches of prominent politicians.

This new edition contains slightly fewer pages than the 1971 edition, but has about the same number of entries (3,000). Although most entries are identical in the two editions, appropriate revisions have been made: statistical information about countries has been updated, closing dates have been added for persons now dead, parts of entries have been revised, and, in some cases, wholly new entries have been added. Few standard political terms are defined or explained.

Major liabilities of the first edition remain: too much in too little space; lack of a pronunciation guide; rapid obsolescence; treatment which may be too advanced for the beginner, but too simplified for the expert; inadequate accessibility to some information in longer entries.

However, the assets of the first edition also remain: succinct, objective political history; relatively complete coverage of the world; easily used format; one-volume convenience package; and the fact that the work was compiled under the direction of a distinguished scholar and commentator. —William C. Robinson. [R: WLB, Dec 74, p. 314; ARBA 75, item 467]

183. Plano, Jack C., and Roy Olton. **The International Relations Dictionary**. New York, Holt, 1969. 337p. $6.95; $3.95pa. LC 69-17657. ISBN 0-03-074675-2(college ed.); 0-03-082843-0(trade ed.).

Topics are arranged within 12 subject matter chapters; thus, terms relating to regional arrangements like NATO or the Arab League can be found in the chapter titled "International Organizations: The United Nations and Regional Organizations." In addition, the index provides an alphabetical approach.

The terms and concepts are clearly defined in simple language suitable for undergraduate students. Most entries offer little historical background, instead emphasizing contemporary meanings. In some cases such an approach has its limitations, such as the entry for "Wars of National Liberation." According to this dictionary the term is synonymous with a recent communist tactical doctrine calling for anti-Western or anti-capitalistic uprisings in the developing countries. Historically speaking, such an interpretation is not complete, since the term was widely used in political literature of the nineteenth century and later by both Lenin and Stalin. Unlike *Dictionary of the Social Sciences* this dictionary does not provide references to pertinent literature; nevertheless, it will be useful for beginning students of international relations as a manageable starting point. Its currency is good and its distillation of a large spectrum of material is valuable. [R: SR, 6 Dec 69; ARBA 70, v.1, p. 92]

184. Plano, Jack C., and others. **Political Science Dictionary**. Hinsdale, Ill., Dryden Press, 1973. 418p. $6.00pa. LC 73-10501. ISBN 0-03-086191-8.

The dictionary's approximately 2,000 key terms, "the working language of political science," are intended to meet the needs of the undergraduate political science student who needs concise, accurate definitions of basic vocabulary relating to these aspects of political science: important political philosophies and ideologies; landmark (political) historical events; major U.S. federal agencies, legislation, and Supreme Court decisions; approaches to the study of political behavior; political theories; political activities; forms, rules, and characteristics; U.S. political institutions and processes; major foreign political institutions and processes; major international organizations; and non-political science terms important to the political scientist.

Unlike Plano's *American Political Dictionary* or *International Relations Dictionary*, the newer work is arranged in straight alphabetical sequence. Both *see* and *see also* references are frequently and appropriately given, although "The Passenger Cases" is found under "T" with no reference from "P." References are made both to main entries and to subjects treated within a main entry. Format is satisfactory, although a wide gutter would facilitate use.

Another major difference between this work and Plano's earlier works is that the significance statements, which provided an intellectual context for most definitions in the earlier works, have been deleted here. Thus, the *Political Science Dictionary* does *not* supersede these earlier works, with their fuller definitions. A word-for-word comparison of entries between these three works mentioned indicates that nearly all definitional statements from the two earlier works have been combined to form the newer work. Definitions in the *Political Science Dictionary* are likely to be more helpful to the student interested in terms of contemporary usage rather than of political history.   —William C. Robinson. [R: ARBA 75, item 468]

U.S. GOVERNMENT

BIBLIOGRAPHIES

185. Wynar, Lubomyr R. **American Political Parties: A Selective Guide to Parties and Movements of the 20th Century**. Littleton, Colo., Libraries Unlimited, 1969. 427p. index. $13.50. LC 75-96954. ISBN 0-87287-011-1.

The compiler, a professor of library science at Kent State University, provides references to over 3,000 titles covering proceedings of party conventions, official papers, unpublished dissertations, periodicals and serials, monographic literature, government documents, and pertinent reference works. The 16 chapters include individual parties and special subjects: Democratic Party, Republican Party, States' Rights Party, Progressive Parties of 1912, 1924, and 1948, Communist and Socialist Movements, Anarchism, Prohibition Movement, and the American Independent Party. A special chapter covers American political parties in the nineteenth century. In addition, separate chapters list reference materials directly related to movements in the United States. An author and subject index completes this comprehensive guide to the study of American political parties, their origin, and their development. [R: AL, Jan 70; ARBA 70, v.1, p. 89]

BIOGRAPHY

186. Morris, Dan, and Inez Morris. **Who Was Who in American Politics: A Biographical Dictionary of Over 4,000 Men and Women Who Contributed to the United States Political Scene from Colonial Days up to and including the Immediate Past**. New York, Hawthorn Books, 1974. 637p. $32.50. LC 76-39620. ISBN 0-8015-8624-0.

A very useful biographical dictionary of political figures; most of them are deceased, while others are still alive but no longer active in politics. The work is a handy, one-volume guide to information about prominent political figures in American politics at the national, state, and local levels.

The general structure of this reference work consists of alphabetical listings for the biographees. Information is included on birth and death dates, place of birth, occupation, elective offices held or appointed posts, or role in the political process, with appropriate dates. Information is sketchy for little-known individuals, and no references or footnotes to additional sources of biographical information are provided. The reference sources at the beginning of this work indicate that standard and highly reliable biographical materials were consulted to prepare this biographical dictionary.

Although it is expensive, it would be a very worthwhile addition to any library. *Who Was Who in American Politics* is a perfect complement to *Who's Who in American Politics*. —Robert P. Haro. [R: Choice, Dec 74, p. 1458; ARBA 75, item 486]

187. Sobel, Robert, ed. **Biographical Directory of the United States Executive Branch, 1774-1971.** Westport, Conn., Greenwood, 1971. 491p. $27.50. index. LC 78-133495. ISBN 0-8371-5173-2.

This biographical directory, arranged alphabetically by surname, is a thorough, well-designed, and well-prepared reference tool. The organization of the data is impressive. There are almost 500 entries, including cabinet heads and presidents and vice-presidents of the Continental Congress. Each biography is detailed, including important dates, pertinent personal information, previous service, religious affiliation, education, and place of death and interment. In addition, each biography contains a brief bibliographic reference to important primary and secondary works that may be consulted for additional information. There are numerous indexes under presidential administrations, heads of state and cabinet officials, other federal government service, state, county, and municipal government service, military service by branch, education, place of birth, and marital information. —Robert P. Haro.
[R: LJ, 15 May 72, p. 1798; ARBA 73, item 423]

188. **Who's Who in American Politics.** 5th ed. 1975-1976. Ed. by Jaques Cattell Press. New York, R. R. Bowker, 1975. 1090p. index. $48.50. LC 67-25025. ISBN 0-8352-0827-3. ISSN 0000-0205.

The fifth edition continues both the strengths and weaknesses of all four previous editions. Its scope remains the same as before. It purports to include the names of men and women, approximately 18,000 in this edition, who "make the American form of government work." Subsumed under this heading are major elective and appointive officials of the federal government—the President, top cabinet officials and chief sub-cabinet officers and Congressmen and Senators; at the state level, listees are governors and their cabinets and members of state legislatures. Locally included officials are mayors of major cities (cut-off population level is not specified) and councillors of the same cities. In addition to governmental figures, the work includes those who hold party offices—e.g., county chairmen and chairwomen (not "chairpersons"), national committeemen and committeewomen.

The consulting editors of the work are Edmund Henshaw of the Democratic Congressional Committee and Paul A. Theis, formerly Public Relations Director for the Republican Congressional Committee. Most of the persons to whom questionnaires were sent came from the offices of these two party functionaries. The consequences are predictable. Officials and officers of the Democratic and Republican Parties are well represented. It is quite otherwise, however, with officials of minor or third parties, who are very sparsely represented.

Several special listings—the President and his Cabinet, State Delegations to the 94th Congress, Governors of the States and State Chairmen—precede the biographical listings. All but the fourth are quite unnecessary. The biographies themselves are very uneven in length; some of them are extremely detailed, while others are terse in the extreme. The editors have clearly not attempted to standardize or rationalize the questionnaire responses.

This work offers some biographical data that are not available in other sources—for example, Marquis's *Who's Who in Government.* The latter work is confined to elective or appointive *governmental* officials. In contrast, Bowker's compilation contains biographical data on major party officers that are not to be found elsewhere. —Richard A. Gray. [R: ARBA 76, item 480]

189. **Who's Who in Government, 1972-1973.** Chicago, Marquis Who's Who, 1972. 785p. index. $49.50. LC 30-29655-PC. ISBN 0-8379-1201-6.

According to the preface, this first edition includes 16,000 listings, in an attempt to record "essential biographical data about key men and women in all branches of the U.S. Federal Government and about a selected list of officials in local, state, and international government as well." In order to facilitate the use of this directory, the editors have added two indexes. In the first, biographees are found within an alphabetical listing of departments, bureaus, offices, agencies, etc. In the second, biographees are listed within an alphabetical arrangement of topics (e.g., Census Statistics, Drug Abuse) that describe the primary subject of the biographee's responsibility.

As the reader may recall, Bowker's *Who's Who in American Politics* has a geographical index. The two volumes complement each other to a certain extent. The Marquis directory provides more comprehensive coverage of government officials (i.e., officials employed in various agencies of the government), while the Bowker publication is stronger in the coverage of politicians, such as officials of both major parties, and also has good coverage of elected officials on state and local levels. Biographical information presented in the two volumes, similar to the usual who's who type, was based on a questionnaire. —Bohdan S. Wynar. [R: LJ, 1 Oct 72, p. 3139; ALA 72; ARBA 73, item 425]

FEDERAL GOVERNMENT

190. Johnson, Donald Bruce, and Kirk H. Porter, comps. **National Party Platforms: 1840-1972.** 5th ed. Urbana, University of Illinois Press, 1973. 889p. $20.00. LC 73-81566. ISBN 0-252-00414-0.

This book enumerates the complete platforms of all the political parties in the United States that responsibly claimed to be national in scope and operation. If they had a significant impact, the compilers included the statements of splinter groups (like the "Dixiecrats") that formed as independent parties after withdrawing from traditional party conventions. With few exceptions, the platforms are drawn from original sources, and none of the platforms have been edited or revised.

The book is divided chronologically, starting with the 1840 presidential campaign and closing with the one in 1972. A brief description of the parties involved in a given campaign serves, in each case, as an historical introduction to the platforms themselves. This compilation gives the serious student or the idle browser an opportunity to trace and compare the principles, goals, and shifting interests of major and minor political parties over the past 132 years. The book does not include an index or bibliography. —Edward J. Bacciocco, Jr. [R: ARBA 75, item 493]

191. Schlesinger, Arthur M., Jr., ed. **History of American Presidential Elections, 1789-1968.** New York, published in association with Chelsea House by McGraw-Hill, 1971. 4v. bibliog. index. $150.00. LC 70-139269. ISBN 0-07-079786-2.

Forth-five eminent scholars undertake to describe and analyze the circumstances and effects of all presidential elections held in the United States since 1789. The format for the coverage of each election is essentially the same; an original descriptive and analytical essay followed by a selection of significant documents relating to the election. The documents have been selected to illustrate the key issues or events of the elections. Among items typically included are party platforms, acceptance speeches or other public statements, and a breakdown of electoral and popular voting results.

The essays are readable and historically accurate synopses of the events before, during, and after each election. When considered as a whole, they provide a rather impressive history of American presidential politics. Reference access to information about each election is facilitated by a good subject index. This publication is useful for gaining rather quickly the flavor and substance of any presidential election. —Gary R. Purcell. [R: LJ, 15 Sept 71, p. 2757; ALA 71; ARBA 72, item 307]

STATE GOVERNMENT

192. Vellucci, Matthew J., Nancy D. Wright, and Gene P. Allen, comps. **The National Directory of State Agencies 1974-1975.** Washington, Information Resources Press, 1974. 601p. $50.00. LC 74-18864. ISBN 0-87815-014-5.

This valuable new directory covers 66 functional agency categories that are common to most state governments. Among the functions included are consumer affairs, corrections, education, highway, library services, motor vehicles, securities, and welfare. Each entry is arranged according to the following format: name of administrator and title; name of bureau, division, etc.; name of overall agency or department; room number and name of building; street address; mailing address; and area code and telephone number. Data for each entry are current to mid-1974. Agencies were asked to confirm, correct, or update their entries; but, in some cases, complete information was not provided and not otherwise available.

The directory has two major parts. The first part is arranged alphabetically by the 50 states and the District of Columbia, and under each state appear entries for the functional agencies. The second part is arranged alphabetically by functional agency, and under each again appear complete data for the state agencies concerned. The directory also includes a list of general information telephone numbers for each state government in the capitol city, and a list of professional associations of state officials by functional area. This latter list includes the name and title of the executive director or secretary of the association, its street and/or mailing address, and area code and telephone number. —LeRoy C. Schwarzkopf. [R: WLB, Sept 75, p. 74; ARBA 76, item 70]

OTHER NATIONAL GOVERNMENTS

193. Shimoni, Yaacov, and Evyatar Levine, eds. **Political Dictionary of the Middle East in the 20th Century.** Rev. ed. New York, Quadrangle/New York Times Book Co., 1974. 1v.(unpaged). illus. $6.95pa. LC 76-175628. ISBN 0-8129-0482-6.

Presents in one alphabetical sequence (in two parts): biographies of important political and historical figures, both local and foreign; articles on chief cities and geographical features, political parties, historical events, issues, concepts, treaties and alliances, ethnic and religious groups; regional relations and policies of countries outside the region; three- to fourteen-page summaries of the individual countries (virtually excluding North Africa west of Libya); and many articles on various aspects of the Arab-Israel conflict, including peace plans and negotiations, the wars, and issues. It consists of the 1972 edition and an 85-page supplement.

The signed articles are all by Israeli specialists. Cross-referencing between articles is so extensive that it mitigates the problem of main entry terminology, which develops when dealing with issues such as "partial settlement" (which could also be entered under "interim agreement," etc.); there are neither cross references from alternate forms in the alphabetic sequence nor an index, which might have contained the variant terminology. Treatment of most subjects is reasonably balanced. However, most articles on the Arab-Israeli conflict exhibit a pronounced Israeli perspective, which often degenerates into an unscholarly bias that colors selection of facts and interpretations of history. The writers have not hesitated to render judgments; generally they adhere to official positions.

The supplement contains new items and continuations from the first edition; updated articles are marked in both sections, so the reader knows when to refer to the other section.

This is an extremely useful work for all students of the region; it contains most of the information most people would need on the post-World War II period, which is the book's main emphasis. —David W. Littlefield. [R: ARBA 75, item 523]

COMMUNISM

194. Kernig, C. D., ed. **Marxism, Communism and Western Society: A Comparative Encyclopedia.** New York, Herder and Herder; distr. New York, McGraw-Hill, 1972— . $40.00/v.; $320.00/set. LC 79-176368. ISBN 0-07-073526-3(set).

This work attempts a comparative analysis between Western thought and that of Marxism and communism in various forms. Redefining the differences between communist and non-communist concepts and doctrines is the essential purpose of the more than 400 articles, written by eminent scholars, covering the humanities, sciences, and social sciences.

For the most part, articles have identical structure, consisting of three parts: Western aspects, Soviet and Marxist aspects, and a critical comparison. Cross references to related material are included within the articles, except for those that are brief, in which case the cross references are appended to the articles. At the end of each article, the author provides a rather comprehensive bibliography, international in scope. Titles in Western languages are not translated, but Russian titles and those of other less familiar languages are transliterated, followed by English translation. There is no general index, but there is a list of "Contents and Cross-References" at the beginning of each volume and an Index of Articles is to appear at the end of Volume 8.

Individuals of major importance rate extensive biographical articles, whereas those of somewhat lesser significance are an integral part of articles about the ideas and movements with which they were associated.

This unique encyclopedia conforms to the highest standards of scholarly research in its successful non-partisan attempt to present and compare interpretations of communist and non-communist thought spanning the spectrum of knowledge. Although the work is still in progress, the impression gained from the first four volumes is that it will be one of the most important works of reference undertaken in recent years by a team of competent scholars. —Bohdan S. Wynar. [R: ARBA 73, item 464]

195. Lazitch, Branko, in collaboration with Milorad M. Drachkovitch. **Biographical Dictionary of the Comintern**. Stanford, Calif., Hoover Institution Press, 1973. 458p. (Hoover Institution Publications, No. 121). $15.00. LC 72-187265. ISBN 0-8179-1211-8.

The Communist International (1919-1943) played an important role in the communist movement until its liquidation by Stalin. The present work, the only biographical dictionary of its leaders, contains 716 biographical sketches of members of the executive committee, speakers at the Comintern congresses, important delegates to congresses, and other members of the Comintern apparatus. The execution of a biographical dictionary of this scope and magnitude required the use of many sources; in general, the work seems to be remarkably well balanced.

The few shortcomings noted are minor. For example, in the article on Mykola Skrypnyk (probably not Nikolai Skrypnik, since this prominent Ukrainian communist seldom used the Russian spelling of his name), one might expect to find more than the simple statement that he committed suicide in July 1933. An explanation of why he committed suicide is in order. Another example: although Shumsky's fate is rather well known, the author states that in 1927 "he completely disappeared, most probably a victim of political police." These minor points certainly do not detract from the excellence of this work. Among other things, this dictionary helps to decode some 350 pseudonyms used by Comintern leaders in their activities. —Bohdan S. Wynar. [R: ARBA 74, item 441]

196. Seidman, Joel. **Communism in the United States: A Bibliography**. Ithaca, N.Y., Cornell University Press, 1969. 526p. index. $22.50. LC 69-12427. ISBN 0-8014-0514-9.

An earlier work, *Bibliography on the Communist Problem in the United States* (Fund of the Republic, 1955), contains some 5,000 books, pamphlets and magazine articles on the subject. Seidman's comprehensive bibliography up-dates this work and for materials listed in the older work Seidman provides more descriptive annotations. All entries are arranged in a single alphabet, with a detailed subject index at the end of the volume. This is by far the most comprehensive and well selected bibliography on this subject and hopefully it can be used as a helpful model for other scholarly works of this nature. —Bohdan S. Wynar. [R: Choice, Apr 70, p. 219; ARBA 71, item 474]

197. Sworakowski, Witold S., ed. **World Communism: A Handbook 1918-1965.**
Stanford, Calif., Hoover Institution Press, 1973. 576p. index. $25.00. LC 70-149798.
ISBN 0-8179-1081-3.

Since 1967 the Hoover Institution has published, on an annual basis, the well-known *Yearbook on International Communist Affairs*, probably the most authoritative one-volume work on the subject. The present handbook offers a more concise treatment of communist affairs from 1918 to 1965.

Organized alphabetically by country, it contains an article on each of the 116 countries in which a communist party was active. Most of the articles include a brief history, plus information on organization and membership, party press organs and records, and congresses; each also has a selective bibliography. These short encyclopedic essays are written by a number of well-known specialists in their respective areas—e.g., John Reshetar, Jr. (Ukraine and the Soviet Union), Walter Kendall (Great Britain), Theodore Draper (Cuba), etc. Witold Sworakowski is Professor Emeritus of Stanford University and for many years served as Director of the Hoover Institution Library. Thanks to him and to the skillfully selected contributors, this handbook is one of the best one-stop sources on the subject. —Bohdan S. Wynar.
[R: ARBA 74, item 444]

INTERNATIONAL RELATIONS

198. **Foreign Affairs 50-Year Bibliography: New Evaluations of Significant Books on International Relations, 1920-1970.** Ed. by Byron Dexter and others. Published for the Council on Foreign Relations. New York, R. R. Bowker, 1972. 936p. index. $35.50. LC 75-163904. ISBN 0-8352-0490-1.

For the last 50 years, *Foreign Affairs* magazine has published bibliographies on international relations every decade. Now, by way of celebrating the magazine's fiftieth birthday, Editor Dexter and some 400 scholars have re-examined the five volumes and selected titles to be reviewed from a fresh, contemporary viewpoint. Annotations of books published between 1920 and 1970 were vetted—e.g., those titles of "transient value." The result is a readable, informative collection of 2,130 new reviews, plus 900 more books cited within the essays (occasionally, the citation should have been reviewed; see the entry for Siegfried's *Canada: An International Power*). Arrangement follows that of the 10-year bibliographies, and the author/title indexes include citations.

Despite an imbalance toward the Western world and *Foreign Affairs'* intrinsic conservatism, this bibliographic "happy birthday" is a valuable reference tool that is also serviceable for collection evaluation. —Peter Doiron. [R: WLB, Nov 72, p. 2934; LJ, 1 Sept 72, p. 2711; ALA 72; ARBA 73, item 468]

199. Grenville, John Ashley Soames. **The Major International Treaties 1914-1973: A History and Guide with Texts.** New York, Stein & Day, 1974. 575p. illus. maps. bibliog. index. $25.00. LC 75-163352. ISBN 0-8128-1654-4.

The author states his intention to provide a "usable collection of such [international] treaties in one volume . . . for students and the general reader concerned with international affairs," and he expresses the hope that this work will fill a gap in the literature where only specialized collections can so far be found. His material is organized both chronologically and regionally; edited texts of the treaties are preceded by historical summaries of the events that led up to them, and, where it was deemed pertinent, partial texts of letters and statements of governments or government officials have also been included. The section on "source references" at the end of the book provides information as to where one may locate the full texts of the various treaties described. There is a detailed subject index.

The author has defined the term "international treaty" broadly, and has used the widest possible latitude in including materials. The *Atlantic Charter*, primarily a declaration of principles, has been included, as has the *Charter of the Organization of American States*.

While the introduction provides a definition of the term and an explanation of the form, structure, and manner of drafting treaties, it also includes a section on treaty vocabulary. Lifting this section out and replacing it with a longer glossary of terms as one of the appendixes would make the work more useful for the general reader and the beginning student. We are given an explanation of such terms as "casus foederis" and "procès-verbal," but it would also be useful to have explanations of such terms as "protocol," "minute," "joint declaration," "statute," and "charter" in the context of international treaties.

All aspects of the international scene have been covered, and for the student whose interest is primarily in the field of current affairs, the final chapter is devoted entirely to the conflicts, treaties, and agreements of 1973. It is to be hoped that this extremely useful work will be followed by supplements. —Margaret Anderson.
[R: Choice, Nov 74, p. 1284; LJ, 15 Feb 74, p. 473; ALA 74; ARBA 75, item 533]

200. Ward, Robert Edward, and Frank Joseph Shulman. **The Allied Occupation of Japan, 1945-1952: An Annotated Bibliography of Western-Language Mater⋅ ls.** Chicago, American Library Association, 1974. 867p. index. $50.00pa. LC 73-8772. ISBN 0-8389-0127-1.

For years to come, this bibliography will be a standard reference work on the Allied occupation of Japan. The editors have selected 3,170 items (books, periodical articles, newspaper articles, government documents and archival materials) representing a "reasonably complete" selection of the more important materials in all the principal Western languages. Most items, however, are in English. The coverage is restricted to materials "which relate at least in part to the planning, staffing, structure, operations, or direct consequences of the occupation and Japanese or foreign relations or reactions thereto."

The annotations are descriptive rather than critical and give a good insight into the subject of the material. A detailed table of contents, author index, and periodical index allow good access to the materials. The items are listed alphabetically in each section and are given complete bibliographic descriptions. The appendix, "List of High Ranking Occupation Personnel," could be useful for scholarly research. —Marty Bloomberg. [R: Choice, Sept 74, p. 919; ARBA 75, item 544]

201. **Who's Who in the United Nations and Related Agencies.** Ed. by Michael Hawkin. New York, Arno Press, 1975. 785p. (Arno Press Who's Who Series). $65.00. LC 75-4105. ISBN 0-405-00490-X.

This biographical directory is more comprehensive than Burckel's *Who's Who in the United Nations* (1951). The Arno work lists some 3,500 U.N. administrators, members of governing boards and commissions, senior delegates of member and observer states, U.N. correspondents, and some representatives of non-governmental organizations.

The following information is provided for each entry: name and position, business address, language spoken, career positions, countries of service, education and professional interests, written books and articles, avocational interests, and home address. Supplementary material includes a U.N. organizational roster, a list of depository libraries, a list of member states, and a list of principal officials and their affiliations with more than 350 U.N. agencies. [R: Unesco, May/June 75, p. 166; LJ, 15 Oct 75, pp. 1908-1909; Choice, Dec 75, pp. 1294-96; ARBA 76, item 471]

CHAPTER 8

LAW

202. Koretz, Robert F., ed. **Statutory History of the United States: Labor Organization.** New York, Chelsea House in association with McGraw-Hill, 1970. 846p. index. $40.00. LC 79-78410.

This study is a work issued in the Statutory History of the United States series. It contains in chronological order the important federal statutes relative to labor organization from the enactment of the Railway Labor Act in 1926 through the Landrum Griffin Act of 1959. The statutes themselves are reproduced, together with Presidential messages, Committee reports, and excerpts from the debates on the floor of Congress. Pertinent court decisions are also included. An editorial commentary prefaces each statutory discussion. This is a useful work, drawing together in one volume the major source material with respect to the legislative background of enactments on labor organization. [Editor's note: *Statutory History of the United States* may be purchased as a set for $120.00.] —Helen M. Burns. [R: WLB, May 71, p. 886; ARBA 72, item 440]

203. Schwartz, Bernard, ed. **Statutory History of the United States: Civil Rights.** New York, Chelsea House in association with McGraw-Hill, 1970. 2v. index. $55.00. LC 79-78410.

This work constitutes a comprehensive survey of civil rights legislation from the ratification of the Thirteenth Amendment to the Constitution through the Civil Rights Act of 1968. The material is presented in chronological order and includes edited legislative source material for each enactment considered. For those statutes enacted during the nineteenth century, the emphasis for coverage is upon the congressional debates. Twentieth century statutes are covered primarily from the congressional committee reports issued in conjunction with the legislative considerations. Major court decisions relative to the enactments are included, and commentary introductory remarks are strategically placed throughout the work. Volume I includes all Constitutional Amendments and Enactments through the Repeal Act of 1894. Volume II covers those laws which have been passed since 1900. This monumental work constitutes a legislative history of the civil rights question as reflected in federal law. —Helen M. Burns. [R: Choice, Jan 71, p. 1497; WLB, May 71, p. 886; ARBA 72, item 442]

204. Stevens, Robert B., ed. **Statutory History of the United States: Income Security.** New York, Chelsea House in association with McGraw-Hill, 1970. 919p. index. $40.00. LC 79-78410.

This volume covers in depth the federal statutes pertaining to income security. It is "an effort to use official documents to tell a crucial aspect of social history; the story of government involvement in income security." Concentration is on income security, which is defined as "cash benefits." However, federal programs for special groups such as railroad employees, public employees, and veterans have been excluded from coverage. Prime consideration is given to the Social Security Act together with its numerous amendments. The presentation is chronological, with an introductory section which surveys the pre-New Deal developments and an Appendix which considers the Nixon Program. This work is published as part of the *Statutory History of the United States*. It covers basic legislative source material. —Helen M. Burns. [R: ARBA 72, item 443]

205. Blackwell, Thomas E. **The College Law Digest, 1935-1970**. Washington, National Association of College and University Attorneys; distr. South Hackensack, N.J., Fred B. Rothman and Co., 1974. 256p. illus. index. $12.00pa. LC 74-79484.

A legal digest is defined as an index to reported cases; arranged by subject and subdivided by jurisdictions and courts, it provides brief, unconnected statements of court holdings or facts of cases. Specializing in a comparatively new area of American jurisprudence, this digest concentrates only on those judicial decisions from 1935 to 1970 that affect institutions of higher education in the United States. Published under the auspices of the National Association of College and University Attorneys, this digest updates the work by Elliott and Chambers published in 1936 by the Carnegie Corporation—*The Colleges and the Courts: Judicial Decisions Regarding Institutions of Higher Education in the United States*. In order to facilitate legal research, over 200 subject headings and subheadings have been developed for this information service; a table of cases, arranged by case name, is provided for ease of access. Dr. Thomas E. Blackwell, lawyer and former vice chancellor at Washington University in St. Louis, is the general editor of this work. —Bernard D. Reams, Jr. [R: ARBA 75, item 564]

206. Brownlie, Ian, ed. **Basic Documents in International Law**. 2nd ed. New York, Oxford University Press, 1972. 284p. index. $8.50; $4.50pa. ISBN 0-19-876024-8.

As an invaluable collection of material, this volume complements existing collections of international legal documents in that its emphasis is toward the current political and law-making trends of the present day and not toward case law. The editor provides a basic selection of relevant and prominent documents relating to International Organizations, the Law of the Sea, Outer Space, Diplomatic Relations, Permanent Sovereignty over Natural Resources, Human Rights and Self Determination, the Law of Treaties, and Judicial Settlement of Disputes. New materials included in this edition are the Vienna Convention on the Law of Treaties, the Declaration of Principles of International Law Concerning Friendly Relations and Cooperation among States, and the Declaration of Principles Governing the Sea-bed and the Ocean Floor, and the Subsoil Thereof, Beyond the Limits of National Jurisdiction. Preceding each document the editor provides introductory notes, with citations to additional literature that contains a more detailed analysis and explanation of the legal issues presented. This volume will prove a useful but general reference source for all library users concerned with the problems of modern international law. —Bernard D. Reams, Jr. [R: LJ, 1 Apr 72, p. 1304; C&RL, Jan 72, p. 45; ARBA 73, item 470]

207. Gamboa, Melquiades J. **A Dictionary of International Law and Diplomacy.**
Quezon City, Philippines, Central Lawbook Publishing Co.; distr. Dobbs Ferry,
N.Y., Oceana, 1974. 351p. $15.00. LC 73-20396. ISBN 0-379-00219-1.

The value of adequate dictionaries in any scholarly field is readily apparent.
As Oliver Wendell Holmes noted in the 1925 Supreme Court decision, *Towne v.
Eisner*, "A word is not a crystal, transparent and unchanged, it is the skin of a
living thought and may vary greatly in color and content according to the circumstances in which it is used." The dictionary will, however, help to establish some
degree of uniformity in the application of words. In few scholarly areas is this need
more evident that in international law and international relations.

Gamboa, a former ambassador for the Philippines to Great Britain, India,
Sweden, Norway, Denmark, and the United Nations, as well as Professor Law at
the University of the Philippines, is admirably well qualified to correct this situa-
tion. The dictionary is, in effect, a revision of the author's earlier work, *Elements
of Diplomatic and Consular Practice: A Glossary*. There are three appendixes: the
Charter of the United Nations, the statutory base of the International Court of
Justice, and the Vienna Convention on the Law of Treaties. —Jerry E. Stephens.
[ARBA 75, item 554]

208. Schwartz, Bernard. **The Bill of Rights: A Documentary History.** New York,
Chelsea House in association with McGraw-Hill, 1971. 2v. index. $59.50. LC 71-
150209. ISBN 0-07-079613-0.

Professor Bernard Schwartz contends that it is impossible to study the American Bill of Rights in a vacuum. A thorough knowledge of the English and American
precedents which shaped the thinking of James Madison and his colleagues is essential. Consequently Schwartz has attempted to present the extensive history of the
Bill of Rights in documentary form. His choise of material is naturally subjective,
but Schwartz, a distinguished professor of law at New York University and author
of many works in legal history, is qualified to make the choice. The documents are
arranged chronologically in eight categories: English antecedents since the Magna
Carta; the Colonial period; the Revolutionary Declarations and Constitutions;
developments under the Articles of Confederation; the state ratifying conventions;
the legislative history of the federal Bill of Rights; and the ratification by the
states. Each of the eight divisions is preceded by a brief but helpful introduction,
as are most of the documents themselves. These brief explanations, placing the
sources in historical perspective, are invaluable for the student, and the excellent
index makes individual items easy to find.

Professor Schwartz has provided a fine reference tool for the study of constitutional, legal, and general American history. This work is absolutely essential
for all public, school, and college libraries, an invaluable reference aid for all students of history. —Nancy G. Boles. [R: ARBA 72, item 441]

CHAPTER 9

GEOGRAPHY

BIBLIOGRAPHIES

209. Alexander, Gerald L. **Guide to Atlases: World, Regional, National Thematic; An International Listing of Atlases Published since 1950.** Metuchen, N.J., Scarecrow, 1971. 671p. index. $19.50. ISBN 0-8108-0414-X.

This checklist of published atlases is quite comprehensive, listing some 5,500 entries. There are several sections. World atlases have been arranged chronologically by date and, within each year, alphabetically by publisher. Regional atlases are usually listed within each continent alphabetically by name of publisher. National atlases are listed under their respective regions; thematic atlases are divided first alphabetically by subject (e.g., economy, geology, etc.), then alphabetically by publisher within each category. Atlases are listed more than once if they cover more than one area or subject. Appended are an index of publishers, an alphabetical language index, and an index of authors, cartographers, and editors.

In a project of this type, one hardly expects to find listings of all new editions. Checking the well-known Hammond atlases revealed many old editions and occasionally incorrect bibliographic descriptions. In terms of languages represented, this checklist covers only 33 languages, and some languages (e.g., Slovak, Korean, and Japanese) are rather poorly represented. Nevertheless, this work serves very well as a first effort. —Bohdan S. Wynar. [R: ALA 71; ARBA 72, item 473]

210. Earney, Fillmore C. F. **Researchers' Guide to Iron Ore: An Annotated Bibliography on the Economic Geography of Iron Ore.** Littleton, Colo., Libraries Unlimited, 1974. 595p. index. $30.00. LC 74-76986. ISBN 0-87287-095-2.

The iron ore industry has been essentially transformed since World War II, and it appears that significant change will continue. This annotated bibliography emphasizes usability and will be useful to researchers—whether business, industrial, academic, or individual—interested in projecting the future of the industry.

The bulk of the entries pertain to the post-World War II period; however, some pre-World War II and retrospective material is included to provide historical perspective. Similarly, most material on steel production and pig iron has been excluded, although some material deemed applicable to iron ore is included. Coverage is limited to English language materials. The bibliography is arranged in three sections—General, Topical, and Regional. Topical sections include, among others, Investments and Ownership, Markets, Transport, Beneficiation Economics, Beneficiation Technology, and Ore Reduction Technology. The regional section is subdivided generally by country or, in the case of the United States, by individual states (some other countries, such as Canada and Australia, are also subdivided). Within classifications, the arrangement is by title; cross references to complete citations are provided where they facilitate use. [R: LJ, 1 Dec 74, p. 3124; ARBA 75, item 569]

211. Harris, Chauncy D., and Jerome D. Fellmann. **International List of Geographical Serials**. 2nd ed. Chicago, University of Chicago, Department of Geography, 1971. 267p. index. (Research Paper No. 138) $5.00; $4.00 series subscription. LC 79-163720. ISBN 0-89065-045-4.

The first edition of this standard directory, published in 1960, contained 1,651 entries. The present edition has been substantially revised and enlarged, listing 2,415 serials from 90 countries. Some 60 scholars cooperated in the preparation of this edition, with the purpose of providing a comprehensive inventory "of all geographical serials, both those currently being published and those no longer active."

As in the first edition, the material is arranged by country with adequate bibliographical description of titles listed. For current serials the compilers provided additional information if known (e.g., frequency of publication, languages used in articles, tables of contents or abstracts, and address of publication). The form of the titles is generally that used in the *Union List of Serials*. Occasionally, the compilers have problems with some foreign titles, primarily in the area of transliteration. Such errors (some typographical) are minor in nature and are often unavoidable in a work of this type. −Bohdan S. Wynar. [R: ARBA 72, item 477]

212. Lock, C. B. Muriel. **Modern Maps and Atlases: An Outline Guide to 20th Century Production**. Hamden, Conn., Archon, 1969. 619p. index. $15.00. LC 70-6153. ISBN 0-208-00869-1.

An evaluative guide to the principal non-textbook materials used in geographical studies. Contents include: The Techniques of Modern Cartography; International Maps and Atlases; National and Regional Maps and Atlases, Thematic Maps and Atlases; and Map Librarianship.

Unfortunately, the coverage of this work is quite uneven, with an obvious emphasis on Great Britain (this book was first published in Great Britain by Clive Bingley) and a rather uninspiring narrative. Nevertheless, it provides comprehensive coverage of 20th century cartography. Bibliographical citations included in individual chapters will assist in locating additional information on topics not fully treated in this work. [R: RQ, Winter 69; ALA 70; ARBA 70, v.1, p. 95]

213. Neal, J. A., comp. **Reference Guide for Travellers**. New York, R. R. Bowker, 1969. 674p. index. $19.95. LC 69-16399. ISBN 0-8352-0227-5.

This comprehensive bibliographic guide to the voluminous travel literature published in English lists 1,947 travel books, guides and official publications. It is divided into eight parts: the world, Africa, Asia, Australia, the Pacific, Europe, North America, and South America. Within each division, entries are arranged by country, region, and city. The sections list standard guide books and special guides first, followed by other suggested readings and official travel publications, including health and medical guides, tourist vocabulary and phrase books, and travel periodicals. Only books that were published before November 1, 1968, and that were submitted for examination by publishers are described. A listing of scheduled 1969 titles is provided in an appendix. Other appendixes include vocabulary and phrase books and travel periodicals. An author-title index, a place index, and a directory of publishers and distributors of travel material are also provided. [R: LJ, July 69; ALA 69; ARBA 70, v.1, p. 101]

214. Walsh, S. Padraig, comp. **General World Atlases in Print, 1972-1973: A Comparative Analysis**. 4th ed. New York, R. R. Bowker, 1973. 211p. index. $12.50. LC 72-13053. ISBN 0-8352-0562-2.

Examining Walsh's fourth edition of his *General World Atlases in Print, 1972-1973*, we have to admit that it has come a long way since the first edition was published in 1966. As the author states in his preface, the purpose of this bibliography is to serve as a practical guide for those involved in the selection of world atlases in the English language. Walsh implies that his work is directed mainly to the average or non-specialist user, but it is a carefully documented critical guide that would be of great use to cartographers, geographers, and librarians.

Walsh surveys 40 major atlases in the first part of the book and discusses 100 inexpensive atlases in the second part. He gives detailed information on the publishers, editors, cartographers, and contributors, as well as availability of the publications. He also cites the purpose and the potential user of each atlas and discusses the index—the scope, contents, and arrangement. There is practical information about a few publishers who change the name of an atlas, but not the contents, and then sell it as a new atlas. Besides listing critical reviews, Walsh has also developed his own rating system. He assigns 25 points for the best atlases available and then rates lesser efforts on a scale down to zero. Although he tries to justify his rating system, we still cannot accept it as a good method of evaluation, since assigning a place on a numerical scale provides an artificial evaluation. We would rather accept his judgment based on experience. In an appendix, Walsh lists discontinued atlases, a scale conversion chart, and a list of atlas publishers.

Librarians involved in selecting atlases have long felt the need for a tool containing all this important information. Somehow, the reviewing media discuss atlases only superficially, and the available critiques are not always authoritative. Because atlases are usually among the more expensive purchases, they should be selected with great care. —Louis Kiraldi. [R: RQ, Fall 73, p. 80; LJ, 1 Sept 73, p. 2426; RSR, July/Sept 73, p. 13; ARBA 74, item 468]

215. Wheat, James Clements, and Christian Brun. **Bibliography of Maps and Charts Published in America before 1800**. New Haven, Conn., Yale University Press, 1969. 215p. maps. index. $30.00. LC 69-15464.

Providing a new and valuable tool for the historian and cartographer, this comprehensive and annotated bibliography of 915 maps represents the first attempt to describe the entire known cartographical contribution of the American press prior to 1800. Included are not only maps and charts published separately, but also those used as illustrations in books and pamphlets and from other sources such as atlases, gazetteers, almanacs, and magazines. Most of the items included pertain to the area that became the United States, but there are also entries covering parts of Latin America, Europe, Africa, the West Indies, and Asia.

Arranged chronologically by region, entries include date of publication, description, size and scale, the publication in which the map first appeared, and the location of existing copies. Included are reproductions of 18 rare maps of the period, as well as a 20-page list of books referred to in this pioneering study. [R: LJ, 15 Sept 69; RQ, Winter 69; ARBA 70, v.1, p. 96]

DICTIONARIES AND GAZETTEERS

216. **Gazetteer of Scotland: Including a Glossary of the Most Common Gaelic Names.** 3rd rev. ed. by R. W. Munro. Edinburgh, Johnston & Bacon; distr. Elmsford, N.Y., British Book Centre, 1974. 353p. $14.95. ISBN 0-8277-2441-1.

The third edition of a standard work that dates back to 1937, this revision adds some 350 entries and updates many previous entries. Some historical and archaeological information has been changed to "conform with modern terminology and discoveries."

Concise identifications are given, with locations stated in miles. The mileage, unfortunately, won't help in planning trips because the distance is given in straight lines and not highway distances.

The entries checked against standard gazetteers proved to be correct and, for the most part, considerably shorter. Many entries in the work are not in standard geographical reference works.

Especially valuable is the glossary of some common Gaelic terms in Scottish place names. The non-Scot, however, will find that an unabridged dictionary is still necessary; the editor considers some terms too common to include in the glossary, even though in the United States the terms are far from common. —William Brace. [R: ARBA 75, item 572]

217. Matthews, C. M. **Place Names of the English-Speaking World.** New York, Scribner's, 1972. 369p. index. $8.95. LC 72-538. ISBN 0-684-12939-6.

Mrs. Matthews has followed her most successful book, *English Surnames*, by another of equal value. In this book she traces the origins and changes of place names from the early history of the English speaking areas of the world. Naturally, Britain and America are to the forefront in her studies. It is the first study of its kind. While the social and historical significance of place names is discussed in considerable depth, the author has produced a history that is vivid and very readable. A large part of the book is devoted to the New World, where the American colonies, the United States, Canada, Southern Africa, Australia, and New Zealand are scrutinized. The book is factual and extremely accurate; standard etymological sources have been well chosen, and there is much original research. The appendixes include a chronological table of events that have influenced place names, and a select bibliography. —P. William Filby. [R: WLB, Dec 72, p. 365; ARBA 73, item 392]

218. Stewart, George R. **American Place Names: A Concise and Selective Dictionary for the Continental United States of America**. New York, Oxford University Press, 1970. 550p. $12.50. LC 72-83018.

This volume contains about 12,000 entries for United States place names, arranged alphabetically, dictionary fashion, in one sequence. Each entry mentions the states in which the place name occurs, followed by a concise explanation as to the origin of the name. Indian names (e.g., Milwaukee) are included. The work is judiciously selective, emphasizing names that people might be expected to question, such as well-known place names, names often repeated, or unusual names. "Obviously obvious" names were eliminated, as were Hawaiian names (not being part of the continental U.S.). This volume replaces the inadequate *American Names: A Guide to the Origin of Place Names in the United States*, a 1947 reprint of a 1902 work.

George R. Stewart is a Berkeley Fellow of the University of California where he has taught for many years. He has written on names at some length, most notably in his earlier book, *Names on the Land*. A past president of the American Name Society, he is eminently qualified to do a book of this kind.

This volume is particularly valuable as a reference source because it is usefully arranged in dictionary fashion; it is intended for the general reader and free of technical terms; it has an excellent bibliography; it is concise, and it annotated every place name I could think of. The book is certainly superior to other recent books of a similar nature, such as Quimby's *Scratch Ankle, U.S.A.*

This volume is a happy combination of sound scholarship, general usefulness, and a pleasing format. It will be the standard work on place names in the United States for some time to come. —Donald Empson. [R: LJ, 1 Nov 70; ALA 70; ARBA 71, item 464]

DIRECTORIES

219. Carrington, David K., comp. **Map Collections in the United States and Canada**. 2nd rev. ed. New York, Special Libraries Association, Geography and Map Division, 1970. 159p. map. index. $8.00pa. LC 72-101336. ISBN 0-87111-190-X.

A revised and updated directory of more than 600 Anglo-American cartography collections housed in academic, public, or special (but not private) libraries. Based on replies to questionnaires distributed by the Geography and Map Division, Special Libraries Association, the compilation represents a 20 percent increase in citations over those in the first edition of 1954.

Arrangement is alphabetical by state or province with such entry information (where applicable) as collection title, address, phone number, name of map librarian or curator, number of staff members, size of collection (to include total number of maps, aerial photographs, globes, relief models, atlases and gazetteers on hand). Annual accessions estimates are quoted. Area and/or subject specializations are listed, as is information on depository responsibilities, extent of service to patrons, interlibrary loans, reproduction facilities available, and publications issued. Data obtained from sources other than the map directory questionnaire are designated by an aster-isk. A brief list of abbreviations most commonly encountered prefaces the directory proper. Summation: a reference work unique in its particular field and of special value to persons engaged in cartographic research. —Lawrence E. Spellman. [R: WLB, Jan 71, p. 504; ARBA 72, item 481]

ATLASES

220. Armstrong, R. Warwick, ed. **Atlas of Hawaii.** Honolulu, University Press of Hawaii, 1973. 222p. illus. maps. bibliog. $15.00. LC 72-91236. ISBN 0-8248-0259-4.

This first atlas of the fiftieth state as a geographical, economic, and social entity was produced through the combined efforts of the University of Hawaii's Geography Department and numerous governmental, industrial, and commercial organizations. The backbone of this paperback volume consists of over 275 maps/ map insets (most colored) and more than 150 illustrations and photographs (colored or black and white). The maps are vivid, excellently drawn, easy to read, and scaled mostly at the approximate ratio of 1 inch to 4.5 miles, or 1:285,000. A significant number portray built-up areas at larger scales. Types include topographic, geologic, and thematic (climate, flora, fauna, archaeology, and population). All maps and diagrams furnish date and source of information. Arrangement is by sub-ject area, and the atlas covers Hawaii's natural environment, culture, and economy with deliberate, but essentially balanced, emphasis on the latter. Brief textual dis-cussions help the reader effectively appreciate and interpret the cartographic imagery. These essays are accompanied by tastefully selected illustrations and photographs whose sole drawback is their rather reduced size. Numerous graphs and tables display statistical data current through 1971. The bibliography is not comprehensive, but it serves as a beneficial basic guide to useful source materials. Approximately 3,300 entries comprise the gazetteer section, which encompasses not only populated places but also names of physical features, objects of man-made culture, deities, plants, and animals; pronunciation is clarified by diacritical marks. Geographical locations are identified by map page number and alphanu-meric rather than geographic coordinates. This is an authoritative, albeit unofficial, atlas of Hawaii characterized by careful scholarship, completeness, and vivacity of presentation. —Lawrence E. Spellman. [R: ARBA 74, item 476]

221. **Atlas of Japan: Physical, Economic and Social.** 2nd ed. Tokyo, International Society for Educational Information; distr. Thompson, Conn., InterCulture Asso-ciates, 1974. 64 + 64p. illus.(part col.). maps. $35.00. ISBN 0-88253-429-X.

In this revised edition, data have been updated to the early 1970s and spell-ing has been "revised into a more Anglicized form." The 73 maps and map insets, which are of excellent cartographic quality, illustrate information about a broad range of areas including geology, agriculture, urbanology, demography, economics, and industry. Textual material accompanying the maps is brief and is in English, Spanish, and French. [R: ARBA 75, item 573]

222. **Britannica World Atlas International.** Ruth Martin Cole, geography ed., and others. Chicago, Encyclopaedia Britannica, 1969. 367p. graphs. maps. index. $35.00.

Britannica World Atlas and Rand McNally's *International Atlas* were published as a joint project. It should be pointed out that this new edition is the most thorough revision of the Britannica atlas since it was first published in 1942. Maps are prepared by Rand McNally; Cartographia, Budapest; Esselte Map Service, Stockholm; George Philip and Son, London; and Teikoku-Shoin, Tokyo. The two atlases are quite similar, but each has its own foreword. The *International Atlas* contains an introductory essay, "Patterns and Imprints of Mankind," by Marvin W. Mikesell, and the Britannica atlas has a section, "World Scene," describing world distribution and political geography, prepared by the Geography Department of Britannica. In this section one finds information on map scales and projections, information on population, distribution and density, languages, climate, natural vegetation, urbanization, agriculture and trade, transportation, and 22 pages of essential information on world political geography. The maps in the two atlases are identical. In conclusion, this is a truly international atlas that observes high professional standards. —Bohdan S. Wynar. [R: BL, 1 Oct 70, p. 113-116; ARBA 71, item 571]

223. Chi-Bonnardel, Regine Van. **The Atlas of Africa.** New York, Free Press, 1973. 335p. illus.(col.) maps. index. $80.00. LC 73-17932.

A geographical, social, and economic overview of Africa and its nations—first of its kind in two decades—prepared primarily by faculty members of the University of Paris and published originally in French by Editions Jeune Afrique with Unesco assistance.

The backbone of the work consists of close to 200 multicolored maps/map insets compiled by L'Institut Géographique National de Paris. These range up to 9" x 12" in size, with scales from 1:1,000,000 (1" is approximately 16 miles) to 1:10,000,000 (1" is about 158 miles). All maps are thus relatively small scale, but they are accurate, cleanly drawn, and easy to interpret. Types include topographic and thematic (population, agriculture, mineral resources, industries, etc.). The unusually extensive, unpedantic text reflects the most current official data available; it emphasizes those geographic, climatic, historical, and economic factors considered critically influential in the cultural and political development of Africa and its peoples from both a regional and a national standpoint. The alphanumeric index is a facile location finder but, with fewer than 6,000 entries, it is rather skeletal. A multilingual glossary of geographic terms will prove helpful to readers of English; the absence of metric conversion tables is regrettable. This is a timely, vitally essential reference work characterized by a high order of scholarship and cartographic portrayal. —Lawrence E. Spellman. [R: LJ, July 74, p. 1792; Choice, June 74, p. 578; BL, 15 Nov 74, pp. 348-49; WLB, May 74, pp. 764-65; ALA 74; ARBA 75, item 576]

224. **The Earth and Man: A Rand McNally World Atlas.** Chicago, Rand McNally, 1972. 439p. illus.(col.) maps. index. $35.00. LC 70-654432. ISBN 0-528-83050-3.

This handsome atlas is divided into three main parts. The first section is a potpourri of information, describing the earth in space, its structure, life on earth, resources, and man on earth. The colorful pictures of man's life on earth are beautifully executed and would be of interest to anyone. But no matter how attractive this part of the publication is, a map librarian might question the necessity of including this type of information in an atlas. A good handbook or encyclopedia can provide this information; an atlas should include maps and closely related information.

The second part consists of 150 pages of maps. These updated maps, although fewer in number, are similar in execution to those in the 1969 edition of Rand McNally's *International Atlas*. It is a pleasure to look up information on these maps; they are vivid, uncluttered and easy to read. The clear printing makes it easy to find rivers, mountains, roads, railroads, localities, and other geographical information. One objectionable feature, however, is that different scales are used for various states and regions of the same continent.

Another poor feature is the way the atlas is indexed. The subject index, while well developed concerning cities and small localities, is very difficult to use to find information on a country. For instance, if someone tries to find a map of Austria, he cannot find "Austria" in the table of contents because it is included in the entry: Europe—Central Europe. The subject index entry for Austria directs the user to the map of Europe, where the map of Austria is rather small, instead of giving the page number of the previously mentioned map of Central Europe, where the map of Austria is quite adequate. Also, the "Index Map" provided is not very clear and is hidden on pages 146-47.

The third part of the atlas deals with geographical facts, figures, and information about the world and the United States. This kind of information is welcome in any atlas.

Since the format is not too large, it is easy to handle. The binding is sturdy and the paper is fine. —Louis Kiraldi. [R: LJ, 1 Dec 72, p. 3890; ALA 72; ARBA 73, item 502]

225. Espenshade, Edward B., Jr., ed. **Goode's World Atlas**. 13th ed. Chicago, Rand McNally, 1970. 315p. maps. gaz. $10.95; $5.95pa. ISBN 0-528-63468-2; 0-528-63470-4pa.

College and university libraries will probably want to have recent editions of all of the available school atlases. *Goode's World Atlas*, an excellent example of the type, compares favorably with Hammond's *Panoramic World Atlas*, the *Aldine University Atlas* and other school atlases. C. B. Muriel Lock, in her book *Modern Maps and Atlases* (Hamden, Archon Books, 1969), calls Goode's "the leading American school atlas . . ." (p. 102). The first edition of the atlas was published more than 40 years ago under the general editorship of the distinguished cartographer, Dr. Goode.

In this 13th edition (edited by Professor Espenshade and a board of distinguished contributors) the coverage has been expanded over that of the 12th edition. Additions include ten pages of thematic maps, a striking double-page "World Portrait Map" depicting land and submarine features of the globe, and eight additional pages in the index of geographical names. This is a physical, political, and economic atlas with worldwide information in the first section. Maps are then arranged sequentially by continent and regions within the continents, leading off with the North American continent. Nine new maps, principally of Canada, appear in this section of the new edition. The introduction contains useful information on map utilization and map reading, including how to understand scales and projections. For each map the projection used and the scale to which it is drawn are indicated.

Projection varies from map to map in order that the most appropriate projection for the accurate depiction of particular information might be used. Sources are indicated for those maps that didn't originate with Rand McNally. The atlas contains beautifully executed physiographic maps by the late Erwin Raisz, and an outstanding "Natural Vegetation" map by A. W. Küchler. Small inset maps of some of the world's principal cities are included, but this coverage, as in most atlases, is far from complete. Maybe some day someone will issue a fairly comprehensive atlas of the cities of the world.

The craftsmanlike offset printing is done using color tinting skillfully to depict land forms and features. Typography has been improved. The atlas is sturdily bound in cloth with strikingly designed covers. The 13th edition of *Goode's World Atlas* is a first-rate, up-to-date atlas. —Frank J. Anderson. [R: ARBA 71, item 572]

226. **Hammond Medallion World Atlas**. Maplewood, N.J., Hammond, 1971. 1v. (various paging). illus.(col.). maps. index. $24.95. LC 71-654313.

More maps for the money is a Hammond hallmark, and this volume emphasizes it. Over 600 maps (accurate, current, and diversified) provide physical, political, and special subject information on every modern country plus each of the 50 states. United States population figures are based on the 1970 census; zip codes are listed for all populated places shown on state maps. A world index of over 100,000 place names (including countries, provinces/states, cities, towns, and major terrain features) is bulwarked by sub-indexes interleaved conveniently with the appropriate map(s). Geographic coordinates are eschewed in favor of a basic alphanumeric locator system. Special sections are devoted to ecology and to Biblical as well as world and United States history. These are vividly illustrated with many colorful diagrams and photos. Text is minimal; the emphasis is on the clear-cut, easy-to-read, well-arranged maps. Summation: superior general atlas providing fast, uncomplicated access to geographical, demographic, and related data. —Lawrence E. Spellman. [R: WLB, Dec 71, p. 363; LJ, 1 Jan 72, p. 59; ARBA 72, item 487]

227. Hsieh, Chaio-min. **Atlas of China**. Ed. by Christopher L. Salter. New York, McGraw-Hill, 1973. 282p. maps. bibliog. index. $17.50. LC 72-8717. ISBN 0-07-030628-1.

Any good atlas contains a great deal of data, but this single-volume work provides an unusually large amount of information. Its 273 monochrome maps, arranged in four categories—Physical (49 maps), Cultural (41 maps), Regional (156 maps),and Historical (27 maps)— display a vast array of general and special aspects of China's land and society. The physical maps treat such topics as the geological structure of the land mass, as well as its climate, soil, and flora and fauna. People, transportation, agriculture, mining, and manufacturing are dealt with in the cultural section. The regional maps, in addition to treating the traditional divisions of China, include plans of cities. Finally, the historical maps, extending from earliest times to the present, add a measure of temporal depth to the work. The maps are complemented by a well-written text. There is a bibliography of predominantly Chinese publications. —John H. Winkelman. [R: NYTBR, 23 Sept 73, p. 40; LJ, 1 June 73, p. 1804; ALA 73; ARBA 74, item 479]

228. **The International Atlas.** Chicago, Rand McNally, 1969. 556p. illus. color maps. index. $35.00. LC Map 77-6543339.

This atlas and the *Britannica World Atlas* were published jointly by Encyclopaedia Britannica and Rand McNally, they are identical except for the 16,000-word introductory essay in *The International Atlas* entitled "Patterns and Imprints of Mankind." Here the major patterns rather than political divisions are discussed. Ten years in the making, this atlas provides a good balance in its coverage; 65 map pages are devoted to Canada and the United States, 47 to Europe, 50 to Asia, and 26 to Africa. The 285 maps include all major geographic areas, most of them are four-color to give a three-dimensional effect of elevation. Only six proportionate map scales are used, ranging from 380 miles to the inch down to 4.7 miles to the inch for principal population centers. Of particular interest are detailed maps (all at 1:1,000,000 scale) of the ubanized regions popularly referred to as developing megalopolises and maps of more than 60 of the world's major metropolitan areas (all at 1:3,000,000 scale). All units of measurement shown on the maps are metric, while scale indicators give both miles and kilometers. Texts are given in four languages (English, German, Spanish and French), and a master glossary provides translations of geographic terms from 52 languages. A comprehensive index contains more than 160,000 place names usually in both English and the local language. These provide location by latitude and longitude rather than by the old alphanumeric grid system. The index also contains historical names no longer in official use. It was produced by computer from a large private geographic data bank developed by Rand McNally. The coverage and the color reproduction in this atlas are much better than in the *National Geographic Atlas of the World* or the old *Encyclopaedia Britannica Atlas*, and its index is much more detailed.
[R: LJ, 15 Nov 69; WLB, Jan 70; ALA 69; ARBA 70, v.1, p. 97]

229. Israel. Department of Surveys. **Atlas of Israel.** Edited by David H.K. Amiran and others. New York, American Elsevier, 1970. 290p. maps. tab. bibliog. $130.00. ISBN 0-444-90740-5.

Published in Israel between 1956 and 1964, this atlas serves as an example for other national atlases. It has 550 colored maps on 71 plates, plus explanatory text in 15 sections covering Israel's historical cartography, geomorphology, geology, climate, flora and fauna, history, population, economic development, education, and all other major aspects of Israel's life and culture. The English edition is more than a simple translation from Hebrew; it has been up-dated, and there are significant changes in the number and quality of maps. The large size of this atlas (19" x 14" x 1½") permits considerable detail. Some of the historical information in this national atlas is biased, but one must admit that, in general, this is a product of sound scholarship. However, it is regrettable that this edition has no subject index. —Bohdan S. Wynar. [R: Choice, Oct 70; Surveying and Mapping, Sept 70, pp. 485-86; ALA 70; ARBA 71, item 401]

230. **Man's Domain: A Thematic Atlas of the World Mapping Man's Relationship with His Environment.** 3rd ed. New York, McGraw-Hill, 1975. 80p. illus.(col.). maps. index. $4.95pa. LC 74-22341. ISBN 0-07-023083-8.

The basic guidebook for the world-lover and student takes the traditional political and physical map (the kind of map we are used to) and transforms it into wonders. While the political and physical aspects are there, we have the benefit of viewing our world in terms of languages spoken, land-forms and physical regions, agriculture, population, climate, precipitation and temperature, and vegetation. A sharp and clear printing job and a readable sans-serif type make even the rather fine print (characteristic of so many mappings) bearable. The world as a whole, North America, Canada, the United States, South America, Europe, the USSR, Asia, Africa, Indonesia and Australasia are viewed separately and in the detail indicated.

The layers and swirls of color, explained in clear legends, make the document a visual as well as an intellectual experience. The publishers are to be commended for maintaining quality while at the same time keeping the cost to a level a student can afford.

The consumer-user of our brief experience in the world is stimulated to quick recognition that the world is small indeed, that its resources are slender and finite, and that man's urgent business is not only understanding his environment, but relating to it as well. —Raymond Paavo Arvio. [R: WLB, May 75, p. 675; ARBA 76, item 527]

231. **The National Atlas of Canada.** 4th ed. Toronto, Macmillan Company of Canada, in association with the Department of Energy, Mines and Resources, and Information, Canada; distr. New York, Books Canada, 1974. 254p. illus. bibliog. $67.50. ISBN 0-7705-1243-7.

This standard atlas of Canada has a long publishing history. The first edition, which appeared in 1906, was published by the Federal Ministry of Interior; the third edition appeared in 1957, and a French edition in 1959. The present fourth edition, published simultaneously in English and French, is considerably updated (up to 1971 in most cases). The emphasis is on physical and economic geography and demography. For historical topics the reader will have to consult Kerr's *Historical Atlas of Canada* (2nd ed., 1966), which we hope will be revised soon. This is the most comprehensive atlas of our northern neighbor. [R: BL, Apr 75, pp. 200-201; ARBA 76, item 534]

232. **Photo-Atlas of the United States: A Complete Photographic Atlas of the U.S.A. Using Satellite Photography.** Pasadena, Calif., Ward Ritchie Press, 1975. 127p. illus. (part col.). $8.95; $5.95pa. LC 75-18099. ISBN 0-0378-04690-X; 0-0378-04692-6pa.

The first of its type in commercial publishing, this work contains over 70 duotone and full-color photomaps of the United States obtained variously by Landsat, Skylab, U-2, and RB57 flights. These range up to 12" by 15" with an approximate scale of 1:1,250,000 (1" on the photomap equals 18 miles on the ground), and each covers about 60,000 square miles or the equivalent of the state of Georgia. All are oriented with the top margin at true (i.e., geographic meridional) north.

Annotations identify major administrative boundaries, mountain ranges, drainage systems, and great metropolitan complexes. Each photomap is accompanied by brief marginal notes treating geographic, geological, and historic highlights of the region portrayed. Arrangement is north to south and west to east, with a double-page index map providing location information. Coverage includes Alaska and Hawaii but does not extend to Puerto Rico, the U.S. Virgin Islands, Guam, or American Samoa. Technical data on the photography/imagery recording means and techniques utilized are excluded.

The basic thrust of the volume is popular and, in this respect, a gazetteer and a reading list would seem appropriate. Clarity is fair to good on the duotone reproductions, excellent on the multi-color enlargements of 10 selected larger city areas to include New York, Los Angeles, Chicago, and San Francisco. This is a regional photo-atlas with high visual appeal, incorporating much useful and precise information on relative shape, size, and location of natural and cultural features in the 50 states. —Lawrence E. Spellman. [R: ARBA 76, item 532]

233. **Rand McNally Cosmopolitan World Atlas.** Enl. "Planet Earth" ed. Chicago, Rand McNally, 1971. 1v. (various paging). illus.(part col.). index. maps. $19.95. LC 72-654253.

Designated the "Planet Earth" edition, this enlarged and revised work contains almost 400 colored maps/map insets up to 12x18", with average scales ranging from 1:2,000,000 to 1:8,000,000. Map types include physical, political, metropolitan area, and oceanographic, and individual maps are devoted to each of the United States and Canadian provinces. Not all maps are oriented with north at the top of the page, and it is frequently necessary to rotate the volume. Cartographic information is as current and complete as is practicable, and the maps are well executed, eye-pleasing, refreshingly non-cluttered, lending themselves to facile and rapid interpretation. A 100-page index locates more than 82,000 populated places, terrain features, and points of interest by appropriate page and alphanumeric coordinates (latitude and longitude figures are not cited).

Brief but informative articles are included on the solar system, the earth's atmosphere and weather, geology, the ocean world and map projections, scales and symbols. These are lavishly illustrated with over 100 diagrams, schematic drawings, and colored photographs (mostly from Apollo missions). Population data cover cities, towns, countries, and major political divisions down to 50,000, except for the United States, where the cutoff is 1,000, although many smaller places are listed. All census sources are identified. This is a superior general reference atlas with exceptionally comprehensive coverage. —Lawrence E. Spellman. [R: ARBA 72, item 489]

234. **The Times Atlas of China.** P. J. M. Geelan and D. C. Twitchett, eds. New York, Quadrangle/The New York Times Book Co., 1974. 144 + 27p. illus.(col.). maps. index. $75.00. ISBN 0-7230-0118-9.

This work contains over 125 colored maps/map insets up to 13½" by 20½" in size, employing scales that average 1:2,000,000 (1" equals approximately 30 miles). Types include topographic, historical, and thematic (demography, climate, resources, etc.). Scale is defined in miles/kilometers, major elevations in meters. A special section shows plans of 36 significant urban areas. Every map is crisply drawn, eminently legible, and attractively tinted. Maps are arranged by province and autonomous region. A 75,000-word text describes these from the standpoint of geographical characteristics, agriculture, commerce, and modes of transportation. The essays are hardly definitive, but each does furnish an excellent overall picture of the land, its inhabitants, and their style of life. Alphanumeric locator indexes are printed in both Chinese characters and English. The main index lists 20,000 entries on populated places and natural features. A brief bilingual glossary is appended, accompanied by helpful notes on transcription based on the Wade-Giles system. This is an unusually comprehensive general atlas of the Chinese People's Republic, with a large number of high-quality maps. —Lawrence E. Spellman. [R: Choice, May 75, p. 376; LJ, 15 May 75, p. 570; ARBA 76, item 535]

235. **The Times Atlas of the World: Comprehensive Edition**. New York, Quadrangle/The New York Times Book Co., 1975. 1v.(various paging). illus.(col.). maps. index. $75.00. LC 75-5875. ISBN 0-8129-0562-8.

A thoroughly revised edition of the standard atlas. The Times of London has been a publisher of atlases since 1895, and this, the fourth *Times Atlas of the World: Comprehensive Edition*, is now in its fifth edition. The Comprehensive Edition is based on the cartography of the previous five-volume Mid-Century Edition (1955-59, 5v.; the maps in this edition carry the copyright dates 1967 and 1968). The new material in this edition includes sections on the moon and artificial satellites as well as a series of highly detailed and up-to-date thematic maps of the world's food, mineral, and energy resources.

The justification for frequently revised editions is the fact that the world itself and our cartographic understanding of it are changing rapidly. Some of the changes since 1972 are re-aligned frontiers (particularly in Africa), new settlements, new states. In addition, plans of many more cities have been included. The introductory plates on world physiography and oceanography have been completely revised to record the latest findings of geological science. —Richard A. Gray. [R: ARBA 76, item 529]

236. U.S. Geological Survey. **The National Atlas of the United States**. Washington, Geological Survey, 1970. 417p. illus. index. $100.00.

Prepared by the Geological Survey with the cooperation of more than 80 federal agencies, this atlas is designed to be of "practical use to decision makers in government and business, planners, research scholars and others needing to visualize country-wide distributional patterns and relationships between environmental phenomena and human activities."

It is the most significant reference work published by the United States government in 1970. Adding to its significance is the fact that it is the first national atlas of the United States. It contains 756 maps of various scales under the following headings: general reference, physical, historical, economic, socio-cultural, administrative, mapping and charting, and the world. Of particular interest to businessmen engaged in international commerce are maps showing foreign service and U.S. foreign trade areas. The economic maps include many that are comparable to those found in the *Rand McNally Commercial Atlas and Marketing Guide*, which has long been unique in this area. The section entitled "Administrative Maps" shows the changing face of regional administration of the federal government as well as public lands such as national parks, forests, and wilderness areas. A detailed subject index is included at the beginning of the atlas, with an index of 41,000 place names at the end. —Sally Wynkoop. [R: ALA 70; ARBA 71, item 581]

237. **World Atlas**. Hallmark Edition. Maplewood, N.J., Hammond, 1971. 2v. graphs. maps. index. $39.95. LC 79-654260.

This two-volume set is one of the most comprehensive Hammond atlases, with luxurious padded binding and a slip-case. The first volume contains a 16-page gazetteer-index of the world, 192 pages of foreign maps, and 128 pages of state maps. The maps are arranged by geographical regions, e.g., Europe, Asia, Pacific Ocean and Australia, Africa, North America, Canada, and United States. Volume two contains a 160-page index with some 100,000 entries incorporating United States zip codes as well as map coordinates; 32 pages of Biblical maps; 48 pages of historical maps; 64 pages of American history maps; and the 32-page environment and life ecology section.

This edition incorporates over 5,000 changes that occurred throughout the world since the last major revision, including updating of political boundaries. This is an authoritative atlas that observes high professional standards.   [R: ARBA 72, item 492]

CHAPTER 10

EDUCATION

BIBLIOGRAPHIES

238. Altbach, Philip G., and David H. Kelly. **American Students: A Selected Bibliography on Student Activism and Related Topics.** Lexington, Mass., Lexington Books/D. C. Heath, 1973. 537p. $25.00. LC 73-7992. ISBN 0-669-85100-0.

This comprehensive bibliography is a revised version of a publication first issued in 1968 under the title *Student Politics and Higher Education in the United States*. Added to this edition is all new material published since 1968 to which a reference could be found, and the scope of coverage has been greatly expanded.

The more than 9,000 entries are arranged in three chapters, the first, and largest, of which is devoted to the subject of student activism in American education. The two other chapters in the bibliography proper list, on a less comprehensive scale, relevant material on minority students in American higher education and on American student characteristics and student life. A short fourth chapter lists published bibliographies on subjects falling within the scope of this work. Each chapter is subdivided into a number of categories, such as general material, theoretical material, historical variables, and sociological aspects, as well as a host of pertinent topics relating to the larger subject. Each category is divided into two sections: books and doctoral dissertations, arranged alphabetically by author; and periodical articles, also alphabetized by author. The format is attractive, the print is clear and readable, and the binding is more than adequate for library use. —Shirley L. Hopkinson. [R: ARBA 74, item 549]

239. Buros, Oscar Krisen, ed. **English Tests and Reviews: A Monograph Consisting of the English Sections of the Seven Mental Measurements Yearbooks (1938-72) and Tests in Print II (1974).** Highland Park, N.J., Gryphon Press, 1975. 395p. index. (An MMY Monograph). $25.00. LC 75-8109. ISBN 0-910674-15-9.

240. Buros, Oscar Krisen, ed. **Foreign Language Tests and Reviews: A Monograph Consisting of the Foreign Language Sections of the Seven Mental Measurements Yearbooks (1938-72) and Tests in Print II (1974).** Highland Park, N.J., Gryphon Press, 1975. 312p. index. (An MMY Monograph). $23.00. LC 75-8110. ISBN 0-910674-16-7.

241. Buros, Oscar Krisen, ed. **Intelligence Tests and Reviews: Monograph Consisting of the Intelligence Sections of the Seven Mental Measurements Yearbooks (1938-72) and Tests in Print II (1974).** Highland Park, N.J., Gryphon Press, 1975. 1129p. index. (An MMY Monograph). $55.00. LC 75-8112. ISBN 0-910674-17-5.

242. Buros, Oscar Krisen, ed. **Mathematics Tests and Reviews: A Monograph Consisting of the Mathematics Sections of the Seven Mental Measurements Yearbooks (1938-72) and Tests in Print II (1974)**. Highland Park, N.J., Gryphon Press, 1975. 435p. index. (An MMY Monograph). $25.00. LC 75-8113. ISBN 0-910674-18-3.

243. Buros, Oscar Krisen, ed. **Personality Tests and Reviews II: A Monograph Consisting of the Personality Sections of the Seventh Mental Measurements Yearbook (1972) and Tests in Print II (1974)**. Highland Park, N.J., Gryphon Press, 1975. 841p. index. (An MMY Monograph). $45.00. LC 74-13192. ISBN 0-910674-19-1.

244. Buros, Oscar Krisen, ed. **Reading Tests and Reviews II: A Monograph Consisting of the Reading Sections of the Seventh Mental Measurements Yearbook (1972) and Tests in Print II (1974)**. Highland Park, N.J., Gryphon Press, 1975. 257p. index. (An MMY Monograph). $20.00. LC 70-13495. ISBN 0-910674-20-5.

245. Buros, Oscar Krisen, ed. **Science Tests and Reviews: A Monograph Consisting of the Science Sections of the Seven Mental Measurements Yearbooks (1938-72) and Tests in Print II (1974)**. Highland Park, N.J., Gryphon Press, 1975. 296p. index. (An MMY Monograph). $22.00. LC 75-8114. ISBN 0-910674-21-3.

246. Buros, Oscar Krisen, ed. **Social Studies Tests and Reviews: A Monograph Consisting of the Social Studies Sections of the Seven Mental Measurements Yearbooks (1938-72) and Tests in Print II (1974)**. Highland Park, N.J., Gryphon Press, 1975. 227p. index. (An MMY Monograph). $20.00. LC 75-8115. ISBN 0-910674-22-1.

247. Buros, Oscar Krisen, ed. **Vocational Tests and Reviews: A Monograph Consisting of the Vocational Sections of the Seven Mental Measurements Yearbook (1938-72) and Tests in Print II (1974)**. Highland Park, N.J., Gryphon Press, 1975. 1087p. index. (An MMY Monograph). $55.00. LC 75-8116. ISBN 0-910674-23-X.

Oscar K. Buros has been producing outstanding reference tools for test users in education, industry, and psychology for over 40 years. His major contribution, *The Mental Measurements Yearbook* (MMY), has been published since 1938.

In 1975, Buros's Gryphon Press issued nine monographs, each dealing with published examinations in one of the following fields: 1) English language and literature; 2) foreign languages; 3) intelligence; 4) mathematics; 5) personality; 6) reading; 7) science; 8) social studies; and 9) vocational counseling. These books consist essentially of reprints, as their subtitles indicate. In addition to extensive test information from *Tests in Print II* (TIP II) and scholarly reviews of examinations from volumes of MMY, each of the monographs contains the following: 1) a list of reviewers; 2) a brief preface; 3) an introduction describing in detail the scope of the book and how it may be used; 4) a classified subject index, reprinted from TIP II, referring to examinations in various fields, including those not covered by the book; 5) a directory of test publishers and a publisher index; 6) a title index; 7) a name index; and 8) a classified subject index limited to material in the book.

These volumes are international in scope, treating examinations available in English-speaking countries throughout the world. All citations in the indexes and cross references are to numbered test entries, not to pages. Running heads and feet are provided in the test and review sections to assist the reader in locating desired material.

Two of the nine books, those in the areas of personality and reading, supplement monographs issued in 1970 and 1968, respectively, and contain material from only the latest edition of MMY. Therefore, they have to be used with the previously published monographs. Buros's other 1975 publications, however, include reprints from all seven issues of MMY and may, consequently, be used independently of his earlier works. It should be noted, however, that none of the pertinent book reviews in MMY have been reprinted in these volumes.

These monographs have been prepared especially for those examiners in specialized fields who lack access to MMY and TIP II. Although they provide not a bit of additional information, the spin-offs are convenient to use, authoritative, and relatively inexpensive (at $20.00 to $55.00 per copy). Purchased individually, the books from which each of these monographs (except for those dealing with personality and reading tests) is derived would cost the reader $312.50. Buros plans to have the material in his 1975 publications supplemented and updated by *The Eighth Mental Measurements Yearbook*, scheduled for 1977, and *Tests in Print III*, to be issued in 1978.   —Leonard Grundt. [R: LJ, 1 Nov 75, p. 2058; Choice, May 75, p. 367; Choice, Dec 75, pp. 1286-88; ARBA 76, items 562-570]

248. Buros, Oscar Krisen. **The Seventh Mental Measurements Yearbook**. Highland Park, N.J., Gryphon Press, 1972 2v. index. $55.00. LC 39-3422. ISBN 0-910674-11-6.

The *Mental Measurements Yearbooks* must be considered among the essential reference works for psychology and for allied areas such as education. Finally attaining the status of a two-volume set of 1,986 oversize pages, this edition treats some 1,157 tests covering a wide variety of skill and ability topics in addition to the domains of personality, vocations, attitudes, and interests. There are 798 new reviews of 546 tests, plus over 19,000 references on all aspects of specific tests and psychometrics—some 144.6 percent more than in the previous edition of the yearbook. To illustrate the editor's thoroughness, information on the noted Rorschach Ink-Blot test may be found in some 27 pages of reference and review material. Four hundred and fifty-four new citations are added to the 3,749 presented in previous editions. Five reviewers present 17 double-columned pages of research, evaluation, and critique. The 12-page list of reviewers reads almost like a professional hall of fame.

Though most users of the yearbooks consult them for test information, note should be made of the extensive treatment of pertinent books on test and measurement topics. Some 664 books published between 1964 and 1970 are reviewed in a 313-page section. An extremely detailed five-page directory and index of periodicals then follows. This is only the first of six indexes, which take up some 144 pages.

All users of these volumes should be thankful that Dr. Buros put aside his "serious consideration to discontinuing the MMY series." No one can estimate the significance of his efforts since the first yearbook was published in 1938. —Bernard Spilka. [R: ARBA 73, item 1533]

249. Buros, Oscar Krisen, ed. **Tests in Print II: An Index to Tests, Test Reviews, and the Literature on Specific Tests.** Highland Park, N.J., Gryphon Press, 1974. 1107p. index. $70.00 ISBN 0-910674-14-0.

The first edition of *Tests in Print* (TIP) was published in 1961. This present edition contains: 1) a comprehensive bibliography of all tests in print as of early 1974 that were published for use with English-speaking subjects, together with over 16,000 references to articles and reviews on the construction, use and validity of specific tests; 2) a directory of 493 test publishers with complete listings of their tests; 3) a title index listing both in-print and out-of-print tests; 4) a cumulative author index to approximatey 70,000 items (tests, reviews, etc.) in TIP II, to the seven issues of *Mental Measurements Yearbook*, to *Personality Tests and Reviews*, and to *Reading Tests and Reviews*; 5) a reprinting of *Standards for Educational and Psychological Tests*; and 6) a "scanning" index for quickly locating tests designed for a particular population. A valuable complement to the *Mental Measurements Yearbook*. [R: ARBA 75, item 1601]

250. Forrester, Gertrude. **Occupational Literature: An Annotated Bibliography.** 1971 ed. New York, H. W. Wilson, 1971. 619p. $15.00. LC 79-149382. ISBN 0-8242-0437-9.

This well-known bibliography, first published in 1946, has been frequently revised and expanded. The 1971 edition lists 4,500 pamphlets and 1,500 books arranged alphabetically under about 500 occupational titles, with brief annotations. A separate section lists 55 series produced by 32 publishers. Other sections list bibliographies and indexes on careers; information about schools and vocational training institutions; charts, posters, and graphic aids; job seeking; counseling services; occupations for the handicapped; textbooks; the counselor's professional bookshelf, and other topics. A directory of publishers and distributors and a brief index of subjects, series titles, and publishers of career series books is appended. Most of the publications are for the use of students in secondary school and early college years. First purchase publications are starred. Criteria used in selecting the literature and in choosing specially recommended titles are described in the introduction. —Christine L. Wynar. [R: ARBA 72, item 574]

251. Gabriel, Astrik L. **Summary Bibliography of the History of the Universities of Great Britain and Ireland up to 1800: Covering Publications between 1900 and 1968.** Notre Dame, Ind., Mediaeval Institute, University of Notre Dame, 1974. 154p. index. (Texts and Studies in the History of Mediaeval Education, No. 14). $18.95. LC 73-79105.

Prepared for the XIIIth International Congress of Historical Sciences, held in Moscow in 1970, this work is one of several that were designed to form a worldwide *Bibliography on the History of Universities.* Professor Gabriel, a faculty member of Notre Dame University, has compiled a selected list of 1,514 books, pamphlets, and periodical articles published between 1900 and 1968, relating to the history of British and Irish universities and colleges up to 1800.

Two preliminary sections list 294 items of general background information on the history of education in Europe and in England up to 1800. The remaining four sections contain entries on English, Scottish, Welsh, and Irish universities and colleges with separate subsections for Cambridge, Oxford, Aberdeen, Edinburgh,

Glasgow, St. Andrews, Maynooth, Trinity College Dublin, and for English, Scottish, and Irish colleges and students on the continent. Entries are arranged alphabetically by author or other main entry within each subsection in order to permit rapid location of an author's publication on a given university or college. All entries are numbered consecutively, however. Author and subject indexes and a list of serials referred to in the bibliography are provided. Entries for books and pamphlets give author, title, place, publisher, date, and number of pages. Those for articles give author, title, periodical name, volume number, date, and inclusive pages.

Although it was planned to be a selective rather than an exhaustive bibliography, the coverage is very thorough, and the work will be a valuable guide to writings and to source materials on the subject. It will supplement and update the bibliography in Rashdall's *The Universities of Europe in the Middle Ages* (Oxford, 1936). —Shirley L. Hopkinson. [R: ARBA 75, item 645]

252. Parker, Franklin, ed. **American Dissertations on Foreign Education: A Bibliography with Abstracts. Volume 1: Canada.** Troy, N.Y., Whitston, 1971. 175p. index. $9.50. LC 73-155724. ISBN 0-87875-013-4.

This publication is a bibliography of 171 dissertations that were accepted by American and Canadian universities from 1907 to the present time and that cover some aspect of education in Canada. It is the first volume of a proposed series which will list dissertations on education in various countries. Of the 171 entries in this volume, 46 include abstracts of varying lengths. Thirty-six of them are taken from *Dissertation Abstracts*, six from Stanford University's *Abstracts of Dissertations*, and one each from the abstracts published by the University of Wisconsin, Ohio State, Pennsylvania State, and Northwestern. Eighteen additional entries include a source reference to *Dissertation Abstracts Index*, but no abstract. The entries with abstracts identify the type of doctorate (Ed.D. or Ph.D.). The others give only the author's name, the title of the dissertation, the name of the university, and the date. The addition to all entries of the degree designation and the source where the citation was located would strengthen the future revisions of the work.

The arrangement is alphabetical by the authors' surnames, and there is a subject index of 124 entries. An article on the Canadian system of education, prepared by William H. Lucow of the Dominion Bureau of Statistics, is included as an appendix. The work serves a useful purpose in bringing together a list of all dissertations on the subject and in reprinting in one volume all of the published abstracts. Additional publications in the series include: Vol. 2, India; Vol. 3, Japan; Vol. 4, Africa; Vol. 5, Scandinavia; Vol. 6, China; Vol. 7, Korea. —Shirley L. Hopkinson. [R: ARBA 72, item 579]

253. U.S. Office of Education. **Bibliography of Research Studies in Education, 1926-1940.** Detroit, Gale, 1974. 4v. index. $165.00. LC 74-1124. ISBN 0-8103-0975-0.

The *Bibliography of Research Studies in Education* was a serial publication issued by the United States Office of Education in its Bulletin series from 1928 to 1941, covering the school years from 1926 to 1940. The 14 annual issues have been reprinted by Gale and bound together in four large hardcover volumes. In all, the set includes 47,866 entries, many of them annotated, covering a wide range of subjects.

Each issue contains from three to four thousand entries, arranged in a classified listing that includes such subjects as educational history, biography, educational
psychology and sociology, tests and measurements, educational theory and practice,
international aspects of education, methods of instruction, special curricular areas
and subjects, teacher training, salaries and professional status of teachers, education
on the several levels, buildings and equipment, vocational education, education of
special groups, educational extension, and libraries and reading. Within each category, entries are arranged alphabetically by author. Each entry gives author, title,
imprint information, date, and number of pages. Unpublished materials are indicated by the abbreviation "ms." Materials available on loan from the Office of
Education library are identified by an asterisk. Some of the annotations were prepared by staff members at the library, others by the person who submitted the
report.

This is a very comprehensive bibliography on educational research, without
parallel for the years covered. The scope is so broad that it will provide references
for scholars in many fields related to education. The coverage of materials on
libraries and reading will be of special interest to librarians. —Shirley L. Hopkinson.
[R: ARBA 75, item 650]

ENCYCLOPEDIAS

254. **The Encyclopedia of Education.** Lee C. Deighton, editor-in-chief. New York,
Macmillan and Free Press, 1971. 10v. bibliog. index. $199.00. LC 70-133143.

This comprehensive work summarizes the achievements in education not only
in this country but also, to some extent, internationally.

The Encyclopedia of Education is well edited and well balanced in the treatment of most subject areas. The preface clearly states the scope of this major undertaking, indicating that "in more than 1,000 articles, it offers a view of the institutions and people, of the processes and products, found in educational practice. The
articles deal with history, theory, research, and philosophy, as well as with the
structure and fabric of education." The most important topics are treated in depth.
As an example, the 45-page article on child development is subdivided into nine
different aspects, starting with overview, effects of infant care, infant-mother
attachment, maternal deprivation, etc. Under "Maternal deprivation" such problems as institutionalization, sensory stimulation, long-term effects of deprivation,
intervention studies, and disadvantaged environments are discussed. Most longer
articles contain bibliographies; thus, the article on child development contains nine
bibliographies, one after each subheading, totaling 264 references for further reading.

The encyclopedia contains many good articles in the area of comparative education; most major countries and their educational systems are represented. There
are several articles pertaining to library education. The one on certification requirements (by Florrinell F. Morton) provides essential information on this subject pertaining primarily to the United States, Great Britain, and Canada, with nothing on
other foreign countries. The article on "Librarians, Education of" (Lawrence A.
Allen) is a good example of a properly presented and well-balanced synthesis.
Unfortunately, this is not the case with all articles. For example, there is a major
article on librarianship consisting of five parts: overview, library administration,

library catalogs, automation in libraries, and library organization. The introduction-overview, written by Caroline Arden Bull, presents a rather simplistic approach with a totally embarrassing discussion on the difference "between the information scientist and the librarian" (see vol. 5, pp. 530-31); her comments on library careers and manpower demands are at best misleading. Other sections in this article are much better, although the section on "Library Catalogs" (by Maurice Tauber) is rather sketchy, with practically nothing on numerous user studies and, frankly, nothing on more recent literature on this subject.

In general this is a well-prepared and authoritative encyclopedia covering a wide range of pertinent topics. In comparison to Monroe's work, it excludes biographical sketches of leading educators, an understandable editorial policy in view of the fact that we now have a number of good sources for biographical information. Excluded also are articles on individual universities, again an understandable fact; this information can be found with ease elsewhere. Most articles have good bibliographies, and the last volume contains a directory of contributors as well as an excellent index with all necessary cross references. —Bohdan S. Wynar. [R: WLB, Dec 71, p. 364; ALA 71; ARBA 72, item 586]

255. **Encyclopedia of Educational Evaluation: Concepts and Techniques for Evaluating Education and Training Programs.** By Scarvia B. Anderson and others. San Francisco, Jossey-Bass, 1975. bibliog. index. $17.50. LC 74-6736. ISBN 0-87589-238-8.

This book was designed to be of use to two types of readers: those who wish a quick reference on a specific topic, and students and program directors who seek a short course on a particular area within the whole subject of program evaluation. The arrangement of articles alphabetically from *accountability* to *variance* provides for the former. The "classification of articles" guide gives an overview of 11 major concept areas by listing under each heading titles of pertinent entries. Headings include program objectives and standards, social context of evaluation, systems techniques, measurement approaches and types, variables, etc. Detailed name and subject indexes provide additional points of access to the information within the entries. The articles, which were written by authorities in the field, are signed by initials which can be identified in the list of contributors. Most articles are three or four pages in length, but some are considerably longer. Each is accompanied by a short, partially annotated bibliography of carefully selected sources and by cross references to other articles. The book also contains a 26-page general bibliography of publications on educational evaluation. Because of the wide range of topics included, this encyclopedia should be of interest to testing officers and teachers of research methods as well as to those immediately involved in program evaluation. —Shirley L. Hopkinson. [R: Choice, June 75, p. 509; ARBA 76, item 591]

256. **Encyclopedia of Educational Research.** 4th ed. New York, Macmillan, 1969. 1522p. $38.95. LC 75-4932.

This new edition of a standard reference work is essentially a new work, rather than a revision of the third edition. The subject content has been designated and the structure designed with the advice of a distinguished Board of Editors appointed by the American Educational Research Association. As in previous editions, contributions are signed and are written by specialists in their respective fields. Many of these contributors are new in this edition, but even repeat articles have been completely rewritten. The lists of selected references for each topic, which formed so valuable a feature of the third edition, have been continued, although the substitution of APA-style name-date citations for the old numbered system of Walter S. Monroe has reduced ease of use for rapid reference work. The latest items cited appear to be 1966, indicating that the time lag is again about three years, and the *Review of Educational Research* must be used for later material.

As with the previous edition, a subject index on yellow stock is inserted in the middle of the book, but it is now a concept rather than a specific entry index, which somewhat reduces its usefulness for reference work. The format includes a content outline with lists of articles in each area, a list of contributors with their articles in each area, an alphabetical list of articles, and a list of abbreviations used. —John Morgan. [R: LJ, 15 April 70, p. 1438; ALA 69; ARBA 71, item 707]

257. Monroe, Paul. **A Cyclopedia of Education**. With a new introductory essay by William W. Brickman. Detroit, Gale, 1968. 5v. illus. $165.00. LC 68-56361.

This work was originally published by Macmillan from 1911 to 1913. It seems likely that while other works will (and must) supplement it, this uniquely comprehensive work will never be totally replaced. The early 1900s was a time of great change in education, and many of the contributors were men who gave direction to that change. The cyclopedia was important in that it stabilized terminology and established a base for further educational development. A book of ideas and not merely of facts, it is strong on theory and the exploration of relationships. Browsing through the volumes, one notes foreshadowings or precursors of such current movements as the library-college, or the university-without-walls.

With comprehensiveness as a goal, the cyclopedia covered philosophy of education, history of education, educational biography, institutions, elementary and secondary education, curriculum, administration, home and foreign school systems, methodology, educational psychology, hygiene, and school architecture. Every subject taught in school was considered in detail. Topics are connected by cross references (a number of which are of the "wild goose chase" variety), and many of the articles are furnished with bibliographies. Although it is arranged alphabetically, the analytical index (end of v. 5) allows the encyclopedia to be used as an exhaustive treatise on a particular aspect of education.

To produce the work, a qualified (and sometimes distinguished) editor was responsible for each of the 15 major areas. John Dewey, for example, was the general editor of the philosophy of education material; he himself wrote 115 articles, some of which are over 6,000 words in length. Altogether more than 1,000 scholars are numbered among the contributors. Monroe, the director, was a member of the Columbia University faculty for 41 years (1898-1938); he was a noted scholar, published numerous writings on the history of education, held many offices, and was most influential in the roster of students whom he trained.

For this reprint, Brickman contributes a new introduction, which gives both a general description of this work and also a bibliographic survey of other educational encyclopedias. The quality of the reprint is good; the binding is not especially sturdy, and there are no guide-letters on the spines of the five volumes. —Joseph W. Sprug. [R: ARBA 71, item 700]

DICTIONARIES

258. Good, Carter V., ed. **Dictionary of Education**. 3rd ed. Prep. under the auspices of Phi Delta Kappa. New York, McGraw-Hill, 1973. 681p. $20.00. LC 73-4784. ISBN 0-07-023720-4.

The first edition of this work was published in 1945, the second in 1959. According to the preface, the dictionary is "concerned with technical and professional terms and concepts in the entire area of education. As a general policy, it has excluded names of persons, institutions, school systems, organizations, places, and titles of publications and journals, except where a movement, method, or plan is represented" (p. ix). Since the present edition adds some 8,000 entries (to make a total of around 33,000), it represents a substantial updating of this well-known dictionary. It should be noted that this edition no longer contains listings of foreign terms (probably because of space limitations; the typeface is very small indeed). —Bohdan S. Wynar. [R: WLB, Sept 73, p. 83; Choice, Oct 73, p. 1162; ARBA 74, item 565]

DIRECTORIES

INTERNATIONAL

259. **Research Centers Directory**. 5th ed. Archie M. Palmer, ed. Detroit, Gale, 1975. 1039p. index. $68.00. LC 60-14807.

The subtitle of this volume accurately describes its first 14 chapters: A Guide to University-Related and Other Nonprofit Research Organizations Established on a Permanent Basis and Carrying on Continuing Research Programs in Agriculture, Business, Conservation, Education, Engineering and Technology, Government, Law, Life Sciences, Mathematics, Area Studies, Physical and Earth Sciences, Social Sciences, and Humanities. The three remaining chapters of the book cover Multi-Disciplinary Programs, Research Coordinating Offices, and addenda not incorporated into previous chapters.

Entries are arranged alphabetically by parent institution, then by name of research center. Independent research organizations are arranged by name, interpolated within the same alphabet. Information provided for each research center is the same—name, address, director's name, phone number, year founded, sources of support, size and type of staff, principal fields of research, research facilities, publications, and library facilities. Obviously, the amount of information provided varies somewhat, depending on the response from a particular institution. An institutional index, an alphabetic index of research centers, and a subject index conclude the directory.

Supplements to *Research Centers Directory* are published periodically. [R: ARBA 76, item 629]

260. Rowland, Howard S., and Beatrice L. Rowland. **The New York Times Guide to Student Adventures and Studies Abroad, 1974.** New York, Quadrangle/The New York Times Book Co., 1974. 550p. illus. index. $4.95pa. LC 72-90454. ISBN 0-8129-0331-5.

Guides to study abroad are abundant, though they are not always kept up to date. This work, however, attempts to guide students to adventurous opportunities abroad as well as to study programs. It begins with a "how to" section containing tips on selecting a program, costs, what to pack, etc. The second section lists opportunities by interest groups: sports, the arts, the sciences, trips, adventuring, exchange programs, working, and learning a language. Finally, a geographical section describes programs and accommodations by country.

Though format varies somewhat, much of the same information is available in the *Whole World Handbook* (Council on International Educational Exchange). Students planning a summer abroad would be wise to consult both of these guides since they provide complementary information. —Sara Lou Williams. [R: Choice, Sept 74, p. 916; ALA 74; ARBA 75, item 664]

UNITED STATES

261. **American Junior Colleges.** 8th ed. Edmund J. Gleazer, Jr., and Jane Follett Cooke, eds. Washington, American Council on Education, 1971. 850p. $18.00. LC 40-33685. ISBN 0-8268-1209-0.

Over 800 junior colleges in the United States recognized by the regional accrediting agencies are described at length in the latest edition of this standard reference work. In addition to the complete descriptions of individual institutions that have characterized earlier editions of this volume, the eighth edition has a number of new features.

For the first time, the book is divided into sections, one listing public institutions, the other, private. Each part is introduced by an essay written especially for the volume. In addition, state systems of junior colleges are also described. These descriptions contain information about governance, financing, extent, and plans of the junior college system. Other new features include each institution's faculty (shown by departments or divisions; rank is noted where applicable).

Published for the first time is a new listing of over 14,000 career programs in hundreds of occupational fields based on an extensive national survey. Also included are lists of special training facilities available to students at the institutions. Most college exhibits contain a statement from the college concerning its most attractive or outstanding program offerings. The fields in which work experience is available are named.

A separate appendix lists two-year programs offered at four-year institutions, with the name of the degree or other award resulting from that program. Other appendixes list housing facilities and religious affiliation of institutions. [R: ARBA 73, item 604]

262. **The College Blue Book.** 14th ed. Vol. 1, **U.S. Colleges: Narrative Descrip-tions.** Vol. 2, **U.S. Colleges: Tabular Data.** Vol. 3, **Degrees Offered by Colleges and Subjects.** Supplemental vol., **Occupational Education.** New York, CCM, 1972. 4v. $84.95 set; $59.85, v. 1, 2, and 3; $29.95/v. LC 24-223. ISBN 0-8409-0301-4(v.1); 0-8409-0299-9(v.2); 0-8409-0300-6(v.3); 0-8409-0282-4(suppl.v.).

The thirteenth edition was published in 10 volumes, while the twelfth edition was in three volumes. The virtue of the thirteenth edition lay in its inclusiveness (since the mere existence of an institution was grounds for listing it) and in the multitude of approaches it offered (by institutions, degrees offered, professional schools, financial aid programs, etc.).

The structure of the present edition has again changed. The first volume (narrative description) offers information on some 3,600 colleges, indicating ad-dress, description, entrance requirements, admission procedure, costs, and collegiate and community environment. A map for each state locates each institution. Arrange-ment is by state and then by the name of institution. The second volume also lists colleges by state, then presents the information in tabular form. The third volume consists of two parts. In the first, under the name of each college (listed alphabeti-cally by state) appears the list of the subject areas for which degrees are offered. Part 2 includes an alphabetical listing of over 2,000 subject areas for which degrees are granted by one or more institution of higher learning. The supplemental volume lists institutions alphabetically by city under state headings. Brief information pro-vided includes name, type of school, contact, accreditation, entrance requirements, and curricula. No narratives are supplied. A large section (240 pages) lists schools by curricula and programs of instruction, while smaller sections list schools by broad area (e.g., medical and dental technology, nursing), give information on financial aid, and list sources of additional information.

The College Blue Book offers a great deal of statistical information—probably more than other directories of this type. There is only one serious drawback: the thirteenth edition was published in 1969, and the present one in 1972. Because statistical information becomes rapidly obsolete, many directories are now published annually, with the result that some of them are more up to date than this compre-hensive work. *The College Blue Book* enjoys a fine professional reputation. [Editor's note: Since the time this review was written, the fifteenth edition has appeared (Macmillan Information, 1975. 3v. $75.00 set).] —Bohdan S. Wynar. [R: ARBA 71, item 719; ARBA 72, item 624; ALA 72; ARBA 74, item 592]

263. Thomson, Frances Coombs, ed. **The New York Times Guide to Continuing Education in America.** Prep. by the College Entrance Examination Board. New York, Quadrangle Books; distr. New York, College Entrance Examination Board, 1973. 811p. index. $12.50; $4.95pa. LC 74-183190. ISBN 0-8129-0271-8; 0-8129-6207-9.

Comprehensive guide to adult courses, academic and vocational, offered at accredited educational institutions in our 50 states. This is the first nationwide directory of college-level institutions and study programs for mature students. It covers a total of 2,281 schools, which offer more than 50,000 courses for adults, including airline ticketing, genetics, oil-burner maintenance, forestry, printing, Swahili, oceanography, court reporting, gunsmithing, disk-jockeying, candlemaking and even bill-collecting. Arrangement is alphabetical by state, with correspondence schools listed separately.

Two particularly valuable sections are those devoted to information about the College Level Examination Program (CLEP) and a list of institutions that award credit on the basis of CLEP examination scores. Also included is a listing of national organizations active in continuing education and a glossary of terms used.

Extremely useful to librarians, educators, and students concerned with adult education. —Theodore Manheim. [R: ARBA 73, item 629]

INDEXES

264. **Comprehensive Dissertation Index, 1861-1972.** Ann Arbor, Mich., Xerox University Microfilms, 1973. 37v. $2495.00; $1995.00 microfiche; $100.00 individual vols. LC 73-89046.

This comprehensive inventory of doctoral dissertations, with a total of 417,000 entries, provides a nearly complete listing of the impressive output of graduate schools in the United States, plus some foreign universities. It is an expanded version of its predecessor, *Dissertation Abstracts International Retrospective Index*, published by University Microfilms in 1970. Other sources were consulted as well—namely, *American Doctoral Dissertations, Index to American Doctoral Dissertations, Dissertation Abstracts International, Dissertation Abstracts,* and *Microfilm Abstracts.* In addition to these Xerox University Microfilms sources, other reference tools were used, especially the Library of Congress's *List of American Doctoral Dissertations Printed in 1912-1932* and H. W. Wilson's *Doctoral Dissertations Accepted by American Universities 1933/34-1954/55.* The new work also contains listings of doctoral dissertations from some 70 universities not completely covered by any of the above-mentioned works.

The first 32 volumes of the set present subject coverage for 22 individual disciplines, and a five-volume author index concludes the set. Five volumes are devoted to education, four to chemistry, three to engineering, three to the biological sciences, two each to psychology, business and economics, language and literature, and astronomy and physics. The following subjects are covered in single volumes: mathematics and statistics, health and environmental sciences, agriculture, geography and geology, social sciences, law and political science, history, communications and the arts, and philosophy and religion. Each volume of the set starts with a 21-page introduction (identical in all volumes), including a complete table of contents, instructions for use, a list of schools covered, a bibliography of sources consulted, instructions for obtaining dissertation copies, etc. The subject index is a computer-produced keyword title index. Each dissertation is assigned to one specific subject area; within that area dissertations are listed by keyword (an average of six separate keyword entries for each, according to the publisher). Individual dissertations are listed under the keyword in their titles, first by date (beginning with the most recent), then alphabetically by school, and finally alphabetically by author. (For the supplement, we would suggest reprogramming the computer to arrange the listing first by school, followed by date, and then author.) Each keyword entry and each entry in the author section provides full information: title, author, degree, date, institution, number of pages, reference to the source from which the citation was obtained, and the order number for dissertations that can be acquired from Xerox University Microfilms.

The use of keyword instead of a traditional subject approach presents several problems. For example, 35 pages (three columns to a page) are devoted to the keyword "economic," 58 pages to "elementary," etc. Even the publishers will admit that the search will be somewhat time-consuming here. In addition, many dissertation titles avoid describing the actual subject matter in simple terms, offering instead a great deal of "sophistication," which quite frequently obscures the real topic under investigation.

In addition to the difficulty of finding a dissertation through one of its keywords, the user must be aware that initial assignment of a dissertation to a discipline is also open to question. As a matter of editorial policy, a given dissertation was placed in only one subject group. Once a dissertation has been placed in the wrong subject group, it is irretrievable except through the author. The introduction provided in each volume indicates that cross references at the beginning of subject sections should help the user locate dissertations on related subjects and disciplines. The cross references can be helpful, however, only if the dissertations have been placed in proper subject categories. As the reviewer in RQ pointed out, this is not always the case.

In spite of its deficiencies, *Comprehensive Dissertation Index* is a monumental undertaking. —Bohdan S. Wynar. [R: LJ, Aug 74, p. 1915; BL, 1 July 74, pp. 1164-65; RQ, Fall 74, pp. 61-62; Choice, July-Aug 74, p. 734; ARBA 75, item 688]

265. **Dissertation Abstracts International: Retrospective Index, Vols. 1-29. Author Index, Vol. 9.** Ann Arbor, Mich., University Microfilms, 1970. 1739p. $225.00. LC 39-21214. ISBN 0-8357-0042-9.

With the publication of this retrospective index, the user now has a single source to the major portion of this well-known abstracting service. The entire set consists of the following volumes: Vol. 1, Mathematics and Physics; Vol. 2, Chemistry; Vol. 3, Earth/Life Sciences; Vol. 4, Psychology, Sociology, Political Science; Vol. 5, Social Sciences; Vol. 6, Engineering; Vol. 7, Education; Vol. 8, Communication, Information, Business, Literature, Fine Arts; Vol. 9, Author Index. The arrangement is under keywords in alphabetical order in columns placed under subject categories. The last volume, an author index, provides UM number information; entries are arranged alphabetically by author of the dissertation plus a brief title. A list of cooperating institutions is also included. [R: ARBA 72, item 572]

BIOGRAPHY

266. **Directory of American Scholars.** 6th ed. Ed. by Jaques Cattell Press. New York, R. R. Bowker, 1974. 4v. index. $148.50 set; $39.50/v. LC 57-9125. ISBN 0-8352-0635-1(v.1); 0-8352-0648-3(v.2); 0-8352-0649-1(v.3); 0-8352-0675-0(v.4); ISBN 0-8352-0804-4(set). ISSN 0070-5101.

These four volumes list approximately 38,000 scholars in the following disciplines: volume 1, history; volume 2, English, speech, and drama volume 3, foreign languages, linguistics, and philology; volume 4, philosophy, religion, and law. Alphabetically arranged entries provide such information as name, birthplace and date, citizenship, discipline, education, past and present professional experience, honors, awards, current membership in professional societies, chief fields of research interest, major publications, and mailing address. There are cross references for scholars with major involvement in several fields.

Two indexes are included to facilitate research and increase usefulness. A geographical index, listing the biographees and their disciplines by state or province and city, is in each volume. The alphabetically arranged biographee index to all four volumes of this edition is included in volume 4.

Criteria for inclusion are (p. ix): 1) "achievement . . . of a stature in scholarly work equivalent to that associated with the doctorate degree, coupled with presently continued activity in such work;" or 2) "achievement as evidenced by publication of scholarly works;" or 3) "attainment of a position of substantial responsibility by reason of achievement" as outlined in numbers 1 and 3. [R: ARBA 75, item 690]

267. **Leaders in Education 1974.** 5th ed. Ed. by Jaques Cattell Press. New York, R. R. Bowker, 1974. 1309p. index. $49.50. LC 32-10194. ISBN 0-8352-0699-8. ISSN 0075-8299.

Leaders in Education serves as a companion volume to the *Directory of American Scholars* (38,000 entries), providing 17,000 biographical sketches of the "who's who" type. This fifth edition includes some 2,000 more entries than the fourth edition, published in 1971. The preface outlines the criteria for inclusion—e.g., professional achievement, research activities, and professional positions held. Most presidents and deans of universities are listed, as well as state and provincial commissioners of education, superintendents of public school systems, key officials in the Office of Education, authors of important books in education, etc.

Our critical comments pertaining to the previous edition (see ARBA 72, item 657) are still valid. *Who's Who in America* and *Directory of American Scho'* s list a number of educators not found in this directory. Our sampling showed that *Leaders in Education* de-emphasizes publications and research activities, providing more details on positions held, memberships, and the credentials stemming from the individual's association with a given institution. A helpful feature in this edition is a new specialty index, which provides listings of 113 different categories—e.g., health administration, higher education, instructional materials (only 17 individuals listed), language arts, etc. Compared to *Outstanding Educators of America* and similar purely commercial and rather unreliable directories, *Leaders in Education* is a carefully edited work. This new edition merits the same high reputation as its predecessors. —Bohdan S. Wynar. [R: ARBA 72, item 657; ARBA 75, item 692]

INSTRUCTIONAL MATERIALS

268. Belch, Jean, comp. **Contemporary Games: A Directory and Bibliography Covering Games and Play Situations or Simulations Used for Instruction and Training by Schools, Colleges and Universities, Government, Business and Management.** Detroit, Gale, 1973-74. 2v. index. $48.00(v.1); $45.00(v.2). LC 72-6353. ISBN 0-8103-0968-8(v.1); 0-8103-0969-6(v.2).

Volume 1, the directory, lists over 900 "decision-making or problem-solving exercises" that the author finds suitable for educational purposes in schools, colleges and universities, government, or business. Excluded are traditional games like chess, checkers (Monopoly is included), card games, games primarily of chance or skill, and athletic sports. Only a few war games and a representative sampling of business and management games are included, but readers are referred to other sources for more comprehensive reviews.

Games are listed alphabetically, and the following information is given for each: subject, age or grade, playing time, mode (manual or computer), date originated, designer, producer, source, price, bibliographic citations for articles or books that describe or evaluate the game, and a brief description. Also included are a subject index, age and grade level index, and a designers' and producers' index with addresses. All are adequately cross-indexed.

Volume 2, the bibliography, lists 2,375 citations to books, articles, scholarly papers, proceedings, directories, and bibliographies relating to games and simulations used in education, government, and business. Classic writings are included, but most of the items were published between 1957 and 1973. Both published and unpublished materials are included. Secondary references lead to sources where items have been reprinted in collections or in other books on the subject. Many of the entries contain annotations that the compiler prepared after personal examination of the materials.

Entries are grouped in five general categories: general information, games in the classroom, business games and management simulations, conflict resolutions, and land use and resource allocation. A sixth section lists reports on research employing or evaluating games and simulations, and a seventh contains entries for directories, bibliographies, and lists on the subject. Classroom games are further classified by subject areas. Within each section or subsection, entries are arranged alphabetically by author. Each entry has been assigned a consecutive item number that is used as a locator device in the indexes. Author, institution, game, and supplementary subject indexes are provided. —Charles Farley and Shirley L. Hopkinson. [R: WLB, Nov 73, p. 263; BL, 1 Dec 73, p. 351; ARBA 74, item 682; ARBA 75, item 697]

269. Hendershot, Carl H. **Programmed Learning and Individually Paced Instruction—Bibliography.** 5th ed. 4114 Ridgewood Dr., Bay City, Mich., the Author, 1973. 1v.(various paging). $30.00 looseleaf; $42.00 with 2 supplements; $54.00 with 4 supplements. LC 73-77783. ISBN 0-911832-05-X.

Carl H. Hendershot is the pioneer in bibliographic control of programmed learning materials. His looseleaf bibliography is the only comprehensive tool in this field. It lists some 3,500 units of instructional materials in programmed or self-pacing format for schools, colleges, business, industry, and adult instruction. The main section lists units under 167 alphabetically arranged subjects (accounting, Braille, chess, dentistry, English, map reading, etc.). Each entry gives the title, authors, publisher's code, approximate length in hours, number of pages or frames, level, price, and other information such as prerequisites, content, date published, and availability of teacher's manual.

The publishers' section is an alphabetical listing of all publishers represented in the bibliography, with their titles. Systems of instruction are listed by publisher in a separate section. These are materials that 1) cover a number of subjects, 2) consist of an extensive instructional package, or 3) are comprehensive in nature.

Machines and devices used in presenting individually paced instruction are listed and described under names of the producers.

A classified bibliography at the end describes books, AV materials, periodicals, miscellaneous equipment and supplies, and associations. An extensive table of contents in the front and tabulated section dividers facilitate use. According to the publisher, the basic volume is to be updated by four supplements, which are to be issued at eight-month intervals. —Christine L. Wynar. [R: WLB, May 74, p. 765; ARBA 75, item 702]

270. Schrank, Jeffrey. **The Seed Catalog: A Guide to Teaching/Learning Materials.** Boston, Beacon Press, 1974. illus. index. $12.95. LC 73-16888. ISBN 0-8070-3164-X.

This huge compendium of references to innovative learning materials on contemporary topics, many of them free or inexpensive, is presented in catalog format, replete with facsimile illustrations from items cited and black and white sketches designed to bring out the "idea seed catalog" motif. Emphasis is placed on nonstandard materials for high school and adult learners, mainly from the fields of the humanities and the communication arts.

The materials cover a wide spectrum of subjects such as crime, human rights, nonviolent action, race prejudice, poverty, aging, the future, technology, ecology, population control, and lifestyles. The listings are grouped under nine categories: publications, organizations, periodicals, audio, film, video, games, multi-media, and devices. The first section, publications, describes books, pamphlets, study packets, and comics. Under organizations are listed the best sources of free or inexpensive help in a number of problem areas such as drug abuse, discrimination, abortion, women's and youth liberation, etc. The section on periodicals presents a number of little-known and unusual magazines and journals. The remaining sections review some 4,000 tapes and cassettes by people such as Asimov, Fuller, McLuhan, Steinem, and Vonnegut, nearly 200 short films, multi-media packages, learning games and simulations, posters, emotionometers, etc. Within each section, entries are arranged in random order, but a fairly detailed index leads to specific titles and subjects. —Shirley L. Hopkinson. [R: LJ, 15 June 74, p. 1692; ARBA 75, item 706]

CHAPTER 11

RECREATION AND SPORTS

GENERAL WORKS

271. Hickok, Ralph. **Who Was Who in American Sports**. New York, Hawthorn Books, 1971. 338p. $9.95. LC 72-158009.

This reliable, fairly detailed volume contains biographical sketches of approximately 1,500 of America's most important and colorful sports figures. As one might expect, athletes from the popular spectator sports dominate the entries. Baseball and football personalities comprise 58 percent of the entries; the former is represented by 635 persons and the latter by 248. Among the 42 sports covered, several are represented by only one or two persons. With few exceptions, all deceased members of the major sports' halls of fame are listed. Some devotees of archery, field hockey, softball, polo, and several other minor sports may question the absence of figures from their specialities.

In addition to athletes and coaches, some well-known broadcasters, managers, sportswriters, officials, and rule-makers are included. The entries give birth and death dates, place of birth, career highlights, records established, life-time averages when appropriate, and the name of the hall of fame to which the athlete was elected. The year in which this honor was bestowed is not listed. References to sources containing additional biographical information on the individuals would have been useful. Index of personalities by sports is included. —Robert van Benthuysen. [R: LJ, July 71, p. 2294; ARBA 72, item 669]

272. Menke, Frank G. **The Encyclopedia of Sports**. 5th rev. ed. London, Thomas Yoseloff; Cranbury, N.J., A. S. Barnes, 1975. 1125p. illus. index. $25.00. LC 73-10529. ISBN 0-498-01440-1.

The fourth edition, published in 1969, contained complete sports records through 1967. The fifth edition continues the records through 1972.

The format remains the same as in the four preceding editions. The major sports of the world are presented alphabetically, and the entry for each gives history, description, basic rules, and names and records of champions. Though the emphasis is on sports in the United States, many sports such as cricket, which is not important in this country, are described, with major attention necessarily being focused on foreign teams, champions, and records.

As have been noted before, this is not an inclusive work of reference for the sporting world. It omits a few sports that are fast becoming very popular. Among these are mountain climbing and sky diving, which seem to be at least as important as some of the minor sports included under the "miscellaneous" heading (such as skate sailing).

On the other hand, Menke's coverage of major U.S. sports remains timely and up to date. This is clear from an examination of the section on baseball, which records numerous post-1967 developments, such as league expansions, mergers, shifts, and new franchises. Despite its neglect of some sports, the current edition of Menke remains a reliably accurate record of all the major team sports played around the world. —Richard A. Gray. [R: ARBA 76, item 698]

273. Ormond, Clyde. **Outdoorsman's Handbook**. New York, Outdoor Life and Dutton, 1971. 336p. illus. index. $6.95; $1.95pa. LC 76-134237. ISBN 0-525-17330-7; 0-525-02893-3pa.

Clyde Ormond, recognized as an outdoor writer of the first order, has prepared this guide for the outdoorsman, be he hunter, fisherman, or hiker and camper. It could very well be included in any bibliography of survival books, because his "how-to" instructions are based on the assumption that the reader is unable or unwilling to buy everything needed at the moment the need arises. Indeed, a hiker who carried enough to meet every eventuality would not be a hiker but the leader of a caravan. Among the many things to be made as needed are: grass or leaf beds that are both dry and comfortable; emergency needles from tin cans; jacks and hoists; survival knives; buttons, emergency whistles, shelters, and foods. Copiously illustrated with line drawings to clarify instructions, this volume is a must for everyone who gets out into the woods for an outing. —Cecil F. Clotfelter. [R: ARBA 72, item 678]

274. **The Oxford Companion to World Sports and Games**. Ed. by John Arlott. New York, Oxford University Press, 1975. 143p. illus. $29.95. ISBN 0-19-211538-3.

In spite of the already voluminous reference literature on this subject, *The Oxford Companion to World Sports and Games* provides a well-balanced presentation of historical background of all major sports, along with descriptions of their rules, procedural matters, lore, and most famous representatives. The introduction points out that the purpose of this volume is to "help the reader understand a sport when he coaches it for the first time." There is a great deal of biographical information, and numerous illustrations enhance the text. Although most sports are covered, the emphasis is British, as one might expect, with only six pages devoted to baseball. Not included here are board and table games, children's games, and folk games. [R: PW, 21 July 75, p. 67; LJ, 15 Sept 75, p. 1618; ARBA 76, item 701]

275. **Rules of the Game: The Complete Illustrated Encyclopedia of All the Sports of the World**. By the Diagram Group. New York, Paddington Press; distr. New York, Two Continents, 1974. 320p. illus.(part col.). index. $14.95. LC 73-20954. ISBN 0-8467-0025-5.

This superbly illustrated guide explains the rules of over 400 active games and sports. Arrangement is in 13 large sections, by type of sport (i.e., Air, Wheels, Water, Combat, etc.). Each sport generally has one to two pages of combined text and illustrations. Many of the illustrations are drawn to scale; all are executed in a visually pleasing manner. In addition to laying down the official rules of each sport, the book illustrates and describes dimensions of playing areas, and gives details of equipment, timing, and scoring procedures. *Rules of the Game* is the best book of its kind available. By comparison, the explanations of rules in such sources as Menke's *Encyclopedia of Sports* (5th ed.; A. S. Barnes, 1975) appear dull and unimaginative indeed. —Marshall E. Nunn. [R: BL, 15 Dec 74, p. 431; LJ, 15 Oct 74, p. 2593; ALA 74; ARBA 75, item 728]

276. Sparano, Vin T. **Complete Outdoors Encyclopedia.** New York, Harper and Row, 1973. 622p. illus.(part col.). index. (An Outdoor Life Book). $15.00. LC 72-90934. ISBN 0-06-013955-2.

This is a compilation of information for outdoorsmen. Nicely illustrated, it devotes almost a third of the text to fishing—equipment, techniques, and the fish themselves, many shown in the color plates. Shooting, hunting, and game animals together are allotted almost the same amount of space with details of types of firearms, habits of wildlife, etc. Considerably less attention is given to camping, boating, archery, hunting dogs, and first aid. There are also lists of sources of information (fish and game departments, state travel agencies, and shooting preserves), plus a fairly good bibliography of recent books on the subjects covered. Quite a few specific brand name products are mentioned, probably because of the availability of good photographs of them.

Some of the older books of this sort, although outdated in many ways, are still quite good and should not be discarded. *The Hunter's Encyclopedia*, edited by Raymond Camp (Stackpole, o.p.) is a favorite for answering a variety of reference questions (such as methods of tanning hides). Other titles include *The Outdoor Encyclopedia* (A. S. Barnes, 1957, o.p.) and the *Outdoor Life Cyclopedia* (Grosset & Dunlap, 1942, o.p.), which are quite valuable for their articles by many of the "greats" in the old outdoor writing field: Townsend Whelen, Jack O'Connor, Ellsworth Jaeger, etc. Still in print is *The Sportsman's Encyclopedia* (Grosset & Dunlap, 1971), which is essentially about games and their playing rules (golf, baseball, etc.). —R. G. Schipf. [R: LJ, 15 Apr 73, p. 1304; WLB, June 73, p. 869; ALA 73; ARBA 74, item 628]

BASEBALL

277. **The Baseball Encyclopedia: The Complete and Official Record of Major League Baseball.** Rev. and updated. New York, Macmillan, 1974. 1532p. illus. $17.95. LC 73-21291.

"Unique, complete, and official one-volume library on baseball"—these words appear on the dust jacket as a description of this massive statistical compilation. The description is accurate. The book is arranged in nine large chapters, the main one of which is "The Player Register," almost 700 pages in length. This chapter is an alphabetical listing of every man who played in the major leagues from 1876 to 1973, except those players who were primarily pitchers (these are listed in another section). Each entry provides basic facts about each player plus his year-by-year batting records. There is a similar register of managers, as well as one for the National Association, baseball's first professional league, 1871-1876. In addition, there are chapters on records, all-star games, playoffs, and World Series highlights and scores. Three appendixes include: information sources, decision of the Baseball Records Committee, and major changes in playing and scoring rules. This is the only reference book that contains such valuable and complete information. The first edition was published in 1969; the current revision updates the material through the completion of the 1973 season. —Marshall E. Nunn. [R: ALA 70; ARBA 75, item 729]

278. **Official Encyclopedia of Baseball**. 5th rev. ed. by Hy Turkin and S.C. Thompson. Cranbury, N.J., A.S. Barnes, 1970. 675p. diagrams. $12.00. LC 63-9369. ISBN 0-498-07539-7.

The most important part of this well-done statistical work is probably the register of all players from the beginning of professional playing down through the 1969 season, with their individual records and records of the series. Much more is included, however, such as a register of umpires, official rules, Hall of Fame data, diagrams of the home parks of all major league clubs, sample player's contract, and many other interesting items. Unfortunately, there is neither an index nor a table of contents, either of which would be helpful in locating information, especially brief articles or tables within the larger sections.

More complete histories of the game and of the various leagues, clubs, and teams are available elsewhere, but the history entered here is sufficient for most purposes. Help in compiling records was provided by both the American and the National League offices. This help, apparently, is the basis for using "Official" in the title, since no other statement of sanction by leagues or commissioners was found. This is undoubtedly the best single volume available with the information required by baseball aficionados. —Cecil F. Clotfelter. [R: ARBA 71, item 778]

BASKETBALL

279. Hollander, Zander, ed. **The Modern Encyclopedia of Basketball**. Rev. ed. New York, Four Winds Press, 1973. 547p. illus. bibliog. index. $14.95. LC 70-81705. ISBN 0-590-17325-1.

If there is one indispensable basketball reference book, this is it. First published in 1969 and now presented in its first revision, Hollander's work is comprehensive, thorough, and accurate. It devotes almost equal attention to the colleges and the pros; emphasis in both sections is on the modern years. The yearly round-ups for college play begin with the 1937-38 season and include all scores in the NCAA and NIT champion games; the rest of the college section includes all-time major college records, profiles of the greatest players and coaches, and year-by-year records of the major colleges from 1938. The pro section has the same type of information, with one important addition: the NBA and ABA all-time register of every player who has appeared in league competition from 1956 to 1972. Miscellaneous sections at the end of the book include players and teams elected to the Hall of Fame, and official amateur rules. Many black and white photographs. —Marshall E. Nunn. [R: WLB, June 73, p. 869; ALA 70; ARBA 74, item 637]

BICYCLING

280. Coles, Clarence W., and Harold T. Glenn. **Glenn's Complete Bicycle Manual**: **Selection, Maintenance, Repair**. New York, Crown, 1973. 339p. illus. $7.95; $5.95pa. LC 70-185100. ISBN 0-517-50092-2; 0-517-50093-0pa.

This is a large-format book for the bicycle fancier and repairman. There are introductory remarks about selecting a bicycle for particular needs and a chapter on the history of cycling and on various popular cycling activities. Most of the book, beginning with taking the cycle out of the crate, is devoted to step-by-step maintenance and repair. Chapters are concerned with maintenance and troubleshooting, and with overhauling the front-wheel hubs, rear-wheel hubs, free-wheel body and sprocket clusters, rear derailleurs, front derailleurs, hanger sets and pedals, brakes, and headsets. Coverage includes American, Japanese, and European cycles. The drawings and photographs, some from factory manuals, are clear and complete. A detailed table of contents adequately substitutes for the lack of an index. Considering the current demand for bicycles, and for bicycle repair manuals and other literature, this excellent manual will be in constant use. —R. G. Schipf. [R: WLB, June 73, p. 870; ALA 73; ARBA 74, item 642]

281. Sloane, Eugene A. **The New Complete Book of Bicycling.** New York, Simon and Schuster, 1974. 531p. illus. bibliog. $12.50. LC 73-9362. ISBN 0-671-27119-9.

Originally titled *The Complete Book of Bicycling*, this completely rewritten and revised new edition of the 1970 work can be considered a classic in the field. Additions to the book include 70 new pages in Chapter 12, which discusses bicycle maintenance; sections on cycling in bad weather, dealing with dogs, tandems, adult tricycles, frames, etc.; new charts, tables, and expanded appendixes. Sloane's first-hand experience in the field of bicycles and bicycling ensures the accuracy and usefulness of the book. [R: Choice, Nov 74, p. 1349; BL, 1 Sept 74, p. 37; ARBA 75, item 744]

BOATING

282. Bradford, Gershom. **The Mariner's Dictionary.** Barre, Mass., Barre Publishers, 1972. 307p. illus. $12.50. LC 72-77971. ISBN 0-8271-7214-1.

This dictionary, which aims to provide some guidance to the lingo of the sailor, has been compiled from the viewpoint of the seaman. (The first edition of this work, under the title *The Glossary of Sea Terms*, was published in 1927.) The language of the sea has become extensive because of the innumerable parts of a vessel, its intricate rigging, the many types of craft, various maneuvers, and the precise way of doing things. Some terms have many meanings, some have different interpretations in different localities, and some are vague at best. Even such commonplace terms as "a fair wind" or "catching a crab" will often start a controversial discussion. This dictionary eliminates some of the confusion. [R: ARBA 73, item 684]

283. **Encyclopedia of Sailing.** By the editors of One-Design and Offshore Yachtsman. New York, Harper & Row, 1971. 468p. illus. $16.95. LC 70-156549. ISBN 0-06-013812-2.

Covers all important aspects of sailing, such as general historical background, sailboats and sailing gear, aerodynamics of sailing, racing and most important sailing competitions, navigation rules, equipment and how to use it, and other practical hints for fans of this sport. The volume is well illustrated with some 250 halftones and line drawings; there is also a rather comprehensive glossary of sailing terms. All in all, this is one of the best recent handbooks on this subject. [R: ARBA 72, item 672]

FISHING

284. McClane, Albert Jules, ed. **McClane's New Standard Fishing Encyclopedia and International Angling Guide**. Enl. and rev. ed. New York, Holt, Rinehart & Winston, 1974. 1156p. illus. bibliog. $40.00. LC 74-6108. ISBN 0-03-060325-0.

While it is nice to have a large selection of books and magazines about fishing close at hand, for quick reference there is no substitute for an excellent encyclopedic reference work. This revised and updated edition is the one to have.

There are 1,156 pages (99 more than in the first edition) with hundreds of line drawings, color photos, and black and white photos. Entries are arranged alphabetically from Aawa, a fish of Hawaiian waters, to Zooplankton. Within the alphabetical arrangement are common terms, technical terms, biographies of persons important to fishing, states and their fishing offerings, both freshwater and saltwater fish, and much more. Fishing in other nations of the world is included, and one can find the names of the famous rivers and lakes listed under the country in which they are located. Definitions and articles vary in length from a few words to many pages, depending on the subject. All articles are written by people well qualified in the subject field; the list of contributors and their qualifications fills six pages. There is also a 19-page bibliography of sources.

All in all, this encyclopedia is undoubtedly the most complete and up-to-date reference work on fishing that can be found. It includes material of value to the biologist as well as to the sportsman. —Cecil F. Clotfelter. [R: ARBA 75, item 761]

FOOTBALL

285. **The Sports Encyclopedia: Pro Football**. By Donald S. Neft, Roland T. Johnson, and Richard M. Cohen. Text by Jordan A. Deutsch. New York, Grosset and Dunlap, 1974. 496p. $14.95. LC 73-21141. ISBN 0-448-11626-X.

Though not really the "complete statistical record on professional football" that it claims to be, this is easily the most comprehensive work on the subject to date.

The main body of statistics begins with 1933, the year in which the standardization of schedules, divisional play, and post-season championship games first occurred (pro football kicked off in 1895, and the NFL was established in 1920, but records were not systematically collected until 1933). It is arranged by significant periods (1933-45; 1946-59; 1960-73) and, within each period, in a year-by-year format. Given for each year are narrative summaries of the season; final team statistics; scores of all games; each player's position, height, weight, interceptions made, and points scored; and other individual records. Also provided are statistical registers with records of single-season and life-time leaders in various categories, championship games, and Super Bowls. The figures seem to be reliable: spot checks of statistics given here correspond with those in Roger Treat's *The Official Encyclopedia of Football* (12th ed.; A.S. Barnes, 1974). A cliche-ridden historical summary of the sport is included. The print is very small and the volume is somewhat difficult to use—an index should be provided in future editions. —Richard J. Kelly. [R: Choice, Feb 75, p. 1756; ARBA 76, item 738]

GAMES

286. **Encyclopedia of Chess.** Compiled by Anne Sunnucks. New York, St. Martin's Press, 1970. 587p. illus. index. $10.00; $4.95pa. LC 78-106571.

International in scope, this volume is the most complete modern-day book in English on chess. Miss Sunnucks, the holder of many championships, has thoroughly researched her subject and with the assistance of ten authorities in the field has compiled a factual, useful tool for the chess world.

Arranged alphabetically, topics covered include biographies of over 500 leading players, the organization of chess in various countries, information about different types of chess, lists of national champions, and results of international tournament play. Chess terms are explained, along with opening plays and illustrations of games. Articles cover such topics as the ancient history of the game, chess libraries, psychology and chess, living chess, computers and chess, the laws of chess, and many others. —Judith Armstrong. [R: LJ, 1 Sept 70, p. 2789; ALA 70; ARBA 71, item 788]

287. Morehead, Albert H., and Geoffrey Mott-Smith, eds. **Hoyle Up-To-Date.** Newly rev. New York, Grosset & Dunlap, 1970. 279p. illus. glossary. $2.95.

Edmund Hoyle (1672-1769) published his first work on card games in 1742. Early titles concerned themselves with individual games such as whist, piquet, quadrille, and others, and it was not until later editions that many games were combined into one volume. Hoyle was widely recognized as an authority on the rules and strategy of cards, and he gave lessons in London. Although his name is carried on in the many editions since his death, many games are included now that were unheard of during his lifetime.

Like the other editions, this volume presents the rules, strategy, purpose and, at times, the mathematical probabilities of achieving certain goals or hands during play. Line drawings and diagrams are included for clarification. A comparison of the present volume with other editions, such as Frey, reveals relatively few significant differences. Rules change in minor points as common usage dictates, or upon the decision of organizations devoted to promoting national and international play, and games are added, or dropped, from one edition to another as popularity waxes or wanes. This is a good edition, but it differs little from relatively recent editions of Hoyle. —Cecil F. Clotfelter. [R: ARBA 72, item 680]

288. **The Official Encyclopedia of Bridge.** New rev. ed. Authorized by the American Contract Bridge League and prepared by its editorial staff. Richard L. Frey, editor-in-chief; Alan F. Truscott, executive ed. New York, Crown, 1969. 768p. $12.50.

This encyclopedia is an authoritative book of information, guidance, and instruction for bridge players. It has been revised to cover up-to-date analyses of the leading and newest techniques, with the full text of the latest contract and duplicate bridge laws. It also gives the newest information on every aspect of bridge in all bridge-playing countries of the world, results of all major tournaments, and biographies of leading players.

Written for both the beginner and the expert, *The Official Encyclopedia of Bridge* furnishes definitions for every term, along with the descriptions and illustrations of every standard bid, recognized convention, and type of play. The historical background of bridge is covered, along with the history of playing cards, and there is material on bridge etiquette and ethics, tournament direction, and bridge clubs and their management. There is a bibliography of books on bridge and a glossary of terms and phrases in six languages. [R: ARBA 70]

289. Scarne, John. **Scarne's Encyclopedia of Games.** New York, Harper and Row, 1973. 628p. illus. index. $13.95. LC 72-79691. ISBN 0-06-013813-0.

Scarne's comprehensive volume organizes instructions for over 1,000 games of chance under 28 chapters. It covers general rules applying to all card games, then describes games under groups such as draw poker, rummy games, bridge, pinochle, hearts, the all-fours group, the stop games, children's and family card games, solitaire, cheating at cards, dice games, chess and checkers, games requiring special equipment, lottery and guessing games, and parlor games. A few diagrams and photos help to explain some games and the use of cards and boards. A glossary of game terms is a very useful addition to the book; a detailed index is also provided.

The text is clearly written and more readable than Hoyle. Scarne includes games for all ages and covers more than card games. —Christine L. Wynar. [R: LJ, 15 Jan 73, p. 180; Choice, Dec 73, p. 1532; ALA 73; ARBA 74, item 685]

HOCKEY

290. Hollander, Zander, and Hal Bock, eds. **The Complete Encyclopedia of Ice Hockey.** Rev. ed. Englewood Cliffs, N.J., Prentice-Hall, 1974. 702p. illus. index. $14.95. LC 73-15019. ISBN 0-13-149913-5.

A good indication of the scope of this volume is to be found in its subtitle, "The Heroes, Teams, Great Moments, and Records of the National Hockey League." One of the most readable books on the subject, this edition covers the activities of the National Hockey League from its founding in 1917 through the 1973/74 season. It also includes, for the first time, complete records of the World Hockey Association. [R: RQ, Summer 75, p. 356; LJ, 1 Jan 75, p. 44; Choice, Apr 75, p. 198; ALA 70; ARBA 76, item 750]

HUNTING

291. Clotfelter, Cecil F. **Hunting and Fishing.** Littleton, Colo. Libraries Unlimited, 1974. 118p. index. (Spare Time Guides, No. 2). $7.50 LC 73-90569. ISBN 0-87287-079-0.

Individual sportsmen, as well as librarians, will find this volume of the Spare Time Guides series to be a useful source of information. Mr. Clotfelter has provided a list of 168 books and 26 large-circulation periodicals, with annotations that describe the kinds of information each book or periodical contains. Listed in separate sections are various national organizations concerned with aspects of hunting and fishing, the publishers of the books included in the bibliography (with addresses), and the names and addresses of manufacturers and suppliers of hunting and fishing equipment. In this one volume, then, is a wealth of information about hunting and fishing, whether the reader wants a general overview of the subject or something very specific. The complete author-title-subject index facilitates use of the guide.

Anyone interested in hunting, archery, firearms, or fishing will be interested in this new book. Not a how-to book, this guide provides information on where to find information. Whether the subject is hunting dogs, trout fishing, fly-tying, handloading ammunition, or bow-hunting for deer, Mr. Clotfelter's guide tells one where to look. [R: LJ, 1 Sept 74, p. 2054; RQ, Fall 74, p. 70; Choice, Oct 74, p. 1106; WLB, June 74, p. 852; ARBA 75, item 721]

292. **New Hunter's Encyclopedia.** 3rd ed. Harrisburg, Pa., Stackpole, 1970. (Repr. of 1966 ed.) 1131p. illus. index. $24.95. LC 66-12713.

Divided into several major sections, the *New Hunter's Encyclopedia* covers more material pertinent to its subject than four or five volumes of more specialized works, without sacrificing very much that is of interest to the probable user. The first seven sections deal with the life histories and hunting information of North American large and small game animals, game birds and predators. Life histories are more extensive and more readable than those found in the various "Fieldbook . . ." series, although some of the more detailed technical points have been omitted. Life histories are adequate for the hunter, the wildlife watcher and amateur biologist, and perhaps even for most college students of biology at the introductory level. A color section of game birds for identification purposes is beautifully done.

Firearms information, in four parts, provides excellent coverage of hunting rifles, shotguns and pistols and their ammunition, with photographs of representative makes and models currently available. Laws governing handguns in the fifty states, Canada, Mexico, Puerto Rico, and the Virgin Islands are discussed in summary form, but the reader should be aware of the possibility, and probability, of changes in laws and of new laws governing rifles and shotguns since the passage of the 1968 Gun Control Act by Congress.

Archery hunting, the preservation of meat and trophies, and the process of tanning game hides complete the information of interest to hunters only. Camping information (recipes for the camp cook, clothing for hunters and campers, bedding and tents and other shelters) is of use to all who enjoy the out-of-doors. The amateur shutter-bug has not been forgotten in this excellent work, but those who delve more deeply into photography will need a more comprehensive and technical publication, since the information here consists primarily of pointers for better hunting and wildlife shots. Federal laws pertaining to wildlife, hunting laws of the states, the Canadian provinces, and Mexico, an extensive glossary of terms and an excellent index complete the volume. The encyclopedia is well bound, well printed, and well illustrated. —Cecil F. Clotfelter. [R: ARBA 71, item 816]

MOTOR RACING

293. Georgano, G. N., ed. **The Encyclopedia of Motor Sport.** New York, Viking, 1971. 656p. illus. (A Studio Book). $25.00. LC 73-162664. ISBN 0-670-29405-5.

Twenty-five writers have contributed to this book, which is divided into four major parts. Part 1, a general introduction, includes information about racing formulas, American racing clubs, and racing specialties. Part 2 describes 161 racing events. Part 3 contains the biographies of more than 350 racing car drivers. Part 4 describes all makes of all car sizes. The extent of coverage of the sport is quite good; there are 1,700 photographs (including 62 excellent color plates), a glossary, and an index. [R: LJ, 15 Jan 72, p. 184; ALA 72; ARBA 73, item 677]

SKIING

294. Scharff, Robert, ed., and the editors of Ski Magazine. **Ski Magazine's Encyclopedia of Skiing.** New York, Harper & Row, 1970. 427p. illus. $15.95. LC 78-123963.

This is a compendium of up-to-date information concerning all aspects of skiing. The book is divided into six major sections: The History of Skiing, Ski Equipment, Principles of Skiing, Ski Competition, Where to Ski (U.S. and foreign countries), and a Glossary, Lexicon, and Listing of Ski Associations. The most important section is the one dealing with ski equipment. This section should be required reading for anyone who has ever skied or dreamed about skiing.

This book, of course, cannot substitute for the experience gained by skiing, but it can be of great assistance. It provides many illustrations showing the step-by-step techniques of skiing, along with clear textual material. The book also offers such hard-to-find information as selecting ski areas for children, and a listing of the steepest, the most challenging, and easy ski runs in North America. There are tips on budget savers, ski lodgings, and other useful bits of information which could otherwise be obtained only from a variety of sources.

The book does not have an index. It does, however, have a very detailed and logical table of contents, which makes the information readily accessible. Unless the publisher plans to revise the book frequently, information dealing with such sections as equipment, technique, ski areas, etc., will be obsolete. A subscription to *Ski Magazine*, of course, would remedy this problem. —Samuel L. Simon. [R: ALA 71; ARBA 72, item 710]

SWIMMING

295. Besford, Pat, comp. **Encyclopaedia of Swimming.** New York, St. Martin's Press, 1971. 235p. illus. index. $7.95. LC 78-157521.

All aspects of competitive swimming and diving are covered in this one-volume encyclopedia. Included are all the names, events, and times of every Olympic, Pan American, European and British Commonwealth champion. There are approximately 200 insightful and pithy biographical sketches of outstanding swimmers, past and present. While the work is international in scope, there is disproportionately wide coverage of the British Commonwealth. The history of swimming and the development of swimming pools could have been treated in greater detail. All entries are arranged in one alphabetical sequence and there is a good name index. Swimming fans will find this a useful potpourri of information, and reference librarians will find it a quick source to settle the argument of who won what event, when and where. —Robert van Benthuysen. [R: ALA 72; ARBA 72, item 706]

TENNIS

296. United States Lawn Tennis Association. **Official Encyclopedia of Tennis.** New York, Harper & Row, 1972. 472p. $15.00. LC 71-181644. ISBN 0-06-014479-3.

Publication of a new and comprehensive encyclopedia of tennis is something of an event, considering the small number of reference books on this subject. The USLTA official encyclopedia, well illustrated with some 250 photos and drawings, covers nearly every aspect of the game—history, equipment, courts, playing fundamentals, rules and etiquette, results of all major championships in the United States and abroad to 1971, lawn tennis greats, a glossary, and an index of subjects. The section on history provides a factual account of the origins and development of the game, records the greats in tennis up to the present, and ends with a summary of the efforts to sanction open competition. It is unfortunate that no effort was made to provide a bibliography for the historical survey, or for any of the other sections.

The biographical section provides sketches of National Lawn Tennis Hall of Fame members, with photos of most of the biographees. Additional brief entries are supplied for foreign players and Americans not elected to the Hall of Fame, plus a list of leading tennis players of today, giving country and date of birth.

None of the names given in the biographical section is listed in the index. Because there are so many separate lists, location of information is sometimes difficult. The table of contents provides a detailed breakdown of section headings, but, alas, the challenge to the reader is great. For example, to locate winners for a particular tournament one must search through one and one-half pages of headings, printed in run-on paragraph style. A better contents section and an index are suggested for future editions. This reference source is more up to date than Brady's *Lawn Tennis Encyclopedia* (Barnes and Noble, 1969). —Christine L. Wynar. [R: Choice, Oct 72, p. 954; LJ, Aug 72, p. 2563; WLB, Dec 72, p. 361; ALA 72; ARBA 73, item 698]

CHAPTER 12

SOCIOLOGY

BIBLIOGRAPHIES

297. Aldous, Joan, and Nancy Dahl. **International Bibliography of Research in Marriage and the Family: Volume II, 1965-1972.** Minneapolis, University of Minnesota Press in association with the Institute of Life Insurance for the Minnesota Family Study Center, 1974. 1530p. index. $35.00. LC 67-63014. ISBN 0-8166-0726-5.

Volume I of the *International Bibliography of Research in Marriage and the Family*, containing 12,850 references to scholarly literature published between 1900 and 1964, arrived in 1967. The second volume, covering the period 1965-1972, includes 12,870 additional items, of which 3,292 appeared from 1900 to 1964. This systematically compiled bibliography, produced with the aid of a computer, lists published research reports, monographs, journal articles, pamphlets, etc., that present empirical data on family life. It is truly international in scope and interdisciplinary in character. The only works intentionally omitted are unpublished theses, legal treatises, materials written in a popular style for the lay public (such as marriage manuals and child-rearing guides), most textbooks, and other secondary sources.

Volume II has been divided into only four major sections: 1) a keyword-in-context (KWIC) index, 2) a subject index, 3) an author list, and 4) a periodical list with 2,547 titles (all in roman characters). A superb introduction by Joan Aldous simplifies use of this excellent reference tool by marriage and family researchers. Unfortunately, no additional book-length volumes of this outstanding work are contemplated.   —Leonard Grundt. [R: ARBA 76, item 781]

298. Straus, Murray A. **Family Measurement Techniques: Abstracts of Published Instruments, 1935-1965.** Minneapolis, University of Minnesota Press, 1969. 316p. $13.50. LC 71-87272.

A collection of abstracts of tests and measurements alphabetically assembled to provide a comprehensive guide to available techniques of measuring characteristics of families. Covers some 300 techniques; the information given about each technique includes a listing of the variables measured, a description of the instrument, an example of the type of interview question or observational unit on which measurement is based, a summary of the evidence on validity and reliability, information on test length and norms, and a bibliography citing studies in which the instrument has been used. Material is indexed by test title, author, and subject. Murray A. Straus is professor of sociology at the University of New Hampshire. [R: ALA 70; ARBA 70, v.1, p. 133]

ENCYCLOPEDIAS AND DICTIONARIES

299. **Encyclopedia of Sociology**. Guilford, Conn., Dushkin, 1974. 330p. illus. bibliog. $5.95pa. LC 73-87072. ISBN 0-87967-055-X.

Sociology has produced an extensive interdisciplinary literature and vocabulary, and ready reference sources have not always kept pace with the expanding literature. There is a particular need for high-quality, current dictionaries like the *Encyclopedia of Sociology*.

This work provides 1,300 concise articles, arranged alphabetically, covering "the language of sociology, the full range of its theories, the institutions of sociology, and the leading figures in both historical and contemporary sociology." Prepared by scholars in the field, the articles treat sociology as an interdisciplinary subject and touch upon psychology, economics, anthropology, political science, education, and history. The value of this source is enhanced by *see* and *see also* references, photographs, suggestions for further readings, and a bibliography. Subject maps throughout the volume outline coverage of 15 major subject areas; these include, among others, methodology and statistics, race and ethnic relations, urban sociology, and social theory. —Peter Hernon. [R: BL, 15 Sept 74, p. 105; Choice, July-Aug 74, p. 734; ARBA 75, item 794]

300. van de Merwe, Caspar. **Thesaurus of Sociological Research Terminology**. Rotterdam, Rotterdam University Press; distr. Portland, Ore., International Scholarly Book Services, 1974. 471p. index. $18.00. ISBN 90-237-6227-4.

Part of the Documentation for Sociological Methods and Techniques project, this thesaurus provides a controlled index vocabulary of 1,600 descriptors and 1,800 unauthorized terms, grouped into 12 main categories. A detailed introduction explains its structure and classification scheme. Terms were chosen from current literature on the basis of frequency of use, effectiveness for information storage and retrieval, and capacity to summarize distinct details of a concept; occasionally, terms were included because they could open up an area of difficult access. Scope notes when needed, and an alphabetical index of all terms, with ample cross references, add to its usefulness. The author plans to issue twice-yearly supplementary notes and a revised edition at the end of 1975. —Laura H. McGuire. [R: ARBA 75, item 795]

ETHNIC STUDIES

301. Cordasco, Francesco. **Puerto Ricans on the United States Mainland: A Bibliography of Reports, Texts, Critical Studies and Related Materials**. Totowa, N.J., Rowman & Littlefield, 1972. 146p. index. $12.50. LC 72-80152. ISBN 0-87471-017-0.

This is an excellent bibliography dealing with the Puerto Rican experience on the American mainland. Too many Americans tend to forget that the Spanish-speaking segment of our society is the second largest minority group—and perhaps the fastest growing one. Preliminary estimates place the number of Puerto Rican residents in the United States at 1.5 million. However, too little is known about this large and growing ethnic minority group.

The purpose of this bibliography is to inform both layman and serious student about the Puerto Rican, from the island experience through migration to the mainland and the resulting problems. Conditions that affect the lives and behavior of the Puerto Rican in schools, in a social setting, in employment, and to a lesser extent, in politics, are the targets for this book.

As a reference book, Cordasco's work is highly successful. The book is organized by subject, with broad headings and more specific sub-headings. Each entry has complete bibliographic information and citations, and some have long notes about their contents, with related source materials and appropriate additional references. The index is restricted to authors. The introduction and foreword are carefully documented. In effect, these two sections sum up the conditions and problems faced by the Puerto Ricans in the United States, particularly on the mainland. Hence, the book is valuable as a resource guide and as an access tool for intellectual inquiry. —Robert P. Haro. [R: ARBA 73, item 736]

302. **The Ebony Handbook**. Ed. by Ebony Editors and Doris E. Saunders. Chicago, Johnson Publishing Co., 1974. 553p. illus. index. $20.00. LC 73-16179. ISBN 0-87485-064-9.

The previous edition of this work was published by the editors of *Ebony* in 1966 under the title *The Negro Handbook*. This work is an enlargement of and improvement upon the older version. In organization, the present work is divided into 20 sections, with an appendix containing miscellaneous information, and a well-organized index. The 20 sections under which information is structured include such standard categories as population, vital statistics, education, economics and business, employment and labor, housing, the press, etc. Each section has its own organizational format to accommodate the peculiar nature of information and data in the topic. The narrative sections are prepared concisely and with an eye to providing the user with quick information. This reference book, a needed addition to sources of information on black Americans, can function as a one-volume reference encyclopedia. —Robert P. Haro. [R: WLB, June 74, pp. 851-52; Choice, July-Aug 74, p. 734; ARBA 75, item 812]

303. Fisher, Mary L., comp. **The Negro in America: A Bibliography**. 2nd ed. rev. and enl. With a foreword by Thomas F. Pettigrew. Originally compiled by Elizabeth W. Miller. Cambridge, Mass., Harvard University Press, 1970. 315 p. index. $12.50; $4.95pa. LC 71-120319. ISBN 0-674-60703-1; 0-674-60702-3pa.

The first edition, edited by Elizabeth W. Miller, was published in 1966. The new edition, which has been considerably enlarged, contains some 6,500 entries for books, serials, articles, pamphlets, and government documents representing, for the most part, a selection of the literature from 1954 to February 1970. Reprints, dissertations, and most newspaper articles are omitted. The entries are arranged under 20 chapters and are subdivided by broad headings. Full bibliographic description is provided for articles; however, the entries for books omit pages. Brief annotations are provided where titles are not self-explanatory. The scope is enlarged to give greater coverage to black history (including historiography), folklore and literature, and biography. Civil rights protest is now in two sections: materials up to 1965 and since 1965. Given more emphasis is the issue of black nationalism, which covers background, theory, Panthers, Muslims, and response and resistance. Other additions and enlargements include black theater, dance, the arts and music, references to language and idiom, and Negro-Jewish relations. The very useful chapter on materials for further research is expanded.

The Fisher/Miller bibliography is much larger than Dorothy Porter's 1,800-entry work (*The Negro in the United States*, Library of Congress, 1970). While Porter emphasizes monographs of current interest to students, teachers, and librarians and is quite strong in areas of cultural development, Fisher/Miller provides more detailed coverage of the social sciences and is oriented to the needs of researchers. [R: ARBA 72, item 731]

304. Hirschfelder, Arlene B., comp. **American Indian and Eskimo Authors: A Comprehensive Bibliography**. New York, Association on American Indian Affairs; distr. New York, Interbook, 1973. 99p. $4.00. LC 73-82109.

A revised and greatly enlarged edition of a bibliography published by the Association on American Indian Affairs in 1970. According to the compiler, the literary contributions of the American Indians and Eskimos have often gone unnoticed because it has been customary "to promote books under the names of the investigators or editors who record or revise materials written or narrated by Natives rather than under the names of the people who deserve the primary credit—the Indians and Eskimos themselves" (Foreword). The purpose of this bibliography, therefore, is to present the American Indians "as they are," through their own writings and narrations, unmediated by non-Indians. All the works cited in this compilation are under the names of Eskimos or Indians who either wrote or narrated them. The bibliography contains about 400 titles by almost 300 Indian and Eskimo authors representing more than 100 tribes. At the outset the compiler includes a tribal index that identifies the tribal affiliation of each author and also lists the Indian organizations that have sponsored various publications. The bibliography itself is arranged alphabetically by author. Each entry contains a descriptive annotation. There is no subject limitation, so the topics covered vary from basketmaking, legends and myths, religion, art, and rituals to accounts of historical events, autobiographies, etc. Although this bibliography will prove to be a welcome reference tool to Indian literature, it does have one major shortcoming: the lack of a subject index makes it difficult to locate materials on specific topics. One must peruse the entire book in order to find specific material. —Anna T. Wynar. [R: ARBA 75, item 805]

305. Jordan, Lois B. **Mexican Americans: Resources to Build Cultural Understanding**. Littleton, Colo., Libraries Unlimited, 1973. 265p. index. $8.50. LC 72-94302. ISBN 0-87287-059-6.

This is a selective annotated bibliography of books and audiovisual materials suitable for young adults in junior high school, senior high school, and college. The topics represented include the Mexican heritage, the Mexican American today, the arts and literature, biography, and fictional stories about Mexican Americans.

The first section contains 751 entries for books, arranged by subject. The audiovisual section describes 277 films, filmstrips, recordings, and other media. All entries provide full bibliographical information and an annotation describing and evaluating the contents of the material. Junior high school level books are designated by the symbol "j" in the entry.

Four appendixes present supplementary information. Brief biographical notes on some Mexican-American personalities who have achieved recognition in sports, entertainment, or government are listed in the first appendix. A directory of the Chicano Press Association and a sampling of Mexican-American periodicals and newspapers is contained in the second appendix. The third appendix is a directory of organizations. In the last appendix there is a list of additional reference sources of a more general nature that provide information about Mexican Americans. [R: Choice, Dec 73, p. 1528; BL, 1 Sept 73, p. 12; ARBA 74, item 735]

306. **Makers of America.** Wayne Moquin, ed. Chicago, Encyclopedia Britannica, 1971. 10v. illus. index. $79.50 (to schools and libraries, plus shipping charges). LC 74-129355. ISBN 0-87827-000-0.

This impressive set is probably one of the most important reference sources on ethnic pluralism in the United States. The material is arranged in chronological order: Vol. 1, The Firstcomers, 1536-1800; Vol. 2, Builders of a New Nation, 1801-1848; Vol. 3, Seekers after Freedom, 1849-1870; Vol. 4, Seekers after Wealth, 1871-1890; Vol. 5, Natives and Aliens, 1891-1903; Vol. 6, The New Immigrants 1904-1913; Vol. 7, Hyphenated Americans, 1914-1924; Vol. 8, Children of the Melting Pot, 1925-1938; Vol. 9, Refugees and Victims, 1939-1954; and Vol. 10, Emergent Minorities, 1955-1970. The set contains 731 selections from letters, diaries, newspaper editorials, and other contemporary sources describing various activities of minority groups, their organizations, important religious groups, etc. *Makers of America* is not a history of immigration in the traditional sense of the term, but a collection of primary sources that will support such a history, showing the diversity of Americans in as many ways and from as many points of view as possible. As it is indicated in the introduction, "*Makers of America* is primarily designed to illustrate issues of ethnic pluralism, immigration, nativism, and race, along with legal, political, social, and cultural matters pertinent thereto. . . . As much as possible the editors have endeavored to call attention to broader issues of American history by the use of readings. . . ." To support such objectives the set is well indexed, with a number of primary and secondary indexes, including ethnic index, proper name index, topical index, author-source index, and illustration index. [R: RQ, Winter 71, p. 169; ARBA 72, item 301]

307. McPherson, James M., and others. **Blacks in America: Bibliographical Essays.** Garden City, N.Y., Doubleday, 1971. 430p. index. $10.00. LC 70-164723. ISBN 0-385-02569-6.

More than a mere enumerative bibliography of the history and culture of black people in the United States, this is a scholarly work of bibliographical essays giving in-depth treatment to over 100 topics, ranging from Africa to the urban lifestyles of blacks up to 1970. More than 4,000 titles are included. The basic organization is chronological, with each topic presented in the form of a self-contained essay. Part one covers general racial prejudices and stereotypes; Parts two through seven cover social, economic, and political developments up to 1970. Part eight is devoted to blacks in literature and the arts during the twentieth century. Each title has sufficient bibliographical information included in the text to allow the user to identify and obtain the book.

This is a unique reference source in that it synthesizes and analyzes the literature of blacks in this country. The index provides a thorough analysis of the text and gives complete listing of the authors and titles mentioned in each essay. —Miles M. Jackson. [R: Choice, June 72, p. 492; ARBA 73, item 733]

308. **Reference Encyclopedia of the American Indian**. 2nd ed. Ed. by Barry T. Klein and Daniel Icolari. Rye, N.Y., Todd Publications, 1974. 2v. $30.00. LC 67-17326.

The first volume, edited by B. T. Klein, includes listings of government agencies, museums, libraries, associations, urban Indian centers, reservations and tribal councils, visual aids, schools, and publications, plus a comprehensive bibliographical section. The bibliography contains approximately 2,500 briefly annotated or unannotated entries in alphabetical and subject sections.

The second volume, edited by Icolari, constitutes a biographical who's who of prominent American Indians as well as non-Indians who are prominent in Indian life and studies. In most cases, the biographical sketches were based on questionnaires and published sources, and the emphasis is on the professional life, rather than the personal life. According to the editor, he "omitted references to family history and offspring" (Introduction).

It is difficult to comprehend why the editors labeled this publication as "reference encyclopedia." There are no articles on Indian life, and there is no relevant statistical and demographic information on Indian tribes in the United States. The first volume is a regular directory of Indian institutions with brief, or sometimes no, annotations. The second volume is a brief biographical dictionary of living people involved in Indian affairs. —Lubomyr R. Wynar. [R: Choice, Apr 74, p. 238; Choice, Dec 74, p. 1459; ARBA 75, item 808]

309. Stensland, Anna Lee. **Literature by and about the American Indian: An Annotated Bibliography for Junior and Senior High School Students**. Urbana, Ill., National Council of Teachers of English, 1973. 208p. index. $3.95pa. LC 73-83285. ISBN 0-8141-4203-7.

The guide is designed principally for teachers of English in junior and senior high schools. Thoughtfully planned and well executed, it is especially useful to school and public libraries and to anyone working with young people. The author, professor of English at the University of Minnesota, provides a selection of 350 titles of books by Indians and many written about Indians from the white man's viewpoint. The annotations contain three main elements: synopsis; critical comments; quotes from reviews by Indian scholars and writers. The bibliography is arranged by subject in nine sections: myths; fiction; drama; biography; history; anthropology; modern life; music, arts, and crafts; and aids for the teacher. Selections include a number of books that present some objectionable images of American Indians. An example is *Flap*, by Clair Huffaker, which is "full of slapstick comedy and many rowdy, drunken, cursing Indians as characters" (p. 62). The author explains in her discussion of criteria for selection that "some of the books in this bibliography give the white man's point of view, which often is not a very accurate picture of the Indian. Yet, in order to understand what happened to the

Indian, it does seem that the reader should understand more of what the white man thought . . ." (pp. 17-18).

The "aids for the teacher" section of the bibliography discusses a few basic materials for background and reference. The study guides section consists, for the most part, of suggested questions for students to consider when reading each of the nine selected books. A biography section sketches lives of 25 of the most prolific American Indian scholars and writers—a welcome change from the typical listing of famous personalities. The basic book collection lists about 40 titles each for junior and senior high school. Appended is a list of sources of information, publishers, and author and title indexes. The lengthy introduction includes a discussion of writings about Indians and Indian stereotypes. --Christine L. Wynar. [R: ARBA 74, item 726]

310. U.S. Library of Congress. **The Negro in the United States: A Selected Bibliography**. Comp. by Dorothy B. Porter. Washington, GPO, 1970. 313p. $3.25. LC 78-606085. (LC 1.12/2:N31)

This bibliography was published to meet the demand for a list of books that can be used to support the many new courses on Negro history and culture that are being taught in high schools, colleges and universities. It is "designed to meet the current needs of students, teachers, librarians, researchers and the general public for introductory guidance to the study of the Negro in the United States." It is a selective bibliography on a wide range of subjects related to Negro history and culture in the United States, with emphasis on recent monographs in the Library of Congress collection. Entries are alphabetical by authors under 23 broad subject headings such as biography, literature, history, art. Includes brief annotations only when the title was not self-explanatory. Indexed by subjects and authors. —Sally Wynkoop. [R: ALA 70; ARBA 71, item 852]

311. Vivo, Paquita, ed. **The Puerto Ricans: An Annotated Bibliography**. New York, R. R. Bowker, 1973. 299p. index. $15.50. LC 73-8825. ISBN 0-8352-0663-7.

This comprehensive bibliography, sponsored by the Puerto Rican Research and Resources Center, Inc., constitutes the first attempt "to present a complete bibliographic overview of Puerto Ricans" (Preface). It is based on the largest collections of Puerto-Ricana, including holdings of the Library of Congress, University of Puerto Rico Library, New York Public Library, and others.

The bibliography is divided into four parts: books, pamphlets, and dissertations; government documents; periodical literature; and audiovisual materials. The guide contains over 2,600 briefly annotated entries, with emphasis on English language materials and dissertations. Book and periodical entries are arranged alphabetically under 21 subject headings, which cover all aspects of Puerto Rican life.

This guide could serve as an example of how to prepare a comprehensive listing on an ethnic or nationality group. The included subject, author, and title indexes facilitate the use of this important work. —Lubomyr R. Wynar. [R: WLB, Dec 73, p. 341; BL, 15 Nov 73, p. 303; ALA 74; ARBA 74, item 734]

312. Wynar, Lubomyr R. **Encyclopedic Directory of Ethnic Newspapers and Periodicals in the United States**. Littleton, Colo., Libraries Unlimited, 1972. 260p. index. $12.50. LC 70-185344. ISBN 0-87287-042-1.

This encyclopedic directory lists and describes 903 publications in 43 languages. Information was provided by a special questionnaire distributed to all known publishers and editors of ethnic publications in this country. Entries are arranged alphabetically in two categories under each ethnic group: publications in the native language and bilingual publications; publications in English. Ethnic groups which publish entirely in English are omitted. Information provided for each publication includes name (with English translation), address, editor, language of publication, sponsoring organization, circulation, frequency, and subscription price. In addition, brief descriptive annotations, based on statements of the editors and on *de visu* examination of individual titles, delineate the scope, content, and purpose of the publications. This directory also contains a useful alphabetical index of titles, an appendix which provides statistical summaries of the publications for each language, and introductory material which describes the intent and methods of the directory and discusses the dearth of reliable research on all aspects of the ethnic press.

WLB indicated that "Dr. Wynar in his review of the bibliographic control of the ethnic press points out the woeful inadequacy of *Ayer's Directory* in this area, as well as the shortcomings of the *Standard Periodicals Directory*. This serves to emphasize the importance of his carefully prepared bibliography. . . ." [Editor's note: The second edition was published in 1976.] [R: WLB, June 72, p. 927; LJ, 15 May 72, p. 1799; ALA 72; ARBA 73, item 28]

313. Wynar, Lubomyr R., with the assistance of Lois Buttlar and Anna T. Wynar. **Encyclopedic Directory of Ethnic Organizations in the United States.** Littleton, Colo., Libraries Unlimited, 1975. 440p. index. $19.50. LC 75-28150. ISBN 0-87287-120-7.

This is the first comprehensive encyclopedic guide to major ethnic organizations in the United States. In all, it includes 1,475 organizations, representing 73 ethnic groups. A separate section provides a selective listing of major multi-ethnic and research-oriented non-ethnic organizations involved in the study of ethnicity. Data provided in this directory are based on a recent comprehensive survey of ethnic organizations in the United States, which was conducted from 1973 through April 1975.

The *Encyclopedic Directory* lists major cultural, religious, fraternal, political, educational, professional, scholarly, youth, and other ethnic organizations. Entries, arranged alphabetically by ethnic groups with the necessary cross references, provide the following information: name of organization, address, phone number, principal officers, staff, date founded, scope, branches, membership, nature of the organization, publications, affiliations, and additional descriptive information.

The emergence of ethnic awareness has resulted in an emphasis on the study of the ethnic heritage of Americans within the curriculum of our universities, colleges, and public schools. The wealth of information contained in this *Encyclopedic Directory* makes it a valuable source of information for governmental agencies, historians, and sociologists engaged in the study of American ethnicity. A comprehensive alphabetical index of names of organizations concludes this important reference guide. [R: ARBA 76, item 394]

LAW ENFORCEMENT AND CRIMINOLOGY

314. Hopkins, Isabella, John K. Maxwell, and Charyl Mattson, comps. **Organized Crime: A Selected Bibliography**. Austin, Criminal Justice Reference Library, University of Texas School of Law, 1973. 99p. index. (Criminal Justice Reference Library Bibliography Series). $15.00.

Because there are few bibliographies that provide broad coverage of organized crime, this bibliography fills a definite void. Publications are arranged within five categories: General Works: Criminal Organizations; Organized Crime Involvement; Organized Crime Control and Prevention; and Reference Materials. Access to specific works is facilitated by a proper name index. The bibliography's worth is the organized treatment afforded many fugitive materials, such as the 1934 Report of the Massachusetts Special Crime Commission. The rapid development and expansion of the literature of organized crime necessitated improved bibliographic control. The interdisciplinary approach of this bibliography should prove useful to both scholars and librarians. It is indeed a fine contribution to the literature. —Jerry E. Stephens. [R: ARBA 75, item 827]

315. Nash, Jay Robert. **Bloodletters and Badmen: A Narrative Encyclopedia of American Criminals from the Pilgrims to the Present**. New York, M. Evans; distr. Philadelphia, Lippincott, 1973. 640p. illus. bibliog. index. $16.95. LC 72-95977. ISBN 0-87131-113-5.

Nash, newspaperman and author of biographies of Dillinger and Hoover, bases this account of about 400 American murderers, gangsters, robbers, etc., on about 5,000 books collected over the past 15 years. The well-written biographies are accompanied by over 300 photographs of the subjects, some of them action shots. Gory tales of mass murder, prison brutality, and the romantic marriage of Belle Starr to a Cherokee Indian gone bad are detailed. A thorough bibliography and an index of criminals and victims are appended. —Frances Neel Cheney. [R: AL, Sept 73, p. 480; WLB, Sept 73, p. 86; LJ, 1 May 73, p. 1471; ALA 73; ARBA 74, item 745]

316. Wright, Martin, ed. **Use of Criminology Literature**. Hamden, Conn., Archon Books, 1974. 242p. index. (Information Sources for Research and Development Series). $13.50. LC 73-19653. ISBN 0-208-01259-1.

The latest in the well-received Information Sources series under the general editorial control of R. T. Bottle and D. J. Foskett, Wright's *Use of Criminology Literature* should be of immediate value to students and scholars in the field. It is the author's purpose to provide a guide to the major literature sources and reference tools; he has accomplished his purpose amply by collecting short chapters on specific topics in the broad field of criminology. Wright, as director of the Howard League for Penal Reform, is himself eminently qualified to direct this brilliant assembly of contributors. Only two of the contributors are located outside the United Kingdom, yet the volume is definitely international in scope. The topics covered range from police literature to alcoholism and crime. The last chapter, "The History of Prisons and Penal Practices," by S. D. M. McConville of the University of Sussex, is alone almost worth the purchase price of the book, as an excellent brief summary statement on penal reform literature. A major contribution to a growing academic and professional field of study. —Jerry E. Stephens. [R: Choice, Oct 74, p. 1116; ARBA 75, item 838]

SOCIAL WORK

317. **Encyclopedia of Social Work.** 16th issue. Robert Morris, ed. New York, National Association of Social Workers, 1971. 2v. $22.50. LC 30-30948. ISBN 0-87101-055-0.

The 1965 *Encyclopedia of Social Work* represented a major change—a transition from the *Social Work Year Book* to an encyclopedic work.

The present edition (under the able editorship of Robert Morris, from the Graduate School for Advanced Studies in Social Welfare, Brandeis University) places the emphasis on societal problems. Articles with a theoretical orientation are balanced by more pragmatic accounts of such topics as housing or family and population planning. An example of a sound theoretical approach is the rather lengthy article on intergroup relations, well documented and including a bibliography. It should be noted that the number of articles is almost twice that of the preceding edition, and that there is much stronger coverage in the areas of health, the economy, and the physical environment. All in all, this well-balanced work will be of interest not only to social workers but to many social scientists as well. —Bohdan S. Wynar. [R: ARBA 73, item 738]

CHAPTER 13

URBANOLOGY

318. Abrams, Charles. **The Language of Cities: A Glossary of Terms**. New York, Viking Press, 1971. 365p. index. $10.00. LC 76-137500. ISBN 0-670-41782-3.

Charles Abrams, who was one of the world's leading urban planners and housing experts, completed this glossary just before his death in February 1970. It was compiled with the assistance of Robert Kolodny. Terms related to the cityscape are defined simply and accurately, giving the historical evolution and current usage of the term, as well as a touch of personal opinion by the author. The glossary, which is liberally cross-referenced, will be of interest to all city-dwellers, be they laymen or professional planners and administrators. —Thomas L. Jenkins. [R: ARBA 72, item 772]

319. Bell, Gwendolyn, Edwina Randall, and Judith E. R. Roeder. **Urban Environments and Human Behavior: An Annotated Bibliography**. Stroudsburg, Pa., Dowden, Hutchinson & Ross, 1973. 271p. index. (Community Development Series). $15.00. LC 72-88982. ISBN 0-87933-016-3.

This bibliography represents a usable source for the field of urban design—that is, the field of relating people and their social activities to physical space. It is divided into three major parts. The first, which deals with the design approaches to the urban environment, includes sections on such topics as perception studies, density and privacy, and the design process. The annotations for each section are arranged chronologically so that the reader can readily determine the sequence of data development under each topic. The major theme of part two is the social sciences approach, and part three presents the framework of the urban environment. A section on other bibliographies is also included, along with a list of key periodicals and journals in the field, an index of annotations, and a subject index. There are approximately 600 annotated entries. This is a very good, well-presented bibliography; it should be of use to architects and urban planners who need to be aware of the human requirements of urban design. —Thomas L. Jenkins. [R: ARBA 74, item 760]

320. Bestor, George C., and Holway R. Jones. **City Planning Bibliography: A Basic Bibliography of Sources and Trends**. 3rd ed. New York, American Society of Civil Engineers, 1972. 518p. index. $9.00pa.

This bibliography, probably the best in the field of city planning, is compiled by two experts in the field. Bestor is an engineer and planner, and Jones is a social sciences librarian and former planning librarian. The bibliography contains 1,837 items, about 75 percent of which are annotated. English language books, technical reports, government reports, and periodicals are included, but not periodical articles or reviews. Full bibliographic information, including price, is given for each item. Furthermore, many annotations contain additional useful bibliographic information, such as lists of titles in series, related reports, etc. The major subject divisions are as follows: the nature and form of cities; the history of cities and city planning; contemporary comprehensive planning; education for planning; general bibliographies; selected services and periodicals in planning and related fields.

The bibliography is technically excellent, well organized, and extensively indexed. It is invaluable for students and for practicing planners, engineers, and government officials. —Thomas L. Jenkins. [R: ARBA 74, item 761]

321. Branch, Melville C. **Comprehensive Urban Planning: A Selected Annotated Bibliography with Related Materials.** Beverly Hills, Calif., Sage, 1970. 477p. indexes. $20.00. LC 73-92349. ISBN 0-8039-0041-4.

This bibliography of 1,500 selected references in comprehensive urban planning is useful to all persons involved in the field, especially researchers, students, and teachers. It incorporates three categories of references: those that deal directly with comprehensive urban planning; those that are closely related to or are subsystems of comprehensive urban planning (for example, land use, transportation systems, and project programming); and environmental or other background materials that underlie comprehensive urban planning and a higher order of municipal management. The references are grouped under the following main headings: Background; Process; Theory; Information-Communication; Research-Analysis; Methodology; Institutionalization; Management, Decision-Making; Effectuation; System Elements; Subsystems; and Particular Forms of Urban Planning. Each reference gives the standard bibliographic data including the Library of Congress catalog card number and a brief annotation.

A section entitled "Related Materials" includes a list of schools in the United States and Canada offering graduate degrees in urban and regional planning, a list of publishers and sources with addresses, and a list of the periodicals referenced with the number of times cited. Subject, author, and title indexes conclude this work.

The references cited provide a good background to the complex field of comprehensive urban planning. Because of the vast number of publications in the field, the work is necessarily highly selective, but Professor Branch's is the only attempt to cover this field. —Thomas L. Jenkins. [R: Choice, July-Aug 70, p. 699; LJ, July 70, p. 2447; ARBA 71, item 867]

322. Whittick, Arnold, ed.-in-chief. **Encyclopedia of Urban Planning.** New York, McGraw-Hill, 1974. 1218p. illus. index. $34.00. LC 73-19757. ISBN 0-07-070075-3.

This encyclopedia represents a major undertaking, bringing together material prepared by 70 leading world authorities in urban planning. The book contains over 400 articles, ranging from brief definitions to long essays, and covering ancient, medieval, Renaissance, and modern planning; transportation and its various forms; planning theories and ideals; social aspects of planning; and the aesthetic aspects of community design. The encyclopedia is most useful for investigating the general theory and practice (history) of urban planning. However, the international emphasis of the encyclopedia is not necessarily an asset to American planners. Foreign planning techniques often cannot be applied to American planning problems because of unique American institutional relationships. On the other hand, the nineteenth and twentieth century planning traditions of 48 foreign countries may be of historical and/or comparative interest. —Thomas L. Jenkins. [R: ALA 74; ARBA 75, item 862]

CHAPTER 14

ANTHROPOLOGY AND ETHNOLOGY

ANTHROPOLOGY

323. Frantz, Charles. **The Student Anthropologist's Handbook: A Guide to Research, Training and Career.** Cambridge, Mass., Schenkman; distr. Morristown, N.J., General Learning Press, 1972. 228p. $5.95; $2.95pa. LC 77-170649. ISBN 0-87073-730-9; 0-87073-731-7pa.

This introduction and guide to anthropology has been written especially for students and beginners although the author, who is a professional, trusts that it will prove useful to fellow professionals and teachers. It is neither a general handbook nor a bibliography, although it is particularly rich in bibliographical and research guides. The introductory chapter gives the historical background and key characteristics of the science and its relevance for the present day. This is followed by a detailed discussion of why and how people become anthropologists, their training, studies and opportunities, the use of museums and field researches, the universities and societies, and even the ethical aspects of the actual practice on the part of professionals. Frantz, who considers anthropology a humanistic discipline closely related to the social and humanistic sciences, feels that its greatest value may be found in its contribution to a general liberal education. Its study is built around the foci of library, fellow students, and faculty, and of these the library is the most important. Accordingly a great part of text describes the use of the library, its catalog, and its resources. Almost all standard reference books, bibliographies, periodicals, etc., that would be of interest to an anthropologist are listed, as well as many otherwise obscure books and articles on methods and techniques. No comprehensive encyclopedia, current bibliography, or up-to-date survey exists in English. For the problem of how best to use the library Frantz offers some interesting comments. Standard classifications (such as LC or Dewey) were developed long before anthropology reached its present dimensions, and today no classification system really works effectively in bringing anthropological materials together. The only improvement in sight may come from some radically different system that makes use of automatic storage and retrieval. He recognizes that the subject entries in the card catalog may be useful and lists some 78 of the more commonly used ones; but he warns that anthropological material may be hidden or ignored under the most diverse headings. All in all, this is an interesting and useful little book. There seems to be nothing comparable to it. —Theodore M. Avery, Jr. [R: ARBA 73, item 764]

324. **A Handbook of Method in Cultural Anthropology.** Edited by Raoul Naroll and Ronald Cohen. Garden City, N.Y., Published for the American Museum of Natural History by the Natural History Press, 1970. 1017p. illus. bibliog. index. $40.00; $15.00pa. LC 78-123703. ISBN 0-231-03731-7; 0-231-03749-Xpa.

Though termed a "Handbook of Method," concern with theory is abundantly evident in this impressive volume and concern for basic philosophical issues continually enters many of the presentations. When 72 first-class scientists contribute to a work such as this, there must necessarily be considerable overlap and, surprisingly sometimes, notable shortcomings. Among the latter would seem to be "a model of role analysis" which still treats the concept as it was handled in sociology and psychology over 20 years ago. No distinction is made between status and position, and the concepts of role expectations, perceptions, and enactments either are not distinguished or are badly confounded. Another weakness is the lack of attention afforded communication, especially of the nonverbal type. Kinesics and proxemics, neither of which appears in the index, are summarily treated in a few lines in the body of one article. Linguistic analysis is essentially ignored. This reviewer soon learned that there was much more in the various articles than was made evident by the index.

Despite these considerations, there can be little doubt that this notable work will remain a central reference source on both method and theory for many years to come. —Bernard Spilka. [R: ARBA 72, item 782]

325. **Handbook of Middle American Indians. Vol. 9, Physical Anthropology.** Ed. by T. Dale Stewart. **Vols. 14 and 15, Guide to Ethnohistorical Sources, Parts Three and Four.** Ed. by Howard F. Cline. Austin, University of Texas Press, 1970, 1975. 3v. illus. $15.00(v.9); $40.00(v.14 and 15). LC 64-10316. ISBN 0-292-70014-8 (v.9); 0-292-70154-3(v.14 and 15/set).

The 15 articles contained in the ninth volume of this set describe the human biology of Middle America using both primary and secondary source material. The authors are recognized authorities in their respective fields, e.g, Juan Comas, Arturo Romano, Santiago Genoves T., Javier Romero, Eusebio Davalos Hurtado, Johanna Faulhaber, G. Albin Matson, Marshall Newman, T. D. Stewart, Mildred Trotter, Oliver Duggins, Nevin Scrimshaw and Carlos Tejada. Articles are arranged chronologically from prehistoric to contemporary times and contain important material on Middle American Indians, on prehistoric human remains, anthropometry, osteopathology, blood groups, physiological studies, physical plasticity and adaptation, psychobiometry and an excellent section related to skin, hair and eyes.

One of the problems relating to multi-volume publication is the unevenness resulting from the different times at which the various articles were submitted and the references used. A scan of the 36-page reference section reveals that most of the notations are pre-1960, which emphasizes the historical and more traditional rather than the "new" physical anthropology with its heavy emphasis on the breakthroughs in genetics; e.g., the latest reference in the article on psychobiometry is 1961, and the latest reference in the article on blood groups is 1966. It may be that current research is not yet available for publication.

Nonetheless there is a wealth of material (thoroughly indexed) on the physical anthropology of Middle America in this volume. Large numbers of foldouts, tables, charts, maps and graphs make immense amounts of data available for observation and analysis, although the binding procedure used makes it difficult to read some of the data of the inner margins. (There is a slip inserted in the volume containing these "difficult to read" lines.) This volume, as well as others earlier published in this series, is an excellent and scholarly reference work and a welcome companion to the *Handbook of South American Indians* earlier edited by Julian Steward.

Volumes 14 and 15 of the *Handbook of Middle American Indians* constitute Parts 3 and 4 of the *Guide to Ethnohistorical Sources*. The *Handbook*, which is under the general editorship of Robert Wauchope, was published under the sponsorship of the National Research Council Committee on Latin American Anthropology, in cooperation with the Middle American Research Institute at Tulane University. Both Volumes 14 and 15 deal with sources in the native traditions. Geography and ethnogeography were covered in Volume 12, and sources in the European tradition comprise Volume 13.

Volume 14 contains the following studies: "A Survey of Native Middle American Pictorial Manuscripts," by John Glass; "A Census of Native Middle American Pictorial Manuscripts," also by Glass in collaboration with Donald Robertson; "Techialoyan Manuscripts and Paintings, with a Catalog," by Robertson; "A Census of Middle American Testerian Manuscripts," and "A Catalog of Falsified Middle American Pictorial Manuscripts," both by John Glass.

Volume 15, also devoted to sources in the native tradition, has the following studies: "Prose Sources in the Native Historical Tradition—(A) A Survey of Middle American Prose Manuscripts" (by Charles Gibson), "(B) A Census of Middle American Prose Manuscripts" (by Gibson and Glass); "A Checklist of Institutional Holdings of Middle American Manuscripts in the Native Historical Tradition," by Glass; "The Boturini Collection," by Glass; "Middle American Ethnohistory: An Overview," by H.B. Nicholson; "Index of Authors, Titles, and Synonyms," by Glass; and "Annotated References," by Glass. The last section of this volume contains illustrations and figures. —Robert H. Amundson and Anna T. Wynar. [R: ARBA 71, item 875; ARBA 76, item 809]

ETHNOLOGY

326. **Handbook of American Indians: North of Mexico.** Ed. by Frederick Webb Hodge. Washington, GPO, 1907-10; repr. New York, Rowman and Littlefield; distr. St. Clair Shores, Mich., Scholarly Press, 1971. 2v. (U.S. Bureau of American Ethnology, Bulletin 30). $82.50.

This handbook is by far one of the most important publications on this subject. Originally published by the GPO, it was reissued by the Smithsonian Institution in 1912 and again reprinted in 1959 by Pageant Books.

This newest reprint, on durable paper with good binding, covers all the tribes north of Mexico, including the Eskimo, and those tribes south of the boundary that are more or less affiliated with those in the United States. Entries provide a brief description of every linguistic stock, confederacy, tribe, subtribe or tribal division, and settlement known in historical sources (or even according to tradition), as well as the origin and derivation of every name represented. Cross references to many forms of names and synonyms, arranged in alphabetical order, are found in the second volume. Under the tribal descriptions, one finds a brief account of the ethnic relations of the tribe, its history, its location at various periods, statistics of population, etc. Accompanying each synonym (the earliest date is usually given), the reader will find a reference to an authoritative source, which thus provides a bibliography of writings pertaining to a particular tribe.

The monumental project of which this handbook is an outgrowth was begun as early as 1873 by Professor Otis T. Mason, and the introduction provides a rather detailed account of its history. All in all, this is an essential sourcebook on the subject. —Bohdan S. Wynar. [R: ARBA 72, item 784]

327. Hill, Edward E. **The Office of Indian Affairs, 1824-1880: Historical Sketches.** New York, Clearwater Publishing, 1974. 246p. index. $18.00. LC 73-16321. ISBN 0-88354-105-X.

This is an invaluable—indeed, a critical—reference tool for anyone engaged in exhaustive research on Indian affairs between 1824 and 1880. The National Archives and Records Service sells a 962-reel set of microfilm, which consists of the correspondence the BIA received between 1824 and 1880—a collection of letters that provides a wealth of information about Indian affairs. Until this book was published, the only complete index to the collection was a looseleaf book in the National Archives. The publication of this book opens up the entire collection to scholars everywhere, since the microfilms can be purchased in single reels, groups of reels, or as a complete set.

The book contains four parts: 1) introduction, 2) unit histories, 3) tribal index, and 4) jurisdictional index. The introduction provides a brief history of the BIA and a description of the nature of the correspondence included in the archives. All of the material is arranged by field unit names (superintendencies and agencies), so the user must know geographical responsibility, tribal responsibilities, and the period of time during which the unit operated. Field units were continually being established, disbanded, and given added or reduced responsibilities. It is essential to read the *entire* introduction. Only then does one know the variety of entries under which relevant data may be found.

The major section of the book consists of a series of brief histories of superintendencies and agencies. Unit histories provide an overview that will help the researcher determine which units may contain relevant data. These histories range in length from two sentences (Neah Bay Agency) to eight pages (California Superintendency, 1849-1880). Each section indicates when the unit was established and disbanded, and also the tribal responsibilities. For larger units with a long history of operation, there is a list of agents and superintendents and the dates of their appointments. One drawback of the book is that some agencies, listed under a superintendency, are not included in the table of contents. It is only through the jurisdictional index that one can find such agencies; but even then reference is to the larger unit and not to the page number on which the history is located.

Two essential indexes are provided—tribal and jurisdictional. The tribal index is important from two points of view. All tribes were controlled by more than one agency or superintendency: e.g., Navajo—Santa Fe Agency, New Mexico Superintendency, and 1877-1880 Colorado Superintendency. The tribal index consists of three elements: 1) an alphabetical tribal arrangement; 2) a heading list indicating *all* the agencies and/or superintendencies that had responsibility for the tribe or band; 3) the page on which the heading unit *begins*. The second value of the index is that it provides the *official* list of Indian tribes *and* bands from the point of view of the U.S. government (BIA).

The jurisdictional index consists of five elements: 1) name of unit and years of operation; 2) years of filing; 3) file heading; 4) reel number; and 5) page. Years of filing indicate the years for which correspondence was filed in the archives; this is frequently less time than the agency was in operation. The reel number refers to the reel(s) in the series that are relevant, and the page number refers to the page in the text on which the unit history is given. —G. Edward Evans. [R: BL, 15 Oct 74, pp. 255-56; Choice, Sept 74, p. 910; ARBA 75, item 804]

CHAPTER 15

STATISTICS AND DEMOGRAPHY

DICTIONARIES

328. Kendall, Maurice G., and William R. Buckland. **A Dictionary of Statistical Terms.** 3rd ed. rev. and enl. Published for the International Statistical Institute. New York, Hafner, 1971. 166p. $12.95. ISBN 0-05-002280-6.

Since the publication of the first edition in 1957, this dictionary has gained a wide reputation as a standard, professionally prepared handbook of basic statistical terminology. This new edition has been substantially enlarged, with the number of entries increased from 1,700 in the first edition to well over 2,500 in the third. Highly recommended for students of statistics and economics as well as for most social scientists. —Bohdan S. Wynar. [R: Choice, Dec 71, p. 1318; ARBA 73, item 770]

329. Webb, Augustus D. **The New Dictionary of Statistics: A Complement to the Fourth Edition of Mulhall's "Dictionary of Statistics."** London, George Routledge and Sons, Ltd.; New York, E. P. Dutton and Co., 1911; repr. Detroit, Gale, 1974. 682p. bibliog. index. $27.50. LC 74-2349. ISBN 0-8103-3988-9.

Mulhall's *Dictionary of Statistics* (4th rev. ed., covering the period ρ to November 1898) was originally published by Routledge in 1899 and reprinted by Gale in 1969. It is one of the best older dictionaries of historical statistics.

Webb's dictionary, supplement to Mulhall's, concentrates on economic and social statistics. The 130 subject-oriented chapters are arranged alphabetically—e.g., Accidents, Agricultural Holdings, Agriculture and Live Stock, Alcohol, Aliens. Most of the statistical tables attempt to cover several countries, but some cover only Great Britain (e.g., Aliens). In most cases, sources are provided, with reference to the 325-item bibliography at the end of the volume. Ample cross references and an excellent index facilitate use of the great body of statistical material. All in all, it is a useful reference book for locating historical statistical information that is not readily available in other sources. —Bohdan S. Wynar. [R: ARBA 75, item 876]

HANDBOOKS

330. Mitchell, B. R., and H. G. Jones. **Second Abstract of British Historical Statistics.** New York, Cambridge University Press, 1971. 227p. index. (University of Cambridge, Department of Applied Economics Monographs, No. 18). $13.75. LC 72-129502. ISBN 0-521-08001-0.

This is a supplementary volume to Mitchell and Deane's *Abstract of British Historical Statistics* (1962) intended as a continuation of that work. Essentially, the earlier work included statistical data beginning with 1938, but there are some series of statistics that began too late for inclusion in the earlier volume.

The purpose of the present volume remains the same—"to provide the user of historical statistics with informed access to a wide range of economic data without the labour of identifying sources or of transforming many annual sources into comparable time series" (Introduction). The following areas are covered: population and vital statistics, labor force, agriculture, fuel and power, iron and steel, nonferrous metals, textiles, transport and communications, building, miscellaneous production statistics, overseas trade, wages and the standard of living, national income and expenditure, public finance, banking and insurance, prices, and miscellaneous statistics. In most cases the cutoff year is 1965, but occasionally there are also earlier years. In this new volume, a few chapters have been rearranged; bibliographical material is included (in the introductory texts) only for topics not covered in the first abstract. [R: ARBA 72, item 792]

INDEXES

331. Ross, Ian C., and John W. Tukey. **Index to Statistics and Probability: Locations and Authors.** Los Altos, Calif., R & D Press, 1973. 1092p. (Information Access Series, Vol. 5). $80.00. LC 72-86075. ISBN 0-88274-004-0.

This fifth volume in the publisher's "Information Access Series" is the fourth part of a five-part comprehensive *Index to Statistics and Probability*. Although it may be used separately, it is primarily intended to complement the *Citation Index*, which is the first part of the index (Volume 2 in the series). Its two main sections include full location and authorship information for all source items in the *Citation Index*. Such information is not provided for the reference items in this or other parts of the five-part index unless the source item is also one of the reference items.

The five-part index covers the great bulk of the literature of statistics and probability, United States and foreign, through 1966. Over 5/7 of the source items come from the primary foreign and domestic journals in these disciplines.

The location section in this volume is arranged alphabetically by the four-letter title code assigned to each journal or series. The full title of the journal or series is also provided. The chronologically arranged entries are identified by the abbreviated code (in 17 characters or less) that is used in the *Citation Index* (i.e., year, author code expressed in three characters, volume number, journal title expressed in four characters, and starting page). The following additional information is provided: ending page, number of references, last name of all authors and their initials, and full titles with accents and diacritical marks removed. This section lists only the number of references; it does not list or identify the items cited by each source.

The second section lists authors alphabetically, and their papers chronologically. Lengthy titles are condensed within a single line. Each title entry also includes the abbreviated location code, which is used in the *Citation Index* as well as in the first section of this volume. —LeRoy C. Schwarzkopf. [R: ARBA 75, item 877]

332. Tukey, John W. **Index to Statistics and Probability: The Citation Index.** Los Altos, Calif., R & D Press, 1973. 1269p. (Information Access Series, Vol. 2). $90.00. LC 72-86075. ISBN 0-88274-001-6.

This second volume in the publisher's "Information Access Series" is the first part in a five-part comprehensive *Index to Statistics and Probability*. This exhaustive five-part index covers the great bulk of the literature of statistics and probability, United States and foreign, through 1966. Over 5/7 of the source items come from primary foreign and domestic journals in these disciplines. The remainder come from a wide variety of sources, including proceedings, *Festschriften*, bibliographies, monographs, theses, lectures, compilations, and technical reports. For the period from 1967 to the present, the author recommends the *Science Citation Index* for coverage of these subjects.

This volume, the *Citation Index*, differs in several aspects from the *Science Citation Index* and similar indexes. Arrangement is alphabetical by four-letter code assigned to the title of the journal, series, or monograph rather than the more usual arrangement (i.e., alphabetical by personal or corporate author). Titles and other information are condensed into abbreviated code designations to a greater extent than in the typical citation index. Information on the cited item includes year, volume, and inclusive pages of the paper. Abbreviated single-line titles are also provided at the beginning and end of the entries for each cited journal to enable the user to decipher the code. Entries for the source items are listed chronologically on one line and designate the following: year, author (expressed in three-character code), volume number, journal title (expressed in four-character code), and starting page. These condensed entries provide no identification problems for journals with volume and page numbers, and especially not for the primary journals, whose four-letter codes are readily recognizable. The front and back inside covers of all volumes contain a list of these primary journals with their codes. However, items that are other than journal articles, such as lengthy numbered technical report series, become unintelligible when compressed to a four-character code. The instructions in the front of the volume provide some help in deciphering the code, but they admit that the reader in many cases will have to refer to Volume 6 for positive identification. The index was prepared in collaboration with a number of distinguished statisticians worldwide. It was produced by computer, and is compactly printed in five columns per page. —LeRoy C. Schwarzkopf. [R: ARBA 75, item 878]

CHAPTER 16

ECONOMICS AND BUSINESS

ENCYCLOPEDIAS

333. **Economics 73/74 Encyclopedia.** Guilford, Conn., Dushkin, 1973. 279p. illus. charts. graphs. bibliog. $5.95pa. LC 72-90094. ISBN 0-87967-012-6.

Planned specifically for those without a background in economics, this encyclopedia is the work of 27 authorities from 21 American colleges and universities. It was first constructed topically and then arranged alphabetically for ease of access.

This rather comprehensive volume contains more than 1,000 relatively short entries, which define technical terms, describe economic theories, practices, and institutions, comment on significant court cases, and furnish capsule biographies of eminent economists, both living and dead. While only those articles exceeding 200 words in length are signed, a full list of contributors and their affiliations appears facing the title page. All entries are in one alphabetical arrangement, with numerous cross references, "item guides," and "subject maps" interspersed throughout the book to obviate the need for a separate index and a topical approach. Item guides accompanying 50 key articles point out specific relationships between individual entries and lead from one to another. Similarly, subject maps under 21 major headings, including "Antitrust Policy," "Business Cycles," "Demand," "Federal Budget," "Labor Movement," "Market System," "National Income," "Theory of the Firm," and "Wages," show in a single display the interrelationships among the different articles pertaining to aspects of the important areas of study. "Consult" references at the end of entries are numerically keyed to items in a classified bibliography of rather recent, English-language publications at the back of the volume.

This handsomely printed paperback has been liberally sprinkled with scores of illustrations, photographs, portraits, cartoons, charts, graphs, and tables. There are few instances of duplication, omission, or inconsistency in the well-edited, accurate, and readable articles. This inexpensive, yet valuable, encyclopedia can be used effectively by laymen and students. —Leonard Grundt. [R: Choice, July-Aug 74, p. 734; BL, 15 Sept 74, pp. 105-107]

334. **Encyclopedia of Business Information Sources: A Detailed Listing of Primary Subjects of Interest to Managerial Personnel, with a Record of Sourcebooks, Periodicals, Organizations, Directories, Handbooks, Bibliographies, and other Sources of Information on each Topic.** By Paul Wasserman and others. Detroit, Gale, 1970. 2v. $47.50/set. LC 79-127922.

The first edition of this work was published in three volumes by Business Guides Company in 1965 under the title *Executive's Guide to Information Sources.*

The introduction of the present work states that it "has been compiled expressly to meet the needs of the executive actually engaged in managing an organization, as well as the needs of researchers and scholars who assist him, and to guide students of business as well. The work is also expected to be of service to those working in libraries who seek specific details with regard to factual information sources, since in every instance a complete citation of each entry is provided, including place of publication, address of sponsoring organization, subscription prices, etc. Throughout the work, English language sources have been cited only, except in the case of statistical sources which rely upon numbers rather than text."

In the first volume, the reader will find a topical approach—e.g., such categories as "banks and banking," "government research," or "fashion industry." The second volume covers geographical regions in the United States and foreign countries. Here the essential information will be found under the name of the country, geographical region, or even major city. Thus, in the first volume under "banks and banking" the reader will find the following categories of material: encyclopedias and dictionaries, handbooks and manuals, bibliographies, abstract services and indexes, trade associations, periodicals, directories, biographical sources, statistics sources, almanacs and yearbooks, financial ratios, and "other sources," a category reserved for miscellaneous information. The listing of pertinent sources is highly selective, limited to the most essential works. If, generally speaking, the first volume covers all essential sources, this is not always the case with the second volume. One finds a number of inaccuracies, some entries are not updated, and a number of important standard works are omitted. Obviously, in a work of this magnitude, it is easy to point out editorial deficiencies and omissions. Probably not all secondary sources were sufficiently consulted, including even the commercial catalogs of some book distributors.

What is important, however, is the general impression of a well-balanced work, with a fairly comprehensive coverage of fugitive material. The new edition has many new subject entries and sources dealing with problems of contemporary interest, especially in such areas as ecology, communication systems, community development, urban redevelopment, etc. Remarkably free of jargon, this guide lucidly exposes most pitfalls awaiting the inexperienced user. —Bohdan S. Wynar. [R: AL, Nov 71, pp. 1113-14; ARBA 72, item 802]

335. International Labour Office. **Encyclopaedia of Occupational Health and Safety.** New York, McGraw-Hill, 1972. 2v. illus. index. $49.50/set. LC 74-39329. ISBN 0-07-079555-X.

The first edition of this encyclopedia, entitled *Occupation and Health*, was published between 1930 and 1934 in accordance with the resolution adopted by the First Session of the International Labour Conference in 1919, the year this organization was founded. It contained 416 articles by 95 contributors from 16 different countries. By 1944, six supplements had been issued, containing 52 additional articles.

The present edition is practically a new work; it contains 900 articles prepared by 700 specialists from 70 different countries. All articles are arranged in one alphabet (with cross references) and they are usually accompanied by additional bibliographical references. They vary in length depending on the relative importance of a given subject. For example, the article on antibiotics is two and a half pages long, the same length as the one on asphalt, but the article on the auto-mobile industry has five pages, subdivided by such specific topics as general intro-duction, hazards and their prevention, automobiles—safe design, etc. Most articles are accompanied by technical data and some illustrations.

This is an indispensable reference work for all those concerned with occupa-tional safety and health, since it provides competent practical information in a form that is not too technical even for those with no specialized technical or medical knowledge. The encyclopedia covers all major aspects of the subject, emphasizing industrial hygiene, accident prevention, occupational and social medicine, toxicology, etc., as related to specific subjects. The treatment of a given topic usually has inter-national dimensions. A most authoritative work. —Bohdan S. Wynar. [R: ARBA 73, item 787]

DICTIONARIES

336. **The McGraw-Hill Dictionary of Modern Economics: A Handbook of Terms and Organizations.** 2nd ed. By Douglas Greenwald and others. New York, McGraw-Hill, 1973. 792p. illus. $22.95. LC 72-11813. ISBN 0-07-024369-7.

The first edition of this work was published in 1965. The present edition con-tains brief but concise definitions of some 1,400 frequently used terms in economic theory and applied economics, plus a description of approximately 225 private, public, and non-profit agencies active in the general field of economics and business, including marketing.

An especially helpful feature of this dictionary is the use of appended refer-ences to both current and original sources of information that can provide more detailed information on a given term. Incorporated in the text are numerous charts and statistical tables, which help clarify the definitions. The McGraw-Hill dictionary provides more in-depth information than Sloan and Zurcher's *Dictionary of Eco-nomics* (5th ed. 1970). Compare, for example, the definitions of fringe benefits or peril points in the two dictionaries. In addition, the McGraw-Hill work is certainly much better than Nemmers' *Dictionary of Economics and Business* (Littlefield, Adams, 1970). All in all, this is one of the best one-volume dictionaries on eco-nomic terminology. —Bohdan S. Wynar. [R: WLB, Sept 73, p. 84; Choice, Oct 73, p. 1168; ARBA 74, item 799]

337. Sloan, Harold S., and Arnold J. Zurcher. **Dictionary of Economics.** 5th ed. New York, Barnes & Noble, 1970. 520p. (Everyday Handbooks) $8.50; $2.50pa. LC 70-118099. ISBN 0-389-00237-2; 0-06-463266-0pa.

The first edition of this well-known dictionary was published in 1949, and the fourth in 1961. The dictionary covers basic terminology of the entire field of economics, traditional as well as modern trends. In other words, the user will find here (in addition to quantitative methods and concepts which, for the most part, relate to productivity and income) economic history and theory, international trade, finance and exchange, international commercial policy, public finance, taxation, money, and credit. On a more selective basis, coverage is also provided for more specialized areas such as business cycles, monopoly and competition, price and wage policies, agricultural and labor economics, industrial organization and management, etc. Added to this new edition is a "Descriptive Classification of Defined Terms," a list of definitions in a classified arrangement. The emphasis is on American terminology. —Bohdan S. Wynar. [R: ARBA 72, item 814]

ATLASES

338. **Oxford Economic Atlas of the World.** Prep. by the Cartographic Dept. of the Clarendon Press. Advisory ed., D. B. Jones. 4th ed. New York, Oxford University Press, 1972. 239p. illus. charts. maps. bibliog. index. $25.95; $8.95pa. ISBN 0-19-894106-4; 0-19-894107-2pa.

World maps (90 pages of them) in modified Gall projections are grouped in 13 sections, and the Statistical Supplement is alphabetically arranged by country. The maps provide a world distribution view of eight commodity groups—crops, livestock, forestry and fishing, fibers and textiles, energy (gas, oil, coal, electricity, nuclear), minerals and metals, transport industries, and manufacturing industries. An introductory section of physical geography includes maps of political units, of the environment (temperature, ocean currents, winds), frost incidence, precipitation, seasonal climates, relief, soils, land use, and economic geology (mineral deposits—nature and origin). Four sections provide information on demography, disease, social and political factors, and communications.

Most maps are based on the period from 1963 to 1965, with comparative figures from 1953 to 1955. International boundaries are those that existed in 1965. Maps also show production/yield of commodities, with tables that indicate information for selected countries.

The Statistical Supplement, including a gazetteer of over 8,000 populated places, specific sites (dams, mines), physical features, and administrative divisions, gives statistics for each country from Aden to Zanzibar. In addition, it shows the relative importance of any commodity in the country's economic profile.

Statistics were obtained from international bodies for maximum comparability; where this was impossible, they were obtained from national associations, private companies, and individuals. —Albert C. Vara. [R: Choice, Sept 72, p. 792; ARBA 74, item 808]

339. **Oxford Regional Economic Atlas: Western Europe.** Prepared by the Cartographic Department of the Clarendon Press. Advisory editors: K. M. Clayton and I. B. F. Kormoss. New York, Oxford University Press, 1971. 96p. (plus index). maps (color). $15.00; $6.95pa. ISBN 0-19-894306-7; 0-19-894307-5pa.

This volume, another in the series of Oxford Regional Economic Atlases, provides up-to-date economic data on 17 European member countries of O.E.C.D., plus Andorra, Finland, Liechtenstein, Monaco, Faeroe Islands, Gibraltar, Malta, and San Marino. The topographical maps are at scales of 30, 50, and 100 miles to the inch. Also included is a section of urban land use plans (at six miles to the inch) for Western Europe's major cities. Most of the thematic maps are at 250 miles to the inch, with the exception of the densely populated areas.

Previously published atlases in this series covered Britain and Northern Ireland, India and Ceylon, Pakistan, the United States and Canada, Africa, and the USSR and Eastern Europe. [R: ARBA 72, item 816]

ACCOUNTING

340. Cashin, James A., ed. **Handbook for Auditors**. New York, McGraw-Hill, 1971. 1v. (various paging). index. $29.50. LC 73-116660. ISBN 0-07-010200-7.

One of the most comprehensive handbooks on this subject, with contributions from some 40 subject specialists. Six major areas of auditing are covered in detail in 52 chapters: Principles, Standards and Branches of Auditing; Evaluation and Programming; Objectives and Audit Procedures; Reviews and Reports; Education and Professional Requirements; Horizons for Auditing. All chapters provide additional bibliographical references, and the volume is well indexed. [R: ALA 72; ARBA 72, item 817]

341. Kohler, Eric L. **A Dictionary for Accountants**. 5th ed. Englewood Cliffs, N.J., Prentice-Hall, 1975. 497p. illus. $19.95. LC 74-1393C. ISBN 0-13-209783-4.

Once again this standard dictionary has been revised, expanded, and updated. Since its first edition in 1952, its ease of use and clear dependable definitions have captured for it a large and enthusiastic audience. Now its fifth edition defines over 3,000 terms and concepts in the fields of accounting theory, methods, and practice, and in related areas of management, law, and finance. Definitions for terms included in earlier editions have, in many cases, been expanded here to present new facets of meaning, and over 200 new terms have been added. It defines phrases as well as single words and abbreviations; illustrations, tables, and charts aid in clarifying concepts and terms. While many definitions are short, explanations of some terms fill several pages. The many cross references make it easy to use. A practical, authoritative source, it gives precise meanings in clear language and is useful for the layman as well as the expert. —Winifred F. Dean. [R: ARBA 76, item 843]

ADVERTISING

342. Graham, Irvin. **Encyclopedia of Advertising**. 2nd ed. New York, Fairchild, 1969. 512p. $20.00. LC 68-14544. ISBN 0-87005-014-1.

This is the second edition of a work first published in 1952, now completely revised and updated. It includes some 1,100 entries grouped according to subject covering all major aspects of advertising, marketing, public relations, publicity, media, and electronics. The articles vary in size from a few lines to several pages. A directory of associations is appended. An index would enhance the use of this otherwise well-organized encyclopedia. [R: LJ, 15 Sept 69; ALA 69; ARBA 70, v.1, p. 155]

COMMERCE AND TRADE

343. Ferber, Robert, ed. **Handbook of Marketing Research**. New York, McGraw-Hill, 1974. 1v.(various paging). illus. index. $34.50. LC 73-12967. ISBN 0-07-020462-4.

Another of the many handbooks published by McGraw-Hill, this is a first in the growing and diversified field of marketing research. Both the *Handbook of Modern Marketing*, by Victor Buell (McGraw-Hill, 1970), and the second edition of the *Marketing Handbook*, by Albert W. Frey (Ronald Press, 1965), had sections devoted to marketing research; but there is no publication comparable to this one.

Composed of four sections, each with a number of chapters written by authorities in the field, the book is designed to provide information on the principal methods used in marketing research and to suggest the solution to a wide variety of marketing problems. The first section includes general introductory material, focusing on the history, ethics, functions, and organization of marketing research. Sections two and three cover the quantitative techniques and the behavioral science techniques of marketing research. Each chapter in the last section describes a type of marketing problem and discusses the various techniques for handling the problem, giving illustrations of the use and presenting both sides of each approach.

The editor states in the preface that the book is designed for those who have only a basic knowledge of mathematics and statistics and who are not specialists in the social sciences; and the book meets these qualifications. Each chapter presents a non-technical approach first, followed by material for the advanced reader. Bibliographies (of varying lengths) follow the chapters. A sampling of these shows that few of them list titles more recent than 1970, which is a weakness in this fast-growing field. The numerous illustrations—mostly charts, graphs, tables, and diagrams—reinforce the factual material of the text. They are well placed and, in most cases, clearly presented, although occasionally the printing of many figures in a small space makes them hard to read. The very detailed index refers not only to specific references but also to general topics. —Peggy M. Tozer. [R: Choice, Nov 74, p. 1283; ALA 74; ARBA 75, item 923]

344. **Handbook of Modern Marketing.** Victor P. Buell, editor-in-chief; Carl Heyel, coordinating editor. New York, McGraw-Hill, 1970. 1v.(sectional pagination). illus. index. $27.50. LC 78-96238. ISBN 0-07-008838-1.

One of the most comprehensive handbooks on this subject, this well-designed volume is composed of 20 sections and 120 chapters, each written by a recognized authority in his field. The handbook has been prepared primarily for producers of foods and services, rather than for wholesalers and retailers, although several sections will be useful to these groups as well. It covers such topics as custom services, packaging, industrial design, legal finance, pricing, control, system selling, brand names, corporate identification, international marketing, and specialty types of marketing such as direct mail, automatic retailing, direct to consumer, and franchising. Most business schools now include courses in related disciplines such as mathematics, statistics, operational research, model building and computer usage, in order to provide background for the quantitative approach in marketing. They also include courses in psychology, sociology, and other social sciences to provide qualitative understanding. Both approaches are incorporated in this handbook, which employs extensive cross references and which includes chapter bibliographies and an index. —Bohdan S. Wynar. [R: ALA 71; ARBA 71, item 932]

FINANCE AND BANKING

345. Davis, William. **The Language of Money: An Irreverent Dictionary of Business & Finance.** Boston, Houghton Mifflin, 1973. 267p. bibliog. $6.95. LC 72-2281. ISBN 0-395-13999-6.

An outstandingly useful and informative dictionary of "terms used regularly by economists, specialists in international finance, accountants, stock market dealers and millionaires." Instead of simply translating, it gets as close as possible to the practical meaning of a word or phrase. It strips away the mystique, verbal one-upmanship and mumbo-jumbo from the jargon in an "unorthodox, simple and often amusing" way. This volume, with its superb introduction on the uses of jargon, is written with a light style rarely found in works of this type. Its author is the former financial editor of the *Manchester Guardian* and present editor of *Punch*, which gives some of the definitions a British flavor.

While it is only one-quarter the size of the *McGraw-Hill Dictionary of Modern Economics* and one-tenth the size of Glenn G. Munn's *Encyclopedia of Banking & Finance*, neither of these standard works, with their serious scholarly approach, can substitute for this book in scope, in readability, or in practical value. —Stanley J. Slote. [R: LJ, 15 Feb 73, p. 537; AL, July/Aug 73, p. 426; WLB, June 73, p. 866; ARBA 74, item 797]

346. **European Financial Almanac, 1974-75.** New York, R. R. Bowker, 1974. 755p. index. $50.00. LC 74-22290.

The *European Financial Almanac, 1974-75,* a major new directory of banks and financial institutions, has been compiled by a team of eight European management and business publishing houses under the direction of Gower Press, England. It is available in four language editions—English, German, French, and Italian. Thirteen European nations are included. Nine are current members of the European Economic Community—Belgium, West Germany, Denmark, France, United Kingdom, Italy, Republic of Ireland, Luxemburg, and the Netherlands. The others are Austria, Switzerland, Norway, and Sweden. It is planned to include Spain and Portugal in the next biennial edition.

The first section of the *European Financial Almanac* is a summary for each country of central banks, issuance of currency, monetary controls, laws and regulations, credit, deposit institutions, savings institutions, insurance, supervisory bodies, non-bank lending, financial markets including stock brokers, some history, and so on. These useful succinct essays, which provide practical insight into diverse banking and monetary structures, were written for each nation by one of its leading authorities on finance. No other directory of banks provides this overview.

Part II, a "Directory of Major Organizations," is arranged geographically. Each of the 1,300 entries gives the name of the organization, including foreign bank branches; head office address; telephone, telex, and telegram information; principal activity; founding date; parent company and/or subsidiaries; officers and executives; number of branches; and accounts for 1971, 1972, or 1973 showing assets, profits, capital, and loans. These entries are categorized into subheads such as banking, savings, non-bank lending, financial institutions, insurance, services, and so on, which reflect the individual financial organization of each country.

Part III, of the *Financial Almanac*, "Who's Who in European Finance," lists 2,500 individuals giving title, business address, phone, past appointments, current appointments as directors or executives in other organizations including the date of appointment, marital status, children, education, publications, and club memberships. This "Who's Who," which is another feature unique to the *European Financial Almanac*, is an alphabetical list by name. Geographic access to these individuals is provided in the third index.

The first index is an alphabetic list of banks, with page citations to the geographical entries in Part II. The second index, an alphabetic list of banks and executive officers, is wholly redundant and should be eliminated. Its function is unclear because its data already exist in the "Directory of Organizations" in Part II.

The *European Financial Almanac*'s innovative features add to the information found in the banking directories of Skinner and Rand McNally or add new information in readily accessible form. —Amity Doering. [R: WLB, Sept 75, p. 74; Choice, July/Aug 75, p. 662; ARBA 76, item 886]

347. Munn, Glenn G. **Encyclopedia of Banking and Finance.** 7th ed. Rev. and enl. by F. L. Garcia. Boston, Bankers Publishing Co., 1973. 953p. $49.75. LC 73-83395. ISBN 0-87267-019-8.

The first edition of this standard work was published in 1924, the sixth in 1962. The present edition has been substantially enlarged. It is some 200 pages longer than the sixth edition, with a total of 4,000 entries arranged alphabetically. Like the previous editions, it contains brief definitions of terms—e.g., checque, cheap money, etc.—and a number of encyclopedic articles on money, credit, banking practices, pertinent business laws and federal regulations, investment, insurance, brokerage, and other topics that require in-depth coverage. Professor F. L. Garcia of Fordham University was in charge of this editorial revision. He should be credited with achieving an excellent balance between the more traditional topics.

The clear presentation and the readability of articles are exemplified in the article on the cost of living index. The one-page, double-column article starts with a definition in terms of popular conception of the expression, followed by a technical presentation of its composition and computation, statistical data, and comparisons to other indexes. The article includes a statistical table showing average standard errors of percent changes in the CPI, based on 1971 data. This particular article has no bibliography, but bibliographies and cross references are appended to many of the longer articles. Munn's work furnishes authoritative and readable information on the whole spectrum of banking and related subjects. —Bohdan S. Wynar. [R: ARBA 74, item 800]

348. Thorndike, David. **The Thorndike Encyclopedia of Banking and Financial Tables.** Boston, Warren, Gorham & Lamont, 1973. 1v.(various paging). index. $47.50.

Intended primarily for investors and bankers, this encyclopedia includes a number of financial tables arranged under five broad sections: mortgage and real estate; compound interest and annuity; interest and savings; installment loans; and investment. It covers a rather impressive range of rates, tables, and terms, with adequate explanations preceding each table. The table of variables shows the variables used to construct each table and the values that are found in the body of the table. There is a glossary, the volume is fully indexed, and the type has been set by computer. [R: Choice, Jan 74, p. 1703; ALA 74; ARBA 75, item 958]

349. Woy, James B. **Investment Methods: A Bibliographic Guide.** New York, R. R. Bowker, 1973. 220p. index. $11.95. LC 73-9607. ISBN 0-8352-0631-9.

Listing articles and book sections pertaining to investment methods, this guide is "intended primarily for use by the individual, nonprofessional investor" (Preface). It emphasizes investment writing that is easily understood by non-professionals.

Articles have been selected from over 30 well-known magazines (*Barron's, Changing Times, Fortune,* etc.) covering the years 1965 to early 1973. The major part of the guide, however, consists of entries taken from chapters of books (some 90 titles) on the subject. About 150 subject headings (or descriptors) are used to identify pertinent investment techniques; most of these are briefly defined. (Example: "Dividend value approach. A method of judging stocks based on the theory that the present work of any stock should be determined by the expected dividend payout over future years.") Under this particular descriptor the author lists two entries from books (one from *Security Analysis* and one from *Encyclopedia of Stock Market Techniques*), plus three articles from periodicals. This bibliography seems to be well balanced. Author and title indexes are included. The book will be useful in most business libraries along with Sheldon Zerden's *Best Books on the Stock Market* (R. R. Bowker, 1972) and Woy's own book, *Investment Information: A Detailed Guide to Selected Sources* (Gale, 1970). —Bohdan S. Wynar. [R: WLB, Dec 73, p. 342; ALA 73; ARBA 74, item 823]

350. Zerden, Sheldon. **Best Books on the Stock Market: An Analytical Bibliography.** New York, R. R. Bowker, 1972. 168p. index. $12.95. LC 72-8275. ISBN 0-8352-0547-9.

This well-annotated bibliography of standard sources is arranged by broad subject categories—e.g., methods of investing, history, biography, books for the beginner, general works, textbooks and reference works, etc. A typical entry provides a complete bibliographical description plus a long (one page or so) description of the contents of the book, often with a quote from its preface. Unfortunately, in the important chapter on textbooks and reference works the editor decided to depart from his usual pattern. Instead of describing each of the 40 titles listed here, he has only provided a bibliographical description plus a one-page general introduction to the chapter as a whole. It is an established fact that reference books in this subject matter vary greatly in their quality, but this chapter lists them all without comment. However, the shortcomings of this guide (which has title and subject indexes) are only minor. —Bohdan S. Wynar. [R: ALA 72; ARBA 73, item 838]

INDUSTRY AND MANUFACTURING

351. Brady, George S. **Materials Handbook: An Encyclopedia for Purchasing Managers, Engineers, Executives, and Foremen.** 10th ed. New York, McGraw-Hill, 1971. 1045p. illus. index. $26.50. LC 29-1603. ISBN 0-07-007068-7.

After 42 years and 10 editions, the *Materials Handbook* can be considered a classic. The first edition (1929) began with a small card index. The eighth edition, published in 1956, described over 9,000 materials. The 1963 edition described 12,000 materials and the latest edition 13,000. The scope has also widened over the years. The first edition was limited to the metal-working industries. The latest edition includes new materials in the electronics, aerospace, and nuclear industries.

The book is in two parts. Part one includes straightforward descriptions of over 13,000 materials, their properties and uses. The materials are listed alphabetically by broad type. When a trade name or sub-type of material is given, such as ablative paint under ablative agents, the term is printed in bold type and indexed in the back of the book. Most terms are indexed only once. Other related references in the volume were not indexed. Part two, "Elements of Materials Economics," contains many tables of physical, mechanical, and economic data. It also contains information prepared with the help of the National Association of Purchasing Management, expressing its concept of the materials-educative work of the Association. The book is easy to use and understand, and it contains much ready information. —R. J. Havlik. [R: Choice, Sept 71, p. 807; ARBA 72, item 838]

352. Lund, Herbert F., ed. **Industrial Pollution Control Handbook.** New York, McGraw-Hill, 1971. 1v.(various paging). illus. index. $29.50. LC 70-101164. ISBN 0-07-039095-9.

   This well-written handbook is intended to be "a communication bridge between the best practical experts on industrial pollution problems and all of the responsible industrial managers." Each chapter was prepared by an authority on that topic. An excellent summary of just what the pollution problem is and how federal, state, and local legislation has come to grips with it is presented in the first three chapters. The next six chapters cover programs of control and research currently being conducted. Ten chapters then discuss in detail pollution control in the steel industry, foundry operations, plating operations, metal fabricating plants, the chemical industry, textile mills, food industries, pharmaceutical industries, the pulp and paper industry, and the aerospace and electronics industry. There are five detailed chapters on control equipment and one on operating costs. A glossary and exhaustive index help to make this another outstanding McGraw-Hill handbook. —H. Robert Malinowsky. [R: ALA 72; ARBA 72, item 770]

MANAGEMENT

353. American Arbitration Association. **A Dictionary of Arbitration and Its Terms: A Concise Encyclopedia of Peaceful Dispute Settlement.** Dobbs Ferry, N.Y., Oceana Publications, 1970. 334p. $15.00. LC 70-94692. ISBN 0-379-00386-4.

   This dictionary is the definitive working tool for the layman, specialist, or student in the field of arbitration. The encyclopedic type information is arranged alphabetically with numerous "see also" references. The comprehensive bibliographies at the end of the work are divided into four subject areas: Commercial Arbitration (U.S.), International Commercial Arbitration, International Public Arbitration, and Labor Arbitration. Besides the standard terms used in the arbitration field cases, legal terms and statutes often appear that would be of interest to the student or arbitrator. At the present time, this is the only major dictionary available on the topic of arbitration (or as the compiler, Katharine Seide, defines it, "peaceful dispute settlement"). —Dwight Burlingame. [R: LJ, 1 Oct 70; ALA 70; ARBA 71, item 1029]

354. Heyel, Carl, ed. **The Encyclopedia of Management.** 2nd ed. New York, Van Nostrand Reinhold, 1973. 1161p. illus. index. $34.50. LC 72-11784. ISBN 0-442-23405-8.

   A completely revised edition of a work published in 1963. Over 200 contributors have prepared a total of more than 300 alphabetically arranged entries. Entries range in size from half-page definitions of terms to 30-page articles on such

topics as electronic data processing or PERT. Among the articles completely new to this edition are those on administrative substations, data processing service centers, management information systems, etc.—a total of 31. Appended to longer articles are selective bibliographies for additional reading, which include references to pertinent journals and to standard texts on the subject. The graphs, diagrams, and statistical tables integrated with the text frequently help the reader understand the more complex technical concepts. As an example of this, the well-written article on job evaluation contains seven such illustrations, including hourly job specification, salaried job specification, office jobs (ratings and total points), etc. A well-rounded work, this is probably the best one-volume compendium on the subject.
—Bohdan S. Wynar. [R: WLB, Dec 73, p. 342; ARBA 74, item 872]

355. Roberts, Harold S. **Roberts' Dictionary of Industrial Relations**. Rev. ed. Washington, Bureau of National Affairs, 1971. 599p. bibliog. $15.00. LC 78-175029. ISBN 0-87179-135-8.

A combination dictionary, short-article encyclopedia, and subject bibliography, it provides "a simple yet accurate explanation of terms and phrases currently used in the field of labor-management relations, brief summaries of important cases, short notes on international unions" and about 2,000 individual bibliographies following selected entries. While the second edition has added a few new entries to the original 3,000, the important change has been the updating and expansion of the bibliographies. About 30 percent of the work is taken up by these bibliographies, which refer to between 6,000 and 7,000 "source references."

This is a "must" work for people dealing in industrial relations, the public wishing to understand the specialized terminology, and students in related fields. While the revised edition is 110 pages longer than the first edition, the first edition will suffice for those interested only in the definitions. It is vastly superior to Becker's *Dictionary of Personnel and Industrial Relations* (1958), which has no references and poor definitions, but it might not be adequate in specialized fields.
—Stanley J. Slote. [R: ARBA 73, item 789]

REAL ESTATE

356. Gross, Jerome S. **Illustrated Encyclopedic Dictionary of Real Estate Terms**. Englewood Cliffs, N.J., Prentice-Hall, 1969. 468p. illus. facsims. forms. $16.00. LC 69-16348.

This dictionary provides definitions of over 2,500 alphabetically arranged terms—terms that deal with policies and programs, legal phrases, technical expressions and jargon. The book also contains sample forms fully illustrated; tables of amortization, taxes, measurements and rates; abbreviations, etc. Friedman's *Encyclopedia of Real Estate Appraising* (Prentice-Hall, 1968) will supplement this volume. [R: ALA 70; ARBA 71, item 1053]

CHAPTER 17

FINE ARTS

GENERAL WORKS

357. Gardner, Helen. **Art Through the Ages**. 5th ed. Rev. by Horst de la Croix and Richard G. Tansey. New York, Harcourt, Brace & World, 1970. 801p. illus. index. $11.95. LC 76-79933. ISBN 0-15-503752-8.

Since the first edition appeared in 1926, Gardner's historical survey has been most popular among high school students and undergraduate students as a readable and well-illustrated narrative of historical development in fine arts, covering a wide range of subjects. Miss Gardner completed the third edition shortly before her death in 1946, and the fourth edition was prepared in 1959 by Sumner Crosby and his colleagues at Yale University. The 1970 edition introduced a number of important changes. It departed from previous editions in its concentration on the arts in Europe and their ancient antecedents, but the arts of Asia, primitive art, and the art of America were still excluded. The text was thoroughly rewritten and updated, and a number of color plates and new illustrative material were added. [Editor's note: The fifth edition was published in 1975 (959p. LC 74-22995. ISBN 0-15-503753-6). It includes new material on primitive and other non-European art forms, and an expanded chapter on the twentieth century. Illustrative material includes 56 leaves of plates.] [R: ARBA 71, item 1077]

BIBLIOGRAPHIES

358. Ehresmann, Donald L. **Fine Arts: A Bibliographic Guide to Basic Reference Works, Histories, and Handbooks**. Littleton, Colo., Libraries Unlimited, 1975. 283p. index. $13.50. LC 74-32452. ISBN 0-87287-070-7.

The need for a new guide to the bibliography of the fine arts has become more and more apparent with the increase of publications in the field. Dr. Ehresmann, professor at the University of Illinois at Chicago Circle, has taken on this task. He defines the scope of his work in the preface: books published before 1900 are not included, since Chamberlin's *Guide to Art Reference Books* covers this period. He includes only classic and standard works between 1900 and 1958, the cut-off date of Chamberlin. His own cut-off date is December 31, 1973, though a few important items of later imprint do appear. He also restricts his list to volumes in Western European languages that deal with at least two major art forms. This excludes some single volumes that form part of a multi-volume series, such as the "Pelican History of Art." Also excluded are books on the minor arts (graphic arts, decorative arts), collecting, and museology, which are to be covered in another bibliography.

The section on books dealing with iconography will be a boon to those who work in this complicated field. The listing of topographical handbooks and national inventories of art and architecture is greater than in Chamberlin and will be of special interest to architecture librarians. The extensive review of this book by Christina Bostick (ARLIS/NA *Newsletter*, Summer 1975) points out some of the anomalies in the bibliography and mentions the inadequacies of the subject index. For example, though there is a section on North American Indian art in the body of the book, the subject index mentions only "North Coast Indian Art, bibliography" under any of the keywords. The table of contents will be much more fruitful for the subject approach. An interesting addition to the bibliography as a whole is a suggested list of books for small libraries, compiled by the author's wife, Julia Ehresmann. This will be useful for checking, surveying, and adding to a small collection. —Julia Sabine. [R: WLB, Oct 75, p. 123; LJ, 1 Oct 75, p. 1810; ARBA 76, item 915]

CATALOGS AND COLLECTIONS

359. McCoy, Garnett. **Archives of American Art: A Directory of Resources.** New York, R. R. Bowker, 1972. 163p. index. $20.00. LC 72-5215. ISBN 0-8352-0598-3.

Founded in 1954, the Archives of American Art is a collection of the personal papers of artists, dealers, collectors, and curators and other primary source material necessary to the scholar involved in art research. This catalog lists and briefly describes the 555 groups of papers that make up the Archives and that are available in microfilm at five regional centers or through interlibrary loan. Entries are arranged alphabetically by name of artist or institution and include the name of owner or donor, types and numbers of items, dates covered by the collection, and general description. A comprehensive index provides access to the many names within the collections. This publication, well done and easy to use, is the only available approach to the Archives. —Marilyn Gell. [R: LJ, 15 Dec 72, p. 3980; ARBA 72; ARBA 73, item 919]

ENCYCLOPEDIAS

360. **The Britannica Encyclopedia of American Art.** Chicago, Encyclopaedia Britannica Educational Corp.; distr. New York, Simon and Schuster, 1974. 669p. illus.(part col.). bibliog. (A Chanticleer Press Edition). $29.95. LC 73-6527. ISBN 0-671-21616-3.

This is the first major encyclopedic work devoted solely to American art. Its broad definition of art includes photography, landscape architecture, handcrafts, industrial design, and even circus wagons, in addition to the usual genres of painting, sculpture, architecture, etc.

The encyclopedia is beautifully laid out with many well-chosen illustrations (both color and black and white). Topical entries, in alphabetical order, include persons, periods, movements, etc., and range in length from several pages to brief paragraphs. Most entries are signed with the initials of the contributors, who are listed at the front of the book.

The main criticism of this encyclopedia stems from its selection of topics for inclusion. The editors' disclaimer in the foreword ("informed readers will note omissions, especially of the work of younger artists whose reputations have yet to stand the test of time") does not excuse many of the omissions. For instance, try to find American Indian art, or any Wyeth other than Andrew. Coverage of artistic styles or movements is also uneven. Romanticism and surrealism are here, but realism and the New Realism (or California School of Realism) are not. Museums and other notable collections of art are included in an appended directory entitled "Guide to Museums and Public Collections."

The lack of an index is a major handicap in using this encyclopedia, but numerous cross references are provided in two ways: 1) within entries, where an asterisk follows a name that is an entry itself; and 2) directly, as in "New York School, see Abstract Expressionism." However, many articles include significant mentions of people or events that do not have entries of their own, and without an index there is no way to locate this material.

Supplementary materials in the *Britannica Encyclopedia of American Art* are a glossary, a guide to entries by arts, a guide to museums and public collections, and a bibliography. The bibliography is in two sections—general works (by subject), and then a bibliography according to entries.

This encyclopedia is an important item because of the wealth of material here that is not in other sources. —Sally Wynkoop. [R: BL, 1 Dec 74, p. 389; Choice, Mar 74, p. 56; ALA 73; ARBA 75, item 996]

361. **Praeger Encyclopedia of Art**. New York, Praeger, 1971. 5v. illus. (some col.). bibliog. index. $150.00/set. LC 75-122093. ISBN 0-275-47490-9.

This five-volume encyclopedia is based on the French encyclopedia *Dictionnaire universel de l'art et des artistes*, published in three volumes by Fernand Hazan in Paris in 1967.

This English edition is copyrighted by Pall Mall Press in London. According to the Preface, "the purpose of this encyclopedia is to provide, within reasonable limitations of space, a comprehensive and authoritative reference guide for both student and general reader—as well as a lively appreciation of the history of world art." There are some 4,000 alphabetically arranged entries (including some 1,000 survey articles) covering periods, styles, schools, and movements. There are 3,000 articles on individual artists from all nations and periods. The text is well integrated with the excellent illustrations (1,700 in color) and there are about 1,000 pictures per volume. Liberal cross references and a general index are included.

Some comparison with the recently published *McGraw-Hill Dictionary of Art* might be in order. The McGraw-Hill work includes 15,000 entries with 2,500 longer articles. The text in the Praeger encyclopedia is arranged in four columns and has about 300,000 fewer words than the McGraw-Hill work. In terms of contributors, the present work seems somewhat better balanced (100 contributors of various nationality backgrounds with many French, as opposed to 125 American and British contributors in McGraw-Hill's dictionary). The emphasis in the two works is on slightly different types of material. For example, it seems that certain topics (e.g., Swedish art or Baroque art) are better documented here; on the other hand, the McGraw-Hill dictionary offers a number of brief articles on art centers or about art techniques not represented in Praeger. In other words, the two works complement and supplement each other. They are not designed for the specialist but contain a wealth of information for the layman. [R: WLB, May 71, p. 883; LJ, July 71, p. 2296; ALA 71; ARBA 72, item 946]

DICTIONARIES

362. Mayer, Ralph. **A Dictionary of Art Terms and Techniques.** New York, Thomas Y. Crowell, 1969. 447p. illus.(part col.). $8.95; $4.95pa. LC 69-15414. ISBN 0-690-23673-5; 0-8152-0371-3pa.

Presents some 3,200 concise definitions of terms encountered in the study and practice of the visual arts and their literature, with emphasis on materials and methods of the artist. Materials are defined in terms of composition, source, use, and characteristic properties; processes and techniques in terms of their practical application and results. Tools and equipment are described and illustrated. The areas covered include painting, drawing, sculpture, printmaking, ceramics and a number of closely related fields. Purely architectural terms are omitted, and there are no separate biographic entries for artists or authors, although some of them are named in entries dealing with schools, periods, and the techniques with which they are associated. The definitions are readable and clear, with references to different spellings, explanations of foreign terms, etc. A short bibliography of especially useful works is appended to this dictionary, which has special interest to commercial artists. Mr. Mayer has an international reputation and is the author of *The Artist's Handbook of Materials and Techniques* and *The Painter's Craft*. [R: SR, 6 Dec 69; LJ, 1 Jan 70; ALA 69; ARBA 70, v.2, p.2]

363. **McGraw-Hill Dictionary of Art.** Edited by Bernard S. Myers; Assistant Editor, Shirley D. Myers. New York, McGraw-Hill, 1969. 5v. illus.(part col.). bibliog. $115.00. LC 68-26314.

This is not an abridgment of the monumental 15-volume *Encyclopedia of World Art*, also published by McGraw-Hill, but an independent work. As one might expect, the dictionary treatment of material is more popular.

This dictionary contains approximately 15,000 entries in alphabetical arrangement, covering all important countries and periods and all major areas of architecture, painting, sculpture, and decorative and graphic arts. There is a wide range of entries, including biographies, definitions, concepts, schools and trends, and description of the major monuments and museums and individual works of art. Depending on the topic, these articles vary in length from 25 to 2,000 words; they were written by a total of 125 contributors. Entries are extensively cross-referenced. For example, biographies are cross-referenced to stylistic articles and general period articles are cross-referenced to individual artists, monuments, and definitions of terms. The text is accompanied by numerous illustrations—1,700 halftones, 400 full color photographs, and 200 line drawings. [R: WLB, Oct 69; LJ, 1 Nov 69; SR, 6 Dec 69; ALA 69; ARBA 70, v.2, p. 2]

364. Myers, Bernard S., and Shirley D. Myers, eds. **Dictionary of 20th Century Art.** New York, McGraw-Hill, 1974. 440p. illus. bibliog. index. $9.95. LC 74-4200. ISBN 0-07-044220-7.

This compact reference work on the art of our century is prepared for students, general readers, and those wanting the basic facts on a modern artist or movement. As clearly stated in the preface, the co-editors carefully selected most of the entries from their earlier work, the five-volume *McGraw-Hill Dictionary of Art* (1969). A few new entries were prepared but most were previously published in the larger work, frequently with a fuller entry. However, the concentration on art history from about 1905 to the contemporary scene is welcome. The editors bring a wealth of expertise to the project, which emphasizes biography. The dates and locations of art works mentioned in the biographic entries appear in parentheses after each title. While not for the specialist or advanced student, this dictionary should be useful in general reference collections in addition to branch and art school libraries. —William J. Dane. [R: ARBA 75, item 999]

365. **Phaidon Dictionary of Twentieth-Century Art.** New York, Phaidon; distr. New York, Praeger, 1973. 420p. illus. $15.00. LC 72-86572. ISBN 0-7148-1557-8.

This listing of over 1,600 individual artists and 140 concepts, groups, and movements is a good basic source of information on twentieth century art. Artists from Europe, South America, and other parts of the world are listed, as well as those painters and sculptors working in England and the United States. Unfortunately, art seems to be rather narrowly defined as painting and sculpture; architecture, photography, other forms, technical terms, and processes are not represented. Entries include standard biographical information, a short description of the artist's work and his relationship to other artists or movements, and, in many instances, a selected bibliography. Representative art works are reproduced in black and white in an appendix. There are, of course, omissions and inconsistencies, as it seems there must be in a work of this type. In general, however, the material is straightforward and well written. In addition, the dictionary includes artists who are difficult to identify from other available sources. —Marilyn Gell. [R: Choice, Nov 73, p. 1360; WLB, June 73, p. 869; LJ, 15 Apr 73, p. 1270; ALA 73; ARBA 74, item 904]

366. **A Visual Dictionary of Art.** Ed. by Ann Hill and others. Greenwich, Conn., New York Graphic Society, 1973. 640p. illus.(part col.). maps. bibliog. index. $30.00. LC 73-76181. ISBN 0-8212-0424-6.

A handy, one-volume compendium of some 4,500 short entries, covering the time span from the earliest period to modern times. The dictionary stresses painting and sculpture, with special emphasis on the non-Western arts. The text is richly illustrated with some 2,000 black and white photographs, plus 250 color plates. As an introduction, 30 essays outline important styles and periods, comprising a brief history of art. Many biographical entries cover lesser-known figures; there is also an analytical index that covers items mentioned in the text of main entries, plus a selective bibliography.

This work is obviously not as comprehensive as the well-known *McGraw-Hill Dictionary of Art* (1969; 5v.) or the 15-volume *Encyclopedia of World Art*, published by McGraw-Hill in 1967. *A Visual Dictionary*, however, is comparable to several of the other one-volume compilations on art. It contains less information on architecture than the *Oxford Companion to Art* (Oxford University Press, 1970; 1277p.; 3,000 entries). Peter and Linda Murray's *Dictionary of Art and Artists* (Penguin Books, 1972; 457p.; $2.65pa.) emphasizes Western art. Nevertheless,

A Visual Dictionary is well edited and contains a great deal of information. [R: Choice, Nov 74, p. 1288; LJ, 15 June 74, p. 1694; ALA 74; ARBA 75, item 1000]

367. Walker, John A. **Glossary of Art, Architecture and Design since 1945: Terms and Labels Describing Movements, Styles and Groups Derived from the Vocabulary of Artists and Critics.** Hamden, Conn., Linnet Books, 1973. 240p. bibliog. index. $10.50. LC 73-3339. ISBN 0-208-01194-3.

The increase in the number of art terms and labels during the past three decades has caused innumerable problems for students, readers of art periodicals, and art reference librarians. Neither card catalog subject entries nor the *Art Index* has been able to keep up with the new art terms. Both an artist and an art librarian, John Walker is admirably qualified to compile this up-to-the-minute, indispensable glossary, which also includes conceptual and theoretical entries.

Alphabetically arranged entries, culled from current publications including journals and exhibition catalogs, provide 378 thorough, yet concise, definitions or explanations, each followed by bibliographies. Painting, sculpture, and architecture are well covered. Labels such as Archigram, Correspondence Art, Destructive Art, Earthwork Architecture, Fluxus, Hermeticism, Indeterminate Architecture, Judd's Dictum, Supermannerism, Usco, Verwischung—as well as the less obscure terms such as Constructivism, Cybernetic, Kinetic, Laser, Op, and Pop—are easily located. A meticulously compiled index, which includes artists, subjects, and exhibitions, also lists *see* references from one term to another. It would have been more convenient if the *see* references had been included in the text of the book rather than in the index, but this is an insignificant point compared to the enormous contribution our British colleague has made towards improving reference services. —Jacqueline Sisson. [R: Choice, Oct 73, p. 1172; WLB, Oct 73, p. 164; LJ, 1 Sept 73, p. 2424; ALA 74; ARBA 74, item 905]

DIRECTORIES

368. **American Art Directory, 1974.** 45th ed. Ed. by the Jaques Cattell Press for the American Federation of Arts. New York, R. R. Bowker, 1974. 457p. index. $32.00. LC 99-1016. ISBN 0-8352-0647-5.

This latest edition of a standard reference tool provides an absolutely essential listing for the field of contemporary art bibliography. It has been expanded by 89 pages over the 1970 edition, and all entries have been updated.

The principal contents are geographic listings of over 3,000 art museums, organizations, and art schools in the United States, Canada, and abroad. In addition, highly useful sections include listings of state art councils, junior museums, art magazines, newspapers carrying art notes, scholarships and fellowships, supervisors of art education in our school systems, and travelling exhibitions. The entries for museums and schools provide quantities of specific information including lists of curators, hours, collection specialties, publications, curricula, and tuition costs. The American Federation of Arts is to be congratulated on the sweep and scope of the 45th edition of this directory, which is fact-packed. This record of current visual art activity in the United States and Canada rates as a major reference book. —William J. Dane. [R: BL, 15 May 74, p. 1014; ARBA 75, item 1007]

369. **Directory of Art and Antique Restoration**. Arthur Porter and Elizabeth Taylor, eds. San Francisco, Directory of Art and Antique Restoration, 1975. 251p. index. $8.50.

This directory of artisans in the United States has five divisions: Antique Restoration, Art Restoration, Parts, Restoration and Repair Services, and Repair of Specific Items. The last section is further divided into such categories as tapestries, quilts, player pianos, needlepoint, drapes, etc. In each of the divisions the craftsmen are listed alphabetically by state and city. This is a new edition of the work first published in 1972; the format is the same, although according to the editors there are 25 percent more entries. Also, the index has been enlarged and there are advertisements for services at the end. Neither the first nor the new edition indicates the criteria used to choose the listings or the method of acquiring information on the listings. A welcome source of information on art and antique restoration services. —Mary D. Malinowsky. [R: ALA 72; ARBA 76, item 960]

INDEXES

370. Havelice, Patricia Pate. **Index to Artistic Biography**. Metuchen, N.J., Scarecrow, 1973. 2v. $37.50. LC 72-6412. ISBN 0-8108-0540-5.

This massive reference guide to biographic information covers 70,000 artists. The compiler used 64 art publications as sources for the listing of international artists active from antiquity to contemporary times. The source books were published between 1902 and 1970 in 10 different languages. The listing is truly international; it includes artists from Iceland, Israel, Norway, Scotland, Japan, Australia, Poland, Argentina, and Brazil, in addition to the more standard entries for European, British, and American artists. Cross references are used for alternate names and for variant spellings, while the information for each artist includes dates, nationality, media, and pseudonyms.

A random checking of a cross section of contemporary and nineteenth century artists proved successful, although a number of the death dates that are omitted could have been found with further research. There are 90 entries under the name of Jones, and well over 200 Smiths listed. Since we are living in a time of aggressive art collecting by institutions and individuals, there is a real need for this type of art research tool; this index immediately takes a place of prominence in the realm of art biography. —William J. Dane. [R: WLB, Oct 73, p. 168; Choice, Nov 73, p. 1356; LJ, 1 Sept 73, p. 2423; ALA 73; ARBA 74, item 913]

BIOGRAPHY

371. Canaday, John. **The Lives of the Painters. Vol. I: Late Gothic to High Renaissance. Vol. II: Baroque. Vol. III: Neoclassic to Post-Impressionist. Vol. IV: Plates and Index**. New York, Norton, 1969. 4v. illus.(part col.). index. $40.00/set. LC 67-17666. ISBN 0-393-04231-6.

Mr. Canaday, the art critic of *The New York Times*, provides a highly readable reference history of Western painting and its artists by means of biographic and critical essays on more than 450 individual painters, Giotto through Cézanne.

Following an over-all chronological pattern, each of 29 chapters groups the artists around a centralizing theme, be it style, genre, or nationality. Each chapter begins with a unifying historical-critical introduction that is designed to guide the reader through the biographies, but is not supported with bibliographic apparatus.

The Lives of the Painters is elegantly produced in four slip-cased volumes. The first three volumes contain the biographies of the painters; the fourth volume contains more than 500 reproductions of the works of each of the artists Mr. Canaday discusses—176 full-page, full-color reproductions and 352 monochrome pictures. Certainly, this work is a challenge to Vasari's *Lives of the Great Italian Painters, Sculptors and Architects.* [R: LJ, 15 Sept 69; NYTBR, 7 Dec 69; SR, 6 Dec 69; ALA 69; ARBA 70, v.2, p. 5]

372. **Creative Canada: A Biographical Dictionary of Twentieth-Century Creative and Performing Artists.** Comp. by Reference Division, McPherson Library, University of Victoria. Buffalo, N.Y., University of Toronto Press, 1971– . index. $15.00/v. In progress. LC 72-151387. ISBN 0-8020-3262-1(v.1); 0-8020-3285-0(v.2).

As indicated in the first volume of this projected series, the purpose of the work is to cover those "creative and performing artists who have contributed as individuals to the culture of Canada in the twentieth century, and who have had this individual contribution recognized in print. The amount of critical acclaim in print has been a guide to the compilers, since it is inconceivable in this era of the media and the message that any artist will be of significance if he has not received critical acclaim in books, journal articles, or newspapers."

According to the stated objectives, authors of "works of the imagination" are included, such as "artists and sculptors, musicians, and performing artists in the fields of ballet, modern dance, radio, theatre, television, and motion pictures; directors, designers, and producers in theatre, cinema, radio and television, and the dance." Excluded are architects, commercial artists, creators of handicraft and patrons of the arts, as well as journalists, historians, etc., "unless they have an established reputation as individual artists in one of the categories listed above."

Each volume contains about 500 entries listed in one alphabetical arrangement. The length of the biographical sketches varies from a few lines to several pages. As stated in the Preface to the second volume, "an artist of some stature producing very little actual material will not have as lengthy an entry as another of equal or lesser importance who has produced a great deal." It is not enough simply to provide inventory-type information and put it into proper perspective. Although this is an interesting work and provides a great deal of detail that will not be found elsewhere, it is out of balance in terms of editorial attention. In addition, an index by profession is an essential ingredient in works of this type. In spite of its deficiencies, this is a unique work. [R: ARBA 72, item 949; ARBA 73, item 920]

ARCHITECTURE

373. Fleming, John and others. **The Penguin Dictionary of Architecture.** Baltimore, Penguin, 1969 (c.1966). 247p. illus. $3.95pa. LC 66-2846. ISBN 0-14-051013-3.

The number of concise low-priced architectural dictionaries on the market is small, and this work is as good as any, as well as being the cheapest. It is aimed at amateur students of architecture and covers architects, terms, materials, ornamentation, styles and movements, and types of buildings. The authors are all authorities, and Pevsner is one of the best-known writers in the field today. They have shown care in their choice of entries, their definitions and their terminology. The work's coverage is very good, including entries corresponding to a third of the architectural entries in such a comprehensive work as the *McGraw-Hill Dictionary of Art* and a significant number not found there, besides. While the illustrations included are nicely drawn, they are sometimes confusing and rather scanty, numbering only 86 small figures. One of the amateur's greatest difficulties in understanding architecture is visualizing the myriad small facets which make up individual buildings. The look and shape of these things are often difficult to convey in words, hence the particular necessity of illustrations in a work of this sort. Many of those in this work are confusing because they show a larger thing without pointing out specifically the smaller part of it which is named in the caption and is the true subject. John Harris and Jill Lever's *Illustrated Glossary of Architecture, 850-1830* (New York, Clarkson N. Potter, 1966) comes closest to fulfilling this need of amateurs to have things "pointed out" to them. Its illustrations have terms in the margins with lines drawn to the part named. This cavil aside, the present work may be recommended for its conciseness and authority. —Dennis North. [R: ARBA 71, item 1104]

GRAPHIC ARTS

374. Beall, Karen F., comp. **American Prints in the Library of Congress: A Catalogue of the Collection.** Baltimore, Published for the Library of Congress by Johns Hopkins Press, 1970. 568p. illus. index. $35.00. LC 73-106134. ISBN 0-8108-1077-9.

This is an outstanding reference book in the field of graphic art. It documents the work of 1,250 artists, listing about 12,000 American prints stretching from Colonial times to today. Over 1,600 illustrations are reproduced in this complete catalog of a great print collection specializing in American graphic art. The informative entries, arranged alphabetically by artists, are followed by lists of the artists' prints owned by the Library of Congress. For each print title is given the date of execution, place of publication, printer, date of publication (if different from execution date), and medium. Print measurements are given in centimeters, followed by analytical notes of considerable research value. The extensive listings for Arms, Pennell, Sloan, and Whistler are nearly catalogues raisonnés for these prolific artists. Indexes for geographic iconography, names, and series, a list of print societies and clubs, and a select bibliography are welcome additions to this outstanding title, which immediately takes a place of major importance in the bibliography of American art history. —William J. Dane. [R: ARBA 71, item 1125]

375. Dreyfuss, Henry. **Symbol Sourcebook: An Authoritative Guide to International Graphic Symbols.** New York, McGraw-Hill, 1972. 292p. illus. index. $28.50. LC 71-172261. ISBN 0-07-017837-2.

Henry Dreyfuss has been collecting and codifying symbols for at least two decades. These have come to him from all over the world and have been stored in a data bank in California, which now contains over 20,000 symbols. It is on this collection that the sourcebook is based. The purpose of the work is to collect and codify graphic symbols "as they are used in all walks of life throughout the world."

The introductory material contains a foreword by R. Buckminster Fuller, an introduction by Dreyfuss, a brief study of "Semantography: One Writing for One World," by C. K. Bliss, and "Isotype: Education Through the Eye," by Marie Neurath. This is followed by a short section on "Basic Symbols." The main section, with more than 6,000 graphic symbols, is organized alphabetically by broad subject, such as Agriculture; Architecture; Business; Chemistry; Communications; Engineering; Folklore; Geography; Home Economics; Manufacturing; Mathematics; Medicine; Meteorology; Music; Photography; Physics; Recreation; Religion. A unit on "Graphic Forms" groups symbols by form only (circles, crosses, etc.), permitting a basis for comparison. Another unit deals with the symbology of color, and there is a most extensive bibliography of related articles and books. A detailed index facilitates use.

One of the aims of this work is to codify and promote the use of symbols as a means of facilitating communication. The author briefly comments on the various national and international standards organizations that have played a significant part in the universal acceptance of symbols.

The task of assembling universally used graphic symbols into a convenient reference source to serve as a practical and easy-to-use guide to symbol information has been successfully accomplished in this book. —Paul A. Winckler. [R: LJ, 15 Mar 72, p. 1002; ALA 72; ARBA 73, item 928]

376. Mason, Lauris, comp. **Print Reference Sources: A Select Bibliography; 18th-20th Centuries.** Millwood, N.Y., Kraus-Thomson, 1975. 246p. $20.00. LC 74-79901. ISBN 0-527-00372-7.

Lauris Mason, dealer in prints, has compiled a long-needed selective bibliography of sources of information that deal with close to 1,300 printmakers within the designated time span. Designed as an aid to research, the work is planned primarily "for the use of collectors, curators, librarians, dealers, auction cataloguers, and print lovers."

The printmakers appear in alphabetical order by last name, in most cases with vital dates included. Each is followed by from one to twenty-two bibliographic entries, the latter being the number for James McNeill Whistler. Cross references are used for variant forms of names. The entries, averaging about three per subject, are arranged by date of publication and include usual imprint information and relevant pagination, when appropriate. Among the items selected for inclusion are a number of out-of-print works as well as some published as late as 1974; reprintings and forthcoming titles are indicated. A frequently cited work is the Library of Congress's *American Prints in the Library of Congress: A Catalog of the Collection*, compiled by Karen F. Beall (1970). Its title notwithstanding, the work appears to be thorough and without conspicuous omissions. This unique reference bibliography provides a sturdy foundation for the growing interest in prints and printmakers and for further efforts in the field. —Donald G. Davis, Jr. [R: Choice, Oct 75, p. 982; BL, 1 Dec 75, p. 530; ARBA 76, item 941]

377. Stevenson, George A. **Graphic Arts Encyclopedia.** New York, McGraw-Hill, 1968. 492p. illus. bibliog. index. $17.50. LC 67-24445. ISBN 0-07-061287-0.

This alphabetical guide for illustration preparation and reproduction defines and describes the terms and techniques of the trade. It covers tools used in the formation of the original image, the kind of image produced and materials used in making the image impression, as well as offering explanation of applications of Xerography, computerized hot metal and cold-composition line castings, programmed process photography and platemaking techniques, and electrostatic screen print. Entries vary in length, depending on the topic; some are short essays. It is not as comprehensive in textual coverage as Strauss's more general *The Printing Industry* (R. R. Bowker, 1967), but it has better and more numerous illustrations. The information is more up to date than that in Edward Allen's comprehensive *Harper Dictionary of Graphic Arts* (1963). A well-selected bibliography, trade and product information, and index conclude this useful and up-to-date handbook for the commercial artist, layout man, and designer. [R: LJ, 15 Jan 69; ARBA 70, v.1, p.17]

SCULPTURE

378. Clapp, Jane. **Sculpture Index.** Metuchen, N.J., Scarecrow, 1970-71. 2v. $32.50(v.1); $37.50(v.2). LC 79-9538. ISBN 0-8108-0249-X(v.1); 0-8108-0311-9(v.2).

This work indexes about 950 sources, including art histories, museum catalogs, and art reference books. Except for a few European museum catalogs, all are in English. Periodical articles and monographs on individual artists are excluded. Locations of original sculptures are indicated, and there is a very impressive 157-page list of public and private collections arranged by country and city. The shorter list (four pages) of names of collections without location may present problems for the searcher.

Although emphasis is placed on work since 1900, sculpture from all periods is included. Volume 1 covers Europe and the contemporary Middle East; volume 2 covers the Americas, the Orient, Africa, the Pacific area, and the classical world.

The index is alphabetically arranged under names of sculptures, by titles and subjects. Nationality and dates are given for sculptors; for their works, the original and present location(s), material used, dimensions in inches, museum identification number, and the sources where illustrations are found. Types of sculpture include portraits, architectural elements, church accessories, and a variety of decorative objects such as masks, jewelry, fountains, and musical instruments. Major subjects include countries, by century (extensively covered) and by major art periods (unevenly covered). Minor subjects cover a very impressive range of people, deities, animals, battles, games, sports, coins, buildings, and themes.

This is a well-made, much-needed reference book that will serve both as a source for illustrations of sculpture and as a general illustration index. —Paul Breed. [R: LJ, 1 June 70, p. 2132; LJ, 15 Apr 71, p. 1352; RQ, Winter 71, p. 173; ALA 71; ARBA 72, item 978]

379. Maillard, Robert, ed. **New Dictionary of Modern Sculpture.** Trans. from the French by Bettina Wadia. New York, Tudor, 1971. 328p. illus. $12.50. LC 70-153118. ISBN 0-8148-0479-9.

A translation of *Nouveau dictionnaire de la sculpture moderne* (first published in 1960 under the title *Dictionnaire de la sculpture moderne*, which appeared under the English title *Dictionary of Modern Sculpture*; New York, Tudor, 1960).

The first edition of this work had biographical and critical sketches of 412 modern sculptors (beginning with Rodin), with 453 illustrations of their works. This revision has about 200 additional artists and an equal number of new illustrations. Articles are initialed by the 34 contributors, a distinguished list including Robert Cogniat, Carola Giedion-Welcker, and Nello Ponente. Biographical information is minimal; emphasis is placed on a sculptor's artistic career, medium, style, and characteristics of work. Important exhibitions are mentioned, along with a few of an artist's best-known works. Usually one or two illustrations appear for each sculptor, but for a few there are none. The brief, succinct descriptions of the salient features of sculptors' works are very well done, but the small space allotted for articles results in truncation (from half a column to three columns) and no bibliographical references are provided.

The dictionary is strictly biographical—there are no articles on movements, countries, or other subjects, and there is no index of subjects or of illustrations. Nevertheless, modern sculptors from all parts of the world are well represented. —Paul Breed. [R: Choice, July-Aug 72, p. 626; ARBA 73, item 939]

380. Richter, Gisela M.A. **The Sculpture and Sculptors of the Greeks.** 4th ed. rev. New Haven, Conn., Yale University Press, 1970. 317p. illus. index. $37.50. LC 70-99838. ISBN 0-300-01281-0.

This is a new edition of a firmly established reference book in the field, the first edition having appeared in 1929. Miss Richter, Curator of Classical Art at the Metropolitan Museum before her retirement, combines knowledge, enthusiasm, and skillful writing in the presentation of her material.

The book is divided into two major sections. Part one discusses the sculpture through a chronological survey, followed by chapters on general characteristics, the human figure, the head, drapery, composition, animals, and technique. Part two covers individual sculptors and their followers in chronological order from the archaic period through the first century B.C. Of special reference value is a twelve-page chronology of outstanding sculptures, an excellent up-dated bibliography, an extensive index to the text, an index to the illustrations, and a list of illustrations indicating the material of the sculptures and their location. The more than 800 illustrations referred to in the main body of the text are gathered at the end of the volume, a very satisfactory working arrangement.

Miss Richter states that she has been able to make many additions and corrections in the text in the light of new discoveries and acquisitions. There also have been additions and improvement in the section of illustrations. Although the discussion is technical and the analysis detailed, one never loses sight of the broad transitional pattern of the five centuries of sculptural development that are covered. The book is of value to both the general reader and the serious student. —Joan E. Burns. [R: ARBA 71, item 1133]

PAINTING

381. **Catalogue de reproductions de peintures 1860 à 1973: et quinze plans d'expositions/Catalogue of Reproductions of Paintings 1860 to 1973: With Fifteen Projects for Exhibitions/Catalogo de reproducciones de pinturas 1860 a 1973: y quince proyectos de exposiciones.** Paris, Unesco; distr. New York, Unipub, 1974. 343p. illus. index. $13.20pa. ISBN 92-3-001123-1.

This is the tenth revised edition (ninth edition, 1969) of the *Catalogue of Reproductions of Paintings 1860–* . Unesco's aim has been to "make masterpieces of painting more widely known by promoting the production and distribution of high quality color reproductions." Reproductions of paintings are chosen on the basis of "the fidelity of the color reproduction, the significance of the artist, and the importance of the original painting." Color reproductions from books, magazines, or portfolios are not included. As of this volume, color plates printed in limited editions, particularly those produced under an artist's supervision, are not listed.

For each painting reproduced in this catalog, the following information is given: 1) for the original painting: the name of the painter, the places and dates of his birth and death, title of painting and date, medium, size and collection of original; 2) for the reproduction: the process used in printing, the size, Unesco's archive number, the printer, the publisher, and the price (usually stated in the currency of the country in which it is published). All entries are arranged alphabetically by artist, and the text is in French, English, and Spanish.

A new feature of the tenth edition is a section of 15 suggested exhibitions, prepared by Professor Damián Bayon. The suggested exhibitions range from impressionism to informalism. Short introductory texts are accompanied by suggested reproductions that are available through this catalog.

The format of the tenth edition is changed to include far more entries per page. All the entries are photoreduced to make a much slimmer volume than the previous editions. Unfortunately, the quality of the binding has not improved.

Overall, this reference volume has proven to be a useful and popular tool. It is important not only because it lists sources where one can get reproductions of well-known paintings, but also because it provides the location of the original paintings and descriptive information about the physical aspects of the painting. —Janice J. Powell. [R: WLB, May 75, pp. 672-73; ARBA 76, item 916]

382. Foskett, Daphne. **A Dictionary of British Miniature Painters.** 2v. New York, Praeger, 1972. illus.(part col.). $135.00. LC 72-112634.

A solid and enduring piece of scholarship, this is also a luxurious production in terms of illustration. To Basil Long's *British Miniaturists* (1929), Miss Foskett has added over 2,000 miniaturists and has extended the period covered by Long to 1910. Volume one lists almost 4,500 names or initials of miniaturists who were native to or worked in Great Britain and Ireland. Biographical and stylistic information in the entries is sufficient and succinct. One hundred fine color illustrations are interspersed in the 600 pages of the first volume, which also contains a brief discussion of miniature materials and techniques, as well as a selective but discriminating bibliography. Volume two is devoted to monochrome illustrations— 967 of them. The illustration list for volume two has thoughtfully been included in both volumes. For collectors, dealers, and scholars, this will be a mandatory acquisition. —Julia M. Ehresmann. [R: LJ, 15 June 72, p. 2172; ARBA 73, item 935]

383. **An Illustrated Inventory of Famous Dismembered Works of Art with a Section on Dismembered Tombs in France: European Painting.** Paris, Unesco; distr. New York, Unipub, 1974. 221p. illus. $23.10. ISBN 92-3-101040-9.

Throughout world history, works of art have been displaced or dismembered by private owners in the course of inheritance disputes, by conquering armies, and by disreputable dealers and collectors. In an effort to find a solution to this problem of dispersal and dismemberment, Unesco commissioned eight renowned art historians to make a study of the situation in each of their countries, and thus to focus world attention on the gravity of the worldwide dispersal, through fragmentation, of some of the greatest works of art.

About 70 of these dismembered masterpieces are illustrated in black and white and discussed in this extremely important pilot study. All of the participants in the project employed a similar format for the presentation of their conclusions. A narrative description of the circumstances leading to the dismemberments is followed by discussions of specific works of art, each including artist, original location, shape, dimensions, paint layer, support, subject, previous history, locations of fragments, suggested reconstitutions and bibliography. Italian, Flemish, French, Spanish, German, and Russian paintings form the core of the text, but two chapters are also included on European manuscripts and French sculpture. Although it is doubtful that the Unesco study will sway nations into sacrificing prized possessions to permit permanent reconstitution of paintings, the study nevertheless is of vital importance to scholars. It is hoped that it will lead to further concentration on this extremely complex area of study. —Jacqueline D. Sisson. [R: Choice, July/Aug 75, p. 672; Unesco, Sept/Oct, p. 281; ARBA 76, item 945]

384. Keaveney, Sydney Starr. **American Painting: A Guide to Information Sources.** Detroit, Gale, 1974. 260p. index. (Art and Architecture Information Guide Series). $18.00. LC 73-17522. ISBN 0-8103-1200-X.

Librarians, scholars, and students have much to look forward to if this first volume of the Gale Art and Architecture Information Guide series is typical of those now in preparation. In addition to providing a selected bibliography of American painting, the guide includes chapters listing major publishers, library research collections, national art organizations, and museums that specialize in or are concerned with the art of the United States.

The annotated bibliography covers general reference sources, general histories and surveys, specialized publications on periods ranging from colonial to modern times, individual artists, source materials, and periodicals. The index lists both authors and artists. Books, exhibition catalogs, collection catalogs, and selected articles from the last five years of *Art News* and *Artforum* are cited. The preface gives no indication of the cut-off date for the entries, but it appears to be the end of 1972.

The ever-present question in such a work is whether only U.S.-born and -trained artists should be listed or whether the coverage should be expanded to include naturalized citizens, foreign-born artists who spent a considerable amount of time in the United States, and American-born artists who were trained abroad or who lived abroad. The author's wise decision was to be inclusive rather than exclusive. As a result of this policy, artists such as Marcel Duchamp are included.

As is true of any selected bibliography, there are omissions, but they are doubtless due to the author's personal evaluation of the published materials. The inclusion of selected articles from two journals seems redundant, since this information is readily available in the *Art Index*. In addition, the fact that the articles were selected means that any serious user of Keaveney's publication will still have to consult the *Art Index* in order to have complete coverage of the available periodical literature.

Even though major bibliographies have appeared in recent histories of American painting, this new bibliography is far more comprehensive. It is an extremely useful, convenient, and valuable addition to the literature of an area of art history that has been undeservedly ignored. —Jacqueline D. Sisson. [R: ARBA 75, item 1028]

385. Muehsam, Gerd, ed. **French Painters and Paintings from the Fourteenth Century to Post-Impressionism.** New York, Ungar, 1970. 646p. illus. (A Library of Art Criticism Series). $25.00. LC 70-98344. ISBN 0-8044-3210-4.

In contrast to other publications dealing with sources and documents, Gerd Muehsam's impressive book is solely concerned with art criticism. A concise, lucid introduction provides background on the history of art academies and the development of art criticism in France.

The entries, arranged chronologically by artist, consist of brief biographical resumes followed by examples of art criticism pertaining to a specific work of art and, in some cases, general criticisms of the artist's total oeuvre. Frequently the selections include statements by the artist and his contemporaries as well as selections from twentieth century critics and art historians. For example, the criticisms of Poussin's paintings are from works by Bellori, Félibien, Voltaire, Reynolds, Stendhal, Ingres, Delacroix, Ruskin, Cézanne, Magne, Gide, Friedlaender and De Tolnay. Regrettably, illustrations are not always included. The entries covering the work of anonymous painters, such as the Master of Aix and the Master of Moulins, are especially successful in illustrating the variety of approaches art historians use to establish or attempt to establish attributions. The task of selecting the materials must have been monumental. Although specialists consulting this valuable reference book will not always agree with all the selections made, there is no doubt that Gerd Muehsam has a scholarly knowledge of the field and its bibliography. The only serious omissions in our opinion are the small number of negative criticisms, incomplete textual and bibliographic information on Charles Sterling's attribution to Quarton of the School of Avignon *Piéta*, and the omission of K. E. Maison's denial of a Daumier attribution for the final painting of *L'Émeute*. This sizable book, which is one of the most important American art reference tools published in 1970, will be consulted by scholars and students in all fields of the humanities. The impressive selected bibliography is an excellent checklist for libraries. —Jacqueline D. Sisson. [R: ARBA 71, item 1119]

386. New-York Historical Society. **Catalogue of American Portraits**. Comp. by Wendy J. Shadwell and Robert Strunsky. New Haven, Yale University Press, 1974. 2v. illus. $50.00. LC 74-79974. ISBN 0-300-01477-5.

Meticulously researched, this catalog of the New-York Historical Society portrait collection of or by Americans is a vital reference tool for research on portraiture and costuming as well as on numerous facets of American cultural, economic, and political history. Executed in various media, the portraits range in artistic quality from the height of portraiture to primitive works whose naivete and unintended humor are totally captivating. Except for a separate section devoted to unidentified portraits, the 2,420 catalog entries and 1,000 illustrations are alphabetically arranged by the sitters' names. Extensive cross-referencing is employed for the portraits of women. The entries are listed according to the person's name at the time the portrait was made with, whenever possible, cross references from maiden names or married names (depending on the marital status at the time the portrait was executed). The sitters and artists are not limited to famous persons nor to New York residents. Portraits of North American Indians are included only if it was possible to determine that the work is an authentic portrait and if the sitter can be identified.

Each entry includes a biography of the sitter, attribution of the work, date, measurements, medium, inscriptions, stylistic analysis, and description. A bibliography usually accompanies each entry. The provenance of the portraits is not as fully developed as one could wish. A sizable bibliography and an artist index complete this catalog of one of the richest collections of American portraiture. The authors are to be commended for their careful planning, which has resulted in an unusually user-oriented format.   —Jacqueline D. Sisson. [R: LJ, 15 Jan 75, p. 114; Choice, Feb 75, p. 1756; ARBA 76, item 918]

CHAPTER 18

APPLIED ARTS AND HOBBIES

GENERAL WORKS

387. De La Iglesia, Maria Elena. **The Catalogue of American Catalogues: How to Buy Practically Everything by Mail in America.** New York, Random House, 1973. 272p. illus. index. $4.95pa. LC 73-5047. ISBN 0-394-70982-9.

Maria De La Iglesia is back with a new collection of mail-order catalogs after her successful *The Catalogue of Catalogues: The Complete Guide to World-Wide Shopping by Mail.* This one describes merchandise of all kinds available from some 750 shops in the United States that sell by mail. Catalog descriptions are arranged alphabetically under 23 subject categories such as antiques, books, cigars and pipes, pets, services and toys. Sections are subdivided where needed. The catalog is well printed, and the use of many photos results in an attractive, as well as an informative, reference book.

A brief comparison with Lyons' catalog shows that some overlapping occurs in types of merchandise covered and, of course, the names of major suppliers. In one instance, where both described the same firm, Northwestern Coffee Mills Store, Milwaukee, Lyons cited the wrong name. Both catalogs are useful. Lyons covers foreign and domestic firms, while De La Iglesia has a selective group of American suppliers with many helpful illustrations. [R: LJ, 1 Feb 74, p. 358; ALA 73; ARBA 75, item 944]

388. Harwell, Rolly M., and Ann J. Harwell. **Crafts for Today: Ceramics, Glasscrafting, Leatherworking, Candlemaking, and Other Popular Crafts.** Littleton, Colo., Libraries Unlimited, 1974. 211p. index. (Spare Time Guides: Information Sources for Hobbies and Recreation, No. 4). $9.50. LC 73-92979. ISBN 0-87287-067-7.

This book is intended for, and includes material for, all craftsmen regardless of experience, skill, or talent. After an initial section that lists books concerned with general crafts, the arrangement of the bibliography is alphabetical by craft. The crafts represented are beads, candles, decoupage, egg decorating, glass, jewelry, leather, metal and wire, mobile and collages, mosaics, paper, pebbles and shells, plastics, pottery and ceramics, toys, and woodworking and carving. There are 474 numbered entries in all. An emphasis was placed on recent books (i.e., 1965 to 1973); however, older classic titles available in many libraries were also included when they contained valuable material. A section on crafts periodicals lists the major national periodicals, and the volume concludes with a list of crafts organizations, a directory of publishers whose books are listed, and an author-title-subject index. This selective bibliography, with its lengthy annotations, will provide guidance to craftsmen and librarians, directing them to the most valuable books in the areas covered. [R: LJ, 15 Nov 74, p. 2954; WLB, Oct 74, p. 185; ARBA 75, item 1035]

389. Osborne, Harold, ed. **The Oxford Companion to the Decorative Arts.** New York, Oxford University Press, 1975. 865p. illus. bibliog. $39.95. ISBN 0-19-866113-4.

The Oxford Companions are well known. This particular volume is similar in structure to its predecessors. It covers a wide variety of subjects—e.g., costume, furniture, jewelry, etc. The coverage is supposed to be international, but not all countries are equally represented, and the emphasis is still on Great Britain, the United States, and the Western European countries. Countries in Asia, including India and China, are mentioned only occasionally, as is also true of the Soviet Union and other countries in Eastern Europe. As always, the material is well documented.   [R: LJ, 15 Nov 75, p. 2133; ARBA 76, item 946]

390. Turner, Pearl, comp. **Index to Handicrafts, Model Making, and Workshop Projects: Fifth Supplement 1968-1973.** Westwood, Mass., F. W. Faxon, 1975. 629p. bibliog. (Useful Reference Series No. 102). $18.00. LC 36-27324. ISBN 0-87305-102-5.

This supplement, which covers the years 1968-1973, lists both books and periodicals. It follows the same guidelines as previous issues—i.e., it excludes needle-work and basic art instruction, and articles indexed in *Reader's Guide*. It does include furniture making, toy making, papier-mâché, pottery, weaving, wood carving, macramé, batik, block printing, candle making, decoupage, enameling, jewelry making, leather work, amateur electronics projects, metal working, woodworking, and general home projects and repair articles. Arrangement is alphabetical under craft, and citations contain complete bibliographical information. In addition to a list of books indexed and periodicals included, there is also a listing of books indexed in the original *Index to Handicrafts* and former supplements that were found in the 1973 edition of *Books in Print*. —Rosemary Henderson. [R: WLB, June 75, p. 751; ARBA 76, item 955]

CRAFTS

CERAMICS

391. Boger, Louise Ade. **The Dictionary of World Pottery and Porcelain, from Prehistoric Times to the Present.** New York, Scribner's, 1971. 533p. illus.(part col.). $22.50. LC 72-123829. ISBN 0-864-10031-2.

This volume has 2,200 entries, which cover basic information about a variety of potteries, styles, and techniques. There are numerous cross references and plenty of illustrations—drawings of makers' marks, characteristic shapes and designs, and color plates that give an idea of the differences in color and glazing. A section of black and white photographs at the end of the volume is a visual overview of the development of world ceramics. This section is followed by succinct but informative notes on these illustrations. The bibliography is divided into the same general categories as these photographs.

Louise Boger is known for earlier books, as well as for answering queries in *House and Garden*. She compiled this book as a "comprehensive and concise guide for the collector and student as well as the general reader." —Julia Sabine. [R: LJ, 1 Jan 72, p. 58; ALA 71; ARBA 72, item 1025]

392. Savage, George, and Harold Newman. **An Illustrated Dictionary of Ceramics: Defining 3,054 Terms Relating to Wares, Materials, Processes, Styles, Patterns, and Shapes from Antiquity to the Present Day.** New York, Van Nostrand Reinhold, 1974. 320p. illus.(part col.). $18.95. LC 73-17999. ISBN 0-442-27364-9.

Except for a list of European factories and their marks, prepared by John Cushion of the Victoria and Albert Museum, this dictionary, unlike most, is totally concerned with the physical piece: its material, pattern, decoration, type, and glaze. The artist and/or manufacturer are identified in the definitions but are not listed by name in the dictionary. Numerous cross references serve two purposes: they avoid duplication and they guide the reader to further pertinent references. General terms such as lid, cover, handle, and spout, not commonly included in dictionaries, have been deliberately listed by the authors, who are respected specialists, in order to establish once and for all a definitive terminology. It is their hope that by so doing they will prevent future misuse of the terms. Cross references from major European terms to their English equivalents are provided throughout this book, which encompasses European, Middle and Far Eastern wares, including figurines, from ancient to contemporary times. Although some American ceramics are listed, coverage of them is not and was not intended to be extensive. Even the briefest perusal of this dictionary reveals solutions for terms that previously required extensive reference work. Even though the authors claim that this publication is not intended for the specialist, it is by far one of the most comprehensive ' d lucid dictionaries in its field. In addition to its excellent coverage of 3,054 terms, the book's typography, layout, and excellent and copious illustrations, some of which are in color, are models of clarity. —Jacqueline D. Sisson. [R: Choice, Sept 74, p. 918; LJ, 1 June 74, pp. 1534-35; ALA 74; ARBA 75, item 1040]

TEXTILES

393. Axford, Lavonne Brady. **Weaving, Spinning, and Dyeing.** Littleton, Colo., Libraries Unlimited, 1975. 148p. index. (Spare Time Guides: Information Sources for Hobbies and Recreation, No. 7). $11.50. LC 75-16436. ISBN 0-87287-080-4.

This work includes annotations for 389 books, alphabetically arranged under handweaving (which includes general books on textiles), spinning, dyeing and resist dyeing (batik and tie-dye), and related crafts (baskets, bobbin lace and sprang, macramé, and rug hooking). In addition, it includes a list of periodicals in the field, a directory of organizations, a directory of supply sources, and a directory of publishers. Books at many different levels are included, though no "play books" are listed. A complete index aids the user and increases the utility of the publication. Annotations are complete, include bibliographical information, and are critical enough to allow the user to select the item needed. —Rosemary Henderson. [R: LJ, 15 Dec 75, pp. 2314-15; WLB, Dec 75, p. 328; ARBA 76, item 947]

COLLECTING

ANTIQUES

394. **The Complete Color Encyclopedia of Antiques**. Rev. and expanded ed. Comp. by The Connoisseur, London. Ed. by L. G. G. Ramsey. New York, Hawthorn Books, 1975. 704p. illus.(part col.). bibliog. index. $37.50. LC 74-7888. ISBN 0-8015-1538-6.

Handsomely illustrated with color plates, this edition has, in some areas, been greatly revised and in many others, not at all. Sections on the Aesthetic Movement, the Arts and Crafts Movement, Art Nouveau, Art Deco, Antiquities, and Ethnographies are totally new. The text of other sections (Arms and Armour; Barometers, Clocks and Watches; Carpets; Coins and Medals; Furniture; Glass; Jewelry; Metalwork; Mirrors; Needlework and Embroidery; Pottery and Porcelain; Prints; Scientific Instruments; and Silver) remains nearly verbatim, except for the commendable addition of descriptions of Far Eastern furniture, glass, and metalwork.

Each section's format consists of historical resumes, including, in some cases, lists of craftsmen, arranged alphabetically by country. Each section has its own glossary. There are some inconsistencies in the methods used to compile terms and names for inclusion in the glossaries, and the quality of indexing varies greatly section by section. Another type of inconsistency is found in the Needlework section, where the resumes of national work (such as Chinese and Greek) are found in the glossary and not in the main text. It is essential that the glossaries and indexes of encyclopedias be inclusive and extremely meticulous. That is not the case in this publication. Also, while the coverage of American and British antiques is good throughout the publication, that of other countries varies greatly and there are some glaring omissions. The sections in the 1962 edition pertaining to books and book binding, painting, drawing, and sculpture have been deleted from the 1975 edition, but the section on prints has been left intact. Again, the coverage concentrates on American and British prints and a total of only four pages is devoted to the Continent.

The list of museums, arranged by types of antiques, continues to be a convenient reference tool. Here again, however, there are serious oversights: the world-renowned glass collection in the Toledo Museum of Art is not mentioned, and no U.S. museums are listed under the category "Japanese Prints." The up-to-date selected bibliography has been re-organized in a more efficient manner and will be a useful basic checklist for libraries. Except for very narrow gutters, the appearance of the new edition has been much improved and, as mentioned above, the revised edition includes new material as well as new illustrations. Even though the text is, in most instances, unchanged, this edition must not be thought of as superseding the 1962 edition, which contains a far greater variety of examples of each type of object. —Jacqueline D. Sisson. [R: LJ, 1 Nov 75, p. 2038; WLB, Dec 75, pp. 326-27; ARBA 76, item 959]

395. Phillips, Phoebe, ed. **The Collectors' Encyclopedia of Antiques**. New York, Crown, 1973. 704p. illus.(part col.). index. $20.00. LC 73-76934. ISBN 0-517-504510.

As the title indicates, this book is aimed primarily at the collector. The subject matter is organized around type, such as arms and armor; bottles and boxes; carpets and rugs; ceramics; clocks, watches, and barometers; embroidery and needlework; etc. Within these categories, treatment is subdivided.

Each of the sections has not only the expected suggestions for further reading, but valuable information on repair and maintenance of the objects, characteristics of fakes and forgeries, and lists of museums in which good examples may be seen by the collector. These lists are necessarily very short, but it is fine to see museum collections noted as sources of study. Some glossaries are included and there is a general index, which works well. The pages are well designed and printed with plenty of black and white as well as color photographs, and numerous clear drawings. Emphasis is on the eighteenth and nineteenth centuries. —Julia Sabine. [R: BL, 1 July 74, p. 1158; Choice, Feb 74, p. 1849; ALA 74; ARBA 75, item 1059]

396. Savage, George. **Dictionary of Antiques**. New York, Praeger, 1970. 534p. illus. (part col.). bibliog. $17.50. LC 75-107216.

Among the general topics covered are: arms and armor, bronzes, carpets and rugs, Chinese art, clocks and watches, gilding, furniture, hausmalerei, ironwork, lighting appliances, mirrors, patina and aging, pewter, Sheffield plate, silver, textiles, and woodcarving. Special articles on styles enable the reader to recognize and date antiques from various periods of the 500 years covered. Articles devoted to European, British, and American antiques and craftsmen are included, with coverage extending to the Victorian and Art Nouveau periods; a separate section on Oriental art traces its influence on Western antiques. There are also sections on preservation, creative techniques, and materials, a total of 1,500 entries. An extensive bibliography, arranged by subject, and a list of makers' marks complete this work. [R: LJ, 1 Dec 70, p. 4158; ALA 70; ARBA 71, item 1141]

COINS AND CURRENCY

397. Hessler, Gene. **The Comprehensive Catalog of U.S. Paper Money**. Chicago, Regnery, 1974. 453p. illus. $20.00. LC 73-6461.

This new, sound, basic catalog of all U.S. federal currency issued since 1861 is illustrated with over 700 facsimiles. Earlier notes are priced in three grades, with average buying price also included. Notes are priced by signature combination and seal color. Numbers are given for issuance, redemption, and outstanding notes, when available. All denominations are clearly illustrated with photographs. Federal Reserve notes are subdivided and priced by Federal Reserve district. Introductory material includes a general history of the United States, a grading guide, and tables of Treasury officials' terms. There is a general rarity table for the national currency by state/territory, but this series is not otherwise detailed. There are good catalogs of fractional currency, encased postage stamps, and error notes. Interesting illustrated data on rejected designs, a good section on counterfeiting, and a brief section on military payment certificates.

This is an excellent work of wide scope, highly praised by U.S. numismatists since its issuance. —Richard H. Rosichan. [R: Choice, July-Aug 74, pp. 736-38; LJ, Aug 74, p. 1926; ALA 74; ARBA 75, item 1066]

398. Hobson, Burton, and Robert Obojski. **Illustrated Encyclopedia of World Coins.** Garden City, N.Y., Doubleday, 1970. 512p. illus. index. $12.95. LC 76-81030.

Not an advanced reference work, this book is most useful for providing an introductory illustrated text to various series and for handy identification of different coins and types. It is a handsome work, copiously illustrated, and designed for the beginning collector. There are not only chapters by country, area, and period, but there are also such helpful categorizations as Anglo-Hanoverian Coinage, Asia Minor, Biblical Coins, Cob Money, Collecting, Counterfeiting, Countermarks and Counterstamps, Cut Money, Debasement, Ecclesiastical Coins, Hoards and Finds, Inflation Coins, Multiple Talers, Odd and Curious, Platinum, Rarities, Siege Coins, and Trial of the Pyx, to name only a fraction. It includes coins that originated in all parts of the world, from ancient to modern times.

Thus, this book is especially useful for answering questions about series that may be well known but that are hard to locate as such in a normal catalog. This book is an encyclopedia, not a catalog. It has a complete table of contents, an index, and an appendix of inscriptions. —Richard H. Rosichan. [R: LJ, 1 March 71, p. 818; ALA 70; ARBA 72, item 996]

399. Krause, Chester L., and Clifford Mishler. **Standard Catalog of World Coins.** 3rd ed. Iola, Wisc., Krause, 1975. 1376p. illus. $19.50pa. LC 75-15251. ISBN 0-87341-006-8.

This gargantuan work is a much updated and expanded version of the two previous editions. It is quite simply an attempt to catalog every coin in the world issued since approximately the early nineteenth century. Logical starting dates are used for each country: 1793 for the United States, George III's accession for England, independence for Spanish America, the revolution for France. This catalog comes closer to success than any previous one. It was produced, as it should have been, by prolonged Herculean labors of compilation and cross-filing, drawing on the contributions of hundreds of people and on much extant, but widely scattered, research and data.

This is a date and mint catalog, and most coins are priced in three grades. "NCLT" (non-circulating legal tender) issues are included as such; exhaustive denomination and country/placename indexes are given. Equivalent Craig/Yeoman numbers are always given, as is metallic content; every type is illustrated with a photograph, usually quite adequately. Mintages are given to the nearest thousand. The mass of data on the most difficult series—German states, China, Indian states, Moslem countries—is impressive. Counterstamps and revolutionary issues are now included; however, the line is drawn with such items as tokens, U.S. private gold, exotic die varieties, and some counterstamps, "offyear" proofs, etc.

Mintmarks, denominational marks, and other identification items in various languages and alphabets are given. Silver and gold metallic content normally includes the fineness.

This is unquestionably one of the most important books for any numismatic library. It is as great an improvement over the two previous editions as the first edition was over previous partial compendia. —Richard H. Rosichan. [R: ARBA 76, item 969]

400. Pick, Albert. **Standard Catalog of World Paper Money**. Munich, Battenberg Verlag; Iola, Wisc., Krause, 1975. 720p. illus. bibliog. $15.00pa. LC 74-19920. ISBN 0-87341-002-5.

This remarkable new opus catalogs all known note issuances of the past 70 to 120 years (depending on the country) by issue and major type. Numerous local, special, revolutionary, and military issues are included. Notes are usually cataloged in two grades, usually VG and VF, and sometimes in VF and Unc. All entries are numbered and coded. Inscriptions are often given and deciphered, and the usual keys to foreign numberings and alphabets are present. There is usually a reduced-size photograph of one denomination of every major issue type. There is a very good bibliography and a basic index.

Although this work is invaluable and unprecedented, certain cautions must be noted. Generally speaking, pre-twentieth-century notes are covered sparsely if at all, although they are outlined briefly in the introduction. The valuations are speculative, affected by supply and demand in a field far less well established than the collecting of coins, and affected also by fluctuating exchange rates. Many items listed are virtually impossible to obtain, particularly in top grades. The rarest items are simply unvalued and rated as to rarity on a three-point scale. The catalog is a basic work and is no substitute for specialized references in the collecting of the notes of one country or region. —Richard H. Rosichan. [R: ARBA 76, item 970]

401. Rosichan, Richard H. **Stamps and Coins**. Littleton, Colo., Libraries Unlimited, 1974. 404p. index. (Spare Time Guides: Information Sources for Hobbies and Recreation, No. 5). $13.50. LC 73-90498. ISBN 0-87287-071-5.

Stamps and Coins includes more than 1,100 entries on numismatics and over 500 entries on philately. Author, title, place and date of publication, publisher, pagination, price, LC card number, and ISBN are provided for most entries. The detailed annotations will help the user distinguish between similar works. Subsidiary or related works are listed under the heading "Other Works Include" within specific subdivisions. Titles listed, regardless of the date of publication, are generally in print and/or readily available from distributors, from coin or stamp dealers, or from most dealers in numismatic or philatelic books.

The final chapters provide separate coverage of the periodicals, organizations, and libraries of the two fields. A publishers' directory lists all publishers whose works were included in the guide, with their addresses. Three indexes—title, author, and subject—complete the work. [R: ARBA 75, item 1052]

402. Taxay, Don, ed. **1971 Comprehensive Catalogue and Encyclopedia of U.S. Coins**. Premier ed. New York, Scott, 1970. 397p. illus. bibliog. $15.00.

By far the most important and comprehensive reference work on U.S. coins published in modern times. Every coin is priced in various grades. Information given includes mintage (when available), rarity on the R1-R8 scale (when applicable), applicable comments on striking, and whereabouts of known specimens for R8 and most R7 pieces.

Taxay differentiates and defines the series thoroughly. Colonial coins intended for America are separated from those of dubious association with the colonies/US; mint essays (patterns) are separated into seven different categories, and cabinet coins are listed in eleven, including regular proofs, offmetal proofs, simulated series, unofficial restrikes, pièces de caprice, etc. Such notoriously misattributed items as the 1913 liberty nickel, 1804 dollar, 1868 "large cent," 1859 and 1860 "transitional" 5-cent and 10-cent, are correctly placed. Private/territorial gold is covered thoroughly, and a final section deals with mint errors, in many cases date by date (including the 1943 bronze and 1944 steel cents). In many cases, clues for positive identification of genuine rarities are given. Die designers are always given. Photo illustrations are bound together in the center of the book.

One defect is the lack of data for pre-1854 proofs in nearly all series, long needed. In addition, there is no reason for such a superb work to lack an index, even though the table of contents is thorough. —Richard H. Rosichan. [R: ALA 71; ARBA 72, item 1003]

COSTUME AND FASHION

403. Wilcox, R. Turner. **The Dictionary of Costume.** New York, Scribner's, 1969. 406p. illus. bibliog. $17.50. LC 68-12503. ISBN 0-684-10660-4.

This illustrated dictionary contains about 3,200 entries pertaining to articles of clothing from all over the world and from all periods of history and includes jewelry, umbrellas, hair styles, underclothing, fabrics, laces, folk costumes, high fashion, academic and military dress, tailoring and dressmaking tools and terms, and brief biographical entries for over 60 well-known figures in the fashion world.

Entries define the term and, in some cases, give historical background. The black-and-white sketches by the author are an important part of this work. With the exception of a very few cases (e.g., animals such as martens, chinchillas, and lambs, which probably could have been omitted), the illustrations are detailed enough to provide a good understanding of the design and decoration of the article. [R: SR, 6 Dec 69; ALA 70; ARBA 70, v.2, p. 13]

GLASS, PORCELAIN, AND POTTERY

404. Kovel, Ralph, and Terry Kovel. **The Kovels' Collector's Guide to American Art Pottery.** New York, Crown, 1974. 368p. illus.(part col.). index. $12.95. LC 74-80295. ISBN 0-517-51676-4.

The authors are already well known to collectors because of their earlier books, including *The Complete Antiques Price List, Dictionary of Marks—Pottery and Porcelain, American Country Furniture 1780-1875,* and others.

The first American art pottery was made in Cincinnati, Ohio, during the 1870s, and the art pottery movement seems to have ended in the late 1920s. This dictionary provides in-depth information about small and larger companies, their lines, marks, and methods of manufacture, individual craftsmen, types of pottery, etc. There are excellent illustrations throughout the text and well-selected bibliographies that will be of substantial assistance to the serious reader interested in more information. [R: ARBA 75, item 1082]

PHOTOGRAPHY

405. Spencer, D. A. **The Focal Dictionary of Photographic Technologies.** Englewood Cliffs, N.J., Prentice-Hall, 1973. 725p. illus. bibliog. $39.95. LC 72-97893. ISBN 0-13-322719-7.

With its distinctly British flavor, this photographic dictionary makes an excellent addition to any reference shelf and complements nicely another worthwhile Focal Press publication: *The Focal Encyclopedia of Photography* (McGraw-Hill, 1970). The two volumes, side by side, fairly exhaust all possible questions on any given photographic term or technique.

The Focal Dictionary is especially handy for quick, lucid, and concise definitions of terminology, with marginal line drawings and diagrams expanding upon the textual explanations. Appendixes include the EMR spectrum, symbols and abbreviations, photographic effects, nomograms, standards, and a bibliography. —Steve Rybicki. [R: ARBA 74, item 1040]

406. Stroebel, Leslie, and Hollis N. Todd. **Dictionary of Contemporary Photography.** Dobbs Ferry, N.Y., Morgan & Morgan, 1974. 217p. illus. $20.00. LC 73-93536. ISBN 0-87100-065-2.

The curious photographer or the inquisitive reference librarian will find here definitions for approximately 4,500 photographic terms currently in use in the field. The book contains words most frequently encountered by the average photographer, as well as less common terms, from the simplest to the highly technical. Terms are defined skillfully and clearly, whether they are uncomplicated words like "dye" or more complex ones like "syzygetic." The format is 10" x 10", with bold type and readable two-column pages. Words have been culled from contemporary photography and its related disciplines (as evidenced in standard texts and reference sources, current magazines, trade publications, glossaries, and thesauri) and from the authors' experience. Both authors are knowledgeable, certified, and practicing photographers; they take sole credit and responsibility for the definitions supplied.

Together, this book and the *Focal Encyclopedia of Photography* (McGraw-Hill, 1970) treat the great majority of photo terms. The book has the potential of becoming a standard reference tool. —Steve Rybicki. [R: ARBA 75, item 1115]

CHAPTER 19

MUSIC

GENERAL WORKS

407. Fuld, James J. **The Book of World-Famous Music: Classical, Folk, and Popular.** Rev. and enl. ed. New York, Crown, 1971. 688p. index. $15.00. LC 65-24332.

First published in 1966, with a fourth printing in 1967, this standard work in its field has now been revised and enlarged. The original edition contained full information about 1,000 songs and other compositions, and the present edition adds another 100 songs.

The author, a notable collector of sheet and other forms of music, has selected the world's most famous melodies and has traced their history back to their original printed sources. All types of music are represented—classical, folk, spirituals, popular songs, hymns, Christmas songs, theatre music—and thus the book is a guide to all the important compositions, composers, operas, ballets, librettists and lyricists. The first line of each piece is quoted with the music in the original key and the words. In compiling this work, the author broke new ground, and much of the information is not to be found elsewhere. The erudite, 81-page introduction is masterly. In it will be found means of determining the date of publication and an excellent discussion on copyright laws. —P. William Filby. [R: ARBA 72, item 1081]

BIBLIOGRAPHIES

408. Brook, Barry S. **Thematic Catalogues in Music: An Annotated Bibliography.** Hillsdale, N.Y., Pendragon Press, 1972. 347p. illus. index. (RILM Retrospectives, No. 1). $18.00. LC 72-7517.

Professor Barry Brook, City University of New York, is the very model of a music bibliographer. He is best known for his efforts in establishing and editing *RILM Abstracts*. In *Thematic Catalogues* he provides control over an area that has been pretty much out of hand. Aside from a modest checklist issued 20 years ago by the Music Library Association, and a 1966 supplement prepared by Professor Brook's students, there has been no general listing of thematics.

We now have this thorough, detailed cumulation of more than 1,450 such indexes: published, unpublished, and in progress, in all formats. Entries are grouped by composer, where appropriate, or otherwise by compiler. Information given includes an account of the thematic material included, plus a full bibliographic description and reference to related works such as revisions in progress, reprints, reviews. The bibliography is prefaced by a valuable essay on the nature, history, and future of thematic catalogs, and is capped with a subject-author index. —Guy A. Marco. [R: LJ, 15 Jan 73, p. 151; Choice, Mar 73, p. 58; ARBA 75, item 1065]

409. Duckles, Vincent, comp. **Music Reference and Research Materials: An Annotated Bibliography.** 3rd ed. New York, Free Press, 1974. 526p. index. $10.95. LC 73-10697. ISBN 0-02-907700-1.

No serious research in music or any of its affiliated areas in traditional academic studies should be attempted without this exceptionally fine volume, in this edition. (If you have the second edition, from 1967, donate it to a smaller college or public library.) It will also save reference librarians quite a bit of time if their patrons know about "Duckles 3," which is 551 entries richer and 141 pages longer than the second edition.

The citations are complete, and the analytic annotations are objective (locations for major reviews are offered for some titles). The entries are then not always of publications equal in value to their companions, but scholars of any age will be sensitive to this and *ipso facto* it might be well to mark both desk and public copies with local call numbers. The former copy then serves as an aid in acquisitions (some jobbers list Duckles numbers almost as an *imprimatur*). If there are no citations in particular fields, this may be an indication that a book or article on the subject has not yet been prepared for research or reference needs. Highly recommended for all serious music collections. —Dominque-René de Lerma. [R: BL, 1 Dec 74, p. 384; Choice, Oct 74, p. 1108; ARBA 75, item 1123]

410. Farish, Margaret K. **String Music in Print.** 2nd ed. New York, R. R. Bowker, 1973. 464p. index. $34.95. LC 73-15721. ISBN 0-8352-0596-7.

The second edition of Ms. Farish's indispensable magnum opus is, in most respects, identical in scope and format to the first edition (R. R. Bowker, 1965) and its supplement (R. R. Bowker, 1968). Farish includes in-print music for solo and ensemble strings, combinations of strings with keyboard, winds, voice, and (in the second edition only) strings with and without other instruments combined with electronic tape. She also includes, as before, trio-sonatas, string-concerted works, and study materials (methods, études, treatises, etc.). The updated publishers' list with agents is invaluable in itself. There is a composer index, a feature previously found only in the supplement (although the earlier index did embrace both the 1965 and 1968 volumes). The entries sometimes overlap, due to the occasional difficulty of verifying, in a work of such large scope, different editions of the same titles. Since many entries in the earlier edition and its supplement have been dropped and new ones added (with yet others differently listed), libraries and scholars should retain all three volumes for historical and bibliographical purposes. (Mozart string quartet titles, for example, dropped 16 of the 1965 entries, retained all four of the 1968 entries, and added nine new entries). Even though Farish's work is not exhaustive for even the publishers whose catalogs she indexes (e.g., C. Fischer still publishes its previously listed edition of Mozart's K. 525), this volume is a very important work. —C. Gerald Parker. [R: BL, 15 May 74, p. 1018; ARBA 75, item 1125]

411. Hixon, Donald L. **Music in Early America: A Bibliography of Music in Evans.** Metuchen, N.J., Scarecrow, 1970. 607p. index. $17.00. LC 74-16407. ISBN 0-8108-0374-7.

A need has long been felt by American scholars and musicologists for extracting the music publications listed in Evans' *American Bibliography* (available in microprint in *Early American Imprints, 1639-1800*). The list is now available in this single volume. The author, however, not content with the simple transcription of Evans entries, has made this bibliography more comprehensible and useful to musicians by changing entries from authors of texts to composers, adding special indexes and short biographies.

The first section lists publications in alphabetical order by composer, compiler, or title. A short title-page transcription and the pagination are given. The second section consists of listings which appear in Evans, but which have not been printed in *Early American Imprints*. A handy biographical dictionary of musicians, authors, editors, and compilers appearing in the index makes up section three. Parts four and five are a composer-compiler index and a title index, respectively. Section six is a list of Evans numbers, which cites page numbers in sections one and two.

Music in Early America is an extremely useful and well-organized bibliography. However, the separate listing of items not available in microprint might have been included in section one for easier reference. Though contents of secular collections are analyzed in section one and indexed in sections three and four, no such consideration is given sacred collections. These minor inadequacies detract very little from the usefulness of this volume and its importance to the study of American music. —Désirée de Charms. [R: LJ, 15 Jan 71, p. 183; Choice, May 71, p. 362; RQ, Spring 71, p. 269; ARBA 72, item 1103]

412. Kagen, Sergius. **Music for the Voice: A Descriptive List of Concert and Teaching Material**. Rev. ed. Bloomington, Indiana University Press, 1969. 780p. index. $17.50. LC 68-27348. ISBN 0-253-33955-3.

A revised edition of a standard reference book first published in 1949. It is a highly selective guide to vocal literature listed by composer (by country of origin for folk songs). Each entry provides such information as the range of the song, its tessitura, the type of voice, publishers who can furnish the music, and a brief annotation. The emphasis is on American material. [R: Choice, Jan 70; ALA 69; ARBA 70, v.2, p. 26]

413. Marco, Guy A. **Information on Music: A Handbook of Reference Sources in European Languages; Volume I, Basic and Universal Sources**. Littleton, Colo., Libraries Unlimited, 1975. 184p. $11.50. LC 74-32132. ISBN 0-87287-096-0.

This selective, annotated bibliography is the first volume of a comprehensive six-volume guide to music reference sources. Volume I, *Basic and Universal Sources*, goes beyond the scope of traditional guides to music reference books and bibliography in that it includes non-music bibliographies where these are essential to a total understanding of music bibliography. Thus, the standard periodical indexes are included, but they are discussed from the point of view of their musical significance. Also, this book is correlated with the third edition of Duckles' *Music Reference and Research Material* (New York, Free Press, 1974). Entries also provide references to Winchell and to *American Reference Books Annual*.

The annotations are clear and precise and the citations are complete, including LC class numbers. The work includes 503 carefully selected books arranged under the following six chapter headings: The Language of Music; Direct Information Sources; Universal Biographical Sources; Guides to Other Sources of Information in General Categories; Lists of Music; and General Discographies. [R: ARBA 76, item 989]

414. Nardone, Thomas R., James H. Nye, and Mark Resnick. **Choral Music in Print, Volume I: Sacred Choral Music.** Philadelphia, Pa., Musicdata, 1974. 656p. $45.00; $32.00pa. LC 73-87918. ISBN 0-88478-000-7; 0-88478-001-5pa.

The field of music bibliography has long needed substantial guides to much of the material in print, and librarians have had to compile files of publishers' catalogs as a partial answer to the needs of their patrons. Guides to limited areas are a partial solution, and several excellent ones are available—e.g., Farish's *String Music in Print.* That entries from publishers' catalogs might be used as the basis of informational blocks to be handled by data processing equipment has recently become a possibility, and now in this volume we have the happy results of one such operation. Some 46,387 entries from more than 300 publishers appear in one alphabetical sequence. Works attributed to a composer have full information listed under his name with necessary title cross references. Anonymous works and folk song arrangements have full information under a title entry, with cross references from variant forms (notably translations of foreign titles) but without references from arrangers and editors. Collections are similarly entered under composer or title depending on their make-up. The contents of a collection may be listed in part or in full, some titles with title cross references for composer collections and composer "analytics" for general collections.

Little editing is done to supplement or correct the information derived from the publishers' catalogs, so caution must be observed in using the volume. Pierre de la Rue appears under both "de la Rue" and "la Rue." Two entries appear under "de Lattre, Roland" rather than Lassus. There is no cross reference from "Handl" to "Gallus."

The introduction is short but well written. Legibly printed on quality paper, the volume is handy to use but undoubtedly will soon need rebinding in a heavily used library. This compilation marks a significant step in the music bibliography field, especially as supplements are planned. [Editor's note: Other volumes in the series are *Secular Choral Music* ($45.00)and *Organ Music in Print* ($32.00). The *1976 Supplement to Choral Music in Print*, published in 1976, has 12,000 new listings.] —John G. Peck, Jr. [R: ARBA 75, item 1132]

DISCOGRAPHIES

415. Rust, Brian. **The American Dance Band Discography 1917-1942.** New Rochelle, N.Y., Arlington House, 1975. 2v. index. $35.00. LC 75-33689. ISBN 0-87000-248-1.

This is another definitive compilation by the dean of jazz/pop discographers. Rust, who has been a jazz player and who has also worked among recordings in the BBC Library, is best known for his *Jazz Records 1897-1942* (London, Storyville, 1970) and *The Complete Entertainment Discography from the Mid-1890's to 1942* (New Rochelle, N.Y., Arlington House, 1973).

The present set lists all the 78rpm records made by 2,373 dance bands. For each disc, information given includes matrix and label numbers, recording dates, arrangers, vocalists, and miscellaneous data. For each band, the personnel are listed with their instruments. An estimated 50,000 records are included, by all the great ensembles (except Glenn Miller and Benny Goodman, who are treated in other discographies by the same publisher). An artist index of about 8,000 names concludes this monumental assemblage. —Guy A. Marco. [R: ARBA 76, item 994]

ENCYCLOPEDIAS

416. Grove, Sir George. **Grove's Dictionary of Music and Musicians.** 5th ed. Ed. by Eric Blom. New York, St. Martin's, 1970 (c.1954). 10v. illus. ports. music. Originally published in 9 vols. in 1954. Suppl. vol. (v.10) published in 1961. $20.00/v.; $7.95/ v.pa. $200.00/set; $79.50/set pa. LC 54-11819rev.2.

Grove's Dictionary of Music and Musicians was first published in 1879-1889 in four volumes. This reprint includes all nine volumes of the fifth edition, plus the supplementary volume published in 1961.

Although it is in need of revision (the sixth edition is in preparation), *Grove's* has long been the standard English language encyclopedia of music. Special emphasis is given to English subjects, but the encyclopedia covers the whole field of music from 1450 and includes musical history, theory, practice, terminology, biography, songs, operas, etc. It does not give opera plots. Articles are signed by specialists. In this edition, periodical articles have been added to the bibliographies. [R: ARBA 71, item 1232]

DICTIONARIES

417. Apel, Willi. **Harvard Dictionary of Music.** 2nd ed. rev. and enl. Cambridge, Mass., The Belknap Press of Harvard University Press, 1969. 935p. illus. plates, music. $20.00; $1.25pa. LC 68-21970. ISBN 0-674-37501-7; 0-671-78142-1pa.

The second edition of this standard and authoritative dictionary, first published 25 years ago, has been thoroughly revised, updated and substantially enlarged. As in the first edition, the emphasis is on the historical point of view; biographical articles are omitted. The definitions cover a wide range of topics: music history, forms, instruments, notation, performance, theory, etc. The second edition gives special attention to compositional techniques, including electronic music and serial music. Individual compositions, representative of every type from every era, are described. A notable feature of this first edition, the bibliography following each article, has been updated and expanded. There are also more illustrations, including drawings of instruments, music examples, diagrams, and charts. Additional features include a list of music libraries and their holdings; the section on historical editions now lists 53 collections of music and briefly describes each volume within each collection. One of the most important reference books published during 1969. [R: LJ, 1 Nov 69; SR, 6 Dec 69; ALA 69; ARBA 70, v.2, p. 23]

418. **Larousse Encyclopedia of Music.** Edited by Geoffrey Hindley. New York, World, 1971. 576p. illus.(some col.). index. $19.95. LC 70-147888.

This work is based on *La Musique: les hommes, les instruments, les oeuvres,* edited by Norbert Dufourcq and originally published in Paris by Larousse. The one-volume work, aimed at a broad spectrum of readers, is beautifully illustrated with some 700 pictures, many of them in color. This volume is superior to the *Golden Encyclopedia of Music* and should find its place in all libraries among other one-volume works such as *The Concise Oxford Dictionary of Music* and *The Oxford Companion to Music*, to mention two 1970 imprints. The English edition, like the French, is divided into six main sections, the first of which deals with non-European musical cultures. Nevertheless, most material of interest to English speaking audiences is here, considerably updated. There is an improved index. [R: ARBA 72, item 1098]

419. Riemann, Hugo. **Dictionary of Music.** 4th ed., rev. and enl. Trans. by J. S. Shedlock. London, Augener, 1908; repr. New York, Da Capo, 1971. 2v. illus.(music). (Da Capo Music Reprint Series). $37.50. LC 75-125060. ISBN 0-306-70025-5.

Today's push toward elimination of foreign language study by librarians is given poor support by the field of music reference, in which so many key works are available only in German, French, or Italian. For example, the Riemann *Lexikon*—perhaps the greatest music dictionary—has been through 12 editions (1882-1967), but only one has been translated into English. The British musicologist John Shedlock translated the revised fourth edition—performing a service whose value is undiminished, though of course we would like to have translations of the newer editions also.

The older Riemanns are still of interest for biographical sketches of persons no longer included (and for the contemporary emphases and preferences they illustrate). And musical scholars still want to read the intriguing, often controversial, views of the author on such topics as major/minor or consonance/dissonance. Although those who are comfortable in German will probably prefer, for general consultation, the fine new twelfth edition (1959-67, 3v.), users restricted to English will find the Da Capo reprint of Shedlock to be a useful shelfmate for later standard works. —Guy A. Marco. [R: ARBA 72, item 1099]

420. Scholes, Percy A. **The Concise Oxford Dictionary of Music.** 2nd ed., edited by John Owen Ward. New York, Oxford University Press, 1969 (c.1964). 636p. illus. $7.50; $4.50pa. LC 64-5946. ISBN 0-19-311307-3; 0-19-311302-3pa.

Musical reference works of broad scope and modest size are usually aimed at penurious students and at individual amateurs wanting a concise home reference source. Anyone with more serious needs or intentions will consult *Grove's Dictionary*, the *Harvard Dictionary of Music*, or *Baker's Biographical Dictionary of Musicians* whenever possible.

The work at hand is, in a sense, a cut-down version of the author's *Oxford Companion to Music*, providing information on the historical, esthetic, and technical phases of music, in addition to defining terms and identifying persons. However, it does this in short articles and with much broader coverage of composers, performers, and conductors than its progenitor. It also escapes most of the idiosyncracies of the former work. In nearly every way, even in price, it is superficially comparable with J. A. Westrup and F. Ll. Harrison's *New College Encyclopedia of Music* (New York, Norton, 1960), but the two are very often complementary in detail, particularly in the biographical articles. Scholes seems to be more accurate in his dates, but Westrup and Harrison give more of them. Although both originated in Britain (Westrup and Harrison as the *Collins Encyclopedia of Music*; London,

Collins, 1959), the British emphasis is much more evident in the present work, again making the two complementary. Westrup and Harrison provide exact dates of birth and death, pronunciations, and musical examples, none of which are in Scholes. On the whole, however, anyone wishing to own this sort of reference work should acquire both. —Dennis North. [R: ARBA 71, item 1235]

421. Scholes, Percy A. **The Oxford Companion to Music.** 10th ed., rev. and reset. Edited by John Owen Ward. New York, Oxford University Press, 1970. 1189p. music. plates. $25.00.

Though it is not without faults, the *Oxford Companion to Music* has long been recognized as a standard reference work in music, particularly for home use. The ninth edition was reprinted five times, with revisions, and this tenth edition is basically a consolidation and resetting of the final text of the ninth edition. It contains 91 new articles, 76 of which are biographical. The basic defect of the work results from Scholes's original approach, which consisted of writing a series of small treatises on various aspects of music and then cutting them up into shorter articles for alphabetical arrangement, with a minimum of editing. Biographical articles and foreign terms are included in the alphabetical arrangement. Paper and typography are excellent. [R: LJ, July 70, p. 2451; WLB, Sept 70; ARBA 71, item 1236]

422. Vinton, John, ed. **Dictionary of Contemporary Music.** New York, Dutton, 1974. 834p. illus. $25.00. LC 73-78096. ISBN 0-525-09125-4.

A handbook of 1,000 general, signed articles on topics, countries, terms, and biographical sketches of composers in one alphabetical arrangement. The sources of information have been composers, composers' associations, information bureaus of various countries, and music specialists. Approximately three-fourths of the entries are biographical sketches of composers who have flourished since the turn of the century. Mr. Vinton defined the scope as concert music in the Western tradition. He has tried to provide insight on contemporary music—the new and the distinctive contributions of this century thus far, rather than the actual "state of the art" of music currently, which would date its reference value too quickly.

This book has the same high editorial standards and thoroughness as Apel's *Harvard Dictionary of Music* (2nd ed.). It has terms not found in Apel and greater coverage of some topics. For example, indeterminacy, third stream, prose music, mixed media, spatial music, computer applications, electronic music, twelve-tone techniques, and texture can be found in Vinton. Jazz, popular music, folk music, and Asian music are treated in general surveys in Vinton. He made the decision to exclude broadcasting, functional music (theater, films, television) and music criticism for want of qualified authors. This reference book is a comprehensive single source for information about contemporary music. —Sharon Paugh Ferris.
[R: WLB, June 74, p. 852; BL, 15 Sept 74, pp. 109-110; LJ, 1 Sept 74, p. 2055; Choice, July-Aug 74, p. 734; ALA 74; ARBA 75, item 1143]

INDEXES

423. Bull, Storm. **Index to Biographies of Contemporary Composers, Volume II.**
Metuchen, N.J., Scarecrow, 1974. 567p. $18.50. LC 64-11781. ISBN 0-8108-0734-3.

Professor Bull (University of Colorado) issued the first volume of this excellent index in 1964. At that time, he cited biographical material on 5,800 composers that was found in 69 sources. The present volume updates the coverage on some 4,000 persons and presents sources of information on about 4,000 others. By inspecting 108 sources for this volume, the author has covered a total of 177 biographical works. Nineteen languages are included among the sources of Volume II, with English accounting for about half the number of works checked.

Format is a straight alphabetical array; information given is nationality, birth/death dates, and abbreviated citations to sources. There is an annotated list of those sources, which in itself is a useful guide to biographical compilations of modern composers. Considerable spot-checking indicates that Professor Bull has done this job very carefully. Dates are correct, and names are given with correct accent markings as needed. Cyrillic names are given with alternate transliterations to account for usage in various sources.

Within its scope limits ("classical" composers born since 1900, or living now whenever born, or deceased since 1950), this is a standard and essential guide.
—Guy A. Marco. [R: ARBA 75, item 1152]

OPERA

424. Kobbé, Gustave. **Kobbé's Complete Opera Book.** Ed. and rev. by the Earl of Harewood. New York, Putnam, 1972. 1262p. index. $12.95. LC 72-82834. ISBN 0-399-11044-5.

Far more than a book of opera synopses, Kobbé's work has long been considered the best and most complete guide to opera available to the general listener. Originally published in 1922, four years after Kobbé's death, the work has been revised six times. Later editions have followed Kobbé's original intention of showing the development of opera, the place of the various composers in that development, and the interrelationship of music and story in the individual operas.

The work is broad in chronological coverage (beginning with Monteverdi's *Orfeo* of 1607 and ending with Britten's *Gloriana*, premiered in 1953) as well as geographically (including composers from all Western countries). It is selective, on the other hand, in including only those works that most English-speaking listeners would be certain to come in contact with. While the book as revised endeavors to show the changes in opera since Kobbé's death in 1918, contemporary repertoire is covered less fully than the older repertoire. The present editor, however, is rumored to be writing a supplementary volume that will cover many of these operas. Changes in opinion about individual operas are recorded, and many older operas that were not performed in Kobbé's time but that have come back into the repertoire have been added—particularly operas from the period before Gluck, who was the first composer discussed in the original work.

Discussions cover 217 operas by 86 composers. Each is described by scene and act; major first performances and revivals are listed; characters and voice roles are enumerated; and some background and criticism of the works is given, as well as plots and musical examples.

The present revision remains substantially the same as the edition of 1954. That edition lost much of the additional material written by Katherine Wright for earlier revisions. New material was added by the Earl of Harewood, who since World War II has been prominent in the British opera world. New data have been added in this revision to the records of performances, and it has often been necessary to make elisions from the discussion of plots to create the needed space. In at least one instance, material thus cut from the text was not cut from the index. The additional performance information dates, for the most part, after the previous revision of 1963, but in some cases it dates to before the 1954 edition. —Dennis North. [R: BL, 15 July 73, p. 1027; WLB, Apr 73, p. 704; ARBA 75, item 1128]

425. Loewenberg, Alfred, comp. **Annals of Opera, 1597-1940.** 2nd ed. Geneva, Switzerland, Societas Bibliographica, 1955; repr. St. Clair Shores, Mich., Scholarly Press, 1971. 2v. index. $48.50. LC 72-166242. ISBN 0-403-01376-3.

Alfred Loewenberg (1902-49) was one of the great men of twentieth century music bibliography, and the *Annals of Opera* was his greatest accomplishment. The first edition, 1943, was universally acclaimed; the second, 1955 (edited by Frank Walker from notes left by the author) improved on it in several ways.

In the Annals we find a chronological listing by date of premiere for some 3,600 operas performed from 1597 to 1939, with three entries for early 1940. Information is given on the first performance, and on the first performances in other countries and languages. There is a general index in the second volume, with indexes by title, composer and librettist.

While far from comprehensive in terms of operas included (Towers lists more than 28,000 in his *Dictionary-catalogue of operas . . .*), the Annals is exemplary in the amount and accuracy of factual material offered. And it does cover virtually every opera of interest to scholars.

Libraries which have even the smallest concern for music history should consider this work essential to their purposes. —Guy A. Marco. [R: ARBA 75, item 1054]

FOLK, JAZZ, AND POPULAR MUSIC

426. Kinkle, Roger D. **The Complete Encyclopedia of Popular Music and Jazz 1900-1950.** New Rochelle, N.Y., Arlington House, 1974. 4v. index. $75.00. LC 74-7109. ISBN 0-87000-229-5.

The title is grandiose, and so is the price, but this is nonetheless a remarkable assemblage of facts that is well worth having. Mr. Kinkle, a musician and record dealer, has obviously put many years into the gathering of data, and he has organized the information neatly.

Volume I presents a good chronology of pop-music events, by year, from 1900 to 1950. For each year we have a list of principal Broadway musicals (with cast, opening date, number of performances, and major songs); a list of leading songs; a list of movie musicals (with cast and songs); and some of the hit recordings (arranged by artist, with record number and flip-side title).

There are two volumes of biographical sketches (pop/jazz people; no attempt to cover classical, country-western, blues) with representative discographies for each person—2,105 sketches in all.

Some 260 pages of the fourth volume offer a valuable listing of discs issued on nine labels, in all important series from the mid-20s through the early 1940s. Each entry cites the performer(s) and names of pieces on both sides of the disc. A "time chart" is provided so that the record listings (which are in manufacturer number sequence) can be matched with release years. Finally, there are indexes to personal names (including those in the chronology discographies), all 28,000 song titles, all 1,200 movie musicals. Accuracy is good, if a spot-check for a set of obscure old favorites can be trusted.

The *Encyclopedia* is recommended as a worthy companion for Nat Shapiro's *Popular Music*, Julius Mattfeld's *Variety Music Cavalcade*, and other standard reference works in this field. —Guy A. Marco. [R: ARBA 75, item 1171]

427. Kinsley, James, ed. **The Oxford Book of Ballads.** New ed. Oxford, Clarendon Press; distr. New York, Oxford University Press, 1969. 816p. $12.00. ISBN 0-19-812133-4.

This is a completely revised edition of the notable collection of English and Scottish ballads made by Sir Arthur Quiller-Couch in 1910. Mr. Kinsley's texts are based on specific single versions of the ballads, and are as close as possible to oral tradition. Nearly 80 ballads are included. Many street ballads and broadsides are included, which might earlier have been regarded as sub-literary but which are a distinctive part of the tradition. James Kinsley is professor of English studies at the University of Nottingham.   [R: ALA 70; ARBA 70, v.2, p. 83

428. Lewine, Richard, and Alfred Simon. **Songs of the American Theater: A Comprehensive Listing of More Than 12,000 Songs Including Selected Titles from Film and Television Productions.** New York, Dodd, Mead, 1973. 820p. index. $15.00. LC 72-3931. ISBN 0-396-06657-7.

Arranged alphabetically by song titles, the first part of this guide attempts to list all songs from 1925 to 1971, with selective coverage for 1900 through 1924. Composer, lyricist, show title, and year are given for each song. Part two, arranged by name of production, includes information about cast and credits and about availability of original cast albums and vocal scores. There is also a chronological list of productions. Indexed by composers and lyricists. [R: BL, 15 July 73, p. 1030; Choice, Oct 73, p. 1168; LJ, 1 Sept 73, p. 2424; WLB, Oct 73, p. 167; ALA 73; ARBA 74, item 1072]

429. Shapiro, Nat, ed. **Popular Music: An Annotated Index of American Popular Songs, Volume 6, 1965-1969.** New York, Adrian Press, 1973. 385p. $18.50. LC 64-23761. ISBN 0-910024-06-5.

The addition of this sixth volume in the series *Popular Music: An Annotated Index of American Popular Songs* now makes it possible to track down almost any popular song that was written during the 50 years from 1920 to 1969. Volume six continues the high standards set in the previous volumes. Like its predecessors, it is easy to use, and it seems to be extremely comprehensive for the years covered.

Each song is listed alphabetically by title under the year of its original copyright. The information given includes alternate titles, author and composer, current publisher, introducing performers, and the first or best selling recordings. In addition, this volume has a title index, a list of publishers with their addresses, and a supplement of songs copyrighted before 1965 that were important during the 1965-1969 period. Volume six also contains Mr. Shapiro's essay "Popular Music, 1965-1969," which describes the special characteristics of the era of The Beatles, Woodstock, Bob Dylan, Neil Diamond, Motown, *Hair*, Johnny Cash, etc. Information about the songs of this diverse but very influential group of musicians and "happenings" makes an already excellent reference tool even more valuable. Other volumes in the series cover 1950-1959(v.1); 1940-1949(v.2); 1960-1964(v.3); 1930-1939(v.4); 1920-1929(v.5). —Karen Burt. [R: ARBA 75, item 1175]

430. Stambler, Irwin, and Grelun Landon. **Encyclopedia of Folk, Country and Western Music.** New York, St. Martin's Press, 1969. 396p. illus. $17.50; $5.95pa. LC 67-10659.

The 500 entries in this biographical dictionary include "classical" folk and country and Western personalities, e.g. Joan Baez and Eddy Arnold, as well as folk rock and country blues artists such as Bob Dylan and Leadbelly. Groups as well as individual performers are included. Entries are in popular style and give music specialty, place and date of birth, a brief summary of the performer's career and notable accomplishments, top hits, etc. In addition to biographies the listings cover some variety shows, such as Grand Ole Opry, definition of a few terms and classes of folk music, and musical instruments. Three brief articles on attitudes toward and development of folk and country music offer little information. Appendixes cover awards and a selective discography of the most popular or representative long-play albums, arranged alphabetically by performers. A bibliography lists articles about performers and some general books on folk and country music. Irwin Stambler is compiler of *Encyclopedia of Popular Music* (St. Martin's Press, 1965). [R: LJ, 15 Nov 69; SR, 6 Dec 69; ALA 70; ARBA 70, v.2, p. 24]

CHAPTER 20

THEATRE

GENERAL WORKS

431. Geisinger, Marion. **Plays, Players and Playwrights; An Illustrated History of the Theatre.** New York, Hart, 1971. 768p. illus. index. $20.00. LC 77-162054. ISBN 0-8055-1091-5.

A copiously illustrated chronological history of the theatre beginning with ancient Greece and Rome. Not as detailed as the Oxford Companion, but it provides basic information accompanied by luscious illustrations of actors, stage settings, theatres, and even playbills.

It is chronologically arranged, with an accent on the English-speaking theatre, although background information on ancient Greece and Rome and the Commedia dell'Arte is provided.

Unfortunately, some of the entries are tantalizing in their brevity. For example, a five-line paragraph on Tennessee Williams precedes far more lengthy discussion of his plays but gives no biographical information on him, discussing only the plays themselves. This defect is offset by two chapters on Russian theatre and American musical comedy, neither of which is handled as well or as extensively anywhere else. [Editor's note: Hart published a revised edition of this work in 1975 ($25.00).] —Judith Rosenberg. [R: ALA 72; ARBA 72, item 1141]

BIBLIOGRAPHIES

432. Drury, Frances Keese Wynkoop. **Drury's Guide to Best Plays.** 2nd ed. by James M. Salem. Metuchen, N.J., Scarecrow, 1969. 512p. index. $17.00. LC 75-5006. ISBN 0-8108-0254-6.

The first edition, published in 1953, included some 1,200 plays available in English. This new edition retains much of the material from the older work and adds new titles. The author listings provide information on the play, publisher, and cast, a plot synopsis, and useful information on current holder of play and royalties. Indexes of co-authors, cast, subject, popular plays, and publishers enhance the practical approach used in this guide. There is also a bibliography of collections of plays. [R: LJ, 1 Jan 70; ALA 69; ARBA 70, v.2, p. 64]

433. Schoolcraft, Ralph Newman. **Performing Arts/Books in Print: An Annotated Bibliography.** New York, Drama Book Specialists, 1973. 759p. index. $32.50. LC 72-78909. ISBN 0-910482-27-6.

A completely revised and updated edition of *Theatre Books in Print*, published originally in 1963 and revised in 1966. The title has now been changed to reflect the enlarged scope of the work, which covers the whole spectrum of performing arts, including the literature of theatre, drama, motion pictures, television, radio, and mass media. The listings are restricted to books readily available in the United States and, with a few exceptions, materials are in English. No plays or collections of plays are included except for collections of Shakespeare's works and scholarly editions of the works of other playwrights, which provide, in addition to the text, a substantial evaluation and criticism of the given playwright's *oeuvre*. It should also be noted that this bibliography lists books on musical theatre; however, it omits works on musical theory or the playing of musical instruments.

The system of classification used here has been adapted from *Theatre Books in Print*; thus, listings are divided into two major sections. The first includes works in print that were published prior to December 31, 1970; the second lists books published during 1971, with the addition of some older imprints previously unknown to the editor. Each section is further subdivided by subject categories: books on theatre and drama; books on technical arts of the theatre; books on motion pictures, television, and radio; and books on the mass media and the popular arts. These parts are, in turn, subdivided by geographical area, historical period, etc. About 12,000 entries are listed in the two sections, and each entry includes author, title, publisher, year of publication, pagination, and price. A brief descriptive annotation (approximately 60 words) is appended to most entries. Author and title indexes and a list of publishers conclude this standard bibliography. —Bohdan S. Wynar. [R: BL, 15 Dec 73, p. 404; ARBA 74, item 1138]

434. Stratman, Carl J. **American Theatrical Periodicals, 1798-1967: A Bibliographical Guide.** Durham, N.C., Duke University Press, 1970. 133p. $8.75. LC 72-110577. ISBN 0-8223-0228-4.

Carl Stratman, editor of *Restoration and 18th Century Theatre Research* and Professor of English Literature at Loyola University, Chicago, has taken on an almost insurmountable task and has proven to be its master. In this first attempt to gather a listing of American theatrical serials published between 1798 and 1967, he has verified 685 titles and located portions of them in 137 libraries in the United States, Canada, and the British Museum.

The bibliography is arranged chronologically by the first year of publication, with titles arranged alphabetically within the year. Each entry contains as much information regarding the publication as can be ascertained and library symbols indicate where the serial may be located. An excellent index serves to make this an even more valuable research tool. —Judith Armstrong. [R: ARBA 71, item 1270]

435. Stratman, Carl J. **Britain's Theatrical Periodicals, 1720-1967.** 2nd rev. ed. New York, New York Public Library, 1972. 160p. index. $11.00. LC 72-134260. ISBN 0-87104-034-4.

This is a completely revised second edition of Stratman's *A Bibliography of British Dramatic Periodicals, 1720-1960*, which was originally published by the New York Public Library in 1962. The original edition listed 674 British dramatic periodicals, increased to 1,235 in the present list. The new edition is similar to the earlier edition in that the list is limited to "periodicals printed in England, Scotland, and Ireland, in the English language."

The word "theatrical" is used loosely, since it includes periodicals primarily devoted to "acting, actors and actresses, ballet, box office, community theatre, dance, drama, magic, managers of theatres, masque, music halls, musical comedy, open air theatre, opera, operetta, pantomime, puppet, scenery, theatre, variety, and vaudeville." No attempt is made to list literary periodicals that deal in part with drama or theatrical material. Each entry gives: "complete title; title changes; editor, or editors, when indicated; place of publication; number of volumes when issued as volumes; number of issues; dates of first and last issues; date of the first issue when the periodical is still in process of publication; frequency of issue, [and] libraries where the periodical is located." The listing is chronological, according to the initial date of publication, with full name and subject index. A scholarly work, indispensable for the study of the British theatre. —Paul A. Winckler. [R: ARBA 73, item 1067]

DICTIONARIES

436. Hartnoll, Phyllis, ed. **The Concise Oxford Companion to the Theatre.** New York, Oxford University Press, 1972. 640p. bibliog. $6.50pa. ISBN 0-19-281102-9.

This paperback edition is based on the third edition of *The Oxford Companion to the Theatre*. Notable changes in this edition are the omission of long articles on individual countries and on technical aspects of the theatre, and the lack of illustrations. The editor states that "every article, however short, has been reconsidered and, in most cases, recast and rewritten in miniature in such a way as to retain the essential facts and still leave room, where necessary, for new material" (Preface). The new material is certainly kept to a minimum; it is mostly reflected in the addition of a date here and there (e.g., Tallulah Bankhead's and John Steinbeck's deaths in 1968, Noel Coward's 1970 knighting, and a sentence on two new Neil Simon plays presented in 1969 and 1970). The extensive bibliography reflects more updating and includes many books with 1967 to 1970 imprints. In sum, this is a useful, accurate, well-organized condensation of the original encyclopedic work. [R: Choice, Mar 73, p. 60; ARBA 74, item 1139]

DIRECTORIES

437. Young, William C. **American Theatrical Arts: A Guide to Manuscripts and Special Collections in the United States and Canada.** Chicago, American Library Association, 1972. 166p. index. $9.95. LC 78-161234. ISBN 0-8389-0104-2.

An extremely important publication for locating primary source material of American and Canadian theatrical personalities including actors, directors, authors, designers, choreographers, composers, critics, dancers and other performers of opera, film, and the circus. Also included are listings of American and Canadian collections containing playbills, theatre history, promptbooks, and posters.

The guide lists the collections of 138 institutions, most of them in the United States. Many of these collections have not been cataloged and do not appear in the

Library of Congress Union List of Manuscripts. The guide is arranged alphabetically by state and then by institution. Most entries indicate the number of pieces in the collection and give a brief description of it. A very good name and subject index facilitates the use of the tool.

Mr. Young's outstanding effort will certainly assist in the documenting of American theatrical history. —Judith Armstrong. [R: Choice, July-Aug 72, p. 630; LJ, 15 Apr 72, p. 1420; RQ, Summer 72, p. 391; WLB, Apr 72, p. 745; AL, Mar 72, p. 319; ALA 71; ARBA 73, item 1065]

INDEXES

438. Guernsey, Otis L., Jr., comp. and ed. **Directory of the American Theater 1894-1971: Indexed to the Complete Series of Best Plays Theater Yearbooks; Titles, Authors, and Composers of Broadway, Off-Broadway, and Off-Off Broadway Shows and Their Sources.** New York, Dodd, Mead, 1971. 343p. $25.00. LC 71-180734. ISBN 0-396-06428-0.

This cumulative index to the Best Plays series has been needed for years. It contains 22,000 names of plays, playwrights, composers, lyricists, and sources, all of which have been checked and re-checked for accuracy. The book is divided into an author (playwright, composer, etc.) section and a title section. Entries are followed by a volume number in italics and the page reference in roman type. This volume will be of tremendous value to the Best Plays series. [R: ALA 71; ARBA 72, item 1146]

439. Sharp, Harold S., and Marjorie Z. Sharp. **Index to Characters in the Performing Arts: Part III—Ballets A-Z and Symbols.** Metuchen, N.J., Scarecrow, 1972. 320p. $11.00. LC 66-13744. ISBN 0-8108-0486-7.

Part I of this series was *Non-Musical Plays: An Alphabetical Listing of 30,000 Characters* (1966, 2 volumes) and Part II was *Operas and Musical Productions* (1969, 2 volumes), by the same authors and publisher.

The work in hand was designed to answer the question, "In which ballet does one find a character named . . .?" In all, 818 ballets are covered and about 3,000 characters are indexed. There are some lapses—for instance, "The Ballerina" of *Petrouchka* is listed under "The Dancer," "The Moor" (in the same ballet) is given as the "Blackamoor"—neither with cross references from the more common name.

The work is in two parts. The first, an alphabetical listing and description of the characters, also includes a five-letter symbol that is the key to the second part. This second part, arranged alphabetically by the symbols, lists the ballets themselves with such pertinent information as number of acts, composer, choreographer, author of book on which based (if any), who did the première performance scenery, decor, and costumes, and where and when the première took place. This work, and its predecessors, will prove invaluable. [Editor's note: Part IV, Radio and Television, was published in 1973 (697p. $15.00. LC 66-13744. ISBN 0-8108-0605-3). It indexes characters in radio and television from the beginnings of these media to 1955 (for radio) and to the Fall 1972 season (for television). Some 20,000 characters from 2,500 shows are included.] —Kenyon C. Rosenberg. [R: WLB, Oct 72, p. 196; LJ, Aug 72, p. 2563; ARBA 73, item 1070]

BIOGRAPHY

440. Highfill, Philip H., Kalman A. Burnim, and Edward A. Langhans. **A Biographical Dictionary of Actors, Actresses, Musicians, Dancers, Managers & Other Stage Personnel in London, 1660-1800.** Carbondale, Southern Illinois University Press, 1973– . illus. $19.85/v.(v.1 & 2); $22.50/v.(v.3 & 4). LC 71-157068. ISBN 0-8093-0517-8(v.1); 0-8093-0518-6(v.2); 0-8093-0692-1(v.3); 0-8093-0693-X(v.4). In progress.

The authors have now completed the first four volumes of their monumental work whose purpose, as stated in the preface to Volume I, is "to provide brief biographical notices of all persons who were members of theatrical companies or occasional performers or were patentees or servants of the patent theatres, opera houses, amphitheatres, pleasure gardens, theatrical taverns, music rooms, fair booths, and other places of public entertainment in London and its immediate environs from the Restoration of Charles II in 1660 until the end of the season 1799-1800." From a study of the volumes under review, it would seem that they have fulfilled that purpose as fully as possible. Saying they have "combed every source that ingenuity could suggest," the authors proceed to enumerate a staggering list of sources (from *London Stage 1660-1800* to all sorts of original and secondary materials).

The entries vary in length from a few lines to several pages, and the information is given in a clear, narrative style, usually in chronological order. Birth and death dates and profession (if known) are given first. It would have been helpful if other standard biographical information had been listed at the beginning of the entry, but, obviously, so little was found about many of the subjects that any standard data format would have been virtually impossible. The series continues to be particularly notable for its drawings, engravings, maps, and theatre plans, which help make a century and a half of the London stage come alive for the reader.

Any collector of original materials of the period will find this set extremely useful for checking names in letters, handbills, prints, etc. This is a truly significant product of years of research, not something thrown together in haste and passed off as a basic reference tool.

Volumes published to date include: *Volume 1: Abaco to Belfille; Volume 2: Belfort to Byzand; Volume 3: Cabanel to Cory; Volume 4: Corye to Dynion.* –Richard M. Buck and William Curtis Young. [R: Choice, Apr 74, p. 234; ARBA 75, item 1188; ARBA 76, item 1045]

441. Vinson, James, ed. **Contemporary Dramatists.** New York, St. Martin's Press, 1973. 926p. (Contemporary Writers of the English Language). $30.00. LC 73-80310. ISBN 0-900997-17-6.

This work is the third volume of the series "Contemporary Writers of the English Language." It contains a massive amount of information. Almost every living dramatist writing in English is included. Each entry includes a biography (not always completely truthful) supplied by the subject, a bibliography of *all* published works (if plays, British and U.S. first production years are given), a list of "theatrical activities" including acting and directing in all media, sometimes a comment by the subject on his own work, *and* a critical essay on the playwright by a contributor whose credentials are listed in the notes. This last section is somewhat peculiar. Apparently the editor was not sure how the critic would

and that have appeared in anthologies, periodicals, biographies, film histories, and mass-market paperbacks. Films are listed alphabetically by title, giving production company and date, director of film, authors of screenplay, source of screenplay if not original, and publication information. Contains a good index. —Judith Armstrong. [R: LJ, July 71, p. 2295; ALA 71; ARBA 72, item 1160]

445. **The New York Times Film Reviews, 1913-1974.** New York, Arno, 1971-1975. 9v. index. $507.00. LC 70-112777. ISBN 0-405-02191-7(set).

The *New York Times Film Reviews* has been updated to include films to 1974 within eight volumes plus a one-volume index. The first eight volumes are a compilation of over 20,000 reviews of films which were evaluated by *Times* critics during the stated period. The cumulative index volume includes a personal name index with complete film credits up to 1974 and citations to *Times* reviews, a title index, and a corporate index. There is also a section of film awards and a "portrait gallery" of 2,000 film actors and actresses. [R: LJ, Aug 71, p. 2481; ALA 71; ARBA 72, item 1168a]

446. Rehrauer, George. **Cinema Booklist.** Metuchen, N.J., Scarecrow, 1972. 473p. index. $11.00. LC 70-188378. ISBN 0-8108-0501-4.

Not only are more and more universities offering courses in film, but even high schools and grade schools are joining the ranks. Educationally, more emphasis is being placed on the use of film in schools and libraries.

Hand in hand with the audiovisual awakening has come increased attention to collection building in libraries. Dr. Rehrauer has gathered 1,600 titles of books and scripts published between 1940 and 1970 that are devoted to films and filmmaking. He has checked them for factual accuracy, presence and quality of illustrations, scope, indexing, and usability. The critical annotations are intended specifically to indicate which books are the best choices, especially when several exist on the same subject.

Items are arranged alphabetically by title, with a separate listing of scripts and periodicals (with addresses). Author and subject indexes are included. —Judith Rosenberg. [R: LJ, 15 Sept 72, p. 2829; WLB, Sept 72, p. 91; ALA 72; ARBA 73, item 1074]

447. Schuster, Mel, comp. **Motion Picture Performers: A Bibliography of Magazine and Periodical Articles, 1900-1969.** Metuchen, N.J., Scarecrow, 1971. 702p. $17.00. LC 70-154300. ISBN 0-8108-0407-7.

This bibliography, based on materials in the Lincoln Center Library, is arranged alphabetically by performer, then chronologically. There is no index, and cross-referencing is kept to a minimum, but the material is self-indexing.

To decide whether a performer should be included, Mr. Schuster has set an arbitrary minimum of four mentions of the individual in articles or books on the film. Thus, many minor actors, foreign actors, and people better known for their endeavors in other areas (such as Ronald Reagan and Pauline Frederick) can be found here. For this reason, also, the range of articles extends into areas other than acting—politics, TV, directing, etc.

Fan magazine articles have been included through the forties because of the lack of any other critical, analytical, or biographical career articles during that time.

Also included is a list of actors eligible for inclusion about whom no material was found.

This is a valuable tool for anyone engaged in research on films or actors. —Judith Rosenberg. [R: ARBA 72, item 1161]

FILMOGRAPHIES

448. Gottesman, Ronald, and Harry M. Geduld, eds. **Guidebook to Film: An Eleven-in-One Reference.** New York, Holt, Rinehart and Winston, 1972. 230p. $6.95; $7.95 text ed. LC 78-160462; 77-167811 text ed. ISBN 0-03-086707-X; 0-03-085292-7 text ed.

A guide to all major aspects of film study, equipment and sources of information, this work contains directory information for film museums and archives, film courses, equipment and supply dealers, distributors, picture and poster sources; a glossary of terms; lists of festivals, awards, organizations; dissertations on film study, film magazines giving some locations of back files, and novels about Hollywood; and annotated bibliographies. [R: ALA 72; ARBA 73, item 1084]

449. Hochman, Stanley, comp. and ed. **American Film Directors: With Filmographies and Index of Critics and Films.** New York, Ungar, 1974. 590p. index. (A Library of Film Criticism). $18.50. LC 73-92923. ISBN 0-8044-3120-5.

The first volume of a proposed series on film criticism, this work includes criticism of the films of 65 outstanding American directors, including most of the films of such luminaries as Alfred Hitchcock, Frank Capra, William Wyler, and Stanley Kubrick. For the most part, the reviews are contemporary with the films, but, in some cases, reviews by later critics are included as well. While most of the reviews show perception of the film as art, some that do not are included, as the author states, "to show what an intelligent director was up against."

The entries are arranged chronologically by review date and alphabetically by director, so that occasionally reviews of the same film are not consecutive. Many of the entries are excerpted, so that only pertinent critical portions remain. At the end of each is the reviewer's name and the source of the piece. A list of directors is included, as well as filmographies of the directors and an author-title index. Several directors whose work is divided between the United States and another country (such as Josef von Sternberg and Fritz Lang) are included, but only their American works are discussed.

This tool will provide ready access to criticism that would otherwise be hard to locate, unless one had access to NYPL's fine collection. —Judith Rosenberg. [R: ARBA 75, item 1210]

450. Lee, Walt, comp. **Reference Guide to Fantastic Films: Science Fiction, Fantasy, and Horror.** Los Angeles, Chelsea-Lee Books, 1972-74. 3v. illus. $29.40pa. LC 72-88775. ISBN 0-913974-04-8(set).

Walt Lee has compiled a three-volume work that attempts exhaustive worldwide coverage of fantastic films, identifying some 20,000 films produced over a period of 75 years. Fifteen years in the making, his *Reference Guide* might be compared in bibliographic significance to work done in the literature of fantasy and sf by Blieler, Day, Tuck, the New England Science Fiction Association, Clareson, and Hal Hall.

For purposes of his *Guide*, Lee defines fantastic films as "motion pictures depicting exceptions to man's natural conception of reality" as explained by common sense or scientific opinion. The films included are listed alphabetically under theatrical release title, television title, original title if different from the above, and translation of original title. The last three are cross-referenced to main listing, as are sequels, other versions of the same story, and closely related titles. Thus, it is possible to locate a film regardless of the name by which it might be known to the researcher. Information following each entry includes some or all of the following: variant title, date of release, country of production, length, cast, credits, character designations, classification, brief content note, and references to reviews. This bibliographical work is accurate, unique in its tremendous scope, and obviously a labor of love. —Mary Jo Walker. [R: LJ, 15 Nov 72, p. 3697; RSR, July/Sept 73, p. 19; RQ, Fall 74, pp. 65-66; ARBA 75, item 1194]

ENCYCLOPEDIAS

451. Spottiswoode, Raymond, gen. ed. **The Focal Encyclopedia of Film and Television Techniques.** New York, Hastings, 1969. $37.50. 1100p. ISBN 0-8038-2268-5.

While calling itself an encyclopedia, this large volume will be most appreciated as a technical manual. Organized in dictionary fashion (1,600 entries) with a visual code to indicate whether the term pertains to film, TV, or both, the book includes the work of the producer, director, cameraman, and editor and describes technical processes. The text is well illustrated throughout. Added to the main body of the text is a general overview, with cross references to the specifics found in the main text. The book is well indexed, and suggestions for further readings are given with individual entries.

Under a general editorial board, approximately 90 highly competent people (almost all British) have made contributions in special areas. The overall competence of the book is clear, and nothing quite like it exists—certainly not in such a compact form. The writing is clear, and remains very readable without losing its scientific stress, so that readers other than technicians can use the book. In criticism, it must be said that, while all differences between U.S. and U.K. systems are noted, apparently there was no U.S. general consultantship. There are national differences and even national prejudices. Further U.S. editorial involvement would be reassuring to technicians on this side of the Atlantic. —Irving Wortis. [R: LJ, 15 Jan 69; LJ, 15 Apr 70; p. 1440; ALA 69; ARBA 71, item 1288]

DICTIONARIES

452. Halliwell, Leslie. **The Filmgoer's Companion.** 4th ed. New York, Hill and Wang, 1974. 873p. illus. bibliog. index. $25.00. LC 75-116875. ISBN 0-8090-4484-6.

This encyclopedic dictionary first appeared in 1966 and has been growing in coverage and accuracy every since. The current edition has been completely reset in a clear, two-column format. Abundant illustrations have been added and, although the offset printing process reduces the quality, the captions for the affectionately selected stills and newspaper advertisements display pungently opinionated observations. The "explanatory notes" have been improved and entries, in most cases, have been expanded, with some commentaries completely rewritten.

Among the distinguishing features of this work are the short essays on film treatments and themes (such as alcoholics, hands, mirrors, pre-credit sequences, student protests), providing the names of selected performers and film titles that treated the subject. In addition to the main entries, there is a list of all films mentioned, a list of fictional screen characters appearing as main entries, a list of all the theme essays appearing as main entries, a list of title changes (American to British and vice versa), a fine list of recommended books, a personal list of 100 favorite films, and an index to the performers appearing in the illustrations.

This work compares in scope and treatment to *The American Movies Reference Book: The Sound Era*, edited by Paul Michael and published by Prentice-Hall in 1969. The main entries in Halliwell are more complete and add personal comment and evaluation. Michael's work provides production and cast credits for film title entries, which is not done in Halliwell's. Directors have more complete film lists in Halliwell. With this edition, an already bright and popular film reference work has become indispensable. —Gerald R. Shields. [R: ARBA 71, item 1285; ARBA 76, item 1052]

453. Sadoul, Georges. **Dictionary of Films**. Trans., ed., and updated by Peter Morris. Berkeley, University of California Press, 1972. 432p. $16.50; $5.95pa. LC 74-136027. ISBN 0-520-01864-8; 0-520-02152-5pa.

454. Sadoul, Georges. **Dictionary of Film Makers**. Trans., ed., and updated by Peter Morris. Berkeley, University of California Press, 1972. 288p. $14.50; $4.95pa. LC 78-136028; ISBN 0-520-01862-1; 0-520-02151-7pa.

These complementary volumes were originally published in France in 1965; this is their first appearance in English.

Films includes about 1,200 entries (in the original languages with cross references from English) that attempt "to give a panorama of world cinema since its origins" (Preface). Each entry includes credit list, running time, short plot summary, and a critical note. For the English edition, Morris has corrected and added to the original entries, and contributed new entries and critical comments of his own—in all cases these changes and additions are indicated. The changing and adding holds true for both dictionaries, each of which is expanded by "some fifteen percent" (Introduction).

Film Makers includes over "a thousand entries devoted to directors, scriptwriters, cinematographers, art directors, composers, producers, inventors," but "no technicians, . . . exhibitors, distributors or exporters" (Preface). The directors' filmographies are the key—each director's entry includes his own filmography (not always complete, although Morris has expanded the originals) and a critical appraisal. The works included in *Films* are not evaluated here, but their inclusion in *Films* is noted by an asterisk. For this reason—and also because neither work has a separate index and each must act as an index to the other—both should be available to gain full value from either.

The one great lack for English-speaking monolinguists is that titles in *Film Makers* are in French. German and Italian have not been translated when the English release title is a simple translation. For example, if one is using the Jean Renoir entry in *Film Makers* to find the listing for a specific Renoir film in the other volume, he must know it by its French title. In *Films*, although the English release titles are cross-referenced to the original language entry, this presupposes that one knows the release title, which is not always the case.

A sampling of the entries in both dictionaries indicated that there are critical comments in most cases, usually the expected ones, to only a few of which one could take exception. Some landmark films such as *Greed* (three columns) and *Intolerance* (two columns) are covered very thoroughly; other entries seem arbitrary: Disney's *Snow White* gets two columns to one for *Wild Strawberries*; *2001* gets one and one-half to one for *The Silence*.

Despite any shortcomings, omissions, errors, or critical misjudgments, these dictionaries are valuable reference tools, are less specialized than either *The American Movies Reference Book* or *The New York Times Film Reviews* (abridged), and supplement any other bibliographies available in English, including the in-progress multi-volume catalog produced under the aegis of the American Film Institute.
—Richard M. Buck. [R: LJ, 1 Oct 72, p. 3138; ALA 72; ARBA 73, items 1096-1097]

DIRECTORIES

455. Limbacher, James L., comp. and ed. **Feature Films on 8mm and 16mm: A Directory of Feature Films Available for Rental, Sale, and Lease in the United States with Serials and Directors' Indexes.** 4th ed. New York, R. R. Bowker, 1974. 368p. index. $16.50. LC 79-163905. ISBN 0-8352-0709-9.

This directory is perhaps one of the most basic and valuable film reference books available today, particularly for areas where extensive film programming takes place. It is essentially an index to the film catalogs of 185 major U.S. distributors of feature films. This new edition is estimated by the compiler to include 95 percent of "all feature films generally available in the United States"—more than 15,000 films that are available for sale, lease, or rent. This represents 5,000 more films than were in the third edition, which was published in 1971. With the current edition, the directory will begin to appear annually. Supplements to the directory also appear five times a year in the magazine *Sightlines*, which is available on a membership or subscription basis from the Educational Film Library Association.

The major portion of the directory is a listing of films by title. They are arranged in alphabetical, word-by-word order with appropriate cross references for films that have been released under more than one title, or that have appeared in different versions. Each entry contains the following information: title, distributor's name or country of origin, the year of original release, running time in minutes, whether it is sound or silent, and whether it is black and white or color, names of the major cast, the director, and a code indicating the distributor and whether the film is available for sale, rent, or lease. Additional information concerning the type of film (documentary, animation, experimental, etc.) and the lack of cast or directors' names is also included where appropriate.

In addition to the feature film listings, the directory also includes a separate listing of 183 film serials titles, two directories of film companies and distributors, a list of film reference works, and an extensive and highly useful index of directors, which lists all of the films available by each. —Richard Akeroyd. [R: AL, Oct 74, p. 497; LJ, July 74, p. 1795; ARBA 75, item 1208]

456. **The New York Times Directory of the Film.** New York, Arno and Random House, 1971. $25.00. LC 70-112777.

An abridgement of the *New York Times Film Reviews, 1913-1968,* which is in six volumes, this directory is comprised of reprints of the original film reviews for films that were selected for the *New York Times* "Ten Best of the Year" lists from 1924 through 1970. Pictures of about 2,000 movie personalities are included. The largest part of the volume is a personal name index, which lists actors, actresses, directors, etc., connected with the film industry, their films (through 1968), and citations to the *New York Times* reviews. A corporate index lists producers and film distributors. [R: LJ, 1 Jan 72, p. 61; ALA 71; ARBA 72, item 1168b]

INDEXES

457. Gerlach, John C., and Lana Gerlach. **The Critical Index: A Bibliography of Articles on Film in English, 1946-1973, Arranged by Names and Topics.** New York, Teachers College Press, 1974. 726p. index. (New Humanistic Research Series). $15.00; $6.50pa. LC 74-1959. ISBN 0-8077-2442-4; 0-8077-2438-6pa.

The Gerlachs have compiled an impressive bibliography/index of magazine articles about film directors, producers, actors, critics, screenwriters, cinematographers, specific films, and 175 topics dealing with the history, aesthetics, and economics of film, the relation of film to society, and the various genres of film. Included are some 5,000 items from 22 primary periodicals published in the United States, Canada, and Great Britain. Selective coverage of about 60 general periodicals (e.g., *American Scholar, Life, New Yorker, Sewanee Review*) is also provided. *Films in Review* was omitted since it has its own decennial indexes. The fact that the index was computer-produced accounts for its unattractive but readable format.

The work is arranged in two main sections: Names (alphabetical) and Topics (hierarchical), with some additional material included in appendixes. A detailed introduction explains the plan and use of the book. A list of topics arranged in hierarchical order and an alphabetical dictionary of topics aid in the use of the Topics section. The appendixes include supplementary reference materials and sources, an essay on criticism, and an essay on the use of the computer in this project.

Without question, the Gerlachs and their computer "assistant" have produced a much needed and useful tool for film collections, researchers, and students. —Christine L. Wynar. [R: Choice, Dec 74, p. 1456; ARBA 75, item 1209]

CHAPTER 22

RELIGION

BIBLIOGRAPHIES

458. Clancy, Thomas H. **English Catholic Books, 1641-1700: A Bibliography.**
Chicago, Loyola University Press, 1974. 157p. index. $8.00pa. LC 74-704. ISBN
0-8294-0231-4.

"The aim of this catalog is to give abridged entries of all English books written
by Roman Catholics and published in the Roman Catholic interest between 1641
and 1700 inclusive" (Introduction). Allison and Rogers performed the same task for
the years 1558 to 1640 in *A Catalogue of Catholic Books in English Printed Abroad
or Secretly in England, 1558-1640* (Arundel Press, 1956). Clancy follows more or
less the same style of entry, adding shelf numbers as well as locations in libraries
and supplying some additional descriptive matter in parentheses where helpful.

The arrangement is by main entry with generous cross references, an index
of publishers, a chronological index, and an index of translators, editors, and compilers. The main body of the work lists 1,139 items, with an additional 381 border-
line items in an appendix. The compiler claims that this is only a "provisional list,"
and, in fact, one wishes that he had visited more libraries; it is, nevertheless, an
important contribution to English language Catholic bibliography and to the growing field of recusant studies. —James P. McCabe. [R: ARBA 75, item 1216]

459. McCabe, James Patrick. O.S.F.S. **Critical Guide to Catholic Reference Books.**
Littleton, Colo., Libraries Unlimited, 1971. 287p. bibliog. index. (Research Studies
in Library Science). $11.50. LC 78-144202. ISBN 0-87287-019-7.

Two basic types of material are covered in this guide: those works that deal
with topics peculiar to the Catholic Church (e.g., the liturgy or other theological
disciplines); and those that deal with issues in the social sciences, literature, and the
arts to which Catholics have traditionally contributed a more or less unique perspective. The five chapters include General Reference Works: Theology and Liturgy;
Humanities; Social Sciences; and History. [R: LJ, 1 Nov 71, p. 3594; WLB, Sept
71, p. 84; Christianity Today, 3 Dec 71, p. 19; ARBA 72, item 1177]

ENCYCLOPEDIAS

460. **Encyclopedia of Theology: The Concise Sacramentum Mundi.** Ed. by Karl
Rahner. New York, Seabury, 1975. 1841p. $32.50. LC 74-33145. ISBN 0-8164-
1182-4.

Rahner, editor of *Sacramentum Mundi: An Encyclopedia of Theology in
Six Volumes* (Herder and Herder, 1968; 6v.), has prepared a highly selective and

condensed version of that important international theological encyclopedia. The concise edition does not include all articles in condensed form, but instead omits about one-third of the articles and deletes large portions of others. Some topics are eliminated totally. About 12 new articles by Rahner have been added. Theological collections should have the complete encyclopedia and will have little need for this condensed version. In many cases, it does present a treatment of topics different from that offered by the *New Catholic Encyclopedia*. —Christine L. Wynar. [R: Choice, Nov 75, p. 1141; LJ, Aug 75, p. 1402; ARBA 76, item 1082]

461. **New Catholic Encyclopedia; Volume XVI, Supplement 1967-1974: An International Work of Reference on the Teachings, History, Organization, and Activities of the Catholic Church, and on All Institutions, Religions, Philosophies, and Scientific and Cultural Developments Affecting the Catholic Church from Its Beginning to the Present.** Prep. by an editorial staff at the Catholic University of America. David Eggenberger, ed. Washington, Publishers Guild, in association with McGraw-Hill, 1974. 520p. illus.(part col.). index. $49.50. LC 66-22292.

Since the articles in the *New Catholic Encyclopedia* were all written before 1965, this *Supplement* is a long-overdue updating of the information contained in the larger work. Longer articles on some of the more contemporary topics could be wished for, and this could be easily accomplished by deleting such non-religious coverage as the seven-page article on space exploration. Nevertheless, there are fine, up-to-date, and impartial articles on abortion, Catholic education, contraception, genetic engineering, infallibility, liturgy, marriage, and pentecostalism. The inclusion of such terms as underground church, institutional church, theology of dissent, women as priests, exclaustration, and laicization illustrates the open and non-partisan style of the articles, which freely acknowledge differences of opinion amor ˜ theologians, try to present all sides of the controversy, and state clearly any official teachings of the Church that bear on the topic. Of the 440 articles, 127 are biographies of notable Catholics and world figures who have died since the publication of the original work. Most of these articles are accompanied by a photograph and a bibliography. The fact that only two of the biographies are of women is perhaps a fault of the editors but may be more a reflection of the real place of women in the Church (in spite of all the ecclesiastical rhetoric to the contrary, some of which may be found in this volume).

In general, the work is a worthy companion to the original work (with the exception of the illustrations, which are inconveniently located and uninspired). —James P. McCabe. [R: BL, 1 Sept 75, pp. 67-69; Choice, Sept 75, p. 818; ARBA 76, item 1085]

462. Rahner, Karl, and others, eds. **Sacramentum Mundi: An Encyclopedia of Theology**. New York, Herder & Herder, 1968-1969. 6v. $135.00. LC 68-25987.

Published simultaneously in English, Dutch, French, German, Italian, and Spanish, this work was prepared by an international community of scholars. Its purpose is to present in-depth articles on the teachings of the Catholic Church. All basic theological areas are covered, plus a number of related disciplines; articles reflect the outlook of Catholic scholarship since Vatican II. Bibliographies are appended to articles and there is a detailed index. The encyclopedia is designed for the specialist and is too erudite and technical for the average layman. [R: WLB, Mar 70, p. 674; ARBA 71, item 1308]

DICTIONARIES

463. **Baker's Dictionary of Christian Ethics**. Carl F. Henry, ed. Grand Rapids, Mich., Baker Book House, 1973. 726p. $16.95. LC 74-83488. ISBN 0-8010-4079-5.

Over 200 evangelical scholars, primarily from the United States, but also from Canada, Great Britain, and Continental Europe, have contributed articles. Their names and qualifications and the titles of articles occupy some 16 pages. Article titles range from "Civilization" (Helmut Thielicke) and "Social Change" (by Jacques Ellul) to "Eschatology and Ethics" (by George E. Ladd) and "Repentance" (by James D. G. Dunn). Entries are firmly rooted in a Biblical understanding of the topics discussed and frequently make reference to pertinent passages from the Bible. Some articles (e.g., "National Council of Churches," "Situation Ethics," and "World Council of Churches") are sharply critical of liberal viewpoints. —A. Robert Rogers. [R: ARBA 74, item 1176]

464. Brauer, Jerald C., ed. **The Westminster Dictionary of Church History**. Philadelphia, Westminster Press, 1971. 887p. $17.50. LC 79-11071. ISBN 0-664-21285-9.

This generally excellent book fills a gap in reference coverage. The LC subject catalog (1950-1971) lists some dictionaries of church history in other languages but no other modern work in English. Winchell and Walford mention dictionaries of a more general nature (e.g., *Oxford Dictionary of the Christian Church*) and some which cover particular periods in church history, but no twentieth century work of comparable scope. In the light of Brauer's comment that coverage emphasizes the modern period, with particularly heavy concentration on the church in the United States, this reviewer found a surprisingly wide range of people and topics from all periods and countries in the generally brief (10 to 30 lines) articles. (There are a few longer articles on major topics with brief bibliographies appended.) Arrangement is alphabetical. There are a few "see" references. Over 140 contributors from various parts of the United States wrote articles which were edited by specialists in early church history, the medieval period, the Reformation, and modern times. Proportionality and factual accuracy appear to be well maintained. The relatively small number of Roman Catholic contributors led this reviewer to examine several articles (including Council of Trent, Ignatius of Loyola, Teresa of Avila, Vatican I and II) for evidence of bias. The impression which emerges is not one of polemic or deliberate distortion, but simply that the compilers are more at home in a liberal and ecumenical Protestant perspective. Vatican II does receive more cordial treatment than Vatican I, but fairness and factuality usually prevail. Church and seminary librarians will find this book indispensable, while reference librarians servicing religion collections in college, university and medium-to-large public libraries should also find it very useful. —A. Robert Rogers. [R: ARBA 72, item 1182]

465. Davies, J. G. ed. **A Dictionary of Liturgy and Worship**. New York, Macmillan, 1972. 385p. $9.95. LC 72-90276.

Few attempts at ecumenical editing have been as successful as this work. Although all of the major Christian denominations are covered, not many terms are neglected. In addition to technical terms, each sect or rite is given an extended article covering the basic worship in each geographical area or branch, information on liturgical books, rituals, prayers, and so forth. The liturgy of each of the sacraments is covered in separate, lengthy articles, and some subjects (e.g., architecture and vestments) are treated in great detail with illustrations. Most of the articles are about one page in length; they are signed and contain bibliographical references. The information is as current and up to date as one could hope for in this rapidly changing field. —James P. McCabe. [R: ARBA 73, item 1108]

466. **A Dictionary of Buddhism.** Ed. by T. O. Ling. New York, Scribner's, 1972. 277p. $7.95. LC 72-37231. ISBN 0-684-12763-6.

The Senior Lecturer in Comparative Religion at the University of Leeds has extracted the entries relating to Buddhism from *A Dictionary of Comparative Religion*, edited by S. G. F. Brandon (New York, Scribner's, 1970) for publication as a separate work. The result is a compilation that retains the high scholarly standards of the original but that brings the material on Buddhism together in somewhat more convenient form. The compiler also hopes to serve the student interested in Southeast Asia through inclusion of entries from the original on such topics as Burma, Cambodia, Laos, Indonesia, and Thailand. Entries are more detailed and technical than those in *A Popular Dictionary of Buddhism*, edited by Christmas Humphreys (London, Arco, 1962; New York, Citadel Press, 1963), though much less so than those in *Encyclopaedia of Buddhism*, edited by G. P. Malalasekere (Colombo, Government of Ceylon, 1961–). Because of the demand for information on Buddhism, *A Dictionary of Buddhism* may serve a special need or as an adjunct to *A Dictionary of Comparative Religion*. —A. Robert Rogers. [R: WLB, Nov 72, pp. 292-93; ARBA 73, item 1109]

467. **Dictionary of Comparative Religion.** S.G.F. Brandon, general editor. New York, Scribner's, 1970. 704p. bibliog. $20.00. LC 76-111390. ISBN 0-684-31009-0.

This concise dictionary covers iconography, philosophy, anthropology, and the psychology of primitive, ancient, Asian, and Western religions. There are articles about the religion of specific groups, such as the Hittites, as well as on practices and philosophies, such as ancestor worship and existentialism. Many entries contain cross references, and short bibliographies are appended to major articles. There is a list of terminology relevant to each major religion. A comprehensive general index guides the reader to subjects that do not have independent entries but that are treated in related articles. [R: LJ, 1 Oct 70; ALA 70; ARBA 71, item 1306]

468. Douglas, James Dixon, general ed. **The New International Dictionary of the Christian Church.** Grand Rapids, Mich., Zondervan, 1974. 1074p. $24.95. LC 74-8999.

The scope of this dictionary is both international and inclusive. People, places, events, movements, and Biblical and theological terms are covered concisely and clearly. The perspective is that of evangelical Protestantism, moderately conservative, but appreciative of other trends and viewpoints. The Scottish editor had the assistance of an American consulting editor. There are signed articles by over 180 contributors, mostly British and American, but with a few from other countries. There is some overlap with *Corpus Dictionary of Western Churches* (Corpus

Publications, 1971), but the Roman Catholic viewpoint of O'Brien's work and its
tendency toward longer articles make coverage and treatment complementary in
many respects. There is also some duplication with the *Westminster Dictionary of
Church History* (Westminster Press, 1971), but Brauer's work is more liberal and
ecumenical in viewpoint, with very extensive North American coverage, including
some noted Canadian churchmen (e.g., Salem Bland) not found elsewhere.

The major rival, however, is the *Oxford Dictionary of the Christian Church*,
edited by F. L. Cross and E. A. Livingstone (2nd ed.; New York, Oxford University
Press, 1974). Some comparisons between *New International* and *Oxford* are in
order. *Oxford* is nearly 50 percent longer and thus has opportunity to be more
comprehensive. Its 245-plus contributors, however, are almost entirely British and
its emphasis on Western European, especially British, Christianity is evident, despite
efforts to extend the coverage of other religious groups (e.g., the Eastern Orthodox
Church) in the second edition. *New International* has better North American and
world coverage in many, but not all, cases. An Anglican and Catholic emphasis
appears in *Oxford*, in contrast to the conservative Protestant viewpoint of *New
International*. Differences in coverage are evident in a number of topics. Generaliz-
ing from those examined, *Oxford* includes more entries, and various aspects of
closely related subjects tend to be treated in separate entries. The *New International*
tends to include related subjects under one entry and has shorter bibliographies.
Both employ cross-referencing. —A. Robert Rogers. [R: ARBA 75, item 1218]

469. Hughes, Thomas Patrick. **A Dictionary of Islam, Being a Cyclopaedia of the
Doctrines, Rites, Ceremonies, and Customs, together with the Technical and Theological Terms of the Muhammadan Religion**. London, 1885; repr. Delhi, India,
Oriental Publishers; distr. Columbia, Mo., South Asia Books, 1973. 750p. illus.
bibliog. index. $17.50.

This antique has a wealth of information on the sciences of Islam: the Koran
(it serves as a dictionary of its terms, has a synopsis of the entire book, and is, in
effect, a subject index of Koranic verses because most articles are larded with relevant quotations from the Koran as well as Hadiths, the oral traditions of the
Prophet); Hadith terminology; philosophy and theology; Islamic law; festivals;
and popular Islam. Other aspects of Arab-Islamic civilization are also included,
such as a 12-page illustrated history of the Arabic script; Arabic dictionaries;
Muslim houses; and dozens of brief biographies.

Aimed at Hughes's fellow Christian missionaries, and at British officials who
were ignorant of Islam but had to deal with it on a daily basis in India, it provides
complete, careful explanations and definitions that presuppose no previous knowledge. Indeed, many of Hughes's articles, which generally range from five to one
hundred lines of this double-columned tome (sometimes more), are much more
comprehensible than the often technical and confusing, albeit highly useful,
scholarship of the *Shorter Encyclopedia of Islam* (Leiden, Brill, 1961), next to
which it should be shelved. Heading terms are either in English for the Christian
who would look up religious subjects in Christian terminology, or in romanized
Arabic, with cross references from the unused form. There is a separate index of
the terms in Arabic script that accompany each article. There are innumerable
cross references between articles. Despite evident Christian bias, Hughes made an
honest effort to provide all the facts, utilizing the latest Western and Eastern

works as well as classical Arabic sources, many of which are cited in the articles. This Indian edition, it should be noted, is complete, in contrast to the 1965 Pakistani reprint (Lahore, 1965), which excised many of Hughes's statements that are offensive to Orthodox Islam.

Hughes's work and the *Shorter Encyclopedia* as yet have not been equalled, let alone surpassed in usefulness. —David W. Littlefield. [R: Choice, Sept 73, p. 944; ARBA 74, item 1177]

470. Neill, Stephen Charles, Gerald H. Anderson, and John Goodwin, eds. **Concise Dictionary of the Christian World Mission.** Nashville, Abingdon Press, 1971. 682p. (World Christian Books). $10.50. LC 76-21888. ISBN 0-687-09371-6.

This carefully edited work appears to be more comprehensive than *The Encyclopedia of Modern Christian Missions: The Agencies* (Camden, N.J., T. Nelson, 1967), which is the only modern book even remotely comparable. The entire period of Christian expansion from 1492 to the present is covered. The editorial viewpoint may be described as international, ecumenical, and liberal. Over two hundred contributors from all over the world have written signed articles (most with bibliographies). The editor is now Professor of Philosophy and Religious Studies at the University College of Nairobi and was formerly Bishop of Tinnevelly.

Countries, leaders, and subjects are treated in concise, yet comprehensive, articles arranged in one alphabet with three types of cross references: from headings not used to those that are used; from small topics without separate articles to larger topics that include the smaller; and from words in the text that are themselves subjects of separate articles (such words being indicated by asterisks). A random check of ten words revealed no blind references. Large and small countries alike are included. Treatment in the samples examined was proportional to each country's importance (e.g., five pages for China and nine lines for Portuguese Guinea). Entries normally include basic facts (area, population, brief history, major religions) as well as matters specifically pertaining to Christian missionary activity. Leaders still alive are not included. Nor are leaders (e.g., Niebuhr, Tillich) without strong missionary identification. There are entries for Carey, Grenfell, Martyn, Mott, Latourette, Ricci, Scudder, and Xavier. Treatment of Vatican II is brief and confined to the missionary aspects. Similar consistency applied to other subjects sampled. —A. Robert Rogers. [R: Choice, June 71, p. 534; LJ, July 71, p. 2296; ALA 71; ARBA 72, item 1184]

471. **The Oxford Dictionary of the Christian Church.** 2nd ed. Ed. by F. L. Cross and E. A. Livingstone. New York, Oxford University Press, 1974. 1518p. $35.00. LC 74-163871. ISBN 0-19-211545-6.

Soon after its initial publication in 1957, the ODCC was recognized as one of the most indispensable one-volume reference works covering the broad spectrum of Christianity. It contained approximately 6,000 entries ranging from just a few lines to about 2,500 words, and nearly 4,500 brief bibliographies. Minor corrections and additions were incorporated in several reprintings, but in many ways this second edition is an entirely new work. The volume has been increased in size by one tenth through the addition of 200 new articles and over 50 additional *see* references. The number of contributors was enlarged from 94 to 247, and the dictionary has been completely reset. Minor, often subtle, changes have been incorporated in many of the articles, and a great many of the bibliographies have been expanded and updated (through 1972). New features include a memoir to Frank Leslie Cross (d. 1968) and a Chronological List of Popes and Antipopes. (Still absent, however, are companion lists of Archbishops of Canterbury and Patriarchs of Constantinople.)

Some of the notable new entries are: Aggiornamento; Coventry; Ecumenical Movement; "Honest to God"; Humanae Vitae; North India, Church of; Orthodox Church; Pacem in Terris; Process Theology, Taize Community; and Vatican Council, The Second. Among the over 60 new biographies are ones on Athenagoras (1886-1972), O. Cullmann, El Greco, G. F. Fisher, M. Heidegger, John XXIII, Martin Luther King, H. R. Niebuhr, M. Noth, Paul VI, A. M. Ramsey, Teilhard de Chardin, and Ralph Vaughn Williams. Coverage of the Eastern Orthodox Church, particularly in its liturgical terminology, has been considerably enlarged, and the inclusion of abbeys and monasteries has been increased, although neither term, per se, is defined. One continuing serious deficiency is the poor coverage of American Christianity. Because 25 entries have been either shortened or deleted, there may be some value in having both editions readily available. —Glenn R. Wittig. [R: ARBA 75, item 1220]

472. Parrinder, Geoffrey. **Dictionary of Non-Christian Religions**. Philadelphia, Westminster Press, 1973 (c.1971). 320p. illus. $10.95. LC 73-4781. ISBN 0-664-20981-5.

This one-volume dictionary contains a large number of brief entries dealing with deities, cults, sacred objects, names and places, philosophies and philosophers, and other terms associated with non-Christian religions throughout history. The stress seems to be on Hinduism, Buddhism, and Islam. There are 242 small drawings that are clear and very well done. The 94 black and white photographs are helpful, but some are dark and lacking in clarity. Three listings of dynasties and a short bibliography are appended.

The entries tend to be short and factual, with a considerable number of cross references added. The language is usually simple and easy to understand, which adds to the ready reference value of the work. The *Dictionary of Comparative Religions* (to which Parrinder contributed) has some of the terms and names, with more information. However, the present work includes many items not found in that dictionary. In addition, its entries are certainly easier to read and therefore will probably be more useful for the layman. Since reference works in religion have tended to include less information on non-Christian religions, this work serves a very useful purpose. —Dennis Thomison. [R: LJ, 1 Sept 73, p. 2424; ALA 73; ARBA 74, item 1178]

HANDBOOKS

473. Child, Heather, and Dorothy Colles. **Christian Symbols Ancient and Modern: A Handbook for Students**. New York, Scribner's, 1973 (c.1971). 270p. illus. index. $17.50. LC 72-2769. ISBN 0-684-13093-9.

Designed for continuous reading as well as for reference, this book in catalog style is topically arranged: symbolism, the Cross, the Trinity, images of Christ, the Virgin Mary, the nativity of Christ, living water, the Holy Spirit, the Eucharist, angels, good and evil, forerunners and followers, symbols of the evangelists, symbols of praise, the Church, categories, and liturgy and crafts. Most of these are further elaborated in the detailed table of contents, which is followed by a list of 33 plates and 114 line drawings, which illustrate variations in symbols in different countries and periods. The text is well written and suitable for the designer and craftsman, the university student, or the educated layman. The bibliography is highly selective. The index is generally good (all topics checked were found in the index); however, sometimes many page references are given under a topic with no indication of where the main discussion of the subject occurs. References to plate numbers are clearly given, but one must turn to the list in the front to find the corresponding page numbers for the plates. Though generally superior to *Church Symbolism*, by F. R. Webber (Cleveland, J. H. Jansen, 1927), this book does lack a list of saints and a glossary of common symbols, which were useful features of Webber. The book is well produced physically, with strong binding and clear typography. The plates are sharp and clear, and the line drawings are good; both reflect a wide range of European and Middle Eastern sources. —A. Robert Rogers. [R: LJ, 15 Mar 73, p. 860; WLB, May 73, p. 794; ALA 73; ARBA 74, item 1180]

474. Mead, Frank S. **Handbook of Denominations in the United States.** 5th ed. Nashville, Abingdon, 1970. 265p. $3.95. LC 70-109675. ISBN 0-687-16568-7.

This 5th edition, a few pages shorter than the 4th, continues the same format in presenting the history, doctrines, organization, and present status of religions in the U.S. More than 250 religious bodies are included, and the text gains accuracy in that it was "read and corrected by denominational authorities." A sampling of known religions suggests that the claim to objectivity is justified. The section on Black Muslims (severely criticized in the 4th edition, cf. *Choice*, March 1965, p. 292) has been thoroughly rewritten. Updating is evident in other areas. Additional information includes a directory of addresses of denominational headquarters, a glossary of terms, a classified bibliography, and an index of proper names. The bibliography could be improved, e.g., the *New Catholic Encyclopedia* (1967) is overlooked although the old (1907) *Catholic Encyclopedia* is listed. In line with its purpose, this is a useful book for concise information about particular religious bodies. [Editor's note: The sixth edition was published in 1975 (320p. $5.95. LC 75-2363. ISBN 0-687-16569-5). It was reviewed in ARBA 76, item 1087.] —Joseph W. Sprug. [R: ARBA 71, item 1318]

ATLASES

475. **Historical Atlas of the Religions of the World.** Isma'il Ragi al Faruqi, ed. David E. Sopher, map ed. New York, Macmillan, 1974. 346p. illus. maps. index. $12.50. LC 73-16583. ISBN 0-02-336400-9.

This book is far more than a collection of maps. There are 20 chapters (prepared by 13 scholars from various parts of the world) that give historical background, illustrated by 65 maps and well over 100 black and white photographs. The chapters, which are signed, vary in length from four or five pages to over 30 pages. The major divisions of the atlas are as follows: religions of the past (Mesopotamia, Egypt, Canaan-Phoenicia, greater Syria, ancient Greece and Rome, Shamanism, Amerindian religions); ethnic religions of the present (traditional religions of Africa, Hinduism, Jainism, Sikhism, Confucianism and Taoism, Shinto, Zoroastrianism, Judaism); universal religions of the present (Theravada Buddhism, Mahayana Buddhism, Chrisitianity, Islam).

The work is well organized for reference purposes. The preface concludes with a short bibliography. The list of contributors and their credentials is followed by the table of contents and a list of maps. Each article contains a select bibliography. There are helpful chronologies for religions of the past and the present. The subject index is reasonably detailed, and there is an extensive index of proper names. The maps (especially for African and Far Eastern religions) break new ground in the field of religious cartography. —A. Robert Rogers. [R: BL, 15 Dec 75, pp. 592-93; ARBA 76, item 1091]

BIOGRAPHY

476. **Who's Who in Religion, 1975-1976.** Chicago, Marquis Who's Who, 1975. 616p. $52.50. LC 75-21777. ISBN 0-8379-1601-1.

The lack of a current biographical dictionary of religious leaders in America has frequently been a source of regret for reference librarians. Not since the early 1940s has there been a general "who's who" approach to the clergy of all denominations as well as to lay persons and teachers.

The present work is limited to religious leaders now active in the United States. The circa 16,000 biographies are distributed over the following categories: church officials, both national and regional, clerical and lay; clergy—leading priests, rabbis, and ministers; professors of religion, theology, or divinity in seminaries and universities; and lay leaders.

Undoubtedly, users will discover both lacunae and unwarranted inclusions, a state of affairs that is almost inevitable in a first edition. Be this as it may, in a field where for so many years there has been literally nothing, the new Marquis volume is most welcome. [R: ARBA 76, item 1093]

BIBLE STUDIES

477. Botterweck, G. Johannes, and Helmer Ringgren, eds. **Theological Dictionary of the Old Testament: Volume I.** Grand Rapids, Mich., William B. Eerdmans, 1974. 479p. $18.50. LC 73-76170. ISBN 0-8028-2325-4.

This is a companion set to the monumental *Theological Dictionary of the New Testament* by Kittel and Friedrich (Grand Rapids, Mich., William B. Eerdmans, 1964-73. 9v.). Successive volumes are scheduled to appear in English about a year after the publication of the original fascicles in German. Words are arranged according to their order in Hebrew (with transliterations). All entries are included in the table of contents in the front of each volume, but it is necessary to know the Hebrew words either in the original script or in transliteration. Other prefatory material in Volume I includes a list of contributors, abbreviations for books and journals, and a transliteration table.

The work is both scholarly and ecumenical. Most of the contributors are European. The articles are generally lengthy and technical in nature, liberally provided with footnotes and bibliographies. All are signed. Cross references within the text are indicated by means of arrows. Each article opens with a contents note.

The article " 'ôth" (pp. 167-88) deals extensively with the subject of signs, opening with a discussion of etymology, number of times used in the Old Testament, and synonyms, and continuing with a brief section on secular usage before concluding with a lengthy discussion of theological usage. There are 165 footnotes in addition to the bibliography for this article.

Volume II was published in 1975. —A. Robert Rogers. [R: Choice, June 75, p. 509; ARBA 76, item 1096]

478. **The Broadman Bible Commentary**. Clifton J. Allen, general ed. Nashville, Broadman, 1969. 12v. $8.00/v. LC 78-93918.

The purpose of this 12-volume commentary is to make the Bible known and understood in the context of modern life. The scholars contributing to this effort are primarily from the Southern Baptist Convention. For each book of the Bible there is an introduction and an outline; a paragraph-by-paragraph interpretation and exposition of the text (the Revised Standard Version is used) is developed within that framework. The introductions deal with questions of purpose, date, authorship, and setting.

A sampling indicates that the work achieves its aim of avoiding extremes in interpretation. Volume 1 contains general articles on the Bible, translations, interpretation, geography, archaeology, the canon, history of Israel, theology of the Old Testament, and contemporary approaches to Old Testament study; it also contains the introductions and commentaries on Genesis and Exodus. In volume 8 there are general articles on the background, canon, theology, and contemporary study of the New Testament, plus introduction and commentary on Matthew and Mark; volume 9 is concerned with the gospels of Luke and John. In addition to bibliographical footnotes in the text, there is a select bibliography at the end of each introduction. No index is included in individual volumes. —Joseph W. Sprug. [R: LJ, 15 Sept 69; ARBA 71, item 1319]

479. Brownrigg, Ronald. **Who's Who in the New Testament**. New York, Holt, Rinehart and Winston, 1971. 448p. illus. maps. $18.95. LC 75-153654. ISBN 0-03-086262-0.

A companion volume to Comay's *Who's Who in the Old Testament* (Holt, 1971), this work deals with fewer names and is able to give more space to each person. The articles on Jesus, Mary, Peter, Paul, and other major figures in the various versions of the Judeo-Christian scriptures are quite long and illustrated with photographs of paintings, statues, landscapes, etc. The biographies usually explain differing doctrines about each person when appropriate and maintain a moderate and objective tone. The value of this work, as of its companion, will depend on a library's need for theological materials and the extent of its holdings in Biblical dictionaries and encyclopedias containing similar information. —James P. McCabe. [R: ALA 72; ARBA 72, item 1194]

480. **The Cambridge History of the Bible**. Ed. by P. R. Ackroyd and C. F. Evans. New York, Cambridge University Press, 1963-70, 1975pa. 3v. illus. bibliog. index. $25.00/v.; $65.00/set; $24.50pa./set. LC 63-24435. ISBN 0-521-07418-5(v.1); 0-521-04255-0(v.2); 0-521-29016-3(v.3); 0-521-09973-0(pa. set).

Contents: Volume 1: *From the Beginnings to Jerome*, edited by P. R. Ackroyd (1970); Volume 2: *The West, from the Fathers to the Reformation*, edited by G. W. H. Lampe (1969); Volume 3: *The West, from the Reformation to the Present Day*, edited by S. L. Greenslade (1963).

This history does not deal directly with the contents of the Bible nor with the science of Biblical scholarship. Rather, it is "an account of the text and versions of the Bible used in the West, of its multiplication in manuscript and print and its circulation; of attitudes toward its authority and exegesis; and of its place in the life of the Western Church." Volume 1 deals with the origin of the text of the Christian Bible, the development of the canon, and the place of the Bible in the early Church. Volumes 2 and 3 concern themselves with the place of the Bible in the Church during the periods indicated, and especially with the various translations, revisions, and printings of the text.

Approximately 50 scholars from all denominations contributed the essays of which each volume is composed. Some articles are highly technical, while others are written in lively narrative fashion with touches of humor. A few articles assume knowledge of Hebrew, Greek, Latin, French, or German, incorporating foreign words or phrases in the text and appending multilingual bibliographies. Also, each volume includes a detailed table of contents, an extensive general index, an index of Biblical references, and from 25 to 50 black and white plates. Volume 3 also contains appendixes on commentaries and other aids to Bible study. There is no table of contents or index for the set as a whole. Recent versions of the Bible (e.g., the *Living Bible* and the *New English Bible*) appeared after this work went into production and therefore do not appear in it. —A. Robert Rogers and James P. McCabe. [R: ALA 70; ARBA 72, item 1195; ARBA 76, item 1097]

481. Comay, Joan. **Who's Who in the Old Testament Together with the Apocrypha.** New York, Holt, Rinehart and Winston, 1971. 448p. illus. maps. $18.95. LC 79-153655. ISBN 0-03-086263-9.

This work duplicates much information that can be found in Bible dictionaries and encyclopedias such as the *Interpreter's Dictionary of the Bible* (Abingdon, 1962), *The New Westminster Dictionary of the Bible* (Westminster, 1970) and the *Encyclopedia Dictionary of the Bible* (McGraw-Hill, 1963). It does give more detail about the important figures in the Old Testament than can be found in most of the aforementioned works, although it also has numerous very brief entries of the type that can be found anywhere.

The work is divided into two parts: the Old Testament and the Apocrypha. Each part has a general introduction followed by a biographical dictionary that lists every name in the work in question. Over 450 photographs and some maps illustrate the biographies. This is a companion volume to *Who's Who in the New Testament*, by Ronald Brownrigg. —James P. McCabe. [R: ALA 72; ARBA 72, item 1198]

482. Davis, John D. **Davis Dictionary of the Bible.** 4th rev. ed. Philadelphia, Westminster Press, 1924; repr. Grand Rapids, Mich., Baker Book House, 1972. 888p. illus. $8.95. ISBN 0-8010-2805-1.

First published in 1898, this important Bible dictionary was revised by its original compiler in 1903, 1911, and 1924. In 1944, a revision by Henry Snyder

Gehman was published under the title *The Westminster Dictionary of the Bible*. In 1954, Baker Book House reprinted Davis's original work with permission of the former publishers. Some 18 reprintings were issued.

The present version (the nineteenth) incorporates several changes—almost 50 pages of photographs and 26 full-color maps. Meanwhile, Gehman has revised and expanded his version (*New Westminster Dictionary of the Bible*; Philadelphia, Westminster Press, 1970), thus widening the differences without eliminating important similarities. The article on "Aaron" is almost word-for-word the same. However, Davis called the etymology "doubtful," whereas Gehman says "probably of Egyptian origin." Gehman gives a phonetic pronunciation. The same scripture references are cited and the same cross references to other articles are given. However, Davis quoted from the Authorized Version and the Revised Version, whereas Gehman uses the Revised Standard Version. Two areas of striking difference are the inclusion of new articles in the text and the use of photographs and maps. Davis has no textual entries for "Dead Sea Scrolls" or "Qumran" while Gehman devotes about two pages to each. The photographs and maps appear to be totally different. Both books are well bound. The typography and layout of Gehman are superior. —A. Robert Rogers. [R: ARBA 73, item 1116]

483. Gehman, Henry Snyder, ed. **The New Westminster Dictionary of the Bible.** Rev. ed. Philadelphia, Westminster Press, 1970. 1027p. illus. maps(part col.). (Westminster Aids to the Study of the Scriptures). $12.95. LC 69-10000. ISBN 0-664-21277-8.

Although somewhat narrow in viewpoint, this revision of the author's 1944 work is a useful source of detailed information on over 5,000 Biblical persons, places, and things. Hundreds of photographs, maps, and charts illustrate the articles, which are of moderate length and which contain an abundance of etymological, historical, political, and geographical detail. Pronunciation is given for each word, but bibliographies are not supplied. References to scriptural passages and occasionally to some major authorities are provided. Frequent cross references and an appended selection of "Historical Maps of Bible Lands" add to the book's reference value.

This work complements rather than duplicates the other recently published, one-volume Biblical dictionaries. It is more detailed than McKenzie's *Dictionary of the Bible* (Bruce, 1965) and Léon-Dufour's *Dictionary of Biblical Theology* (Desclée, 1967), but it is not quite as thorough or scholarly as the *Jerome Biblical Commentary* (Prentice-Hall, 1968).

The main value of the work probably lies in its readily available factual content and not in its interpretations, which are the work of one man and which reflect traditional Protestant viewpoints more extensively than Jewish or Catholic viewpoints. Information is lacking on some of the more current scriptural developments in such areas as hermeneutics, for which there is no article; eschatology, for which there are six lines; hope, which is not included (although faith and charity are); and immortality and the resurrection, which receive sketchy treatment. However, Gehman does consider relevant archaeological discoveries of the past 30 years and includes information about such topics as the Dead Sea Scrolls and Qumran. On the whole, this revision represents a considerable improvement over the previous text. The book is well bound and typography and layout are superior. —James P. McCabe. [R: LJ, 1 Sept 70; ALA 70; ARBA 71, item 1322]

484. Kittel, Gerhard, and Gerhard Friedrich, eds. **Theological Dictionary of the New Testament.** Geoffrey W. Bromiley, translator and editor. Grand Rapids, Mich., Eerdmans, 1964-1973. 9v. $20.50(v.1); $22.50/v.(v.2, 9); $25.00/v.(v.3-7); $18.50(v.8).

This dictionary is a study of theologically significant terms. As with other disciplines, there has been much progress in Biblical studies in recent times; volumes produced after the fourth (in German, 1942) naturally reflect more of the discoveries of modern research, especially Qumran. It is recognized that the contributions vary in worth, that this work does not replace a full commentary, and that some of the conclusions are subject to debate. Even so, this is a most significant publication for the understanding of the Bible; it is an indispensable starting point for serious study of the ideas of the New Testament. Since the first fascicle appeared (in German, 1932), this work has been regarded as a classic, as one of the best products of Protestant scholarship of this or any century. There has been praise for the accuracy of translation and quotation in Bromiley's rendition. Articles and bibliographies have not been updated; they must be supplemented by later research.

Articles vary in length: one or two pages for less significant terms; booklet length for such words as "agape" (love, 34p.) or "hamartia" (sin, 50p.). The longer articles, packed with information and bibliographical leads, are preceded by a contents note. Some of the longer articles have been edited and issued separately in a series called "Bible Key Words." Examples of terms (in the Greek form) that receive more extensive treatment are church, lord, death, god, time, judgment, demon, teacher, righteousness, glory, power, peace, bishop, work, prayer, life, etc. These terms impress one with the desirability of using this work as a starting point in investigating a particular topic from the viewpoint of Biblical theology. —Joseph W. Sprug. [R: ARBA 71, item 1324]

485. Layman, Charles M., ed. **The Interpreter's One-Volume Commentary on the Bible.** Nashville, Abingdon Press, 1971. 1386p. illus. maps.(part col.). index. $17.50; $19.50(thumb-indexed ed.).

This new commentary, based on the Revised Standard Version of the Bible, includes the books of the Apocrypha. It is the result of many years of research and the work of 70 Bible scholars from the United States, Canada, and Great Britain. Designed for use by laymen, ministers, librarians, and anyone studying the Bible, it includes commentary on historical background, scope, and significance of each book of the Bible; many general articles; full color maps; and many sketch maps, drawings, and photographs. Two indexes (to scripture references and to subjects) further enhance the usefulness of this valuable work. [R: WLB, Oct 71, p. 193; ALA 71; ARBA 72, item 1199]

486. Léon-Dufour, Xavier, ed. **Dictionary of Biblical Theology.** 2nd ed., rev. and enl. New York, Seabury, 1973. 712p. (A Crossroad Book). $19.50. LC 73-6437. ISBN 0-8164-1146-8.

This dictionary is a preeminent one for Biblical theology. The French original—*Vocabulaire de théologie biblique*, which was published in 1962 and enlarged in 1968—has been highly praised. The English translations followed in 1967 and 1973, and the dictionary has been or is being translated into 11 other languages as well.

The differences between the two editions are considerable. Among the 40 new articles are those on adultery, anguish, city, conscience, dreams, farewell speeches, perfume, responsibility, salt, and violence, as well as one on Jesus Christ (a topic strangely missing from the first edition). Most of the original articles have been revised and/or corrected by their respective authors. Fuller and more detailed cross references have been added at the end of each article. The index (or more precisely, the reading guide) that has been added arranges a large number of the articles under three major theological divisions. The new work is almost 100 pages longer.

Due to an editorial mix-up, the analytic table of all terms discussed in the dictionary still appears separately at the back of the volume, instead of being interspersed alphabetically as announced in the foreword (and as is actually done throughout the first ten pages). Uncommon abbreviations are used for the Books of the Bible. —Glenn R. Wittig. [R: Choice, Mar 74, pp. 62, 64; ARBA 75, item 1230]

487. **Oxford Bible Atlas.** Ed. by Herbert G. May, with the assistance of G. N. S. Hunt, in consultation with R. W. Hamilton. 2nd ed. New York, Oxford University Press, 1974. 144p. illus.(part col.). maps. index. $9.95; $4.95pa. ISBN 0-19-211556-1.

The book is divided into four main parts. The first is a historical introduction by H. G. May entitled "Israel and the Nations." It is illustrated by 58 black and white photographs (including some taken in 1973) and two sketches. Two tables of dates aid in relating key personages to events. The second part consists of 26 colored maps (usually with text on the same or facing pages). Topography, climate, historical periods, and archaeological sites are covered. The next section, by R. W. Hamilton, is devoted to "Archaeology and the Bible"; it contains 31 black and white photographs and one sketch. The "Gazetteer" at the end is really more of an index to the maps.

Although it is less comprehensive than Aharoni's *The Macmillan Bible Atlas* (New York, Macmillan, 1968), Grollenberg's *Atlas of the Bible* (Camden, N.J., Nelson, 1965) or Negenman's *New Atlas of the Bible* (Garden City, N.Y., Doubleday, 1969), the Oxford atlas is modestly priced in hardcover and is also available in paperback.

Comparison with the 1962 edition reveals several changes. The type is smaller. The paper is whiter and no longer glossy. There are several new photographs (generally, the photographs are not as crisp and clear as those in the first edition), and there are some significant changes in the text. —A. Robert Rogers. [R: BL, 1 Dec 74, pp. 389-90; WLB, Nov 74, p. 245; ARBA 75, item 1232]

488. **The Zondervan Pictorial Encyclopedia of the Bible.** Gen. ed., Merrill C. Tenney, assoc. ed., Steven Barabas. Grand Rapids, Mich., Zondervan, 1975. 5v. illus.(part col.). index. $79.95. LC 74-6313.

Although there have been several one-volume dictionaries/encyclopedias of the Bible in recent years, the number of multi-volume sets has been much smaller. For over half a century, Hastings' *Dictionary of the Bible* (New York, Scribner's, 1898-1904; 5v.) was the standard work. The scene began to change with the appearance of *The Interpreter's Dictionary of the Bible* (Nashville, Abingdon Press, 1962;

4v.) and the store of readily available Biblical information is now greatly enhanced by *The Zondervan Pictorial Encyclopedia of the Bible*.

Zondervan is the product of extensive collaboration. There are contributions from 238 scholars, mainly from the United States but also from Great Britain, Canada, Australia, New Zealand, South Africa, and Israel. All but the very shortest of the 7,500 alphabetically arranged articles are signed. There are 32 pages of full-color maps with index (at the end of Volume 5), 48 pages of full-color plates (some in each volume), and literally hundreds of black and white photographs, sketches, and maps. Although the colored maps are easy to find and the black and white illustrations are in close proximity to the appropriate articles, the color plates are neither numbered nor cross-referenced from the pertinent articles. This is a pity, because it would be easy to overlook the 71 superb color photographs of coins when reading the article and to conclude that the black and white sketches and photographs are all that the encyclopedia has to offer. Other plates containing significant information could likewise be missed in a hasty search.

Some comparisons are made with *The Interpreter's Dictionary of the Bible*. *Zondervan* is more lavishly illustrated and the colors in the plates are more vivid. However, *Interpreter's* does number its color plates and make references from the articles. Map coverage overlaps but does not completely duplicate. *Interpreter's* maps (at the end of Volume 1) are not separately indexed and are sometimes less detailed than those in *Zondervan*. Both give Hebrew words and, where appropriate, Greek. Both have valuable articles on supplementary topics, such as the alphabet. Both have bibliographies at the ends of all but the shortest articles, but *Zondervan* tends to cite mainly English language sources, whereas *Interpreter's* makes frequent citations from other languages. *Interpreter's* gives rather detailed and explicit directions on how to use the set. *Zondervan* gives a good list of abbreviations but little in the way of explicit guidance for use.

It is when one examines viewpoint that the differences become even more important. *Zondervan* is conservative, with an effort to state other opinions. *Interpreter's* is more liberal. Comparison of the articles on "Jonah" revealed sharp differences over date and authorship. *Interpreter's* merely states that "the book is now mostly held to have been written *ca.* the fourth century B.C. by an unknown writer. . . ." *Zondervan* discusses the problem at length, noting various viewpoints, and concludes by giving reasons for accepting the traditional view that the book was written by "Jonah, the son of Amittai, who lived in the 8th century B.C." The *Zondervan* bibliography is longer, with 12 items.

Zondervan can be particularly valuable for its supplementary information and alternative viewpoints. —A. Robert Rogers. [R: ARBA 76, 1104]

CHAPTER 23

PHILOSOPHY

489. **The Encyclopedia of Philosophy**. Paul Edwards, editor in chief. New York, Macmillan, 1967; repr. New York, Macmillan, 1973. 8v. in 4. index. $99.50.

A four-volume reprint of the eight-volume original, which was published in 1967. Approximately 1,500 articles attempt to cover philosophy in its entirety—both Eastern and Western—including relevance to other disciplines. Some articles are of such length that they could constitute small books, and most have prodigious bibliographies. More than 500 philosophers from throughout the world have contributed to this work, and their names, brief credentials, and major publications are provided.

Biographical coverage of ancient, medieval, and early modern philosophers is generally good. That of contemporary philosophers is better for Western Europe, North America, and India than it is for the Soviet bloc and the People's Republic of China. There are excellent articles on philosophical movements, major ideas, the philosophies of various disciplines, and the history of philosophy in various countries. Articles of particular interest include those on philosophical bibliographies, dictionaries, encyclopedias, and journals.

The integrated approach has been preferred to a series of short articles, and subtopics can be located by use of the detailed index in Volume 8. Although the type size has been reduced, the print is still very easily read. This is a valuable, definitive encyclopedia. [R: ARBA 75, item 1237]

490. Potter, Karl, comp. **The Encyclopedia of Indian Philosophies. Volume 1: Bibliography of Indian Philosophies**. Published for American Institute of Indian Studies. Delhi, India, Motilal Banarsidass; distr. Columbia, Mo., South Asia Books, 1970 (1971). 811p. index. $25.00. LC 70-911664. ISBN 0-8426-0112-0.

This bibliography, a listing of over 9,200 sources of Indian philosophies, inaugurates a projected multi-volume scholarly work titled *The Encyclopedia of Indian Philosophies*. The preface states that the encyclopedia is an endeavor by an international team of scholars to present the contents of Indian philosophical texts to a wider public than has hitherto been possible. This bibliography, with additions and revisions, will constitute, in effect, the table of contents for the subsequent volumes. Each of these will deal with the literature of one of the systems of Indian thought and will attempt to provide a definitive account of current knowledge about each of the systems of classical Indian philosophy.

The scope of this bibliography also reflects the intended coverage of the encyclopedia, which will provide an account of works of Indian literature that are 1) of philosophical interest throughout; 2) theoretical rather than practical in their intended function; and 3) polemical or at least expository in a context where defense of one view among alternatives is appropriate. Thus, this bibliography attempts to utilize distinctions drawn from both Western and Indian understanding of the scope of philosophy. Works that are clearly theological or religiously sectarian have been excluded. Similarly, classics such as the Upanishads, the Pali and Jain canons, the Prajna-Paramita literature, etc., are omitted since, although they contain the philosophical material, they are not sustainedly polemical and systemically philosophical throughout. Also omitted, because they are not pertinent to the scope of this bibliography, are recent books and articles that are by Indian authors but that are devoted primarily to topics in Western philosophy.

The compiler does not claim that this bibliography is exhaustive. The heavy representation of Bengali material was due to the ready and quick cooperation of the team from the National Library in Calcutta.

The bibliography is divided into three parts: part one, a chronological listing of Sanskrit texts and authors whose dates are known; part two, an alphabetical listing of Sanskrit texts and authors whose dates are unknown; and part three, secondary literature arranged by genre. Parts one and two are comprised of listings of all Sanskrit works known to the compiler to exist in some form or other. Publications pertaining to a Sanskrit work are listed in chronological order of appearance under that work's title. Editions, translations, commentaries, etc., are indicated. A very thorough and comprehensive index is divided into three categories—names, titles, and topics. This first volume of the encyclopedia can be used independently as a bibliographical guide. —Sharad Karkhanis. [R: Choice, Dec 70, p. 1356; ARBA 73, item 1125]

491. Wiener, Philip P., editor-in-chief. **Dictionary of the History of Ideas: Studies of Selected Pivotal Ideas.** New York, Scribner's, 1973-74. 5v. illus. index. $40.00/v.; $200.00/set. LC 72-7943. ISBN 0-684-13293-1(set).

In view of the interdisciplinary character of the curriculum in academia, this interesting work seems to be timely and long overdue. Its major emphasis is on intellectual history. Over 300 articles included in the five-volume compendium describe significant ideas in Western thought, demonstrating the interrelationships of intellectual concepts in different disciplines. The reader will find, generally speaking, three types of articles: cross-cultural studies limited to a given century or period; studies that trace the origin of certain thoughts from antiquity to the present time; and finally, studies that trace the evolution of an idea in the writings of its leading proponents. Each article is signed (contributors are well-known authors from various countries), and each concludes with a bibliography that lists not only the works referred to in the text but also some standard titles pertaining to a given topic. At the end of each article are a number of helpful cross references that direct the reader to related material. There is a separate index volume.

As indicated above, the interdisciplinary character of this work emphasizes intellectual history. Thus, a number of articles deal with literature and the arts, philosophy, history, religion, science, mathematics, and the broad spectrum of social sciences. There are many articles of particularly contemporary significance— academic freedom, civil disobedience, and social attitudes toward women, to name only a few. As Philip P. Wiener indicates in the preface, "the purpose of these studies of the historical interrelationships of ideas is to help establish some sense of the unity of human thought and its cultural manifestations in the midst of a world of ever-increasing specialization and alienation. These cumulative acquisitions of centuries of work in the arts and sciences constitute our best insurance against intellectual and cultural bankruptcy. Taking stock of the ideas that have created our cultural heritage is a prerequisite of the future growth and flourishing of the human spirit" (Vol. 1, p. vii). We think that these objectives have been achieved in this work. —Bohdan S. Wynar. [R: LJ, 1 Nov 73, p. 3250; Choice, Oct 73, p. 1173; RSR, July/Sept 73, p. 26; WLB, Sept 73, p. 83; ARBA 74, item 1198]

CHAPTER 24

MYTHOLOGY, FOLKLORE, AND POPULAR CUSTOMS

MYTHOLOGY AND FOLKLORE

BIBLIOGRAPHIES

492. Ziegler, Elsie B. **Folklore: An Annotated Bibliography and Index to Single Editions.** Westwood, Mass., Faxon, 1973. 203p. (Useful Reference Series No. 100). $12.00. LC 73-77289. ISBN 0-87305-100-9.

The compiler states that "the purpose of this book is to aid librarians, teachers and researchers of folklore in locating appropriate folklore for story hours, reading units, social studies units, voluntary reading and analysis" (Introduction). The book is arranged in six parts: annotated title bibliography, subject index, motif index, country index, type of folklore index, and illustrator index. Each entry in part one presents a full description: title, author, illustrator, imprint, date, pages, and synopsis. A list of headings used in each of the five indexes is also given for each title, plus cross references to different versions of the tales. Over 400 separately published stories are indexed. The format is well designed and easy to use. The special indexes for motifs, countries, etc., are excellent timesavers for anyone searching for specific types of tales. —Christine L. Wynar. [R: ARBA 74, item 1209]

DICTIONARIES AND HANDBOOKS

493. **Brewer's Dictionary of Phrase and Fable.** Centenary Edition. Rev. by Ivor H. Evans. New York, Harper & Row, 1971. 1175p. $15.00. LC 79-107024. ISBN 0-06-010466-X.

This British work has a long history, the first edition having been published in 1870. Three more recent editions were published in 1959, 1963, and 1970 by Cassell and Company in Great Britain and Harper & Row in this country.

The present edition is based on that of 1963, but the editor, as he explains in the Preface, "sought to return more closely to Dr. Brewer's original conception by discarding entries, e.g., Artesian Wells, which seemed to have little claim to be in a dictionary of Phrase and Fable. Words which have no particular 'tale to tell' have also been deleted, as well as numerous words and technical expressions, etc., for an explanation of which the average reader would naturally turn to the household dictionary, general encyclopedia, or specialized reference book." Thus, this dictionary includes primarily colloquial and proverbial phrases in a wide range of subjects (archaeology, history, religion, the arts, the sciences, etc.), as well as biographical and mythological references, fictitious characters, and other hard-to-find information. In this edition, there are many more Americanisms, and repetitions have been largely eliminated by comprehensive cross-referencing. Nevertheless, we would recommend that libraries also keep the old edition, since some of the material that was dropped in this new edition may occasionally be useful. [R: ARBA 72, item 1224]

494. Briggs, Katharine M. **A Dictionary of British Folk-Tales in the English Language, Incorporating the F. J. Norton Collection. Part A, Folk Narratives. Part B, Folk Legends.** Bloomington, Indiana University Press, 1970-71. 4v. bibliog. indexes. Part A, 2v., $40.00. Part B, 2v. $40.00. Complete set of 4v., $70.00. LC 70-97241. ISBN 0-253-31715-0(pt.1); 0-253-31716-9(pt.2); 0-253-31717-7 (pt.3); 0-253-31718-5(pt.4).

In the British Isles, the study of folklore developed slowly. The latter part of the nineteenth century saw collections of local legends of some north and west counties, but these were mostly amateurish rather than scholarly projects. Not until the appearance of *A Dictionary of British Folk-Tales* has the British material been brought together in any kind of organized fashion. Dr. Briggs, who is recognized as the outstanding student of the British folk-tale today, has previously published, with Ruth L. Tongue, *Folktales of England*. This was a selection of surviving tales drawn from oral sources along with scholarly apparatus.

The work reviewed here is an ambitious collection of British folk-tales from various printed and manuscript sources. Many have been found in obscure county collections, in general periodicals like *Notes and Queries*, and in other sources where they have lain buried. Among the unpublished sources have been the manuscript and tape collections of F. J. Norton, Ruth L. Tongue, the School of Scottish Studies, and the Irish Folk-Life Commission. Part A consists of folk narratives, or tales told primarily for entertainment. They are presented full-length or in summary, with reference to the immediate, original, and parallel sources. Arrangement is by type, following the universally used Aarne-Thompson system: fables, fairy tales, jocular tales, novelle, and nursery tales. Legends comprise the two volumes of Part B; unlike the narratives, these are tales that were believed and told as true by the folk narrator. Their arrangement is by subject: black dogs, bogies, devils, dragons, fairies, ghosts, and giants. Legendary material cannot be fitted into the Aarne-Thompson scheme. The legend, being a supposedly true account, is not embellished in the telling, as the narrative frequently is, and Dr. Briggs has tried to restrict Part B to those tales that reported what was actually believed. In order to hold the collection to a manageable and publishable length, she has excluded those tales of the British Isles in the Celtic, Gaelic, Irish, and Welsh languages, admitting only those handed down in English. Tales differing only in slight detail have also been omitted. About 850 narratives are included in Part A and over 1,200 legends in Part B. Whether given in their original form or in summary, they are written well, are authoritative, and are fully documented. Each of the two parts includes a bibliography, a motif or classified index, and an index of story titles. The most complete collection of the British folk-tale yet published. —Rolland E. Stevens. [R: LJ, 1 Oct 70; Choice, Dec 70, p. 1353; LJ, Aug 71, p. 2480; ALA 71; ARBA 72, item 1225]

495. Leach, Maria, ed. **Funk & Wagnalls Standard Dictionary of Folklore, Mythology, and Legend.** New York, Funk & Wagnalls; distr. New York, T. Y. Crowell, 1972. 1236p. index. $17.95. LC 72-78268. ISBN 0-308-40090-9.

This is a one-volume, but complete and uncut version of *Funk & Wagnalls Standard Dictionary of Folklore, Mythology, and Legend,* published in two volumes in 1949-50. The significant feature of this new edition is a key to the 2,405 countries, regions, cultures, areas, people, tribes, and ethnic groups presented or discussed in the book. As is well known, this dictionary offers comprehensive coverage of customs, beliefs, songs, tales, heroes, dances, games, etc., for the various cultures of the world, including survey articles with bibliographies on individual regions and on special topics. [R: ARBA 73, item 1133]

496. **The New Century Handbook of Greek Mythology and Legend.** Ed. by Catherine B. Avery. New York, Appleton-Century-Crofts, 1972. 565p. illus. $9.95. LC 75-183796. ISBN 0-13-611996-4.

This encyclopedic dictionary of figures from ancient Greek mythology has been extracted from a larger work, *The New Century Classical Handbook* (1162p., 1962). The text is very readable and is intended to entertain as well as instruct. Some of the articles have been prepared by the late Jotham Johnson and by professors Abraham Holtz and Philip Mayerson. The book contains approximately 900 entries; those on the principal 14 gods and heroes, such as Apollo, Athena, Heracles or Zeus, are long and detailed, with 400 or more lines each. Attractive, small illustrations are reproduced from authentic vase paintings. Each page is provided with a guide to pronunciation. In the final analysis, this is a popular compilation: no bibliography, few references to sources, and little or no critical analysis of the subject material. The book should be particularly useful for school assignments, but its value for serious students is limited. —Theodore M. Avery, Jr. [R: Choice, Oct 72, p. 954; ARBA 73, item 1134]

497. Tripp, Edward. **Crowell's Handbook of Classical Mythology.** New York, Thomas Y. Crowell, 1970. 631p. illus. $11.95. LC 74-127614. ISBN 0-690-22608-X.

Original sources used in the compilation of this handbook have included most of the major writers of classical antiquity, usually in versions most familiar to modern readers. Citations refer to editions in the Loeb Classical Library. Coverage, though less complete than in monumental works such as Roscher's *Ausführliches Lexikon der griechischen und römischen Mythologie,* appears to be more comprehensive than in Oswalt's *Concise Encyclopedia of Greek and Roman Mythology* (Follett, 1969) or the Greek and Roman sections of *Larousse Encyclopedia of Mythology* (Prometheus, 1959).

The arrangement is alphabetical by specific subjects. Cross references are fairly plentiful. Complete information is given under the main entry, with shorter accounts under other headings. It is easier to use than Larousse. There are maps and family trees, but no other illustrations, in marked contrast to Oswalt (which must average almost one per page) and Larousse (which even has a few color plates). Pronunciations are given in a separate "Pronouncing Index" (p. 611-631). Though not glamorous in appearance, this volume is sturdily bound, generously leaded, and printed in very readable type on good quality paper. —A. Robert Rogers. [R: LJ, 1 Dec 70, p. 4159; ALA 70; ARBA 71, item 1351]

INDEXES

498. Ireland, Norma Olin. **Index to Fairy Tales, 1949-1972: Including Folklore, Legends & Myths in Collections.** Westwood, Mass., Faxon, 1973. 741p. (Useful Reference Series, No. 101). $18.00. LC 26-11491. ISBN 0-87305-101-7.

Compiled as a continuation of Mary Huse Eastman's *Index to Fairy Tales, Myths and Legends* (Boston, Faxon, 1926. Supps. 1937, 1952), this work begins where Eastman's second supplement stops. Some 406 collections have been indexed, under titles and subjects. Included are all the fairy tales, folklore, legends, and myths of all countries that appear in these collections. Authors have been included only when specifically mentioned in the collections being indexed. Main entries are under titles. Comprehensive subject headings have been chosen with the needs of children's librarians in mind. The ALA filing rules are followed in arrangement of entries. The extensive subject indexing is an innovation and a major improvement over Eastman. Cross references (both *see* and *see also*) enhance the usefulness of the book, which should be an immense timesaver for busy reference and children's librarians. —A. Robert Rogers. [R: LJ, 1 Dec 73, p. 3544; WLB, Dec 73, p. 340; ALA 73; ARBA 74, item 1206]

POPULAR CUSTOMS

499. Gregory, Ruth W. **Anniversaries and Holidays.** 3rd ed. A revision of the work by Mary Emogene Hazeltine. Chicago, American Library Association, 1975. 246p. bibliog. index. $10.50. LC 74-23163. ISBN 0-8389-0200-6.

The precursor of this work was Mary Hazeltine's *Anniversaries and Holidays*, 2nd ed. (Chicago, ALA, 1944). For many years librarians have regretted that Hazeltine's very useful book was completely obsolete. Indeed, the need for a complete revision was urgent. The world today is a completely different place from what it was in the 1940s. Most of the nation states existing today did not exist then, and each of today's nation states has its own anniversaries and holidays, to cite only one reason for a revision.

The revision by Ruth Gregory follows the organization of her model. Like the earlier work, the revision is divided into three parts: the "Calendar of Fixed Dates," arranged calendrically (January through December); the "Calendars of Movable Days," subdivided according to the Christian, Islamic, and Jewish calendars and the festivals of the Eastern and Western worlds; and a bibliography of books about anniversaries and holidays.

The Calendar of Fixed Dates constitutes the body of the book (146p.). Set forth month by month and day by day, the entries very briefly describe the reason why each day is special to someone, somewhere. Example: "July 3—Idaho Admission Day. Idaho became the 43rd state on July 3, 1890."

Part II (Movable Days) is theoretically more complicated. For example, the differences in calendrical systems (Julian, Gregorian, Jewish, Islamic) are important and their implications for dating have to be explained. The explanations are good as far as they go, but in many instances they should go further. The great Christian movable feast, Easter, is not, as it should be, elucidated in terms of how Easter Sunday is fixed each year.

The bibliography is a sound, workable, and thoroughly updated tool containing complete citations. The index is sufficiently detailed to provide access by all pertinent points of reference—people, places, political units, etc. —Richard A. Gray. [R: ARBA 76, item 1108]

500. Myers, Robert J., with the editors of Hallmark Cards. **Celebrations: The Complete Book of American Holidays.** Garden City, N.Y., Doubleday, 1972. 386p. illus. bibliog. index. $8.95. LC 77-163086.

Arranged chronologically by holidays from New Year's Day to Christmas, this useful, attractively designed volume will serve both the reference librarian and the reader seeking information about "the notable holy days and holidays currently observed in America: how and why these special days originated, their history, and past and present observances." Complete chapters on 45 holidays are followed by supplementary information on 15 more of lesser importance, such as Sweetest Day, Groundhog Day, and Armed Forces Day. "Other Holidays at a Glance," a two-page chronological listing, serves as a guide to essentially regional celebrations—Admission Day (Arizona, California, and Hawaii), Leif Ericson Day (Minnesota), Coptic Christmas, and Wright Brothers Day, among others. Included in the detailed accounts of the major holidays are the often-sought-for fabrications of Parson Weems, the custom of hot cross buns, and the change in wording of The Pledge of Allegiance. A selected bibliography is included, and there is a good index. To be used in conjunction with the more comprehensive, but outdated, *American Book of Days*. —Charles R. Andrews. [R: LJ, 1 Dec 72, pp. 3889-90; ALA 72; ARBA 73, item 1139]

501. Post, Elizabeth L. **The New Emily Post's Etiquette.** 14th ed. New York, Funk & Wagnalls, 1975. 978p. illus. index. $11.95; $12.95 thumb-indexed. LC 74-14667. ISBN 0-308-10167-7; 0-308-10168-5 thumb-indexed.

Revised to meet modern-day needs, this edition of the classic etiquette book now discusses such topics as obscene phone calls, doggy bags, and what to do about unmarried couples as weekend guests. A useful, unstodgy, and up-to-date approach to etiquette. As is pointed out in the preface, Emily Post's 1922 definition of etiquette is still valid today: its purpose is "to make the world a pleasanter place to live in, and you a more pleasant person to live with" (p. vii). [R: BL, 1 Apr 75, p. 781; WLB, June 75, p. 757; ARBA 76, item 1109]

CHAPTER 25

LINGUISTICS AND PHILOLOGY

BIBLIOGRAPHIES

502. McMillan, James B. **Annotated Bibliography of Southern American English.** Coral Gables, Fla., University of Miami Press, 1971. 173p. index. $7.95. ISBN 0-87024-183-4.

McMillan has done an admirable job of assembling more than 1,100 pertinent references to the regional speech of the southeastern United States. While the major dialect boundaries do not generally coincide with political borders, this identification of the area, below the Ohio River-Mason-Dixon Line as far west as the longitude of Texarkana, makes good sense in terms of general cultural history and of the older traditions of defining "Southern" dialects.

The items in this collection range from the most catholic (Mencken's American Language series) to treatments of individual words ("poorboy" in the oilfields), from social dialects (numerous recent studies of black language) to the areal. It is unlikely that any accessible or authentic piece of linguistic Dixiana has been omitted from this book; there is even ample coverage of place names, personal names, metaphorical language, and, of particular significance, literary dialect. Amateur and professional dialectologists will be well served by this bibliography, which could be the model for similar up-to-date lists for other regions of the country. —Robert Parslow. [R: LJ, 15 Dec 71, p. 4083; ARBA 72, item 1236]

503. Shibles, Warren A. **Metaphor: An Annotated Bibliography and History.** Whitewater, Wis., Language Press, 1971. 414p. index. $12.50. LC 72-157087. ISBN 0-912386-00-2.

"This is the only extensive bibliography on metaphor. . . . Every major article, book, dissertation, etc. in every major language and field of study has been included. . . ." Such a bold claim invites attempted disproof. Both BIP and the LC subject catalog (1950–date) were checked. The only book that even came close was *Diktens bildspräk*, by Jan Thavenius (Lund, 1966, 47p.). Several tests of thoroughness were then applied. Names of a few noted philosophers, literary critics, and creative writers were searched. Gilbert Ryle, I. A. Richards, Northrop Frye, Ezra Pound, T. S. Eliot, Benedetto Croce, René Wellek, W. K. Wimsatt, Ludwig Wittgenstein, C. S. Lewis, and Cleanth Brooks were all there— and many more. Plato and John Dewey seemed to be notable omissions, but a quick effort to check their works (through indexes) did not reveal any writings specifically on metaphor, though some of Dewey's *Art as Experience* might be related. The omission of F. R. Leavis and Ivor Winters was noted but not explored.

The "Background" section of the bibliography at the end of the article on metaphor in the *Encyclopedia of Philosophy* was checked. This section contained nine references by nine authors. Shibles included eight of the authors and furnished 21 references. For the "Theory of Metaphor" section, the *Encyclopedia* had nine references by eight authors. Shibles, this time, had included all eight—and had given 27 references.

The book has other virtues. In addition to the annotated bibliography (arranged alphabetically by author), there is a three-part index of nearly 100 pages. Part one lists 24 noted works on metaphor. Part two is a general index of names and terms. Part three is an index of concepts that begin with the word "metaphor" (e.g. "metaphor as ambiguous"). The author's introduction is the least useful part. —A. Robert Rogers. [R: ARBA 72, item 1237]

504. Stankiewicz, Edward, and Dean S. Worth. **A Selected Bibliography of Slavic Linguistics, Volume 2.** The Hague, Mouton; distr. New York, Humanities, 1970. 530p. index. $41.75. (Slavistic Printings and Reprintings, XLIX, 2) LC 65-26005.

The series "Slavistic Printings and Reprintings," edited by C. H. Van Schooneveld of Indiana University, has gained considerable professional reputation over the years. The present volume, no exception, is a well-balanced work with appropriate attention to bibliographical detail. The introductory section, West Slavic, enumerates general and special studies, then discusses the Lechitic group and relationships to South and East Slavic languages as well as to non-Slavic languages, and onomastics. This is followed by sections devoted to individual languages: Polish, Pomeranian, Polabian, Lusatian, Czech, Slovak, Belorussian, Russian, and Ukrainian. The conclusion of the work consists of a bibliography of bibliographies and history of research, covering general and comparative studies, and South, West, and East Slavic languages. There is a helpful list of abbreviations and a detailed index at the end of the volume.

In sections dealing with individual languages, the arrangement of material is by topic (e.g., synchronic studies, diachronic studies, the standard language and its history, texts, orthography and orthoepy, dictionaries, onomastics, dialectology, stylistics and poetics, versification, and relationships to other Slavic and non-Slavic languages). There are no annotations, but many entries provide references to published reviews. The material in general is well selected, covering the most important monographs and articles in scholarly periodicals. In short, a well-executed work. —Bohdan S. Wynar. [R: ARBA 72, item 1239]

INDEXES

505. **Words and Phrases Index: A Guide to Antedatings, New Words, New Compounds, New Meanings, and Other Published Scholarship Supplementing the Oxford English Dictionary, Dictionary of Americanisms, Dictionary of American English and Other Major Dictionaries of the English Language.** Compiled by C. Edward Wall and Edward Przebienda. Ann Arbor, Mich., Pierian Press, 1969-1970. 4v. $19.95/v.; $75.00/set. LC 68-68874. ISBN 0-87650-001-7.

Intended to supplement the *Oxford English Dictionary*, the *Dictionary of American English on Historical Principles*, and other major English language dictionaries, this computer-produced index "cites words, compounds, phrases, definitions, and additional information which is often not available in major dictionaries." Entries are in alphabetical order on a word-by-word basis; phrases are listed under the first word other than an article. Citations refer to passages in selected sources where the word or phrase is used in context. This work will serve as a timesaver for linguists. [R: C&RL, Mar 70, p. 112; ALA 70; ARBA 71, item 1377]

ENGLISH LANGUAGE DICTIONARIES

COMPREHENSIVE

506. **The American Heritage Dictionary of the English Language.** Ed. by William Morris. Boston, Houghton Mifflin and American Heritage, 1973. 1550p. illus. $8.76 (thumb-indexed). LC 76-86995. ISBN 0-395-09066-0.

"First published in the fall of 1969, and continuously revised since then," this much-touted dictionary has continuously revised its dust jacket blurb, but not much else, naturally. It has also changed in binding from blue to red, and the editors have added some illustrations on a few pages that had none—total illustrations number about 4,000. All well and good, for it is a fine dictionary. The editors can be faulted, however, for not correcting a few minor errors in the 1969 edition, such as the airport code for Washington, D.C., which is listed as DCA, while, more explicitly, DCA is the code for Washington, D.C., National Airport. There are two airports in Washington.

Also, there is an individual entry for *founder* (to become disabled), but *founder* (one who casts metals) and *founder* (one who establishes) must be located under the definitions for the various meanings of *found*. Introductory, prefatory, and appended material remains virtually unaltered, except for a change in major offices in the American Heritage Publishing Company. Dates of death are not included for Harry Truman or Lyndon Johnson, though less recent events, such as the resignation of Harold Wilson as British Prime Minister and the establishment of Bangladesh have been noted. United States population statistics are those for 1970, but foreign population is further off. —Frances Neel Cheney. [R: ALA 69; ARBA 74, item 1219]

507. **Funk & Wagnalls Comprehensive Standard International Dictionary: Bicentennial Edition.** Chicago, J. G. Ferguson Publishing Co., 1973; distr. New York, Crowell, 1974. 1929p. illus.(part col.). $49.95. LC 74-150152. ISBN 0-308-10109-X.

The editor of this dictionary is Sidney I. Landau, and the chairman of the Editorial Advisory Board is Allen Walker Read, professor of English at Columbia. The consulting editors and members of the editorial staff, listed on pages ii and iii, include a number of distinguished scholars and lexicographers as well as representatives from business and industry.

In terms of its scope, this dictionary belongs to the family of comprehensive abridged dictionaries, with a vocabulary range of approximately 175,000 entries. Entries include not only colloquialisms, slang, synonyms and antonyms, etc., but also personal and place names, scientific and technical vocabulary (on a selective basis), and, to warrant the use of "international" in the title, a selected number of foreign language terms in general use, as well as British, Canadian, Australian, and Scottish terms. In word treatment the American spelling is stressed, with British variations noted. The etymologies present a very concise history of the word with reference to origin, form changes, and semantic development. Greek roots are given in the Roman alphabet. The dictionary also contains a number of small black and white illustrations, and there are several plates and numerous illustrations in the "Encyclopedic Supplement." This supplementary material (420 pages) covers a wide variety of linguistic subjects—e.g., grammar and usage, quotations, almanac-type information on the United States and other countries, and even a section on writing business letters. Most of this information can be readily found in other sources.

An evaluation of this dictionary should stress, first, that its vocabulary is well selected, with clear definitions and the minimum etymology necessary for home or school use. Like most other abridged dictionaries, this work is not prescriptive but descriptive, reflecting standard usage. The format is handy, and the volume is thumb-indexed for easy use. Consequently, this abridged dictionary will be of substantial assistance in homes and to the general reader. —Bohdan S. Wynar. [R: ARBA 75, item 1251]

508. **The Oxford Illustrated Dictionary.** 2nd ed. Text ed. by J. Coulson and others. Rev. by Dorothy Eagle. New York, Oxford University Press, 1975. 998p. illus. $20.00. ISBN 0-19-861118-8.

It is difficult for me to review a general English dictionary without automatically comparing it with my trusted vade mecum, *The American Heritage Dictionary*—especially when the work under scrutiny is illustrated and purports to be something of an encyclopedia.

The present work, as is typical of Oxford University Press publications, is tastefully designed and printed; the black and white illustrations are clear and aptly chosen; and one would think that the 998 pages with 35 to 50 entries each would have practically any term or name in ordinary use. Perhaps I chose the wrong one for my first test: Charles Martel. He appeared under neither "Charles" nor "Martel," whereas the AHD entered him under the former, with a cross reference under the latter. But I must admit that, at times, the Oxford work gives a bit more; e.g., Friedrich August *Kekulé von Stradonitz* is identified as "the formulator of ring structure of benzene"; whereas AHD calls him merely a "German chemist." In general, however, it would seem from checking back and forth on terms covered by both that the AHD gives as much in the way of definition and explanation as does the work at hand, which indeed is presented as a "dictionary and encyclopaedia." Certainly the AHD far surpasses it in sheer number of illustrations; and the AHD use of photographs allows for portraits, while the work reviewed has only line drawings and seems to average about one on every other page. Appendixes present lists of Roman and Holy Roman emperors, some popes, British rulers and prime ministers, etc. The relatively small format (23 cm.) with its three-columned pages might be attractive, but, considering the price of this book, I would still opt for the AHD in spite of its hoary age of six years. —Francis J. Witty. [R: LJ, July 75, p. 1309; WLB, Oct 75, p. 121; Choice, Nov 75, p. 1141; ARBA 76, item 1117]

SCHOOL AND COLLEGE

509. **The American Heritage School Dictionary**. Boston, Houghton Mifflin; New York, American Heritage, 1972. 992p. illus. $8.95. LC 72-75557. ISBN 0-395-13850-7.

The 35,000 entry words defined in this new school dictionary were selected from a computerized corpus. The designers of *The American Heritage School Dictionary* (AHSD) set out to identify, in an objective way, words that are actually encountered by students in American schools in grades 3 through 9. A survey of 107 educators produced a list of the books of all kinds most used in their schools. One thousand titles were ultimately selected, and from these books the initial corpus of English words was developed. It is not surprising to find "dope" and "pot" defined in terms of drug use, but not words such as "rip off." Roberts' *The Third Ear: A Black Glossary* could profitably be used to supply definitions for some of the slang and street language cleaned out of the AHSD. The AHSD provides short, but accurate and uninhibited, definitions for the few words on sex and human biology that are included. Nevertheless, drawings and other illustrations have been discreetly selected; furthermore, taboo words and popular graffiti seem to be absent. Overall, the selection of words covers all areas and topics and should be satisfactory for most classroom work for grades 3 through 9, although, obviously, many words will have to be located in unabridged dictionaries.

The page format is clear and well designed. The wide pages allow for two columns of type plus a yellow center column for small photos and drawings. No maps are included. Heavy black type is used for entry words, which are shown with syllabication marks. Pronunciation respellings are given; a pronunciation key is printed at the bottom of each left-hand page. Examples are supplied where these are useful for illustrating figurative senses and multiple senses of words. Definition by example is also employed where needed. Most variants are separately entered. Some homophones are noted as an aid to spelling. Geographic (country names, capital cities, names of seas and mountain ranges, etc.) and biographic entries are included on a highly selective basis. Notes providing some additional information on the origin and use of certain words are sometimes used as fillers for the center illustration column on each page. These are illuminating bits that should interest students; more often, however, the additional space in the column is left blank. Selection of a few additional illustrations or extension of notes would have been useful in these instances.

The AHSD is a comprehensive desk dictionary for young people that is well edited, attractively produced, and sturdily bound at a reasonable price. Its main purpose is to serve as a students' dictionary in the classroom, but it should find wide use in homes and libraries as well. –Christine L. Wynar. [R: ARBA 73, item 1164]

510. **Macmillan Dictionary for Children**. William D. Halsey, editorial director. Christopher G. Morris, ed. New York, Macmillan, 1975. 724p. illus.(part col.). $10.95. LC 74-24661.

This large-size volume for the early intermediate grades through junior high contains about 30,000 entries printed in large type with many small, clear, color illustrations. Entry words are written as children ordinarily see them—no diacritical marks or syllable division—thus making them easy to identify and locate. Plurals that are spelled differently (*elves*) are entered separately as well as being noted under the singular (*elf*). Names of places (countries, states, planets) are included, as are organizations. Contractions (*don't, we'll*) and common phrases (*double-cross, comic-strip, navy blue*) are also listed separately. Definitions, part of speech, plurals, pronunciation, and sample sentences are given. There are also "language notes" for many words that give background or usage. The relatively simple pronunciation key appears on alternate pages for easy references. The introductory material is particularly good; it is simply worded and clearly explains what a dictionary is and how to use one. This work is also published in a school text edition, with a different introduction, as the *Macmillan Beginning Dictionary*. —Eleanor Elving Schwartz. [R: BL, 1 Oct 75, pp. 261-62; ARBA 76, item 1121]

511. Thorndike, E. L., and Clarence L. Barnhart, eds. **Thorndike-Barnhart Advanced Dictionary**. Garden City, N.Y., Doubleday, 1973. 1186p. illus. $9.50. LC 73-77962. ISBN 0-385-07543-X. (Text edition available from Scott, Foresman.)

512. **Webster's Intermediate Dictionary: A New School Dictionary**. Springfield, Mass., G. & C. Merriam, 1972. 50+910p. illus. $6.50. LC 70-38974. ISBN 0-87779-179-1.

These two dictionaries are presented for the teenage student; the former specifies (on the dust jacket) "grades 7—12," while the latter states "edited for young teenagers."

The Webster deceptively notes "illustrations in color," but all illustrations are black and white, with a negligible number with some blue shading. Since it uses blue for guide words and letters, this is no added burden in the printing, and it is neither an aesthetic nor an illustrative aid.

The Webster boasts of "over 57,000 entries," the Thorndike of "55,000 main entries and 95,000 total entries." The printing of the Webster is in two columns with an unimpressive, heavy sans serif for entries and the above-mentioned use of blue. The Thorndike uses three columns, with tastefully chosen typefaces for both entries and definitions. The latter is by far the more attractive and the more complete work, with all entries arranged in one alphabetic order; thus, there are no extra lists as in the Webster, where the list of vice-presidents includes pronunciations of the names—e.g., Humphrey / ˈhəm(p)frē!! Fortunately, the Thorndike lists him in the H's and pronounces his name as "hum' frē."

Since there have been a rather large number of lexicographical studies over the past few years—particularly on words used in school books and recommended school readings—there is hardly a problem about what words to choose for such dictionaries. It seems rather to be a problem of what aids should be given and how they should be presented. In this reviewer's opinion, the Thorndike is a long way out in front: it has etymologies; it is generous with examples of usage; it obviously has more entries and more illustrations; and last of all, it is a better-looking book altogether. If one begins (appropriately) with "A," one finds "aardvark" as the eighth entry in Webster; but it is the fifteenth in Thorndike. But go to "B" and find "babel"; it is the eighth entry in Webster, but the seventeenth in Thorndike. In price there is a $3.00 difference between the two, but the Thorndike is well worth that difference. —Francis J. Witty. [R: RSR, Jan/Mar 73, p. 11; ARBA 74, items 1229-1230]

513. **Webster's New Collegiate Dictionary**. Springfield, Mass., G. & C. Merriam, 1973. 1536p. $9.95; $11.95 thumb-indexed. LC 72-10966. ISBN 0-87779-319-0; 0-87779-320-4 thumb-indexed.

The origins of this desk dictionary date back to 1898. From 1963 to 1972 the dictionary was titled *Webster's Seventh New Collegiate Dictionary*. This eighth edition, based on *Webster's Third New International Dictionary* and numerous Merriam-Webster citation files, contains 152,337 entries plus separate sections for 6,051 biographical and 12,485 geographical entries, 566 foreign words and phrases, a list of colleges and universities, signs and symbols, and a handbook of style. A handy index at the end of the dictionary quickly reveals the location of such items as a table of Easter dates or a table of metric measures and English equivalents. Introductory matter includes explanatory notes on the use of the dictionary and an essay by W. Nelson Francis, "The English Language and Its History." The page format is condensed but the type, in double columns, is clear and legible; 892 small line drawings are fitted into the text. Each entry word is printed in boldface, followed by pronunciation, functional labels, inflected forms, etymology, usage, and sense division. Some 24,000 phrases, including 3,093 quotations from authors, are added to show how certain words are used. The editors state that 1,875 synonyms and antonyms are provided for words believed to be of interest to dictionary users.

Webster's is comparable in terms of number of entries to *The Random House Dictionary of the English Language, Collegiate Edition*. Each of these dictionaries contains words not found in the other. However, Webster's contains more words of recent origin or importance, such as Chicano, Black Panther, charge-a-plate, Wankel engine. *Webster's New Collegiate Dictionary* is an up-to-date and well-edited desk dictionary. —Christine L. Wynar. [R: BL, 1 Nov 73, p. 251; WLB, June 73, p. 866; Choice, Sept 73, p. 952; RSR, July/Sept 73, p. 26; ARBA 74, item 1223]

514. **Webster's New Elementary Dictionary**. Springfield, Mass., G. & C. Merriam, 1975. 612p. illus. $4.95. ISBN 0-87779-275-5.

This elementary dictionary is suitable for students in grades 4—6 and is part of a series of three Webster school dictionaries—elementary, intermediate, and students' dictionaries. Vocabulary entries were chosen "chiefly on the basis of their occurrence in textbooks and supplementary reading in all subjects of the elementary-school curriculum" (p. 31); specific word lists or studies are not cited. The more than 25,000 entries are printed in large boldface type; definitions printed in medium face are clear and well leaded. Guide words are at the top of each two-column page; pronunciation keys are printed on the bottom. About 1,200 pictorial illustrations in black and white are placed throughout the dictionary, but these are not of special quality. In fact, some sketches do not adequately distinguish the items. Entries contain the word in bold (centered periods mark syllables), pronunciation between slant lines, part-of-speech labels, senses, a verbal illustration of usage in angle brackets. Some entries also show synonymous cross references. About 200 etymologies, identified by square brackets, are provided, but they are hard to locate. The appearance of the pages and the structure of the entries offer little attraction to the student. Information is presented in a traditional manner and, because of the numerous devices and markings used in the entries, the student needs special instruction in order to use the dictionary. A brief introduction to the use of the dictionary is provided, but few youngsters will be able to benefit from it without guidance. Lists of abbreviations, states, large cities, nations, presidents, and symbols are appended.

Comparison of Webster's elementary dictionary with *Macmillan Dictionary for Children* (Macmillan, 1975) is inevitable. In terms of number of entries and general vocabulary selection, the two are close, with Macmillan slightly in the lead (e.g., Macmillan contains 30,000 entries). However, the unique structure of Macmillan's entries brings dictionary use much closer to the skill levels and needs of children. The main entries show the words undivided, immediately provide meanings, offer an abundance of illustrative sentences geared to children's experiences, and leave the formal part-of-speech labels, etc., to the end. Definitions are not as terse as those in Webster. The appearance of the Macmillan pages in terms of selection of paper, type style, and general layout is far superior to Webster's and is a pleasure to look at and read. Finally, there is no contest when it comes to comparison of illustrative matter. Macmillan's 1,000 color drawings are larger and more detailed. The selection of illustrations is also integrated to real-life activities and not static representations, a feature that marks all aspects of the Macmillan dictionary. Etymologies are easily spotted between heavy horizontal blue lines. This device encourages browsing. No special appendixes are added, but the introduction to use of the dictionary is written and designed to attract the student and encourage his participation in learning about words. More than one dictionary is needed in schools but, as a first choice, Macmillan is a winner. Webster represents a traditional dictionary that is informative but highly formal in style and that requires special instruction before young children can use it. —Christine L. Wynar. [R: ARBA 76, item 1123]

515. **Webster's New World Dictionary of the American Language**. 2nd college ed. Ed. by David B. Guralnik. Cleveland, Collins-World, 1974. 1692p. $8.95; $9.95 thumb-indexed. LC 74-5544.

Webster's New World Dictionary of the American Language was prepared as a new second college edition in 1970; it maintains its currency through biennial updating. The 1974 revision is the second updating of the dictionary under the "continuous revision" program; consequently, it contains only minor changes and no increase in pages. The college edition is a well-prepared desk dictionary known for its numerous etymologies, especially for American place names, and for the marking of entries that are considered to be Americanisms. —Francis J. Witty. [R: LJ, 1 Feb 75, pp. 280-81; WLB, Feb 75, p. 461; ARBA 76, item 1125]

516. **The Xerox Intermediate Dictionary**. William Morris, ed. New York, Grosset & Dunlap, 1973. 800p. illus. $7.95; $9.95 thumb-indexed. LC 73-75574. ISBN 0-448-02849-2; 0-448-02905-7 thumb-indexed.

This is one of the best dictionaries of its class to have crossed this reviewer's desk. Except that the columns of the dictionary proper are not justified, the work is well printed; its 1,400 illustrations are clear and are tastefully and perceptively chosen; and excellent articles on its use, on pronunciation, and on Greek and Latin roots precede the actual dictionary entries. The definitions have been composed in clear, readily understandable English, and, for the most part, stand up well under the critical eye of the reviewer—e.g., there is no nonsense about the distinction between "bi-" and "semi-". I would mildly object to the first definition of *organ* as "A musical instrument made up of a keyboard and pipes through which air is blown," since most users of an intermediate dictionary are probably much more familiar with the electronic instrument. However, I am sure that most organists would rejoice at the definition's exclusiveness. But one out of more than 34,000 entries hardly merits the quibbling. It should be added that this dictionary is also published for school and library use as *The Ginn Intermediate Dictionary* by Ginn and Company. —Francis J. Witty. [R: BL, 15 June 74, pp. 1114-15; ARBA 75, item 1255]

HISTORICAL

517. Burchfield, R. W., ed. **A Supplement to the Oxford English Dictionary, Vol. 1: A-G.** New York, Oxford University Press, 1972. 1331p. $50.00. ISBN 0-19-861115-3.

The well-known 12-volume OED was published from 1884 to 1928, with a supplement (Volume 13) published in 1933. Shortly after World War II, it was decided to prepare a revised version of the 1933 supplement and, after preliminary preparations, in 1957 R. W. Burchfield took over as editor. Since that time, nearly 100 readers, contributors, and consultants have been engaged in extracting over a million quotations from works of all kinds. They have made forays into the written English of the United States and Canada, Australia, New Zealand, South Africa, and India. Approximately one-fourth of this projected three-volume supplement will be new words; the remaining three-fourths will be words that have new meanings. Words like "canned" (music) and "usherette," excluded from the 1933 supplement because they were not fully established, have now been added, along with literary-based words like "Babbitt" and "bandersnatch," anthropometric terms like "ectomorphy," and words that have evolved out of recent world events, like "Biafran." The first of the three volumes of the revised supplement has now been published, while two additional volumes—covering the rest of the alphabet—are planned for publication "over intervals of not more than three years." The concluding volume will contain a bibliography. [R: LJ, 15 Dec 72, p. 3981; ALA 73; ARBA 73, item 1160]

518. **The Compact Edition of the Oxford English Dictionary: Complete Text Reproduced Micrographically.** New York, Oxford University Press, 1971. 2v. $90.00/set. LC 72-177361. ISBN 0-19-861117-X.

The publisher has micrographically reduced the $300, 13-volume OED to a compact, two-volume form, with four pages of the original fitted onto one new page. A rectangular magnifying glass is supplied with this edition. The quality of reproduction is excellent. [R: LJ, 15 Mar 72, p. 1002; ARBA 73, item 1161]

519. Morris, William, and Mary Morris. **Dictionary of Word and Phrase Origins.** New York, Harper & Row, 1962-1971. 3v. $10.00/v. LC 62-10842. ISBN 0-06-111260-7(v.1); 0-06-111201-1(v.2); 0-06-013068-7(v.3).

Designed to supplement the *American Heritage Dictionary of the English Language*. This standard, widely popular reference book is a treasury of hard-to-find information; it provides little-known stories about everyday words and expressions. Arranged in convenient alphabetical order, these capsule accounts range from the earliest years of our language to current teen-age slang. Entries vary in length depending on the popularity of the expression and on the background material assembled by the compilers. Quite frequently, definitions are selected for wit (e.g., Churchill's definition of a fanatic: "one who can't change his mind and won't change the subject").   [R: Choice, Dec 68; ARBA 70, v.2, p. 50; ARBA 72, item 1252]

520. **The Shorter Oxford English Dictionary on Historical Principles.** Prep. by William Little, H. W. Fowler, and Jessie Coulson. 3rd ed. Rev. and ed. by C. T. Onions. New York, Oxford University Press, 1973. 2v. $60.00; $65.00 thumb-indexed. ISBN 0-19-861126-9; 0-19-861127-7 thumb-indexed.

This is an authorized abridgment of the *Oxford English Dictionary*. The first edition was published in 1933, the second in 1936, and the third in 1944. This third edition has been reprinted 13 times with some corrections and revisions, most recently in 1972. The present edition, according to the publisher's note, incorporates two new features: "The etymologies of all words in the body of the Dictionary have been revised by Dr. G. W. S. Friedrichsen, former colleague of the late Dr. C. T. Onions; this major undertaking represents more than eight years' work by Dr. Friedrichsen. The second main feature is the inclusion of a fresh set of Addenda, drawn chiefly from the material assembled for the new Supplement to the *O.E.D.* (the first volume of which was published in the autumn of 1972), and presenting notable accessions to the English language in the period since *O.E.D.* appeared. The entries in the main text of the Dictionary remain essentially as they were, pending the completion of the Supplement to the *O.E.D.* towards the end of the present decade." Thus, the new material is based primarily on the first volume of the Supplement (letters A-G) plus the card files for letters H-P and Q-Z.

The introduction's claim that "the etymologies of all words have been revised and for the most part rewritten, ultimately on the basis of the material presented in the *Oxford Dictionary of English Etymology* (1966), which embodies recent research on the etymologies of English and of the other languages concerned" (p. xii) is not necessarily true for all cases. A comparison of etymologies in the 1970 printing with those in the 1973 printing shows that many, but not all, have been revised. Also, many of these revisions are only of a remedial or supplementary nature. Secondly, an updated addenda list (pp. 2598-2672) indeed has many new words; it has almost twice as many pages as the 1970 printing. But the larger type size for the 1973 printing probably accounts for a substantial part of this increase. Obviously, a complete revision of the SOED can be undertaken only after the three-volume Supplement has been completed.

The excellent quality of typography and paper makes the SOED very easy to use. The fact is that it provides a larger amount of information about the history of the word than any other dictionary of comparable size (163,000 words, combinations, and idiomatic phrases), and it contains some material not in the OED. Many libraries probably already have purchased *The Compact Edition of the Oxford English Dictionary*, a micrographically reproduced complete set in two volumes, published in 1971. This abridgment is a valuable reference work either by itself in smaller libraries, or in conjunction with the micrographically reproduced OED for libraries that do not have an original set. —Bohdan S. Wynar. [R: BL, 1 Nov 74, pp. 298-99; Choice, July-Aug 74, pp. 740-41; RQ, Summer 74, p. 364; WLB, Feb 74, p. 508; ARBA 75, item 1252]

SLANG

521. Wentworth, Harold, and Stuart Berg Flexner, comps. and eds. **Dictionary of American Slang.** 2nd supplemented ed. New York, Thomas Y. Crowell, 1975. 766p. bibliog. $12.95. LC 75-8644. ISBN 0-690-00670-5.

In 1960 the first edition of this work was published. In 1967, the publisher issued a revised edition consisting of the original Wentworth/Flexner vocabulary in one alphabetic sequence, followed by a 48-page supplement prepared by Flexner alone. The present "second supplemented edition" consists of the original 1960 dictionary in one sequence, and the 1969 Flexner supplement that has, in turn, been augmented by insertion of new slang terms coming into vogue in the late 1960s and early 1970s. The supplement that was 48 pages in length in 1967 is now 88 pages. Ergo, the new matter in this edition is exactly 40 pages.

An examination of the newly augmented supplement shows that it does indeed record some very recent coinages. An example: "Barbie Doll," to designate a typical all-American WASP conformist of either sex. This slang phrase is dated by Flexner as 1972. Slang, as Flexner carefully points out, always appears first in oral discourse. Only later does it find its way into print. Therefore, all dated references to first uses in print are to be construed as only approximate indicators of the date of invention.

That Flexner and his new associates, Sheila Brantley and Herbert Gilbert, are really *au courant* is nowhere more evident than in their inclusion of slang terms for which we are indebted to Richard M. Nixon and his Watergate confederates. Perhaps that President's most creative contribution to American civilization consists in his invention, or at least popularization, of such terms as "go the hang-out road (or route)" and "stonewall it." —Richard A. Gray. [R: LJ, Aug 75, p. 1404; ARBA 76, item 1129]

SYNONYM AND ANTONYM

522. Sisson, A. F. **Sisson's Synonyms: An Unabridged Synonym and Related-Terms Locater.** West Nyack, N.Y., Parker, 1970 (c.1969). 691p. $12.95. LC 74-77314. ISBN 0-13-810630-4.

This is a more scholarly work than most of the standard books of synonyms— Webster, Allen, Crabb, etc.—in that the synonyms include extremely esoteric terms; for example, under *hotel* can be found such words as *imaret* and *xenodochium*, and under the entry *hook* are found *hamate* and *uncinate*. No index is provided, but the work is arranged alphabetically. There are numerous cross references, although there are no definitions, discussions, or analogous terms or antonyms. —Marjorie P. Holt. [R: ALA 70; ARBA 72, item 1257]

523. **Webster's New Dictionary of Synonyms: A Dictionary of Discriminated Synonyms with Antonyms and Analogous and Contrasted Words.** Springfield, Mass., G. & C. Merriam, 1973. 909p. $8.95. ISBN 0-87779-141-4.

A revision of the work that first appeared in 1942, this work is an alphabetically arranged thesaurus of words with definitions, synonyms, antonyms, and closely related terms, which also includes quotations from respected authors to aid in correct usage. Every device is provided to make consultation easy: thumb-indexing, caption guides, explanations of symbols and abbreviations at the foot of each page, an abundance of clear cross references, and precise and authoritative definitions. However, care should be exercised in its use: a string of words after an entry does not necessarily consist of true synonyms—e.g., "biennial: *biannual, semiannual"; the word marked with the asterisk (complete entry with definitions, etc.) should be consulted. If we look under "biannual," we find that the three terms are "frequently confused" and that "semiannual" is "unequivocal, since it means half-yearly." The typography is tastefully chosen both for aesthetics and for clarity, and the binding is serviceable. The introduction on the history of English synonymy is substantially the same as in the former editions, but it is recommended reading for the reference librarian who has not yet perused it. —Francis J. Witty. [R: ARBA 75, item 1254]

FOREIGN TERMS

524. Carroll, David. **The Dictionary of Foreign Terms in the English Language.** New York, Hawthorn Books, 1973. 212p. $9.95. LC 70-39281.

Frequently used terms in French, German, Latin, Spanish, Japanese, Gaelic—approximately 7,000 terms from almost 30 languages—are listed in one alphabet and defined. Each word or phrase is succinctly defined and, when necessary for clarification, the term is used in a sentence. Language of origin is indicated by an abbreviation, but no pronunciation is given. Words that have been assimilated into English are in roman type, rather than in the italics used for strictly foreign terms. Commonly used abbreviations of foreign terms are appended in a separate section. Those who need a quick definition (with no etymological background) of foreign terms used in English will find this to be a most helpful reference source. [R: WLB, Oct 73, p. 163; LJ, 15 Mar 73, p. 857; BL, 1 Dec 73, p. 351; Choice, Dec 73, p. 1525; ALA 73; ARBA 74, item 1217]

525. Mawson, C. O. Sylvester. **Dictionary of Foreign Terms.** 2nd ed. Rev. and updated by Charles Berlitz. New York, Thomas Y. Crowell, 1975. 368p. $9.95. LC 74-12492. ISBN 0-690-00171-1.

This dictionary contains some 15,000 words and phrases from more than 50 languages. It is a revision of the venerable *Dictionary of Foreign Terms Found in English and American Writings of Yesterday and Today*, which appeared in 1934. The new material included in this second edition should make it more useful to the current generation.

Much has happened to the English language, especially the American variety, in the last 40 years. This edition reflects the foreign influences upon American English that have resulted from the expansion of the language into all parts of the world since World War II. Additions include words and phrases from the Far East, especially Japan, and from African and American Indian languages.

Rather than relying principally on literature, the second edition reflects many areas of human endeavor, including cuisine, law, the military, business, the fine arts, and diplomacy. Nevertheless, it is fortunate that the material derived from classical and modern literature has been retained. Since the decline and virtual disappearance of liberal education, even the well-educated reader of today must turn to a reference of this type for the meanings of Greek, Latin, French, or German expressions that an earlier generation would have recognized.

Entries are arranged alphabetically letter-by-letter, including articles and prepositions. Except for Greek, all entries are in the Roman alphabet. —Stanley Joe McCord. [R: Choice, Sept 75, p. 818; WLB, June 75, p. 753; LJ, 15 Apr 75, p. 748; BL, 15 Jan 75, p. 476; ARBA 76, item 1118]

ARCHAIC

526. Craigie, Sir William Alexander, and A. T. Aitken. **Dictionary of the Older Scottish Tongue from the Twelfth Century to the End of the Seventeenth; Founded on the Collections of Sir William A. Craigie.** Chicago, University of Chicago Press, 1931-1975. In 4v., 27pts. $47.50/v.; $190.00/set; $13.50pa./pt.(pts.1-26); $16.00pa. (pt.27).

This monumental undertaking began publication in 1931. The language, as expressed in standard subject headings, is the Scottish dialect of English, not the Celtic language of Scotland. The articles for each word are extensive and contain complete documentation for usages. Although it is similar in presentation to the OED, the two-column format and clear, tasteful typography of this work make it much easier for consultation. —Francis J. Witty. [R: ARBA 72, item 1251]

GRAMMAR AND USAGE

527. Barnhart, Clarence L., Sol Steinmetz, and Robert K. Barnhart. **The Barnhart Dictionary of New English Since 1963.** Bronxville, N.Y., Barnhart/Harper and Row, 1973. 512p. $12.95. LC 73-712. ISBN 0-06-010223-3.

This record of the English language from 1963 to 1972 consists of some 5,000 entries, selected from half a billion words printed in British, American, and Canadian books and periodicals during the time period. Technical dictionaries were not consulted, since the aim was to list those words that have entered the common vocabulary. Pronunciation is provided when necessary, following a pronunciation key based on the IPA. Concise definitions are given, along with part of speech and the single usage label "slang." Meanings for entries used in more than one sense are given in order of frequency (in the editors' judgment).

Quotations are used to show the word in an actual context, to supply additional details about the word's connotation, to point out the range of use in different times and places, and to indicate the type of writing in which the word appears. The source (including author) is indicated after each quotation; names of publications are spelled out and dates are given in full, for the reader's convenience.

Since 1963 marks the end of the record of new English in comprehensive dictionaries currently available, this new work becomes an essential source of information on the English language as it is now spoken and written. [R: LJ, 15 Sept 73, p. 2536; RSR, July/Sept 73, p. 26; ALA 73; ARBA 74, item 1234]

528. Bernstein, Theodore M. **Miss Thistlebottom's Hobgoblins: The Careful Writer's Guide to the Taboos, Bugbears and Outmoded Rules of English Usage.** New York, Farrar, Straus and Giroux, 1971. 216p. index. $6.95. LC 78-143299. ISBN 0-374-21043-8.

Without the subtitle, this tongue-twisting title gives no clue to the fact that it is a novel way of attacking the kinds of rules concerning English which are no longer relevant or which never were really important or necessary. Topics under attack include syntax, idioms, and dicta concerning such thorny grammatical problems as ending the sentence with a preposition, *got* versus *have*, *but* used as a preposition or a conjunction, etc. For the guidance of reporters and copyreaders, there is also a "Don't List" from the *New York Herald Tribune*. Also appended is Ambrose Bierce's *Write It Right* and William Cullen Bryant's *Index Expurgatorius*. The author has written a number of books on the subject of language. This handy little volume contains some information that might not be easily found in other sources. —Marjorie P. Holt. [R: LJ, 15 June 71; ALA 71; ARBA 72, item 1260]

529. Follett, Wilson. **Modern American Usage.** Ed. and completed by Jacques Barzun, in collaboration with Carlos Baker and others. New York, Warner Paperback Library, 1974. 528p. $1.95pa. ISBN 0-446-78119-3.

First published in hardcover in 1966, this very welcome, handy volume comes to us now in paperback. Follett spent his life studying language and its usage and, during his last years, he composed this work, which was then published posthumously. It consists mainly of a lexicon of American usage, the entries of which can easily be controlled through the "Inventory of Main Entries" in the introductory material; cross references are generously supplied throughout. Appendixes covering "shall/will, should/would" and punctuation complete the volume.

Mention should be made of the delightful introduction by Follett; it is probably the best *apologia*, to this reader's knowledge, of traditional grammatical concepts and of the attitude that there is a right way and a wrong way to express thoughts in one's native tongue. In an age when, on the one hand, information specialists are desperately trying to store data for retrieval under precise terms, and, on the other, we are faced with dictionary-compilers who accept anything so long as it is used, it is exceedingly refreshing to peruse an author who has the courage to speak out against these lexicographical "Charlie Browns." —Francis J. Witty. [R: ARBA 75, item 1288]

FOREIGN LANGUAGE DICTIONARIES

ARABIC

530. Madina, Maan Z., comp. **Arabic-English Dictionary of the Modern Literary Language.** New York, Pocket Books, 1973. 791p. $2.50pa. ISBN 0-671-78656-3.

This pocket dictionary is basically an abbreviation and rearrangement of the standard *A Dictionary of Modern Written Arabic*, by Hans Wehr (Cornell University Press, 1961), the best to date. The abbreviation consists of: 1) cramming everything together, separating root entries by lines, in contrast to Wehr's liberal spacing even between subentries; 2) replacing Wehr's romanization by complete vocalization of Arabic words, which this reviewer much prefers; 3) deleting many synonyms and near-synonyms which, though often useful, more often confuse the novice—Madina seems generally to have chosen English terms with which the user can most readily use his imagination to catch the sense of the Arabic words, especially important since context is vital in Arabic; 4) deletion of many phrases and sentences provided in Wehr, particularly those that can be translated—Madina leaves in those that cannot be translated literally to learn their meanings; 5) omitting rare words. Wehr's entries are arranged so that the verb forms of the various root expansion patterns are brought together first, followed in succession by nominal forms arranged by length, verbal nouns of forms II-X, and active-passive participles. Madina puts all these together with their verbal stems, which this reviewer prefers—though when there are many derivatives of verb form I, it takes extra concentration to locate the desired item because they are crammed together. The English and Arabic printing and arrangement of the text are fully as readable as in Wehr, or even more so. Generally, most users have lost little or nothing in Madina's version, so it should replace Wehr for most purposes; Wehr's great expense need be borne only by libraries with great demand for it. —David W. Littlefield. [R: LJ, 15 Dec 73, p. 3620; ARBA 74, item 1245]

CHINESE

531. Lin Yutang. **Chinese-English Dictionary of Modern Usage.** Hong Kong, Chinese University, 1972; distr. New York, McGraw-Hill, 1973. 1920p. index. $47.50. LC 72-3899. ISBN 0-07-099695-4.

Dr. Lin Yutang has summed up a lifetime of knowledge and experience in this monumental work. Its predecessors were two other notable works: *Chinese-English Dictionary*, by Herbert A. Giles (1892) and *Chinese-English Dictionary*, by R. H. Mathews (1932).

Among the features of Dr. Lin's work are: 1) entries that relate the successive meanings of the words; 2) a convenient romanization system; 3) an index system that, among other things, reduces the 214 Kanghsi radicals to only 50; 4) the inclusion of levels of speech (e.g., "derogatory," "courteous," "facetious," etc.); 5) a list of characters from the regular to the simplified and from the simplified to the regular.

The basic principle of the work, according to the author, is contextual semantics—i.e., the imperceptible changes of meaning due to context. The influence of past usage on the present is pointed out, and there is an emphasis on the spoken language. Supplementary material includes directions for using the dictionary; a numerical index of characters; an explanation of cycles; lists of Chinese dynasties, geographical names, and common English and Chinese names; the 214 radicals; and an English index. —Suzine Har Nicolescu. [R: ARBA 75, item 1264]

CZECHOSLOVAKIAN

532. **Dictionary of the Czech Literary Language.** Slovnik Spisovneho Jazyka Ceskeho. Praga, Ceskoslovenske Akademie Ved, 1958-1966; distr. University, University of Alabama Press, 1971. 4v. $20.00/v. LC 66-16431. ISBN 0-8173-0850-4(v.1); 0-8173-0851-2(v.2); 0-8173-0852-0(v.3); 0-8173-0853-9(v.4).

This is by far the most comprehensive dictionary of Czech literary language, published by the Czechoslovak Academy of Science. No etymologies or complete historical definitions are given, but vocabulary is adequately explained in terms of contemporary use. In addition, the secondary definitions remind us somewhat of those provided in the *American Heritage Dictionary of the English Language*. [R: ARBA 72, item 1283]

FRENCH

533. Mansion, J. E., ed. **Harrap's New Standard French and English Dictionary; Part One, French-English.** Rev. and ed. by R.P.L. Ledésert and Margaret Ledésert. New York, Scribner's, 1972. 2v. $25.00/v.; $39.50/set. LC 72-2297. ISBN 0-684-13006-8(v.1); 0-684-13045-9(v.2).

After 25 years of research, M. and Mme. Ledésert present Part One (French-English, in two volumes) of *Harrap's New Standard French and English Dictionary*. Not only have all articles been revised to reflect current usage, but the *New Standard* contains 50 to 60 percent more material than the original. Terms that are the result of developments in science and technology are included, and there are also large numbers of idioms, slang expressions, and "franglais" words.

The very readable preface gives detailed information on criteria, orthography (English versus American), and use of the dictionary. It also reveals, in an interesting sidelight, the perils of presenting handwritten copy to the typesetter.

Entries provide pronunciation, utilizing the International Phonetic Alphabet; part of speech; translation; variant meanings; and examples. In addition, specialized meanings (Bot., Nau., etc.) are so identified, as are archaic, obsolescent, and literary words, vulgar terms, and colloquialisms and slang expressions.

Part two of the *New Standard* (the English-French part) is not yet available. Until it is published, part two (English-French) of *Harrap's Standard French and English Dictionary* must be used. [R: ALA 73; ARBA 73, item 1193]

534. **Nouveau Petit Larousse.** New York, Larousse & Co., 1972. 1790p. illus. (part col.). maps. $14.95.

This new edition has been substantially updated in both the language section and the "arts, letters, sciences" section, the latter commenting on men, their works, and current events in all areas. In all, there are 70,500 articles, lavishly accompanied by photographs, line drawings, and maps.

All entries are, of course, in French. Those in the language section provide pronunciation (IPA system), part of speech, gender, and a definition (often with examples of use). In the second section, individuals are identified, with their dates and often a short resume of major accomplishments or writings. Geographical names are located ("Little Rock, v. des Etats-Unis, cap. de l'Arkansas; 132,000 h. Bauxite"), with greater detail provided for the more important entities. There is still a section of pink pages in the middle, defining Latin and foreign phrases.

With its addition of 2,500 words, its new maps, and its signalling of acceptable usage, pronunciation, etymology, and synonyms and antonyms, this new edition of the most famous one-volume "dictionnaire encyclopédique" is an important tool for francophiles and the libraries serving them. [R: ARBA 73, item 1195]

GERMAN

535. Farrell, R. B. **Dictionary of German Synonyms.** 2nd ed. New York, Cambridge University Press, 1971. 403p. index. $18.50; $7.95pa. LC 77-134623. ISBN 0-521-08018-5; 0-521-09633-2pa.

At first glance, one is tempted to wonder at the need for another English-German dictionary; however, the present text is so conveniently different in its presentation from the ordinary English-German dictionary that this second edition is well warranted. The special difficulties of the English-speaking learner of German are taken into account. Only the words that can cause confusion in the linguistic interchange are treated, but these are treated fully and clearly with copious examples. In fact, the work might be likened to an English-German "Fowler" combined with a synonym dictionary. For example, under "Bad, Evil, Wicked," the terms *schlecht, schlimm, arg, übel, böse* are treated with uncommon fullness, with an additional warning paragraph on adverbial usage. Although there are no cross references within the dictionary itself, all of the synonyms appear in a "List of Words Treated," and there is also a "German Word List" at the very end. Thus, the synonyms "evil" and "wicked" would have been found in the former list. The excellent typography is an added advantage to make the work easily consulted. –Francis J. Witty. [R: ARBA 72, item 1275]

536. Messinger, Heinz. **Langenscheidt's Comprehensive English-German Dictionary.** Berlin, Langenscheidt; distr. New York, Optimum Book Marketing, 1972. 1104p. $27.50. ISBN 0-88254-050-5.

The dust jacket tells us that there are 120,000 entries; but then it also states that there are 1,134 pages. The work is a large, well-bound quarto with three columns to a page; it is easy to consult, with its entry words in heavy roman, meanings in a clear, legible type, and eye-catching cross references. Altogether it represents a fine job of printing and proofreading. The work is presented as "a new dictionary for the 1970s," with the statement that "great attention has been given to the exhaustive treatment of key words" which have "crowded into the vocabulary" in the 1960s. Its stated aim is to "take a middle course between Langenscheidt's

Muret-Sanders and the *College English-German Dictionary*, profiting from the merits of both works." The introductory explanations are set out in parallel columns in German and English. Appendixes cover abbreviations, names, numerals, temperature conversion, weights and measures, and irregular verbs. Like most English-foreign language dictionaries of the reviewer's acquaintance, this one sometimes is not mutually exhaustive in its treatment of synonyms; e.g., under "grave clothes" we find only *Totengewand*; under "shroud" we find *Leichentuch*, *Totenhemd*. But this is a difficult area to cover exhaustively, even with the aid of a computer. The stated "middle course" followed by the compiler makes the work practical in size without taking too much away from its comprehensiveness. On the whole this dictionary is highly regarded. —Francis J. Witty. [R: LJ, 15 June 73, p. 1904; ARBA 74, item 1252]

537. **The New Cassell's German Dictionary: German-English, English-German.** Rev. by Harold T. Betteridge. Based on the editions by Karl Breul. New York, Funk & Wagnalls; distr. New York, T. Y. Crowell, 1971. 632p. $8.95. LC 58-7924.

This "all purpose" dictionary was first published in 1958; since that time it has undergone several revisions. The last revised edition was published in 1965. The present edition again introduces a number of new definitions, many new scientific terms, etc., thus maintaining its currency. *Cassell's* emphasizes current usage, omitting obsolete words and out-of-date material. It is by far one of the best bilingual dictionaries—a good competitor to the Langenscheidt family. [R: ARBA 72, item 1277]

538. Schöffler, Herbert. **The New Schöffler-Weis German and English Dictionary: English-German/German-English.** Completely rev., greatly expanded, and fully updated by Erich Weis and Erwin Weis. Chicago, Follett, 1974(c.1968). 562+ 500p. illus. maps. $6.95. LC 73-90689. ISBN 0-695-80458-8.

This is another example of a frequent phenomenon these days: the "Americanized" bilingual dictionary originally published in the country of the foreign language; consequently, the English-German section comes first. The work is quite comprehensive and up to date, incorporating the broad coverage of Schöffler and the pedagogical emphasis of Weis. Meanings are treated fully, with examples of usage and clear explanations. The triple-column format might not appeal in every case, nor will the heavy italic used for the main entries in the German-English section; but, in general, the work is easy to handle. Extras include a short historical atlas of Germany and the usual lists of abbreviations, weights and measures, proper names, etc. Strongly endorsed in the foreword by the Chairman of the University of Chicago's Department of Germanic Languages and Literatures, it appears an excellent tool where a one-volume, bilingual dictionary will suffice. —Francis J. Witty. [R: ARBA 75, item 1270]

INDONESIAN

539. Echols, John M., and Hassan Shadily. **An English-Indonesian Dictionary.**
Ithaca, N.Y., Cornell University Press, 1975. 660p. $29.50; $9.95pa. LC 72-5638.
ISBN 0-8014-0728-1; 0-8014-9859-7pa.

Indonesian is the national language and the only official language of the
largest country in Southeast Asia and the most widely taught Southeast Asian
language in American and Australian universities. Thus, the absence for so long
of a good, basic, modern Indonesian-English dictionary is to be wondered at.
Since the authors of this dictionary published their *Indonesian-English Dictionary*
(2nd ed.; Cornell University Press, 1963), the companion volume has been eagerly
awaited. This dictionary is more specifically an American English-Indonesian
dictionary, with American spelling and standard American pronunciation indicated.
The new orthography jointly adopted by the governments of Indonesia and
Malaysia has been employed throughout, and the major features of the new spelling
system are briefly described in the introduction.

The dictionary has been prepared specifically for Indonesians, although the
preface and introduction are in English. The abbreviations used to indicate parts
of speech and special usages are mainly in Indonesian, although some English
abbreviations are used. Sentences and colloquial phrases illustrating variant uses
of English words are generously employed. The authors have, however, incorporated
some devices to make the dictionary useful to English speakers; the dictionary will
no doubt be the standard English-Indonesian dictionary for many years, and perhaps
decades, to come. —Charles R. Bryant. [R: LJ, July 75, p. 1306; ARBA 76,
item 1150]

ITALIAN

540. Reynolds, Barbara, comp. **The Concise Cambridge Italian Dictionary.** New
York, Cambridge University Press, 1975. 792p. $19.95. LC 74-77384. ISBN 0-
521-07273-5.

This dictionary, as its title suggests, is a concise version of the well-regarded
Cambridge Italian Dictionary. While primarily designed for the English speaker, it
is equally proficient at rendering English into good, current Italian. Barbara
Reynolds has made a sincere attempt to preserve the swing and syntax of modern
Italian in translating from English; the emphasis, however, is on British usage, and
many Americanisms have been omitted. Little attempt is made at etymology in
this shortened format, and pronunciation is supplied only in cases in which the
person having reasonable acquaintance with Italian would feel some doubt. The
three-column format compensates for the compact size of the volume, and the
print, although small, is quite clear.

Syllabication is provided for all polysyllabic words. Parenthetical abbreviations (e.g., mil., mus., geo.) indicate the specialized uses to which certain words
are put. Elements of dialect are found scattered throughout, including words
peculiar to Tuscan or Sicilian usage. The compiler has a tendency to translate
rather than to define, but a concise Italian reference grammar and several useful
tables are appended as aids to comprehension. Overall, the *Concise Cambridge*

Italian Dictionary is a very commendable reduction of a large, highly technical work into a convenient and portable volume. It provides an extremely competent rendering of colloquial (British) English into the *lingua parlata* of mainstream contemporary Italian. —Bruce A. Shuman. [R: Choice, Sept 75, p. 821; WLB, June 75, p. 754; LJ, 15 Apr 75, p. 747; LJ, 15 Mar 75, p. 570; ARBA 76, item 1154]

LATIN

541. **Dictionary of Medieval Latin from British Sources: Fascicule I, A–B.** Prep. by R. E. Latham, under the direction of a committee appointed by The British Academy. New York, published for The British Academy by Oxford University Press, 1975. 231p. bibliog. $44.50pa. ISBN 0-19-725948-0.

The efforts that led ultimately to a definite commitment to this dictionary on the part of the British Academy began in 1913, when R. J. Whitwell first expressed the need for such a work. After repeated delays, disappointments, and false starts, punctuated by two world wars, in 1963 the Academy launched the project.

The dictionary seeks to record every Latin word used by British medieval authors from 400 to 1520. Fascicule I, covering only letters A and B, consists of 231 pages, a fact which betokens a truly massive work when completed. The first component in Fascicule I is a bibliography of all sources used in the dictionary for lexical verification and documentation, very much in the manner of the *Oxford English Dictionary*. The sources are cited in the dictionary proper by coded abbreviations. The vocabulary scope of the work embraces words that are unquestionably medieval Latin, but it also includes classical Latin words when medieval British authors used them in set phrases that were foreign to classical Latin writing.

An entry usually consists of the ML or CL word, an English translation, and then a chronologically arranged series of quoted excerpts illustrating the use of the word in British medieval writing. The excerpts are keyed to the sources listed in the bibliography.

If a word is pure medieval Latin, it appears without parenthetic designation. If it is classical Latin, it bears the appropriate designation—i.e., (CL). Other words, neither ML nor CL, also appear in the dictionary, though very infrequently—for example, Anglo-Saxon (AS) or Old French (OF) words. Such words are those of vernacular origin that medieval writers occasionally adopted for use in an otherwise strictly ML literary context.

This monumental project, launched under impeccable scholarly auspices, promises to be a major contribution to lexicography. [R: ARBA 76, item 1149]

542. Glare, P. G. W., ed. **Oxford Latin Dictionary**. Oxford, Clarendon Press, 1968– ; distr. New York, Oxford University Press, 1968– . 8fas. $18.75pa./fas. (fas.1&2); $17.00pa. (fas.3); $24.00pa. (fas.4); $27.25pa. (fas.5). ISBN 0-19-864209-1(fas.1); 0-19-864215-6(fas.2); 0-19-864216-4(fas.3); 0-19-864217-2(fas.4); 0-19-864218-0 (fas.5). In progress.

Latin-English dictionaries previously have been largely translated or adapted from European dictionaries, which have themselves been in part derivative. This dictionary is independent of all other dictionaries, being the first on this scale and based on a fresh and thorough reading of all the available sources. It follows, generally speaking, the principles of the *Oxford English Dictionary*, and its formal layout of articles is similar. Within each section or subsection, quotations are arranged chronologically, the first example showing, where practicable, the earliest known instance of that particular definition or usage. The dictionary is designed to give a full account of the meaning and use of words occurring in Latin from the beginnings to about 200 A.D. A major work of scholarship that will support the interpretive studies of our classical heritage.

The work will be complete in eight fascicles. The first fascicle, "A–Calcitro," includes a list of references and other aids to the reader; it was published in 1968. Other fascicles include: Fascicle 2: "Calcitro-Demitto"; Fascicle 3: "Demiurgus-Gorgoneus"; Fascicle 4: "Gorgonia-Libero"; and Fascicle 5. [R: SR, 17 May 69; ARBA 70, v.2, p. 53]

POLISH

543. Bulas, Kazimierz, and Francis J. Whitfield. **The Kościuszko Foundation Dictionary. Vol. I, English-Polish. Vol. II, Polish-English.** The Hague, Mouton; distr. New York, Humanities Press, 1969. 2v. $23.00/set.

The first volume of this dictionary was published in 1959 and the second in 1961; both were published in Poland's Millennium Series by the Foundation. This is the most comprehensive dictionary of this type on the market; it is already listed in all standard reference sources, including Winchell. The most comprehensive dictionary of the Polish language is a Warsaw publication (planned in 12 volumes) by the Polish Academy of Sciences—*Slownik jezyka polskiego*, but it is still in progress. [R: ARBA 71, item 1389]

RUSSIAN

544. Smirnitsky, A. I., and others, comps. **Russian-English Dictionary.** Newly rev. ed. New York, Dutton, 1973. 766p. $13.95. LC 58-5989. ISBN 0-525-19520-3.

"Smirnitsky" has long been accepted in this country as the best standard dictionary for college and school use. Now in its ninth edition, it still retains its usefulness as a general all-purpose dictionary, with a total vocabulary of some 50,000 words. This new edition is the first completely reset version since the third edition (published in 1958), although it retains the same number of words.

In 1972 a new *Oxford Russian-English Dictionary* was published, edited by B. O. Unbegaun. The Oxford work contains about 70,000 entries, including colloquial vocabulary and idioms and a selected number of scientific terms. A comparison between the two dictionaries reveals that the *Oxford Russian-English Dictionary* gives more English equivalents for Russian words; also, it defines about 20,000 more words, and the grammatical information accompanying entries seems to be better structured. Nevertheless, both dictionaries are reliable, and both serve their stated purpose well. Choosing between them will be largely a matter of personal preference. —Bohdan S. Wynar. [R: ARBA 75, item 1275]

545. Wheeler, Marcus. **The Oxford Russian-English Dictionary**. Ed. by B. O. Unbegaun. New York, Oxford University Press, 1972. 918p. $18.00. ISBN 0-19-864111-7.

This work is intended as a general-purpose dictionary of Russian as it is written and spoken. It is designed primarily, though not exclusively, for the use of those whose native language is English. It contains about 70,000 entries, including colloquial vocabulary and idioms, as well as some scientific and technical terms of a more general nature. Entries include illustrative phraseology and indications of principal grammatical features. Commonly used abbreviations are provided in a separate appendix. As indicated in the acknowledgments, the author and editors used several standard Russian dictionaries—e.g., Ulshakov, Smirnitsky, and *Slovar' Russkogo Yazyka*, compiled under the auspices of the Russian Language Institute of the Academy of Sciences (Moscow, 1957-1961).

As a general dictionary for a beginning student of the Russian language, this dictionary will suffice. Advanced students, however, will want to use more comprehensive dictionaries, including the Soviet work mentioned above. —Bohdan S. Wynar. [R: ARBA 73, item 1196]

SERBOCROATIAN

546. Benson, Morton, comp. **Serbocroatian-English Dictionary**. Philadelphia, University of Pennsylvania Press, 1971. 807p. $27.50. ISBN 0-8122-7636-1.

Contains approximately 60,000 words and over 100,000 phrases and idioms. It should be noted that this dictionary lists both Ekavian (Eastern) and Jekavian (Western) forms. The illustrative phrases are given only in the Eastern variants. The glosses are in American English. In addition to everyday vocabulary, this work includes, on a selective basis, some scientific and technical terms as well as obsolete words and regionalisms that occur frequently in literature. Emphasis is on the contemporary language. This dictionary will be of substantial assistance to universities and to students of the Serbocroatian language. [R: LJ, 15 May 72, p. 1797; Choice, July-Aug 72, p. 623; ARBA 73, item 1202]

SPANISH

547. **Simon and Schuster's International Dictionary: English/Spanish, Spanish/English**. Tana de Gámez, ed. in chief. New York, Simon and Schuster, 1973. 884+1605p. $10.95; $15.95 (indexed). LC 71-180718. ISBN 0-671-21507-8; 0-671-21267-2 (indexed).

This is a worthy newcomer to the competitive field of Spanish-English dictionaries. On first glance, its 200,000-plus entries packed into a lightweight, readable, and inexpensive volume make this work a potential bargain for the individual and the institutional buyer alike. More fundamentally, the Simon and Schuster stands on its own special merits—namely, balance and insight. Both of these qualities stem from the makeup of the editorial staff and the list of contributors, which helps to assure that European and American English and Spanish receive balanced coverage. Not only is there sufficient attention to idioms and regionalisms, but also British pronunciation is distinguished from the American.

280 / Linguistics and Philology

Pronunciation is indicated in the International Phonetic Alphabet. The editors have sought to reflect current usage regardless of the dictates of the Spanish Royal Academy or other bodies. This descriptive policy extends to vulgarisms and international terms of sophistication, such as "ciao" or "gemütlich." While they have done a creditable job of providing exact equivalents in most cases, the editors have attempted to "convey the spirit as well as the meanings of words." To this end, the dictionary focuses on literary and folk expressions, versatile terms (e.g., "get," "*poner*") and false cognates, and bolsters these with frequent examples of usage. Finally, the editors have reduced the introductory sections to a minimum, yet filled them with enough information on grammar, verbs, and pronunciation so as not to encumber the text with too many symbols or details. On the strength of its format, balance, and depth, the Simon and Shuster deserves consideration by anyone in the market for a complete Spanish-English dictionary. —John Robert Wheat. [R: Choice, Dec 74, p. 1534; ALA 73; ARBA 75, item 1279]

548. **The University of Chicago Spanish Dictionary**. Comp. by Carlos Castillo and Otto F. Bond. Rev. ed. by D. Lincoln Canfield. Chicago, University of Chicago Press, 1972. 202+233p. $6.50; $1.95pa. LC 78-177425. ISBN 0-226-09671-8; 0-226-09672-6pa.

This new version of the popular Chicago Spanish-English dictionary (1st ed. 1948) consists mainly of additions rather than changes. Reviser Canfield has sought to improve and update the original, but the New World emphasis and the reliance on standard word sources remain the same. The addition of 2,000 entries, mostly technological terms or regionalisms (and mostly English), raises the total to 32,000 with few deletions. Canfield has supplemented the auxiliary data on Spanish pronunciation, grammar, etc., with sections on monetary units, adjectives of nationality, and especially New World Spanish and its regional dialects. A section of common phrases that had appeared in later printings of the old edition has been dropped. The most significant editorial changes are 1) a more precise labeling for Spanish-American regionalisms where formerly just the symbol "Am." was employed, and 2) the addition of "parenthetical identifying expressions" to distinguish between multiple definitions for certain words. The latter are particularly useful for such catch-all favorites as "get" or, in Spanish, "*correr*." The new Chicago dictionary perpetuates the criteria that made its predecessor a classic in the schoolroom and the suitcase. The much-needed revision has made it a better and more current source of standard vocabulary at no significant increase in price, at least in the paperback edition. —John Robert Wheat. [R: ARBA 74, item 1261]

CHAPTER 26

JOURNALISM

549. Burack, A. S., ed. **The Writer's Handbook.** Boston, The Writer, 1975. 847p. index. $14.95. LC 36-28596. ISBN 0-87116-0919-9.

With the recent proliferation of "where to sell it" books, it's good to have an old standby, a familiar and reliable source. Now in its newly revised and enlarged 1975 edition, *The Writer's Handbook* tells not only what and how to write, but where to sell the finished product. A host of already successful and recognized authors, experts in their field, have contributed chapters of instruction and advice based on their own working and selling experience. Of the book's 100 chapters, 40 appear here for the first time. Part IV, the juicy part for unpublished writers with manuscripts ready to go, lists 2,500 markets for novels, articles, short stories, poetry, fillers, children's literature, and other special fields such as stage and TV plays. Also included are publishers' editorial requirements, payment rates, addresses, etc., leading American literary agents, and writers' organizations. The information is updated regularly. The chapters are a compilation of the best articles from *The Writer* magazine, well known among practicing authors.

The book differs sharply from its best competitor, *The Writer's Market*, in that it combines instruction with the market sources. As such, the beginning and unpublished writer should consider it as a first reference, and even the oldsters can pick up a tip or two. But if a collection is to be thorough and up to date, both titles must be included.   —Steve Rybicki. [R: ARBA 76, item 1168]

550. Kent, Ruth K. **The Language of Journalism: The Glossary of Print-Communications Terms.** Kent, Ohio, Kent State University Press, 1970. 186p. bibliog. $5.00; $1.95pa. LC 71-100624. ISBN 0-87338-091-6; 0-87338-092-4pa.

This handy dictionary for journalism students and newcomers to the craft concentrates heavily on printers' jargon. This makes it valuable for its intended audience, whose educations too often don't deal with the mechanical aspects of journalism.

Its weakness comes in the area of words and phrases commonly used by reporters and editors to describe the process by which a daily newspaper is produced. Such words as "take," "move," and "add" are given limited meanings that don't reflect their day-to-day usage in journalism, and some common words like "backshop," "frontshop," and "insert" don't appear at all.

The dictionary's strong bibliographic section includes not only an extensive bibliography but notes on traditional, modern general, and specialized sources of information. Common abbreviations rate a special section in the work, which also features a 17-page etymological study of selected words and phrases. Words whose histories appear in the etymology are specially designated in the body of the dictionary. —Steve Wynkoop. [R: RQ, Fall 71, p. 81; Choice, Sept 71, p. 811; ALA 71; ARBA 72, item 1301]

551. Price, Warren C., and Calder M. Pickett. **An Annotated Journalism Bibliography: 1958-1968.** Minneapolis, University of Minnesota Press, 1970. 278p. $12.75. LC 70-120810. ISBN 0-8166-0578-5.

This annotated bibliography on journalism updates a similar work by W. C. Price entitled *The Literature of Journalism: An Annotated Bibliography*, published in 1959. It is rather broad in scope and covers all aspects of the field of journalism. Types of materials include historical works; autobiographies of journalists; management of the press; techniques of journalism; magazines; the foreign press and international communication facilities; journalism education and vocational guidance; political, economic, and social reporting and corresponding; photography and cartoons; general news and features, and works in the allied areas of communication that carry useful journalistic information. Also included are works that are non-journalistic in content whose authors were engaged in the practice of journalism at the time they were written.

Entries are limited to those printed in the English language. In spite of the fact that the title of this work limited the entries to works that appeared between 1958 and 1968, about 10 percent of the entries listed were published before 1958. The arrangement of this bibliography is alphabetical, with a subject index as the key to individual entries. This is the major difference between this work and Price's earlier bibliography, which was grouped by subject headings. The alphabetical arrangement is simple to use, yet a subject division of the test might have been more helpful for reference use. Omitted from this bibliography is one useful work by Ross and Herman entitled *English Language Bibliography on Foreign Press and Comparative Journalism*. —George V. Hodowanec. [R: LJ, 15 Nov 70; ARBA 71, item 1405]

CHAPTER 27

LITERATURE

GENERAL WORKS

552. **Contemporary Literary Criticism: Excerpts from Criticism of the Works of Today's Novelists, Poets, Playwrights, and Other Creative Writers, Volume 1.** Ed. by Caroline Riley. Detroit, Gale, 1973. 385p. $25.00. LC 76-38938.

This is the first volume of a new Gale series that is similar in format and scope to Gale's successful and useful Contemporary Authors series. The 200 entries contain excerpts from criticism of writers drawn roughly from the past 25 years. Writers included are novelists, poets, playwrights, and other creative writers who are now living or who have died since January 1, 1950. Certain international writers such as Borges, Sartre, Anouilh, etc., are included, but the major emphasis is on writers in English. Indexes to the authors and the critics quoted will be included in later volumes. The five or six critical excerpts for each author usually run to several paragraphs, which are taken directly from fully identified sources: either books, journals, or reviews. There may be some value in this set for undergraduate use, although it will probably be utilized as a slightly sophisticated crib source rather than as a survey of the aim and reputation of the writers, which the compilers probably intend it to be used for. The graduate student and specialist will find the set of less value, since they will need more than is made available here. Still, this is a strong effort, and the cumulative evaluation of the work should be positive. A useful complement to Moulton's *A Library of Literary Criticism.* —Charles Mann. [R: Choice, Oct 73, p. 1162; RSR, July/Sept 73, p. 21; LJ, Aug 73, p. 2264; ALA 73; ARBA 74, item 1283]

553. Daiches, David, ed. **The Penguin Companion to English Literature.** New York, McGraw-Hill, 1971. 575p. $10.95. LC 77-158061. ISBN 0-07-049275-1.

Similar in structure to the Penguin volume on European literature, this handy guide offers fairly comprehensive coverage of the literary achievements of the entire English-speaking world, with the exception of the United States and Latin America. (Both these areas are dealt with in a separate volume.) It should be noted that in addition to covering English literature from Saxon times to the present, this volume offers biographical sketches on prominent philosophers, scientists, historians, and others who have made some contribution to the literature. All in all, this is a well-balanced work, prepared by a number of distinguished scholars. It should be of interest to libraries of all types, but it can also be recommended for home use. [R: ARBA 73, item 1303]

554. **The Penguin Companion to Literature: Volume 2, European.** By A. K. Thorlby and others. Baltimore, Penguin Books, 1969. 906p. index. $3.95.

This second volume of *The Penguin Companion to Literature* "deals with all the literature of Europe with the exceptions of Britain and the ancient classical world." The contributors (listing all of them takes up nearly five pages) have composed their entries in the light of the following questions: "Which are the more important European authors? Which are their main works? What, briefly, are these about? What editions and translations are available? What critical commentaries are to be recommended?" Some philosophers ("important for literary reasons") and some historians (of "some degree of literary standing") have been included in this very extensive list of literary authors. Also included are important literary movements, such as Acmeism and Dada; general subjects, like French literary criticism in the nineteenth and twentieth centuries, are also treated.

The alphabetically arranged entries cut across country and time, so that the last item is *Stefan Zweig*. Many authors whose works have not been translated into English are included. The "index" is actually a guide to entries by language and country, where the arrangement is chronological within each category of language (Albanian, Austrian, Basque, etc.). Under French, in this guide, we find ten pages of around 400 items, beginning with "Roland, Chanson de–late 11th cent.–epic poem," and ending with "Sagan, F.–1935- –novelist." A ready tool for opening an investigation of an author, a work or a subject.

Other volumes in the series are: *Volume 1, English and Commonwealth; Volume 3, American and Latin American; Volume 4, Classical and Byzantine, Oriental and African.* –Denton May. [R: ALA 71; ARBA 71, item 1428]

555. **Webster's New World Companion to English and American Literature.** Ed. by Arthur Pollard. New York, World; distr. New York, Crowell, 1973. 850p. $15.00. LC 72-12788. ISBN 0-529-05080-3.

Signed articles by more than 80 contributors give biographical information about more than 1,100 English and American authors and mention, however briefly, some 6,000 individual works. Entries are alphabetical. There are some cross references. There are also some general articles (e.g., "Hymns," "Middle English Literature"). There is an "Appendix of Secondary Bibliography" (pp. 759-850). The articles are drier and more factual in tone than those in A. C. Ward's *Longman Companion to Twentieth Century Literature* (New York, Longman, 1973) and there are no separate entries for noted literary works, fictional characters, etc. Of course, the period of time covered is much different. A sound, useful work, which carries its coverage of some contemporary authors into the early 1970s. –A. Robert Rogers. [R: LJ, 15 Nov 73, p. 3365; WLB, Dec 73, p. 339; ARBA 74, item 1282]

BIBLIOGRAPHIES

556. Altick, Richard Daniel, and Andrew H. Wright. **Selective Bibliography for the Study of English and American Literature.** 5th ed. New York, Macmillan, 1975 (c. 1974). 168p. $3.95pa. LC 74-2642. ISBN 0-02-302100-4.

The fourth edition of this standard guide was published in 1971. Like it, this fifth edition is divided into major sections which cover all aspects of English and American literature. The helpful essay on the use of scholarly tools is still retained and compensates, in some measure, for the meager or non-existent annotations. Some entries have been updated and new titles have been added. [R: Choice, May 75, p. 367; ARBA 72, item 1343; ARBA 76, item 1180]

557. Kennedy, Arthur G., and Donald B. Sands. **A Concise Bibliography for Students of English.** 5th ed. Rev. by William E. Colburn. Stanford, Calif., Stanford University Press, 1972. 300p. index. $10.00; $5.00pa. LC 77-183889. ISBN 0-8047-0804-5; 0-8047-0813-4pa.

The fourth edition of this standard work was published in 1960, prepared by Donald B. Sands after Professor Kennedy's death. It contained over 5,000 entries, grouped into 228 categories.

The present edition follows the format and structure of the fourth edition, with some changes that should be noted here. The material in languages other than English is kept to a minimum, along with material in ancillary fields and works of narrow specialization. As in previous editions, works devoted to single authors do not appear, with the exception of periodicals devoted to single authors. The areas of linguistics and folklore (well represented in the previous edition) receive only token coverage here, since it includes "only basic works in these areas, and only those of most interest to students of literature" (Preface). This is well justified in view of the large volume of material published in both areas in the last decade.

All in all, Mr. Colburn has done an outstanding job in updating this work. It will continue to be of substantial assistance to all students of English and American literature. Obviously, the major criticism of this edition, which applies also to the previous one, is the fact that bibliographical citations do omit publisher, and sometimes even place of publication, for monographic works. Apparently English majors don't think such information is important. We do. —Bohdan S. Wynar. [R: ARBA 73, item 1232]

558. Parks, George B., and Ruth Z. Temple, eds. **The Romance Literatures: A Bibliography.** New York, Ungar, 1970. 2v. indexes. (The Literature of the World in English Translation, Vol. 3). $45.00. LC 70-98341. ISBN 0-8044-3239-2.

This is the third volume of the series, published in two parts. The first two volumes of the series covered Greek and Latin literature and Slavic literature. Part 1 of this volume includes Catalan, Italian, Portuguese and Brazilian, Provençal, Rumanian, Spanish, and Spanish American literature; part 2 is devoted entirely to French.

The first part contains the general reference section repeated and expanded from volume one of the series. The individual literatures begin with a general section, and the translations are then divided according to appropriate chronological periods. As in the other volumes of the series, "literature" is given a broad interpretation, so that the work includes literary history and criticism, history, philosophy, theology, law, and science in addition to belles-lettres. Since these volumes are the result of cooperative scholarship, the various literatures show uneven treatment, but this is frankly admitted in the editors' preface. The placement of some linguistically problematic authors, especially in the Rumanian section, raises the question of consistency. Many of these authors write in French and English, and this is noted (e.g., Peter Neagoe, who writes in English; Mircea Eliade, who writes in French and lives in the U.S.; and Eugene Ionesco, who was brought up in France and has written in French). Eliade and Neagoe are listed under Rumanian literature, but Ionesco is given a cross reference to French literature. In general, the cross references are adequate, although none was found from "Guillaume" or "Chanson de Guillaume" to the entry "William, Song of".

Part 2 divides French literature into a general class with chronological divisions and "French Literature of Other Countries" consisting of Belgium, Switzerland, Canada, Louisiana, The West Indies, and Africa. The two individual volumes (parts) have their own indexes.

The coverage, as in the other volumes of the series, is quite comprehensive and the printing and binding are excellent. —Francis J. Witty. [R: ARBA 71, item 1422]

ENCYCLOPEDIAS

559. **Cassell's Encyclopaedia of World Literature.** Rev. and enl. ed. General ed., John Buchanan-Brown. New York, William Morrow, 1973. 3v. $47.95. LC 73-10405. ISBN 0-688-00228-5.

The first edition of this title, published in 1953, was rapidly acclaimed a standard ready reference tool; this new edition should have the same reception.

The first volume, subtitled "histories and general articles," includes essays on the literatures of various lands and languages (e.g., Finnish literature, Basque literature), genres (morality play, essay, epigram, etc.), and literary terms. The two remaining volumes are devoted to biographies only. There is a galaxy of entries, from virtually all inhabited continents. One is pleased to encounter such moderns as Solzhenitsyn, Isak Dinesen, and Alan Ginsberg, as well as such oldsters as Huigh Groot and Su Shih.

Each entry gives place and date of birth, place and date of death (and place of burial, if different), and spouse. Following these details is a biographical essay that concludes with a catalog of works and a bibliography of biographical and/or critical works. Every essay and entry in all three volumes is signed by the contributor; all contributors are scholars, and most are British. —Kenyon C. Rosenberg. [R: Choice, June 74, p. 577; ARBA 75, item 1315]

560. **Encyclopedia of World Literature in the 20th Century.** Wolfgang Bernard Fleischmann, General Editor. New York, Ungar, 1967-1971. 3v. illus. $34.50(v.1); $36.50(v.2); $46.00(v.3). LC 67-13615. ISBN 0-8044-3092-6(v.1); 0-8044-3093-4(v.2); 0-8044-3094-2(v.3).

561. **Encyclopedia of World Literature in the 20th Century: Volume 4, Supplement and Index.** Ed. by Frederick Ungar and Lina Mainiero. New York, Ungar, 1975. 462p. illus. index. $48.00. LC 67-13615. ISBN 0-8044-3091-8.

Based on the well-known German encyclopedia *Lexikon der Weltliteratur im 20. Jahrhundert* (Herder, 1960-61, 2v.), this encyclopedia will adequately meet the needs of the general public, especially in the area of European literature.

In comparison to the German work, this encyclopedia is substantially enlarged and updated, contains brief bibliographies, and occasionally has new quotations of critical comments about major writers.

Arrangement of the 1,300 entries is alphabetical. In general, the well-written, readable articles on all aspects of contemporary literature are rather brief, with the exception of those on national literature, on literary movements, etc. Information presented is well documented with primary and secondary sources. For example, the article on Ukrainian literature, written by a specialist, Professor G. Luckyj of Toronto University, is a balanced presentation of this little-known branch of Slavic literature. It contains up-to-date information plus a sufficient bibliography of most of the important works on the subject. The same is true of biographical articles on lesser-known persons, such as the Polish poet Tuwim and the Nigerian novelist Amos Tutuola. There are some scattered black and white portraits.

The passage of four years brought to world prominence new writers who either were not included or were given insufficient attention in the basic three-volume set. These have occasioned the supplementary volume. In general, its articles maintain the same high standards. At the end of this volume is an index that covers all four volumes. [R: LJ, 15 Jan 68; C&RL, July 68; Choice, June 68; ARBA 71, item 1426; ARBA 72, item 1315; ARBA 76, item 1185]

562. Ivask, Ivar, and Gero von Wilpert, eds. **World Literature since 1945: Critical Surveys of the Contemporary Literatures of Europe and the Americas**. New York, Ungar, 1973. 724p. index. $25.00. LC 72-79930. ISBN 0-8044-3122-1.

The present work, much smaller in scope than Ungar's *Encyclopedia of World Literature in the 20th Century*, provides a well-balanced survey of developments in individual literatures since the end of World War II, thus serving as a complement to the larger work. Twenty-eight countries are covered, and most of the contributors are leading scholars in their respective fields. The presentation is condensed but clear, and the text is well documented. At the end of each article are selective bibliographies of secondary works and of major works in English translation.   [R: WLB, Nov 73, p. 259; ARBA 74, item 1284]

DICTIONARIES

563. Beckson, Karl, and Arthur Ganz. **Literary Terms: A Dictionary**. New York, Farrar, Straus and Giroux, 1975. 280p. $3.95pa. LC 75-4507.

A revised and enlarged edition of the authors' earlier *A Reader's Guide to Literary Terms* (1960), this encyclopedic dictionary should be welcome to those who teach English. Three major changes mark this edition: each term is clearly boldfaced, guidewords are supplied at the top of each page, and bibliographical references follow many entries. Those who suffered with the miserable format of the first Beckson and Ganz will be pleased with this new easy-to-use arrangement. Larger than its predecessor by 46 pages and some 200 entries, this volume retains the same clarity in its definitions, adding such terms as "black humor," "Blooms-bury Group," "romance," "anti-hero," "Angry Young Men," and "kitsch." Numerous entries have been expanded and improved: e.g., "romanticism," "satire," "tragedy," and "stream of consciousness"; "symbolism" has become "symbolist movement." Among the terms unwisely dropped are "solecism," "tour de force," "colophon," "revenge tragedy," and "spoonerism." The earlier edition had a surprisingly weak explanation of "science fiction"; it has not been improved by substituting *Childhood's End* for *Brave New World*. Nevertheless, *Literary Terms* still lives up to its publisher's encomium: ". . . clear, reliable, comprehensive, entertaining." A word to the wise—keep your 1960 edition. —Charles R. Andrews. [R: Choice, Dec 75, p. 1286; LJ, 1 Apr 75, p. 654; WLB, Nov 75, p. 268; ARBA 76, item 1184]

564. Lazarus, Arnold, and H. Wendell Smith. **A Glossary of Literature and Composition**. New York, Grosset and Dunlap, 1973. 343p. illus. index. $3.95pa. ISBN 0-448-00022-9.

This paper-bound book was initially published as Part I of the same authors' *Modern English*, which met with some praise upon its publication in 1971. In this new format the "Glossary" has been revised and expanded. Definitions range from brief statements to lengthy articles. Before proceeding further, it should be noted that *A Handbook to Literature*, long and familiarly known as Thrall and Hibbard, covers much the same ground; it is now available in paperback in a third edition considerably revised and expanded (1,360 entries, 600 of them new) by C. Hugh Holman (Odyssey Press, 1972).

What special advantage Lazarus and Smith offer with their *Glossary* is found in their bibliographic footnotes to each entry, which lead the reader to quite recent material on some of these very old topics. This feature adds a glow of freshness to the book and perhaps gives it a more contemporary feel than "Thrall and Hibbard" (now "Holman") imparts. Also, one must make an obligatory bow to H. W. Fowler's *A Dictionary of Modern English Usage* (Oxford, 1965) which is idiosyncratic and old-fashioned, but indispensable.

New entries in Lazarus and Smith include: "graffiti," "Great Books," "great chain of being," "kinetic," "Kitsch," "whichmire." On the whole, there is a more pronounced emphasis upon composition words: "revising," "paragraph," "tension," and the like, so that for straight-out desk usage, Lazarus and Smith is direct, fresh, and pertinent—and, with its very useful references for further reading, it is an aid to research. —Charles Mann. [R: ALA 71; ARBA 74, item 1279]

565. Myers, Robin, comp. and ed. **A Dictionary of Literature in the English Language from Chaucer to 1940**. New York, Pergamon, 1970, 1971. 2v. illus. index. $50.00/set. LC 68-18529. ISBN 0-08-016143-X(set); 0-08-012079-2(v.1); 0-08-016142-1(v.2).

According to the Preface, "the aim of this work is to provide in a single volume, bibliographical and biographical details of some 3,500 authors who have used English as their medium . . . with reference to other bibliographical studies. . . . The definition of literature is a wide one. It includes not only great poets, dramatists and novelists, but also such writers as might be considered to form part of the literary history of their time, together with select examples of such semi-literary genres as the detective story and the romantic novel, too numerous and too ephemeral to be fully documented in a work of this nature. Certain non-literary writers, too, scientists, historians, economists, lawyers and statesmen, who have much influenced the thought of their day, or who have written excellently, have an undoubted place in literary history and are included in the dictionary. The user will find a selection of these peripheral literary figures who are often the very ones that the librarian finds most in demand." We have quoted this long excerpt from the Preface because it not only shows the scope of this work but may indirectly explain its usefulness as a handy reference book in this hard-to-define area.

All entries are arranged in one alphabet; each entry consists of full name and title, biographical note, and a list of biographical sources consulted or suggested for further study. Then follows a list of the first editions of separately published literary works in chronological order. When appropriate, important collected editions are also listed. The second volume serves as a complete title-author index. In examining certain listings for individual literary figures, it might be safe to assume that the author relied heavily in his selection on such standard works as *The Cambridge Bibliography of English Literature*. Other entries, such as the listing for the famous anthropologist James George Frazer or the economist John Keynes, had to be located in a number of different sources. Actually, it is in this area that the real value of this work lies. Obviously, the reader might be somewhat disappointed at not finding Percy Williams Bridgman, who was not only a brilliant physicist and author of many classic works on the philosophy of science, but who was also a newspaper correspondent and the author of books on public affairs. There are many other omissions of this nature. Nevertheless, it is almost an impossible task to provide complete coverage in this peripheral area, where so much must depend on interpretation. —Bohdan S. Wynar. [R: WLB, Jan 71, p. 500; ARBA 72, item 1384]

566. Shipley, Joseph T., ed. **Dictionary of World Literary Terms: Forms, Technique, Criticism.** Completely rev. and enl. ed. Boston, Writer, 1970. 466p. $12.95. LC 75-91879. ISBN 0-87116-012-9.

Earlier editions (1943, 1953) of this work had the title *Dictionary of World Literature*. Since its first appearance, this dictionary has been regarded as important, especially for its contributions to theoretical aspects of literary criticism. Many revisions were made in the 1953 edition, and many more are apparent in this new publication, to which more than 260 authorities contributed.

The 1970 edition marks the first time that the book has been arranged in parts: Part I (the major section) contains the treatment of terms, forms, types, definitions, techniques and genres; Part II contains critical surveys of American, English, French, German, Greek, Italian, Latin, Medieval, Russian and Spanish criticism; Part III includes selected lists of critics and works from 25 additional countries. There has also been some shifting of material (e.g., "Voice and Address" has been reentered under "Narrator"). Many of the more obscure or archaic terms (Aeolist; Anacephaloeosis; etc.) have been removed. New terms (Absurd, Theatre of the; Black humor; Happening; Pornography; Science fiction; etc.) have been added. Rewriting is evident throughout, more cross references have been added, and the bibliographies have been updated. Style of writing is generally more abstractly refined than in, for example, *A Handbook to Literature* (Thrall and Hibbard). It is recommended that all three editions of this work be retained. —Joseph W. Sprug. [R: RQ, Winter 70, pp. 172-3; ARBA 71, item 1429]

567. Ward, A. C. **Longman Companion to Twentieth Century Literature**. 2nd ed. New York, Longman, 1975. 597p. $16.50. ISBN 0-582-36205-9.

The first edition of this work was published in 1973. The second edition updates the entries for novels and plays, fictional characters, literary categories and terms, and, of course, authors.

Despite its title, which suggests a scope similar to that of *Encyclopedia of World Literature in the 20th Century* (New York, Ungar, 1967-75; 4v.), the work is confined essentially to those twentieth century literary artists who wrote in English. Many important modern European writers whose works have been at least partially translated into English are not included (e.g., Günter Grass). For Anglo-American literature, however, the work is a worthwhile supplement to such works as W. R. Benet's *The Reader's Encyclopedia* (2nd ed.; New York, Crowell, 1965). —Richard A. Gray. [R: ARBA 76, item 1190]

BIOGRAPHY

568. Richardson, Kenneth, ed. **Twentieth Century Writing: A Reader's Guide to Contemporary Literature**. New York, Transatlantic, 1970. 751p. index. $15.00. LC 70-431735.

Some 34 editors and contributors assisted in this project, which primarily covers literature in the English language. Some other nationalities are represented, but to a much smaller extent. Approximately 1,200 writers are included. The length of articles on individual writers varies; in this respect, some writers of minor importance receive more attention than, for example, Nabokov (23 lines). One can note many omissions, and the information provided is not always accurate. Nevertheless, this compilation includes entries for minor writers who are not treated in similar compilations. [R: LJ, 1 Oct 70; ALA 70; ARBA 71, item 1421]

DRAMA

BIBLIOGRAPHIES

569. Stratman, Carl J. **Bibliography of Medieval Drama**. 2nd ed., rev. and enl. New York, Ungar, 1972. 2v. index. $35.00. LC 78-163141. ISBN 0-8044-3272-3.

This updating of the 1954 edition is arranged in 10 sections (General Studies, Festschriften, Liturgical Latin Drama, English Drama, Byzantine Drama, French Drama, German Drama, Italian Drama, Low Countries' Drama, Spanish Drama) plus addenda and a general index of subjects and authors of works listed. Within sections, the entries are arranged chronologically instead of alphabetically, as they were in the first edition. This is helpful for historical research, but it puts a greater responsibility on the index.

The work has been planned as an aid to students of English drama and does not supplant bibliographies exclusively concerned with medieval drama in any of the countries represented. According to the preface, 5,000 entries have been added since the 1954 edition. Each entry includes full author, complete title, place, publisher, date, pagination, indication of any significant bibliographies included, and symbol of library location (including that of manuscripts). Although there are no annotations, the items considered most important by the editor are asterisked.

The bibliography is an important, but quite special, reference tool that should be available to all students of the history of European drama. —Richard M. Buck. [R: ARBA 73, item 1245]

ENCYCLOPEDIAS

570. Gassner, John, and Edward Quinn, eds. **The Reader's Encyclopedia of World Drama**. New York, Thomas Y. Crowell, 1969. 1029p. illus. bibliog. $15.00. LC 69-11830. ISBN 0-690-67483-X.

Designed as a ready-reference book, this one-volume encyclopedia concentrates on drama "as literature, not as theater." Entries focus primarily on plays, their authors, and their literary characteristics.

Entries fall into four categories. One of these is national drama, where under the name of each country, there is a historical survey of the development of that nation's drama from its origins to its most contemporary forms. In most cases, a brief bibliography is appended, with works primarily in the English language. Another category covers the significant playwrights from the standpoint of either literary merit or importance to national drama. Playwrights are treated in separate entries, which provide biographical sketches, list important works, and give some critical evaluations. Entries in the third category, covering plays, generally include a precis of the main action and critical commentary. And, finally, all the major dramatic modes and many minor ones are discussed in articles of varying length, depending on the relative importance of the topic. All articles are initialed; there are some 95 contributors.

An appendix includes basic documents in dramatic theory but, unfortunately, there is no index. This work is quite readable and has well-balanced international coverage. It is intended for a general audience. [R: SR, 6 Dec 69; LJ, 15 Feb 70; ALA 69; ARBA 70, v.2, p. 65]

571. Matlaw, Myron. **Modern World Drama: An Encyclopedia**. New York, Dutton, 1972. 960p. illus. index. $25.00. LC 71-185032. ISBN 0-525-15902-9.

This comprehensive work on twentieth century drama is apparently the sole responsibility of the author, save for the research sources and specialists mentioned in the preface, in which Matlaw also notes that the contents reflect "my own tastes and attitudes." In scope, entries cover geographical areas, biographies of playwrights (no producers, directors, or actors), names of plays (some with full plot outlines, many without), and modern technical terms such as "absurd." The articles are well cross-referenced, except that the small-caps indication for cross-referencing is used only the first time the word is used in any particular article. In addition to the main A-Z entries, there are a character index and a general index. In the general index, where the playwright's name in parentheses follows the play title, small caps are not used to show which playwrights have their own entries, although the play titles are so differentiated!

From a rather careful examination of selected entries, it seems that new European playwrights fare rather better than American, but the emphasis is essentially on the standard moderns from Ibsen to O'Neill, and even here the decisions as to whether to provide full or brief coverage seem peculiarly arbitrary. Of the Europeans, Ionesco rightly has a major entry, and *Amédée, Rhinoceros,* and *The Killer* have full plot summaries, but *Exit the King* and *The Pedestrian in the Air* do not; Gombrowicz has an entry, but Handke is mentioned only under Austria; Pinget has an entry, but his plays do not have separate entries. Most of the major avant-garde playwrights have entries, but they are not treated as fully as the naturalists. Of the Americans, both Kopit and *O, Dad, Poor Dad* . . . have entries, but there are no entries for Rochelle Owens, Israel Horovitz, or Sam Shepard, or for any of their plays—all these and many others must be traced through the general index to the "United States" article. Musicals are slighted even more—there are entries for very few American musicals except *My Fair Lady.* Hardly any musical playwrights are separately listed, and no composers that I could find.

Most consistently exasperating is Matlaw's arbitrary choice of which plays to plot in full, with no indication in the general index as to which plays have been given the full plot treatment. Despite the limitations, this is the only reference work of its kind. It should be valuable for library reference, especially as a supplement to the *McGraw-Hill Encyclopedia of World Drama*, which is easier to use because all main entries are under the playwright. —Richard M. Buck. [R: WLB, Sept 72, p. 90; ALA 72; ARBA 73, item 1242]

572. **McGraw-Hill Encyclopedia of World Drama**: An International Reference **Work in Four Volumes.** New York, McGraw-Hill, 1972. 4v. $129.00. LC 70-37382. ISBN 0-07-079567-3.

This is the first specialized encyclopedia on this subject in the English language. Its coverage of biographical materials far exceeds that of such one-volume works as, for example, *The Reader's Encyclopedia of World Drama*, by Gassner and Quinn (T. Y. Crowell, 1969). There are, however, foreign-language encyclopedias that are more comprehensive, including the well-known 10-volume Italian set *Enciclopedia dello spettacolo*.

The *McGraw-Hill Encyclopedia of World Drama* is a major achievement. According to the introduction, the objective of this work is to bring "into focus the accomplishments of the world's major dramatists. It also touches on many of the lesser figures. . . ." In general, the two types of dramatists covered in this work can be roughly classified as "major" and "lesser." Each article about a major drama-tist is divided into several sections—factual discussion of the author's life, short synopses of several if not all of his plays, comprehensive listings of his entire body of work, and bibliographical information. Scattered among the biographical entries in the text are about 100 abbreviated non-biographical entries—dramatic terms, theater movements and styles, anonymous plays—which serve as useful collateral material. The entries for 300 "major" dramatists provide, in addition to the informa-tion mentioned above, a complete chronology of the writer's scripts, describing types of plays, the earliest publication, and date and place of the first production. There are listings of some 600 "minor" playwrights with less extensive information. Thus, there are some 900-plus "author" entries, and 100 articles providing defini-tions of terms. Some 2,000 photographs, many full page or half page, are integrated in the text. The length of the "author articles" varies from about 12 or 13 pages to one or two paragraphs. An index to play titles is appended in the fourth volume.

It should be pointed out that this encyclopedia covers what we may call "dramatic literature." Its main objective is to cover individual plays and playwrights rather than to dwell on the relationships between drama as literature and drama as theater. Michael Kirby, who provided a long review for this encyclopedia in the *New York Times Book Review*, indicated that in this encyclopedia " 'drama' means only 'dramatic literature.' 'Encyclopedia of Plays and Playwrights' would have been a much more accurate title. . . . This mirrors the literary approach to drama that still dominates our schools and colleges." We think, on the contrary, that the objectives of this work are clearly defined and that the editors have a right to concentrate on drama as dramatic literature, especially since there are many other reference works covering such topics as staging, directors, actors, etc. Nevertheless, it might have been unwise to limit this work to individual playwrights. What disturbed this reviewer is the lack of survey-type articles on trends in dramatic writing and on the historical development of drama in individual countries. Gassner and Quinn, in the work mentioned above, rightly point out that drama as a universal phenomenon is deeply rooted in the culture of the community (we would add "and of a particular nation") as well as in the experience of the individual. The latter aspect is covered well in the McGraw-Hill work. The synthetic approach, defining drama in terms of its historical and cultural milieu, is missing. Missing also are extremely important playwrights from Eastern cultures—from such countries as China, Japan, etc. Western playwrights are well represented, even including playwrights from such countries as Russia, Poland, and the rest of Eastern Europe (with the exceptions of Rumania, Ukraine, Bulgaria, and, to our surprise, even some of the Scandinavian playwrights).

For all practical purposes, this comprehensive and well-executed work is primarily concerned with the European tradition. —Bohdan S. Wynar. [R: NYTBR, 26 Nov 72, pp. 46-48; ALA 72; ARBA 73, item 1243]

HANDBOOKS

573. Anderson, Michael, and others. **Crowell's Handbook of Contemporary Drama**. New York, T. Y. Crowell, 1971. 505p. $10.00. LC 79-158714. ISBN 0-690-22643-8.

A convenient one-volume guide to "developments in the drama in Europe and the Americas since the Second World War—or, in the case of Spain, since the Civil War. The emphasis is entirely on written drama, not on theater." It includes: 1) surveys of modern drama in various countries in fairly long overview studies; 2) biographical sketches and critical appraisal of the career and work of many playwrights; 3) descriptive and critical evaluation of the more important and representative plays, and 4) brief presentation of theorists, directors, movements, and companies that have had an influence on dramatic form.

Fourteen authorities have contributed material on the drama and dramatists of Czechoslovakia, Scandinavia, Finland, France, Germany, Austria and Switzerland, Great Britain, Hungary, Italy, Latin America, Poland, Spain and Portugal, and the United States. Entries are arranged alphabetically in unsigned articles. In some entries, bibliographical information is given for additional sources, but this is not a strong point in this work. Emphasis is on the overview of the drama in various countries, and on the biographical information. An authoritative and useful source for critical appraisal of present-day drama and dramatists, reflecting "the central importance of social criticism and political ideology in the drama of many nations today." —Paul A. Winckler. [R: ARBA 72, item 1317]

INDEXES

574. Breed, Paul F., and Florence M. Sniderman, comps. and eds. **Dramatic Criticism Index: A Bibliography of Commentaries on Playwrights from Ibsen to the Avant-Garde.** Detroit, Gale, 1972. 1022p. $28.00. LC 79-127598. ISBN 0-8103-1090-2.

According to the preface, this selective index is a result of the examination of "approximately 630 books and over 200 periodicals." There are "nearly 12,000 entries in English on 300 or more American and foreign playwrights, the majority of them from the twentieth century." Entries are arranged alphabetically by playwright, with a general section followed by an alphabetical listing of works. The commentaries cited under each heading range from major articles and chapters of books to one or two pages from a longer work. Few play reviews are included, unless no other comment was found for the particular work. There are three supplementary indexes: play titles, critics (which lists play title and playwright criticized), and books indexed (which is the only place where full citation of the books is given). Although no cut-off date for inclusion is noted, the latest date found for either books or periodicals indexed was 1969.

The index is admittedly selective and could already be supplemented—but it seems to be the best bibliography of its kind available. Only *Modern Drama: A Checklist of Critical Literature on 20th Century Plays* (Adelman and Dworkin, Scarecrow, 1967) is comparable to it. The 1967 index is less extensive, though it does include articles in languages other than English and is certainly not superseded by this work. The *Dramatic Criticism Index* is a helpful reference tool for libraries that hold even a few of the books and periodicals indexed. —Richard M. Buck. [R: LJ, 1 Dec 72, pp. 3888-89; WLB, Dec 72, pp. 362-63; ALA 72; ARBA 73, item 1240]

575. Keller, Dean H. **Index to Plays in Periodicals.** Metuchen, N.J., Scarecrow, 1971. 558p. $17.00. LC 72-142236. ISBN 0-8108-0335-6.

576. Keller, Dean H. **Index to Plays in Periodicals: Supplement.** Metuchen, N.J., Scarecrow, 1973. 263p. $8.50. LC 72-142236. ISBN 0-8108-0586-3.

Keller's first volume lists over 5,000 plays from about 100 periodicals, mostly English language, which extend back to the mid-nineteenth century. Entries, arranged alphabetically by author, include the author's full name and date(s), title of play, number of acts, citations to periodical sources, name(s) of translator(s), and language (if not English). There is a title index.

The reference value of the supplement is greatly increased by the addition of complete runs of 37 periodicals to the 16 complete runs of titles included in the basic volume. New acquisitions include several foreign titles—namely, *L'Avant-Scène,*

Mesures, *Das Wort*, and *Il Dramma*. Other additions include little magazines such as *Blast*, *Chimera*, *Glebe*, *Mask*, *Smoke*, and two important titles of the 1920s, *Smart Set* and *Transatlantic Review*. The 2,334 plays indexed in this supplement are arranged in the same way as in the basic volume, and the title index is retained.

This title will be useful, along with *Play Index*, *Chicorel Theater Index to Plays . . .* , and similar works. *Play Index* covers only plays in collections. *Chicorel*, in its first two volumes alone, lists about 21,000 plays in nearly 1,000 anthologies but includes only 16 to 18 periodical titles. Both *Play Index* and *Chicorel* emphasize plays that have appeared in recently published anthologies. —Rolland E. Stevens and Frances Neel Cheney. [R: LJ, Aug 71, p. 2480; RQ, Fall 71, p. 81; ALA 71; ARBA 72, item 1319; ARBA 74, item 1296]

577. Ottemiller's Index to Plays in Collections: An Author and Title Index to Plays Appearing in Collections Published between 1900 and mid-1970. Ed. by John M. Connor and Billie M. Connor. 5th ed. rev. and enl. Metuchen, N.J., Scarecrow, 1971. 452p. index. $12.00. LC 71-166073. ISBN 0-8108-0447-6.

The fourth edition of this standard work on the subject analyzed 814 collections and was published in 1963. The present edition retains the same basic features, adding 233 collections published from 1963 through mid-1970. There is one exception in terms of previously established format. In the case of production dates, when a play has never been performed or when no performance date has been found, publication is given in parentheses. If an exact date of production cannot be determined, an approximate date is given and indicated by a question mark, as in previous editions. With the completion of this volume, *Ottemiller's Index* now covers, in all its editions, 3,049 different plays by 1,444 authors. [R: ARBA 72, item 1320]

578. Palmer, Helen H., and Anne Jane Dyson, comps. **European Drama Criticism. Supplement I, To January 1970. Supplement II, Through 1972.** Hamden, Conn., Shoe String, 1970, 1974. $6.50(suppl. 1); $8.50(suppl. 2). LC 67-24188. ISBN 0-208-01044-0; 0-208-01422-5.

The basic volume, *European Drama Criticism: Interpretations of European Drama*, was published in 1968 and is a comprehensive listing of criticism which appeared in books and periodicals, in English and foreign languages, from 1900 to 1966. *Supplement I* updates the basic bibliography to 1970 and *Supplement II* further updates it through 1974.

The index includes criticism of the dramatic works of outstanding European playwrights and is arranged alphabetically by playwright. A playwright's works are entered alphabetically under his/her name with sources of criticism appearing alphabetically by critic's name under each work. Quality of criticism was not a consideration for inclusion. Cross-references are provided for pseudonyms, joint authors, and foreign language titles. Main entries give full bibliographic information. There is a "List of Books Indexed," a "List of Journals Indexed," and an index which includes plays and playwrights, giving date(s) for the latter, if known. Criticism of Shakespeare's plays has not been included, as a number of bibliographies are devoted exclusively to criticism of his works.

European Drama Criticism is a companion title to *American Drama Criticism* by the same compilers. —Peggy Jay. [R: WLB, Oct 74, p. 182; Choice, Nov 74, p. 1286; ARBA 72, item 1321; ARBA 75, item 1324]

579. **Play Index 1968-1972: An Index to 3,848 Plays.** Estelle A. Fidell, ed. New York, H. W. Wilson, 1973. 403p. $20.00. LC 64-1054. ISBN 0-8242-0496-4.

This latest supplement to the *Play Index* covers 3,848 plays. The format is the same as for previous volumes, with Part I devoted to the author, title, and subject index. Author entries list play title, publisher, copyright date, pagination, brief plot outline, number of sets, acts, and actors. If the play also appears in an anthology, reference is given to that volume. Title entries refer the user to the author's name for the more complete entry. Subject entries are arranged by author and then title. Specific play forms, such as puppet plays, are also listed under the form heading. In addition to the usual *c* indication for children's plays for the elementary grades, a *y* is now used for plays for grades 7 to 10.

Part II contains cast analyses for sex and number of characters. An additional section has been added here for "Variable Cast," where the sex of the characters is interchangeable. Part III gives the full bibliographic listing of the anthologies, and Part IV provides complete addresses for publishers and distributors. Other volumes in the *Play Index* series cover 1949-1952; 1953-1960; and 1961-1967. —Judith K. Rosenberg. [R: ARBA 74, item 1295]

FICTION

BIBLIOGRAPHIES

580. Adelman, Irving, and Rita Dworkin. **The Contemporary Novel: A Checklist of Critical Literature on the British and American Novel Since 1945.** Metuchen, N.J., Scarecrow, 1972. 614p. $17.00. LC 72-4451. ISBN 0-8108-0517-0.

This is a welcome addition to the shelf of bibliographies of fiction criticism. In the preface, the compilers carefully define their scope and limits as selective coverage from scholarly journals, excluding book reviews unless they are of unusual merit—or they are the only critical material available. Novelists who wrote before 1945 are included if they continued to publish significant works after 1945 or achieved most of their recognition after that date. A sampling of the nearly 200 leading British and American novelists who fit these guidelines did not uncover any omissions: all the major writers appear to be there. The inclusion of novels published before 1945 by writers who met the guidelines might lead one to expect to find works of criticism also, but this is generally not the case. Most of the books and periodical articles cited are from the 1950s and 1960s.

Areas of apparent overlap with other bibliographies are frequently more apparent than real. For example, Volume I of Gerstenberger's *The American Novel* has six entries for *Studs Lonigan*, by James T. Farrell (several from the 1930s), and Volume II has 10 entries from the 1960s. The work under review has 21 entries, only five of which are duplicates of those in Volume I *and* II of Gerstenberger. Likewise, *The American Novel: Sinclair Lewis to the Present*, by Blake Nevius, is less inclusive even for its stated area of coverage, omitting such writers as John Cheever, Herbert Gold, and James Purdy, all of whom are included by Adelman and Dworkin. Coverage outside the United States is not even attempted in the works cited above, whereas the book under review not only has leading British novelists like John Braine, Ivy Compton-Burnett, Graham Greene, Iris Murdoch, George

Orwell, and Evelyn Waugh, but, for good measure, tosses in a few Canadians like Morley Callaghan, Hugh MacLennan, and Mordecai Richler. —A. Robert Rogers. [R: ALA 73; ARBA 73, item 1246]

581. Barzun, Jacques, and Wendell Hertig Taylor. **A Catalogue of Crime.** New York, Harper & Row, 1971. 831p. index. $18.95. LC 75-123914. ISBN 0-06-010263-2.

The subtitle on the dustjacket (but not on the title page) describes this book as "Being a Reader's Guide to the Literature of Mystery, Detection, & Related Genres." This bibliography or catalogue raisonné includes some 7,500 works in 3,476 numbered entries covering the period 1870-1970. There are six separate sections: 1) novels of detection, crime, mystery and espionage; 2) short stories, anthologies, periodicals and plays; 3) biography and criticism, including a subsection on the literature of Edwin Drood; 4) the literature of actual or true crimes; 5) the literature of Sherlock Holmes; and 6) ghost stories, supernatural stories and psychical research. There is a detailed index of 105 pages. Many of the entries are annotated both descriptively and critically. Basic bibliographical information is provided, although there is a special code for publishers' names. The detailed introduction sets the scope of the work, including a long discussion of this composite genre.

Although this work must be considered as a basic guide to the literature of the genre of mystery writing, it is selective and perhaps more representative of the compilers' taste than of their scholarly attitudes. Many of the annotations (although delightful to read) seem to lack academic objectivity. This work will be more useful for the reader of mystery stories than for the student of this genre. Furthermore, the work must be treated as a bibliography and not as a selection aid, since many, many entries are out of print. Paperbacks are generally ignored. —John Phillip Immroth. [R: LJ, July 71, p. 2293; ALA 71; ARBA 73, item 1248]

582. Bleiler, Everett F., ed. **The Checklist of Fantastic Literature: A Bibliography of Fantasy, Weird and Science Fiction Books Published in the English Language.** Chicago, Shasta, 1948; repr. Naperville, Ill., FAX, 1973. 452p. $10.00.

Forrest J. Ackerman, professional sci-fi fan and collector, once called Bleiler's *Checklist* "the single greatest contribution ever made in the field of fantasy enjoyment." For nearly 25 years, much of the time out of print and selling for $50 or more on the o.p. market, this pioneering work has served dealers, collectors, and fans as a sort of bible in a field in which authentic scholarship is scarce. Bleiler omitted all magazine material, concentrating instead on about 5,300 books of prose fiction published in English from 1764 to 1947. His definition of fantasy has been questioned; some of the works he omitted are considered generic to the field. Bleiler, however, was a careful scholar and listed no book that he had not looked at personally or that he could not verify in Library of Congress or British Museum catalogs. Because fiction of this type is often issued in privately printed editions and frequently ignored in national bibliographies, the wonder is that he did not omit more titles. Works included are arranged by author, with complete and accurate bibliographical information plus lists of contents where applicable. A title index and an annotated list of 65 reference works complete the volume.

In 1963 Bradford Day issued *The Supplemental Checklist of Fantastic Literature*, which updated Bleiler, citing some 3,000 novels that had appeared in the pulps before 1947 but that were not published in book form until later. Day's supplement is now out of print; until someone attempts another revision, Bleiler's *Checklist* remains the only book-length bibliography of comparable scope available in fantasy fiction today. —Mary Jo Walker. [R: RQ, Summer 73, p. 403; ARBA 74, item 1297]

583. Clareson, Thomas. **Science Fiction Criticism: An Annotated Checklist.** Kent, Ohio, Kent State University Press, 1972. 225p. index. (The Serif Series: Bibliographies and Checklists, No. 23). $7.00. LC 71-181084. ISBN 0-87338-123-8.

Sci-fi continues its hi-fi soar. Clareson's 820 critically annotated entries attest to sci-fi's growing popularity and Clareson's own scholarship. Developed from a two-part bibliography first published in *Extrapolation* (May and December, 1970), *Science Fiction Criticism* covers books and articles in nine categories. Arranged alphabetically by author, the areas covered include such things as "Literary Studies," "Visual Arts," "Futurology, Utopia, and Dystopia," and "Specialist Bibliographies, Checklists, and Indices." Two indices complete the volume: entries, and authors mentioned. Unfortunately, they are geared to section and entry numbers instead of just to pages, forcing readers into a kind of double step—i.e., referring to the table of contents at the same time. Running heads would simplify searching.

Clareson has compiled an invaluable combination of retrospective and current materials. —Peter Doiron. [R: Choice, Nov 72, p. 1113; LJ, July 72, p. 2374; ALA 72; ARBA 73, item 1250]

584. Hagen, Ordean A., comp. **Who Done It: An Encyclopedic Guide to Detective, Mystery and Suspense Fiction.** New York, R. R. Bowker, 1969. 834p. $21.50. LC 69-19209. ISBN 0-8352-0234-8.

Provides bibliographic information on some 50,000 American and British mystery novels published from 1841 to 1967. Arrangement is alphabetical by author. Includes indexes to heroes, villains, detectives, locales, a subject guide to mysteries, a geographical guide to scenes of the crimes, a dictionary of heroes, villains and heroines, a selected list of mystery anthologies and collections, and other information making it probably the most comprehensive reference tool on the subject. [R: LJ, 15 Oct 69; ALA 69; ARBA 70, v.2, p. 66]

ENCYCLOPEDIAS

585. Tuck, Donald H., comp. **The Encyclopedia of Science Fiction and Fantasy through 1968: A Bibliographic Survey of the Fields of Science Fiction, Fantasy, and Weird Fiction through 1968; Volume I: Who's Who, A-L.** Chicago, Advent, 1974. 286p. $20.00. LC 73-91828. ISBN 0-911682-20-1.

The first volume in this projected three-volume encyclopedia consists of "Who's Who, A-L," and their works. In an 8½ x 11-inch, two-column format, it presents an alphabetical listing of science fiction authors, editors, anthologists, and artists. Entries under each personality include a brief biographical sketch, with detailed bibliographical information on all forms of their published work through 1968. Tables of contents are given for most anthologies and collections, and books and short stories that comprise connected series are noted.

Volume II, to be issued in 1976, will continue with "Who's Who, M-Z," followed by a title index of all books, paperbacks, and other publications mentioned in the who's who sections. Volume III, planned for publication in 1977, will provide a checklist of magazines and series, a separate listing of paperbacks by title, author, and publisher, a cross-reference section on pseudonyms, plus bibliographies on such general subjects as flying saucers, ghosts, and utopias. Supplements, to be published at five-year intervals, are planned to keep the coverage up to date.

Science fiction buffs already know this work, by reputation at least, although not all may be fortunate enough to have seen a copy. First issued in 1954 in a duplicated edition entitled *A Handbook of Science Fiction*, revised and enlarged in 1959, it is a classic in its own time and is probably the most comprehensive reference work on science fiction and fantasy ever attempted. The earlier editions, now virtually unobtainable, are collectors' items. —Mary Jo Walker. [R: ARBA 75, item 1330]

DICTIONARIES

586. Freeman, William. **Dictionary of Fictional Characters**. Rev. by Fred Urquhart. Boston, The Writer, Inc., 1973. 579p. index. $10.00. LC 73-18065. ISBN 0-87116-085-4.

Originally published in Great Britain in 1963, this newly revised edition indexes over 20,000 fictional characters from novels, short stories, poems, plays, and operas written in the English language during the last six centuries. These characters were gleaned from over 2,000 works by approximately 500 British and American authors. Practically all the works of Shakespeare, Dickens, Hardy, Kipling, Wells, Jane Austen, and the Brontës are accounted for. But there are some real oddities. For instance, a work of Fanny Hurst is included, but one finds no entry for Huxley's *After Many a Summer Dies the Swan*, nor for any of the operas of Benjamin Britten. There is no mention of Norman Mailer or Gertrude Stein or Edward Albee or Robert Ruark. But we do encounter Thomas Love Peacock, Nora Hoult, and M. Pickthall. Despite these and other lapses, this effort answers many questions.

The dictionary is arranged in three parts. The main section is alphabetically arranged (by fictional character's name), indicating that character's relationships to the important personae of the work. Also given is the title of the work in which these characters appear, plus the author and first date of publication. The remaining two indexes are devoted to authors and titles, respectively. The first of these gives page citations to the works listed under the author's name, while the title index gives only the name of the author. —Kenyon C. Rosenberg. [R: BL, 15 Nov 74, p. 350; LJ, July 74, p. 1795; ARBA 75, item 1326]

INDEXES

587. Hall, H. W., ed. **Science Fiction Book Review Index, 1923-1973**. Detroit, Gale, 1975. 438p. index. $45.00. LC 74-29085. ISBN 0-8103-1054-6.

This is a complete record of all books reviewed in science fiction magazines from 1923 to 1973. Beginning in 1970, coverage was extended to include reviews of science fiction in selected general magazines, library magazines, and amateur magazines (fanzines). The book is divided into five parts: the index of books reviewed (a few title entries are included), the directory of magazines indexed, a listing of indexes to science fiction magazines, an editor index, and a title index. In all, citations are given to about 14,500 reviews from 216 magazines. Each title is listed under its author, and a listing of all reviews and reviewers is given immediately below. Excerpts from the reviews are not included.

Since the first magazine devoted exclusively to science fiction, *Amazing Stories*, began publication in 1926, the period covered by this index comprises almost the entire history of SF as a separate literary genre. The usefulness of the work is thereby enhanced. The major practical limitation to the usefulness of this book undoubtedly lies in the fact that most libraries would be unlikely to own the magazines mentioned in the citations; many of them are collectors' items now, and at the time of their issue they were considered unworthy of shelf space.

Science fiction has been fortunate in having more than its share of indexes and bibliographers. This work is another indication of that fact. Anyone interested in serious SF scholarship should have access to this book. —Martin Andrews.
[R: LJ, 1 Sept 75, p. 1535; WLB, Nov 75, pp. 267-68; ARBA 76, item 1206]

588. Siemon, Frederick. **Science Fiction Story Index, 1950-1968**. Chicago, American Library Association, 1971. 274p. $4.50pa. LC 70-162470. ISBN 0-8389-0107-7.

Indexers of science fiction undoubtedly are plagued with more than the usual number of indexing problems and decisions. Besides the major questions of time and scope and format, they must decide how they will define science fiction. Wherever the lines are drawn, someone will be displeased.

In the present guide, Siemon indexes over 3,400 short stories, novellas, novels, and poems in 237 anthologies. Although such writers as Saki and H. P. Lovecraft are represented, Siemon has concentrated on anthologies of pure or hard-line science fiction, covering approximately 90 percent of those published in the United States and England from 1950 through 1968. Periodical fiction is not indexed here, and Siemon has also excluded volumes produced in limited editions and books not readily identifiable as anthologies.

The guide consists of three clearly defined and easy-to-use sections. The first lists stories alphabetically by author. The second, which can double as a buying aid, describes the anthologies indexed, giving complete bibliographical information for each, plus reading level and in-print status. Price is not indicated. The third section, an alphabetical listing by titles, refers the user to the author section or directly to the anthology in which the story appeared. Comprehensive and definitive within its scope, *Science Fiction Story Index* may be used alone in general reference collections. Libraries serving science fiction fans, however, will need to supplement it with W. R. Cole's *A Checklist of Science Fiction Anthologies*, which covers 1927 through 1963, and Bradford M. Day's *Index to Science Fiction Magazines 1926-1950*, and *1951-1965*. —Mary Jo Walker. [R: AL, Oct 71, p. 1015; LJ, 15 Oct 71, p. 3314; WLB, Oct 71, p. 190; RQ, Winter 71, p. 180; ALA 71; ARBA 72, item 1326]

BIOGRAPHY

589. Vinson, James, ed. **Contemporary Novelists**. New York, St. Martin's Press, 1972. 1422p. (Contemporary Writers of the English Language). $30.00. LC 75-189694.

This is a comprehensive guide to biographical information for about 600 living English language authors of novels and short stories, similar in style to *Contemporary Poets of the English Language*. It is arranged alphabetically by author. Each entry contains a brief biography, full bibliography, a comment by the writer (for over half the entries writers did choose to comment), and a signed critical essay on the writer's body of fiction. It is very up to date, listing, for example, Joyce Carol Oates's *Wonderland* (New York, Vanguard, 1971; London, Gollancz, 1972). However, it is not sufficiently current to show that Wallace Stegner won the Pulitzer Prize for Fiction in 1972 for *Angle of Repose*. Authors who have written novels but who are not usually thought of as novelists (e.g., Mark Van Doren) are included. Authors are from African countries, the Caribbean islands, India, and, of course, Australia, Great Britain, and the United States. —Sally Wynkoop. [R: ALA 73; ARBA 73, item 1236]

POETRY

BIBLIOGRAPHIES

590. Coleman, Arthur. **Epic and Romance Criticism: Volume One, A Checklist of Interpretations 1940-1972 of English and American Epics and Metrical Romances**. Searington, N.Y., Watermill Publishers, 1973. 387p. $13.75. LC 73-75805. ISBN 0-88370-001-8.

Drawn from over 500 periodicals and from hundreds of monographs and books, *Epic and Romance Criticism* brings together for the student, teacher, and scholar over 20,000 bibliographical entries on the subject of poetic epics, metrical romances, and sagas.

Some scholars may be surprised at the number of books and articles cited, for Coleman has dilated the definition of epic. Since epics reflect the age in which they were produced, Coleman argues in an introduction, "they grow with the world, and like the world change their form and character—while their spirit remains constant." Coleman defines epic or heroic verse as "poetry which depicts large concerns covering a particular epoch of human history and civilization, with a marked tendency to see something universal about these concerns, in a style notably serious, earnest, and dignified." This definition enables him to view as epics not only *Beowulf*, the *Nibelungenlied*, and *Paradise Lost*, for example, but also a number of modern works ranging from Conrad Aiken's *Kid* to Eliot's *The Waste Land*, Hopkins' *The Wreck of the Deutschland*, Pound's *Cantos*, W. C. Williams' *Paterson*, and, in an appendix, Robert Penn Warren's *Brother to Dragons*. The inclusion of criticism on these latter works may prove helpful in establishing further continuities between the modern and earlier literary periods.

Epic and Romance Criticism is a welcome research tool. However, the exclusion of criticism in foreign languages (although many French, German, Scandinavian, and Slavic-language periodicals were consulted for articles in English) is unfortunately but another example of an insularity that all too frequently characterizes American and English literary criticism. —Jim Wayne Miller. [R: LJ, July 73, p. 2067; RSR, July/Sept 73, p. 23; ALA 73; ARBA 74, item 1273]

ENCYCLOPEDIAS

591. Preminger, Alex, ed. **Princeton Encyclopedia of Poetry and Poetics**. Enl. ed. Princeton, N.J., Princeton University Press, 1975. 992p. $27.50; $7.95pa. LC 63-7076. ISBN 0-691-06280-3; 0-691-01317-9pa.

The first edition of this standard book on the subject was published in 1965. It is an authoritative and scholarly encyclopedia, international in scope; its discussions of literary movements and genres deal exclusively with theory. Terms used in criticism are defined, including some used in prose and in the fine arts. Omitted are articles on individual poets or poems and allusions. The impressive total of the first edition was some 1,000 signed articles in 906 pages. This "enlarged edition" consists of a page-by-page reprint of the first edition, with a supplement of some 75,000 words. The supplement covers some new topics, such as "Computer Poetry," and provides information on subjects left out of the first edition, such as "Harlem Renaissance." All essays in the first edition as well as in the "enlargement" are written by prominent authorities on this subject. The *Princeton Encyclopedia* is certainly a landmark book; adding a supplement to the first edition was probably more economical than resetting the entire text. —Bohdan S. Wynar. [R: Choice, Oct 75, p. 983; WLB, Sept 75, p. 70; ARBA 76, item 1213]

INDEXES

592. Smith, William James, ed. **Granger's Index to Poetry**. 6th ed., rev. and enl. New York, Columbia University Press, 1973. 2223p. $80.00. LC 73-4186. ISBN 0-231-03641-8.

The long history of this standard source is well known to most librarians. The first edition was published in 1904, the fifth in 1962. In preparation for the sixth edition, the editor consulted a number of reference librarians; the result was a substantial enlargement of the work. Thus, the present edition indexes a total of 514 volumes of anthologized poetry, including not only 114 new works or new editions, but also most of the anthologies that appeared in the fifth edition and the 1967 supplement. The structure of the index remains the same: title and first-line index, author index, and subject index. [R: WLB, Dec 73, p. 339; ARBA 74, item 1304]

BIOGRAPHY

593. Vinson, James, ed. **Contemporary Poets**. 2nd ed. New York, St. Martin's Press, 1975. 1849p. $35.00. LC 78-165556. ISBN 0-099007-20-6.

The first edition of this biographical dictionary was published in 1971 under the title *Contemporary Poets of the English Language*. It is universal in its coverage of some 1,100 living English language poets.

This second edition bears a shortened title—simply *Contemporary Poets*. It is nearly one-third longer than its predecessor, but its entries number only 800; coverage of each poet included is more comprehensive. Arrangement is alphabetical by name. Entries include information of the "who's who" variety, a bibliography of the poet's works, an autobiographical note about the poet's verse, and a short, signed critical article about the poet's work. [R: WLB, Nov 75, p. 267; ALA 72; ARBA 72, item 1388; ARBA 76, item 1214]

QUOTATIONS

594. **The International Thesaurus of Quotations.** Comp. by Rhonda Thomas Tripp. New York, Thomas Y. Crowell, 1970. 1088p. $9.95; $11.95 thumb-indexed. LC 73-106587. ISBN 0-690-44584-9; 0-690-44585-7 thumb-indexed.

The quotation dictionary has two main uses: to identify remembered or partially remembered quotations and to learn of appropriate quotations on a topic or theme. Of the two, the first use is much more frequent in the average library. This dictionary, however, is compiled primarily for the second use. It supplies writers, speakers, and browsers with quotations to fit a given idea. This function is fulfilled admirably by the arrangement of some 16,000 quotations under the ideas they express rather than under key words within the quotation, the method used by most other dictionaries. The selection is wide, thoughtful, and modern. More than 6,000 are of this century, including favorites from Eric Hoffer, John Kennedy, Walter Lippmann, Pearl Buck and numerous other current speakers and writers.

A comparison with six of the standard quotation dictionaries indicates that a maximum of 30 percent of its quotations can be found in any of them. Proverbs are included, but not slogans, old saws, and familiar phrases like "till Hell freezes over" or "an apple a day keeps the doctor away." Citations to sources are complete. In addition to an index of authors and sources and an index of the topics and ideas under which the quotations are arranged, there is a 294-page index of key words to help the user identify a particular quotation. This is less complete than we could hope for, often listing a quotation under only one of its significant words. Reference from the index to the quotation is to category and specific entry in the main section. *The International Thesaurus of Quotations* is of value in supplying both old and more recent quotations on a theme and in containing a large number of quotations not found in other dictionaries. —Rolland E. Stevens. [R: ALA 70; ARBA 71, item 1435]

595. Magill, Frank N. **Magill's Quotations in Context**. Second Series. New York, Harper & Row, 1969. 1340p. index. $11.95. LC 69-15317. ISBN 0-06-003659-1.

The first edition of this work was published in 1966 and reviewed in *Library Journal* (April 15, 1966). The Second Series contains 1,500 additional quotations from the classics of poetry, drama, fiction, and non-fiction. Information about the context is given for each entry; a full explanation of who said what, when, where and why. Both the quotations and the background information are longer in this new volume than in the first and much longer than in other quotation books. The quotations are almost exclusively literary in their origin and interest. There are three indexes. Two of these appear ahead of the text: a list of quotations arranged, as are the full entries themselves, alphabetically by the first significant word, and a key-word index, helpful when the reader cannot remember a quotation verbatim, but can recall an important word or identifying phrase. An author index is at the end of the book. Obviously, this work is not as comprehensive as Bartlett, Stevenson, or *The Oxford Dictionary of Quotations*, but it will be useful primarily because of the special aids for interpretation, which give it an educational value beyond that of other quotation books. [R: SR, 17 May 69; ALA 70; ARBA 70, v.2, p. 63]

CHILDREN'S LITERATURE

GENERAL WORKS

596. Fisher, Margery. **Who's Who in Children's Books: A Treasury of the Familiar Characters of Childhood.** New York, Holt, Rinehart and Winston, 1975. 399p. illus.(part col.). index. $22.95. LC 75-5463. ISBN 0-03-015091-4.

A delightful compendium of information on about 1,000 characters in children's books. Despite the noted author's disclaimer that this "is not intended primarily as a reference book," it can be used as such, if the compiler's own statements are kept in mind. This is not meant to be inclusive; nursery rhyme and fairy tale figures as well as real historical persons who appear in fiction are excluded. Few minor characters appear unless essential to the plot or famous on their own.

It might also be noted that there is some British bias. Many English series (e.g., Biggles) that are hardly known in the United States are included, while equally well-known American series (e.g., Miss Pickerell, Encyclopedia Brown) are not. There are also many scenes from BBC-TV programs not known abroad.

The entry arrangement is alphabetical, but by the first word of the name as it appears in the original work: Miss Eglantine Price under M, Laura Ingalls (no Wilder given) under L, Great-Aunt Dympha under G, and so on. When groups are presented under family names, relationships are carefully explained.

Good information is charmingly presented, ranging from the Bobbsey Twins and Little Lord Fauntleroy (Cedric Errol) to Little Pear and Bilbo Baggins. The volume has approximately 400 illustrations, 16 of them full-page and in color. Pictures are primarily reproductions of book illustrations, but they also include stills from motion picture and TV versions of the works, title pages, and authors. —Eleanor Elving Schwartz. [R: LJ, 15 Dec 75, p. 2315; ARBA 76, item 1198]

BIBLIOGRAPHIES

597. **Children's Books in the Rare Book Division of the Library of Congress.** Library of Congress. Rare Book Division. Totowa, N.J., Rowman and Littlefield, 1975. 2v. $100.00. LC 75-9605. ISBN 0-87471-579-2.

Since the establishment of the Library of Congress Rare Book Division in 1927, its acquisition of rare children's books has resulted in a fine collection of some 15,000 volumes. It is the pre-eminent collection of Americana in children's books. The printed catalog of the collection records temporary cards not available in other LC printed catalogs or printed cards and adds a selection of some 1,000 items housed in the Children's Book Section. The latter titles are representative of each year's books to 1973. Criteria for these titles, selected by Virginia Haviland, are importance of author and illustrator, quality of design, and significance of a title in representing trends in the children's book field.

The catalog is arranged in two sections: authors and chronological list. The complete catalog card, reduced in size, is reproduced three columns per page in the authors volume and all authors are listed in a single alphabet. The editor points out that the catalog thus acts as a supplement to the Library's rare children's book collection card file (and shelf arrangement), which separates "well-known" authors' cards from the author file and the chronological file. (Well-known authors' cards are filed in a separate file.) Most of the entries in the catalog are for American imprints, but some English titles are represented, as well as a small number of foreign language books from other countries. The chronological volume omits the portion of the cards below the collation area, or below notes if those are important (e.g., "imperfect copy"). The chronological entries begin with updated items. The first dated book is 1635, Edmund Coate's *The English Schoole-Master*. Entries for the twentieth century (about 2,300) represent only 76 of the 493 pages, with nearly two-thirds of that space devoted to the period 1900 to 1950.

The catalog will serve as an excellent finding list for eighteenth and nineteenth century Americana, but it is obviously not as complete from 1900 forward. —Christine L. Wynar. [R: ARBA 76, item 1197]

598. Haviland, Virginia, comp. **Children's Literature: A Guide to Reference Sources, First Supplement.** Washington, Library of Congress, 1972. 316p. illus. index. $3.00. LC 66-62734. ISBN 0-8444-0022-X.

This guide updates the basic volume, *Children's Literature: A Guide to Reference Sources* (1966), which lists materials published through 1965. This supplement covers publications issued from 1966 through 1969, although it does include older items that were not available to the compilers in 1966.

Works were selected for inclusion "on the basis of their estimated usefulness to adults concerned with the creation, reading, or study of children's books." Two new sections have been added to the framework of the earlier *Guide*: "The Publishing and Promotion of Children's Books" and "The Teaching of Children's Literature." This supplement increases emphasis on foreign books, on books concerned with minorities in the United States, and on children's book illustration. "Entries are annotated to indicate the relative importance and value as well as the usefulness and interest of the items described." Library of Congress call numbers follow each title. There are cross references to other entries in this supplement and to entries in the basic volume, when appropriate. An author, title, and subject index is preceded by a directory of professional associations and agencies whose published material is listed.

The compilers anticipate publishing additional supplements about every five years and occasionally revising the basic work. —Peggy Jay. [R: ARBA 73, item 169]

599. Rosenberg, Judith K., and Kenyon C. Rosenberg. **Young People's Literature in Series: Fiction; An Annotated Bibliographical Guide.** Littleton, Colo., Libraries Unlimited, 1972. 176p. index. $7.50. LC 72-93401. ISBN 0-87287-060-X.

This is a guide to fiction books in series for readers in grades 3 to 9. This work covers over 1,400 titles of young people's fiction from 1955 to date, supplementing Frank Gardner's *Sequels* (Library Association, 1955). Omitted are series of consistently low quality, including the Bobbsey Twins and the Hardy Boys. Evaluative annotations consider plot content, depth and believability of characterization, writing style, and book format. The arrangement is by author, with individual titles listed in their logical sequence within the series. Following the bibliography is an individual title index and a series title index. [R: ARBA 73, item 167]

600. Rosenberg, Judith K., and Kenyon C. Rosenberg. **Young People's Literature in Series: Publishers' and Non-Fiction Series; An Annotated Bibliographical Guide.** Littleton, Colo., Libraries Unlimited, 1973. 280p. index. $10.00. LC 73-75237. ISBN 0-87287-058-8.

With the publication of this volume, the two-part set *Young People's Literature in Series* is complete. The first volume, covering fiction series, was released in December 1972. *Young People's Literature in Series* is designed to help identify the various titles published in series for young people and to provide descriptive and evaluative information about each series. The two volumes contain 7,451 entries—1,428 in the fiction volume and 6,023 in the publishers' and non-fiction volume.

Arrangement is alphabetical by series title or, in the case of untitled author series, by author. The bibliography aims to list all individual volumes of a given series. Annotations refer to a series as a whole and comment on format, durability, reading level, illustrations, indexes, bibliographies, and wherever possible, overall writing style. [R: WLB, Nov 73, p. 260; BL, 1 Dec 73, p. 352; ARBA 74, item 1316]

601. Shaw, John Mackay. **Childhood in Poetry Supplement.** Detroit, Gale, 1972. 3v. index. $87.50. LC 67-28092. ISBN 0-8103-0476-7.

Subtitled "A Catalogue, with Biographical and Critical Annotations, of the Books of English and American Poets Comprising the Shaw Childhood in Poetry Collection, Library of The Florida State University, with Lists of the Poems That Relate to Childhood, Notes, and Index." This is a three-volume supplement to the five-volume base set published by Gale in 1967. The purpose of the original work was to index the 100,000 poems appearing in the 10,000-book Shaw Collection. The supplement contains all new matter on 60,000 poems from over 8,000 books added to the collection since 1967. (These titles range from works published in 1790 to books published in 1970.) Included are the works of both major and minor English and American poets who wrote for and/or about children. Anthologies, biographies of poets represented in the collection, pertinent reference works, and important child-related periodicals are also listed.

The annotations, arranged alphabetically by author, take up the first two volumes and half of the third volume. Volume three also contains a Short Title List and Key and a Keyword Index. The Short Title List records alphabetically by author the title of each book analyzed in the main part of the set. It lists the item number, author, title, and year. The Keyword Index is designed to be used in conjunction with the Short Title List in order to identify the author. Full information is provided in the main text, Annotations. Each entry lists the author and his dates, item number (for each book), title, date, place and publisher, edition, collation, size in centimeters (height and width), cover material and stamping, and any inscriptions. Cites typical passages from the book and, for many books, lists individual poems under the heading "Volume Also Contains." Poets whose poems are identified in collections are listed with *see* references to specific item numbers. In all, this monumental undertaking provides access to an abundance of poems for and about children. —Christine L. Wynar. [R: ARBA 73, item 168]

602. Welch, d'Alté A. **A Bibliography of American Children's Books Printed Prior to 1821**. Barre, Mass., Barre Publishers, 1972. 516p. index. $45.00. LC 77-163898. ISBN 0-8271-7133-1.

This carefully compiled and comprehensive bibliography of American children's books prior to 1821 was first published in six parts in *Proceedings* (American Antiquarian Society, April 1963, October 1963, October 1964, October 1965, April 1967). The compiler prepared notes for revisions prior to his death in 1970 and the edited version published in 1972 contains the corrections and additions. Introductory matter consists of acknowledgments recognizing the distinguished gallery of book collectors associated with Welch's project. A chronological history of American children's books sketches the development of publishing, citing the earliest and most famous titles, authors, and publishers. The most important part of this section is the "Method of the Work," which describes the scope, explains the entry form, abbreviations, and method of collation, and lists the location of symbols used in the bibliography. Locations are cited for books in 18 private collections and 185 libraries, including two Canadian libraries and the British Museum.

"The bibliography is primarily concerned with narrative books written in English, designed for children under fifteen years of age. They should be the type of book read at leisure for pleasure. . . . Books written about or by children, treatises on education or how to rear children are avoided. . . . Broadsides, sermons, books of advice, catechisms, primers, and school books are excluded" (Introduction). Entries for books of poetry, jokes and riddles, natural history, games, as well as narrative books, are included in the bibliography.

Arrangement is by author (when known) with his works listed alphabetically. Books by anonymous or unknown authors are listed under title. Each book with a separate title is numbered. Books first published in England are listed citing the first English edition. Entries give author and his dates, title, edition, place and publisher or printer, year, collation, size, any signatures, a description of binding and any other outstanding features, plus notes on missing pages or mutilations. Location symbols are included. The bibliography records 1,478 separate titles. At the end is an index of printers, publishers (with their dates and city), and imprints. Book numbers are listed in chronological sequence under each name. Welch's work is a significant contribution to the study of the history of American children's books. —Christine L. Wynar. [R: ARBA 73, item 170]

INDEXES

603. Brewton, John E., Sara W. Brewton, and G. Meredith Blackburn, III. **Index to Poetry for Children and Young People, 1964-1969: A Title, Subject, Author, and First Line Index to Poetry in Collections for Children and Young People.** New York, H. W. Wilson, 1972. 575p. $20.00. LC 71-161574. ISBN 0-8242-0435-2.

Brewton's *Index to Poetry for Children* is the standard reference tool in this area. The main volume (1942) indexes 15,000 poems by 2,500 different authors from some 130 collections under 1,800 subject headings. The First Supplement (1954) adds 7,000 poems by 1,300 authors from 66 collections. The Second Supplement analyzes 8,000 poems by 1,400 authors from 85 collections. This new volume indexes 11,000 poems by 2,000 authors from 117 collections published since the cutoff date of the Second Supplement (1963) through 1969. Following the well-developed pattern of the previous volumes, it is a thorough index of titles, subjects (2,000 separate headings), authors, and first lines. Scope is similar to that of the previous indexes, covering books of poetry for young children through senior high school age—although more books are included for the grades 7 through 12. To reflect this shift in emphasis, a more inclusive title has been chosen (. . . *for Children and Young People*).

The elementary school level titles still predominate over books for grades 7 through 12, running about 4 to 1, and selections are still based on votes of consulting librarians and teachers. The titles tend toward a traditional style, although some newer names are noticeable. For senior high school use, the index is quite limited. A check against poetry anthologies and collected poems of American and English authors in *Senior High School Library Catalog*, 10th ed., shows that not all of the titles listed in the catalog are included in Brewton. Some omissions are L. Hughes' *New Negro Poets USA*, W. Lowenfels' *The Writing on the Wall*, R. Schreiber's *31 New American Poets*, G. Brooks' *In the Mecca*, and individual volumes of collected poems by Crane, Deutsch, Moore, etc. The coverage of children's anthologies and the collected poems by individual poets is better.   —Christine L. Wynar. [R: ARBA 73, item 186]

604. Kreider, Barbara. **Index to Children's Plays in Collections.** Metuchen, N.J., Scarecrow, 1972. 138p. $6.00. LC 72-3008. ISBN 0-8108-0494-6.

Not since ALA's *Subject Index to Children's Plays* has there been a volume specifically dedicated to children's plays. Ms. Kreider has filled the gap with her index of juvenile play collections published between 1965 and 1969. She has indexed 25 of the 31 collections published during those years—by title, subject, theme, type of play, famous personalities in the plays, historical period, geographical area, special occasion or holiday, and special form or cast. The author (main) entry lists title, collection(s) the play is in, and the number of characters.

In a separate section, the author lists plays by character analysis: female, male, mixed, and puppet casts, and then by the number of characters required in each play. This will prove invaluable for group leaders who need plays to fulfill special cast requirements. The author also lists complete bibliographic information on the collections indexed, as well as a directory of their publishers.

Because it is the first new play index in recent years, and because of its many subject headings and cast analyses, this will prove important to many collections, large and small. —Judith K. Rosenberg. [R: ARBA 73, item 187]

605. Silverman, Judith. **Index to Young Readers' Collective Biographies: Elementary and Junior High School Level.** 2nd ed. New York, R. R. Bowker, 1975. 322p. index. $14.95. LC 75-834. ISBN 0-8352-0741-2.

In updating her earlier edition (R. R. Bowker, 1970), Ms. Silverman has followed the same format: alphabetical listing of biographees, followed by birth and death dates, nationality, occupation, and symbols for the works in which they are included. This new edition encompasses 249 newly indexed volumes (although no cut-off date for inclusion is mentioned), plus the 471 in the original work, thus swelling the total of biographees to 5,833.

Several improvements over the previous edition have been made, notably an index of the titles of the books included therein, with a list of their contents. This index should help the book selector choose new items whose coverage does not duplicate titles already in their collections. Out-of-print editions have been indicated. In the Subject Listing of Biographees, 20 new areas have been added. Also appended are a key to publishers and an index to the subject headings; the latter seems rather superfluous, since it simply repeats the headings in exactly the same order as they appear in the Subject Listing.

While this is a well-presented and well-researched project, a few bugs remain to be ironed out in the next edition. In the case of sports or entertainment figures most commonly known by a nickname, the nickname is used for the entry, followed by the full name in parentheses. But there is no "see" reference from the full name. Nevertheless, this is a tremendously worthwhile project. —Judith K. Rosenberg. [R: RQ, Fall 75, p. 81; WLB, Sept 75, p. 76; ARBA 76, item 1200]

BIOGRAPHY

606. Commire, Anne. **Something About the Author: Facts and Pictures About Contemporary Authors and Illustrators of Books for Young People.** Vol. 1. Detroit, Gale, 1971. 233p. illus. index $15.00. LC 70-127412.

Volume one of this new biographical series includes lengthy, easy-to-read sketches covering over 200 authors and illustrators of juvenile books. Each sketch follows the general format of Gale's *Contemporary Authors* series, giving full name with pseudonyms in parentheses, personal data (dates, marriages, education), career, list of writings, work in progress, sidelights, and a photo of the author. An index of illustrators is at the front. The lists of writings appear to be nearly complete. The "sidelights" written by each author provide some interesting comments on the writer's background, his inspiration for certain books, and other activities of importance to the author. The book is copiously illustrated not only with photos of the writers but with well-chosen illustrations (some in color) from the published works of the authors and illustrators. The text is set in clear 10-point type in double columns. The quality of this new biographical series, both editorially and graphically, is superior to other directories in this field. Marquardt and Ward's *Authors of Books for Young People* and their *Illustrators of Books for Young People* contain many more entries, but there is no comparison to the fullness of information and quality of bookmaking offered by Gale's new series. Gale has promised that additional volumes in the series, which will substantially increase the number of entries, will appear at regular intervals. Young people who are curious about their favorite authors or who are required to produce some biographical data for a class assignment will find much useful information in this new dictionary. The illustrations will make the search for information easier and more appealing to children. [R: WLB, Sept 71, p. 86; AL, Dec 71, p. 1225; ARBA 72, item 156; ARBA 73, item 188]

607. Doyle, Brian, comp. **The Who's Who of Children's Literature.** New York, Schocken Books, 1970 (c.1968). 380p. $10.00; $3.95pa. LC 68-28904. ISBN 0-8052-3290-7; 0-8052-0307-9pa.

An unchanged reprint of the 1968 edition. The guide is in two parts: authors and illustrators. The first part is an alphabetical list of under 200 British and American authors "who constitute the heritage of juvenile literature." Some European authors whose works are well known in translation are included. In addition to the early writers, some important contemporary names are provided. The entries give place and date of birth, education, career, and summary of the most important juvenile works. Similar information is given for about 50 names in the second section on illustrators. Reproductions of 104 illustrations and some stills from film versions of children's books provide interesting comparisons of illustrations by different artists for the same books. The biographical guide is a welcome addition to children's literature reference tools. It is, however, surprising that some important omissions occur in the classified, selective bibliography. Arbuthnot's *Children and Books* is listed in the old 1947 edition; no mention is made of Haviland's *Children's Literature: A Guide to Reference Sources* (Library of Congress, 1966). —Christine L. Wynar. [R: LJ, 15 April 70; ALA 69; ARBA 71, item 145]

608. **Third Book of Junior Authors.** Ed. by Doris de Montreville and Donna Hill. New York, H. W. Wilson, 1972. 320p. illus. index. $12.00. LC 75-149381. ISBN 0-8242-0408-5.

This latest compilation in the Junior Authors Series continues the work of Stanley J. Kunitz and Howard Haycraft in *The Junior Book of Authors*, 2nd ed. (rev. 1951), and that of Muriel Fuller, in *More Junior Authors* (1963). After a two-year study preliminary to listing some 1,200 candidates, 255 sketches of authors and illustrators of books for children and young people were selected by the editors, in consultation with advisory committee members.

The format is appealingly readable, with names and cross references in an alphabetical sequence. Usually covering one page, the autobiographical or biographical excerpt is preceded by birthdate, a photograph, the authorized signature. The statements, representing a variety of styles, reflect the background for the artist's or writer's creativity, often recapturing much of the remembered child. Erik Christian Haugaard's comment is perhaps representative: "I write my books because birds must sing, as dogs are meant to bark. I write for children who were born east of the sun and west of the moon. . . ."

Taken together these statements represent a kind of collective insight and appreciation into the process of creation and the sources of inspiration; they also reflect many different values behind modern writing for children. Editorial additions provide listings of awards as well as selected works written and/or illustrated. Some older authors included in this edition are Frank Baum, Lucy Boston, "Crockett Johnson," Sterling North; among contemporary writers are Betsey Byars, Tom Feelings, Nat Hentoff, Ib Spang Olsen, Inger and Lasse Sandberg, Charles

Schulz, and Brinton Turkle. The index lists all the authors and illustrators included in each of the series volumes.

The title continues to convey an impression not entirely favorable to the total life work of the contributors: not "junior." However, this reference tool will continue to be useful. —Clara O. Jackson. [R: SLJ, Sept 72, p. 49; ARBA 73, item 190]

AMERICAN LITERATURE

GENERAL WORKS

609. Bradbury, Malcolm, Eric Mottram, and Jean Franco, eds. **The Penguin Companion to American Literature.** New York, McGraw-Hill, 1971. 384p. $9.95. LC 70-158062. ISBN 0-07-049277-8.

Another volume in this well-designed and well-executed Penguin Companion series. The product of some 20 scholars, this work presents in one alphabet biographical sketches of most important writers in the United States and Latin America, with special emphasis on the younger generation. In addition, short but well-documented essays trace the development of both literatures from the earliest period to the present. A good example of a well-balanced and at the same time concise treatment is the article on "Little Magazines" or the one on "The New Humanism," the name given to the literary and philosophical writings of a group of conservative critics, notably Irving Babbitt, Norman Foerster, Paul Elmer More, and others in the late 1920s. There is also a brief, but adequate, article on Negro literature, although its bibliography is perhaps *too* brief. All in all, this excellent volume will be of interest to all students of literature who need an inexpensive and professionally prepared one-volume handbook. [R: ARBA 73, item 1269]

610. Burke, W. J., and Will D. Howe. **American Authors and Books, 1640 to the Present Day.** 3rd rev. ed. Rev. by Irving Weiss and Anne Weiss. New York, Crown, 1973. 719p. $12.50. LC 62-11815. ISBN 0-517-501392.

American Authors and Books, first published in 1943, has become a standard reference source for those interested in American *belles lettres*. This new edition has been thoroughly updated and revised, a commendable job. Entries are very brief and not really biographical in the usual sense. Entries for persons provide birth (and, where applicable, death) dates, birthplace, occupation (e.g., anthropologist, author), and titles and years of publications. In addition to entries for authors, this guide provides information on illustrators, periodicals, publishing companies, editors, etc. Title entries sometimes give a synopsis of the work but often provide only authors' names; *see* references are provided from pseudonyms to real names.

It should be noted that it encompasses more than literary figures or literature per se—e.g., there are entries for Craig Claiborne, H. W. Wilson, William Langer, John Holt, and Louis Shores. There are omissions and errors (e.g., only 10 novels are listed under the entry for the Lanny Budd series, but the entry for Upton Sinclair lists the eleventh novel), but these are exceptions to the overall high quality of this work. In all, this compilation is the most thorough work of its kind. —Sally Wynkoop. [R: WLB, Mar 73, p. 611; RSR, July/Sept 73, p. 21; ARBA 74, item 1308]

611. Curley, Dorothy Nyren, Maurice Kramer, and Elaine Fialka Kramer, eds.
Modern American Literature. 4th rev. and enl. ed. New York, Ungar, 1969. 3v.
index. (Library of Literary Criticism). $60.00. LC 76-76599. ISBN 0-8044-3046-2.
　　This has been much improved since it was first published in 1960, meagerly
following in the opulent tradition of C. W. Moulton's *A Library of Literary Criticism*.
The present edition covers some 300 authors from the early 1900s to the present,
alphabetically arranged. For each entry there is a bibliography and selection of
British and American criticism. The new edition includes about 100 more new
writers than the third edition (1964) and more recent excerpts have been added
to the entries for some two-thirds of the authors. In addition, comprehensive bibliographies of the works of all authors are at the end of each volume. This work
deserves a place as a standard reference source.　[R: LJ, Sept 69; Choice, Sept
69; ARBA 70, v.2, p. 72]

612. Leary, Lewis. **Articles on American Literature, 1950-1967**. Durham, N.C.,
Duke University Press, 1970. 751p. $20.00. LC 70-132027. ISBN 0-8223-1239-X.
　　Leary's new index of periodical articles on U.S. writers and writing supplements his earlier work, *Articles on American Literature, 1900-1950*. The new index
follows the same format as its predecessor. Entries are arranged alphabetically by
authors' names, with miscellaneous articles grouped under 25 broad categories such
as Humor, Indian, Negro, and Theater. Nearly 1,000 authors are represented, some
by one article, others by many pages of references. Although literary figures predominate, such writers as Bernard Berenson, William James, Thomas Jefferson, and
Frederick Jackson Turner are included. On the other hand, few science fiction
writers are represented. Some authors who appeared in the preceding work have
been dropped from the present one, indicating that they attracted little scholarly
interest during the period. Others, such as Fitzgerald, Hemingway, and K. A. Porter,
show substantial gain in literary popularity. Altogether, the new index cites approximately 20,000 articles from more than 500 American and foreign periodicals, as
compared with about 16,500 in the preceding volume—evidence of a tremendous
increase in scholarly publication during the past two decades.
　　Other differences in the two volumes are more technical. The form used
in citations has changed. Entries used to follow standard MLA order; now they
resemble those in the Wilson indexes. Authors' life dates have been omitted.
Where applicable, pseudonyms follow real names; cross references to these would
have been helpful. Despite minor faults or omissions, Leary's work renders an
invaluable service to American literary scholarship and will save researchers and
librarians much drudgery.　—Mary Jo Walker.　[R: WLB, Oct 71; LJ, 15 Mar
71, p. 945; ALA 71; ARBA 72, item 1342]

613. Rees, Robert A., and Earl N. Harbert, eds. **Fifteen American Writers Before
1900**. Madison, University of Wisconsin Press, 1971. 442p. index. $12.50. LC 77-
157395. ISBN 0-299-05910-3.
　　Seventeen bibliographic essays actually comprise this fine collection. In
addition to those on the 15 American authors, there are two essays designed to
encompass authors and literary movements of the South, old and new. Except
for these two essays, each chapter follows a format similar to that of *Eight American Authors* and *Fifteen Modern American Authors*: bibliography, editions,

manuscripts and letters, biography, and criticism. The authors so treated are Adams, Bryant, Cooper, Crane, Dickinson, Edwards, Franklin, Holmes, Howells, Irving, Longfellow, Lowell, Norris, Taylor, and Whittier. The choice both of authors and of their critics is open to criticism, as the editors mention in the preface, but the quality of the writing in this volume attests both to the contributions of these authors to our literature and to the perspicacity and sense of order of their critics. Indeed, one learns more from these essays than simply what a given author has written and what has been written about him. One also learns of the problems of selecting reliable bibliographies and editions of the authors' works, of the "scholar-adventurers" sifting through manuscripts and other personal papers, of the effect of the vicissitudes of fortune on an author's reputation. In short, to read such essays as these is to see a select group of American writers in their fullness, tempered by expert judgments which should, as the blurb claims, "promote further excellence in critical studies." *Fifteen American Authors before 1900* is a tool for reading or thoughtful consultation; its format and name-only index demand such an approach. —Edwin S. Gleaves. [R: Choice, June 72, p. 493; LJ, 15 Feb 72, p. 670; ALA 72; ARBA 73, item 1265]

614. Spiller, Robert E., and others, eds. **Literary History of the United States.** 4th ed., rev. New York, Macmillan, 1974. 2v. bibliog. index. $19.95. LC 73-14014.

It is no easy task to ascertain the true history of *Literary History of the United States*; the best single chronicle of its various editions appears in the preface to the second bibliographical supplement (page 1037 of the bibliography volume of the present edition). The fact that this preface and much of what follows appear intact is suggestive of one important overriding fact about LHUS, fourth edition; it is mainly a reprint. The only thing new in the bibliography volume, for example, is the index, and it is new only in the sense that the contents of the original bibliography volume (1948), Supplement I (1959), and Supplement II (1972) all appear in one index.

The history volume does include some new material—but not much. It reprints the third edition (which had reprinted most of previous editions) up through page 1391. Actual revision begins in the second part of "End of an Era," and begins to cut new ground with the section "Mid-Century and After," which includes the chapters "The New Consciousness," "Poetry," "Drama," and "Fiction"—about 60 pages in all. The reader's bibliography which follows has been revised, and the index incorporates the new and revised materials, excepting the bibliography.

LHUS still stands as the definitive literary history of this century, and its bibliography is still useful—though challenged by the rush of new bibliographical reviews and research and criticism. But it is well to remember that most new editions of LHUS have come more as updates than as actual revisions. —Edwin S. Gleaves. [R: ARBA 75, item 1339]

BIBLIOGRAPHIES

615. Blanck, Jacob, comp. **Bibliography of American Literature**. Comp. for the Bibliographical Society of America. New Haven, Conn., Yale University Press, 1954– . $27.50/v. (v.1-4); $30.00/v. (v.5-6). LC 54-5283. ISBN 0-300-00310-2(v.1); 0-300-00311-0(v.2); 0-300-00312-9(v.3); 0-300-00313-7(v.4); 0-300-01099-0(v.5); 0-300-01618-2(v.6).

Begun in 1954, this monumental work will be the standard bibliography on the subject when it is complete. The first five volumes were published over the years 1954 to 1969. The complete set of eight or nine volumes is expected to cover about 300 authors who died before 1930 and to contain approximately 35,000 numbered entries alphabetically arranged by author. For each author, all first editions, fully collated, are presented in chronological order; subsequent editions incorporating textual changes are briefly described; and a selected list of bibliographical, critical, and biographical works is included. The sixth volume of *Bibliography of American Literature* covers Augustus Baldwin Longstreet to Thomas William Parsons and includes 35 authors.

Blanck, a former bibliographer in Americana at the Library of Congress and author of many bibliographies, is preparing this title under the direction of the Bibliographical Society of America. [R: Choice, July-Aug 74, p. 733; ARBA 70; ARBA 75, item 1335]

616. Gohdes, Clarence. **Bibliographical Guide to the Study of the Literature of the U.S.A.** 3rd ed., rev. and enl. Durham, N.C., Duke University Press, 1970. 134p. index. $5.75. LC 79-110576. ISBN 0-8223-0234-9.

The third edition of this well-known guide lists books that will help the professional student of the literature of the United States in the acquisition of information and techniques of research. It is also designed for college teachers of American literature and for reference librarians, as well as for graduate students who are preparing theses. As in previous editions, the material is in classified arrangement. The 35 chapters cover all important aspects of American literature, with numerous cross references to related subjects. All entries provide complete bibliographical descriptions, but not pagination, and many reference books include brief annotations with occasional critical comments.

Although this guide is not as comprehensive as Kennedy and Sands' *A Concise Bibliography for Students of English* (5th ed., Stanford University Press, 1972), the selection of material and coverage is somewhat better than in Altick and Wright's *Selective Bibliography for the Study of English and American Literature* (5th ed., Macmillan, 1975).

In conclusion, one may assume that Gohdes's guide may have somewhat broader appeal to graduate students and faculty, primarily because it also includes well-selected titles for the study of American social and intellectual history, journalism, philosophy, architecture, painting, and music. —Bohdan S. Wynar. [R: ARBA 71, item 1442]

617. Jones, Howard Mumford, and Richard M. Ludwig. **Guide to American Literature and Its Backgrounds since 1890**. 4th ed., rev. and enl. Cambridge, Mass.,
Harvard University Press, 1972. 264p. index. $10.00; $2.75pa. LC 72-85143. ISBN
0-674-36753-7; 0-674-36754-5pa.

The third edition of this well-known work was published in 1964. The general
structure of this new edition remains unchanged. The book is arranged in two main
parts: Backgrounds (whose seven chapters include general guides, general reference
works, general histories, special aspects, literary history, etc.) and Reading Lists.
This second section is subdivided first by period (1890-1919; 1920-1972), and then
by subject. Each new subdivision is introduced by a brief sketch of pertinent characteristics, followed by a list of suggested readings.

The new edition has been only moderately updated. Nevertheless, this is one
of the more popular guides on the subject, and it will serve students well along with
other similar works—e.g., the bibliographic guide by Altick and Wright, *Selective
Bibliography for the Study of English and American Literature* (Macmillan, 1975)
or the more comprehensive work by Arthur G. Kennedy and Donald B. Sands,
A Concise Bibliography for Students of English (5th ed., Stanford University Press,
1972). —Bohdan S. Wynar. [R: ARBA 73, item 1266]

618. Rubin, Louis D., Jr., ed. **A Bibliographical Guide to the Study of Southern
Literature**. Baton Rouge, Louisiana State University Press, 1969. 368p. (Southern
Library Studies Series). $12.50; $3.25pa. LC 69-17627. ISBN 0-8071-0302-0; 0-
8071-0139-7pa.

This work is intended as a comprehensive guide to the study of Southern
writers from the Colonial period to the present. The checklists, contributed by 100
specialists, were edited by Mr. Rubin, a professor of English at the University of
South Carolina.

The guide is organized in two parts. Part I, general topics, includes 23 special
bibliographies with introductory comments (e.g., general works on Southern literature, humorists of the old Southwest and twentieth century drama). Part II, individual writers, provides a brief introductory note followed by a checklist of critical
books and articles for each of 135 writers. An appendix contains materials on 68
additional writers of the Colonial South, by J. A. Leo Lemay. This comprehensive
work supplements and extends the bibliographies in Jay B. Hubbell's *The South
in American Literature, 1607-1900*.   [R: LJ, 15 Nov 69; WLB, 7 Dec 69; ALA
69; ARBA 70, v. 2, p. 74]

FICTION

619. Dickinson, A. T., Jr. **American Historical Fiction**. 3rd ed. Metuchen, N.J.,
Scarecrow, 1971. 380p. $11.00. LC 78-146503. ISBN 0-8108-0370-4.

Originally published in 1956 and revised and enlarged in 1963, this title has
again been enlarged and improved. The number of titles listed has risen from 1,224
to 2,440; the subject index, now separate from the author-title index, is more
detailed; and the publication dates of titles included now extend from 1917 (as
previously) to 1969. Noteworthy or significant novels pre-dating 1917 are select-
ively included (works by Cooper, Hawthorne, the early Dreiser, etc.).

The list, covering Colonial times to the late 1960s, is arranged by historical period, and brief descriptive annotations point out the historical bearing.

By using a broad definition of "historical novel"—a novel that centers upon an identifiable time, place, person, event, or other aspect of the cultural landscape—the compiler includes a number of titles set in times contemporary with the author (*The Great Gatsby*, *Of Mice and Men*, *The Naked and the Dead*). Despite this latitude, the field marked out by Coan and Lillard's *America in Fiction*—fiction of merit that reflects some aspect of American life—is not seriously infringed upon. The two titles complement each other; both are necessary for the study of American history and life. —David Rosenbaum. [R: WLB, Oct 71; ARBA 72, item 1354]

620. Eichelberger, Clayton L., comp. **A Guide to Critical Reviews of United States Fiction, 1870-1910.** Metuchen, N.J., Scarecrow, 1971. 415p. index. $11.00. LC 77-149998. ISBN 0-8108-0380-1.

621. Eichelberger, Clayton L., comp. **A Guide to Critical Reviews of United States Fiction, 1870-1910, Volume II.** Metuchen, N.J., Scarecrow, 1974. 351p. index. $10.00. LC 77-149998. ISBN 0-8108-0701-7.

For the first work, 30 English, Canadian, and American periodicals were searched for evaluative reviews of American fiction for the period covered. Because of the regional character of some of the periodicals, many obscure works are listed, some of which do not appear in Wright's *American Fiction 1851-1875* and *1876-1900* or in Blanck's *Bibliography of American Fiction*. Arrangement is alphabetical by author with an index of titles and an appendix of anonymous and pseudonymous works.

Volume II, published under the same title as the original work, is supplementary to it. Authors are listed alphabetically with cross references for pseudonymous and anonymous works. Under the author's name, individual titles are listed, followed by bibliographical references to journals reviewing the book. Approximately 9,000 references to critical notices are included, which expands the listing for the two volumes to over 20,000 items. This is an admirable work in concept, organization, and inclusiveness. —James P. McCabe and Paul Z. DuBois. [R: LJ, 1 Jan 72, p. 59; WLB, Oct 74, p. 183; LJ, Aug 74, p. 1926; ARBA 72, item 1355; ARBA 75, item 1341]

POETRY

622. Malkoff, Karl. **Crowell's Handbook of Contemporary American Poetry: A Critical Handbook of American Poetry since 1940.** New York, Crowell, 1974. 338p. index. $10.00. LC 73-14787. ISBN 0-690-22625-X.

Mr. Malkoff opens with a 43-page "Short History of Contemporary American Poetry." His divisions within this essay help define the scope of the handbook: Contexts; From Imagism to Projectivism; Three Major Poems; Beat Poetry; The New York Poets; The Confessional Poets; The New Black Poetry; Deep Imagism; The Formal Poets. The following major portion of the book lists alphabetically some 70 American poets (e.g., Ashbery, Blackburn, Ferlinghetti, Lowell, Plath, Wakoski, and Wilbur) along with schools and movements of poetry. Each poet is given a birth date and place of birth and is discussed in varying lengths depending on whether his or her poetry lends itself well to illustrating new techniques, theories, and themes that are unique to new American poetry. At the end of each author entry is a selected bibliography and at times a selection of articles about the poet. Within these entries on poets or schools or movements of poetry are cross references sending the reader back to the introduction or to another poet.

The many people admitting absolute ignorance or at least confusion when confronted with contemporary poetry can now turn to this handbook. The introduction itself is worthy of private publication as a concise overview of American poetry since 1940 that "attempts to reinterpret the relation of man's inner world to the perceptual world . . ." (p.3). Given the limits Mr. Malkoff has set (his work is limited to American poets "who have not commercially published books of poetry before 1940," p. viii) and his purpose, which is "to enable readers to make judgments rather than to make judgments for them" (p. ix), he has clearly accomplished what he set out to do. —Jon M. Warner. [R: ALA 74; ARBA 75, item 1342]

BRITISH LITERATURE

BIBLIOGRAPHIES

623. DeLaura, David J., ed. **Victorian Prose: A Guide to Research.** New York, Modern Language Association of America, 1973. 560p. index. $15.00; $6.50pa. LC 73-80586. ISBN 0-87352-250-8; 0-87352-251-6pa.

This is the third research guide in Victoriana sponsored (and in this case published as well) by the Modern Language Association. This volume, on non-fictional prose, is edited by David J. DeLaura, winner of the MLA award for his article on Arnold and Carlyle, and a specialist in the field of Victorian studies. The scope is wide-ranging and thorough: minor figures are covered more fully than in the preceding volumes, yet attention to major figures remains sound. A section each is devoted to Macaulay; the Carlyles, Thomas and Jane; Newman; Mill; Ruskin; Arnold; Pater. Minor literary critics of the period are covered separately. An extensive section on religious prose covers the Oxford Movement and Victorian churchmen; non-believers are discussed in the final chapter. All writers and movements are examined from the standpoint of biographical material, bibliography, criticism, ideas, and influence. The evaluations are conscientiously balanced and objective.

As in all monumental studies of this kind, there are some omissions. The most serious case is that of Thomas DeQuincey, whose major contribution is in his prose; he therefore belongs within the province of this volume, although he may as easily be linked with the Romantics in spirit as with the Victorians in chronology. Less serious, because the authors' main contributions lie in other fields, is the omission of Lewis Carroll's mathematical writings; George Bernard Shaw's art, drama, and music criticism; A. E. Housman's classical papers. In no case, however, can one complain of total neglect; hardly a writer of the period escapes some mention, insofar as he relates to discussions of the major figures.

The 12 scholars who have combined their learning in this distinguished contribution to scholarship continue the same tradition of excellence as the preceding guides to research. The index, meticulously accurate and thorough, covers persons but not titles; it enhances the book's value. —Dorothy E. Litt. [R: LJ, 1 Mar 74, p. 643; ARBA 75, item 1372]

624. Dick, Aliki Lafkidou. **A Student's Guide to British Literature: A Selective Bibliography of 4,128 Titles and Reference Sources from the Anglo-Saxon Period to the Present.** Littleton, Colo., Libraries Unlimited, 1972. 285p. index. $11.50. LC 77-189255. ISBN 0-87287-044-8.

The main purpose of Dr. Dick's bibliography is to provide students of English literature with a conveniently structured, selective guide not only to the most important authors and their writings, but to literary criticism, reference works, and complete editions. Basic reference books are listed first, followed by chapters covering Old English, Medieval, Renaissance, Restoration, Nineteenth Century, and Twentieth Century. These chapters first list bibliographies and criticism pertaining to a period as a whole. Following these general works, each genre is listed alphabetically and divided into: works pertaining to the genre as a whole, and individual authors or works of unknown authorship. Entries for individual authors are divided into four parts—chronological list of important works; reference books; complete or important editions; and literary criticism. An author and subject index concludes the work. [R: LJ, July 72, p. 2375; ALA 72; ARBA 73, item 1296]

625. **English Literature, 1660-1800: A Bibliography of Modern Studies.** Comp. for Philological Quarterly. Princeton, N.J., Princeton University Press, 1950– ; repr. New York, Gordian, 1974– . $16.50/v.(v.1, 5, 6); $22.50(v.2); $17.50(v.3). LC A-51-6808. ISBN 0-691-06033-9(v.1); 0-87752-163-8(v.2); 0-87752-164-6 (v.3); v.4, o.p.; 0-691-06184-X(v.5); 0-691-06185-8(v.6).

A photoprint compilation of the annual bibliographies that appear in *Philological Quarterly.* The "more significant books, articles, and reviews" on Restoration and eighteenth century English literature are listed and supported by a thorough index to authors, editors, and reviewers. Articles and books are often summarized and criticized.

The six volumes that have been published to date include: Volume 1, 1926-1938; Volume 2, 1939-1950; Volume 3, 1951-1956; Volume 4, 1957-1960; Volume 5, 1961-1965; Volume 6, 1966-1970. Volume 4 is apparently out of print; other volumes are being reprinted by Gordian. A continuing set that is of particular value to active research programs but that is also appropriate for the undergraduate and the layman. [R: ARBA 73, item 1295; ARBA 75, item 1374]

626. Howard-Hill, T. H. **Bibliography of British Literary Bibliographies.** Oxford, Clarendon Press, 1969; distr. New York, Oxford University Press, 1969. 570p. index. (Index to British Literary Bibliography, No. 1). $27.25. LC 70-390421. ISBN 0-19-818134-5.

This first volume of the projected three-volume set records enumerative and descriptive bibliographies, published in English since 1890, that are potentially useful to the student of literary works published in Britain from 1475 to date. It includes some 5,000 listings of bibliographies published separately in serial form, or as parts of other works. It is divided into seven main sections: General and

Bibliographies of and Guides to British Literature; General and Period Bibliographies; Regional Bibliographies; Presses and Printing; Forms and Genres; Subjects (from Accounting to Witchcraft); and Authors (pp. 239-508). Each section or subsection is arranged chronologically by date of publication. Entries provide adequate bibliographic description and include annotations and, occasionally, references to published reviews. A detailed index of names and subjects and many cross references are provided.

Volume 2 will cover Shakespeare; the final volume will cover bibliography and textual criticism. This is the most thorough and up-to-date bibliography now available. [R: LJ, 1 Sept 69; ARBA 70, v.2, p. 82]

627. Mellown, Elgin W. **A Descriptive Catalogue of 20th Century British Writers.** Troy, N.Y., Whitston, 1972. 446p. index. $17.50. LC 79-183301. ISBN 0-87875-022-3.

The *Descriptive Catalogue*, arranged alphabetically, lists "all the British writers who, born after 1840, published the larger part of their work in England or Ireland after 1890 or thereabouts and who have been the subject of bibliographical study." Mellown has also included birth and death years as well as pseudonyms. For those writers who have been the subjects of intensive bibliographical study, the author entry consists of three main sections: primary (bibliographies of writings by the author); secondary (critical or biographical studies about the author); and general (short bio- and/or bibliographical pieces appearing in 15 "general bibliographies," such as the CBEL, the NCBEL, and *Who's Who*). For writers of lesser stature, the entries usually list only those general bibliographies in which they are included. Although the emphasis is clearly on "imaginative writers and writers in the humanities," the better-known writers in the sciences and the social sciences are dealt with. Mellown nowhere mentions a general cut-off date for his entries, but it appears to be 1970, with some 1971 titles included. —Charles R. Andrews. [R: WLB, Oct 72, p. 199; LJ, 1 Oct 72, p. 3137; ALA 72; ARBA 73, item 1298]

628. **The New Cambridge Bibliography of English Literature.** Ed. by George Watson. Cambridge, Cambridge University Press, 1969– . $69.50(v.1); $55.00/v. (v.2-4). ISBN 0-521-20004-0(v.1); 0-521-07934-0(v.2); 0-521-08535-7(v.4).

A revision and substantial expansion of *The Cambridge Bibliography of English Literature*, edited by F. W. Bateson (Cambridge, Cambridge University Press, 1940. 4v. and suppl.). This new five-volume set is comprised of: Volume 1, 600-1660; Volume 2, 1660-1800; Volume 3, 1800-1900; Volume 4, 1900-1950; Volume 5, Index (not yet published). This monumental work aims to list and classify the whole of English studies, as represented by the literature of the British Isles, analyzing both primary and secondary sources. The *New Cambridge Bibliography of English Literature* is confined to authors native to, or mainly resident in, the British Isles, but no nationality or language restrictions are imposed on secondary materials (mainly biography and criticism).

Each of the first four volumes represents a literary period, which is divided by form (drama, poetry, etc.); these form divisions are in turn subdivided by individual authors and special topics. The author subdivisions list bibliographies and collections, primary material, and secondary material. Excluded are unpublished doctoral dissertations, "ephemeral journalism, encyclopaedia articles, reviews of secondary works, brief notes of less than crucial interest to scholarship, and sections in general works such as literary histories." The most important contribution to English studies, second only to the *Oxford English Dictionary*. [R: WLB, Dec 74, p. 316; Choice, Jan 75, p. 1609; LJ, 1 Jan 75, p. 45; BL, 15 Jan 75, p. 516; ARBA 72, item 1381; ARBA 75, item 1375; ARBA 76, item 1260]

DRAMA

629. Logan, Terence P., and Denzell S. Smith. **The Predecessors of Shakespeare: A Survey and Bibliography of Recent Studies in English Renaissance Drama.** Lincoln, University of Nebraska Press, 1973. 348p. index. $15.00. LC 72-75344. ISBN 0-8032-0775-1.

The eight essays in this volume do an invaluable service for the student of English Renaissance drama. They provide a succinct yet full survey of the significant criticism and scholarship printed between 1923 and 1965 on the life and works of seven major writers (Christopher Marlowe, Robert Greene, Thomas Kyd, Thomas Nashe, John Lyly, George Peele, Thomas Lodge) and 18 anonymous plays ranging from *The Rare Triumphs of Love and Fortune* to *The Tragical History of Guy Earl of Warwick*. In addition, the editors provide a brief summary of each scholarly article concerning eight minor figures of the period: Breton, Farrant, Forsett, Hughes, Kempe, Legge, Porter, and Wilson.

Each of the essays on the major writers is divided into four parts: 1) a critical survey of general biographical and critical studies of the author and his works; 2) a critical survey of the criticism and scholarship on the individual plays and poems, amounting to a fully annotated bibliography of the more important works; 3) a canon, including apocrypha, of the dramatist's works, with discussions of dates and a critique of the texts and editions; 4) a complete bibliography supplementing the works already mentioned in the previous sections. Particularly valuable and readable are Robert Kimbrough's essay on Marlowe and Joseph Houppert's on Lyly. However, the most impressive work in the volume is the essay by Anne Lancashire and Jill Levenson on the anonymous plays. Their fine summary and synthesis of a diverse and miscellaneous body of material is a feat for students to admire for years to come. The book as a whole represents careful work and is a necessary tool for the student of Renaissance drama. —Robert L. Welker. [R: LJ, Aug 73, p. 2299; Choice, Oct 73, p. 1168; ARBA 74, item 1358]

FICTION

630. Dyson, A. E., ed. **The English Novel.** New York, Oxford University Press, 1974. 372p. (Select Bibliographical Guides). $11.25; $3.95pa. ISBN 0-19-871033-X; 0-19-871027-5pa.

With the help of an admirable list of British and American contributors, A. E. Dyson here covers all major British novelists from John Bunyan to James Joyce; the only serious complaint is the exclusion of Virginia Woolf. The guide is intended for the serious scholar of English literature, specifically the novel.

Each critic follows the same format in discussing his author: a citing of authoritative texts; a sampling of representative criticism found in published essays, journals, and books; the kinds of biographies to be found and how (or whether) they illumine the artist's fiction; the presence, if any, of the author's own record in letters and diaries and the quality of editions available; the bibliographies that will offer access to other, possibly unmentioned, critics; and finally, background readings that make historical and philosophical suggestions to augment literary understanding. Each essay concludes with a bibliography listing all sources mentioned in the essay.

As a guide, this reference work is helpful in several ways. First, the chapters are similar in format, enabling the user to identify easily the kind of information he seeks. Second, because the contributors are critics themselves, they attempt to discuss schools of critical thought as well as the specific persons who initiated the schools. Third, an attempt is made to define the artists and their milieu, as well as the critical reaction to their work. And fourth, as an unexpected asset, this guide gives suggestions for needed research and does not hesitate to cite gaps in knowledge (e.g., "no modern collection of Bunyan," "no adequate study of Defoe's religious thought," "need for a fully annotated, definitive edition of *Gulliver's Travels*," "no entirely satisfactory edition of *Tom Jones*," "no large-scale bibliography of Jane Austen," etc.).

The English Novel makes no pretense at being exhaustive. As the editor states, "the contributors to this book are concerned with mapping territory, pointing to landmarks, suggesting routes." For the serious student of the English novel, this is a practical, functional, and worthwhile guide. —Sharon S. Peterson. [R: WLB, Oct 74, pp. 181-82; LJ, July 74, p. 1792; ARBA 75, item 1376]

631. Palmer, Helen H., and Anne Jane Dyson, comps. **English Novel Explication: Criticisms to 1972.** Hamden, Conn., Shoe String Press, 1973. 329p. index. $12.50. LC 73-410. ISBN 0-208-01322-9.

This work is a supplement to Bell and Baird's *The English Novel* (Swallow, 1959), which covered the subject through 1957; hence, this volume covers criticisms essentially from 1958 to 1972. A few items that were overlooked by Bell and Baird and that were published earlier than 1957 are included here.

The arrangement is alphabetical by author, then by title; under title, criticisms are arranged alphabetically by author. There are three appendixes: a list of the books indexed, a list of the journals indexed, and an author/title index. Unfortunately, the fact that there is no table of contents makes it difficult to find the appendixes. Another minor difficulty stems from the omission of the quotation marks that should set off journal article titles.

Still, insofar as Bell and Baird's work is generally considered indispensable, so will this supplement be necessary. —Kenyon C. Rosenberg. [R: LJ, 1 Sept 73, p. 2424; WLB, Dec 73, p. 339; Choice, Dec 73, p. 1531; ALA 73; ARBA 74, item 1364]

POETRY

632. Reiman, Donald H., ed. **The Romantics Reviewed: Contemporary Reviews of British Romantic Writers; Part A, The Lake Poets.** New York, Garland, 1972. 2v. $98.34. LC 72-11860. ISBN 0-8240-0509-0.

633. Reiman, Donald H., ed. **The Romantics Reviewed: Contemporary Reviews of British Romantic Writers; Part B, Byron and Regency Society Poets.** New York, Garland, 1972. 5v. $98.33. LC 72-11860. ISBN 0-8240-0510-4.

634. Reiman, Donald H., ed. **The Romantics Reviewed: Contemporary Reviews of British Romantic Writers; Part C, Shelley, Keats, and London Radical Writers.** New York, Garland, 1972. 2v. index. $98.33. LC 72-11860. ISBN 0-8240-0511-2.

Although issued as three distinct sets, this is actually one nine-volume work; and although it is not labeled on the spine, the index to all volumes appears at the end of Part C, Volume Two. The primary purpose of the work is to include "all contemporary British periodical reviews of the first (or other significant) editions from 1793 [to] 1834" (p. xxxi) of works by Wordsworth, Coleridge, Byron, Shelley, and Keats. Some other contemporary writers such as Godwin, Southey, Hazlitt, and Mary Wollstonecraft Shelley are secondarily included. The editor admits, with the following qualification, that this work does not include *all* reviews: "That is, all are included that I was able to identify and for which we were able to locate an original text that could be reproduced in facsimile" (p. xxxi).

Each of the three parts is arranged alphabetically by the name of the periodical in which reviews appeared, with the reviews in chronological order. Obviously, the main drawback is that the reviews are not by poet and poem. To find all reviews of a particular work it is necessary to use the index, which does not contain entries for specific reviews except under name of the author.

There are definitely technical and editorial problems in this work, and librarians should be aware of that. However, it is the most comprehensive work of its kind. —Sally Wynkoop. [R: Choice, July/Aug 73, p. 744; ARBA 74, items 1365-1367]

OTHER NATIONAL LITERATURES

AFRICAN LITERATURE

635. Herdeck, Donald E. **African Authors: A Companion to Black African Writing, 1300-1973.** Rockville, Md., Black Orpheus Press, 1973. 430p. illus. $27.50. LC 73-172338. ISBN 0-87953-008-1.

This volume provides entries for 594 African authors. Each entry contains a discussion of the author's most important works, a list of biographical and critical sources, and usually a photograph or drawing of the author. Appendixes include a chronological arrangement of the authors, an arrangement by genre, another according to medium used, and listings of authors by African language(s) and by country of origin. Major publishers, journals, and bookshops devoted to African literature are also listed.

The editorial execution of *African Authors* is better than that of *Who's Who in African Literature*, but its coverage of contemporary literature is not as comprehensive as that found in *A Reader's Guide to African Literature*. [R: LJ, 15 Jan 73, p. 151-2; ALA 73; ARBA 74, item 1403]

636. Zell, Hans, and Helene Silver, eds. **A Reader's Guide to African Literature.** New York, Africana, 1972. 218p. index. $12.50; $4.95pa. LC 76-83165. ISBN 0-8419-0018-3; 0-8419-0019-1pa.

In the relatively new field of African studies, much-needed reference works like this volume are just beginning to appear. This work lists 820 works by black African authors south of the Sahara writing in English and French. Reference materials, anthologies, and critical works are included. Designed to supplement existing bibliographies on this subject, this work has two new features: annotations and extracts from book reviews. The editors, focusing on contemporary African literature, have excluded writings in Portuguese and Arabic as well as those of North African and white South African writers. The arrangement of the work tends to be somewhat confusing—e.g., the section "Bibliography" is subdivided into bibliographies, anthologies, and critical works, while the section "Writings in English" is subdivided by country. Nevertheless, the information is accurate and up to date, the annotations are clear, and the biographies are particularly valuable as supplementary material. A statement of the availability of a work is given in each entry. [R: AL, May 72, p. 559; ALA 72; ARBA 73, item 1346]

CANADIAN LITERATURE

637. Toye, William, ed. **Supplement to the Oxford Companion to Canadian History and Literature.** New York, Oxford University Press, 1973. 318p. $11.50. ISBN 0-19-540205-7.

Although some biographical articles on major authors who died before 1967 (e.g., Frederick Philip Grove, E. J. Pratt) have been reprinted from Norah Story's *The Oxford Companion to Canadian History and Literature* (Oxford University Press, 1967), most of the information deals with the years 1967 through 1972. It is, thus, a true supplement, and not a work that supersedes or that can stand alone on the reference shelves. Unlike the original, which was the work of one person, the supplement includes signed articles from 37 contributors, most of whom are on the faculties of major Canadian universities. One notable feature (missing in the original) is the attention given to children's books in both English and French. Literature in French generally receives proportionately greater emphasis. Both the original and the supplement contain articles of monographic length on topics like "Fiction in English," "Literary Magazines in French," "History Studies in English," "Political Writings in French," etc. Both have numerous cross references from the names of individuals to the appropriate sections of these monographic articles. Both the biographical and the topical articles are rich in bibliographical citations, often accompanied by critical comments. These two volumes are a goldmine of useful information for all reference librarians whose patrons are interested in Canadian history or literature. —A. Robert Rogers. [R: Choice, Apr 74, p. 240; LJ, 1 Apr 74, p. 1020; ARBA 75, item 1412]

FRENCH LITERATURE

638. Osburn, Charles B. **Guide to French Studies: Supplement with Cumulative Indexes.** Metuchen, N.J., Scarecrow, 1972. 377p. index. $11.00. LC 68-12638. ISBN 0-8108-0493-X.

Half the references listed in this supplement complete the basic volume (*Research and Reference Guide to French Studies*, Scarecrow, 1968; reviewed in *French Studies*, 25, 1971, No. 2). The remaining items have been published since 1968. All citations in this work are to studies of a reference nature—bibliographies, indexes, biographies, surveys—that will aid research in French language and literature and related topics. Users can not only explore sources for literature (including an up-to-date listing of items about the detective story), but can also find points of orientation in allied fields (cinema, television, radio).

The author and subject indexes in this supplement also index the basic volume, and the subject index includes numerous cross references (for example, "calligraphy," see also "paleography" and "autographs"). Students of French language and literature will find Osburn's guide to be their basic source for beginning research. —Marcia Jebb. [R: ARBA 73, item 1350]

GERMAN LITERATURE

639. Smith, Murray F., comp. **A Selective Bibliography of German Literature in English Translation, 1956-1960.** Metuchen, N.J., Scarecrow, 1972. 403p. $12.00. LC 76-157727. ISBN 0-8108-0411-5.

Planned as a second supplement of *A Critical Bibliography of German Literature in English Translation, 1481-1927* (2nd ed. 1938, repr. 1965) and its *Supplement Embracing the Years 1928-1955* (1965) by Bayard Quincy Morgan, this work is far more complete than its only rival, *German Literature in the United States, 1945-1960*, by W. Lamarr Kopp (Chapel Hill, University of North Carolina Press, 1967). Whereas Kopp lists only 900 works by 270 authors for the whole 15 years, Smith appears to have included between 3,000 and 4,000 works by some 1,500 to 2,000 authors for only five of those years. Smith uses the term "literature" in a very broad sense, as did Morgan. Smith makes no attempt to rate the quality of the translations, a practice Morgan abandoned after 1927, though it is still retained in the reprint of his basic work.

The arrangement is alphabetical by author and then by English title. Whenever available, the original German title is given in parentheses. Names of translators are also usually given. Place, publisher, date, paging, and size are included as well as the source or sources from which information has been taken (principally LC, BNB, and *Index Translationum*). The introduction gives a very detailed statement of scope, methodology, and problems. —A. Robert Rogers. [R: WLB, June 72, p. 930; ARBA 73, item 1351]

GREEK AND LATIN LITERATURES

640. Gwinup, Thomas, and Fidelia Dickinson. **Greek and Roman Authors: A Checklist of Criticism.** Metuchen, N.J., Scarecrow, 1973. 194p. $7.00. LC 72-10156. ISBN 0-8108-0560-X.

Students in search of the key to the world's classical heritage will find this comprehensive bibliography of recent criticism on Greek and Roman authors an invaluable aid. The authors have provided accurate listings of general criticism on some 70 ancient masters (Aeschylus to Xenophon) as well as particular criticisms of an author's individual works. Author entries range in length from two pages up to 15 pages (for Plato). The nearly 4,000 entries were acquired through the use of diverse bibliographies and through original research by the authors.

This work complements the *International Bibliography* of the Modern Language Association. The latter covers some ancient literature, such as Egyptian and Sanskrit, and includes medieval and Neo-Latin, but it excludes all of classical Greek and Latin literature as such. Only items written in English are included. This clear, concise, and comprehensive checklist is a fine companion to the handbooks and histories of the classical age. —Doris L. Gustafson. [R: WLB, June 73, p. 867; RSR, July/Sept 73, p. 24; Choice, Oct 73, p. 1164; LJ, 15 June 73, p. 1904; ALA 73; ARBA 74, item 1413]

641. **The Oxford Classical Dictionary.** 2nd ed. Edited by N.G.L. Hammond and H. H. Scullard. New York, Oxford University Press, 1970. 1176p. index. $30.00. ISBN 0-19-869117-3.

The first edition of this standard work was published in 1949. The introduction to the first edition stated that "it is designed to cover the same ground, though on a different scale, as the well-known dictionaries by Sir William Smith on Greek and Roman antiquities and on Greek and Roman biography, mythology, and geography." The eighth edition (1914) of Lübker's *Reallexikon* was taken as a general model, but with certain modifications in principle and with certain differences in emphasis.

The present work is intended to be less purely factual than Lübker. It devotes more space to biography and literature, less to geography and bibliographical information, aiming, in this latter respect, at no more than referring the reader to the best works, in English and foreign languages, on the various subjects. A special feature is the inclusion of longer articles designed to give a comprehensive survey of the main subjects and to place minor characters, places and events, the choice of which has been necessarily selective, against their appropriate literary or historical background.

The second edition follows the same format; there is a little more emphasis on the archaeological background, some longer articles have been abbreviated a little (to make room for new additions), and the later Roman empire receives more comprehensive treatment. As in the first edition, most articles are brief, contain bibliographical references (up to 1968), and provide well-balanced coverage of most aspects of Greek and Roman culture. There is no separate article on *Aeneid* and other important works of literature, but all writers and poets are represented.

Some readers may prefer *New Century Classical Handbook* (Appleton-Century-Crofts, 1962) and for a more detailed treatment, one still has to consult *Pauly's Real-Encyclopädie der classischen Altertumwissenschaft*. All in all, however, this is one of the best one-volume sources on the subject. —Bohdan S. Wynar. [R: ARBA 71, item 1427]

HUNGARIAN LITERATURE

642. Tezla, Albert. **Hungarian Authors: A Bibliographical Handbook**. Cambridge, Harvard University Press, 1970. 792p. index. $25.00. LC 74-88813. ISBN 0-674-42650-9.

This annotated bibliography of 4,646 items is a companion volume to Tezla's *Introductory Bibliography to the Study of Hungarian Literature* (Harvard, 1964). It lists, with full bibliographical data, first and subsequent editions of works by 162 major Hungarian-born authors. The selection spans the period from 1450 to date and basically reflects the consensus of Hungarian and foreign experts and literary critics. Of course, one always could argue for the inclusion or elimination of one or another author. Tezla's high reputation, earned by his earlier work, together with the acknowledged participation of such Hungarian scholars as T. Klaniczay, S. Kozocsa, S. Lukácsy and K. Bor, lend the work an unusual authority.

The tome opens with a long list of abbreviations, symbols, and Hungarian bibliographical terms and phrases. The introduction indicates that the systematic review for the book of primary and secondary sources was concluded with August 1, 1965. The main body of the volume is divided into two parts: authors from 1450 to 1945, and authors from 1945 to the present—a division apparently suggested by the sociopolitical and ideological changes that have taken place in Hungary since World War II. Sections for most authors include a concise biographical sketch, as well as entries describing first editions, subsequent editions, biographies, bibliographical sources, and criticism pertaining to the particular author. On-the-spot research and interlibrary loans are facilitated by the addition of the international library location symbols (Gardner system) for each entry. Five appendixes supply information concerning (A) recent published studies on Hungarian literature (1960-1965); (B) literary awards, societies and serial publications mentioned in the biographical sketches of authors; (C) scholarly and literary periodicals used as sources of information for the main entries; (D) identification of authors by major literary periods and trends; and (E) codes and full names, with addresses, of source libraries in the United States and Europe. A name index to authors, compilers, editors, etc., enhances the usefulness of this excellent research tool. —Ivan L. Kaldor. [R: ARBA 71, item 1499]

ORIENTAL AND EASTERN LITERATURES

643. **Dictionary of Oriental Literatures**. Ed. by Jaroslav Prusek. New York, Basic Books, 1974. 3v. $40.00/boxed set. LC 73-82742. ISBN 0-465-01649-9.

This three-volume set is somewhat more comprehensive than the *Guide to Eastern Literatures*. It contains about 1,600 brief articles on individual authors, important literary movements and trends, genres, etc. Each of the volumes covers one or two specific regions: East Asia (Vol. 1), South and South-East Asia (Vol. 2), and West Asia and North Africa (Vol. 3).

Intended for the non-specialist, the dictionary can also be recommended for undergraduate students interested in comparative literature. More in-depth treatment will be found in numerous specialized works devoted to one geographical area or national literature, but such works serve an entirely different purpose and audience. [R: LJ, 15 Oct 74, p. 2592; ARBA 75, item 1316]

644. Lang, David M. **A Guide to Eastern Literatures**. New York, Praeger, 1971. 500p. index. $15.00. LC 79-157114.

This guide provides a concise, up-to-date survey of Near, Middle and Far East literatures, with a separate chapter for each nationality including Arabic, Indian, Chinese, Japanese, and Korean. As an example, the chapter on Jewish literature has the following structure: historical and cultural background (subdivided by such topics as Jewish culture in Spain, the Middle Ages, Jewish literature in Italy, the Haskalah, the Zionist Movement, etc.), followed by brief biographical sketches of important individual writers. Each chapter has a selected bibliography that will help the reader locate additional sources of information. There are several contributors for specific areas, and the information presented is not readily available elsewhere in such a compact form. [R: ALA 72, ARBA 72, item 1437]

SLAVIC LITERATURES

645. **Modern Slavic Literatures: A Library of Literary Criticism; Volume I, Russian Literature.** Vasa D. Mihailovich, ed. New York, Ungar, 1972. 424p. index. $20.00. LC 75-163143. ISBN 0-8044-3176-0.

646. **Modern Slavic Literatures: A Library of Literary Criticism; Volume II, Bulgarian, Czechoslovak, Polish, Ukrainian, and Yugoslav Literatures.** Igor Hajek and others, eds. New York, Ungar, 1972. 736p. $27.50. LC 72-170319. ISBN 0-8044-3177-9; 0-8044-3175-2(set).

These two companion volumes on twentieth century Slavic literatures follow the format of other volumes in the Library of Literary Criticism series (American, British, German, and Romance literatures).

The preface to Volume I points out that "the critical selections represented here were chosen mainly with the idea of giving a balanced perspective of the authors' achievements and, where appropriate, of including extended remarks on individual works—such as Pasternak's *Doctor Zhivago* and Sholokhov's *The Quiet Don*—as well as overviews of the writers' careers." The 69 Russian writers represented in this volume range from the internationally known Chekhov and Pasternak to such writers as Pogodin, Platonov, and Balmont. The selections of critical comments were chosen from a variety of sources (e.g., book reviews, introductions, full-length critical studies, etc.), with an emphasis on material published in English. Nevertheless, foreign journals are represented.

Volume II surveys the works of nearly 200 writers. For many of these authors nothing has been available in the English language until publication of this volume.

Critical excerpts cover such writers as Čapek and Hašek of Czechoslovakia, Gombrowicz and Andrzejewski of Poland, Franko of the Ukraine, and Andrić and Krleža of Yugoslavia.

Like the other volumes in this series, *Modern Slavic Literatures* will be helpful for students of the literature or for study of comparative literatures. —Bohdan S. Wynar. [R: ARBA 73, item 1359]

SPANISH LITERATURES

647. Foster, David William, and Virginia Ramos Foster, comps. and eds. **Modern Latin American Literature**. New York, Frederick Ungar, 1975. 2v. index. (A Library of Literary Criticism). $38.00. LC 72-81713. ISBN 0-8044-3139-6.

Modern Latin American Literature proposes to present "twentieth-century Latin American writers through the eyes of leading critics in their own countries and abroad, with particular stress on their reception in the United States." This two-volume compilation of international critical commentary follows the style of other volumes in Ungar's "Library of Literary Criticism" series by including critical excerpts in English on 137 Latin American writers. The excerpts were extracted from monographs, encyclopedias, periodicals, and newspapers; about half are translations from Spanish and Portuguese sources and the remainder come mainly from English language publications.

The main body of the work is arranged alphabetically by the author being reviewed. The criticisms for each author are then arranged chronologically. Each volume includes an alphabetical list of all the writers reviewed as well as a list of the authors by country of origin. Volume II concludes with a cross-reference index to authors and an index to critics.

This outstanding compilation fills a tremendous void in Latin American literary criticism. In the past, critical sources for contemporary Latin American literary figures have been extremely elusive for a variety of reasons: the scarcity of Latin American periodicals in the United States, the diffuseness of critical reviews in the world press, and the lack of indexing. These volumes, by providing translations into English of many previously unavailable reviews and by offering the user a selected bibliography of sources, should help alleviate the situation. As a unique synthesis of literary criticism in the field, *Modern Latin American Literature* will be a valuable reference and research tool. —Laura Gutiérrez-Witt. [R: Choice, Oct 75, pp. 978-80; LJ, 1 Sept 75, pp. 1534-35; WLB, Nov 75, p. 268; ARBA 76, item 1301]

CHAPTER 28

SCIENCE AND TECHNOLOGY—GENERAL

GENERAL WORKS

648. Thornton, John L., and R. I. J. Tully. **Scientific Books, Libraries, and Collectors: A Study of Bibliography and the Book Trade in Relation to Science.** 3rd ed., rev. London, Library Association; distr. Detroit, Gale, 1971. 508p. illus. index. $21.00.

Thornton's guide to scientific literature (first published in 1954 and revised in 1962) has become the classic bibliographical history of science. Twelve revised and updated chapters survey the production, distribution and storage of scientific literature from the pre-Gutenburg era through the mid-twentieth century. Six of these chapters discuss scientific authors and their publications; the remainder of the volume provides introductory commentary on scientific societies, the periodical literature, scientific libraries—private and public—and scientific publishing and bookselling. In addition, Chapter 9 is a useful survey of guides to the literature, current and retrospective bibliographies, and other control tools. There is, naturally, a tendency to emphasize the bibliography of Continental Europe and Britain. However, the authors give reasonable coverage to significant U.S. bibliographies, books, libraries, and publishers.

Each chapter is supplemented by extensive footnotes, and the volume as a whole is capped by an 85-page bibliography—much expanded from the second edition. A detailed index completes the organization structure. Considering the myriad details and the titles and dates incorporated in text and footnotes, the overall design has typographical clarity and readability. The authors suggest that "the professional historian of science will find little new in these pages." However, no other source supplies such a convenient compendium of scientific bibliography and associated data. —Laurel Grotzinger. [R: LJ, July 72, pp. 2360-61; ARBA 73, item 1364]

BIBLIOGRAPHIES

649. Deason, Hilary J., comp. **The AAAS Science Book List: A Selected and Annotated List of Science and Mathematics Books for Secondary School Students, College Undergraduates, and Nonspecialists.** 3rd ed. Washington, American Association for the Advancement of Science, 1970. 439p. index. $10.00. LC 74-105531. ISBN 0-87168-201-X.

The first edition of this standard guide on the subject was published in 1959, and the second edition in 1964. The third edition, substantially enlarged, will probably be as useful as previous editions. All bibliographical descriptions are complete, including prices and LC numbers; annotations are descriptive and quite adequate. As in the previous editions, the material is arranged under broad subject categories; there is also a list of publishers represented in this volume. Listings are current as of 1969, and one occasionally finds 1970 imprints. The general editorial work is excellent. For all practical purposes, this is one of the best guides on this subject. The only criticism of this otherwise well-prepared guide is the omission of certain other bibliographical guides. For example, *Science Reference Sources*, 5th edition, by Jenkins, is not listed, nor is Malinowsky's *Science and Engineering Reference Sources*. Both publications had good reviews and certainly should have been included. [R: WLB, Oct 71, p. 193; ARBA 72, item 1456]

650. **ISIS Cumulative Bibliography: A Bibliography of the History of Science Formed from ISIS Critical Bibliographies 1-90, 1913-65.** Ed. by Magda Whitrow. London, Mansell, in conjunction with the History of Science Society, 1971. 2v. $88.00. ISBN 0-7201-0183-2.

These two massive volumes are merely the beginning of a major publishing project launched by the History of Science Society. The aim of the project is to offer a complete index to George Sarton's ISIS, the unique quarterly devoted to the history of science. Between 1913 and 1965, ISIS printed 90 brilliant critical bibliographies of scientists. The cumulation and grouping of the entries of these bibliographies according to an ingenious system of subdivisions have resulted in a list of more than 40,000 titles relating to over 10,000 personalities and institutions. Volume 1, Part I and Volume 2, Part I contain, in alphabetical sequence, entries describing publications (including reference works, monographs, pamphlets, and magazine articles) dealing with the life and work of an individual scientist (subject entries), and also new editions and re-issues of his works (author entries). Where the number of entries under one personality warrants, convenient subdivisions are applied (e.g., bibliographies, life and work, large scale works, forerunners, biography, portraits, texts, etc.). In Volume 2, Part II (Institutions) efforts have been made to use entry forms which comply with the *Anglo-American Cataloging Rules*. International organizations have been entered under the English form of the name, with references from other versions. Close adherence to LC rules of cataloging, filing, and transliteration makes the contents of these extremely well organized volumes even more accessible. In summary, the *ISIS Cumulative Bibliography* easily qualifies for the title of the most significant research tool in the area of the history of science; its importance can be paralleled only by that of the bibliographical treasurehouse George Sarton offers in his own works. –Ivan L. Kaldor. [R: ARBA 73, item 1365]

651. Kyed, James M., and James M. Matarazzo. **Scientific, Technical, and Engineering Societies Publications in Print 1974-1975.** New York, R. R. Bowker, 1974. 223p. index. $17.50. LC 74-5094. ISBN 0-8352-0727-7.

The purpose of this listing is "to provide bibliographic and sales information for material not normally covered in standard publication-finding tools" (p. vii). Two hundred fifty organizations were asked to submit publications lists; the 151 that responded are listed in alphabetical order. A comparison of the list of 151 societies with PTLA's list of publishers reveals very little duplication. It would have been helpful if the compiler had listed the other 100 societies that were originally contacted; in the preface, the compilers state that some of them reported that they do not publish anything at all, and a list of those would be helpful.

Under the name of each society, publications are listed in one of three categories—books, periodicals, and nonprint materials. Book titles are listed alphabetically under subject headings supplied by the society (an exception is monographic series, which are listed in numerical order). Where applicable, author, edition, publication date, order number, and price are listed for titles. Periodicals and nonprint materials are also listed alphabetically by title. Author and keyword indexes complete the volume.

This is a worthy venture that we hope will continue on some regular basis. The compilers state that the "growth in the number of works published by these societies has created a bibliographic void which this volume hopes to fill" (Preface); it does indeed fill the void. —Sally Wynkoop. [R: LJ, Aug 74, p. 1927; Choice, Dec 74, p. 1458; ARBA 75, item 1430]

652. Stillwell, Margaret Bingham. **The Awakening Interest in Science during the First Century of Printing, 1450-1550: An Annotated Checklist of First Editions Viewed from the Angle of Their Subject Content.** New York, Bibliographical Society of America, 1970. 399p. index. $25.00. LC 78-114982.

This checklist is arranged in two parts. Part one is an author list of 900 selected titles arranged under six subject categories: astronomy, mathematics, medicine, natural science, physics, and technology. Entries provide full bibliographic description, lists of references, and occasional citations to monographs. Part two contains an analytical list of editors, places of printing, and names of printers and translators. Stillwell needs no introduction. Her *Incunabula and Americana, 1450-1800: A Key to Bibliographical Study* is well-known; and this checklist retains the author's high professional standards. —Bohdan S. Wynar. [R: LJ, 1 Dec 70, p. 4158-9; ARBA 71, item 1515]

ENCYCLOPEDIAS

653. **McGraw-Hill Encyclopedia of Science and Technology.** 3rd ed. New York, McGraw-Hill, 1971. 15v. illus.(part col.). index. $35.00/v.; $410.00/set. LC 70-116670. ISBN 0-07-079798-6.

This one-of-a-kind encyclopedia, intended for high school and undergraduate students, has adequate general coverage of all areas of science and technology. It is also useful for advanced researchers who may need some information on a topic not in their field. The first edition of the encyclopedia was published in 1960 and the revised edition (with only minor changes) in 1966. At that time, *The Booklist* described this encyclopedia as "the first modern multivolume encyclopedia aimed at authoritative comprehensive coverage of the physical, natural and applied sciences."

The present edition, substantially expanded and revised, contains some 7,600 articles written by more than 2,500 scientists and engineers. All major articles are signed. Most longer articles begin with a definition of the subject, followed by a detailed discussion of certain aspects of a given topic, with a brief bibliography appended. There are many helpful cross references in the text, but, unfortunately, pronunciation of scientific terms is not indicated. This lack of pronunciation is, in our opinion, a major failing; even general encyclopedias usually provide this information. The overall format of double columns is good, and many drawings, diagrams, graphs and charts convey additional information.

We examined a number of specific topics and subject areas and found this encyclopedia to be well balanced, with accurate and up-to-date information presented in readable form. Most articles examined were readable at the non-specialist level; however, the length of an article was not always proportionate to the subject. For example, eight pages were devoted to paleobotany and only three to paleontology. The topical index, however, devotes only one-third as many individual articles to paleobotany as it does to paleontology. Nevertheless, *McGraw-Hill Encyclopedia* provides much more information on more specialized topics than do general adult encyclopedias. Hundreds of articles discuss special aspects of science and technology that are not covered in *Americana* or even *Britannica*.

The index volume is praiseworthy. It contains a list of contributors and two indexes: an analytical index and a topical index. The analytical index (130,000 entries) is excellent and easy to use, though some illustrations, tables, maps, and color plates are not indexed. The topical index includes 130 topics under which all 7,600 titles of articles are listed. This provides an excellent method of checking to see if the general information on a topic is covered in the encyclopedia.

Two well-designed booklets, *Reader's Guide* and *Study Guide*, serve as an introduction to the use of the encyclopedia both as a reference work and as a means of studying a given subject through the various articles. —H. Robert Malinowsky and Bohdan S. Wynar. [R: ARBA 71, item 1520]

DICTIONARIES

654. Collocott, T. C., ed. **Chambers Dictionary of Science and Technology.** New York, Barnes & Noble, 1972. 1328p. illus. $27.50. LC 72-180608. ISBN 0-389-04482-2.

For over 30 years the *Chambers Technical Dictionary* has been acknowledged as one of the most comprehensive single-volume dictionaries of its kind. This book is a completely revised and expanded edition of this classic. The dictionary now covers dozens of new fields ranging from Acoustics to Zoology. The definitions have been re-examined by competent authorities and there are additions, revisions, and deletions. Most of the new words, however, come from the newly developed directions of scientific activity. The terms are arranged alphabetically in letter-by-letter order with compound or modified words grouped under the first component, although a few biological terms (such as respiration, aerobic; respiration, anaerobic; respiration, external; and respiration, internal) have been inverted. Each definition is labeled to indicate its field. If a term is used in more than one field, the definitions are arranged alphabetically by the label (i.e., *Acous., Bot., Inst.,* etc.). Trade names, when used, are also noted. The volume has many appendixes, including "Table of Chemical Elements," "Periodic Table," and tables of classification for "Igneous Rocks," "Sedimentary Rocks," "The Plant Kingdom," and "The Animal Kingdom."

Most important are tables of physical concepts and standard values in SI (Système International d'Unités), the new international metric system. All in all, this dictionary achieves its goal, which is to reflect "honestly and adequately the level of vocabulary required by those interested in understanding the scientific and technological developments and problems in our lives today." —Robert J. Havlik. [R: Choice, July-Aug 72, p. 623; WLB, Nov 72, p. 293; ALA 72; ARBA 73, item 1370]

655. Godfrey, Lois E., and Helen F. Redman, eds. **Dictionary of Report Series Codes.** 2nd ed. New York, Special Libraries Association, 1973. 645p. $24.50. LC 72-87401. ISBN 0-87111-209-4.

This long-awaited, indispensable guide to the alphanumeric codes used to identify technical reports includes 25,500 codes related to the various agencies of the Department of Defense, the Atomic Energy Commission, their contractors (including industrial, educational, and professional organizations), agencies of the U.S. government, and similar agencies of foreign governments. The second edition (1st ed., 1962) has doubled the number of entries cited and reflects the phenomenal increase in the report literature, which is now estimated to encompass as much as half a million publications a year. The new edition also reflects the fact that report literature is now published in the social as well as in the hard sciences.

Introductory material gives a history of the use of report series codes, how designators are assigned, the components of codes (which generally consist of a combination of letters and/or numbers and a serial number), and a brief discussion of the evolution and proliferation of the codes. Other preliminary and useful data include a glossary, a bibliography of articles on technical codes, hints for code searches that are not answered by this volume, and sources of the codes included here. The bulk of the text is divided into three color-coded sections: 1) "Reference Notes—48 explanations of series designations or of the practice of the assigners in expanding on a series designation." 2) A list of report series codes, arranged by the first letter found in the code, with identification of the related agency (e.g., "NTO-(Number)-" is the code for reports from the Department of Laboratory Medicine at the University of Connecticut in Hartford). Many but not all of the codes are acronyms, and certain combinations of letters coincidentally stand for several different sources. However, this section will provide the known alternatives for any given combination of letters. 3) Corporate entries with related report series codes—e.g., Bell Telephone Labs., Inc., N.Y.C.: BTL-(Number)-(Letter).

Because of their complexity, their non-standardized format and publication criteria, and the lack of effective bibliographical control, reports are often ignored by patrons and librarians alike. They are, however, an increasingly used and respected means of communication, since they often contain primary and secondary information not necessarily available elsewhere. The code number serves as the most precise method of recall, and this volume provides essential information about the generation of those code numbers. —Laurel Grotzinger. [R: Unesco, July-Aug 73, p. 235; ARBA 74, item 1439]

656. **McGraw-Hill Dictionary of Scientific and Technical Terms**. Daniel N. Lapedes, Editor-in-chief. New York, McGraw-Hill, 1974. 1v.(various paging). illus. $39.95. LC 74-16193. ISBN 0-07-045257-1.

It is impossible in today's world not to come in contact with the vocabulary of science and technology. The development of new fields such as nuclear engineering, molecular biology, and aerospace adds new words and terms to the vocabulary. The *McGraw-Hill Dictionary of Scientific and Technical Terms* is a new major compendium of almost 100,000 terms in current use. The dictionary emphasizes the definitions of the terms rather than their pronunciation, word derivation, and syllabication. The style is clear and understandable and the depth of the definition varies with the complexity of the term and the subject itself. The definitions are supplemented by over 2,800 illustrations.

The definitions were written by an outstanding editorial staff and group of consultants, and the following McGraw-Hill publications were also consulted: *Condensed Computer Encyclopedia*, by Philip Jordain; *Artists' and Illustrators' Encyclopedia*, by John Quick; *Electronics and Nucleonics Dictionary*, by John Markus; *Blakiston's Gould Medical Dictionary*; and *Standard Handbook for Mechnical Engineers*, edited by Theodore Baumeister and Lionel Marks. Each term is classed in one or more of 102 clearly defined fields. The terms, which appear in boldface, are alphabetized letter-by-letter and are followed by the abbreviation of the subject field and one or more definitions. When a word is used in more than one field, the fields are listed alphabetically. There are numerous *see* references as well as informal notes such as "Also known as . . .", etc. Chemistry definitions may include either an empirical formula or a line formula, whichever is appropriate. The 26-page appendix contains numerous pages of conversion tables to international measurement systems as well as mathematical tables, tables of constants, symbols and abbreviations. Most unusual, however, is the revised "Taxonomy of Bacteria," which reflects the changes that occurred when the eighth edition of the standard *Bergey's Manual of Determinative Bacteriology* was published while this dictionary was in press. The new "Taxonomy" corrects the old system, which was used throughout the text. This dictionary will become a "must," and the use of computer composition will insure the ease of updating future editions. —Robert J. Havlik. [R: ALA 74; ARBA 75, item 1434]

BIOGRAPHY

657. **Dictionary of Scientific Biography**. Charles Coulston Gillispie, editor-in-chief. New York, Scribner's, 1970– . $40.00/v. LC 69-18090.

Published under the auspices of the American Council of Learned Societies, this monumental dictionary is projected in 14 volumes, 12 of which have been published to date. Closely patterned after the *Dictionary of American Biography* and the *Dictionary of National Biography*, it covers all periods from classical antiquity to the present and includes only deceased scientists. Selection criteria are influenced by "contributions to science . . . sufficiently distinctive to make an identifiable difference to the profession or community of knowledge." Although the scope is international, some countries (India, China, Japan) are not as well represented as Western countries because of the limited availability of scholarship, as acknowledged in the preface. When complete, it is estimated that the dictionary will include about 5,000 names.

Entries first give places and dates of birth and death (when known) and a very brief summary of the individual's contributions to science. The body of each article presents in-depth coverage of the subject's career and scientific accomplishments; personal biography is intentionally minimized. Articles vary in length, but all have selective bibliographies which include both primary and secondary references. The article on Aristotle runs to 31 pages, two of which are devoted to bibliographical information. Although balanced selection of Eastern scientists has been precluded, an eleventh century Chinese mathematician and astronomer, Shen Kua, is discussed in 25 pages, nearly three pages of which are bibliography. Not all subjects receive such lengthy treatment, but the remote past is not skimmed in favor of more recent developments.

Even though the *Dictionary of Scientific Biography* is still incomplete, it has already established itself as an indispensable work for serious science scholars as well as for the science historian. It is a well-balanced, scholarly biographical dictionary that could be a model for disciplines that still lack retrospective biographical coverage.   [R: WLB, Oct 70; LJ, July 70; ALA 70; ARBA 71, item 1532; ARBA 75, item 1439; ARBA 76, item 1329]

CHAPTER 29

MATHEMATICS

658. Burington, Richard S. **Handbook of Mathematical Tables and Formulas.** 5th ed. New York, McGraw-Hill, 1973. 500p. illus. index. $6.95. LC 78-39634. ISBN 0-07-009015-7.

According to the author, "this book has been constructed to meet the needs of students and workers in mathematics, engineering, physics, chemistry, science, and other fields in which mathematical reasoning, processes, and computations are required." It consists of two parts. The first part includes the main formulas and theorems of algebra, geometry, trigonometry, calculus, vector analysis, sets, logic, matrices, linear algebra, numerical analysis, differential equations, some special functions, Fourier and Laplace transforms, complex variables, and statistics. The second part consists of tables of logarithms, trigonometry, exponential and hyperbolic functions, powers and roots, probability distributions, annuity, and other tables.

The readers to whom this book is directed will find it useful—particularly the part on mathematical tables. However, some chapters of part one might be incomprehensible to beginners. For example, the sections on plane areas and volumes by double integration (page 67) are vague because no explanation is given about the limits of integration; the same is true of the section on homomorphic correspondence (page 148); and the definition of convex surface (page 117) is not exact. The chapter on partial differential equations is short (a little over two pages) and is therefore of little use to any reader. Despite the above, the book is a useful publication. —Elie M. Dick. [R: WLB, Mar 73, p. 613; ARBA 74, item 1450]

659. Dick, Elie M. **Current Information Sources in Mathematics: An Annotated Guide to Books and Periodicals, 1960-1972.** Littleton, Colo., Libraries Unlimited, 1973. 281p. index. $12.50. LC 72-075143. ISBN 0-87287-047-2.

This bibliographic guide to recent materials in mathematics supplements Parke's *Guide to the Literature in Mathematics and Physics*, published in 1958. It lists and describes the most important monographs published in English from 1960 to 1972, providing full bibliographical descriptions and annotations for some 1,600 titles. The material is arranged in 33 main chapters (e.g., General Elementary Mathematics; Algebra and Trigonometry; Calculus, Analytic Geometry and Vector Analysis; Set Theory, Logic and Foundations, etc.). Essential works are coded to reviews in *Mathematical Reviews*, and some titles are recommended for purchase by university and college libraries.

In addition to monographic material presented in the classified arrangement shown above, there are chapters on reference books, periodicals, and the most important professional organizations and publishers. [R: RSR, Apr/June 73, p. 18; WLB, June 73, p. 870; ARBA 74, item 1446]

660. **The Universal Encyclopedia of Mathematics.** Foreword by James R. Newman. New York, Simon and Schuster, 1969. 598p. diagr. $4.95pa. LC 63-21086. ISBN 0-671-20348-7.

This paperback edition of a work originally published in 1964 will now be available to a larger audience. Based on a German work, Joseph Meyer's *Grossen Rechenduden* (1964), it covers all the major mathematical functions, including arithmetic, algebra, applications, geometry, trigonometry, special functions, series and expansions, differential calculus, and integral calculus. Suitable for college and high school students. [R: Choice, Dec 64; ARBA 70, v.2, p. 104]

CHAPTER 30

ASTRONOMY

661. Howard, Neale E. **The Telescope Handbook and Star Atlas.** Updated ed. New York, Thomas Y. Crowell, 1975. 226p. illus. index. $14.95. LC 75-6601. ISBN 0-690-00686-1.

An excellent handbook covering the observational aspects of amateur astronomy. The work is a companion volume to the author's useful guide for constructing amateur telescopes, the *Standard Handbook for Telescope Making*. Howard, an outstanding amateur astronomer, has produced this revised and updated edition of his very successful handbook that first appeared in 1967.

The new handbook is an excellent introduction for the novice astronomer. Chapters cover types of telescopes; the celestial sphere; observing the planetary system, double and variable stars, comets and meteors, star clusters and nebulae; and celestial photography. Of special note are the 14 star charts prepared for handy use at the telescope. Useful appendixes include: a gazetteer of 234 named stars, a list of visual binaries, long and short period variables, nebulae and clusters down to magnitude 12, periodic comets, annual meteor showers, and a complete Messier Catalog arranged by central meridian transit (i.e., by season). Tables for converting Sidereal to Universal Time, Universal Time to U.S. Time, astronomical symbols, Greek alphabet, and an instructive glossary round out Howard's basic primer. An excellent bibliography for the novice will point the way to more advanced astronomical works.

The work is marred by a few errors in the updating. The updating consists of new NASA photos, correcting the astronomical coordinates to the 1970 epoch, and revising the lists of eclipses and comets. Most of the errors in this section appear to be the result of careless editing. For instance, the November 1975 Total Eclipse of the Moon is not noted at all, and the April 1976 Annular Eclipse of the Sun occurs on the 29th of the month and not the 19th, as the author states. Even with these occasional errors, the work is an extremely useful book for basic astronomical reference. —Ralph L. Scott. [R: ARBA 76, item 1337]

662. Kopal, Zdenek. **A New Photographic Atlas of the Moon.** New York, Taplinger, 1971. 310p. illus. $20.00. LC 72-125480. ISBN 0-8008-5515-9.

This superb atlas is an updated version of a 1965 lunar atlas by the same author. Included are a number of excellent recent telescopic pictures made with a large telescope at Pic-du-Midi in France, and a selection of the best of the recent space photographs.

Written by an eminently qualified astronomer who has directed lunar mapping projects, the book describes the history of such mapping, the mechanical and geometrical aspects of the Moon's motion, the evidence for a lack of atmosphere, and especially the geography and structure of the Moon's surface.

The text starts with the earliest telescopic discoveries of Galileo in 1610, and ends with the most recent data from instruments left on the Moon's surface by the Apollo astronauts. The lunar craters and maria are described with regard to their sizes and distribution. Their probable origin is due, in some cases, to meteoric or comet impacts and, in other cases, to volcanic action. Of course, the structure and age of the Moon rocks are discussed in detail, taking into account the chemistry and crystal structure of the returned Moon rocks. The scientific description occupies about one-quarter of the book. The remainder is devoted to the 200 pictures and their explanatory captions. Of particular interest are the extraordinary detail of the well-known craters Copernicus and Plato, and the complete photographic coverage of the Moon's far side, which is invisible from earth. —Edgar Everhart. [R: ARBA 72, item 1484]

663. Lewis, H.A.G., ed. **The Times Atlas of the Moon.** London, Times Newspapers Ltd.; distr. New York, New York Times, 1969. 110p. maps. illus.(part col.). index. $25.00. ISBN 0-7230-0006-9.

A handsome quarto volume with a misleading title, since detailed map coverage of the lunar surface is limited to the Near Side only. The backbone of this work consists of more than 60 carefully drawn and attractively colored maps up to 13" x 23" in size and scaled approximately 1" to 20 miles. They are based on U.S. Air Force 1:1,000,000 lunar charts, with additional information furnished by the U.S. Army Topographic Command, NASA and the U.S. Geological Survey. Printed in the United Kingdom by the prestigious cartographic firm of Bartholomew, each map is beautiful to contemplate, with relief intimated by subtle shading, the shadows depicted as though illumination is emanating from a westerly direction. Where data are available, contour lines are shown. Spot elevations are indicated in meters. All major and many minor topographical features, with the exception of crater-contained rilles (clefts), are clearly delineated and labeled. A geographic coordinate grid is superimposed on each map. Legends contain graphic scales graduated in statute miles and kilometers.

The text portion of the atlas includes information on techniques of lunar flight, lunar landscape characteristics, geology of the Moon, mapping methodology and a discussion of Far Side topography. Accompanying and elucidating these fact-filled essays are numerous stunning color photographs and explanatory drawings.

Indexing is by named feature; location is indicated by latitude and longitude rather than by an alphanumeric system, which many non-technical readers would probably find easier to use. The best of its kind to date in an area of interest certain to expand conspicuously. —Lawrence E. Spellman. [R: ARBA 71, item 1546]

664. Moore, Patrick, ed. **The Concise Atlas of the Universe.** New York, Rand McNally, 1974. 192p. illus.(part col.). charts. graphs. index. $19.95. LC 74-421. ISBN 0-528-83031-7.

A revised and updated presentation of the *Atlas of the Universe* (Rand McNally, 1970) is a joy to behold and even more of a value. The exploration of the Moon dominated the 1970 volume; this has been reduced to essentials and the *Concise Atlas* has been updated in such areas as the Russian Moon lander, the

Comet Kohoutek, and Pioneer 10 photos of Jupiter. (The original volume, a 272-page edition, still in print and useful; this newer edition is directed to the general public.)

Like the 1970 edition, the new volume is organized in four main sections: 1) Atlas of the Earth from Space; 2) Atlas of the Moon; 3) Atlas of the Solar System; and 4) Atlas of the Stars. The valuable "Catalog of Stellar Objects" is included as well as a "Glossary of Terms Used in Astronomy" and an index. The index generally works, though it has flaws; Kohoutek is not listed, although it is noted in the text.

The index is detailed and the sections are distinct in their coverage. Part 1, which deals with the Earth from space, includes the Earth's magnetosphere and atmosphere, weather systems, and space panoramas; Part 2 includes all relevant data on the Moon including the landscape, Moon maps, and the "conquest" of the Moon; Part 3 has 50 pages devoted to the solar system, including the Copernican revolution, the planets, asteroids, comets, meteors, etc.; and Part 4 has 60 pages on such topics as stellar evolution, the star clusters and nebulae, galaxies beyond our own, star maps, etc. The maps, photography, diagrams, and charts and drawings are superbly executed and alone are well worth the price of the book. In addition, the narrative accompanying each illustration is lucid, concise, and—amazingly—readable. —Laurel Grotzinger. [R: ARBA 75, item 1447]

665. Whipple, F. L., and Charles Lundquist, eds. **Smithsonian Astrophysical Observatory Star Atlas of Reference Stars and Nonstellar Objects**. Prep. by the staff of the Smithsonian Astrophysical Observatory, with an intro. by Joseph Ashbrook. Cambridge, Mass., MIT Press, 1969. 1v.(looseleaf). $18.50. LC 75-84659. ISBN 0-262-19061-3.

This atlas consists of 152 loose charts 11" x 14", boxed for handling convenience. They graphically pinpoint the coordinates of over a quarter of a million stars along with various kinds of nonstellar objects. This project was begun in 1957, and no other undertaking of this kind is planned before the year 2000. Stars are shown on the charts as solid circles or dots, their visual magnitudes being indicated by their size or by special symbols. Variable and double stars, and stars without known proper motions, are also indicated by special symbols. Galaxies, globular clusters, and planetary nebulae are plotted to scale as open circles and ellipses so that their angular diameters and orientations (in the case of galaxies) are visually apparent. Objects from Dreyer's *New General Catalogue* (NGC) and *Index Catalogue* (IC) are plotted as small diamonds. The primary source of the stellar positions was the *Smithsonian Astrophysical Observatory Catalogue* (1966). The positions of the nonstellar objects were gathered from a number of sources, including the Shapley-Ames catalogue, the Palomar Sky Survey, and the NGC and IC. Explanatory text is provided with the atlas, along with an alphabetical list of the named stars (and their positions) and several tables and figures that cover the entire sky and serve to index the individual charts and show how they fit together. [R: ARBA 70, v.2, p. 106]

CHAPTER 31

CHEMISTRY

666. Bard, Allen J., ed. **Encyclopedia of Electrochemistry of the Elements, Volume I– .** New York, Marcel Dekker, 1973– . 495p. illus. charts. bibliog. index. $60.00/v.; $50.00/v. subscription. LC 73-88796. ISBN 0-8247-6093-X.

The purpose of this multivolume encyclopedia (15 volumes estimated by the publisher) is to provide a critical, systematic, and comprehensive review of the electrochemical behavior of the chemical elements and their compounds. This new and unique reference work is designed to bring together in one convenient source the descriptive aspects of inorganic and organic electrochemistry. The encyclopedia is divided into two parts: Part I, Inorganic Electrochemistry; Part II, Organic Electrochemistry. The initial volumes will cover the inorganic elements and their compounds. The basic classification of elements and their compounds is the same as that used by *Gmelins Handbuch der anorganischen Chemie*.

Each chapter, written by a leading authority on the particular subject, is divided into five sections: 1) Introduction and Standard Potentials; 2) Voltammetric Characteristics; 3) Kinetic Parameters and Double-Layer Properties; 4) Electrochemical Studies; 5) Applied Electrochemistry. The first section discusses introductory material and the standard potentials in aqueous, nonaqueous and fused salt mediums. Polarographic and other voltammetric research is presented in the second section. The third section explores such topics as rate constants, exchange current densities, transfer coefficients, potential of zero charge, and double-layer capacities. The fourth section surveys the electrochemical reactions of the element and its compounds, reaction mechanisms, reaction orders, current efficiencies, oxidation and reduction products, passivation phenomena, oxide films, and anodization. The last section discusses the use of electrochemistry in the isolation and/or purification of the element, the electrochemical production of compounds, and the use and behavior of the element and its compounds in electrochemical devices. At the end of each chapter is an extensive bibliography covering references to the primary literature on all data and reactions. Volume 1 covers the following elements and their respective compounds: Ar, At, Ba, Br, Ca, Cd, Cl, He, I, Kr, Mn, Ne, Pb, Ra, Rn, Sr, and Xe. —Robert K. Dikeman. [R: ARBA 75, item 1450]

667. **Concise Chemical and Technical Dictionary.** 3rd enlarged ed. Ed. by H. Bennett. New York, Chemical Publishing, 1974. 1175p. illus. $35.00.

No technical library should lack this dictionary, first published in 1947 and since expanded to list about 75,000 definitions. H. Bennett, who is also the editor of *Chemical Formulary*, added some 15,000 new entries—new trademark products, chemicals, drugs and terms.

A special feature of this work is the compilation of thousands of trade names of proprietary products in chemistry and related trades. Since this is a "concise" dictionary, brevity rather than extended definition has been the rule. For those who need more detailed treatment of a subject, a short list of references is attached.

Other useful features are the names of formulae of radicals occurring in organic compounds, the pronunciation of chemical words, and appendixes that cover conversion tables, indicators, important ring systems, and various symbols. The dictionary will be useful to scientists and technicians as well as to technical librarians. —Vladimir T. Borovansky. [R: WLB, Feb 75, p. 461; ARBA 76, item 1342]

668. **The Condensed Chemical Dictionary.** 8th ed. Revised by Gessner G. Hawley. New York, Van Nostrand Reinhold, 1971. 971p. $28.50. LC 75-133848. ISBN 0-442-23237-3.

This eighth edition of an outstanding chemical dictionary appears 52 years after the first edition. It is intended to be a brief, quick reference aid, leaving more detailed discussions to the *Encyclopedia of Chemistry*. "Three distinct types of information are presented: 1) technical descriptions of chemicals, raw materials, and processes; 2) expanded definitions of chemical entities, phenomena, and terminology; and 3) description or identification of a wide range of trademarked products used in the chemical industries." For each chemical the name, synonym, formula, properties, source or occurrence, derivation, grades, containers, hazards, uses, and shipping regulations are given, as appropriate. Trademarked materials are keyed to a list of manufacturers. New in this edition are brief biographies of many early chemists; official threshold limit values on toxic and flammable materials; short descriptions of leading chemical and engineering societies, names and addresses of numerous trade associations and technical institutes; and special attention to products and problems of current environmental concern. The introduction should be read thoroughly. —H. Robert Malinowsky. [R: ARBA 72, item 1487]

669. Dean, John A., ed. **Lange's Handbook of Chemistry.** 11th ed. New York, McGraw-Hill, 1973. 1v.(various paging). illus. index. $22.50. LC 73-6553. ISBN 0-07-016190-9.

Related groups of factual data are presented within the following sections: mathematics, inorganic chemistry, analytical chemistry, electrochemistry, spectroscopy, organic chemistry, thermodynamic properties, physical properties. Improvements over the tenth edition include self-instructional sections developed for the areas of pH measurement, use of statistics, separation and chromatographic methods, and x-ray methods. New material is introduced on emission and absorption lines for arc, spark, flame, and atomic absorption (with sensitivities and detection limits), formation constants of metal complexes with organic and inorganic ligands, anion and cation selectivity coefficients for ion-exchange resins, Hammett and Taft substituent constants, and mass absorption coefficients for x-ray lines for every element. Expanded coverage is provided in the more traditional areas of heats and free energies of formation, entropies and heat capacities, x-ray emission spectra and K and L absorption edges, critical properties, limiting equivalent ionic conductances (aqueous), table of nuclides, ionization potentials of elements, solubility products, acid dissociation constants, electrode potentials, bond energies, atomic and ionic radii, and reference pH buffers for water (H_2O and D_2O), aqueous-organic solvents, and biological media. —John R. Riter, Jr. [R: ARBA 74, item 1458]

670. Gordon, Arnold J., and Richard A. Ford. **The Chemist's Companion: A Handbook of Practical Data, Techniques and References.** New York, Wiley, 1972. 537p. index. $17.95. LC 72-6660. ISBN 0-471-31590-7.

Subtitled "A Handbook of Practical Data, Techniques and References," the book is divided into nine chapters. It covers properties of atoms and molecules, spectroscopy, photochemistry, chromatography, kinetics and thermodynamics, various experimental techniques, and mathematical and numerical information including the definitions, values, and usage rules of the newly adopted International System of Units (SI Units). The chapter on spectroscopy seems especially well done.

Also included is a variety of hard-to-classify but frequently sought information such as names and addresses of microanalysis companies and chemistry publishers, descriptions and commercial sources of atomic and molecular models, and safety data for hazardous chemicals. More than 500 references are given.

The volume has a tremendous range of material that should be of about equal utility to the working chemist, the research scientist, and the classroom teacher. Indeed, several of the chapters could be profitably read simply to increase one's understanding of modern concepts in chemistry, as well as to find out specifically about superacids, freons, chi-square tests, etc. —John R. Riter, Jr. [R: Choice, Oct 73, p. 1164; ALA 73; ARBA 74, item 1459]

671. Hampel, Clifford A., and Gessner G. Hawley, eds. **The Encyclopedia of Chemistry.** 3rd ed. New York, Van Nostrand Reinhold, 1973. 1198p. illus. index. $39.50. LC 73-244. ISBN 0-442-23095-8.

The third edition of this excellent one-volume encyclopedia exhibits the quality and usefulness of its predecessors, which were edited by Clark and Hawley. The new senior editor is well known for his work with other one-volume reference books in chemistry. Although many articles remain unchanged, or nearly so, the extensive additions and revisions reflect advances and new emphases since the second edition was published in 1966. Of particular interest are new topics in environmental chemistry and the chemistry of life processes including, for example, biomaterials, genetic code, psychotropic drugs, and sea water chemistry. The maintenance of approximately the same number of articles (more than 800) was accomplished by deletion of those of less interest to chemists, such as Mössbauer Effect, and by appropriate combination of topics previously listed under two or more separate headings. An especially noteworthy improvement is the inclusion of bibliographic references to additional literature on specific topics. An accurate and detailed index is provided. —Julie Bichteler. [R: WLB, Nov 73, p. 264; ARBA 74, item 1460]

CHAPTER 32

PHYSICS

672. Besançon, Robert M., ed. **The Encyclopedia of Physics.** 2nd ed. New York, Van Nostrand Reinhold, 1974. 1067p. illus. index. $37.50. LC 73-17022. ISBN 0-442-20691-7.

The 344 articles in this encyclopedia, which are designed to give uniform coverage, are written on three different levels: those on the main divisions of physics are intended for readers with little background in the subject; those on the subdivisions are aimed at readers with more knowledge, and those on the more finely divided areas are geared toward readers with fairly sound backgrounds in both physics and mathematics.

This plan seems to be rather successful in the execution. There are a number of sections on mathematical techniques such as vector physics, tensors and tensor analysis, Fourier analysis, and a rather terse section on differential equations in physics. Descriptions of chemistry and chemists written by physicists are often the source of mild amusement; the results here, however, are a pleasant surprise— the Chemical Physics section is particularly succinct. One might wish for even a small discussion of a topic such as flames, which has no index entry; this subject must have been judged to be beyond the periphery of physics proper.

The articles sampled on each of the three levels provide appropriate weighted combinations of introductory material, references for further study, and clear and sometimes even provocative suggestions as to where future research in some areas may be headed. All teachers of beginning students will remember new insights that they have gained into a subject by looking at things from the perspective of the beginner; and so it is here with many of the first-level articles.

Among the numerous contributors are many leaders in their areas. One finds that equations, figures, and diagrams all seem to have been carefully set. The binding is strong, which is good, because the volume would seem to be in for a lot of use. —John R. Riter, Jr. [R: WLB, Dec 74, p. 318; ARBA 75, item 1456]

673. Gray, Dwight E., coordinating ed. **American Institute of Physics Handbook.** 3rd ed. New York, McGraw-Hill, 1972. 1v.(various paging). illus. index. $49.50. LC 72-3248. ISBN 0-07-001485-X.

This internationally accepted physics handbook "continues the philosophy of supplying authoritative reference materials—including tables of data, graphs, and bibliographies—selected and described with a minimum of narration by leaders in physical methods for research." Many revised and rewritten sections have also been included. One cannot say enough about this handbook, which has become the bible among physics handbooks. Each of the nine sections covers a field of physics in logical sequence from definitions and concepts through the many subtopics of that particular field. As with past editions, this one has excellent format, and good tables, charts, and graphs, all documented. The index helps the user locate the specific material needed. —H. Robert Malinowsky. [R: ARBA 73, item 1402]

674. Gray, H. J., and Alan Isaacs, eds. **A New Dictionary of Physics.** 2nd ed. New York, Longman, 1975. 619p. illus. $35.00. ISBN 0-582-32242-1.

Substantially revised, updated, and expanded, Longman's *New Dictionary of Physics* will be an invaluable tool for students, teachers, scientists, and the general reader in need of relatively simple explanations of the terms and concepts used in contemporary physics.

The dictionary, which is alphabetically arranged, covers all branches of physics. It reflects all modern developments in particle physics, solid-state physics, and closely related fields.

The first edition's lengthy articles on the elements were dropped in order to accommodate new materials. Some key concepts are still treated at length, but most technical terms are given brief definition. Even with this new feature, the new edition is 65 pages longer than the first. The problem of British terminology for the American user has been almost completely solved by the new developments in solid-state technology and elimination of terms like "valve" or "vacuum tube," etc.

Each article consists of a self-contained description of the subject, accompanied, in some cases, by a diagram. Articles on leading physicists give brief biographical information, useful to a reader who comes across names in using the literature of physics. All quantitative information is given in SI units, and 16 tables, which give a wide range of information, are at the end of the dictionary. —Vladimir T. Borovansky. [R: Choice, Nov 75, p. 1142; WLB, Sept 75, p. 72; LJ, 1 Apr 75, p. 654; ARBA 76, item 1350]

675. Thewlis, J. **Concise Dictionary of Physics and Related Subjects.** Elmsford, N.Y., Pergamon, 1973. 366p. $16.50. LC 72-10122. ISBN 0-08-016900-7.

The well-known editor of the *Encyclopaedic Dictionary of Physics* (1961 to 1964, with supplements) has produced this new dictionary of more than 7,200 entries, based in part on the older work. Intended primarily for students and non-specialists, the *Concise Dictionary* should also be useful for the researcher interested in aspects outside his immediate specialty. The briefly defined terms come not only from physics but also from meterology, mathematics, photography, astronomy, crystallography, and many other subject areas. Thus, one finds definitions of tornado, granitic layer, extracorporeal circulation, pasteurization, Banach space, and colour photography (British spelling is used throughout). Criteria for inclusion of such terms are not clear. Appendixes include brief metric conversion tables, values of general physical constants, and the periodic table with a list of elements and symbols. Extensive cross references are a strong point.

Although this dictionary will be a useful addition to physics reference materials, it does suffer from more than its share of typographical errors and inconsistencies. Inconsistency can be illustrated by the several approaches taken in treating synonyms. Double entry is often used (for example, the definition for Heaviside layer: "Kennelly-Heaviside layer: E-layer" is repeated under "E-layer: Heaviside layer: Kennelly-Heaviside layer" and under "Kennelly-Heaviside layer: Heaviside layer: E-layer"); alternatively, such synonymous terms may be given no entry at all, may be described as "Another name for . . . ," or may be indicated by a *see* reference. —Julie Bichteler. [R: WLB, Dec 73, p. 340; ARBA 74, item 1470]

CHAPTER 33

NATURAL HISTORY AND BIOLOGY

GENERAL WORKS

676. Bottle, R. T., and H. V. Wyatt, eds. **The Use of Biological Literature**. 2nd ed. Hamden, Conn., Archon, 1971. 379p. index. (Information Sources for Research and Development). $18.50. ISBN 0-208-01221-4.

One of the best introductions of its kind. The literature of biology assumes a shape in 20 bibliographic chapters. Multiple changes in biology information caused the authors to rewrite and thoroughly revise the first edition (1966). Ecology, genetics, and teaching/laboratories now have whole chapters, and bibliographies have been updated (although not as much as one might have hoped). New questions have been added to the exercises, and the illustrations have been retained. Bottle and colleagues adequately survey the field: government publications, patents, abstracts, bibliographies, and such subjects as taxonomy, zoology, and agriculture. The index is impaired due to a decision to cite only important abstracts and reference books.

British this book is, but American libraries and budding biologists will find it viable. —Peter Doiron. [R: ARBA 73, item 1407]

677. Smith, Roger C., and W. Malcolm Reid. **Guide to the Literature of the Life Sciences**. 8th ed. Minneapolis, Minn., Burgess, 1972. 166p. index. $8.50. LC 74-181748. ISBN 0-8087-1964-5.

This revision of Smith's *Guide to the Literature of the Zoological Sciences* (7th ed., 1967) continues its tradition as a manual primarily useful for students of the zoological and botanical sciences, despite the authors' claim that it has appeal for specialists. Although it is not intended as a comprehensive bibliography, its lists still cover the major reference sources quite adequately, with special emphasis on abstract journals, primary research journals, and taxonomic works. Particularly valuable to the student is the opening chapter on literature problems of the scientist; it ranges from texts in the field through special literature concerns (review journals, translations, irregular serials, etc.) to sources of research funds, literature on the teaching of biology and, as in all chapters, library assignments. In addition, a chapter on the mechanics of library organization and classification of materials, one on bibliographic form and forms of literature, and a brief description of search methods and the preparation of scientific papers, supply the novice with necessary information for effective use of the literature.

The book appears reduced in coverage, but this is largely due to the page design and the authors' compression of material rather than to any loss of information. Many sections have new and/or additional information and the bibliographies have been updated to cover material dating through 1971. The organization has been modified from that used in the previous edition, but a detailed index solves this problem and answers the criticism that the order of the contents seems somewhat random. —Laurel Grotzinger. [R: ARBA 73, item 1408]

BIBLIOGRAPHIES

678. Smit, Pieter. **History of the Life Sciences: An Annotated Bibliography.** New York, Hafner Press, 1974. 1036 cols. + pp. 1037-1071. index. $55.00. LC 74-12091. ISBN 0-02-852510-8.

The bibliography originated as an extension of those parts of Sarton's *Guide to the History of Science* (Waltham, Mass., Chronica Botanica, 1952) that deal with the life sciences. It is intended to serve primarily the historian of science, but also scholars in biology and medicine, and librarians. Over 4,000 entries containing full bibliographical information for all entries are included; summary reviews are given for nearly all the entries. Coverage is highly selective for the earliest writings and extends to publications issued through mid-1971.

The physical organization of the volume is somewhat unusual. Also, since the chapter listings in the table of contents do not correspond exactly to the chapter numbering in the text, the user will encounter some difficulties. The entries are set out in double columns on each page and each column is numbered; in contrast, the pages, not the columns, of the index are numbered. In addition to the two main chapters, there is a separate section—"Selected List of Biographies, Bibliographies, etc., of Famous Biologists, Medical Men, etc., Including Some Modern Reissues of Their Publications"—plus an index of personal names. The "Selected List" is labelled Chapter III in the text but is not identified as a chapter in the table of contents.

Chapter I, General References and Tools, contains four main subsections treating philosophy and methodology of history, comprehensive works on the history of science and civilization, comprehensive bibliographies and biographical dictionaries, and recommended encyclopedias, chronologies, historical dictionaries, taxonomic indexes, and other reference works.

Chapter II, Historiography of the Life and Medical Sciences, the main portion of the bibliography (columns 149-862) contains first a brief list on the philosophy of the life sciences, followed by a section on historiography, ancient and medieval periods, chronological and ethnographical (columns 157-558), and historiography, Renaissance and later periods, according to subject (columns 559-862). The "Selected List" cited in the text as Chapter III lists entries in alphabetical order by author without any subdivisions (columns 863-1036). The index of personal names is on regularly numbered pages. It is unfortunate that title references were not added to listings for prolific authors; some of these require an extensive search in order to locate the desired title.

The retrospective bibliography, which is international in coverage, will be a valuable addition to the bibliographical sources on the life sciences. —Christine L. Wynar. [R: ARBA 76, item 1354]

ENCYCLOPEDIAS

679. Gray, Peter, ed. **The Encyclopedia of the Biological Sciences.** 2nd ed. New York, Van Nostrand Reinhold, 1970. 1027p. illus. map. tab. bibliog. index. $29.95. LC 77-81348. ISBN 0-442-15629-4.

Updated and slightly expanded, the second edition has the same purpose as the first (1961): "to provide succinct and accurate information for biologists in those fields in which they are not themselves experts." Thus it is a valuable reference for the generalist librarian. The editor wisely excluded the applied biological sciences but does include what he describes as "developmental, ecological, functional, genetic, structural, and taxonomic aspects" of biology—thereby giving it a wide subject base. The signed topical articles average two to three pages in length, but biographical entries are brief—often only half a column—and lack references. The coverage is uneven, but the explanations are lucid and seem relatively complete—although comparison with other encyclopedias is recommended. References, as a source for further data, are quite undependable; for example, an entry under *Ebenales*, a relatively small order, has 27 citations while Platyhelminthes, a major phylum, has only four references. The illustrations are limited in number and poorly reproduced, as is the text, which is printed in a small type. Despite these limitations, Gray has produced the only comprehensive, one-volume biological encyclopedia in the field today. —Laurel Grotzinger. [R: LJ, 15 Mar 70; Choice, Sept 70; ARBA 71, item 1573]

680. Gray, Peter. **The Encyclopedia of Microscopy and Microtechnique.** New York, Van Nostrand Reinhold, 1973. 638p. illus. bibliog. index. $34.50. LC 73-164. ISBN 0-442-22812-0.

An impressive list of dictionaries and encyclopedias in the biological sciences is credited to Dr. Gray's editorship. He now adds to the list this excellent new encyclopedia on microscopy and microtechniques.

This book is completely new and not an updating of Clark's *Encyclopedia of Microscopy* or Gray's own *Microtomist's Formulary and Guide.* It is comprised of nearly 175 articles prepared by over 180 expert contributors; articles are arranged alphabetically, from Acanthocephala to Zoom Microscopes. They range from short articles to long articles on Polychrome Staining Formulas and Fixative Formulas, which provide tables and numerous formulas and solutions. Bibliographies are appended to almost all the articles. All types of microscopes are covered (including instruments that use photon and electron beams) as are all methods of preparation (including dispersion, grinding, sectioning, incineration, and others). Since the microscope has so many diversified uses today, the book will be of value to workers in many fields and professions. The extensive and detailed index, which provides access to many subjects covered in the more specialized articles, will be heavily used. —R. J. Havlik. [R: ARBA 74, item 1476]

DICTIONARIES

681. Chinery, Michael. **A Science Dictionary of the Animal World.** New York, Watts, 1969. 288p. illus.(part col.). $4.95. LC 68-17109.

682. Chinery, Michael. **A Science Dictionary of the Plant World.** New York, Watts, 1969. 264p. illus.(part col.). $4.95. LC 68-17110.

Though not strictly speaking a set, these companion volumes are so similar in scope and treatment that they are best considered together; what is true of one is true of the other. Each is an alphabetic listing of the more common terms and major taxonomic groups of one of the kingdoms of living organisms, with definitions that vary from a single word to several pages; most terms are also illustrated. A concluding phylum-by-phylum survey, arranged in natural systematic sequence, helpfully brings together information on related forms that is dispersed by the artificial, if handy, alphabetic arrangement of the main text. The definitions are inconsistent in quality, being sometimes unclear or circular in wording, but the illustrations compensate by their consistent appropriateness, clarity, and attractiveness; they are certainly the most valuable feature of these books. The text is printed in two columns, in a small but clear typeface with adequate white space; the illustrations, both black and white and colored, are well reproduced. There are no indexes, but numerous cross references provide an adequate substitute. Originally published in Great Britain in 1966, both books use mostly European forms as examples, which may somewhat limit their use in American libraries. Of scant value to scholarly collections, these dictionaries will be useful to high school and undergraduate students and to amateur naturalists. —Paul B. Cors. [R: ARBA 71, items 1615-1616]

683. Gray, Peter. **Student Dictionary of Biology.** New York, Van Nostrand Reinhold, 1973. 194p. $8.95; $3.95pa. LC 73-742. ISBN 0-442-22815-5; 0-442-22816 3pa.

Dr. Gray has provided a necessary service to students of biology in this simply arranged and easily used reference work. The book, which contains approximately 8,000 entries, is very comprehensive. It includes a pronunciation guide for each entry and Latin names of genera commonly found in textbooks. A further feature is the inclusion of roots, which allows the student to use the root as the key to a term that has been forgotten or is only vaguely recalled. The detailed cross references allow the user to find easily other words referring to the concept. An invaluable reference work for the novice. —John C. Jahoda. [R: WLB, Nov 73, p. 264; LJ, 1 Nov 73, p. 3249; ARBA 74, item 1477]

684. King, Robert C. **A Dictionary of Genetics.** 2nd ed. rev. New York, Oxford University Press, 1974. 375p. illus. $5.95pa. ISBN 0-19-501902-4.

The first edition of this dictionary was published in 1968. For the present edition, the compiler has added 700 new terms and has updated the appendixes. The *Dictionary of Genetics* lists 5,000 terms found in the genetic literature as well as related terms from psychology, physics, mathematics, and chemistry. The definitions are clear and concise and, in many instances, include appropriate diagrams, tables, and chemical formulas for biological compounds. In the appendixes, Professor King provides a valuable chronology of events in genetics since 1590, a comprehensive listing of periodicals cited in the literature of genetics, cytology, and molecular biology, a list of laboratories engaged in studies of human genetics in Canada and the United States, a list of teaching aids (16mm motion picture films, filmstrips and film loops), and, finally, a list of gene localizations and other properties of human chromosomes. This dictionary will be useful to students as well as to laymen interested in genetics. [R: Choice, Sept 75, p. 818; ARBA 76, item 1356]

685. Leader, Robert W., and Isabel Leader. **Dictionary of Comparative Pathology and Experimental Biology.** Philadelphia, W. B. Saunders, 1971. 238p. bibliog. $14.00. LC 72-118591. ISBN 0-7216-5659-5.

The Leaders believe that man is not as different from other animals as is often inferred. In this dictionary they attempt to assemble terms that focus attention on biological and behavioral characteristics which exist in multiple forms throughout the animal kingdom. Perhaps the most helpful word included is one they coined, "anoman," intended to designate "animals other than man." It can substitute for such vague expressions as "lower animals" or the inaccurate phrase "man and animals."

While the book is intended for professionals and, therefore, omits general terms already well covered in standard medical dictionaries, it does provide expanded definitions in instances in which knowledge of comparative animal data is of special significance (e.g., leukemia and zoonosis). Also, to keep the book a manageable size, they refrain from extensive definitions—in some cases, by inserting references to books or symposia that deal with the particular topic. Many of the references have 1969 or 1970 dates. Much of the information in the book is presented in tabular form, although most of the tabulated material is also covered individually in the text. Other unique inclusions are: terms used by experimental behaviorists, including about 300 entries; and information concerning the husbandry, breeds, genetic characteristics, and diseases of such common laboratory animals as rats, mice and rabbits. Anticipating the ecological importance of "anoman" pathology in the near future, as man tries to better assess and control his environment, they have also included material on invertebrate pathology. The book will be an invaluable aid to biologists, physicians, veterinarians, laboratory animal scientists, medical students, veterinary students, graduate students, and teachers of high school biology. —Brower Burchill. [R: ARBA 72, item 1508]

CHAPTER 34

BOTANY

BIBLIOGRAPHIES

686. Swift, Lloyd H. **Botanical Bibliographies: A Guide to Bibliographic Materials Applicable to Botany.** Minneapolis, Burgess, 1970. 804p. index. $28.50. LC 70-106633. ISBN 0-8087-1960-2.

This excellent guide to bibliographies of botany and of the manifold subjects allied to botany covers a stupendous range. It is divided into five main parts. Part I, General Bibliography, includes sections on library classifications, periodicals, book reviews, and abstracts. Part II, Background Literature for Botany, includes sections on mathematical and physico-chemical background literature as well as on life-science background literature. Part III, Botanical Literature, includes general and reference literature, taxonomic botanical literature, plant-kingdom literature, and ecological and physiological botanical literature. Part IV, Literature of Applied Areas of Plant Study, includes literature of economic aspects of plant study and literature of plant cultivation. Part V, Literature of Areas Auxiliary to Botany, includes bibliographic keys for literature on style, botanical illustration, photography, foreign works, etc. No book of this size can be definitive and Dr. Swift states in his preface that his offering is "a guide and not a catalog. It enumerates selected lists and catalogs, but is not a compendium for their data . . . The guide is planned primarily for beginning graduate students in botany, but it should be useful to all classes of users of botanical literature." —Elizabeth C. Hall. [R: ARBA 71, item 1582]

DICTIONARIES

687. Coon, Nelson. **The Dictionary of Useful Plants.** Emmaus, Pa., Rodale Press, 1974. 290p. illus. index. $10.95. LC 74-14947. ISBN 0-87857-090-X.

To laymen gardeners, Nelson Coon is a well-known writer of books and magazine articles pertaining to plants, both cultivated and wild. The book under review is an outgrowth of his research for two of his previous books, *Using Plants for Healing* (1963) and *Using Wayside Plants* (1969), both published by Hearthside Press.

The main part of this dictionary is devoted to native and escaped plants of the United States, arranged alphabetically under plant families (which number well over a hundred). Under each plant family are arranged, also alphabetically, the genera, species, and varieties. The data for each plant include a multitude of useful and fascinating facts—description, habitat location, and current and historic uses (in food, medicine, and crafts, with frequent notes on the customs of the American Indian). There are numerous line drawings of the plants discussed. Preceding the dictionary section of the book are several chapters with titles such as "Dye Plants of the United States," "Poison Plants of the United States," "Medicinal Plants and Their Uses," etc. All told, there is an abundance of facts and fancy, presented in a chatty, informal style. —Elizabeth C. Hall. [R: WLB, Mar 75, p. 530; ARBA 76, item 1373]

688. Howes, F. N. **A Dictionary of Useful and Everyday Plants and Their Common Names; Based on Material Contained in J. C. Willis: A Dictionary of the Flowering Plants and Ferns (6th Edition, 1931).** New York, Cambridge University Press, 1974. 290p. $13.75. LC 73-91701. ISBN 0-521-08520-9.

A Dictionary of Useful and Everyday Plants and Their Common Names is also a dictionary of products from plants. The late F. N. Howes, the author and former Keeper of the Museum, Royal Botanic Garden, Kew, compiled this dictionary to complement the seventh edition of J. C. Willis's *Dictionary of Flowering Plants and Ferns* (Cambridge University Press, 1966). The seventh edition, though revised and enlarged, was restricted in its scope to generic and family names; therefore, Howes undertook the task of enlarging and updating the more general information of the sixth edition into this new dictionary. For more than 70 years, Willis's work had been the most comprehensive plant dictionary available. Because of Howes, the encyclopedic approach of the early editions of Willis remains available. The eighth edition of Willis was published in 1973.

Howes' emphasis is on common names, trade names, and economic or commercial plant products throughout the world where English is spoken. Definitions of such words as "grafting" and "germination" are given, but, in general, botanic terms and Latin names are left to other dictionaries or manuals of classification. The entries for common names or plant products give Latin names, country of each plant's origin, and practical uses. For such terms as "aquarium plants," "bee plants," "Bible plants," "bonsai," "classification," "gourds," "snakebite remedies," "tannin," and "timber," Howes provides concise but comprehensive essays, a unique and most helpful type of entry. In these essays, he lists plants that are, for example, suitable for aquariums, mentioned in the Bible, most popular to dwarf, and so on, as well as providing citations to published articles and books that readily open avenues to further research. A bibliography of major botanic dictionaries and manuals, titled "Some Useful Reference Works," concludes the dictionary. Howes' work will be a welcome and respected addition to standard reference tools. —Amity Doering. [R: LJ, 1 Dec 74, p. 3124; ARBA 75, item 1463]

689. Usher, George. **A Dictionary of Plants Used by Man.** New York, Hafner Press, 1974. 619p. $15.95. LC 74-2707. ISBN 0-02-853800-5.

All plants and trees used for commercial purposes are listed according to their botanical families. Usher used the classification adopted in Willis's *Dictionary of the Flowering Plants* (8th ed. revised by H.K.A. Shaw). The main reference for each plant (in italics) includes a brief description of its genus, total number of species included in it, authorities for the name, vernacular name, country of origin, and uses. Botanical descriptions have not been included. The reader may also find a plant by its vernacular name (in capitals) and learn the genus. This arrangement facilitates use by laymen, students, and scholars.

Usher, author of *Dictionary of Botany* and *Textbook of Practical Biology*, is a recognized plant pathologist and teacher. The book was originally printed in Great Britain in 1973. F. N. Howes' *Dictionary of Useful and Everyday Plants* is limited to plants that occur only in English speaking countries, while Usher's is worldwide in scope. The undergraduate and graduate student may find it useful to combine the factual content of Usher's book with the *Oxford Book of Food Plants* (B. E. Nicholson and others), for its very clear colored illustrations, which show the plant parts most involved in food production at relevant stages of maturity. Usher's book is more inclusive, however, since it is not limited to food plants. —Doris Flax Kaplan. [R: ARBA 76, item 1374]

690. Willis, J. C. **A Dictionary of the Flowering Plants and Ferns.** 8th ed. Rev. by H. K. Airy Shaw. New York, Cambridge University Press, 1973. 1245p. index. $35.00. LC 72-83581. ISBN 0-521-08699-X.

First published in 1897, this important botanical dictionary at first included concise entries (A to Z) on family and generic names, common names, and botanical terms and products. The seventh edition eliminated much of that material but did attempt to include every published generic name from 1753 onwards.

This eighth edition provides substantial additions and amends many of the errors in the 1931 (seventh) edition. One new feature is an alphabetical list of accepted plant family names with their equivalents in Bentham and Hooker's *Genera Plantarum* and in the latest edition of Engler's *Syllabus*. The list of generic names in this work includes all variant spellings and intergeneric hybrids. In many cases, brief characteristics of subfamilies are given. This comprehensive and recognized reference tool is well known to botanists and is important to scholarly collections of science materials. —Andy Armitage. [R: ARBA 74, item 1495]

HANDBOOKS

691. Krochmal, Arnold, and Connie Krochmal. **A Guide to the Medicinal Plants of the United States.** New York, Quadrangle/The New York Times Book Co., 1973. 259p. illus. bibliog. index. $12.50. LC 72-83289. ISBN 0-8129-0261-0.

All will be well, so long as readers *strictly* observe the warning given in this book: "Self-medication with wild plants is highly risky. Many of them are poisonous in the wild, unprocessed form. . . . We urge and warn our readers to avoid treating ailments themselves through use of the information we have presented in this book." If the warning is disregarded, all will probably not be well. As a guide to native plants that are believed to have medicinal virtues, this offering is attractive, interesting, and useful. The number of plants discussed is 272. The common and botanical names of each are listed, together with a brief description, information about where it grows, which parts are harvested and when, and uses. The brief and simple descriptions are usually inadequate to identify the plants, but they serve well as checks and are supplemented by line drawings and half-tones. Variant names and scientific terminology are included in the index. This is a useful reference book by responsible, knowledgeable authors. —Elizabeth C. Hall. [R: Choice, July-Aug 74, pp. 738-40; LJ, 1 Apr 74, p. 1018; ALA 74; ARBA 75, item 1466]

ATLASES

692. Edlin, Herbert. **Atlas of Plant Life.** New York, John Day, 1973. 128p. illus.
(col.). maps. index. $10.00. LC 73-4361. ISBN 0-381-98245-9.

This continent-by-continent presentation of plant distribution throughout
the world is profusely embellished with full-color illustrations and maps. Additional
chapters deal with climate and plants, and with the spread of plants by man.
Although common plant names are used in the nontechnical text, a table at the
end of the book lists vernacular names with their Latin equivalents. A fascinating
and informative book for grade and high school students. —Elizabeth C. Hall.
[R: LJ, 1 Dec 73, p. 3569; ALA 73; ARBA 74, item 1505]

FLOWERS

693. Fitter, Richard, and Alastair Fitter. **The Wild Flowers of Britain and Northern
Europe.** New York, Scribner's, 1974. 336p. illus.(col.). index. $10.00. LC 74-3756.
ISBN 0-684-13880-8.

This excellent field guide to the wild flowers of Britain and Northern Europe
should serve as a model for other handbooks. Richard Fitter and Alastair Fitter
have presented expert information in a format that any beginner can readily use in
identifying wild flowers. In addition to the standard "Index of English Names" and
the "Index of Scientific Names," they have provided visual keys arranged by the
shapes of the flowers (or leaves, in the case of trees and shrubs), with page references
to plants of like characteristics. The unique visual-indexing format, which is followed
throughout the book for all plant families, is a real asset to identification.

The guide describes more than 2,000 species of native flowering plants, including marine vegetation and widely established alien herbaceous plants and trees in
northwest Europe. Over 1,000 of these are illustrated. All except marine plants are
in color. Excluded are grasses, sedges, rushes, ferns, some plants on the periphery of
the area in the west of Finland, and alpine plants descending down-river in the
neighborhood of Munich. In one of the appendixes, a section on ecology describes
plants typical to various soils by the amount of moisture available. A map at the
beginning of the book indicates the locations of the types of soils found in this area
of Europe. The nations within the scope of this book are Britain (including the Isle
of Man and the Channel Islands), Ireland, France, Belgium, Luxemburg, Germany
(including the Faroes), the Netherlands, Denmark, Norway, Sweden, and Iceland.
There is an appendix on plant photography. The authors urge their readers not to
pick specimens but to rely on photography, in order to protect not only the
endangered species but all plants. Other appendixes deal with additional species,
introduced shrubs, aggregates, further reading, and British botanical societies.

This is a well-planned, carefully made, unique, and useful field guide. The
book's color illustrations are also a testimony to the printer's art. —Amity Doering.
[R: Choice, Sept 75, p. 816; LJ, 15 Apr 75, p. 745; ARBA 76, item 1389]

694. Hutchinson, John. **The Families of Flowering Plants Arranged According to a New System Based on Their Probable Phylogeny.** 3rd ed. New York, Oxford University Press, 1973. 968p. illus. index. $62.50.

This is a great and scholarly work, the result of a long lifetime of study by one of the most outstanding botanists of the twentieth century. In 1926 Dr. Hutchinson, of the Royal Botanic Gardens, Kew, England, published the first volume of the first edition, which was followed in 1934 by the second volume. In 1959 appeared the second edition. The 1973 edition does not depart drastically from the evolutionary sequences presented in the previous ones. The change in the position of the family *Lythraceae* is the most notable change. New features include 67 drawings as well as notes on the chief orders, additional keys, and miscellaneous notes. In addition, for the first time, the parts dealing with the Dicotyledones and the Monocotyledones are contained in one volume.

At the time of Dr. Hutchinson's death the third edition was in page proof. The proofs were checked and minor corrections and emendations were made by Dr. William T. Stearn of the British Museum and by Dr. Bernard Verdcourt of the Royal Botanic Gardens, Kew. Botanical science does not stand still, as is well illustrated by the number of plant classification systems proposed both before and after Linnaeus. Two of the best known of these are those of Bentham and Hooker (1862-1883) and Engler and Prantl (1887-1898). One cannot expect everyone to agree with all of Dr. Hutchinson's views, but no botanical library should be without this outstanding contribution. —Elizabeth C. Hall. [R: ARBA 75, item 1477]

695. Klimas, John E., and James A. Cunningham. **Wildflowers of Eastern America.** New York, Knopf, 1974. 273p. illus.(col.). bibliog. index. $17.95. LC 74-942. ISBN 0-394-49362-1.

696. Orr, Robert T., and Margaret C. Orr. **Wildflowers of Western America.** New York, Knopf, 1974. 270p. illus.(col.). bibliog. index. $17.95. LC 74-943. ISBN 0-394-49363-X.

The logical approach to assessing these two works is to treat them as a set, and we would recommend that library catalogers consider entering them under a title entry: Wildflowers of America: vol. 1, Eastern America; vol. 2, Western America.

The volumes, identical in pattern, are descriptive guides based on a special identification system similar to that developed by the Royal Horticultural Society, whereby flowers are keyed by a symbol representing a color grouping. In this case, the color groupings for flowers are: white-green; yellow-orange; red-pink; blue-violet; and brown. Each is represented by a special symbol. The text is set out by color groupings identified by running titles at the head of the page; the plant descriptions are arranged numerically by plate numbers. The plates, in turn, are also keyed by the color-grouping symbols repeated as running heads; further sub-division is provided by season (for Eastern America) or by locale (for Western America).

The volume for Eastern America contains an introductory chapter that is equally applicable to the Western American volume. It discusses the definition of wildflowers, when and where to look for them, the source for common names, and folklore and uses. A "how to use this book" explanation appears in both volumes.

Both volumes then have identical pictorial representations for identification of flower parts and leaves, and a duplicated glossary.

The texts are arranged non-alphabetically by the most widely used common name. For each flower is given its proper name, its family, a botanical description, and a paragraph of general information. Each color grouping begins with a simplified key relating the plants to the drawings of flower parts and leaves, to their season (for Eastern America) or to their habitat (for Western America). The key is followed by the superb color photographs, 304 for Eastern America and 291 for Western America.

Each volume then has a section describing the plant families included and a useful and informative chapter of wildflower recipes. The volume for Eastern America, in addition, has a section giving edible parts of plants and a separate listing of poisonous and potentially poisonous plants, the lack of which in the Western America volume leads one to believe either that Western America wildflowers won't harm you if you ingest them, or that no one would eat them anyway. Both volumes have short select bibliographies and dual indexes of both common and proper names.

Other than the fact that either volume is perhaps a little heavy to pack for a hike through the woods, they are both extremely useful and easy to use. The organization of the books makes it quite easy to identify any particular wildflower. One imagines that the pair shall remain the standard work on United States wildflowers for some time to come. —David St. C. Skene-Melvin and Ann Skene-Melvin. [R: ALA 74; ARBA 75, items 1478-1479]

697. Polunin, Oleg. **Flowers of Europe: A Field Guide**. New York, Oxford University Press, 1969. 662p. illus. 192 plates; map. bibliog. $15.00. LC 70-410049. ISBN 0-19-217621-8.

Describes 2,600 common wild flowers in Europe. Arrangement is by families and entries provide adequate identification with information on habitat and uses. Some 1,000 plants are illustrated by color photographs in appendix. Includes also a glossary and lists of common French, German and Italian names of well known species. A more comprehensive work for the United States is Rickett's *Wildflowers of the United States* (McGraw-Hill, 1966-75). [R: WLB, Nov 69; SR, 6 Dec 69; Choice, Dec 69; ARBA 70, v.2, p. 121]

698. Rickett, Harold William. **Wildflowers of the United States**. New York, McGraw-Hill, 1966-75. 6v.plus index. illus. index. $69.50/v.(v.1, 2, 5); $47.50(v.3); $72.00(v.4); $74.50(v.6); $32.50(index). LC 66-17920. ISBN 0-07-052614-1(v.1); 0-07-052630-3(v.2); 0-07-052633-8(v.3); 0-07-052636-2(v.4); 0-07-052640-0(v.5); 0-07-052643-5(v.6); 0-07-052647-8(index).

Published for the New York Botanical Garden, these volumes provide the most comprehensive treatment of the subject available. The first six volumes are: Volume 1, The Northeastern States; Volume 2, The Southeastern States; Volume 3, Texas; Volume 4, The Southwestern States; Volume 5, The Northwestern States; and Volume 6, The Central Mountains and Plains. An index volume, which lists both the common and botanical names for each flower, concludes the set. Each of the first six volumes is arranged in broad categories and subdivided according to genus and species. A wealth of detailed yet comprehensible information about flowers and their habitats is offered. Botanical terms are explained and both Latin and common names are listed. Illustrations include many line drawings and thousands of strikingly beautiful color photographs, many showing the flowers in their natural habitats. [R: SR, 6 Dec 69; ARBA 70; ARBA 74, item 1519]

TREES

699. Bean, W. J. **Trees and Shrubs Hardy in the British Isles.** 8th ed. fully rev. George Taylor, general ed. London, John Murray, 1970; distr. New York, Scribner's, 1974. 2v. illus. index. $25.00/v. ISBN 0-7195-1790-7.

First published 60 years ago, this monumental work is in the truest sense a classic, indispensable to every serious student of temperate-region trees and shrubs. Among the several outstanding dendrologists Great Britain has produced, none outshines—and probably none equals—William Jackson Bean. From 1883 until his death in 1947 he was employed at the Royal Botanic Gardens, Kew, for many years as curator in charge of all living plants, and before that in charge of the Arboretum. Bean lived at Kew; he knew intimately every tree and shrub of the vast collection there. His Kew experience was fortified by his many travels and by the unexcelled opportunity he enjoyed of corresponding with and meeting others who shared his interests. Bean's is a facile pen. His writings are not rehashes of the writings of others, nor are they merely skeletons of botanical terminology, lacking the flesh of simple descriptive English. Every description breathes of his intimate knowledge of the plant of which he writes, but his facts have been carefully checked against library and herbarium records. He writes clearly and succinctly, so that even non-experts can understand.

These two new volumes—the first two of the most welcome eighth edition—well reflect the capabilities of the team that for the past decade has been engaged in bringing Bean's work up to date. It is a tribute to their integrity that they have succeeded in adding descriptions of new plants, updating certain information about others, and most importantly, bringing nomenclature into line with modern botanical thinking. To have done less would have failed their purpose, to have done more would have been as disastrous as for a modern artist to over-paint a Gainsborough or a Titian. But they have given us Bean as Bean was—unchanged in character or spirit, but reflecting changes necessitated by the passing years. No better horticultural book has ever been revised. —Elizabeth C. Hall. [R: ARBA 75, item 1490]

700. Johnson, Hugh. **The International Book of Trees: A Guide and Tribute to the Trees of Our Forests and Gardens.** London, Mitchell Beazley, Ltd.; distr. New York, Simon and Schuster, 1973. 288p. illus.(part col.). index. $29.95. LC 73-3974. ISBN 0-671-21607-4.

According to the publisher, *The International Book of Trees* is the first fully illustrated book to include all the major garden and forest trees of the temperate world. Mr. Johnson, a freelance writer, is also author of *The World Atlas of Wine*.

The present compendium is not a reference book in the strict sense of the word, but rather a collection of essays. The first section contains 29 articles on general subjects such as the history of trees, how to maintain them, etc., copiously illustrated with color photographs and graphic material. The second and third sections are reserved for articles on conifers (26 articles) and broadleaf trees (56 articles). The book concludes with the "Reference Section and Index," which consists of a number of brief articles on such topics as tree pests and diseases, rates of tree growth, etc., along with a glossary of Latin and Greek terms.

Many reference books on this subject are already available, including specialized works limited to a particular region or to particular types of trees. Johnson's compendium is very readable and beautifully illustrated. It will appeal to the layman as a general orientation guide. For more in-depth information, however, the reader will have to look elsewhere. [R: ALA 74; ARBA 75, item 1491]

MOSSES AND FUNGI

701. Miller, Orson K., Jr. **Mushrooms of North America**. New York, Dutton, 1972. 360p. illus.(col.). index. (A Chanticleer Press Edition). $19.95. LC 72-82162. ISBN 0-525-16156-1.

Miller, following in the footsteps of Alexander H. Smith, has produced a comprehensive field guide to mushrooms of North America. Its aim is to satisfy the needs not only of amateur mycologists but of students of biology. In all, 680 species are included; however, detailed descriptions are given for 422. Pictorial keys, 72 in number, are provided to simplify identification. The introductory section contains some general instructions on collecting and studying mushrooms, information on names, characteristics, fruiting of mushrooms, and mushroom toxins.

The numbered detailed descriptions are arranged under five groups. For each species in the group, an entry gives the Latin name, abbreviations for names of individuals as discoverers, edibility and frequency of occurrence, and basic physical description. This description covers cap size in millimeters, shape and appearance, gills, length of stalk, spore size, color in Melzer's solution and color of spore print, distribution, and species that are related or that have a similar appearance. At the end are color plates keyed to each of the 422 entries, a small collection of recipes, glossaries, a bibliography, and an index. At the outset is a handy picture key to aid in identifying major groups.

The guide covers more species than A. H. Smith's *The Mushroom Hunter's Field Guide* (rev. and enl. ed.; University of Michigan Press, 1963), and it is more detailed in its scientific description. However, it would take a dedicated mushroom hunter indeed to carry this heavy tome on a trip; its main use will lie in identifying specimens at home or in the classroom. The color plates are clear and sharp. [R: WLB, Jan 73, p. 448; ALA 72; ARBA 74, item 1522]

702. Mycological Society of America. Mycological Guidebook Committee. **Mycology Guidebook**. Ed. by Russell B. Stevens. Seattle, University of Washington Press, 1974. 703p. illus. bibliog. index. $15.00. LC 73-17079. ISBN 0-295-95313-6.

This definitive and indispensable manual, the combined work of a host of eminent mycologists, is intended for those who teach introductory mycology. Part I covers field observations of fungi and discusses techniques of collecting and preserving; Part II deals with the taxonomic groups; Part III covers the ecological aspects; Part IV, entitled "Fungi as Biological Tools," surveys fungus physiology and genetics. Most useful is the information offered in the appendixes, such as the quarantine and shipment of biological materials, culture collections, stains, reagents, media, and films and film loops. As stated in the preface, "the key objective . . . is not drastically to alter mycology courses but to provide resources whereby instructors may substantially improve them." —Elizabeth C. Hall. [R: Choice, Sept 74, p. 972; ARBA 75, item 1488]

703. Snell, Walter H., and Esther A. Dick. **A Glossary of Mycology**. Rev. ed. Cambridge, Mass., Harvard University Press, 1971. 181p. illus. bibliog. $8.50. LC 77-134946. ISBN 0-674-35451-6.

First published in 1936 under the title *Three Thousand Mycological Terms*. This is a completely revised edition, with some 7,000 terms defined. It will supplement Ainsworth and Bisby's *Dictionary of Fungi* (5th ed., 1963). [R: Choice, Sept 71, p. 813; ARBA 72, item 1517]

GRASSES

704. Hitchcock, A. S. **Manual of the Grasses of the United States**. 2nd ed. rev. by Agnes Chase. Washington, GPO, 1950; repr. New York, Dover, 1971. 2v. illus. index. $6.00pa.(v.1); $4.00pa.(v.2). LC 70-142876. ISBN 0-486-22717-0(v.1); 0-486-22718-9(v.2).

A welcome reprint is this second revised edition of a monumental work on the native and introduced grasses of the United States (published by the U.S. Government Printing Office in 1950 as U.S.D.A. Misc. Publ. No. 200). The first edition was published in 1935. Professor Hitchcock was the Chief Botanist in charge of systematic agrostology for the U.S. Department of Agriculture, and Agnes Chase was Research Associate, U.S. National Museum, Smithsonian Institution—both recognized authorities on the enormous and vastly important group of plants, the grasses. This unabridged republication includes 1,199 line drawings, identification keys, comprehensive descriptions of each species and variety (with scientific and vernacular names), range of distribution, the common uses, and over 200 pages devoted to synonymy—names of grasses that have previously appeared in botanical literature. This definitive work is invaluable to both the amateur and the professional botanist. —Elizabeth C. Hall. [R: ARBA 72, item 1532]

CHAPTER 35

ZOOLOGY

ENCYCLOPEDIAS

705. Burton, Maurice, and Robert Burton, eds. **The International Wildlife Encyclopedia.** New York, Marshall Cavendish Corp.; distr. New York, Purnell Library Service, 1969-1970. 20v. illus. index. $179.50. lib. binding. LC 78-98713.

Published simultaneously in England and the United States, this 20-volume encyclopedia aims to cover all animal life throughout the world. Each 8½" by 12" volume contains about 140 pages (the set is continuously paged). All volumes are lavishly illustrated with many full-page color photos, smaller photos, drawings, and distribution maps—a total of some 2,500 illustrations. The text, in three-column arrangement, is clearly printed and well edited. Entries are specific—e.g., amoeba, anchovy, badger, pack rat. Two indexes are contained in Volume 20—an animal index and a systematic index. The animal index is especially important for locating, as an example, the names of all bees that are included. Entries range in length from one page to four or five pages. Each article includes information on the geographic distribution (a small map is provided for many of the animals). At the end of each article the scientific classification according to class, order, family, genus and species is printed in bold face. Articles are broken down under such rubrics as breeding, conservation, feeding habits, habitat, enemies and defense, life cycles, and distribution.

The text is highly informative but at the same time makes enjoyable reading. The photographs, a delight to the eye, reveal a good amount of additional information about the animals. A close-up shot of a bearded lizard eating a stag beetle is nearly like being present at the meal. If small animals are shown larger than life size, the photograph is accompanied by a scale in millimeters and inches or by an indication of the number of times the subject is enlarged. A few photographs of ultra-tiny details, such as the teeth on an abalone's radula, were obtained by using a deep field scanning electron microscope (SEM). Most of the pictures show the animal, close up, in his natural habitat, which adds to the educational value of the work.

The International Wildlife Encyclopedia is quite similar to *The Illustrated Encyclopedia of the Animal Kingdom* (Danbury Press, 1970). The latter is arranged by animal groups and has a simpler, less detailed text. The index in the former work, however, is better, and the illustrations are all as good as those in the *Illustrated Encyclopedia*—perhaps even somewhat better. While specialists will prefer a work such as *Grzimek's Animal Life Encyclopedia* (Van Nostrand Reinhold) for its more thorough treatment, *The International Wildlife Encyclopedia* is a good choice for general readers and certainly will be a valuable reference source in schools. —Christine L. Wynar. [R: ARBA 73, item 1458]

706. **Grzimek's Animal Life Encyclopedia**. Bernhard Grzimek, editor-in-chief. New York, Van Nostrand Reinhold, 1972-75. 13v. illus.(part col.). index. $29.95/v.; $325.00/set. LC 79-183178. ISBN 0-442-22944-5(v.1); 0-442-22942-9(v.2); 0-442-22943-7(v.3); 0-442-22933-4(v.4); 0-442-22938-0(v.5); 0-442-22939-9(v.6); 0-442-22934-8(v.7); 0-442-22935-6(v.8); 0-442-22936-4(v.9); 0-442-22930-5(v.10); 0-442-22931-3(v.11); 0-442-22932-1(v.12); 0-442-22938-0(v.13).

Originally published in Germany in 1967, this encyclopedia has now been published in an English edition. The 13 volumes include: Volume 1, Lower Animals; Volume 2, Insects; Volume 3, Mollusks and Echinoderms; Volume 4, Fishes 1; Volume 5, Fishes 2 and Amphibians; Volume 6, Reptiles; Volume 7, Birds 1; Volume 8, Birds 2; Volume 9, Birds 3; Volume 10; Mammals 1; Volume 11, Mammals 2; Volume 12, Mammals 3; Volume 13, Mammals 4. Volume 1 contains two introductory chapters for the whole set, summarizing basic concepts of zoology.

Articles were prepared by nearly 100 international authorities in various specialties, and a list of these contributors to the series is at the beginning of each volume. Material in each volume is arranged by animal orders and families. The text discusses the evolution of each group of animals and indicates physical description, range and habitat, feeding and mating habits, and other behavioral characteristics. Articles vary in length from less than a page to a full chapter. The writing is highly descriptive and detailed, presenting a large amount of information in concise form. As is almost inevitable in works of multiple authorship, there are occasional repetitions, conflicting interpretations, and differences in approach (e.g., a few contributors tend to focus on European or North American representatives of the group of animals being described, while others have no geographic emphasis). Overall, the accounts are accurate, up to date, and accessible to the non-specialist.

Illustrations consist of line drawings and color plates (both photos and paintings). The effectiveness of the latter is occasionally diminished by poor placement and reproduction from dirty or poor plates. At the end of each volume is a systematic classification index to the volume, showing page numbers as well as references to color plates. There is also a detailed index that includes common and scientific names. An additional feature is a four-way animal dictionary in English, German, French, and Russian. A common name can be located in any of the languages and the corresponding word is provided in each of the other three languages. A short selective bibliography of English and German titles is appended. [R: LJ, July 72, p. 2375; Choice, June 75, p. 512; ALA 72; ARBA 73, item 1459; ARBA 75, item 1523; ARBA 76, items 1403-1407]

707. **The Illustrated Encyclopedia of the Animal Kingdom**. 2nd English ed. New York, Danbury Press (Grolier), 1972. 20v. illus.(most col.). maps. charts. index. $99.50. LC 71-141898. ISBN 0-7172-8100-0.

This major reference set was first published by Fabbri of Milan in 1968 as *Gli animali e il loro mondo*, edited by Antonio Valle; the first English-language edition under the current title was published by Danbury in 1971 under the editorial direction of Percy Knauth. This revised second edition has been edited by Herbert Kondo and Jenny E. Tesar, with the advice of a group of outside consultants. The pictorial matter, which constitutes about 60 percent of the total content, has remained essentially the same in all three editions, but the text has undergone extensive rewriting.

The coverage is the entire animal kingdom from the amoeba to man, but, as is typical of comprehensive zoological works for the non-specialist, there is a pronounced emphasis on the larger, more colorful forms. This is easily demonstrated by the contents: Vol. 1, General introduction to vertebrates; Vols. 2-6, Mammals; Vols. 7-8, Birds; Vols. 9-10, Reptiles and amphibians; Vol. 11, Fishes; Vols. 12-13, Arthropods other than insects; Vols. 14-16, Insects; Vol. 17, Mollusks; Vols. 18-19, Other invertebrates; Vol. 20, Endangered species and the general index. This distribution bears no relationship to absolute numbers of species or individuals in the various phyla, but it does quite accurately reflect economic importance and predictable reader interest, if not exactly vindicating the claim in the advertising matter that this work is "a complete library of all the animals . . . in the world." Some imbalances of treatment within groups are also apparent—e.g., about one and three-fourths volumes of the five devoted to mammals are given over to the carnivores, while the far more abundant (both in species and in individuals) rodents rate only about half a volume. Similarly, the sharks are given a more extended and detailed treatment, at the expense of some other orders of fishes, than their actual importance would seem to warrant. Both examples doubtless reflect the peculiar fascination that large dangerous creatures have for the average man, a phenomenon that may be readily observed at any zoo.

The illustrations, mostly photographs but including some paintings and drawings, are almost without exception outstanding, and the printing is of very good quality. Certainly it is the illustrations that are the work's greatest asset; they will answer many reference questions, but at the same time they provide a temptation to mutilation that librarians should be aware of.

The concise text covers the morphology, behavior, and distribution of the animals treated, without extensive detail or use of difficult terminology. The first edition's over-pedantic style alternated with occasional cuteness and anthropomorphism; that edition included long meaningless lists of names of species without descriptions. Moreover, in at least some volumes of the first edition, an inexcusably high percentage of the picture captions contained misidentifications, some so far wrong as to be ludicrous. The second edition has a much more readable and straightforward style, useless lists have been omitted, and the erroneous captions have been corrected. While some taxonomic interpretations presented are not universally accepted, overall the work is accurate and up to date. Both the substantive and the stylistic changes are so extensive—and were so urgently needed— that they provide ample explanation for the appearance of this second edition only one year after the publication of the first.

Each volume is indexed separately, and the whole work is covered by the general index in the final volume. The indexes are another area in which this edition has been significantly improved from the first edition, both in being more analytic in content, and in having a more useful physical format. A serious weakness which has not been corrected in this edition is the total lack of bibliographic references that would lead the interested reader to more specialized treatises.

The page design is pleasing, and the printing is clear and acceptably free from typographical errors. The binding is sturdy enough for library use, and the attractive pictorial covers will draw the attention of prospective users.

The work is not too difficult for better students in the upper elementary grades, nor too simple for the college undergraduate or the general adult reader without a background in biology. —Paul B. Cors. [R: ARBA 73, item 1461]

HANDBOOKS

708. Gosner, Kenneth L. **Guide to Identification of Marine and Estuarine Invertebrates, Cape Hatteras to the Bay of Fundy.** New York, Wiley-Interscience, 1971. 693p. illus. bibliog. index. $29.95. LC 70-149971. ISBN 0-471-31897-3.

The title accurately defines the scope of the work: it consists of a series of illustrated keys, arranged in systematic order, to all species of invertebrates recorded from the shore and shallow sea along the northeastern coast of the United States. Introductory chapters briefly discuss the physical and biotic environment of the region and some basic techniques of handling invertebrate specimens; there are also short descriptions of the general characteristics of all major taxonomic groups included. The author has consulted numerous specialists (listed in the acknowledgments in preparing the text. To cover so much material in a single volume, the work is necessarily terse in style and highly technical in language. References are appended to the end of each chapter. General and systematic indexes are included. Main users of this guide will be the graduate student and the professional zoologist, but it is not beyond the comprehension of the undergraduate or the serious amateur. The extensive bibliographies are of considerable reference value in their own right. —Paul B. Cors. [R: LJ, 15 Apr 72, p. 1388; ALA 71; ARBA 73, item 1463]

ATLASES

709. Jarman, Cathy. **Atlas of Animal Migration.** New York, John Day, 1972. 124p. illus.(col.). index. $10.00. LC 72-1748. ISBN 0-381-98129-0.

710. Nayman, Jacqueline. **Atlas of Wildlife.** New York, John Day, 1972. 124p. illus.(col.). index. $10.00. LC 78-38034. ISBN 0-381-98162-2.

These companion volumes are very similar in scope and format. Each is a handsomely illustrated introduction to its subject, written for the adult layman seeking a basic knowledge of the topic, but useful also with at least the better student from the middle school level up. The use of the term "atlas" is perhaps a bit misleading. While each book contains numerous good maps as part of the illustrative matter, neither is primarily a collection of maps; rather, maps, paintings and text are complementary. Both have good indexes but lack bibliographies.

Atlas of Wildlife begins with a short chapter covering zoogeography in general, particularly in relation to the concept of continental drift. This is followed by chapters on the seven major regions (Palaearctic and Nearctic are here regarded as distinct, and Antarctica is also treated separately). A concluding chapter considers island faunas. Appended is a world map locating major wildlife parks and refuges.

Atlas of Animal Migration also begins with a chapter summarizing current thought on its topic, discussing the reasons for and mechanisms of migration and animal navigation; it then considers the principal migratory groups individually. Both true migration (i.e., cyclic movements between areas over regular routes, such as those of typical migratory birds) and emigration (i.e., sporadic unidirectional mass movements like those of locust swarms) are included, though the emphasis is on the former, as it should be. Two final maps locate migratory bird refuges in the United States and bird migration watchpoints in Europe. –Paul B. Cors. [R: RSR, Jan/Mar 73, p. 17; ARBA 74, items 1530 and 1531]

BIRDS

711. Campbell, Bruce. **The Dictionary of Birds in Color.** American consultant editor, Richard T. Holmes. New York, Viking Press, 1974. 352p. illus.(col.). (A Studio Book). $22.50. LC 73-17954. ISBN 0-670-27225-6.

An authoritative author and compiler and a topic of major interest to thousands of individuals occasionally come into happy conjunction and produce an excellent reference book: *The Dictionary of Birds in Color* is such a volume. This is a scholarly, comprehensive text that deals with more than a thousand different species distributed in six main geographical regions of the world: the Palaearctic, the Nearctic, the Oriental, the Australasian, the Ethiopian, and the Neotropical. The author provides a general introduction, which describes the six faunal regions, origins and species, bird anatomy, and classification; this last section includes an annotated sequence of orders and families developed first by Sir Landsborough Thomson and used widely by J. L. Peters and his successors. Each entry in ʻʼ is section briefly notes the relationship of orders and families, gives key physical characteristics, and cites examples. This section also includes a few line drawings that illustrate some of the exemplary species.

The bulk of the volume consists of an alphabetical dictionary arranged by the scientific general bird names—printed in boldface type. Entries, which average 150 to 200 words, include the common English name, approximate length in inches, and the zoogeographical region where the species breeds. The descriptive entry also notes breeding and wintering distribution and breeding habitat, gives colors of adults of both sexes, briefly comments on habits and behavior (including displays, voice, and principal foods), and usually cites each breeding season and details of nest, eggs, incubation, and fledglings. Complementing this section (and preceding it in physical placement) is a unique collection of color photographs. Although some artificial light was occasionally used in order to gain the needed clarity, the plumage of each bird is represented with considerable accuracy due to the excellent printing and processing used by the publishers. Access to these photographs is gained through the dictionary section, where each entry has a reference, also in boldface type, to the accompanying illustration. Each plate notes the scientific name.

For the average user, numerous cross references from the common names to the correct scientific terminology are provided in the dictionary section. No special index is needed because of this extensive cross referencing, but a brief glossary and some abbreviations and notes are included in the opening pages of the volume. British spelling is used throughout.

The volume is well bound and the excellent paper, typography, and design give it overall quality. It makes it "possible for ornithologists and bird lovers alike to study the detailed beauty of nearly every living [bird] family in its natural surroundings in full-colour photographic close-ups." —Laurel Grotzinger. [R: BL, 15 Apr 75, pp. 871-72; Choice, May 75, pp. 367-68; WLB, Mar 75, p. 529; ARBA 76, item 1416]

712. Clements, James F. **Birds of the World: A Check List.** New York, Two Continents, 1973. 522p. illus. maps. bibliog. index. $15.00. LC 73-22744. ISBN 0-8467-0032-8.

At last the long need for a simple, complete list of the world's bird species has been fulfilled, by three books! In addition to Clements, there are similar listings by Ernest P. Edwards, *A Coded List of Birds of the World* (1974; available from the author, Sweet Briar, Va. 24595) and Edward S. Gruson, *Checklist of the World's Birds* (Quadrangle, 1974; not seen by the reviewer). These books should all be of great use to taxonomists, museum curators, and the many bird watchers who keep world lists of birds they have seen.

Clements has the advantage over Edwards of having considerable space between species for penciling in notes, undoubtedly one of the heaviest uses these three books will enjoy. It also gives more complete range descriptions, often naming all the countries each bird occurs in, rather than just having alphabetical symbols for the large faunal areas of the world, as Edwards does. Edwards lists 8,908 species, Clements 8,904, a remarkably close total considering the widespread disagreements that exist among bird classifiers. Both books could profit from more complete indexes. Unless one has a more than superficial familiarity with accepted phylogenetic ordering and nomenclature of birds, just having an index to genus names and English names for orders and families is not sufficient. Edwards has a system of alphanumeric codes that may find much use among scientists who plan to use computers for storing ornithological information. Edwards also plans to issue revised editions.

Taxonomic specialists will no doubt find many faults with both books, even as they do with each other, but this is to be expected in a field that is unavoidably subjective, judgmental, and open to individual interpretation. The publication for the first time of a simple world list of all birds is long overdue and most welcome. This reviewer prefers Clements because of its more attractive format, the space it provides for writing, and its more detailed information on bird distribution. —Henry T. Armistead. [R: ARBA 75, item 1502]

713. Peterson, Roger Tory, Guy Mountfort, and P. A. D. Hollom. **A Field Guide to the Birds of Britain and Europe.** New rev. ed. In collaboration with I. J. Ferguson-Lees and D. I. M. Wallace. Boston, Houghton Mifflin, 1974. 344p. illus.(part col.). index. (The Peterson Field Guide Series). $10.00.

Since the first edition of this title appeared in 1954, it has become the most popular handbook for the field identification of European birds, both in English and in translation into a dozen other languages. This revision (called the third edition everywhere except the title page) is not a complete rewriting of the second edition (1965), but it shows numerous small changes throughout. The geographic area covered (the British Isles, Iceland, the Faeroes, Continental Europe east to 30° longitude, and the islands of the Mediterranean except Cyprus) is unaltered, and the sequence of families and species remains that of 1965, despite some changes recommended in the current taxonomic literature. There have been some changes in nomenclature, both common and scientific, and many changes in distribution data—over half the range maps have been redrawn, several species have been changed from accidental to regular status, and a few questionable occurrences have been dropped. Two more color plates have been added (covering those species that have been moved from accidental to regular status), the list of accidentals has been substantially expanded, and the index has been redone; the selective bibliography has been omitted. This work remains a basic reference, although it is no longer alone in its subject area; the third edition has been sufficiently updated to justify its acquisition to replace the earlier versions. —Paul B. Cors. [R: ARBA 76, item 1429]

FISHES

714. Wheeler, Alwyne. **Fishes of the World: An Illustrated Dictionary**. New York, Macmillan, 1975. 366p. illus.(part col.). $27.50. LC 75-6972. ISBN 0-02-626180-4.

Alwyne Wheeler, a noted British marine biologist and consultant to Unesco, has succeeded in preparing an excellent dictionary on fishes. This illustrated work contains 500 color photographs, 700 line drawings, and descriptions of over 2,000 species of fish.

In addition, the introduction presents a brief and pertinent analysis of the various categories of fish, thus providing the user, and especially the layman, with a general overview of living fishes found in the waters of the earth. A glossary of terms adds to the usefulness of this dictionary.

The 500 color plates, which are grouped in a special section, are arranged in a systematic order by families, so that closely related groups are brought together. Within each family group the plates are arranged alphabetically.

The dictionary section also utilizes an alphabetical arrangement. Separate entries for families are also included and are cross-referenced to the genera.

Each fish species is under its scientific name, although vernacular names are also given and cross-indexed. Entries provide information on geographical range, size, habitat, commercial use, biological data, and behavior patterns. The dictionary is of value not only to the professional but also to the amateur ichthyologist. —Anna T. Wynar. [R: ARBA 76, item 1437]

INSECTS

715. Borror, Donald J., and Richard E. White. **A Field Guide to the Insects of America North of Mexico**. Boston, Houghton Mifflin, 1970. 404p. glossary. bibliog. index. illus.(part col.). (The Peterson Field Guide Series, No. 19). $5.95. LC 70-80420.

Here is another member of the excellent, pocket-sized Peterson Field Guide Series, sponsored by the National Audubon Society and National Wildlife

Federation. An identification guide written primarily for the layman naturalist, it includes, in addition to detailed specific descriptions, basic information on the structure, habits, and importance of 579 insect families and brief notes on other arthropods such as millipedes, centipedes, spiders, mites, and ticks. The more than 1,300 drawings, of which 142 are in color, are of high quality and accurately depict, as to scale and detail, the important members of North American insect families; these include dragonflies, grasshoppers, crickets, cockroaches, bugs, aphids, beetles, bees, flies, moths, and butterflies. Most helpful are the introductory chapters on collecting, mounting, and preserving insects, on keeping insects in captivity, and on the screen projection of living insects. This authoritative and attractive field guide should serve to stimulate entomological interest among both adults and youngsters. —Elizabeth C. Hall. [R: Choice, July-Aug 70, p. 699; ALA 70; ARBA 71, item 1629]

716. Linsenmaier, Walter. **Insects of the World**. Tr. from the German by Leigh E. Chadwick. New York, McGraw-Hill, 1972. 392p. illus.(col.). index. $25.00. LC 78-178047. ISBN 0-07-037953-X.

Linsemaier is first a painter, then an entomologist, so it is not surprising that the 160 color plates are this book's most striking feature; many of them, both in rendering and in reproduction, rank among the finest colored illustrations of insects ever published. However, this is no mere picture book for the dilettante, since the extensive and accurate text provides an excellent conspectus of the huge and complex class Insecta, useful both to the professional zoologist and to the serious amateur naturalist. Following a general introduction on insect biology, the various orders are taken up in detail, with salient points illustrated both by the color plates and by numerous black and white drawings within the text. The arrangement is systematic, except that social insects and aquatic insects are each treated in separate chapters. The emphasis is on the insect as a living organism; economic and medical aspects of entomology are not overlooked, but they are not emphasized. There is a slight bias toward the two orders that contain the greatest number of strikingly beautiful species—Coleoptera and Lepidoptera—but not to the point of imbalance. Two minor weaknesses must be noted: the separation of the captions from the plates to which they refer is awkward, and the indexing could be somewhat fuller. —Paul B. Cors. [R: LJ, 1 Mar 73, p. 755; ALA 73; ARBA 74, item 1560]

717. Swan, Lester A., and Charles S. Papp. **The Common Insects of North America**. New York, Harper and Row, 1972. 750p. illus.(part col.). bibliog. index. $17.50. LC 75-138765. ISBN 0-06-014181-6.

This introduction to the insects of the continental United States and Canada is written for the reader with some background in general biology but no previous special knowledge of the subject. While technical terminology is necessarily used, the terms are carefully defined and the amateur naturalist should have no difficulty understanding the concepts presented. A brief general section on insect biology is followed by concise accurate accounts of about 2,400 species (most illustrated by a black and white drawing; eight illustrated by a color painting). The emphasis is is noticeably on species of economic importance, both harmful and beneficial. Appendixes include charts of insects arranged by geological periods, orders, and families. There is an adequate glossary and an extensive bibliography, and there are good indexes to common and scientific names and to subjects. One slightly questionable practice is the providing of common names for all species, some of which are coinages (e.g., "guttate scymnus") of little use, but this is a minor weakness.

The only similar work, Donald Borror and Richard White's *A Field Guide to the Insects of America North of Mexico* (Houghton Mifflin, 1970), is a guide for identification of families, with few individual species described; the two titles complement rather than duplicate each other. A most useful introduction to a complex subject. —Paul B. Cors. [R: ALA 72; ARBA 73, item 1476]

718. Watson, Allan, and Paul E. S. Whalley. **The Dictionary of Butterflies and Moths in Color.** New York, McGraw-Hill, 1975. 296p. illus.(col.). bibliog. $39.95. LC 74-30433. ISBN 0-07-068490-1.

This excellent book contains 405 color photographs. "In this book we have illustrated examples of nearly every currently accepted family of the insect group Lepidoptera . . ." (p. vi). The quality of the photographs is good. Many of them illustrate specimens, some with 20, 25, or more species. Others show wild, live examples of one species only.

The dictionary section of the book (pp. 147-296) is an alphabetical arrangement with some 2,000 entries listing genera and families. Within these two groups selected species are also described, stressing unusual ones and/or those illustrated in the photo plates. These are conveniently referenced to the plate number if illustrated. The bibliography is good, and there is a helpful glossary also. Both authors are associated with the Department of Lepidoptera of the British Museum. which has the biggest collection of these insects in the world. —Henry T. Armistead. [R: ARBA 76, item 1442]

MAMMALS

719. Dorst, Jean. **A Field Guide to the Larger Mammals of Africa.** Boston, Houghton Mifflin, 1970. 287p. illus.(part col.). maps. bibliog. index. $8.50. LC 72-120835.

Though not one of Houghton's Peterson Field Guides, this work follows the format of that excellent series. For each species, a concise description emphasizes identifying characteristics of physical appearance, habitat, and behavior. There is also a range map for each, and a colored painting (by Pierre Dandelot) with field marks pointed out. For hard-to-separate species, a list of similar species is given, and distinguishing features are carefully indicated. The geographical area covered is mainland Africa south of the tropic of Cancer. Only those species that can be readily identified in the field are included, emphasizing game animals, carnivores, and primates; most rodents and insectivores are excluded, as are all bats and marine mammals except the dugong. The author is frank to admit that the exact distribution of many species is still speculative, and that no attempt has been made to unravel the systematic tangles of some groups (especially mongooses and small antelopes). Common names for most species are given in French and German and, where appropriate, Afrikaans and Swahili. For its purpose, "identification of mammals in the wild," this work has no competitor. —Paul B. Cors. [R: ALA 70; ARBA 71, item 1632]

720. Mochi, Ugo, and T. Donald Carter. **Hoofed Mammals of the World**. new ed. New York, Scribner's, 1971. 268p. illus. bibliog. index. $9.95. LC 75-169790. ISBN 0-648-12382-7.

When this book was first published in 1953, its combination of scientific informativeness, in Carter's precise, accurate text, and artistic excellence, in Mochi's superb illustrations, made it an immediate success, and it has long been a choice collector's item. It is now back in print, and remains an outstanding work; it is still the only good general handbook of the ungulates in English, covering all living species, many subspecies, and a few recently extinct forms; and Mochi's illustrations still arouse the greatest admiration—nominally silhouettes, each being knife-cut from a single piece of black paper, they are astonishingly detailed, three-dimensional and lifelike. The principal change in this edition is in format: the awkward folio size of the original has become a more convenient standard octavo, with the illustrations dispersed in the text rather than on separate plates. Textual revision consists of a new introduction, updating of African and Asian geographical names, and changes in the nomenclature of some species. The bibliography is unaltered, but the index is a welcome new feature. This splendid combination of art and science belongs in all academic and public libraries, though libraries owning the original edition may not find it absolutely essential to acquire this reissue. —Paul B. Cors. [R: ARBA 72, item 1584]

721. Truitt, Deborah, comp. **Dolphins and Porpoises: A Comprehensive, Annotated Bibliography of the Smaller Cetacea**. Detroit, Gale, 1974. 582p. index. $45.00. LC 73-19803. ISBN 0-8103-0966-1.

This work attempts to list everything ever published on dolphins and porpoises, defined as all members of the families Delphinidae and Platanistidae except the genera Feresa, Globicephala, Orca and Pseudorca. Perhaps it does not include everything, but it does contain some 3,549 entries, ranging chronologically from 560 B.C. through 1972, citing books, the report literature, and journal articles. Most of the titles are scientific works, but fiction, mythology, and even children's stories are included. The arrangement is by subject; there are 15 major categories, most of them subdivided into smaller subject areas, for a total of 72 sections; under each, the subarrangement is first chronological, then alphabetical by author. Titles in the roman alphabet are cited in the original language; titles in non-roman alphabets are translated into English. Each entry includes a concise but complete bibliographic description; most include a brief descriptive annotation as well. Works not seen by the compiler are so indicated, with a note on the basis for their inclusion if the title does not make this obvious. There are indexes of authors, taxonomic names (including some vernacular names if these are all that appear in the work indexed), and subjects. This comprehensive, well-organized, and well-printed book completely supersedes the few earlier works of similar scope. —Paul B. Cors. [R: LJ, 1 Nov 74, pp. 2832-34; ARBA 75, item 1521]

722. Walker, Ernest P., and others. **Mammals of the World**. Rev. for 3rd ed. by John L. Paradiso. Baltimore, Johns Hopkins University Press, 1975. 2v. illus. bibliog. index. $37.50. LC 74-23327. ISBN 0-8018-1657-2.

Mammals of the World is the long-awaited third edition of the late Ernest Walker's classic and highly acclaimed mammalogical work. This revision by John L. Paradiso differs from earlier editions in that the third volume, which was a classified bibliography of worldwide literature, has been dropped because of the monumental task of updating it.

The present edition includes more than 2,000 black and white photographs and descriptions of 1,050 genera of mammals, with 270 new photographs by such wildlife photographers as Leonard Lee Rue, III. Ten new genera are included, and most material has been updated. John Paradiso, chief of the branch of biological data, Office of Endangered Species, U.S.F.W.S., has spent more than five years updating and revising this monumental work.

The text describes the size, weight, coloration, food, mating habits, care of the young, and economic importance of each genus. Also included are descriptions of interesting behaviors. Many of the animals are photographed in their natural habitat, although the text still includes many photographs of stuffed specimens, museum skins, or captive animals when better material could not be found. This is especially true of the rarer species. In this respect, the edition is a major improvement over earlier editions. Distinctive features such as webbed claws, snouts, tails, and skeletal features are illustrated. Of special interest are descriptions of various endangered species such as rhinos, leopards, whales, wolves, and the vicuña. Each volume is indexed, and a 24-page world distribution chart greatly aids in locating any genera in the world.

No other single work includes such diverse information on the world's mammal fauna in such a readily accessible format. —John C. Jahoda. [R: Choice, Oct 75, p. 984; BL, 1 Dec 75, pp. 528-29; ARBA 76, item 1446]

REPTILES AND AMPHIBIANS

723. Cochran, Doris M., and Coleman J. Goin. **The New Field Book of Reptiles and Amphibians**. New York, Putnam, 1970. 359p. illus. photos.(part col.). bibliog. index. (Nature Field Book). $5.95. LC 69-18168. ISBN 0-399-10292-2.

This is the most comprehensive identification manual yet published in its subject area, providing, as it does, concise and accurate, yet not overly technical, descriptions of every species and subspecies, native and naturalized, of amphibian and reptile so far recorded within the United States (including Alaska and Hawaii). While its intended audience is primarily the amateur naturalist, it will be useful to professional herpetologists as well, especially for its information on distribution and systematics; the treatment of subspecies, in fact, is more appropriately the concern of professional taxonomists than of amateurs.

The textual descriptions are brief but adequate, but the book's use for field identification is hampered by inadequate illustrations; many forms described are not illustrated at all, and for those that are, the black-and-white photos don't always show markings clearly, while the color photos are too small (mostly about 3.5 by 5.5 cm.) and too few (96) to suffice. There are glossaries for each of the six categories. For first purchase, the corresponding titles in Houghton Mifflin's Peterson Field Guide Series (Roger Conant, *A Field Guide to Reptiles and Amphibians of the United States and Canada East of the 100th Meridian*, 1958; and Robert C. Stebbins, *A Field Guide to Western Reptiles and Amphibians*, 1966) are preferable because of their superior colored illustrations, but this will be a necessary supplemental work. —Paul B. Cors. [R: Choice, Oct 70; ALA 70; ARBA 71, item 1634]

724. Conant, Roger. **A Field Guide to Reptiles and Amphibians of Eastern and Central North America**. 2nd ed. Illus. by Isabelle Hunt Conant. Boston, Houghton Mifflin, 1975. 429p. illus.(part col.). maps. index. (The Peterson Field Guide Series, No. 12). $6.95; $4.95pa. LC 74-13425. ISBN 0-395-19979-4; 0-395-19977-8pa.

This much-expanded edition is an important handbook for the amateur herpetologist. It identifies species and subspecies of turtles, crocodiles, alligators, lizards, snakes, salamanders, newts, frogs, and toads. Each family and genus is introduced with a brief description, followed by information on distinguishing features, habitat and range for each species, and a brief note on the appearance and range of subspecies. Handy information on such things as collecting and transporting of specimens, care in captivity, and first aid for snakebite is also included.

The expansion over the first edition (1958) is noticeable in many ways. Geographically, the range has been extended into western Texas as well as into the western parts of the states to the north and adjacent Canada—that is, beyond the 100th meridian (the first edition covered east of the 100th only). This was done in order to close the gap between the first edition and R. C. Stebbins' *Field Guide to Western Reptiles and Amphibians* (Boston, Houghton Mifflin, 1966), number 16 of the Peterson Field Guide Series. This expanded range, as well as new species within the range of the first edition, has increased the number of species from 391 to 474. The second edition has 48 plates (32 in color) as compared to 40 plates in the first. This edition includes measurements in both inches and metric equivalents, which the earlier edition did not.

The things that remain the same are good. The authority (Dr. Conant is a well-known expert on herpetology), the careful organization, and the comprehensiveness are good recommendations for this edition as a fine basic reference for identification of North American reptiles and amphibians. —David Isaak. [R: ARBA 76, item 1448]

725. Ernst, Carl H., and Roger W. Barbour. **Turtles of the United States**. Lexington, University Press of Kentucky, 1973. 347p. illus.(part col.). maps. bibliog. index. $22.50. LC 72-81315. ISBN 0-8131-1272-9.

This is the first comprehensive work in more than two decades on the turtles of the United States (including Hawaii) and the adjacent oceans; it will undoubtedly be the standard reference for some time to come. After a short introduction on general characteristics of turtles, the bulk of the work consists of detailed species accounts emphasizing ecology, behavior, and conservation, including a distribution map and good photographs. There are about 500 illustrations, of which 60 are color photographs. The data, which are derived both from the authors' own researches and from a thorough search of the literature, reflect recent taxonomic thought. Appendixes include a discussion of the evolution of American turtles; notes on the care of turtles in captivity; a list of the parasites, symbionts, and commensals reported from the species included; a glossary of scientific names; and an extensive bibliography emphasizing, but not strictly limited to, the period 1950 through 1970. The good index covers subjects and common and scientific names. Overall, the treatment is thorough enough for the professional zoologist, but it is within the understanding of the amateur naturalist who has a good basic knowledge of vertebrate zoology. —Paul B. Cors. [R: ALA 73; ARBA 74, item 1562]

726. Glut, Donald F. **The Dinosaur Dictionary.** Secaucus, N.J., Citadel Press, 1972. 218p. illus. $12.50. LC 70-147825. ISBN 0-8065-0283-5.

It seems only inevitable that the wide popular interest in dinosaurs would generate some sound and usable reference books for those who wish to find detailed scientific information about these prehistoric creatures. Glut's *The Dinosaur Dictionary* is such a work. It is an alphabetical listing of nearly all genera of dinosaurs currently known to paleontologists, with cross references to similar genera. The entries describe the classification, tell when and where it is known to have existed, and list the skeletal remains by which it has been identified. In some cases, the date and place of discovery are noted. Several black and white photos or drawings appear on every page; while these are not as exotic as the color illustrations in some popular works and books for young readers, they are informative. Drawings are provided to illustrate bone fragments, skulls, and reconstructions. —Christine L. Wynar. [R: ALA 73; ARBA 73, item 1460]

MOLLUSKS

727. Abbott, Robert Tucker. **American Seashells: The Marine Mollusca of the Atlantic and Pacific Coasts of North America.** 2nd ed. New York, Van Nostrand Reinhold, 1974. 663p. illus.(part col.). bibliog. index. $49.50. LC 74-7267. ISBN 0-442-20228-8.

This second edition is substantially larger in size and broader in scope than the original edition of 1954, and is now aimed at the needs of the research malacologist rather than the amateur shell collector, though it is not beyond the comprehension of the serious amateur who has mastered the basic concepts and terminology of molluscan biology. It is a complete catalog of all the marine mollusks of North America (including nudibranchs and cephalopods, which are not normally thought of as "seashells"); approximately 2,000 species are described in detail, and 4,500 more are listed without descriptions. The geographic area covered is not clearly described, but it is essentially Canada, the continental United States (including Alaska), Bermuda, and northwest Mexico (Baja California, Sonora, and Sinaloa); however, some West Indian and even Brazilian species are included. The text is supplemented by about 4,000 black and white photos and drawings, and 24 well-done colored plates; there is a 65-page index of generic, specific, and common names. The extensive bibliography of the first edition has been replaced with a brief list of the major references used by the author in compiling the work. This will be a basic reference for all research libraries in the field, and, though very expensive, it should also be considered by public libraries in areas where there is an interest in shell collecting. —Paul B. Cors. [R: ARBA 75, item 1522]

CHAPTER 36

ENVIRONMENTAL SCIENCES

728. Ciaccio, Leonard L., ed. **Water and Water Pollution Handbook.** New York, Dekker, 1971. 4v. illus. bibliog. index. $27.50/v. LC 78-134780. ISBN 0-8247-1104-1(v.1); 0-8247-1116-5(v.2); 0-8247-1117-3(v.3); 0-8247-1118-1(v.4).

The first part of this work covers environmental systems, including the chemical, physical, and biological characteristics of water resources, estuaries, irrigation and soil waters, wastes and waste effluents. Waste treatment, effects of pollution, self-purification, and mathematical modeling are all discussed. Part two deals with the chemical, physical, bacterial, viral, instrumental, and bioassay techniques needed in analyzing water. The handbook is intended for all those with a vested interest in water environment. The editor, Head of Environmental Sciences and Technology at G.T.E. Laboratories, Inc., has brought together the specialized knowledge of over 40 researchers in preparing this outstanding handbook. —H. Robert Malinowsky. [R: ARBA 72, item 767]

729. Durrenberger, Robert W., comp. **Dictionary of the Environmental Sciences.** Palo Alto, Calif., National Press Books, 1973. 282p. illus. $7.95; $4.95pa. LC 78-142370. ISBN 0-87484-186-0; 0-87484-150-Xpa.

Considering the current interest in the environment, which is reflected in civic activities as well as in the curricula of many universities and colleges, this handy dictionary with its multidisciplinary approach will be helpful to the novice. It covers a wide range of topics, providing about 4,000 concise definitions; illustrations and diagrams are incorporated in the text. Some of the definitions are rather popular (e.g., those for cash crop and storage capacity), but, in general, this dictionary will do. Appended is a geologic time scale and a table of conversion factors. [R: ALA 73; ARBA 74, item 1568]

730. **The Energy Directory.** New York, Environment Information Center, 1974. 418p. $50.00. LC 74-79869.

The Energy Directory is a relatively comprehensive effort to list government agencies, private industries, and public interest groups concerned with the resolution of energy problems and the carrying out of energy supply and conservation responsibilities. While the 1,899 entries in the directory would seem to provide good coverage of the American energy establishment and some international organizations, many private and public entities within the scope of the work don't appear. As a well-organized starting point for persons trying to wend their way through the American energy establishment, the work is a valuable tool. The compilers admit to the directory's incompleteness in their foreword, and it has valuable features that compensate for that weakness.

Chief among the directory's assets are the brief descriptions of the functions and energy interests of many of the governmental agencies and professional, trade, and non-governmental organizations listed in the directory. Also of value is a listing of telephone numbers—right down to the president's or director's extension number, in many cases.

It is easy to enumerate specific agencies and companies that have been left out. There are some weaknesses in the directory. International corporations based outside the United States aren't listed (most striking among those omissions is British Petroleum, with its large Alaskan holdings) and many small, independent oil operators aren't listed (for example, Gary Oil Company, which operates the massive Bell Creek oil field in Wyoming). Nevertheless, it is important to point out that *The Energy Directory* does fill a void and fills it very well, if one is aware of its limitations.   —Steve Wynkoop. [R: ARBA 75, item 1548]

731. Environment U.S.A.: A Guide to Agencies, People, and Resources. Comp. and ed. by The Onyx Group, Inc. Glenn L. Paulson, advisory ed. New York, R. R. Bowker, 1974. 451p. index. $15.95. LC 73-20122. ISBN 0-8352-0671-8.

The compilers have attempted to put together a comprehensive handbook for researchers in the environmental fields. More than a fourth of the volume consists of lists of government agencies (state and federal) and private environmental organizations. The latter includes both citizen organizations, arranged by state, and trade and professional associations in an alphabetical list. This is followed by a list of almost 800 environmental consultants, both individuals and firms, arranged by state. Subject specialties of the consultants are given. An indication of whether they are free or paid is also provided for many of them.

There are lists of environmental officers or presidents of the companies on the Fortune 500 list, the 50 largest utility companies, and the national labor unions. There is a state-by-state list of educational programs in environmental fields and another of environmental libraries; a short article on environmental careers, by Odom Fanning; one on fund raising, by Joseph Willen; and a longer one on environment and the law, by Angus MacBeth.

A list of environmental conferences and conventions for 1974 is included. The annotated list of nearly 500 films provides purchase and rental information, but it unfortunately does not give age level or intended audience. There is a geographical listing of newspapers and radio and television stations, with the name of the environmental or science editor, but it is really too short to be useful. It includes approximately two newspapers, one radio and one television station for each state, with, for example, no television stations listed for Los Angeles, San Francisco, or Denver.

A 65-page selected bibliography of books, reports, and articles provides an introduction to the several fields of environmental concern. It is not annotated. This is followed by a worldwide list of about 200 periodicals, with addresses but no annotations. They are not necessarily the same journals from which articles were selected for the bibliography.

There is a subject classified index of the federal agencies that appear at the beginning of the book (where they are listed by department), and an alphabetical index of government and private organizations and consultants. Other parts of the book are not indexed.

The Onyx Group, Inc., is identified only as "a group of people with varied backgrounds in the environmental and publishing fields . . ." The advisory editor is listed in the text as a consultant, the other names on the title page are not identified. No selection criteria are given for the consultants, the organizations, or the films. The list of private environmental organizations does not differentiate membership groups from those that may be industry sponsored. Future editions will, perhaps, include the qualifications of the compilers and their selection criteria. In the mean-time, this handbook will fill a gap for teachers and researchers in many areas. —David W. Brunton. [R: LJ, 15 June 74, p. 1692; WLB, Oct 74, p. 186; Choice, Dec 74, p. 1458; BL, 15 Dec 74, p. 429; ARBA 75, item 1549]

732. **McGraw-Hill Encyclopedia of Environmental Science.** New York, McGraw-Hill, 1974. 754p. illus. charts. graphs. index. $24.50. LC 74-13065. ISBN 0-07-045260-1.

Put briefly, this encyclopedia is authoritative, complete, and easy to use. It is probably the best general work on the environment. While at least a nodding acquaintance with scientific terminology is needed in order to comprehend many of the articles, the encyclopedia doesn't "talk down" to the reader. The articles are crisply written but convey an ample amount of information. Each article is almost a mini-lecture on a different aspect of the environmental sciences. Many of the articles have multiple authors. For example, the article on sea water has 15 authors— each a specialist in some aspect of sea water. The articles are signed, and there are large bibliographies.

The encyclopedia is well illustrated, and the numerous charts, graphs, and tables help to summarize information.

The work does not repeat some articles from the *McGraw-Hill Encyclopedia of Science and Technology*, but much of the material is new. It is valuable to have the environmental material in a separate volume, for several reasons. First is the interest in the topics covered. The encyclopedia will be valuable to students trying to get an overview of the environmental sciences. Second, by combining all the works in one volume and providing extensive cross-indexing, the authors can point out to the reader where the environmental sciences overlap and can broaden his appreciation of the approaches that many disciplines are taking to common con-cerns. The third is the cost factor. This single volume, available at a reasonable cost, has the potential of becoming a key resource tool for environmental sciences information.

In a world where the base for growing renewable resources is shrinking and non-renewable resources are being quickly depleted, a work that deals with the science of protecting and conserving the earth's life-support systems is especially needed. McGraw-Hill has made a positive contribution to stretching man's knowl-edge of this vital area. —Steve Wynkoop. [R: ARBA 75, item 1533]

733. Sarnoff, Paul. **The New York Times Encyclopedic Dictionary of the Environment.** New York, Quadrangle Books, 1971. 352p. illus. $10.00. LC 74-178736. ISBN 0-8129-0203-3.

Would-be environmental activists who have been holding back because they don't understand what the scientists are talking about have lost their last excuse. Using an easy-to-read, opinionated style, Sarnoff, ecological projects consultant at Hofstra University, zips along from "abatement" to "zooplankton." The text is amply illustrated. Sarnoff takes the blame "for errors of omission and commission," and it should be noted that the work contains at least one blind reference, a minor fault in a work containing more than 2,000 entries. "PPM" is referred to, and while "parts per million" is defined, "PPM" is not.

This encyclopedic dictionary, suitable for use in senior high schools, could be a valuable adjunct to materials used for introductory environmental sciences courses. But, even though it is not too complex for beginners, this work should be a valuable reference tool for professional use. Sarnoff unravels the jargon that often stands in the way of effective multidisciplinary action, throwing in enough lighthearted commentary so that even the most dour researcher can keep his perspective and sense of humor while trying to figure out why ecologists insist on calling lake shores and seashores "littoral zones." Besides these pluses, buying the 40 percent recycled paper book saves a portion of a tree and boosts the recycling business. —Steve Wynkoop. [R: ARBA 72, item 750]

734. Winton, Harry N. M., comp. and ed. **Man and the Environment: A Bibliography of Selected Publications of the United Nations System 1946-1971**. New York, Unipub; New York, R. R. Bowker, 1972. 305p. index. $12.50. LC 72-739. ISBN 0-8352-0536-3.

This bibliographic guide includes some 1,200 numbered entries arranged under subject categories—e.g., natural resources and the earth sciences, geography, geology, geophysics, seismology, mineral resources, oceanography, etc. Some of the broad subject categories are further subdivided by more specific topics (e.g., under mineral resources we find General, Laws and Regulations, and Iron Ores). Most publications listed here are still in print. In addition to reference works, included are monographic works, proceedings, and surveys, plus periodical literature. Most entries have brief descriptive annotations and the volume is well indexed with separate title and subject indexes.

The author's familiarity with the subject provides us with a well-designed volume on this timely subject. —Bohdan S. Wynar. [R: WLB, Nov 72, p. 294; LJ, Aug 72, p. 2564; ARBA 73, item 1487]

CHAPTER 37

EARTH SCIENCES

ENCYCLOPEDIAS

735. Fairbridge, Rhodes W., ed. **The Encyclopedia of Geochemistry and Environmental Sciences.** New York, Van Nostrand Reinhold, 1972. 1321p. illus. index. (Encyclopedia of Earth Sciences Series, Vol. IVA). $49.50. LC 75-152326. ISBN 0-470-25141-7.

This volume of the "Encyclopedia of Earth Science Series" covers the chemistry of the earth and its compositional evolution. Minerals are mentioned briefly but will be covered in more detail in a separate volume. Environmental science is included with geochemistry because of the geologist's current concern about the pollution of our air and water. The detailed entries provide clear, concise discussions, with all the needed chemical and mathematical notations, graphs, charts, and illustrations needed. This is a highly recommended encyclopedia for those in the fields of geochemistry, geology, and chemistry. References for additional reading and cross references to other entries in this volume and to entries in other volumes of the series are included at the end of each discussion. This makes it mandatory to have the complete series: Volume 1, *Encyclopedia of Oceanography* (1966); Volume 2, *Encyclopedia of Atmospheric Sciences and Astrogeology* (1967); Volume 3, *Encyclopedia of Geomorphology* (1968); and Volume 4B, *Encyclopedia of Mineralogy and Economic Geology*, in preparation. Other volumes will cover petrology and structure, sedimentology, stratigraphy, and world regional geology. —H. Robert Malinowsky. [R: ARBA 73, item 1500]

GEOLOGY

736. Challinor, John. **A Dictionary of Geology.** 4th ed. New York, Oxford University Press, 1974. 350p. $13.00. ISBN 0-19-519719-4.

The first edition of this work was published in 1961, the fourth in 1973. It is one of the best dictionaries on this subject, with good definitions and many quotations from geological literature that illustrate the usage of a given term. In this respect, Challinor is superior to Whitten and Brooks' *The Penguin Dictionary of Geology* (1972). Both works are essentially British, but this should not restrict their usefulness in this country. The recent edition of Challinor is considerably updated and the text has been reset. It continues to provide a helpful list of prefixes and suffixes used in the geological vocabulary, plus a well-prepared classified index of terms. [R: BL, 15 Mar 75, p. 774; Choice, Mar 75, p. 44; ARBA 76, item 1471]

737. Gary, Margaret, Robert McAfee, and Carol L. Wolf, eds. **Glossary of Geology.**
Washington, American Geological Institute, 1972. 1v.(various paging). bibliog.
$22.50. LC 72-87856. ISBN 0-913312-00-2.

The first comprehensive dictionary in this subject area, with 14,000 definitions, was published in 1957 by the National Academy of Sciences under the title
Glossary of Geology and Related Subjects. The second edition, published in 1960,
had 18,000 entries. The present work, by far the most comprehensive, contains
33,000 entries, thus indirectly indicating the substantial diversification in the
development of geology in the last decade. The emphasis is on the current or preferred meaning of a term rather than on its original usage or historical development.
In terms of scope, it encompasses several subdisciplines of geology, such as astrogeology, engineering geology, geochemistry, geomorphology, meteorology,
mineralogy (some 4,000 mineral names are defined), paleontology of the invertebrates, stratigraphy, structural geology, etc. All entries are presented in one alphabet, with numerous cross references listed at the end of a definition. Several definitions provide citations to the standard works on a given subject, and full citations
for references used in the text are given in a bibliography at the end of the volume.
This is by far the most comprehensive dictionary on the subject. [R: ARBA 74,
item 1579]

HYDROLOGY

738. Geraghty, James J., and others. **Water Atlas of the United States.** 3rd ed.
Port Washington, N.Y., Water Information Center, 1973. 1v.(unpaged). illus. maps.
$35.00. LC 73-76649. ISBN 0-912394-03-X.

A good general visual guide to the water situation in the United States, including Alaska and Hawaii. The information is presented in 122 maps arranged on a
common base, so that the data can be compared from map to map. The data cover
all aspects of precipitation, surface water, and ground water, plus new material on
water pollution, water quality, water conservation/recreation, and water law. The
text that accompanies each map defines the subject (e.g., water hardness) and gives
facts and statistics necessary to cover the subject.

A good companion to water facts in tabular form as presented in the *Water
Encyclopedia*, a Water Information Center publication issued in 1970. —Dederick C.
Ward. [R: Choice, Sept 74, p. 919; WLB, Apr 74, pp. 674-75; ARBA 75, item 1567]

739. Giefer, Gerald J., and David K. Todd, eds. **Water Publications of State
Agencies: A Bibliography of Publications on Water Resources and Their Manage-
ment Published by the States of the United States.** Port Washington, N.Y., Water
Information Center, 1972. 319p. $39.50. LC 72-75672. ISBN 0-912394-04-8.

A bibliography of retrospective and currently available water resources publications of 335 state agencies in the 50 United States as supplied by lists from the
agencies to the editors. Arrangement is by state, then by issuing agency. There are
no subject or author indexes, but, in most cases, the simple arrangement of the
book precludes one's need of them. Federal government reports (except "cooperative" ones) are omitted, as are reports of agricultural and interstate agencies.
Publications of the water resources research centers established by Public Law

88-376 are included. Since state libraries are depositories for these reports, a list of the libraries and their addresses is appended. Price and out-of-print information are included if supplied by the agency.

State publications are elusive because publication and distribution policies change with administrations, and many reports are not copyrighted. For these reasons, many reports do not appear in the Library of Congress' *Monthly Checklist of State Publications*. Some are found in the Department of the Interior's *Selected Water Resources Abstracts*, but this bibliography is also incomplete, and it is retrospective only to 1968. The editors tried to fill gaps in the lists they received from the reporting agencies by doing independent research in the libraries of the University of California, Berkeley.

This compilation is a time-saver. It identifies many reports that appear only on the individual state lists and not in the standard indexes previously mentioned. Hopefully, the bibliography will be updated every few years. —Dederick C. Ward. [R: ARBA 73, item 1509]

740. Todd, David Keith, ed. **The Water Encyclopedia: A Compendium of Useful Information on Water Resources**. Port Washington, N.Y., Water Information Center, 1970. 550p. $27.50. LC 76-140311.

Dr. Todd, Professor of Civil Engineering at the University of California, Berkeley, has produced, in cooperation with the Water Information Center, an important reference publication in the area of water resources data, facts and statistics. The organization of the volume is based on the valid premise that data in this field are found in numerous, widely scattered sources—sources difficult to identify and locate. Nine major chapters cover 1) climate and precipitation; 2) hydrologic elements; 3) surface water; 4) ground water; 5) water use; 6) water quality and pollution control: 7) water resources management; 8) agencies and organizations involved in the area of water resources; and 9) constants and conversion factors relating to water configurations. As a result of this sweeping approach, the publication is a useful and relatively convenient handbook of information from dozens of specialized sources. The index, although not lengthy, attempts to "facilitate the rapid location of specific data"—the terminology is clear and readily understood by the layman.

The major weaknesses of the volume lie in the time span of source materials as well as in their incomplete identification if one wishes to pursue newer reports. Some of the data are based on materials dating to the 1950s, and a citation that simply says "House of Representatives, U.S. Congress" is frustrating. However, this handbook (it is *not* an encyclopedia) does fill a reference gap in a field of considerable import. —Laurel Grotzinger. [R: Choice, Nov 71, p. 1164; RQ, Summer 71, p. 365; LJ, 15 May 71, p. 1697; ALA 71; ARBA 72, item 1596]

METEOROLOGY

741. **Climates of the States in Two Volumes: A Practical Reference Containing Basic Climatological Data of the United States.** By Officials of the National Oceanic and Atmospheric Administration, U.S. Department of Commerce. Port Washington, N.Y., Water Information Center, 1974. 2v. illus. maps. charts. bibliog. $39.50. LC 73-93482. ISBN 0-912394-09-9.

The National Climatic Center of the National Oceanic and Atmospheric Administration (NOAA) issues a valuable series entitled *Climatological Data* (C55.214) by states. The series is monthly with separate annual summaries; it is not a depository Item. The Water Information Center, Inc., a commercial publisher, has conveniently combined in two volumes the reports of the official series issued during the last decade. Volume I covers the Eastern states and Puerto Rico/ Virgin Islands; Volume II includes the Western states.

Each state section contains a general summary of climatic conditions followed by detailed tables of temperature, precipitation and freeze data. Accompanying the data are maps showing temperature, precipitation, and locations of stations as well as miscellaneous information on snowfall, sunshine, and occurrence of tropical storms. Acknowledgment to the official NOAA documents is given in the "General Reference Notes" at the end of each volume.

Although the work is specialized, the informed layman can benefit from the introductory essays on the climate of each state; they are readable and include a bibliography.

Because of its suitability for easy use, it will be a valuable reference source for students and scholars in the atmospheric, environmental, and agricultural sciences. However, it would clearly have been in the public interest if the federal government had issued this compendium and distributed it to libraries as a depository Item. —Joe Morehead. [R: BL, 1 May 75, pp. 919-22; Choice, Feb 75, p. 1759; ARBA 76, item 1477]

742. Ruffner, James A., and Frank E. Bair, eds. **The Weather Almanac.** Detroit, Gale, 1974. 578p. illus. charts. maps. $17.50. LC 73-9342. ISBN 0-8103-1049-X.

According to the old saying, "Everyone talks about the weather, but no one does anything about it." Documents librarians have frequently felt this way about the plethora of weather data in reports and records prepared by various agencies of the U.S. government. James Ruffner and Frank Bair have done something about it by gathering this material between two covers. Much of the information published here has been gathered and printed directly from government reports and records. The material has been grouped into these major sections: U.S. Weather, in Atlas Format; Storms and Severe Weather Information; Retirement and Health Weather; Air Pollution; Marine Weather; Be Your Own Forecaster; Record Setting Weather; Round-the-World Weather (including climates of the world and weather records for 550 cities of the world); and finally, Weather of 108 Selected U.S. Cities. Although the maps, charts, safety rules, and data are available from the U.S. Weather Service or the National Oceanic and Atmospheric Administration (NOAA), this almanac is a time-saving and handy one-stop reference. The section on Retirement and Health Weather was specially prepared for the book and is unavailable in other publications. —Robert J. Havlik. [R: ALA 74; ARBA 75, item 1568]

743. **Weather Atlas of the United States.** (Original title: Climatic Atlas of the United States). Climatic maps prep. by John L. Baldwin. Washington, U.S. Environmental Data Service, GPO, 1968; repr. Detroit, Gale, 1975. 262p. illus. $17.50. LC 74-11931. ISBN 0-8103-1048-1.

This atlas is a redesigned reprint of an edition originally issued by the U.S. Environmental Data Service. Its purpose is to depict the climate of the United States in terms of the distribution and variation of such climatic measures as the mean, normal and/or extreme values of temperature, precipitation, wind, barometric pressure, relative humidity, dewpoint, sunshine, sky cover, heating degree days, solar radiation, and evaporation. The map projections have been standardized to allow for the accurate comparison and correlation of the various climatic measures.

The atlas contains 271 maps and 15 tables. The Gale reprint is a redesign of the original edition from its oversized 21¾ by 16 inches to a more convenient and conventional 8½ by 11 inch format. —Robert K. Dikeman. [R: RQ, Fall 75, p. 84; ARBA 76, item 1479]

MINERALOGY

744. Roberts, Willard Lincoln, George Robert Rapp, Jr., and Julius Weber. **Encyclopedia of Minerals.** New York, Van Nostrand Reinhold, 1974. 693p. illus. (col.). $69.50. LC 74-1155. ISBN 0-442-26820-3.

The *Encyclopedia of Minerals* is an authoritative and completely up-to-date compendium of information on the mineral kingdom. It provides chemical, physical, crystallographic, x-ray, optical, and geographical data on over 2,200 authenticated mineral species. The mineral names are arranged alphabetically so as to be available to a wide audience not familiar with the more refined structural/chemical arrangements of the researcher. For each mineral is given: crystal system, class, space group, lattice constant, three strongest diffraction lines, optical constants, hardness, density, cleavage, habit, color-luster, mode of occurrence, and the best reference in English (i.e., most complete and handiest). The latter feature is an outstanding bibliographic aid not available in former compilations.

As mineralogists know, many mineral species are described in the published literature by conflicting data. In this volume, the compilers have chosen to include what they believe to be the most correct data from a variety of sources. The phrase "inadequately described mineral" is used to accompany mineral names when tentative data are the only kind presently available.

Because minerals can be so well documented visually, the encyclopedia contains nearly 1,000 spectacular full-color photomicrographs by Julius Weber, of the American Museum of Natural History. Weber chose this method to illustrate minerals because photographs of micro-crystals offer a wealth of details not captured by the naked eye, and because specimens of similar or equal quality are available to all mineral collectors.

This definitive and beautifully illustrated reference volume will quickly gain wide acceptance by a broad audience of scientists, museum curators, students, teachers, and mineral collectors at all levels. —Dederick C. Ward. [R: ARBA 75, item 1573]

CHAPTER 38

PSYCHOLOGY

BIBLIOGRAPHIES

745. **The Harvard List of Books in Psychology.** 4th ed. Comp. by the psychologists in Harvard University. Cambridge, Mass., Harvard University Press, 1971. 108p. index. $2.75pa. LC 71-152700. ISBN 0-674-37601-3.

This is a classic reference work for persons interested in determining what a set of top scholars consider the seminal works in the field. Though there are 40 more citations here than in the third edition, this does not indicate that almost half of the list is composed of new entries. As with any collection of this nature, the scholar in a special area will wonder why one work is included while others, which he considers of prime significance, are left out. In addition, perusers will ask where psychology ends and allied fields such as sociology begin. For example, leaving out a work such as Talcott Parsons' *Social Structure and Personality* might seem arbitrary or an oversight. The list is by no means intended to be comprehensive. In sum, it is a carefully selected and clearly annotated collection of both classic and contemporary works in the field which should be of significance to those interested in gaining a perspective on psychology.   —Bernard Spilka.
[R: Choice, Sept 71, p. 810; ARBA 72, item 1609]

746. Watson, Robert I., Sr., ed. **Eminent Contributors to Psychology: Volume I, A Bibliography of Primary References.** New York, Springer, 1974. 469p. $24.00. LC 73-88108. ISBN 0-8261-1450-4.

An impressive amount of scholarly and painstaking effort has gone into the production of this selected bibliography. It lists 12,000 publications produced by 538 individuals living between 1600 and 1967—an average of 23 references per person, with a range from 1 to 80.

The bibliography has several laudable purposes. Its goal is to make available for quick reference a list of the major publications of eminent contributors to psychology without the inconvenience of accumulating lengthy lists from such standard sources as *Psychological Index* and *Psychological Abstracts*. It serves also as a handy verification source for the most commonly cited papers in the field. For psychologist readers it is a source to turn to for references on a particular theme that they can associate with the name of an individual (e.g., intelligence with Binet). The editor's own personal interest in producing this bibliography is a desire to increase the popularity of work in the history of the behavioral sciences by making it somewhat more convenient to pursue.

The procedures for ascertaining eminence of the contributors to psychology, for selection of references, and for their collection and verification are all explained in careful detail. In fact, these complex procedures have been the topic of several journal articles, which are cited for further reading. The 538 individuals selected for their contribution to psychology include 228 psychologists per se, while the remainder are from the fields of philosophy, biology, psychiatry, anthropology— 22 categories in all. The most important works of each person were chosen from the editor's personal files, a large number of historical works, bibliographies, biographies, Festschriften, and collections of papers from various countries and branches of science, social science, and the history of science. Selections for 349 of the contributors were evaluated by 239 specialists who are particularly knowledgeable about one or two of the contributors. Approximately 70 percent of the total references included were examined directly for accuracy, and the majority of those remaining were doublechecked in sources other than those used originally to generate the reference.

The contributors are listed alphabetically with full name, dates of birth and death, the country (or countries) where their principal work was done, along with their major field of endeavor and their eminence rating score derived for this bibliography. Collections of complete and selected works and letters are identified in separate chronological order, followed by intermingled books and articles also in chronological order. The publications included are current through early 1972.

Suggestions, corrections, and additions are welcomed by the editor, who plans to list at least the corrections in the *Journal of the History of the Behavioral Sciences* if no other edition of this volume is published. The second volume is described as containing more than 50,000 selected secondary references to the work of the same contributors to psychology. —Lorraine Schulte. [R: ARBA 75, item 1579]

747. Weinberg, Martin S., and Alan P. Bell, eds. **Homosexuality: An Annotated Bibliography**. New York, Harper and Row, 1972. 550p. index. $15.00. LC 70-160653. ISBN 0-06-014541-2.

The editors are both with the Institute for Sex Research founded by Alfred C. Kinsey at Indiana University. They urge the reader "to develop a critical attitude, to jump to no conclusions on the basis of one book or article, and, at the same time, to maintain an objectivity which will allow him to consider seriously others' views and findings" when reviewing these 1,265 numbered books and articles in the English language, some of them translated. Titles, published from 1940 to 1968, are classified under three broad categories— physiological, psychological, and sociological considerations—with appended author and subject indexes. Entries were selected from such indexes and catalogs as *Cumulative Book Index, Cumulated Index Medicus, Excerpta Medica, Library of Congress Catalog, Psychological Abstracts, Sociological Abstracts,* and *Subject Guide to Books in Print, 1968,* all searched under such subjects as homosexuality, lesbianism, sexual perversion, and sodomy. Also, 112 standard journals in anthropology, criminology, the law, psychology, and sociology were examined, as well as the extensive collection of vertical file materials in the Institute for Sex Research library. Dissertations were listed when considered significant. Abstracts prepared by nine graduate and two undergraduate social science students at Indiana University (under the editors' supervision) admittedly do not possess the same degree of comprehensiveness, but they are informative enough to allow the user to determine whether or not he wishes to consult the original. All are recorded "to conform to the most stringent of bibliographic standards."

Belles-lettres, all popular magazines (except *Sexology*) and newspaper articles are excluded, while limited coverage is given to law and criminology, to popular works in religion, social work and counseling, to medical cases, federal government employment directives, pedophilia, transvestism, exhibitionism, material in homophile publications, and parts of general works on human sexuality. A commendable reference feature is the section giving cross references to related titles, appended to the main lists of titles found under such sub-topics as etiology, assessments, the homosexual community, societal attitudes toward homosexuality, and homosexuality and the law, which augment the detailed subject index. There is also an author index. When viewed in comparison with the nine other bibliographies and dictionaries listed in a concluding section, the need for the present volume for serious students is immediately apparent. Well searched, well selected, well recorded. —Frances Neel Cheney. [R: ALA 72; ARBA 74, item 1634]

ENCYCLOPEDIAS

748. **Encyclopedia of Psychology**. Ed. by H. J. Eysenck, W. Arnold, and R. Meili. New York, Herder and Herder; distr. New York, Seabury Press, 1972. 3v. $75.00/ set. LC 79-174154. ISBN 0-8164-9119-4.

This three-volume encyclopedia, prepared with the cooperation of some 300 contributors, was published simultaneously in several languages. The articles vary in length (the longest is about 4,000 words) and the bibliographies that are appended reflect an international approach. Among the 5,000 entries are 300 major articles; briefer articles are usually reserved for biographical sketches (although there are exceptions, such as the article on Pavlov), or for definitions of terms. Some of these shorter definitions seem inadequate, and the coverage provided for terms is not always the best. Dictionaries such as English and English's *A Comprehensive Dictionary of Psychological and Psychoanalytical Terms* offer much more. Also, many leading psychologists are not represented in the biographical sketches.

This encyclopedia is not a definitive work on the subject. But because it is the first attempt so far to provide an encyclopedic treatment, it will be useful as a handy compendium. —Bohdan S. Wynar. [R: LJ, 1 Dec 72, p. 3889; WLB, June 72, p. 933; Choice, Dec 73, p. 1526; ALA 72; ARBA 74, item 1602]

749. Goldenson, Robert M. **The Encyclopedia of Human Behavior; Psychology, Psychiatry, and Mental Health**. Garden City, New York, Doubleday, 1970. 2v. $24.95. LC 68-18077. ISBN 0-385-04074-1.

Some insatiable achievement-oriented enthusiast is reported to have said "the difficult we do right away; the impossible takes a little longer." Goldenson's herculean efforts tell us such a task may take considerable time. Many previous efforts up to the level of the eight-volume *Encyclopedia of the Social Sciences* are deficient in special areas and often of little use to the expert. In like manner, Dr. Goldenson's work must fall short of its avowed goals.

Knowledge is growing at disciplinary interfaces, and it is here that this encyclopedia runs into serious difficulty. The decision to stay in the mainstream of an area necessitates losing much information of importance to psychologists and psychiatrists. It is literally impossible to define where the efforts of the latter end and those of sociologists, anthropologists and other social scientists begin. To illustrate, terms such as "alienation," "anomia," and "anomie" are either ignored or poorly treated in the present work.

If, however, we attempt to stay within the center of psychology, just as the clinical domain seems exceptionally well treated, so is the perceptual one seriously slighted. We find listed among the references, the seminal works of Ames, Bruner, Sherif (Brunswik is left out), but no index citations are made to these scholars or their views—Transactional Functionalism, Directive-State Theory, Hypothesis Theory, Probabilistic Functionalism and Frame-of-Reference Theory. Similarly, considerations of Perceptual Defense and Vigilance are not present. One can match these with weaknesses in the motivational area (e.g., Surgency, Regnancy, Succorance, Nurturance) and with learning—the distinction between primary and secondary stimulus generalization.

It is not difficult to multiply similar examples, but pebble-picking an effort such as this is really the height of trivialization. Goldenson has accomplished more than could have been expected of one man, or even one computer. In addition, the depth and clarity of the writing afforded the many concepts presented here cannot be lightly treated. A number of articles include case histories and illustrations. There is a good general index. For lay persons and professionals alike, this encyclopedia may offer a valuable entrée to the field of behavioral study.
—Bernard Spilka. [R: ALA 70; ARBA 71, item 1662]

750. **Psychology 73/74 Encyclopedia.** Guilford, Conn., Dushkin, 1973. 311p. illus. charts. graphs. bibliog. $5.95pa. LC 72-90092.

Over 1,000 relatively short articles, liberally illustrated with graphs, diagrams, and photos on every page, treat the language of psychology and the full range of its theories, practices, and institutions.

The encyclopedia was first constructed topically to insure comprehensiveness, and the material was later arranged alphabetically. Many *see* and *see also* references tie together related material, and comprehensive "subject maps" display in outline form the interrelationship among articles for each of 12 major areas of psychological study. Each author also includes "consult" references for further reading. These are primarily recent publications that will be especially useful to non-professional readers, but professional journals and classic works are cited as well. The suggested further readings are conveniently grouped in a classified bibliography at the end of the volume.

Most of the articles are extremely readable and are refreshingly devoid of social science and super science jargon. Since the publisher's intention was to produce a work that would be of most value to non-professional readers, the authorities writing articles for the encyclopedia were chosen for their experience in helping people with no training in psychology to understand the field.

Within the editorial limitation on article length, an attempt was made to insure that every article be as complete as possible, but certain editorial decisions also had to be made on what should be excluded. Professionals in psychology could not turn to this encyclopedia for a discussion of "logotherapy," "monoamine exidase inhibitors," "method of constants," or "Ganzheit," but it might serve them as a handy, concise reference for information outside of their immediate specialties and as a source of a large amount of biographical information. Considerably less biographical information is included in the three-volume *Encyclopedia of Psychology*, edited by H. J. Eysenck and W. Arnold (New York, Herder and Herder, 1972). Geared primarily to a professional audience, this encyclopedia is generally more comprehensive and does include such topics as logotherapy, etc. The articles in *Encyclopedia of Psychology*, however, do demand greater familiarity with professional psychological terminology.

The publisher indicates in the preface that the revision for the next edition is already under way, although there is no definite commitment to annual publication as the title might imply. —Lorraine Schulte. [R: Choice, July-Aug 74, pp. 734-36; BL, 15 Sept 74, pp. 105-107; ARBA 75, item 1582]

DICTIONARIES

751. Kinkade, Robert G., ed. **Thesaurus of Psychological Index Terms**. 1974 ed. Washington, American Psychological Association, 1974. 362p. $12.00. LC 74-13190.

The uncontrolled proliferation of psychological terminology in the past decades has been an annoying source of difficulties and problems for psychologists in theoretical and applied fields as well as for professionals in related areas. In responding to this problem, the American Psychological Association has published its *Thesaurus* which, for the users, represents an authorized systematic list of terms in the discipline and thus, indirectly, an attempt at codification.

The volume is divided into three sections, each serving a different purpose. The Relationship Section forms the essential part; here each alphabetically listed term is cross-referenced and presented with its broader, narrower, and related concepts. In order to facilitate rapid selection of a search term, as well as verification of its spelling, thesaurus terms are listed alphabetically in the Alphabetic Section. In the Hierarchical Section, the concepts, represented by 17 major classification categories used in *Psychological Abstracts*, are placed at the highest level. Subsequently, all associated concepts are listed hierarchically as subcategories; the hierarchical structuring of terms was produced by computer and is listed in descending order, based on broader and narrower term designation. The technical aspects related to the development of the *Thesaurus* (such as the selection of candidate terms) are described in the introductory part. No definition or explanation of the meaning of any listed psychological term is provided. Evidently, the user is expected to be familiar with the conceptual spheres within the discipline.

The *Thesaurus* is a highly technical reference instrument. It is an essential guide for many search and indexing operations. The attempt of the American Psychological Association to stabilize terminology in psychological sciences is commendable. —Miluse Soudek. [R: ARBA 76, item 1495]

752. Wolman, Benjamin, ed. **Dictionary of Behavioral Science**. New York, Van Nostrand Reinhold, 1973. 478p. $22.50. LC 73-748. ISBN 0-442-29566-9.

This comprehensive dictionary, which briefly defines some 20,000 terms, was compiled and edited by Dr. Wolman, a well-known author of several psychology books. Some 30 consulting editors also participated in this project. The scope of the dictionary is rather broad. It covers psychology, psychiatry, psychoanalysis, neurology, psychopharmacology, endocrinology, and related disciplines. Among the categories of psychology covered are experimental and developmental psychology, personality, learning, perception, motivation, and intelligence. In terms of applied psychology, the reader will find here definitions of terms used in diagnoses and treatments of mental disorders, and in social, industrial, and educational psychology. In general, definitions are brief but adequate for a beginning student. Some terms have a number of different definitions depending on their use in a particular discipline (see, for example, "functional unity").

In addition to definitions of terminology, there are some biographical sketches, primarily of leading psychologists. The length of an article does not necessarily reflect the relative importance of a given individual. Compared to older works, however—e.g., English and English's *A Comprehensive Dictionary of Psychological and Psychoanalytical Terms* (McKay, 1958)—it is not only more up to date but also much more comprehensive. —Bohdan S. Wynar. [R: ALA 73; ARBA 74, item 1604]

INDEXES

753. Grinstein, Alexander. **The Index of Psychoanalytic Writings, Volumes X–XIV**. New York, International Universities Press, 1971-75. 5v. index. $150.00/set. LC 56-8932. ISBN 0-8236-2570-2(v.X); 0-8236-2571-0(v.XI); 0-8236-2572-9 (v.XII); 0-8236-2573-7(v.XIII); 0-8236-2574-5(v.XIV).

The Index of Psychoanalytic Writings was originally an expansion and updating of J. Richman's *Index Psycho-Analyticus, 1893-1926* (London, Hogarth Press, 1928). In its three sets, the *Index* presents a complete bibliography of topics in the area of psychoanalysis from its origins through 1969. The first five volumes, covering the literature through 1952, were published in 1956-60; the four additional volumes list the literature through 1959 (published 1964-66). The present supplementary volumes bring the *Index* up to date by providing a comprehensive non-evaluative listing of psychoanalytical literature from 1960 through 1969.

Volumes X–XIII include: 1) books, articles, monographs and pamphlets that deal with psychoanalysis or that apply psychoanalytic thinking to other fields, in any language during the above-mentioned period; 2) relevant materials published before 1960 that had been omitted from previous volumes of the *Index*; 3) books, articles, monographs, and pamphlets published from 1960 through 1969 by members of the International Psycho-Analytical Association, even when not obviously analytic; 4) all abstracts and reviews appearing in "official" psychoanalytic journals in English, and in "official" foreign language journals as available. Volume X contains an appendix of English translations of works of Sigmund Freud as listed in all preceding volumes of the *Index*. Volumes X–XIII are arranged alphabetically by authors (A—Z), and under each author alphabetically according to the title in the original language; the English translation always follows all foreign language titles.

Volume XIV, the subject index to this third set, is based on titles and broad general concepts dealt with in given publications. Because of the author arrangement of the *Index*, the instructions to this cross-index of subjects should be read carefully if one is to have full access to a specific topic throughout the volumes.

Using this extensive and fundamental reference work, one has to admire the immense work put into it. This set is worth its price, and its usefulness extends to many disciplines. —Miluse Soudek. [R: ARBA 76, item 1503]

BIOGRAPHY

754. Nordby, Vernon J., and Calvin S. Hall. **A Guide to Psychologists and Their Concepts.** San Francisco, W. H. Freeman; distr. New York, Scribner's, 1974. 187p. illus. index. (A Series of Books in Psychology). $8.00; $3.50pa. LC 74-11165. ISBN 0-7167-0760-8; 0-7167-0759-4pa.

Forty-two psychologists were selected by virtue of the viability and influence of their ideas on the contemporary psychological scene. These are nineteenth and twentieth century American and European psychologists who represent every field of psychology, including among them medical doctors who specialize in psychiatry. The essence of their theories is distilled for quick reference and presented with a brief biographical sketch for the general reader and the student with a minimal background in psychology. Excluded are historical figures whose activities do not bear on the contemporary psychological scene, along with important experimental and applied psychologists whose contributions have been primarily practical rather than of an original, theoretical nature. The 400 concepts identified with these psychologists are printed in the text in boldface or italics and listed alphabetically in the subject index. A short bibliography of the most important published works of each psychologist is also included with each sketch.

The authors cite in their introduction a number of sources that give more complete accounts of the various concepts and theories described in this guide, which is not intended to be exhaustive. The biographical information tends to be more personalized and anecdotal than that found in two comparable brief psychology reference sources recently published: *Psychology '73/'74 Encyclopedia* (Guilford, Conn., Dushkin, 1973) and *Dictionary of Behavioral Science*, edited by Benjamin B. Wolman (New York, Van Nostrand Reinhold, 1973). These two sources present comparable information in a more abstracted and synthesized manner, rather like a curriculum vita, highlighting only the major events in the lives of these personalities. The biographical information selected by all three sources is slightly different in each case. Based on a brief sample, the concepts and theories identified with the 42 psychologists in Nordby and Hall's guide seem more numerous and more specific. One finds in the *Dictionary of Behavioral Science* approximately half of the concepts identified by Nordby and Hall, and only one-third of these are accessible through *Psychology '73/'74*. Because of the orientation of this work, concepts and theories are more precisely and consistently attributed to the psychologists who originated them. A second edition of the work is planned. —Lorraine Schulte. [R: LJ, Aug 75, p. 1402; BL, 22 Sept 75, pp. 197-98; RQ, Fall 75, pp. 76-77; Choice, Jan 75, p. 1700; ARBA 76, item 1504]

PARAPSYCHOLOGY AND THE OCCULT

755. Cavendish, Richard, ed. **Encyclopedia of the Unexplained: Magic, Occultism and Parapsychology.** New York, McGraw-Hill, 1974. 304p. illus.(part col.). bibliog. index. $17.95. LC 73-7991. ISBN 0-07-010295-3.

The editorial approach of this much needed reference work is one of "sympathetic neutrality" toward three overlapping categories: parapsychology, magic and the occult, and divination. Consultant J. B. Rhine, noted expert and author on psychic research, stresses that much of this information has previously been hidden from the layman and that now the reader can decide for himself about the topics, which range from systems that have no reliable proof to those that have accumulated a body of evidence.

Because of space limitations, there is a concentration on the nineteenth and twentieth century West. Arrangement is alphabetical; length of articles varies greatly, but many of the longer ones are signed by authorities on the subject and are accompanied by bibliographies. The helpful index of names and book titles occasionally misses briefly mentioned people. The article on yoga fails to mention Swami Yogananda, who brought yoga to the United States, and his world organization, Self-Realization Fellowship. The bibliography of over 500 books and articles, which is otherwise complete, fails to mention his books and, for some reason, those of L. Ron Hubbard. There is no mention of Scientology, although, according to the preface, the encyclopedia does not shy away from exposés. The societies that are included are mostly those of European origin.

Tiny flaws aside, this up-to-date, interestingly written, and beautifully illustrated work will throw much light on many previously unknown or little known secrets and research. —Margaret Kaminski. [R: LJ, Aug 74, p. 1925; WLB, Dec 74, p. 318; ALA 74; ARBA 75, item 1604]

756. White, Rhea A., and Laura A. Dale, comps. **Parapsychology: Sources of Information Compiled under the Auspices of the American Society for Psychical Research.** Metuchen, N.J., Scarecrow, 1973. 303p. index. $7.50. LC 73-4853. ISBN 0-8108-0617-7.

This comprehensive book provides many sources of information on parapsychology. There are 282 annotated entries of the best books in the field, covering 24 topics (e.g., altered states of consciousness, critical review of literature, experimental research, mediums and sensitives, precognition and retrocognition, survival, unorthodox healing). The books were selected on the bases of scientific merit as well as interest value, and they should help beginning and serious students and librarians to select materials wisely from the mass of literature currently published. The annotations accurately reflect the contents of the books and are clearly written. Other important contributions of this source book are the sections that describe 1) parapsychological topics in encyclopedias; 2) parapsychological organizations, including their addresses and functions; 3) parapsychological periodicals, including addresses and information pertaining to their editorial policies; 4) various sources of scientific recognition of parapsychology (e.g., academic institutions that have sponsored courses and research); and 5) a glossary of terms. Other sources of information include very detailed indices of names, topics, books and periodicals in the field, and bibliographical references. This source book is clearly the best to date; it provides a wealth of information for persons with differing interests and levels of experience in parapsychology. —Gregory T. Fouts. [R: WLB, Nov 73, p. 263; ARBA 74, item 1619]

CHAPTER 39

MEDICAL SCIENCES

BIBLIOGRAPHIES

757. Andrews, Theodora. **A Bibliography of the Socioeconomic Aspects of Medicine.** Littleton, Colo., Libraries Unlimited, 1975. 209p. index. $10.00. LC 74-34054. ISBN 0-87287-104-5.

Divided into two major sections, general reference sources and source material by subject area, this bibliography presents 569 annotated references to socioeconomic aspects of medicine. Social, political, and economic implications are the linking factors to medicine. Limited to mostly American sources, the books are mainly those written after 1969.

Entries are complete with pagination, price, and book numbers. The length of annotation varies from two sentences to several paragraphs. The information is complete enough to indicate audience, useful material and facts, and the purpose of the author. Occasionally, an annotation reflects the annotator's personal opinion.

Government publications are included as well as general information sources. The 65 periodicals listed represent a good cross section of the area. Under source material by subject area appear health care delivery; ethics; hospital and nursing homes; mental health; drug abuse, alcoholism, and tobacco; the environment; and patent medicine, quackery, and questionable belief. But don't expect to find malpractice or dying. In all, this title is intended for use by laymen, librarians, and personnel involved in the health sciences field. —Roylene G. Cunningham. [R: ARBA 76, item 1511]

758. Walters, LeRoy, ed. **Bibliography of Bioethics, Volume I.** Detroit, Gale, 1975. 225p. index. $24.00. LC 75-4140. ISBN 0-8103-0978-5.

This is the first volume in a projected series of current bibliographies on the new and interdisciplinary subject of bioethics. The volume covers references from 1973 on medical ethics, research ethics, and social questions relating to biomedical and behavioral technology. The bibliography was compiled at the Center for Bioethics, Kennedy Institute at Georgetown University, with funding mostly from the National Library of Medicine. The listing includes 800 items published in both print and non-print media in English. Included are court decisions, laws, films and audio tapes in addition to journal and newspaper articles, letters to the editor, and monographs.

There is a bioethics thesaurus that has 479 searchable terms, with cross references from other common synonyms. Also included are a subject entry section, a list of journals cited (with ISSNs), a title index, and an author index. In the subject entry section, each reference includes full bibliographic information and a list of descriptors. One unusual aspect of the section is the coordination of subject headings so that articles on Human Experimentation on the Mentally Retarded are separated from articles on Human Experimentation on Prisoners. The system takes up more room, but it could make the bibliography easier to use.

This is the beginning of an important series of works that will be useful to anyone concerned with ethics and human beings—that is to say, to anyone. —Shirley B. Hesslein. [R: LJ, 15 Dec 75, p. 2316; ARBA 76, item 1520]

ENCYCLOPEDIAS

759. Larson, Leonard A., ed., and Donald E. Herrmann, asst. ed. **Encyclopedia of Sport Sciences and Medicine**. Under the sponsorship of the American College of Sports Medicine, the University of Wisconsin, and in cooperation with other organizations. New York, Macmillan, 1971. 1707p. $45.00. LC 70-87898.

This publication, which is international in scope, summarizes the scientific literature of this interdisciplinary field and serves as a definition of the sports medicine field, which is somewhat in the development stage.

The encyclopedia contains over 1,000 signed articles that present data on all the influences that affect the human organism before, during, and after participation in sports. Since the editors felt that any force, stress, or environmental factor that influences the human being in such instances is within the scope of sport sciences and medicine, the context of physical activity has been enlarged to include the social, emotional, physical, and intellectual characteristics, abilities, and capabilities of the individual independently, the individual within the group, and the group as a whole. Consequently, the coverage of the encyclopedia is quite broad. Such areas as the environment, emotions and the intellect, drugs, prevention of disease, safety, rehabilitation, and physical activity and the handicapped individual are included, along with the more obvious areas. Some detailed information is also included regarding individual sports—the basic skills required, evaluation, and skill measurement.

Over 500 writers, authorities in science and medicine, contributed to the encyclopedia. Numerous approaches, including experimental, clinical, and theoretical approaches, were used. For instance, certain articles have been written theoretically because of a lack of research data.

The publication is impressive and well-written and it has considerable value as a general reference book. It is organized in 10 general areas. References are included in most cases. Articles vary in length from about a quarter of a page to two or three pages. The detailed subject index makes it easy to locate material on specific topics. The author index includes the names of authors of the articles and also the names of the authors in the citations. The publication is unique in that no other work of this kind and scope is available. —Theodora Andrews. [R: ARBA 72, item 1636]

DICTIONARIES

760. **Black's Medical Dictionary.** 30th ed. By William A. R. Thomson. London, Adam & Charles Black; distr. New York, Barnes and Noble, 1974. 934p. illus.(part col.). $13.50. ISBN 0-7136-1441-2.

Since 1906, *Black's Medical Dictionary* has been a standard and authoritative dictionary source in medicine. It has been designed both as a quick reference for the medical profession and as a medical educational tool for the layman.

The present edition has been completely reset by computer-based typesetting. Prior to this edition, the last complete resetting was in 1951, when the twentieth edition was produced. Thus, in addition to the usual updating practices, several important changes are obvious in the thirtieth edition.

(1) The text has been radically and comprehensively revised. As indicated in the preface, the sections on burns and scalds, clothing, dermatitis, duodenal ulcer, eczema, exercise, and Menière's disease, for example, have been rewritten, and new sections have been added on a wide range of subjects, including aversion therapy, hearing aids, irritable colon, mushroom-workers' lung, and prostaglandins, as well as a selection of important new drugs that have been introduced since the last edition appeared.

(2) All the 441 black and white illustrations have been, for the first time, incorporated on the text pages instead of on separate plates.

A good and worthwhile investment indeed! —Ching-chih Chen. [R: Choice, Jan 75, p. 1602; ARBA 76, item 1522]

761. **Blakiston's Gould Medical Dictionary.** 3rd ed. New York, McGraw-Hill, 1972. 1828p. illus. index. (A Blakiston Publication). $14.00. LC 78-37376. ISBN 0-07-005683-8.

A new computer-produced edition of a classic medical dictionary, *Blakiston's Gould Medical Dictionary* is the latest of a series that began in 1890 with *A New Medical Dictionary* by Dr. George M. Gould. This edition is completely revised, with updated definitions and a new arrangement. It has been customary in medical dictionaries to list definitions by category, such as "operation," "disease," or "syndrome." In this volume, "Paget's disease" appears under "P," "fenestration operation" under "F." Eponyms are identified, and basic biographical data are given. Each of the more than 7,000 entries is provided with pronunciation, brief etymology, form for dividing, and a clear, brief definition. There are frequent cross references. There are 26 plates, and the appendix covers such areas as anatomical tables, phobias, and weights and measures. Medical, dental, and pharmacological terms are included. —Shirley B. Hesslein. [R: ARBA 73, item 1557]

762. Magalini, Sergio. **Dictionary of Medical Syndromes.** Philadelphia, Lippincott, 1971. 591p. $18.00. LC 73-109956. ISBN 0-397-50278-8.

This work presents information about individual syndromes or "symptom complexes" from every branch of medicine. There are approximately 1,800 separate entries, and the following information is usually given: synonyms, symptoms and signs, etiology, diagnostic procedures, therapy, prognosis, and bibliography. The information is presented in this order because the author feels that this best corresponds to the doctor's approach to his patient.

The material for the dictionary was said to be collected from about 10,000 medical articles and more than 50 textbooks. Many of the names of medical syndromes are eponymic—that is, they are named after a person, usually the discoverer. This volume is not limited to eponyms, but it does include a large number of them. The arrangement is alphabetical; also included is an alphabetical index where synonymous names appear, making the use of cross references in the text unnecessary.

There are at least two other works that are somewhat similar to this dictionary. The first that comes to mind is Jablonski's *Illustrated Dictionary of Eponymic Syndromes and Diseases and Their Synonyms* (Saunders, 1969), which is quite similar but which is limited to eponymic entries only and has no index. It is illustrated, however, and Magalini's work is not. The other work is Kelly's *Encyclopedia of Medical Sources* (Williams and Wilkins, 1948), which is also limited to eponymic entries but which has an index with other entries. All three of the works attempt to include original literature references. The Magalini work seems to be more complete than the others; it should be valuable particularly for physicians, students, medical librarians, researchers, and medical writers. —Theodora Andrews. [R: ARBA 72, item 1637]

763. **Stedman's Medical Dictionary: Illustrated**. 22nd ed. Baltimore, Williams and Wilkins, 1972. 1533p. illus. index. $19.95. LC 78-176294. ISBN 0-683-07919-0.

A new edition of a classic medical dictionary, which has been updated with the help of the computer. *Stedman's Medical Dictionary* began in 1911; this is the 22nd edition, thoroughly up to date and complete. Thirty-one color plates and illustrations are scattered throughout, and there are 11 appendixes. The updating is massive: 7,199 new entries and 24,877 revised definitions. *Stedman's* continues to group definitions by category, but for assistance in locating terms, Appendix 11 is an alphabetic index to subentries, for checking the categories that words relate to. "Germ," for instance, relates to six categories, including "cell," "disease," and "theory." Eponymic terms are cross-referenced to diseases and syndromes, and biographical information is briefly mentioned. An excellent reference tool for the technical medical vocabulary which includes pharmacological and dental terms as well as the purely medical.

Choosing between this and *Gould* may really be a matter of taste. The differing arrangements are equally easy to use. *Stedman's* seems to cover more material, but the extra terms are the very specialized ones. The vocabulary in *Gould* seems to be a fraction less technical. —Shirley B. Hesslein. [R: ARBA 73, item 1558]

764. Thomas, Clayton L., ed. **Taber's Cyclopedic Medical Dictionary**. 12th ed. Philadelphia, F. A. Davis, 1973. 1v.(various paging). illus. $9.50; $10.95 thumb-indexed. LC 62-8364. ISBN 0-8036-8303-0; 0-8036-8302-2 thumb-indexed.

This work maintains the high quality of earlier editions. Because the type for this edition was set by computer, which allows for last-minute additions, the material is unusually up to date. New tables and illustrations have been included, and obsolete terms have been dropped. For these definitions older editions must be consulted. The dictionary is intended for all persons concerned with the promotion of health, care of the sick, and prevention of disease. Areas covered are medicine in general, nursing, diagnosis and treatment, drugs, foods, chemistry, and many allied sciences. Most definitions are concise, but a few take up a column or more. The extensive appendix section presents such material as a list of poison control centers in the United States and Canada, a table for radiological emergencies, dietary information, a five-language outline for basic medical diagnosis and treatment, physiological standards for blood, and many other useful lists and tables. *Dorland's* and *Stedman's* dictionaries are more complete and scholarly, but this work contains much useful information in a somewhat simpler presentation. —Theodora Andrews. [R: ARBA 74, item 1643]

765. Thomson, William A. R. **Thomson's Concise Medical Dictionary**. Edinburgh, Churchill Livingstone; distr. New York, Longman, 1973. 439p. $7.00. ISBN 0-443-00940-6.

With considerable experience as a physician and editor of a medical journal, Thomson has produced a dictionary of interest to all health sciences personnel, especially students. The outstanding feature of this volume is that it has short concise definitions of most words that such individuals are likely to encounter during their studies and daily routines. It is excellent for quick reference and can be carried in the laboratory coat pocket. This is one of the few medical dictionaries written and produced in Britain. There are numerous references to B.P. 1968 (*British Pharmacopoeia*, 1968), B.P.C. 1968 (*British Pharmaceutical Codex*, 1968), and B.P. Commission; if they are available, the *Pharmacopoeia* and *Codex* can provide additional information on chemical compounds, such as description, structural formula, identification, preparation, actions and uses, dose, etc. Anatomical terms constitute a large percentage of the entries; this is perhaps wise, considering the current lack of emphasis on memorization in the health sciences curricula. The format is good; typographical errors are minimal. The print size is adequate and boldface type is used effectively. Pronunciation, syllabication, and etymology are not indicated, and there are no illustrations. However, derivations are given for some of the more important prefixes and suffixes used in medical terms. Abbreviations have been reduced to a minimum. There are two appendixes: one consists of tables of arteries, muscles, nerves, and veins; the other covers weights and measures. —James E. Bobick. [R: ARBA 75, item 1625]

FAMILY MEDICAL GUIDES

766. Andelman, Samuel L. **The New Home Medical Encyclopedia**. New York, Quadrangle Books; distr. New York, Harper and Row, 1973. 4v. illus. $29.95. LC 71-116070. ISBN 0-8129-0260-2.

The foreword, by Dr. Walter C. Alvarez, sets the tone for this new medical encyclopedia for laymen; it discusses the frequent communication gap between physicians and patients and stresses the need for up-to-date concise information presented with a minimum of technical jargon.

Individual articles vary in length from a few lines, for a simple definition, to several pages. The article on burns, for example, gives a one-column description of the physical changes caused by first, second, and third degree burns, a one-page section on first aid for burns, and a section on "how a doctor treats burns," followed by a section on skin grafts. Under the heading "cancer," there is a general discussion, then sections on "what is cancer," "why does cancer start," "foods, drugs and cancer," "how cancer is transmitted," and "treatment of cancer." This is followed by discussion of the individual types of cancer.

There is no index, but there are many *see* references to related articles. The illustrations are helpful. Some are simple line drawings explaining anatomical features, others are photographs of pertinent histological or physiological conditions. Charts of nutritional values and similar tabular matter are set off in colored blocks.

The absence of the condescending attitude so often found in medical books for the layman is to be welcomed. The overall impression of this encyclopedia is a very good one. —Suzanne K. Gray. [R: ARBA 74, item 1668]

767. **The New Illustrated Medical Encyclopedia for Home Use: A Practical Guide to Good Health**. Ed. by Robert E. Rothenberg. New York, Abradale Press, 1974. 4v. illus.(part col.). index. $50.00. LC 67-14553. ISBN 0-8109-0284-2.

The questions that patients or their families would like to ask are often not asked, frequently because patients are afraid to impose on the busy doctor's time; and even those questions that are asked sometimes remain unanswered, because the doctor's explanation is not fully understood. But knowledge of one's medical problem and access to accurate information about health and disease are rights that everyone has.

Recognized medical specialists have collaborated with Dr. Rothenberg in this encyclopedic compilation of such questions, with succinct, authoritative answers. Medical terms are clearly explained at the end of the fourth volume, which also contains a detailed index. The extensive table of contents in the first volume outlines the whole set. It is thus very easy to locate individual items. Each cha~*er starts with cross references to related topics, considerably enlarging coverage of each subject.

Senior citizens will appreciate the large readable type in this revised edition. Illustrations are exceptionally attractive and informative.

This is not a do-it-yourself medical book; helpful explanations of conditions and problems of health and disease at all stages of human existence are expertly presented. Information is current and coverage remarkably wide. Useful for health educators and students as well as consumers of health care. —Harriette M. Cluxton. [R: ARBA 76, item 1545]

768. Wagman, Richard J., ed. **The New Concise Family Health and Medical Guide**. Chicago, Ferguson; distr. Garden City, N.Y., Doubleday, 1971. 404p. illus. index. $12.95. LC 77-171358. ISBN 0-385-08075-1.

Here is an authoritative, easy-to-follow, popular family medical book. The eight chapters are: staying healthy and attractive through the years, nutrition and weight control, the environment and health, skin and hair, medical emergencies, disease, alcohol, and drugs. The first chapter is 106 pages. The chapter on disease is 168 pages. The book is liberally illustrated with photographs as well as with several dozen color illustrations, diagrams of systems and organs of the body, etc. This guide is quite contemporary in outlook, emphasizing many uniquely modern health hazards such as noise pollution from snowmobiles and jets, pesticides, smog, and mercury. There is a lot of commonsense advice about everyday living: how to take care of one's hair, proper exercise, use of drugs, alcohol and smoking, what to eat, personal hygiene, sports, and so on. Altogether this is a non-technical, reliable, and authoritative family health reference work, easy to read or consult. The family medical book is a popular genre; Wagman's guide should rank with the more successful. —Henry T. Armistead. [R: ARBA 73, item 1591]

PHARMACOLOGY

769. **National Formulary XIV.** 14th ed. Prep. by the National Formulary Board with the Approval of the Board of Trustees, by authority of the American Pharmaceutical Association. Washington, American Pharmaceutical Association; distr. Easton, Pa., Mack, 1975. 1123p. illus. index. $24.00. LC 55-4116. ISSN 0084-6414.

This publication (known as the NF) and the *United States Pharmacopeia* (the USP) are the two compendia that list drugs with official status in the United States. The publications do not duplicate one another; official drugs are designated as either USP or NF. In recent years, the publications have come out at about the same time and at approximately five-year intervals. The compendia are produced by volunteer medical and pharmaceutical scientists, and their basic aim is to set forth standards of identity, strength, quality, purity, packaging, storage, and labeling of drug and related articles. A primary objective of official compendium standards is to ensure uniformity of drug products from lot to lot and from manufacturer to manufacturer.

The largest section of the book (about three-fourths of it) is made up of short monographs (about half a page in length) on each of the therapeutic agents. They are arranged alphabetically by generic name. The rest of the book presents sections on 1) General Tests, Processes, Techniques, and Apparatus; 2) Reagents, Test Solutions, and Volumetric Solutions; and 3) General Information. There is also an interesting section on the history of the *National Formulary*.

The first edition of the NF appeared in 1888, although the USP was established in 1820. It is of note that, although there have long been two official U.S. compendia, most countries have only one or have adopted that of another country. It is likely that this is the last edition of the NF to be prepared as it has been. Steps have recently been taken to unify the two drug standards, setting compendia under one organization; the first supplement to the current USP and the first supplement to the fourteenth edition of the NF have been published as a composite listing. —Theodora Andrews. [R: ARBA 76, item 1552]

770. Osol, Arthur, and Robertson Pratt. **The United States Dispensatory.** 27th ed. Philadelphia, Lippincott, 1973. 1287p. bibliog. index. $30.00. LC 73-2673. ISBN 0-397-55901-1.

This monumental work is a new edition of an old classic. Basically, the dispensatory presents a collection of articles, alphabetically arranged, about individual drugs. Articles are longer than in most drug compendia—one page to several pages, as compared to about half a page in the *U.S. Pharmacopoeia* or the *National Formulary*. The articles contain such information as: chemical, generic, and brand-name nomenclature; chemical structure; a summary of method of synthesis or other form of preparation; pharmacologic action; therapeutic uses; contraindications; untoward effects; warnings and precautions; drug interactions; dosage; and dosage forms. There are also general articles on classes of drugs, such as antibiotics, antihistamines, etc. The work is planned to provide pharmacists with a source of information so that they may better help the physician, other health professionals, and their patients with proper information on the use of drugs. Much of the information included came from scientific journals, and the references are included in the text.

The older editions of the U.S.D. (up to the 26th) were much larger volumes. The reduction in size was brought about by deleting older drugs, botanical descriptions, and explanations of physical and chemical tests and assays for drugs. The older editions are sometimes consulted for this material. —Theodora Andrews. [R: ARBA 74, item 1684]

VETERINARY MEDICINE

771. Miller, William C., and Geoffrey P. West. **Encyclopedia of Animal Care.** 10th ed. Baltimore, Williams and Wilkins, 1972. 1026p. $20.25. LC 73-157555. ISBN 0-7136-1335-1.

Since its first appearance in 1928, this work (presently published in Britain as *Black's Veterinary Dictionary* and modeled after the well-known *Black's Medical Dictionary*) has become established as the standard handbook of British veterinary procedure for the farmer and animal breeder. "The revision for this new edition covers several developments in veterinary medicine, animal husbandry, public health matters and techniques. . . . The results of the Swann Committee's recommendations have been incorporated. . . . The sections on brucellosis and salmonellosis in cattle have been extended, as have those dealing with rabies and diseases of cats. . . . New entries include those on metabolic profile tests, L-forms of bacteria, pheromones, dog ticks, 'oulou fato' and ulcerative spirochaetosis of pigs. . . . The prevention of disease as well as first-aid has received attention. . . ." Arrangement is alphabetical. The lack of an index is compensated for by ample cross references, though there are a few blind and circuitous references. The style of writing is clear and concise, but it may seem a bit stilted to many American readers. Any compendium of this sort must be supplemented by reference to periodical literature for the newest developments. [R: ARBA 74, item 1691]

CHAPTER 40

AGRICULTURAL SCIENCES

AQUARIUMS

772. Hoedeman, J. J. **Naturalists' Guide to Fresh-Water Aquarium Fish**. New York, Sterling, 1974. 1152p. illus.(part col.). maps. bibliog. index. $30.00. LC 72-95209. ISBN 0-8069-3722-X.

This substantial volume, a revised and expanded translation of the fifth Dutch edition, focuses primarily, as the title suggests, on the natural history and taxonomy of aquarium fishes in their native habitats; it is only secondarily a guide to their care and breeding in the aquarium. It is in two parts: a clear and thorough summary of all aspects of fish biology, designed for the reader who lacks an extensive background in zoology (including a short chapter on the fundamentals of aquarium maintenance); and a systematically arranged survey of more than 1,100 species of fish that are or have been available to aquarists in Europe and the United States. A few cold-water species are included, but the emphasis is predominantly on warm-water forms of tropical origin. The species accounts vary in length from a sentence or two to several pages and are quite consistently clear and accurate; the infrequent ambiguous statements are, perhaps, attributable to the problems of translation.

Most accounts include a photo of satisfactory quality; occasionally the colors (especially where they are structural, not due to pigmentation) are not lifelike or there is insufficient contrast between the subject and the background. Some lack of correlation between photos and text was noted.

The bibliography is largely confined to taxonomic publications. The index, which includes subjects and common and scientific names, is, in part, also a glossary, incorporating brief but adequate definitions of scientific terms. It is very thorough, but not analytical, as there is no indication of which page reference under the name of a species refers to the main account and which refers only to passing mention. In a few instances, it is necessary to search under both common and scientific names (e.g., piranha and Serrasalmus) to locate all references to a genus or species. Since no cross references are provided, this could cause the reader who does not know both names to miss some data. However, despite these occasional, and relatively minor, flaws, this is an important reference, containing a vast amount of information that will be useful to both ichthyologists and aquarists. —Paul B. Cors. [R: Choice, Oct 74, p. 1160; WLB, Oct 74, pp. 185-86; LJ, Aug 74, p. 1926; ALA 74; ARBA 75, item 1668]

BEVERAGES

773. Lichine, Alexis. **Alexis Lichine's New Encyclopedia of Wines & Spirits.** 2nd ed. New York, Alfred A. Knopf, 1974. 716p. illus. maps. bibliog. index. (A Borzoi Book). $20.00. LC 74-7734. ISBN 0-394-48995-0.

Wine merchant Lichine has here produced *the* definitive basic book about wines, in a revision of his well-received 1967 book. His superb and well-written introductory material covers history, health, cellars, vinification processes, and viticulture. The main body is alphabetical in arrangement and self-indexing. He covers geographic areas with the types of vines, wines, aperitifs, and locally applied technical terms (much more of the latter for this revision). Sketch maps have been reduced in size to accommodate more text, but for good maps one should consult Johnson's *World Atlas of Wine* (Simon and Schuster, 1971).

Most entries are long, especially for French and German wine-growing areas, and chateaux or specific appellations are also given their own alphabetical entries. Appendixes include classifications of Médoc, Pomerol, Graves, St. Emilion, and other Bordeaux areas (including Bourg and Blaye for the first time), plus German wines, a new feature; container information; tables of spirit strength and conversions; updated vintage charts through 1973; pronouncing glossary; and a good historical bibliography through 1973. In fact, all parts of the book have been thoroughly revised through 1973. Other changes: upgrading of wine qualities (e.g., the Italian Abruzzi has changed from 1967's "pleasant but unimportant" to 1974's "agreeable"); new material on the United States (from 31 columns to 54, plus three more maps); many additional entries; and primary measurements now in "hectares" instead of the previous edition's "acres." This is a well-organized book that is also very enjoyable to read. —Dean Tudor. [R: WLB, Jan 75, pp. 357-58; LJ, 1 Jan 75, p. 45; BL, 15 Mar 75, p. 774; ARBA 76, item 1562]

774. Simon, André L. **The International Wine and Food Society's Encyclopedia of Wines.** New York, Quadrangle; distr. New York, Harper and Row, 1973. 312p. illus. maps. bibliog. $12.50. LC 72-85052. ISBN 0-8129-0303-X.

This is the legacy left behind after Simon died in 1970, when he was well past the age of 90. It had been developed from a number of his previous books, such as *A Dictionary of Wines, Spirits and Liqueurs* (Citadel, 1963), itself based on a 1935 *Dictionary of Wine*, and his 1970 edition of *A Wine Primer*, often revised and now available as a Penguin paperback in 1973. He opens with a brief 50-page description on wines of the world, then presents his 200-page "gazetteer," followed by 40 pages of maps. The 7,000 entries are either vineyard names or place names that correspond to types of wine; hence, great wines and *vins ordinaires* are given equal prominence. They are in alphabetical order, with adequate cross references. Each entry on the double-column pages has about three lines to describe: 1) the corresponding map number; 2) its correct designation in terms of its country's laws and regulations (e.g., France's A.O.C. "Pomerol"); 3) its location in terms of its largest neighbor; 4) a half dozen words or so about its quality (e.g., "ordinary to fair light white dessert wine"); and 5) the country of origin. Its main value, then, lies in the rapidity with which it identifies a wine, distinguishing it from others with a similar name.

The quantity and brevity of the entries make this book more a dictionary than an encyclopedia. There are defects: the maps are so small and sketchy as to be virtually useless except to identify a particular wine as indeed coming from a particular country (but from where within?); although a good description of Argentinian wines is presented (one of the few in print), the map is indecipherable, since all of the Western Hemisphere is reduced to a 5 inch by 8 inch plate—and on magenta paper, yet; and there are no general entries, as found on the labels of inexpensive wines such as "Hautes Côtes." Johnson's *World Atlas of Wine* (Simon and Schuster, 1971) has better maps, identifies "Hautes Côtes," and provides a non-descriptive gazetteer for its many illustrations and color maps. Simon's book lacks both illustrations and color. The information provided in these two is, of course, duplicated. Thus, the choice is either Johnson for a subject arrangement, large maps, and illustrations, or Simon for a dictionary of wine names. —Dean Tudor.
[R: BL, 15 Nov 73, p. 303; WLB, Sept 73, p. 79; LJ, July 73, p. 2104; ARBA 74, item 1698]

COSMETICS

775. Winter, Ruth. **A Consumer's Dictionary of Cosmetic Ingredients: Complete Information about the Harmful and Desirable Ingredients Found in Men's and Women's Cosmetics.** New York, Crown, 1974. 236p. $3.95pa. LC 73-91516. ISBN 0-517-514753.

Recent FDA regulations require that cosmetic manufacturers list ingredients on labels. The purpose of this book is to allow the consumer to look up specific cosmetic ingredients and to determine their origins, functions, and safety. The terminology and depth of description are designed for the average consumer, for whom the *Merck Index* would be too detailed and technical. References are given from chemical names to more common names. The definitions tell what the ingredient is, what it comes from, what it is used for, and any advantages or disadvantages (allergies, poisons, side effects, effects on lab animals, danger to children). The emphasis is definitely on the harmful effects; this book may turn many people on to making their own cosmetics at home. Winter is the author of *The Consumer's Dictionary of Food Additives* (Crown, 1972). —Nancy Tudor.
[R: WLB, Nov 74, p. 246; LJ, 15 June 74, p. 1700; ALA 74; ARBA 75, item 940]

DOMESTIC ANIMALS

776. **The Complete Dog Book: The Photograph, History, and Official Standard of Every Breed Admitted to AKC Registration, and the Selection, Training, Breeding, Care and Feeding of Pure-Bred Dogs.** 15th ed. New York, Howell Book House, 1975. 672p. illus. index. $7.95. LC 72-88163. ISBN 0-87605-461-0.

This edition of the American Kennel Club's official publication lists breed standards, revised and corrected as of May 1, 1975. Arranged by dog groups—sporting, hounds, working, terriers and non-sporting dogs—listings for each breed follow a standard format: a brief history of the breed, followed by the official standard (general appearance; head, neck, and chest; legs and feet; tail; coat; color; movement; weight and height at shoulders). Under each subhead disqualifying deviations are given.

The book concludes with a long, 100-page section on caring for a dog, advice on first aid, a glossary, and an index. The index is important because the main listing is categorical by group.

The Complete Dog Book is the main tool used by judges at dog shows. The AKC's standards are carefully worded to allow a precise determination of any dog's good and bad points. Considering that interest in dogs is both high and constant, a current edition of the book should be in every public library. [R: BL, 1 Dec 75, p. 493; ARBA 76, item 1564]

777. Dangerfield, Stanley, and Elsworth Howell, eds. **The International Encyclopedia of Dogs**. With special contributions by Maxwell Riddle. New York, McGraw-Hill, 1971. 480p. $19.95. LC 70-161547. ISBN 0-07-015296-9.

The editors describe this book as an international work, stating that contributors were commissioned from the appropriate countries to write with authority on breeds, kennel clubs, shows, and specialist subjects. A list of contributors is at the front; American articles are written by Maxwell Riddle, an AKC judge and newspaper columnist. The book was produced by Rainbird Reference Books, Ltd., London, and published in the United States and Canada by McGraw-Hill in association with Howell Book House.

The encyclopedia covers dog care; training and management; diseases; all breeds recognized by Kennel Clubs of America, United Kingdom, Canada, Australia and New Zealand; some breeds from other countries; genetics and biology; international shows, and other topics. Arrangement is alphabetical beginning with Aberdeen Terrier and Abortion, ending with Yorkshire Terrier and Zygoma. British spellings and names are used, with cross references under alternative names. Small caps are used within articles to signal related articles where additional information may be found. Every page contains one or more black and white photos or sketches, over 600 in all. A photo accompanies almost every article on a particular breed. In addition, 126 full-color plates present champions of nearly every important breed. The double-column pages are easy to read, entries are simple to locate, and the whole is handsomely illustrated. Articles on various breeds discuss the origin, development, and use of dogs, physical characteristics, and special traits, qualities, or defects; articles end with a summary: essentials of the breed. While the articles are highly informative, they are well written and do not display the impersonal, dull writing characteristic of over-edited reference works. This is an attractive and easy-to-use reference book covering a wide range of topics of interest to dog lovers and experts. —Christine L. Wynar. [R: ALA 72; ARBA 72, item 700]

778. Hamilton, Ferelith, ed. **The World Encyclopedia of Dogs**. New York, World, 1971. 672p. illus. index. $20.00. LC 72-158530.

Ferelith Hamilton, editor of the encyclopedia and editor of *Dog World*, was assisted by Arthur F. Jones, editor of the *American Kennel Gazette*, and 120 contributors, who are fully identified in a section at the back. The encyclopedia consists of articles on each of 280 breeds, arranged alphabetically under seven major divisions: working dogs, other working and utility dogs, gundogs, hounds, terriers, toy dogs, Spitz or Nordic dogs. British names are used for the breeds; names used in other countries are shown in parentheses and are also listed in the index. The articles vary in length but follow the same sequence: history and development, color, care, character, and the salient points of the official Standards. The articles tend to provide a great deal of historical background and reflect individual contributors' knowledge of the breed. Controversial issues are sometimes pointed out, (e.g., origin of the mastiff). For each breed, several photos are provided to display the development of the breed, to portray the salient points of male and female animals, usually champions, and puppies at the age when they are likely to be purchased. In addition, the editors have illustrated as many as possible of the breeds with head studies, front and side views, of leading pedigree dogs. While many of the 1,100 illustrations (mostly photos) are clear and good-looking, some are technically of poor quality. The emphasis is decidedly on informative rather than on aesthetic factors.

In addition to the main sections on breeds, there are articles containing general information, such as evolution of the dog, basic canine anatomy, and the dog in the home. The closing articles cover nutrition, diseases, showing and championship systems, and the dog in use and in sport. A list of national kennel clubs, a glossary, notes on contributors, and an index are at the end. Of special interest is the historical survey of books on dogs and the list of books arranged by breed. These two bibliographic aids are severely limited in their usefulness since only author, title, and date are given. With very small effort, the editors could have provided place and publisher for the benefit of all who need to search for these materials.

In summary, the encyclopedia is a sound work covering more breeds in greater detail than is generally found in reference books; however, the classified arrangement will necessitate additional searching to locate some information.
—Christine L. Wynar. [R: ARBA 72, item 701]

779. Henderson, G. N., and D. J. Coffey, eds. **The International Encyclopedia of Cats.** New York, McGraw-Hill, 1973. 256p. illus.(part col.). $17.95. LC 72-10958. ISBN 0-07-027163-7.

Cat lovers, owners, and breeders will appreciate this non-technical, authoritative encyclopedia, which covers every aspect of owning and caring for cats. Photographs (over 60 in color and 100 in black and white) of exceptionally fine quality enhance the visual appeal of this fine volume on the cat.

The more than 700 alphabetical entries contain explicit and useful advice on buying, breeding, grooming, genetics, the cat in the home, sickness, and health. There are descriptions and photographs of all well-known breeds, newly developed species, and the larger wild cats, plus articles on the role of the cat in different countries, periods, religion, art, music, literature, legend, and lore.

Encyclopedic in format, with many cross references (but no index), it includes articles on such diverse topics as achondroplasia (defective cartilage formation before birth); brain disorders; diaphragmatic hernia; the Jaquarondi (which has a remarkable resemblance to the family that includes badgers, martens, weasels and otters); parasites; the Royal College of Veterinary Surgeons; tongue disorders; and warts. The line drawings liberally scattered throughout the volume consist primarily of anatomical bisections and silhouettes of the cat structure and skeletal makeup.
—Judy G. Caraghar. [R: ARBA 74, item 1705]

780. Hope, C. E. G., and G. N. Jackson, eds. **The Encyclopedia of the Horse**. New York, Viking, 1973. 336p. illus.(part col.). $22.50. LC 72-90351. ISBN 0-670-29402-0.

This comprehensive encyclopedia covers the history of the various breeds of horses in each country from prehistoric times to the present. Arrangement is by broad headings, and entries cover the role of the horse in film, on stage, in art, and in literature. Each breed is illustrated in large color photographs. There are also numerous illustrations of the horse's anatomy and of equipment related to the horse and to horsemanship. Details of horse sporting events are included as well as lists of events and their winners. [R: WLB, Nov 73, p. 265; LJ, 15 Sept 73, p. 2560; ALA 73; ARBA 74, item 1706]

781. Pond, Grace, ed. **The Complete Cat Encyclopedia**. New York, Crown, 1972. 384p. illus.(part col.). bibliog. index. $15.00. LC 72-77778. ISBN 0-517-50017-5.

Provides all the essential information on U.S. and British standards for cat breeds, plus articles on a wide variety of topics such as nonpedigree cats, genetics, evolution, the cat in the home, boarding, the governing bodies of the cat fancies, anatomy, nutrition, diseases, vetting at shows, breeding, breed numbers (American, British, and Canadian), legends, show judging, and many others. Each article is written within a consistent format and is generously illustrated with photographs, some of which are in color, and drawings. [R: LJ, 15 Dec 72, p. 3981; ALA 72; ARBA 73, item 1480]

FOODS AND COOKING

782. Beard, James, and others, eds. **The Cooks' Catalogue**. New York, Harper and Row, 1975. 565p. illus. bibliog. index. $16.00. LC 75-6329. ISBN 0-06-011563-7.

The subtitle reveals the extent of this cooks' treasure: "A critical selection of the best, the necessary and the special in kitchen equipment and utensils. Over 4,000 items including 200 extraordinary recipes plus cooking folklore and 1,700 illustrations produced with the assistance of the world's leading food authorities." After an introduction (by James Beard) and a three-page section on how to use the book, utensils are discussed under such headings as measuring and cleaning tools; knives, sharpeners, and cutting boards; grinders, crushers, etc.; multipurpose machines; stovetop utensils; oven utensils; roasting and broiling pans; baking pans for batters; pastry baking; and specialty cookware (seafood, eggs, ice-cream, coffee and tea, health food equipment, etc.).

Information provided for each item includes a description (material, size, price) immediately beneath the clear black and white photograph, followed by a detailed paragraph on the item's particular usefulness and any defects it may have. These paragraphs are eminently readable.

The bibliography is a "sampling of books of unusual merit and practical value"; it includes cookbooks, reference books, and books for reading. Each entry gives title, author, publisher, date of publication, and a one- or two-sentence description. Interspersed throughout the book are recipes and kitchen hints—an invaluable addition that will make the book an essential purchase for all serious cooks as well as for the reference departments that serve them. A list at the back of the book gives the manufacturer of each item, plus the manufacturer's item number; an alphabetical list of manufacturers and their addresses follows this. A recipe index and a general index conclude the book. —Ann J. Harwell. [R: LJ, 15 Dec 75, p. 2324; ARBA 76, item 1568]

783. Jacobson, Michael F. **Eater's Digest: The Consumer's Factbook of Food Additives.** Garden City, N.Y., Doubleday, 1972. 260p. illus. index. $5.95. LC 75-186030.

As recently as 1969, the subject of food additives was not considered an "in" topic. However, with the publication of Ruth Winter's *Poisons in Your Food* (Crown, 1972); the meeting of the First White House Conference on Food, Nutrition, and Health; the FDA actions on cyclamates, food coloring, and saccharin; and the rise of the organic and natural food cult—it now seems as if everyone is reading the labels on the foods they buy. And now we have the definitive reference guide to those funny-named chemicals they have been slipping in our hot dogs, beer, and baby foods all these years.

The author, who has a Ph.D. in microbiology from M.I.T. and who is a Naderite, has put together an excellent, non-hysterical factbook that begins with an overview of the subject, with a clear explanation of the "whys" of additives and the means of testing them. The major portion with the greatest reference value is an alphabetical approach to the additives—defining each, giving its use, possible effects, and test results, and providing references to both technical and non-technical articles related to each substance. Another section gives a close-up of a number of common foods such as chili con carne, corned beef hash, and margarine, breaking down the actual ingredients for each.

The appendixes include a list of additives that have been banned, a glossary of terms, and chemical formulas of additives. This is a timely reference work that, in most cases, states its sources. However, what may be GRAS (Generally Recognized as Safe) today could be found by the FDA to be a killer tomorrow. You are what you eat! —Andy Armitage. [R: LJ, Aug 72, p. 2562; ALA 72; ARBA 73, item 1651]

784. Johnson, Arnold H., and Martin S. Peterson. **Encyclopedia of Food Technology.** Westport, Conn., Avi, 1974. 993p. illus. index. (Encyclopedia of Food Technology and Food Science Series, Vol. 2). $65.00. LC 74-14129. ISBN 0-87055-157-4.

This volume is far more than an encyclopedia. A more descriptive title might have been "a dictionary, handbook, manual, and encyclopedia of food and food technology." While food processing methods and technology are fully covered for more than 250 subjects, each article usually provides other useful information concerning the particular food item. Such additional information might include a brief history of the origin and past uses of the item, past methods of processing the item, crop value ranges of the item, and so forth. The subjects covered range from "acidulants" and "acorns" to "yogurt" and "zero milk." Also included are general interest topics such as "bacteriology," "cholesterol," "hydrogenation," "nationality foods," "nutrition," "soul food," and "taboos and food prejudices," to name a few.

Two extra advantages that distinguish this title are biographical information for men and women in the field and a section on achievement awards given by the food industry. The planning and the gathering of information (from 235 individuals outstanding in the field of food technology and its related disciplines) are said to have taken two years. This volume is so rich in details and up-to-date information that it is certainly well worth the time spent. A detailed index and the generous use of cross references and "see" references increase the usefulness of this encyclopedia. An excellent volume to complement and, in some instances, to replace the now somewhat dated *Encyclopedia of Food*, by Artemas Ward. —Elma M. Stewart. [R: BL, 1 Dec 75, pp. 527-28; ARBA 76, item 1574]

785. Kraus, Barbara. **Calories and Carbohydrates**. New York, Grosset & Dunlap, 1971. 322p. illus. $7.95; $1.75pa. LC 70-119037. ISBN 0-448-01982-3.

An alphabetical listing of 7,500 brand names and basic foods with their caloric and carbohydrate contents. For basic foods, the first entries are for the fresh product weighed with seeds as it is purchased in the store, then for the fruits in small portions as they may be eaten or measured. These entries are followed by the processed products, canned, dehydrated, dried, and frozen. This basic plan, with some modifications, is followed for fruits, vegetables, and meats. The book also includes beverages and other liquids. In almost all entries, when data were available, the U.S. Department of Agriculture figures are shown first. The Department of Agriculture values represent averages from several manufacturers and are shown for comparison with the values from individual companies or for use where particular brands are not available. All brand-name products have been italicized and company names appear in parentheses. Cross references facilitate use. All in all, this is a well-prepared compilation. [R: LJ, 1 Oct 71, p. 3114; ALA 71; ARBA 72, item 1724; ARBA 74, item 1716]

HORTICULTURE

786. Angier, Bradford. **Field Guide to Edible Wild Plants**. Harrisburg, Pa., Stackpole, 1974. 256p. illus.(col.). $4.95. LC 73-23042. ISBN 0-8117-0616-8.

Author of a number of books on the subject of camping and living in the out-of-doors, Angier has prepared this field guide, arranged alphabetically by common name. Each plant description includes family, other names, appearance, distribution, and edibility on one page. The facing page contains a multi-color illustration of roots and crown (if edible), stalk, leaves, fruit, and seeds. The pictures are useful in identifying the plant and are an attractive addition. The information should be accurate and helpful to the layman or student. Nutrition information is given in only a few instances, so it adds little to the book. It should also be noted that this type of information is not readily available and represents a needed subject of research. The instruction to eat some foods "dripping with butter" is a dangerous suggestion. There is no index. The book is a good reference for students and the general public. —Doris Flax Kaplan. [R: LJ, 1 Nov 74, p. 2830; ALA 74; ARBA 75, item 1465]

787. **Exotic Plant Manual: Fascinating Plants to Live With—Their Requirements, Propagation and Use.** Alfred Byrd Graf, ed. East Rutherford, N.J., Roehrs Co.; distr. New York, Scribner's, 1970. 840p. illus. index. $27.50. LC 77-115116.

This is a substantial contribution to the understanding of a vast variety of plants cultivated by Americans in homes, offices, stores, greenhouses, and outdoors in warm parts of the United States. A distillation of the best from Graf's vast and scholarly *Exotica III*, it presents more than 4,200 excellent black and white and color pictures of exotic plants, from *Abelia* to *Zygopetalum*. In addition to pictures, the book contains sound descriptions and cultural and other information about every plant illustrated. There are chapters on many subjects of interest, including detailed, reliable recommendations regarding environments and cultural practices, such as watering, fertilizing, propagating, etc. There are chapters on horticultural curiosities, on carnivorous plants, on aquatics, on fruited and berried plants, and much more—all very helpfully illustrated. There is a glossary, a common name index and a generic name index. This is an outstanding contribution to the literature of exotic plants and the part they play in contemporary American horticulture. —Elizabeth C. Hall. [R: Choice, Sept 71, p. 808; LJ, 1 May 71, p. 1597; ALA 71; ARBA 72, item 1536]

788. Hay, Roy, and Patrick M. Synge. **The Color Dictionary of Flowers and Plants for Home and Garden.** Compact ed. Published in collaboration with The Royal Horticultural Society. New York, Crown, 1975. 584p. illus.(col.). $6.95pa. LC 76-75086. ISBN 0-517-524562.

This dictionary of flowers and plants is accompanied by bold colored plates. It will supplement the *Dictionary of Gardening*, prepared by the Royal Horticultural Society, which has no colored plates. The plates have been arranged into six main sections: alpine and rock garden plants; annual and biennial plants; greenhouse and house plants; hardy bulbous plants; perennial plants; trees and shrubs (with climbers and conifers separately grouped within the section). Preceding the photographs are general cultural notes for each section and some helpful techniques on photographing flowers for vivid color and composition. The 2,048 brilliant color plates, in the first 344 pages, are alphabetical by the botanical names within the six main sections. Each of the six plates per page is accompanied by a number and the correct botanical name.

The last 200-plus pages of the volume are the dictionary text, arranged alphabetically by the botanical name with complete cross references from the common names. Here a compact, complete description of the plant is given, noting the identification, flowering time, foliage, soil, hardening, pruning, geographic location, color, and illustration number referring to the plate for the color illustration. This new comprehensive collection of plants in color, published by the Royal Horticultural Society, is of outstanding quality in the handbook size. —Mary Clotfelter. [R: ARBA 76, item 1587]

789. Healey, B. J. **A Gardener's Guide to Plant Names.** New York, Scribner's, 1975(c.1972). 284p. $3.95pa. LC 72-1202. ISBN 0-684-14439-5.

As the title indicates, this is a handbook of plant names; it gives the common names as well as the scientific names. The introduction points out the importance of using and understanding the scientific names and terms. Most reference sources and business firms refer to plants by scientific names rather than by common name. There is a brief history of plant nomenclature. Plants listed are those that grow in open gardens with temperate summer and winter conditions; large trees and shrubs are excluded. In the first part of the book is a list of the most common names and their botanical equivalents in alphabetical order by the common name.

Two-thirds of the book is devoted to the botanical names of the genera and their species (family names) arranged alphabetically by the generic name. Notes and the derivation of the generic names are given along with description of the plant, colors, hardiness, conditioning, recommended varieties, and suggested landscape uses. A glossary of specific names or epithets, a list of typical personal and commemorative names, the family groups, and a glossary of botanical terms conclude the volume.

The book is very readable, well organized, compact, comprehensive, and accurate. As a handbook-type of reference guide, it is a book the horticulturist, botany student, and amateur gardener will enjoy using. —Mary Clotfelter. [R: ARBA 76, item 1588]

790. Pirone, Pascal P. **Diseases and Pests of Ornamental Plants.** 4th ed. New York, Ronald Press, 1970. 546p. illus. index. (An Official Publication of the New York Botanical Garden). $13.50. LC 74-110556. ISBN 0-8260-7175-9.

The years since the third edition of this comprehensive reference book have seen many changes in the control of diseases and pests in plants. A major change, for example, is that DDT has been removed as a control measure. In the use of all other pesticides, those that are recommended first are the ones least harmful to man and animals.

The book is arranged in two parts. Part I, diseases and pests in general, gives an excellent summary of the various diseases and pests plus their general control. Part II, diseases and pests of particular hosts, is the key section of the book. Here, arranged by botanical name of host, are listed all ornamental plants from flowers and grasses to shrubs and trees. For each one, the various diseases and pests are described fully along with their recommended control. Numerous illustrations, descriptive footnotes, and diagrams make this an extremely useful book for professional and amateur gardens, arborists, nurserymen, landscape architects, floriculturists, greenskeepers, and the layman. A comprehensive index covers scientific as well as common names of plants, diseases, and pests. —H. Robert Malinowsky. [R: Choice, June 71, p. 534; ALA 71; ARBA 72, item 1548]

791. Wyman, Donald. **Wyman's Gardening Encyclopedia.** New York, Macmillan, 1971. 1222p. illus.(part col.). $17.50. LC 69-18250.

Among available one-volume encyclopedias of gardening, this is by far the best and most up-to-date. It will serve most amateurs very well and will prove helpful even to those with professional backgrounds. As is usual with the writings of this author, the coverage is selective rather than inclusive, which is both advantageous and disadvantageous. It permits ready comprehension of the particular species and varieties of each genus that Dr. Wyman, a horticulturist of much experience and wise judgment, believes most widely meritorious, but leaves unsatisfied the seeker of information about numerous plants which are, in the author's opinion, less worthy. As is to be expected from one who so long managed the plant collections of The Arnold Arboretum, the discussions of hardy trees and shrubs are especially meritorious and, on the whole, more reliable and helpful than those of many plants in other categories, although the latter are by no means poor or unacceptable. The botanically inclined will regret the omission of the names of many of the families to which the genera discussed belong, information that is often helpful in determining methods of cultivation.

Occasionally one finds rather puzzling entries, the most noteworthy perhaps being *Stectorum glaucum*, for which the complete entry is: "1 foot. Zone 5. Rosettes of foliage 3 in. across; oblanceolate leaves, brownish spotted at tips; flowers an inch long and red, borne in 2-3 in. panicles. Native to Central Europe." No mention of what the plant *is*. Annual? Biennial? Herbaceous perennial? Bulb? Woody plant? No indication of how hardy it is, or how to grow, propagate it, or employ it in the garden. Perhaps *Stectorum* is a figment of the author's imagination. I find no reference to it in Willis's authoritative *Dictionary of Flowering Plants and Ferns*, published in 1966, which lists the names of all genera of flowering plants and ferns published since 1753. If Dr. Wyman's imagination is to be credited as author of a new genus (albeit without Latin description), we must then commend that faculty for providing not only a description of a non-existent plant, but also the pronunciation of its nonexistent name (given as stec-TOR-um). (Could the plant referred to be *Sempervivum tectorum glaucum*?) Despite all this, and some blatant typographical errors, here is a welcome addition to the list of available garden books.
—Elizabeth C. Hall. [R: ARBA 72, item 1550]

CHAPTER 41

ENGINEERING AND TECHNOLOGY

CHEMICAL ENGINEERING

792. Considine, Douglas M., ed. **Chemical and Process Technology Encyclopedia.** New York, McGraw-Hill, 1974. 1266p. illus. index. $35.00. LC 73-12913. ISBN 0-07-012423-X.

This one-volume encyclopedia covers many facets of chemical and process technology—inorganic, organic, and physical chemistry and chemical, metallurgical, and process engineering. Arranged alphabetically, it includes many cross references. Topics include equipment, materials, processes, products, and theory. There is a substantial subject index that includes, for example, some 120 references under steel and two references to barbiturates. In addition to the expected traditional topics, there is material that will be of interest to rather diverse groups of workers: medicinal chemists and metallurgists, electronics engineers, and design specialists. The few entries tested almost at random yielded rather detailed and extensive discussions. Many entries include brief bibliographies. The illustrations seem to be helpful and are of good quality. —John R. Riter, Jr. [R: Choice, Dec 74, p. 1453; ALA 74; ARBA 75, item 1755]

793. **Elsevier's Dictionary of Chemical Engineering.** Comp. by W. E. Clason. New York, American Elsevier, 1969. 2v. $50.00/set. LC 68-54865. ISBN 0-444-407146-6 (v.1); 0-444-40715-4(v.2).

The first volume of this two-volume dictionary, *Dictionary of Chemical Engineering and Laboratory Equipment*, deals with the terminology for apparatus and component parts used in chemical laboratories and in the chemical and allied industries. Apart from the purely chemical apparatus, attention has also been given to installations. The second volume, *Dictionary of Chemical Engineering: Processes and Products*, gives terminology of processes and methods used in chemical engineering as well as terminology concerning raw material, its processing and finished products. Commonly known chemicals are not included. Each volume has a basic table that gives the English terms with their equivalents in French, Spanish, Italian, Dutch, and German. [R: Choice, Oct 69; LJ, 1 Nov 69; ARBA 70, v.2, p. 158]

CONSTRUCTION

794. Harris, Cyril M., ed. **Dictionary of Architecture and Construction.** New York, McGraw-Hill, 1975. 553p. illus. $35.00. LC 74-30219. ISBN 0-07-026756-1.

Not many dictionaries devoted to architecture and construction are available. Since the fields have expanded and developed during the past decades, this well-bound and well-printed volume is welcome. It includes common abbreviations used in the construction industry, definitions of modern terms, tools, machinery, etc., as well as more traditional terms used in architectural history.

The numerous black and white illustrations found in the margins vary in style; some resemble the line drawings found in Bannister Fletcher (*History of Architecture on the Comparative Method*), others look like illustrations to a technical manual. There are plenty of *see* references, which help define variant names and terms. —Julia Sabine. [R: WLB, Nov 75, p. 266; Choice, Nov 75, p. 1142; ARBA 76, item 938]

795. Putnam, R. E., and G. E. Carlson. **Architectural and Building Trades Dictionary**. 3rd ed. Chicago, American Technical Society, 1974. 510p. illus. $9.25. LC 74-75483. ISBN 0-8269-0402-5.

This third edition of a very comprehensive dictionary has been completely updated since the 1955 publication of the second edition. Definitions have been revised where necessary and many new terms have been included. The clear, simple line drawings, diagrams and photographs illustrating many of the definitions are well placed in relation to the text and successfully expand the meaning of many of the terms. The section of legal terms has been retained and an alphabetical listing of building material sizes has been added. This is a thoroughly useful volume for students, professionals, and the general public. —Joan E. Burns. [R: ARBA 75, item 1021]

796. Scott, John S. **A Dictionary of Building**. 2nd ed. Baltimore, Md., Penguin Books, 1974. 392p. illus. $2.50pa. ISBN 0-14-051015-X.

Everyone from the home handyman to the professional builder will find this inexpensive volume of value. This dictionary is an alphabetical list of terms dealing with men, materials, and methods associated with building proper, both traditional and modern. The terms are classified under carpentry; drawing office practice; electrical, joinery, mechanical engineering; painting; plastering; floor and wall tiling; plumbing; quantity surveying; and conversion and working of timber. Because this subject is close to civil engineering, cross references to *A Dictionary of Civil Engineering*, also published by Penguin, are made when necessary. A list of abbreviations and conversion factors is also given. The cross references between English and American terms make the work valuable to both countries. The illustrations of tools of the trade also add value to the work. —Robert J. Havlik. [R: ARBA 75, item 1760]

DATA PROCESSING AND COMPUTER TECHNOLOGY

797. Chandor, Anthony, with John Graham and Robin Williamson. **A Dictionary of Computers**. Middlesex, England, Harmondsworth; distr. Baltimore, Md., Penguin Books, 1970. 407p. $2.45pa. LC 79-497304. ISBN 0-14-051039-7.

This new Penguin reference book provides an excellent introduction to computer terminology. Precise definitions are supplied for some 3,000 words, phrases and acronyms, which include such intriguing technical terms as "graceful degradation," "flip-flop," "output bus driver," and acronyms such as PERT,

COBOL, and ALGOL. In addition to the definitions, there is a concise general article, "Introduction to Computers," which explains in simple terms what computers are and how they are used. Interspersed with the definitions are some 70 general articles, varying from one to several pages in length, that explore specific topics. These topics fall into two groupings: those for the layman (digital computers, systems analysis, programming); and those for the technical reader (character recognition, flowcharting, real time). Several select references are given at the end of most articles for further study. Detailed cross-referencing is supplied and, in any definition, all words defined elsewhere are italicized the first time that they are used.

Considering the importance of the computer in all areas of contemporary society, this pocket book has a high utility. It will appeal to the unsophisticated layman interested in learning about computers; to professionals in fields such as accounting, librarianship, and banking; to engineers who are increasingly dependent upon the services of the computer; and to young technicians in the computer industry who are eager to improve their competence. The textual material is of high quality and is eminently clear and readable. —Alan M. Rees. [R: Choice, Dec 70, p. 1355; ARBA 71, item 125]

798. **Encyclopedia of Computer Science and Technology: Volume 1, Abstract to Amplifiers.** Jack Belzer, Albert G. Holzman, and Allen Kent, exec. eds. New York, Marcel Dekker, 1975. 497p. illus. $60.00. LC 74-29436. ISBN 0-8247-2251-5.

Like the *Encyclopedia of Library and Information Science*, the present work is projected in many volumes (at least 15, according to executive editors Belzer, Holzman, and Kent). There are other similarities between these two encyclopedias in progress: both have the same publisher and they share one name among their executive editors, Allen Kent.

The *Encyclopedia of Computer Science and Technology* finds its raison d'être in the fact that hitherto there has been no encyclopedic survey of computer science addressed to the broad spectrum of its component subfields. One major category of potential users consists of the various kinds of computer scientists, such as program analysts, operations researchers, mathematicians. Secondly, it is addressed to those who use the products of computer technology, a category that definitely includes librarians. Thus, the first volume, the only one issued so far, has two articles on abstracting and indexing services that relate in very specific terms how the computer is used in their preparation. [R: ARBA 76, item 1626]

799. Meek, C. L. **Glossary of Computing Terminology.** New York, CCM Information Corp., 1972. 372p. $12.95. LC 72-80206. ISBN 0-8409-0014-7.

An excellent source for information about computers and all aspects of the computer field, this glossary has clear, well-written explanations. It is primarily a glossary of computer and computer-associated terms, but it also has a 67-page Equipment Numerical Listing, which is especially useful to the reference librarian trying to find his way through the computer numerical soup. The equipment listings offer two approaches: by name of equipment, and by number.

Each term in the glossary is accompanied by a reference symbol that indicates the source from which the definition originates. Each meaning or nuance of a term is represented, and examples are provided for added clarity. In the case of hardware, the description of an item includes its function and capability. Some cross references are provided. The book could be even more useful if it included synonyms and antonyms whenever possible. Otherwise an excellent source for information. —Donald P. Hammer. [R: ARBA 74, item 1619]

800. Sippl, Charles J., and Charles P. Sippl. **Computer Dictionary and Handbook.** 2nd ed. Indianapolis, Howard W. Sams, 1972. 778p. illus. $19.50. LC 70-175572. ISBN 0-672-20850-4.

In the few short years since 1966, when the first edition of this glossary was published, it has become one of the stand-bys in the computer field. This second edition includes 22,000 definitions as against 8,500 in the previous volume. In addition, many new and useful features have been added.

The definitions are well written and clear, and they include much explanatory material. Multiple definitions are given when appropriate. Acronyms and abbreviations are given in the main list of terms, but, in some cases, they are also found under special headings in appendixes. A great many cross references are included and many times a definition is repeated under varying forms of an expression. The terms are arranged letter by letter (thus, "check, instruction" follows "checking, sequence").

About a third of the book consists of appendixes, which provide brief information about many different facets of computer systems and related areas. Most of this information is textbook data on such subjects as computer system principles and procedures, computer systems personnel, management science, model building techniques, operations research, number systems, flowcharting, and computer languages.

Some of these appendixes, however, tend to make the book confusing to use. Definitions of some words appear both in the appendixes and in the main dictionary of terms. This is especially true of mathematical definitions, statistical definitions, acronyms, and abbreviations. The last two are even divided into several groups within an appendix. The user must refer to several places to find these terms or, in some cases, all the definitions of some terms.

In spite of that defect, this dictionary is a highly recommended source for both definitions and basic computer information.

The *Computer Dictionary*, published by Howard W. Sams in 1974, is a stripped-down copy of the *Computer Dictionary and Handbook*, the difference being that the *Computer Dictionary* is a reprint of only the original dictionary. The advantage of this reprint, even though it is two years old and lacks updating, is that for less than half the price one gets a good pocket dictionary without a lot of material that is available in many other sources. —Donald P. Hammer. [R: WLB, May 73, p. 796; ARBA 74, item 1782]

801. **The Way Things Work Book of the Computer: An Illustrated Encyclopedia of Information Science, Cybernetics, and Data Processing.** New York, Simon and Schuster, 1974. 245p. illus. index. $8.95. LC 74-11702. ISBN 0-671-21900-6.

Intended as a quick source of information on the theoretical and practical aspects of computers, this volume is one of a "way things work" series. Designed for both the uninformed and the sophisticated reader, it supplies narrative explanations, simple two-color diagrams, and mathematical equations. The reader can choose the explanation most appropriate to his talents.

As stated in the preface, "the book describes the practical applications that have grown out of the theoretical principles, including the use of the computer in many major technological projects that would be impossible without its invention."

Some of the topics covered include communication, automation, information theory, cybernetics, documentation, number systems, logic elements, storage devices, programming, printers, time-sharing, data banks, artificial intelligence, etc.

In spite of its claims, however, it is not a simple book to understand—a certain amount of sophisitication is required of all readers. An unnecessary annoyance is the very poor typesetting, which uses eight-point type for the narrative explanations. The illustrations in the book are excellent, but the pages of narrative are crowded and poorly designed. Nevertheless, the book contains a great deal of information that is otherwise scattered throughout the literature and therefore hard to find quickly. —Donald P. Hammer. [R: ARBA 75, item 1779]

ELECTRICAL AND ELECTRONICS ENGINEERING

802. Engineering Index, Inc. **Engineering Index Thesaurus.** New York, CCM Information Corp., 1972. 402p. $19.50. LC 72-78325. ISBN 0-8409-0011-2.

More than 11,800 terms or descriptors, primarily in the fields of plastics and electrical/electronics engineering, are identified and cross-referenced in this new thesaurus. It will be a useful manual for libraries, indexers, and information specialists in establishing vocabularies. The thesaurus is similar in format to two previous thesauri published by the Engineers Joint Council—*Thesaurus of Engineering Terms* (TET), 1964, and *Thesaurus of Engineering and Scientific Terms* (TEST), 1967. Even though EIT stresses terms in plastics and electrical/electronics engineering, considerable terminology is included from the fields of aeronautics; astronautics; chemical, civil and mechanical engineering; fluid and solid mechanics; mathematics; nuclear, plasma and solid-state physics; optics; statistics and systems engineering— a fact which makes this more than just a micro-thesaurus. Terms are listed in sets, each consisting of a main term followed by cross reference to broader, narrower, or related terms. Good format and clear type make this an easy-to-use reference work. —H. Robert Malinowsky. [R: ARBA 73, item 1693]

803. Shiers, George. **Bibliography of the History of Electronics.** Metuchen, N.J., Scarecrow, 1972. 323p. index. $9.50. LC 72-3740. ISBN 0-8108-0499-9.

Although the history of electricity goes back for thousands of years, it has been only in the last 100 years that electrical science (and subsequently electronics) has developed into the important field it now is. Today hardly anyone is untouched by radio, television, radar, computers, or industrial electronics.

This bibliography contains 1,820 descriptive annotations of books, articles and reports associated with the history of electronics and telecommunications. The references may be grouped into three sections: 1) chapters on general works, encyclopedias, guides, serials, and indexes; 2) general subject histories and biographies of such inventors as Bell, Crookes, de Forest, Joseph Henry, and Vladimir Zworykin; and 3) specific subjects ranging from broadcasting, electromagnetic waves, and solid-state electronics to television and facsimile. The articles cover the history from the 1860s to the 1950s. An author and subject index is also provided.

Users of the book will range from the electronics amateur to the professional historian of science. The organization of the work is clearly set forth in the introduction, and the short summary of the contents of each chapter helps to show the relationship between sections and subjects. —Robert J. Havlik. [R: ARBA 73, item 1690]

MECHANICAL ENGINEERING

804. Considine, Douglas M., ed. **Encyclopedia of Instrumentation and Control.** New York, McGraw-Hill, 1972. 788p. illus. index. $33.50. LC 77-116661. ISBN 0-07-012424-8.

With contributions from 124 scientists and engineers, this encyclopedia is designed to be a "bridge between the underlying principles and the techniques of applying instruments and controls to whatever work there is to be done." In addition to the usual subject index, there is a "classified index," which allows the user to learn which entries pertain to some larger field of study. For example, one may look under "oceanography" in this index and be referred to such entries as "fathometer" and "sonar." Cross references are placed wherever needed in the text and many of the entries have lists of references for further reading. This work is *not* "profusely illustrated" and many users will, perhaps, be disappointed in not finding pictures of things such as the above-mentioned fathometer. The illustrations that are present, mostly drawings, seem adequate to their tasks.

A number of entries were compared to similar entries in the *McGraw-Hill Encyclopedia of Science and Technology* (1971 edition). Most of these comparisons show that the present work is generally more informative, but there are exceptions, even when the entry is by the same person. This is a fairly comprehensive and handy compilation of material about instrumentation and control. It is authoritative and attractively produced. —R. G. Schipf. [R: ARBA 73, item 1720]

TRANSPORTATION

805. Allen, Jon L. **Aviation and Space Museums of America.** New York, Arco, 1975. 287p. illus. $12.00. LC 73-91258. ISBN 0-668-03426-2.

A well-conceived and excellently executed reference book that will have value for the aviation scholar and air enthusiast. The tourist interested in aerospace history will also find the book of interest. The concise history or background is given for each of 54 United States museums and three Canadian museums, along with details on exhibits and the types of aircraft or space vehicles on display, and occasional information about a museum's plans for expansion. Each entry provides information on location of a museum and how to get to it by car, schedule of operating hours year round, and admission charges, if any. The entries are well illustrated. An appendix provides a list of organizations and publications concerned with aviation history. —Alexander S. Birkos. [R: LJ, 15 Oct 75, p. 1906; ARBA 76, item 64]

806. Angelucci, Enzo. **Airplanes: From the Dawn of Flight to the Present Day.** New York, McGraw-Hill, 1973. 287p. illus.(part col.). bibliog. index. $14.95. LC 72-12755. ISBN 0-07-001807-3.

This is a history of the flying machine from the time of Leonardo da Vinci to the drawing boards depicting the space shuttle and other aircraft of the future. The book is a translation of *Gli Aeroplani* (Milan, Italy, Arnoldo Mondadori Editore, 1971). Over 900 illustrations discuss aircraft types from early wing studies to the space shuttle and short-takeoff-and-landing craft (STOL). Operational and experimental aircraft, both military and civilian, are discussed in detail to outline the current state-of-the-art. Color illustrations and black and white photographs are abundant, and various technical data are given for each illustration. These data include the nomenclature, height, weight, length, wing spread, speed, and number of crew. There is also a chronology of World War II, which emphasizes its impact on aviation. In addition to an extensive bibliography, there is a general index and an index by nation of aircraft illustrated. Excellent for ready reference and browsing. —Steven J. Mayover. [R: Choice, May 74, p. 55; LJ, 1 Feb 74, p. 350; ALA 74; ARBA 75, item 1819]

807. Cors, Paul B. **Railroads.** Littleton, Colo., Libraries Unlimited, 1975. 152p. index. (Spare Time Guides: Information Sources for Hobbies and Recreation, No. 8). $10.00. LC 74-31396. ISBN 0-87287-082-0.

Besides being Chief, Technical Processing, University of Wyoming Library, Cors has long been a collector of railroad books and has reviewed new railroad books for *Library Journal.* He is well qualified to compile a selective, annotated list of 259 (mostly in-print) recommended books. Because railroad books interest many library users, but are reviewed neither well nor widely in standard selection tools, Cors's guide should be helpful. E. T. Bryant's *Railways: A Reader's Guide* (Archon, 1968) offers a reasonably comparable treatment for the British and European railways that are excluded here. Together, these two works cover the domestic and foreign railroad materials likely to interest Americans.

Limited to English language books on railroads in Central and North America (plus Hawaii), *Railroads* also excludes model railroads as well as non-adult books, most fiction, publications of railroads, guidebooks to individual museums, and funicular railways and monorails. However, scope is still quite broad; included are general works on railroading, locomotives, rolling stock, trains, stations, railroads by geographic region, tourist and industrial lines, street cars, interurbans, and rapid transit. Even rail museums, societies, and periodicals receive attention. Criteria for inclusion emphasize in-print materials plus those which the author has found to be valuable. Although his work is basically an annotated bibliography. Cors provides the reader with a good general introduction to the railroad literature. The index is useful and there is a directory of publishers. Following the bibliographic citation (full title, place of publication, frequency, indication of special features, plus LC card number), annotations describe and evaluate the material. Within each chapter arrangement is hierarchical, usually East to West, and not alphabetical.

While differing with the author on a few specifics, the reviewer believes that Cors's judgment and his familiarity with the railroad literature are excellent. He writes well and the book is attractively designed so that it is legible and easy to use. Since it is often difficult to locate reviews of railroad books, Cors might have given reviewing more explicit attention. For example, *Railroad History* has the most and best book reviews. A *guide* to a subject, as opposed to an annotated bibliography, should include a variety of information sources (i.e., railroad phonorecords, maps for train-watching, sources of railroad photos, names and addresses of the several individual railroad historical societies, etc.) to meet the varied needs of patrons. And if specialist book stores are as important as Cors indicates, then a listing of them would have strengthened the work. —William C. Robinson. [R: LJ, 15 Nov 75, p. 2127; ARBA 76, item 1670]

808. Georgano, G. N., ed. **The Complete Encyclopedia of Motorcars, 1885-1968.** New York, Dutton, 1969. 640p. illus.(part col.). indexes. $30.00. LC 68-22674. ISBN 0-525-08351-0.

No other volume on automotive history has ever come close to the comprehensiveness of this work, which lists some 4,100 makes of automobiles from all over the world. Arrangement is alphabetical, usually with an illustration of at least one model of the marque (there are some 2,000 photographs altogether). Information given includes country of manufacture, dates, corporate details, descriptions of some models, and occasionally notes on prices, number made, etc. Specialists have noted some omissions, errors, and inconsistency in cross references (for example, the Adams-Farwell is listed only under Adams but is frequently referred to as the Farwell). A glossary, cast largely in British terms, and several indexes (Personalities; Component Manufacturers and Agents; Sporting Events) are included. The editor was assisted by a staff of consultants from all over the world. —Walter C. Allen. [R: ARBA 71, item 1813]

CHAPTER 42

MILITARY SCIENCE

BIBLIOGRAPHIES

809. Bloomberg, Marty, and Hans H. Weber. **World War II and Its Origins: A Select Annotated Bibliography of Books in English.** Littleton, Colo., Libraries Unlimited, 1975. 311p. index. $13.50. LC 74-81959. ISBN 0-87287-089-8.

It is difficult to review a select bibliography because the qualifier "select" defines the entries as those chosen by the authors. Other authors would undoubtedly have made other choices in many areas. So one must be content to say that these two authors selected well, annotated their selections, limited the choices to books in English, and stuck to the core of subject, which meant skirting the flood of fringe books on unit histories, escape accounts, and all non-information presentations. There are more than 1,600 entries, arranged in 12 subject chapters. Bibliographic entries are complete, including author, title, place of publication, publisher, date, and pagination. A reviewer also has great difficulty, however, when he finds his own book omitted for one that seems clearly inferior. But who said war was fair? —David Eggenberger. [R: Choice, July/Aug 75, p. 660; WLB, June 75, pp. 756-57; RQ, Fall 75, pp. 70-71; ARBA 76, item 289]

810. Higham, Robin, ed. **A Guide to the Sources of British Military History.** Sponsored by the Conference on British Studies. Berkeley, University of California Press, 1972. 630p. $25.00. LC 74-104108. ISBN 0-520-01674-2.

An outstanding bibliography compiled by Higham with the assistance of a score of American, British, Canadian, and other experts in the field. Subject oriented, the work ranges from English defense policy to military developments to strategic and tactical historical accounts, with special emphasis on the economic, scientific, and technological background thereof. Each of the chapters is prefaced by an explanatory essay of greater length and more in-depth informational value than are customarily found in most full-fledged bibliographies. Entries following the essays are for published works, journal articles, unpublished official works (to include staff studies), government documents, private papers, manuscripts and archival materials. Within each category, entries are numbered consecutively, arranged alphabetically by author, editor, or other source, and include standard minimal bibliographic data. All titles are conveniently italicized. Updating addenda help the reader identify those works and articles issued just prior to going to press. The vast majority of citations cover material published only in English, although some few major untranslated works of foreign origin and especial interest are noted. —Lawrence E. Spellman. [R: Choice, May 72, p. 353; ARBA 73, item 347]

811. Higham, Robin, ed. **A Guide to the Sources of United States Military History.** Hamden, Conn., Archon Books, 1975. 559p. $27.50. LC 75-14455. ISBN 0-208-01499-3.

This well-planned, useful volume is modelled on the longer *Guide to the Sources of British Military History*, but it takes into account technology and science as well as modern military and naval medicine. It begins with the European background of American military affairs and proceeds chronologically from Colonial Forces 1607-1766 to the Department of Defense and its components 1945-1973. Eighteen author/experts assisted Professor Higham, who is editor of the journals *Military Affairs* and *The Aerospace Historian.*

After contributing general sources to the introduction, each author had about 4,500 words and 300 entries to survey the broad sources in his field (or period), cover key subtopics, list applicable archives, and suggest further research. The plan worked very well. The volume ends with a 12-page bibliographic essay on museums as historical resources.

As with all solidly compiled and well-manufactured source books, this one is expensive. But such books will not get any less costly in the foreseeable future. —David Eggenberger. [R: ARBA 76, item 1675]

812. Nebenzahl, Kenneth. **A Bibliography of Printed Battle Plans of the American Revolution, 1775-1795.** Chicago, published for The Hermon Dunlap Smith Center for the History of Cartography at the Newberry Library by University of Chicago Press, 1975. 159p. index. bibliog. $12.00. LC 74-16679. ISBN 0-226-56958-6.

A listing and description of the battle plans of the War of Independence. Over 200 maps are cataloged in chronological order and are provided with an excellent index and supplemented with a list of cartobibliographies and references consulted. Maps relating to the Revolutionary War have been taken from many different types of publications, such as broadsides and almanacs published both in the colonies and in England. The emphasis is on published material, since the bibliography does not include manuscript maps.

The volume is the work of one of the nation's foremost authorities on rare books and maps, Kenneth Nebenzahl, and is the outgrowth of research he has done for other books. It is published under the auspices of the Hermon Dunlap Smith Center for the History of Cartography at Newberry Library. The union list (partial) is compiled from first-hand sources and is presented in a format consistent with the principles of the Anglo-American Cataloging Rules. Additional information, primarily of a military nature, is added to satisfy questions about variant editions, related battles, and copy description.

A first-rate bibliography, the volume is of primary importance to the military historian. It is nonetheless an excellent addition to the cartographic bibliography. It will be of limited use in most libraries because it does not contain any maps and because its approach is limited. —William Brace. [R: ARBA 76, item 313]

813. Ziegler, Janet. **World War II: Books in English, 1945-1965.** Stanford, Hoover Institution Press, 1971. 223p. index. (Hoover Bibliographical Series, No. 45) $10.50. LC 74-155297. ISBN 0-8179-2451-5.

With a listing of 4,519 entries of nonfiction works (monographs but not periodical articles), this guide provides a rather impressive coverage of the subject.

Entries are not annotated, but there are notes indicating different editions or even editions of the same work published under a different title. There are eight major chapters, e.g., military aspects of the war, political aspects, economic and social aspects, etc., subdivided by appropriate topics. There is an author-series index. This is by far the most comprehensive listing of pertinent material in English about World War II. The detailed index enhances the usefulness of this guide. [R: LJ, 15 Nov 71, p. 3746; ALA 71; ARBA 72, item 1833]

DICTIONARIES

814. Harbottle, Thomas Benfield. **Dictionary of Battles.** Rev. and updated by George Bruce. New York, Stein & Day, 1971. 333p. $12.50. LC 76-150604. ISBN 0-8128-1364-2.

This substantial revision of a well-known work briefly describes the geography, tactics, and results of decisive battle from earliest recorded history to the late 1960s throughout the world. Emphasis is definitely on the Western world, particularly Western Europe. Many cross references and alternative names for battles provide easy location of information in both old and newly added entries. The index must be used also, however, since many battles, particularly the recent ones, do not have independent entries, but are grouped under the name of a country or a war. [R: LJ, July 71, p. 2293; ALA 71; ARBA 72, item 1834]

815. Quick, John. **Dictionary of Weapons and Military Terms.** New York, McGraw-Hill, 1973. 515p. illus. bibliog. $25.00. LC 73-8757. ISBN 0-07-051057-1.

A copiously illustrated compendium of military hardware from the dawn of history to the present, with succinct definitional notes on the development, physical characteristics, and use of such hardware. Over 1,200 black and white photographs, judiciously selected and of high clarity, portray mankind's martial armory from the earliest edged weapons to the latest nuclear missile. The geographic span is international, with special emphasis on the United States and its NATO allies. Also included are military terms used in intelligence, training, combat, and logistical operations. Technical words and phrases are defined, as well as acronyms, code names, and slang expressions of all the armed services. Cross-referencing is extensive. The source of each photograph is indicated.

Summation: accurate, well-written, and wide-ranging reference work of particular interest to instructors, students, and hobbyists concerned with military history. —Lawrence E. Spellman. [R: BL, 1 Oct 74, p. 196; ARBA 75, item 1838]

ALMANACS

816. Dupuy, Trevor N., Grace P. Hayes, and John A. C. Andrews. **The Almanac of World Military Power.** 3rd ed. New York, R. R. Bowker, 1974. 387p. illus. maps. index. $25.00. LC 74-7578. ISBN 0-8352-0730-7.

The noted military historian Trevor N. Dupuy and his associates have expanded and updated this valuable reference work, which provides essential information on the strategic situation and defense structure of 154 countries throughout the world, both large and small. Divided into 10 regions, such as North America and Western Europe, the almanac provides a survey describing the military geography of the region, discusses its strategic significance and regional alliances, and includes a chronology of recent intra- and extra-regional conflicts. The survey is followed by a section for each country within the region, which summarizes its power potential statistics (including area, population, total armed forces, GNP, and military budget); describes its defense structure, military assistance programs, and alliances; and analyzes its politico-military policy and strategic problems. Detailed statistics on the armed forces of each of the countries include strength, organization, and armament; in most cases, the information is current as of mid-1974. The uncolored maps that are provided for each region and country are considerably improved from previous editions, being larger and providing more detail. A glossary of military terms includes operating characteristics of major types of aircraft, ships, and armaments. —LeRoy C. Schwarzkopf. [R: BL, 15 Oct 75, p. 323; WLB, May 75, p. 675; ARBA 76, item 1677]

ATLASES

817. Banks, Arthur. **A Military Atlas of the First World War.** Commentary by Alan Palmer. New York, Taplinger, 1975. 338p. illus. maps. index. $29.95. LC 77-179660. ISBN 0-8008-5242-7.

For the close student of the military history of World War I, this very complete collection of maps, charts, diagrams, and tables relating to the slaughter of 1914-1918 will be a necessity. The organization and scope of the book are shown by the following list of sectional headings: The Pre-War Situation; War on the Western Front in 1914; War on the Eastern Front in 1914; The Gallipoli Campaign; The War in 1915; The War in 1916; The War in 1917; The War in 1918; The Peripheral Campaigns; Weapons; The War at Sea; The War in the Air.

Although detailed maps of battles and campaigns predominate, the work has numerous features not commonly associated with atlases, an example of which is the technical explanation of how the Royal Navy overcame the German U-Boat menace by relentless surface tracking and, consequently, exhausting the German submarines' batteries. Such technical explanations as this appear routinely throughout the book as parenthetic adjuncts to maps.

The maps are clearly drawn in such a manner as to render the chaotic movements of armies intelligible even to those innocent of military knowledge. [R: ARBA 76, item 296]

818. Young, Peter, ed. **Atlas of the Second World War.** Cartography by Richard Natkiel. New York, Putnam, 1974. 288p. illus. maps. index. $17.95. LC 73-78626. ISBN 0-399-11182-4.

This reference work covers every important aspect of the military operations of the war, including battles and campaigns on land and sea and in the air. Arranged according to major theaters or campaigns, and within these by major battles, the book also provides succinct explanatory texts to accompany the 215 detailed maps. Longer narrative introductions precede each main section and provide more general information regarding the forces, the commanders, and the tactical, geographical,

and logistical problems involved. Though still somewhat brief, these sectional introductions enable the reader to have enough of an overview so as to be able to understand the sequence and importance of the subsequent battle and campaign maps.

A check of the maps with other sources reveals them to be quite accurate.
The text pertaining to each of the maps provides good capsulized descriptions.
Interspersed, where appropriate, are informative balance charts that show the relative strength of opposing forces. Photographs relating to the area covered are also
included, lending an aura of realism to the maps and text.

The work is comprised of the following sections: "Germany Strikes in the
West," "The War in the Mediterranean," "The North African Campaign," "Operation Barbarossa," "The Japanese Offensive," "The Italian Campaign," "The Pacific
War," "The Burma Campaign," "Russia Fights Back," "The War in North-West
Europe," "The Naval War," "The War in the Air." The index is well done; within
the alphabetical sequence, military forces are arranged by nationality, and within
this grouping by theater and size of unit.

One could wish for longer and more detailed explanatory texts, but, on the
whole, this is an excellent work with clear, concise, and precise maps and texts. A
good succinct bibliography would have been an excellent addition. —Hans H. Weber.
[R: LJ, 1 Oct 74, p. 2477; Choice, Dec 74, p. 1462; ALA 74; ARBA 75, item 1843]

AUTHOR-TITLE INDEX

Awakening interest in science during the
first century of printing, 1450-1550, 652
Awards, honors and prizes, 25
Axford, L. B., 393

Bair, F. E., 742
Baker, C., 529
Baker's dictionary of Christian ethics, 463
Bakó, E., 109
Baldwin, J. L., 743
Banks, A., 817
Banno, M., 90
Barabas, S., 488
Barbour, R. W., 725
Bard, A. J., 666
Barnhart, C. L., 511, 527
Barnhart, R. K., 527
Barnhart dictionary of new English since
1963, 527
Barzun, J., 529, 581
Baseball encyclopedia, 277
Basic documents in international law, 206
Bauer, A., 29
Beale, S., 16
Beall, K. F., 374
Bean, W. J., 699
Beard, J., 782
Beckson, K., 563
Belch, J., 268
Bell, A. P., 747
Bell, G., 319
Belzer, J., 798
Bennett, H., 667
Benson, M., 546
Berlitz, C., 525
Bernstein, T. M., 528
Besançon, R. M., 672
Besford, P., 295
Best books on the stock market, 350
Bestor, G. C., 320
Betteridge, H. T., 537
Bibliographia Canadiana, 156
Bibliographical guide to the study of
Southern literature, 618
Bibliographical guide to the study of the
literature of the U.S.A., 616
Bibliography of . . . American children's
books printed prior to 1821, 602;
American literature, 615; bioethics,
758; British history, 157; British
literary bibliographies, 626; Canadian
bibliographies, 104; Latin American
bibliographies, 124; maps and charts
published in America before 1800,
215; medieval drama, 569; printed
battle plans of the American Revolution,
1775-1795, 812; publications issued by
Unesco or under its auspices, 38;

Bibliography of (cont'd) . . . research studies
in education, 1926-1940, 253; the history
of electronics, 803; the socioeconomic
aspects of medicine, 757
Biggerstaff, K., 87
Bill of Rights, 208
Biographic dictionary of Chinese communism,
1921-1965, 88
Biographical dictionaries and related works,
51
Biographical dictionary of . . . actors, actresses,
musicians, dancers, managers and other
stage personnel in London, 1660-1800,
440; Republican China, 89; the Comintern,
195
Biographical directory of librarians in the
United States and Canada, 78
Biographical directory of the United States
executive branch, 1774-1971, 187
Biographical history of blacks in America
since 1528, 151
Biographical register of the Confederate
Congress, 148
Birds of the world, 712
Birnbaum, E., 85
Blackburn, G. M., 603
Blacks in America, 307
Black's medical dictionary, 760
Blackwell, T. E., 205
Blakiston's Gould medical dictionary, 761
Blanck, J., 615
Bleiler, E. F., 582
Blom, E., 416
Bloodletters and badmen, 315
Bloomberg, M., 809
Boatner, M. M., 141
Bock, H., 290
Boger, L. A., 391
Bond, O. F., 548
Book collector's handbook of values, 18
Book of world-famous music, 407
Bookman's glossary, 15
Bookman's guide to Americana, 19
Books for college libraries, 74
Books for secondary school libraries, 76
Books on Asia from the Near East to the
Far East, 85
Boorman, H. L., 89
Borror, D. J., 715
Botanical bibliographies, 686
Botterweck, G. J., 477
Bottle, R. T., 676
Boutell's heraldry, 174
Bradbury, M., 609
Bradford, G., 282
Bradley, V. A., 18
Brady, G. S., 351
Branch, M. C., 321
Brandon, S. G. F., 467

SUBJECT INDEX